D0871950

The History of Menshevism

LEOPOLD H. HAIMSON, *General Editor*

HOOVER INSTITUTION PUBLICATIONS 117

The Mensheviks

THE HOOVER INSTITUTION
on War, Revolution,
and Peace

Edited by Leopold H. Haimson

The Mensheviks

FROM THE REVOLUTION OF 1917
TO THE SECOND WORLD WAR

With Contributions by David Dallin, George Denicke,
Leo Lande, Boris Sapir, and Simon Wolin

Translated by Gertrude Vakar

THE UNIVERSITY OF CHICAGO PRESS
CHICAGO AND LONDON

This volume is one of a series arising from the
work of the INTER-UNIVERSITY PROJECT ON THE
HISTORY OF THE MENSHEVIK MOVEMENT

Leopold H. Haimson, general editor of the
History of Menshevism series, has been with
the Russian Institute of Columbia University
since 1963.
[1974]

THE UNIVERSITY OF CHICAGO PRESS, CHICAGO 60637

The University of Chicago Press, Ltd., London

© 1974 by The University of Chicago

All rights reserved. Published 1974

Printed in the United States of America

International Standard Book Number: 0-226-31222-4

Library of Congress Catalog Card Number: 73-87302

To the memory of two cherished collaborators
Julia Abramovna Kamermacher and Gertrude Vakar

Contents

Preface

Leopold H. Haimson

This volume was conceived well over a decade ago as one of the major tasks of the Inter-University Project on the History of the Menshevik Movement. The project, launched in 1959, was itself the offspring of an unusual collaboration between the then already fast dwindling Menshevik émigré community and professional historians teaching at a number of American universities. These historians were moved by the challenge, and the urgency, of sponsoring a collective effort to record the history of a party that had played so great a role in the development of Russian Marxism and the three major revolutions that Russia experienced in the early twentieth century—only to have had its voice muffled in the years that followed, or altered, however subtly, by the conditions of émigré life.

One of the project's most immediate aims was to collect and preserve the various written records of the history of the Menshevik movement that still lay scattered, often in highly perishable form, in Europe and the United States. But the directors of the project also considered it their task to fill out these records—however difficult it might be to do after so many years had passed—by searching and recording the memories of the survivors of the Menshevik movement still within their reach. To this purpose, these survivors were encouraged to write memoirs, ranging in scope from recollections of episodes in the history of menshevism in which they had been centrally engaged to full-length autobiographies that would set these activities in the context of their authors' personal development and of the changing social milieus in which their lives had moved.

This gathering of memoir materials was supplemented by interviews conducted by a number of American scholars associated with the project. These interviews, too, ranged considerably in scope, from the recording, sometimes over many sessions, of full-blown life histories to more specific inquiries about particular political actions and events. In recording the life histories, an effort was made to reconstruct as fully as possible the psychological pressures and social circumstances that had conditioned our respondents' development from childhood and youth through their years of political involvement. But even in our more circumscribed interviews, we sought to probe, below the level of rationalization, into the motivations that underlay certain critical political decisions.

All these materials were made available to a number of professional scholars associated with the project, and eventually deposited, for more general use, in an archive on the history of menshevism established at Columbia University. But in addition to making such materials available to Western scholars—whose interpretation of the history of the Menshevik party would necessarily reflect, in part, values and viewpoints different from those that had animated its members—the initiators of the project also considered it their task to engage some of their Menshevik associates more fully in the reconstruction of their party's history.

To the obvious objection that any studies of this kind—conducted by participants in the very events they would seek to recount—would necessarily reflect the passions they had once engaged and fall short of the ideal of objective history, an equally facile counter could be offered: All historical writing necessarily reflects the viewpoints and values of those who engage in it; and ultimately, as L. J. Henderson once put it, all "facts," not to speak of the relations ascribed between them, are "data in a conceptual scheme." However, the project's decision to encourage its Menshevik associates to write their own history was motivated by a more positive consideration: that the historiographies of all the great revolutionary conflicts of the modern age, most notably those of the Great English and French revolutions, have drawn much of their vitality precisely from the articulation and confrontation of the viewpoints that were once represented in these revolutions—viewpoints that, even while undergoing periodic changes as they were passed on from generation to generation, have remained integral components of the cultural traditions of the countries concerned.

The real question that faced us was whether such vitality of expression could still be infused into the viewpoints that were to be brought out in the works of our Menshevik associates in view of the break that had occurred in Russia's cultural tradition as a result of the revolution and its aftermath. Or whether, in the thin air of fifty years in the emigration, these viewpoints had not become calcified and the memories and values we sought to evoke turned into stereotypes.

We could draw comfort from the fact that, of all the currents in the Russian post-revolutionary emigration—and indeed of all the political emigrations in modern European experience—the Mensheviks had proved by far the hardiest. Through these years of wars and upheavals, and of the enforced migrations that they imposed upon survivors of the Menshevik party—from Russia to Germany, from Germany to France, and eventually to the United States—these survivors had managed, to a remarkable degree, to keep a social community and a political culture in being. As our studies were being launched, the journal they had founded in Berlin in 1922 was celebrating its fortieth year of publication!

Still, in an effort to meet the problems admittedly posed by discontinuity of experience, physicial displacement, and the sheer erosion of time, we adopted for the historical studies of our Menshevik associates two principal working rules: One of these was that, as much as possible, each contributor should concentrate on chapters and events in the history of menshevism in which he had been directly involved, and that he should do so, not on the basis of memory alone, but with the assistance of all the primary sources bearing on his experience that the project managed to collect. (In some cases these were documents that the contributors had themselves drawn up, or helped to edit, during the period in the party's history that they were now to reconstruct.) It was hoped that in this fashion a vital interplay would be set off between document and memory: that the source materials scrutinized would revive or sharpen the author's remembrance of things past—his recall of what he and those around him had once experienced and felt—and that memory, in turn, might fill out the gaps, and illuminate the obscurities, of the often fragmentary records.

The other working rule we sought to follow in the preparation of each of the major contributions of our Menshevik associates was to have them discussed at biweekly seminars regularly attended by the project's director and research fellows, invited American and European scholars pursuing research interests bearing on our own, as well as ten of the survivors of the Menshevik leadership in the emigration who were most closely associated with our work (Rafael Abramovich, Gregory Aronson, Lydia Dan-Zederbaum, David Dallin, George Denicke, Boris

Dvinov, Leo Lande, Boris Sapir, Solomon Schwarz, and Simon Wolin).
Pulling together as it did genuine common interests and widely different skills, viewpoints, and backgrounds, this seminar provided an
effective catalyst for wide-ranging and often free-wheeling discussion
of work in progress, and especially for questioning and probing the
memories of the Menshevik participants in an effort to reach—beyond
the level of rationalization and facile explanation—for an understanding of why certain positions were taken and certain actions performed
or left unperformed. It should also be noted that the Menshevik
survivors who participated in these seminars had themselves been
identified during the periods under discussion with different political
currents and factions in the Menshevik movement (from defensism to
internationalism, from the Menshevik "left" to the Menshevik "right"),
and consequently had assumed at crucial times in the party's history
quite different, and often sharply conflicting, political stands. For this
reason, our seminars also provided a natural setting for the confrontation not only of individual memories but also of conflicting values and
points of view—and ultimately for reconsideration, to some degree at
least, of positions once so militantly held. The records of these often
heated discussions were eventually transcribed, and the contributors
whose work had been discussed were encouraged to revise their drafts
on the basis of the queries, criticism, and suggestions they had received.

These, in substance, were the approaches we used to guide the work
of our Menshevik contributors, and it will be for our readers to judge
how effective they have been. Many of the contributions submitted
were eventually deposited in mimeographed form in major research
libraries in Europe and the United States (to date, some thirty such
studies have been distributed in this form). Others have been issued, or
still remain to be issued, in our project's Russian-language series. Two
of them, Solomon Schwarz's book on 1905 and the present volume,
were eventually translated for inclusion in the English-language series
on the history of menshevism that our project is publishing under the
aegis of the Hoover Institution and the University of Chicago Press.

The present volume is intended to serve several purposes: in part, it
is to be regarded as a collection of historical studies, in the strict sense,
of the Menshevik party's trials from the Revolutions of 1917 to the
outbreak of the Second World War (when this party largely ceased to
function, even in emigration, as an organized political entity); in part,
it seeks to bring together the recollections of the contributors about
political developments and events in which they were directly engaged; and, last but not least, it is to be regarded as a final statement of
the value judgments, the reflections, the reconsiderations of survivors
of a now extinct political movement.

The authors of the various sections of the volume all played an active and continuing role in the affairs of the Menshevik party. But during the years under review they held quite different factional sympathies and often assumed, on major issues, conflicting political positions. To illustrate the point, let us review the political biographies of the two oldest contributors to the volume whose involvement in Russian social democracy, by the time of their deaths, had spanned half a century.

David Dallin (1889–1962), who contributed the introduction to, and most of the chapters on, the period between the October Revolution and the launching of the New Economic Policy (NEP), was throughout these years one of Martov's closest collaborators and a leader of the internationalist faction, which after the October Revolution assumed a dominant position in the Menshevik party. An active member of Menshevik organizations since the age of eighteen, when he matriculated in the juridical faculty of the University of Saint Petersburg, Dallin suffered his first political arrest in 1910 and was compelled to pursue his academic studies abroad, graduating from the University of Heidelberg in 1913 with a doctorate in economics. The outbreak of the First World War thus found him in political exile, and in the Russian political emigration he assumed from the outset a militant stand, somewhat on the left flank of the Zimmerwald center. Dallin remained an uncompromising Internationalist after his return to Russia in the spring of 1917, and it was as a representative of Martov's, then minority, faction that he was elected, for the first time, at the August "Unification" Congress, to the Menshevik party's Central Committee. The major realignment within the party after the October Revolution brought him to the fore as a spokesman of the new Internationalist majority bloc, and in this capacity he faithfully followed its line of condemning the authoritarian features of the Soviet regime while opposing, equally resolutely, foreign intervention and White "reaction." Throughout the period of the civil war and War Communism, Dallin maintained this balanced position in his pronouncements as a deputy to the Moscow Soviet, his addresses to congresses of Soviets and trade unions, and his articles in the Menshevik press. As late as 1920, he was advocating support of the war effort against Poland, while censuring some of its "imperialist" features as well as the severe political repressions that were already stifling the life of the Menshevik party and all other "democratic" opposition in Soviet Russia.

Yet, even during these years, there already appeared in Dallin's writings a distinctive note of pragmatism. (Actually, this pragmatism was as basic to his temperament as the militance that so often caused him to take uncompromising, indeed dogmatic, stands, only to sharply reverse himself when his insistent sense of reality told him he had reached an impasse.) At the time, Dallin's natural pragmatism was expressed in increasingly vocal skepticism not only about the "socialist achievements" of the Soviet regime (about this, almost all Menshevik Internationalists could agree), but also about its socialist "potential" for the future. In an article in *Kharkovskaia Mysl'* in 1919, and an address to the Eighth Congress of Soviets in December 1920, he focused his fire on the economic policies of the Soviet regime, predicting catastrophe unless the "utopian" and arbitrary features of these policies and their implementation were promptly repudiated. This criticism was soon partly met with the adoption of the New Economic Policy. This turn in economic policy was to be accompanied, not by the liberalization of political life that Dallin and his fellow Mensheviks viewed as its logical and necessary extension, but by a further tightening of political controls: 1921, the year of the launching of the NEP, also brought the systematic suppression of Menshevik organizations and the wholesale arrests of their leaders.

Late in 1921, shortly after his release from a brief prison term, Dallin emigrated to Berlin, where he joined the Zagranichnaia Delegatsiia RSDRP (Delegation of the RSDRP Abroad) and became one of the editors of its journal, *Sotsialisticheskii Vestnik*. At this time he was already becoming openly doubtful about the major economic assumptions of orthodox Marxist doctrine and the likelihood of their confirmation not only in Soviet, but also in Western contemporary experience; and he articulated these doubts in print. But although his revisionism drew him into some vigorous exchanges with Martov, and especially with Dan, about the "revolutionary" and "socialist" prospects in contemporary Western Europe (see Wolin's section of this book), Dallin continued, until the late twenties, to endorse the modulated position toward the Soviet regime and the leftist stance in the international socialist movement upheld by the majority of the Zagranichnaia Delegatsiia. The era of the five year plans brought more fundamental changes in Dallin's political stand. A bitter critic of the "general line" of forced draft industrialization and collectivization even before the great purges, he now began to advocate so unrelenting a struggle against the Soviet regime that he felt impelled, in 1934, to break with his old comrades on the Zagranichnaia Delegatsiia. Dallin held uncompromisingly to this position, and he rejoined the Zagranichnaia Delegatsiia only in 1939 when, together with Boris Nicolaevsky and Rafael Abramovich, he was able to organize a new "centrist" bloc that, in practice if not always in theory, effected a rapprochement with the old Menshevik right.

Thus, by the outbreak of the Second World War, David Dallin's life journey had taken him from a position well on the left of the spectrum of European social democracy to one well on the right. And the discerning reader should be able to detect the mark of this journey in his retrospective account of the earlier, more radical, period in his political life that he recounts in this book. I should note, however, that Dallin wrote this account at a time when he was already mortally ill, and knew it: Perhaps partly for this reason, many of its pages appear to me pervaded with a mellowness, indeed a philosophic streak, unusual in so combative a spirit. Dallin remains faithful in these pages to the memory of old comrades-in-arms, faithful to the quality of feelings and dreams once shared. Yet, more often than not, he manages to be equally generous to old political adversaries (at least within the Menshevik party), equally perceptive of their qualities of mind and spirit, and of the quality of *their* dream. And in his judgments about a past that he had at least partly outlived—if not repudiated—he succeeded remarkably, it seems to me, in striking a balance between the skepticism, indeed the greater conservatism of outlook that he had reached in his later years, and the reexperiencing—the reliving—of the views, the emotions, the intellectual and moral assumptions that had given his earlier life its shape and its tone.

If in his later years David Dallin was gradually but steadily pulled from the left to the right of the international socialist movement, George Denicke (1887–1964), who contributed the other chapters in this volume on the period of War communism, followed far different and more circuitous paths. Denicke was a relative latecomer to the ranks of the Menshevik movement. As a student, freshly arrived from Kazan, at the Petersburg Technological Institute, he had been irresistibly pulled during the heady summer of 1905 by the appeals of bolshevism: by Lenin's sweeping conception of the democratic revolution and the dictatorship of the proletariat and peasantry, and by the opportunities for activism and romantic self-affirmation that the Bolshevik center then so richly afforded its most gifted young followers. By the early fall of 1905, Denicke had become one of the "responsible" agitators of the Petersburg Kollegiia of Agitators—"responsible," at the age of eighteen, for all the workers in the Narva district, including the many thousands at the giant Putilov Works. Almost as vertiginously, he had been drawn into the higher reaches of the Bolshevik center, to the company of those brilliant representatives of the Bolshevik generation of 1905—Bazarov, Bogdanov, Lunarcharsky—who so irresistibly combined his own penchants for *both* romantic voluntarism and "scientific" realism. Even in this company, Denicke's publicistic gifts had been quickly recognized, and he had worked in the electoral campaigns to the first two Dumas, contributing a pamphlet echoing Lenin's denunciation of the "bourgeois" opportunism of the Kadets and of their readiness to "make a deal" with the autocracy. Denicke's involvement with bolshevism did not withstand the shock of the defeat of Russia's first revolution and his consequent disillusionment with Lenin's stubbornly optimistic prognoses about its course. But even after this break, he did not join the Menshevik movement, electing instead to identify himself, for over a decade, as a nonfactional Social-Democrat. In the light of this political background, the position that Denicke assumed, when, somewhat reluctantly, he finally joined the Menshevik party, well after the outbreak of the Revolution of 1917, may at first seem puzzling if not paradoxical. For in both word and practice, he was from the outset one of the most consistent and militant champions of revolutionary defensism. In his public activity in Kazan, where he served as deputy chairman of both the city's Soviet and its Committee of Public Organizations, he sought to act as a veritable bridge between these two local organs of the "dual" power (and between the "lower" and "upper" reaches of the society that they respectively purported to represent). And in his writings in the Party press, he took pride, then as in later years, in having been one of the first and most unqualified advocates of coalition at the national level.

Yet, however paradoxical, there was a psychological, if not a political, consistency between the position that Denicke assumed in 1917 and his earlier attraction, in 1905, to Lenin's views. This psychological consistency was reflected in Denicke's discomfort, throughout his political career, with the conception, embedded in orthodox Marxist doctrine in Russia, of a two-stage revolutionary process: the proposition that in Russia a bourgeois revolution must necessarily precede— and be separated by a proper, historically determined, interval from— the eventual socialist revolution. A corollary of this proposition, which many Mensheviks entertained even more rigidly after than before the "intoxications" and eventual defeats of 1905, was that a socialist party should not attempt to seize, or even share, the reins of political authority during the first stage of this revolutionary process; indeed that it should refrain from assuming any such responsibilities until, in accordance with the inexorable laws of historical development, the "objective prerequisites" for the establishment of socialism had been fully achieved. When in 1917 the leaders of the Menshevik party finally opted for coalition, many of them did so hesitantly, guiltily, and only because of the realization—in the face of the rapid disintegration of existing political authority—that unless they now agreed to assume some of the responsibilities of power, they might soon be compelled to take it all.

Denicke never really shared this orthodox Menshevik conception of the revolutionary process. For one thing, he was never really convinced—in 1917 and the period of War communism any more than in 1905—that the Russian bourgeoisie was a significant revolutionary force, and therefore (although he occasionally paid lip service to the conception) that the Russian revolution should be viewed, at any of its stages, as primarily a bourgeois revolution. For one thing, Denicke was by temperament a Bohemian, and he never had much sympathy or respect for those representatives of the bourgeoisie he did encounter, both in Russia and in Western Europe. But, more important, there was nothing about his experience in Petersburg, and especially about his life in Kazan, before and after 1905, that could persuade him that any of the driving forces of the Russian revolution—any of the major elements of Russian society that were dedicated to its genuine transformation—were to be identified in any significant way with a "bourgeoisie." In 1905, this sense had induced Denicke to accept readily Lenin's conception of dictatorship of proletariat and peasantry. In 1917, with almost a decade of experience of Kazan public life behind him, this same sense would induce him to assert, unhesitatingly, that the "democratic" elements of Russian society (even the ostensibly "nonsocialist" ones) and the workers and soldiers represented in the Kazan Soviet could and should be drawn together in the defense and consolidation of a truly democratic order.

Inherent in Denicke's sense of what could, and should, be done—without hesitation and without delay—was, as I have already suggested, a perception *in the Russia of his own time* of the outline of a democratic society, and of a democratic intelligentsia to lead it in the building of a freer and more equitable political and social order. But I should add that Denicke's sense of the dangers, as well as the opportunities, that this society now faced also reflected a more voluntaristic view of political power per se—a more generous view of the significance of political authority and of the *uses* to which it could be put—than Russian orthodox Marxism, at least in its most conservative streak, allowed.

Denicke had continued to be concerned with the problem of political authority even during the decade of relative political noninvolvement that had followed his break with the Bolsheviks. This problem had provided much of the intellectual focus of the historical studies in which he had engaged during these years. Indeed, in 1915—in the setting of the military defeats and of the rapid disintegration of the political and moral authority of the tsarist regime—he had embarked on a vast study, never completed, of the decline of legitimate authority in the late Roman Empire.

It was partly with these visions of disintegration—in the old world and the new—that Denicke had greeted the collapse of the czarist regime. Thus, from the very outbreak of the Revolution, he was especially sensitive to the fissures that it exposed in Russian society, and especially conscious of the pressures that these fissures, as well as the additional stresses caused by the cruel experience of the war, were imposing on the fragile structure of political authority. But these, in his view, were precisely the difficulties that a resolute exercise of political authority should now seek to overcome, drawing on whatever prestige and moral weight could still be drawn by *officially, publicly*, assuming its vestments. Thus it was that from the outset of the Revolution, Denicke was a militant champion of coalition—of the view that the socialist parties should assume, without delay, some of the official prerogatives of power. Thus is was, after October, that, far more decisively than most of his comrades in the Menshevik party, he insisted on opposing to Lenin's dictatorship of Soviets the moral and political prestige of the Constituent Assembly, seeing in this assembly the *symbol*, if not the reality, of the authority around which to rally the democratic society he believed in.

The attitudes I have described were admittedly idiosyncratic—indeed, from a political point of view, Denicke never fitted very comfortably within the Menshevik party. In 1917 and in its immediate aftermath, however, they drew him close to two major figures in this heterogeneous party. One of them was Iraklii Tsereteli, who drew—partly perhaps from the political experience of Georgian social democracy—a comparable vision of the makings of a democratic society and of the ways in which political authority could be used to establish it and hold it together. The other major figure in menshevism to whom Denicke felt intellectually and emotionally close during these years—even if he did not share all of his political instincts—was A. N. Potresov, of whom he speaks with much understanding and empathy in this book. With Potresov, Denicke shared, above all, a sense of identification with the intellectual traditions and mores of the Russian intelligentsia, and an insistent belief—however Marxist dogma chose to deflate it—in the centrality of this intelligentsia's role in making a democratic revolution and building a democratic society in Russia. Even though after the Bolshevik seizure of power Denicke refused to join Potresov in his journey into the political wilderness, this affinity of attitudes, including the distaste he shared with Potresov for the qualified support that the Menshevik party chose to offer the Soviet regime after the outbreak of the civil war, caused Denicke to feel almost as uncomfortable with his party's political direction throughout these years.

But Denicke's personal, if not political, sympathies during this period were not confined to the Mensheviks, or even to the members of the "democratic" camp with whom he politically identified himself. Even after the summer of 1918, when the members of this camp became the objects of large-scale repressions, he did not break his old friendships with several prominent figures in the Bolshevik party, in particular Bukharin. And his observations about the moral pangs that some of his Bolshevik friends underwent even as they steeled themselves to commit the political acts that he so resolutely condemned were never wholly devoid of his unique combination of detachment and imaginative empathy. Although at the time Denicke probably did not feel such empathy for Lenin, this quality is not absent in the characterization and evaluation that Denicke offers of him in this book. Symptomatically, his most generous comments in this regard focus on Lenin's efforts to preserve some kind of political authority and order in Russia.

Lest the reader be confused by this last remark, I should emphasize that Denicke himself was never a supporter of order and political authority for their own sake—independently of the uses to which they were put. He wanted to use political power decisively and to the full, but only consistently with the kind of democratic and equitable political and social order in which he believed. To the end of his days, such an order, in his eyes, bore practically as little resemblance to the "bourgeois" values and institutions that he encountered during his years of wandering abroad as they did to the Soviet Russia he left in 1922. Indeed, Denicke never fully absorbed the reformist ethos that became dominant in European social democracy during the interwar period, and to the end he greeted with unflagging interest and hope the new currents that periodically emerged on the left of the international socialist movement. He lifted his face to every new political and intellectual breeze that blew his way, and continued to be irresistibly attracted by the estranged, the downtrodden, the uprooted whom he encountered on the paths he had to travel.

I have dwelt at such length on the diverse political backgrounds of the two deceased contributors to this volume because they dictated, in part, my own approach to my role as editor. I mentioned earlier that, from the outset, my colleagues and I considered that, while intended to serve in part as a historical monograph in the strict sense, this volume should draw on the individual memories of its contributors in its reconstruction of the events in which they had been engaged as well as provide a vehicle for their final reflections and value judgments—from a half-century's distance—about the political experience that they had undergone.

The first guideline clearly to be drawn from this conception was that while encouraging in the preparation of the book a full and scrupulous use of all available historical sources, I should studiously refrain from any attempt to impose on the contributors the historical judgments and conceptions of historical development that I had drawn from my own very different background and experience. By the time I could undertake my editing work, such restraint appeared all the more indicated in view of the fact that two of the major contributors, David Dallin and George Denicke, had already passed from the scene.*

The conception of the purposes of this book also suggested similar restraint in handling the occasional chronological and thematic overlaps of individual accounts. As we have seen, the contributors had been identified during the periods they recount with different currents in the Menshevik party, and their historical reconstructions were at least partly drawn on the basis of quite different mental sets—quite different experiences and attitudes. Under the circumstances, it appeared to me important, even at the risk of taxing the reader's patience, to allow their respective judgments of certain personalities and events to appear in this volume side by side.

Before closing this preface to what is clearly to be the last major contribution by survivors of the Menshevik movement to the reconstruction of their party's history, I wish to express, on my own behalf and that of the Menshevik Project, our appreciation to all those who, notwithstanding many difficulties and trials, helped bring off this

---

*The reader will find, in however narrow a chronological compass, a statement of my own view of the trials of the Menshevik party after the October Revolution in a short monograph devoted to the period from the Bolshevik seizure of power to the dissolution of the Constituent Assembly, which is to appear as a companion volume to this study. This account was originally intended to serve as a bridge between David Dallin's and George Denicke's respective contributions to this book, which, due to their deaths before they could complete their task, left something of a chronological gap in the coverage of these crucial months. The "bridge" I sought to write turned out to be far too long, however, and the interpretations offered in it too different from those of the other contributors to be suitable for inclusion in this book; hence the decision to publish it under separate cover.

unusual effort. First and foremost I wish to pay tribute to the project's Menshevik associates, and particularly to the late David Dallin and George Denicke, who displayed extraordinary fortitude—extraordinary *muzhestvo*—in persisting in their effort to complete their contributions at a time when their health was already rapidly failing.

I also wish to acknowledge the project's special debt to two other collaborators to whose memory this volume is dedicated. Julia Kamermacher-Kefali served throughout the decade it took us to complete our major task as the secretary of the Menshevik Project. The intelligence, the patience, the devotion that she so abundantly displayed throughout these years probably helped more than any other factor to keep the project functioning smoothly and the various strong personalities associated with it in mutual harmony and good spirits. Gertrude Vakar, who is identified as the translator of the volume, in fact contributed much more to its possible merits: With her sure sense of the economy and precision of language, she helped me to tighten the contributions to the volume through two exhausting rounds of editorial work and managed to render a political language, not always distinguished by clarity or elegance, in accessible and even graceful English prose. My own life has been the poorer for the death of these two remarkable women.

Finally, I must express our appreciation to those individuals and insitutions who so generously contributed aid and counsel at various stages of the project: to the members of its advisory committee, and the universities they represented (in particular, California, Chicago, Columbia, Harvard, Indiana, and Washington) for their assistance in getting the project under way; to the Ford, Rockefeller, and Atran foundations, which helped keep the project afloat financially for the better part of a decade; and last but not least, to The Hoover Institution and The University of Chicago Press, who have so patiently overseen the long process of gestation and the eventual publication of our labors.

I.   The Mensheviks in 1917

Leo Lande

Introduction

On the evening of 24 October 1917, the Bolshevik Military-Revolutionary Committee of the Petrograd Soviet of Workers' and Soldiers' Deputies announced that "despite all sorts of rumors" it did not intend to seize power but only to "defend the interests of the Petrograd garrison and of democracy from counterrevolution."

On the morning of 25 October, the same MRC issued a triumphant communiqué:

> The provisional government has been deposed. The state power has passed to the organ of the Petrograd Soviet of Workers' and Soldiers' Deputies—the Military-Revolutionary Committee, which stands at the head of the proletariat and garrison of Petrograd. [1]

No battles had been fought in the short interval between the two communiqués. The Bolsheviks had met no armed resistance in Petrograd. That night it was brought home to the provisional government that it had forfeited the trust of "Soviet democracy" and that no part of the garrison would come to its aid.

The cabinet was still in session at the Winter Palace, in touch by phone and telegraph with the city, the provinces, and the Stavka (general headquarters). Not until midnight did some Bolsheviks invade the palace and arrest the ministers. The premier, A. F. Kerensky, escaped from Petrograd, hoping to meet the troops he had called out and to return to the capital at their head. A week later, his mission a failure, he went into hiding.

Actually, the Bolsheviks were not yet in control even in Petrograd, let alone in the provinces. Yet on the very next day there was not in the entire country a single agency acting in the name of the provisional government. Not a single group of any authority asserted itself, even briefly, in a limited territory, to oppose the Soviet of People's Commissars and lay claim to governing the country.

The Menshevik leaders, both of the right and left, had expected and feared the Bolshevik seizure of power. While aware of the masses' enthusiasm for the Bolsheviks' promises, they also believed that the Bolsheviks would not be able to negotiate a "democratic" peace with Germany, resolve the economic crisis, and introduce a socialist order. They predicted that the Bolsheviks would have to surrender to Germany and that this might lead to Russia's involvement in the war against the Western Allies. They foresaw that the soldiers, once demobilized, and the peasantry, once in possession of land, would turn against the Bolsheviks; and that the attempt to implant socialism in a backward country would be resisted by the peasantry and most of the urban population. Only by "blood and iron" would a Bolshevik government be able to rule. Having cut itself off from democratic elements, it would "inevitably turn into the worst kind of dictatorship, a minority government relying on bayonets, repressing the free will of the people, for it quite rightly does not believe in its own ability to fulfill all the promises of peace, bread, and freedom."[2] Yet even "blood and iron" would not keep the Bolsheviks in power: the Red terror would pave the way for a reactionary regime and White terror.

In many provincial cities the workers were still pro-Menshevik. Even in Moscow and Petrograd not a great many, and few mature ones, had taken part in the overturn as members of the Red Guard. It was obvious, however, that in the capitals the workers on the whole favored the Bolsheviks and would support the Soviet of People's Commissars, which had so easily overthrown the disappointing provisional government.

The Mensheviks distinguished between "advanced workers" who shared their views and were "trained in traditional Marxist theory" and the masses "blindly" embracing maximalist slogans. We read in one of the first appeals of the Central Committee of the Russian Social-Democratic Labor Party (United) (RSDRP[0])[3] to come out after the overturn, "To the Workers of Petrograd": "*Conscious workers* must firmly dissociate themselves from the Bolshevik venture. They must explain to the working masses the duplicity and demagoguery of the Bolsheviks, who have won over *the working masses* by flattery and unrealizable promises."[4] The existence of pro-Bolshevik sentiments among Moscow and Petrograd workers was admitted even by the Right Mensheviks, including the groups that still hoped for the restoration of the provisional government.

Under such conditions, the Menshevik organizations of these cities would not have taken part in armed action against the Bolsheviks even had they had a sufficient following. They visualized the struggle rather as competition for influence over the workers. They also hoped that the Social-Democratic elements among the Bolsheviks would prevail over the maximalists who supported Lenin. There seemed to be no other way to overcome Lenin peacefully, to avoid a civil war and the terrorist reactionary regime that was likely to follow it.

Gaining time was of the essence—time for the masses to sober up and for the Bolshevik opposition to get the better of Lenin. Therefore "recognition" of the Sovnarkom as the legal government had to be withheld, but without opposing to it another new government,[5] to keep up the appearances of negotiations about a central government and prolong the indefinite situation. Under cover of the talks and of various organizations that called on the local population to "rally" around them until a new government was formed, provincial authorities could still operate freely wherever Mensheviks were influential and yet maintain with the Sovnarkom the minimal contact necessary even under the prevailing conditions of extreme decentralization and administrative chaos.

Some Mensheviks favored a government of all socialist parties including the Bolsheviks; others, a socialist government without them; still others, a "broad coalition." Even so, their polemics caused no serious organizational rift since all agreed in their assessment of the situation. Iu. O. Martov, the leader of the Internationalist wing, observed that even most Right Mensheviks tended to be very cautious about fighting the Bolsheviks, for fear of taking part in destroying the proletariat.

The Mensheviks and all other democratic socialists in Russia never again rose to power after their defeat in October. It is, however, an open question whether their hopes were entirely illusory and their strategy entirely unrealistic. The anti-Bolshevik tide they had foreseen did begin to rise among the workers toward the end of 1917. In November the revolt against Lenin in the Bolshevik party surpassed their expectations and almost split the leadership that had just carried out a successful overturn. What the Mensheviks had not foreseen was Lenin's surrender to Germany, the willingness of imperial Germany to recognize and support his regime, and the terrorism that was to outrage the world.

1

The Basic Currents in Menshevism

The First World War had caused profound disagreements in all the socialist parties of Europe: the Mensheviks had divided into Internationalists and Defensists (*Oborontsy*). The former predominated among the émigrés and took part in the Zimmerwald and Kienthal conferences of the European socialist groups of the left. The entire Menshevik center abroad, the so-called Secretariat Abroad of the Organizational Committee of the RSDRP, [1] took the Internationalist stand, as did, in Russia, the Menshevik faction of the Duma and many Party members in Siberian exile (for example, F. I. Dan and I. G. Tsereteli).

Many among the factory workers of Petrograd and the Party intelligentsia in Russia favored defensism. Menshevik Defensists played a leading role in creating and guiding the "Workers' Groups" attached to the War Industries committees. [2] As these groups grew into militant centers of struggle for the workers' interests and of active political opposition to the tsarist regime, they gradually gained acceptance even among the Menshevik Duma members and other Menshevik Internationalists in Russia. By 1917 the dissention between Menshevik Internationalists and Defensists had lost much of its sharpness, [3] though not in émigré circles.

Some minor factions on the extreme left flank of menshevism, for instance the so-called Initiative Group (*Initsiativnaia Gruppa*) in Petrograd, did keep away from the Workers' Groups. So did the extreme right of the Defensists, clustered around Potresov and the paper *Den'*: the growing radicalism of the groups seemed to them extremely dangerous at a time when winning the war should be considered the main national objective.

The February Revolution naturally united those Menshevik Defensists who had accepted the Zimmerwald idea of peace without annexations and indemnities and those Menshevik Internationalists who now wanted to defend revolutionary Russia. This new bloc of "Revolutionary Defensists" became the "center" that dominated the Party from February to October, determined the policy of the Soviets, and to some extent the government's. [4] Its efforts to end the war were opposed by the extreme Defensists, whose leader, Potresov, had evolved a complex Marxist explanation for his stand.

A. N. Potresov had been one of the founders of the Party and one of the "young" editors of *Iskra*. Yet in 1917, when Lenin was the Bolshevik leader and Martov the undisputed leader of the Menshevik Internationalists, Potresov did not become the head of the Defensist wing of menshevism. Though most of the 222 delegates at the Party Congress of August 1917 were Defensists, only nine voted for a resolution offered by Potresov. [5]

Toward the end of 1917, the Potresovites vainly tried to split the party. P. Ia. Golikov, an outspoken supporter of Potresov, active in the Menshevik organization of Petrograd Province, actually ended his speech at the December Congress with the words, "Hail to a split." In the elections to the Constituent Assembly in Petrograd and Kharkov the Potresovites had their own list of candidates, separate from the Party's; in Moscow, many prominent Mensheviks sympathized with them. [6] Yet there are hardly any references in the contemporary press to provincial Menshevik organizations supporting Potresov. (One of the few exceptions is the weekly *Mysl'*, which began publication in Astrakhan in October.) [7]

But it would be a mistake to judge the specific weight of Potresov's movement merely by the number of people who supported it at Party congresses or in the executive organs of Soviets. Other factors came into play: Potresov's role in the history of the Party, his brilliant intellectual gifts, his influence among the Menshevik workers of Petrograd; finally, the sympathies of the Menshevik ministers in Kerensky's last cabinet, who were spiritually closer to Potresov's group than to the Revolutionary Defensists and the majority of the Party's Central Committee.

Standing entirely outside the Party organization though headed by G. V. Plekhanov, the founder of Russian social democracy, the group Edinstvo ("Unity") was still more extremely Defensist. For them, winning the war was not the main but the *sole* task of the moment. Consequently this group and the Menshevik party, including the Revolutionary Defensists, shunned each other. *Rabochaia Gazeta* of 25 May 1917 commented on the "bad joke" history had played on Plekhanov: "She had caused him—he who had been the first to map out the correct path to a revolution—to oppose the revolutionary movement with all the weight of his authority during the war; and when the revolution had come, without him and despite him, [history] set him aside from the struggle, leaving him only one solace: griping."

No representative of *Edinstvo* became a member of the Executive Committee of the Petrograd Soviet, although the committee gave key positions to the relatively small, extremely Defensist-minded group of *Trudoviki and Narodnye Sotsialisty* (NSs).[8] In July 1917, when invitations to the Unification Congress of the RSDRP were sent to all Social-Democratic organizations, Plekhanov's group was not included.[9] It simply played no role in the fortunes of menshevism at that time.

Serious opposition to the Revolutionary Defensists emerged from the left only in May 1917, when Martov and his followers returned from abroad. Menshevik Internationalists gained influence in the organizations of Moscow, Kharkov, and the Donets Basin, among others. In the early summer a "Central Informational Bureau of Menshevik Internationalists" was formed. (Comprising some twenty members, it was rather like a discussion club operating on a high intellectual level.) There was also a "Secretariat of the Central Bureau of Menshevik Internationalists,"[10] which does not seem to have functioned very regularly.

The Party daily, *Rabochaia Gazeta*, was first published jointly by the Mensheviks' Organizational Committee, or OC (*Organizatsionnyi Komitet*, or *OK*, as the Menshevik Central Committee (CC) was called until the August "Unification" Congress), and the Party's Petrograd organization. But Martov soon persuaded the latter to dissociate itself from this newspaper because of its promotion of defensism. From issue no. 63, 24 May the Petrograd Organization no longer appeared on the masthead.[11] The Revolutionary Defensists and the Menshevik Internationalists also sent separate delegations to the so-called Third Zimmerwald Conference in Stockholm (Ermanskii and Martynov represented the Internationalists).[12]

At the Unification Congress (see Appendix A), on 24 August, Martov announced in the name of twenty-six delegates that they would take part in the elections of the Party's new Central Committee and present candidates for it, but "reserved the right to criticize the Party's decisions to the masses." Tsereteli objected that no one who thus refused in advance to recognize the authority of the CC should run for election to it. So many of Martov's own comrades in the Menshevik Internationalist faction (delegates from Petrograd, Moscow, Odessa, Tver, and Tula among them) disagreed with his stand that he was able to speak for only twenty-six members of his faction out of a total of about sixty. Nevertheless, he won. After long negotiations, the congress accepted a compromise suggested by Abramovich: not to vote at all on Tsereteli's resolution to enforce Party discipline but start electing the CC right away. And not only Martov but also Martynov and Semkovskii, who had supported him, were among the eight Internationalists elected to the CC.

The unusual compliance of the congress can partly be explained by Martov's personal glamor and authority: most of the delegates did not want the Party to lose him. But the congress may also have given in to him because the Revolutionary Defensists had come to doubt their own views about Kerensky's government and the future of the revolution. Their new attitude would become manifest after the congress, during the Kornilov affair and the ensuing governmental crisis. By September the Central Committee was passing resolutions concerning the government that Martov could approve. Within three weeks he would be selected as the official spokesman for the Menshevik faction of the Democratic Conference, and Tsereteli, for the minority, would criticize its stand. Thus it is quite possible that at the congress many Revolutionary Defensists may already have felt some sympathy for Martov's position—enough at least to recoil from facing him with the option of changing it or leaving the Party. A sense of basic agreement on ultimate aims helped the congress to disregard the factional, almost schismatic, declarations of Martov and his group.

Martov also got his way within the group of the twenty-six adamant Internationalists he had led at the congress. Its left flank demanded a clean break with the Defensists and withdrawal from the Party, which had just reaffirmed its support of them. But Martov's charm and authority kept the group together (besides, he had just won his followers the right to oppose the majority publicly). The extremists did not secede. They were still in the Party at the time of the overturn, notwithstanding inevitable and often sharp clashes during September and October. Despite murmurings about his stand on Party discipline, and his own considerable intolerance toward those who did not share his views, Martov also remained throughout these months the ideologist and leader of the more moderate Menshevik Internationalists. [13]

A few Internationalist organizations to the left of the Menshevik Internationalists preferred not to belong to the Menshevik party after the Unification Congress. Their large daily, *Novaia Zhizn*, founded by

Maxim Gorky in 1917, was militantly Internationalist; it attacked the Revolutionary Defensists and urged the government and the Soviet to adopt an active policy to end the war through the combined efforts of the warring countries' popular masses. At the same time, it firmly dissociated itself from the demagogy of the Bolsheviks. This was the only mass newspaper for which Martov wrote during the revolution. Other Menshevik Internationalists, e.g., Dallin and Rozhkov, as well as some Bolsheviks, Krasin and Krestinskii, also contributed to it.

Novaia Zhizn was ostensibly the ideological center of the "United Internationalists," or "United Social-Democrats (Internationalists)," but the various groups supporting it had no common organizational center. The "Central Bureau of the United S-D Internationalists," which sometimes signed public statements, had no formal authority. It believed that it represented only the "advanced," "conscious," elements of the Russian labor movement and hoped that these elements would eventually merge with a reunited RSDRP. In June the *Novaia Zhizn* coterie, making use of the presence in Petrograd of provincial delegates to the Congress of Soviets, had called a meeting of those S-Ds among them who were not yet reconciled to the RSDRP's division into Bolsheviks and Mensheviks. The meeting, on 18 June, elected an "Organizational Bureau to Prepare the Convocation of a Social-Democratic Unification Congress." The new bureau was housed in the *Novaia Zhizn* building. [14]

The "United Social-Democrats Internationalists" took part in preparing the Menshevik Unification Congress, and their representative N. Stroev was elected to its Presidium. As it turned out, however, the congress did not meet the expectations of these groups. It reaffirmed the Party's Defensist stand: continued participation in the coalition government, and preservation of the fighting capacity of the army. "Struggle for peace" was mentioned only in general terms. "All the elements of the bourgeoisie" willing to support "a resolute democratic policy" were to be drawn in to help solve the problems of the revolution. The editors of *Novaia Zhizn* and twelve provincial delegates, noting that the congress had not met its task of "creating a united, revolutionary, and Internationalist party of the working class," refused to join the "united" party formed at the congress, leaving the final decision to the organizations that had delegated them. Consequently they did not vote in the elections to the Central Committee. [15] A resolution, offered by Avilov, received the votes of twenty delegates representing 14,000 members, [16] out of the total of 222 delegates representing 207,000.

Only a few of these groups later joined the Mensheviks. One of them was the group under the leadership of A. P. Pinkevich that ran the "Free Labor" circles in various cities of the Petrograd region. The organization of the Moscow S-D Internationalists ("Moscow United Social-Democratic Organization") decided at its conference on 8 September to remain independent—that is, not to join the Menshevik organization in the city. For the Mensheviks this was a disappointment. Internationalists predominated in their own Moscow organization, and relations were so friendly that in June the Moscow Mensheviks had included many S-D Internationalists in the list of RSDRP candidates for the city Duma. At the Unification Congress, both the Mensheviks and the delegates of the Moscow Internationalists had been so sure of imminent union that two of the latter, N. Rozhkov and V. Iakhontov, had been elected to the Central Committee of the Party. In September Rozhkov chose to leave his organization and remain in the CC; Iakhontov left the CC. Soon, however—in early October, when a conference of the Moscow S-D Internationalists rejected his proposal to support the Menshevik ticket for the Constituent Assembly—Iakhontov and fourteen other delegates (of a total of sixty) walked out and joined the Menshevik organization. [17]

The Moscow United Social-Democratic Organization, as we have noted, was an organization of the "United S-D Internationalists" and operated in competition with the regular Bolshevik and Menshevik organizations in the city. Other "United" organizations, or organizations of "Uniteds," had been established *instead* by regular, if independent-minded, S-D organizations in an effort to overcome, on a local scale, the schism between Bolsheviks and Mensheviks. All currents in social democracy were usually represented in these, and Revolutionary Defensists actually predominated in most. During 1917, "United" organizations continued to operate only until local Bolsheviks, yielding to Lenin's pressure, succeeded in subordinating them to the Bolshevik Central Committee, or, if they failed to do so, created in competition with them new Bolshevik organizations, often with the help of soldiers of local garrisons.

Of the fifty-two organizations represented at the All-Russian Menshevik Conference in May 1917, twenty-seven had been listed as "Menshevik" and twenty-five as "United." [18] In mid-July, the CC published a list of provincial Party papers; twenty of them were Menshevik and only thirteen "United." Of the latter, nine were in Siberia and only four in European Russia—in Odessa, Vitebsk, Ufa, and Elizavetgrad. [19] Important organizations like those of Rostov-on-the-Don and Nizhnii Novgorod, placed among the "United" in May, figured as Menshevik in July.

The Unification Congress, which nominally created the "United Party," basically represented only Menshevik organizations. The old Menshevik Organizational Committee became the Central Committee of the RSDRP(0). Formally, all Menshevik organizations from 27 August 1917 were parts of the new RSDRP(0). In practice, however, the "United" ones that had existed earlier either split or were supplanted by Menshevik ones. In some provincial capitals of European Russia the process of disintegration of the "United" organizations was slower, and independent Bolshevik and Menshevik organizations were not formed until shortly before the October overturn. In Odessa, for instance, this occurred only in October 1917. In Riazan, the Bolsheviks withdrew from the "United" organization on 4 October. In Penza, they left the provincial conference of the RSDRP(0) on 9 October when, according to Bolshevik sources, "considerable masses of workers and soldiers still trusted the Mensheviks and SRs." In Pskov, the provincial Social-Democratic conference on 28 September drew up a list of candidates for the Constituent Assembly with a Menshevik Defensist heading the list, a Menshevik Internationalist in second place, and a Bolshevik in third. [20]

Outside the main centers of the labor movement, Bolsheviks could be found in United organizations even after October. In Vologda, the pro-Bolshevik members of the United organization—probably few in number—supported the demand for a government of all the socialist parties. In Mogilev, despite a visit by L. Kaganovich in the early fall, the "Bolshevik faction" decided "not to split the United organization." The split occurred only after the October overturn, and the faction was subordinated to the Bolshevik CC on 20 December. [21]

Yet the word "United," which had been added to the Menshevik party's name, had become patently inaccurate even before the "Unification" Congress closed. It could be defended only from a formal point of view, [22] and was used mainly in official documents; in the press and in public appeals it was soon replaced by the old, unambiguous "Menshevik." When *Vpered* became the organ of the CC after the latter moved to Moscow in early 1918, the paper was described as the organ of the RSDRP (Menshevik). On 13 April 1918, after the Bolsheviks had changed the name of their party to "Communist," the Menshevik CC decided to return to the old designation "RSDRP," without the addition of either "Menshevik" or "United." [23]

The wish for unity had run strong in the labor movement throughout the "February" period, and it was not to die easily even after October. At bottom, it sprang from the belief that the working class had to remain united if it were to fulfill its historical role. Therefore, although it increasingly clashed with reality, all parts of Russian social democracy in 1917 had paid some lip service to the masses' yearning for a single, united labor party. The Bolsheviks, intent on preserving the unity of the "left-Zimmerwald" position, had confined themselves to inviting the Menshevik Internationalists to participate in their Sixth Congress. [24] The *Novaia Zhizn* group, as we have seen, had taken part in setting up the Menshevik's Unification Congress, though their own utopian aim was to unite into one party the Bolsheviks, the Menshevik Internationalists, and those Defensists who would submit to the probable Internationalist majority of this improbable party. The Menshevik Internationalists had sent greetings to the Bolshevik Sixth Congress, despite Martov's old mistrust of Lenin. Indeed, their left wing had dreamed of a party that would "chop off its long tail of confirmed reformists and rabid social-patriots"—though aware that this was "easier said than done" [25] and that they themselves would not be bold enough to perform the amputation.

In the Menshevik camp only Potresov and his followers had opposed from the outset the idea of a single party, denying its progressive role. Potresov had not recovered from the shock he had received in 1915, when the German invasion had "aroused even the most stagnant elements of bourgeois society" but "awakened nothing in the proletarian masses," no response worthy of the "most revolutionary class of today's society." The "class instinct" of the Russian workers had not inspired the right conduct; nor could this instinct be trusted to correct the position of their Social-Democratic party. At heart, the Russian worker was still a backward peasant; his class instinct had not turned into "a developed class consciousness that would help him to take part in building a new state order." The reason, according to Potresov, lay in "Russia's heartbreaking history since the sixteenth or seventeenth century," which had made Russian society a mixture of Europe and Asia, and the Russian civic movement "a kind of grimace of history ...resembling the triumphal procession of European civilization on some Fiji Island." This explained the "strange stand of the Russian proletariat in the matter of the country's defense," which revealed abysmal indifference to the country's fate. [26] Potresov begged his comrades to resist the dream of party unity: it fed on a common history, but despite "the seeming identity of the basic theoretical premises of Marxism" no program could be worked out on which Defensists and Internationalists could agree. He ridiculed those who imagined that "unity can be invented." The pursuit of impossible unity would only put the Mensheviks in the company of the "flatterers of the proletariat" who corrupted the masses by "catering to all their low instincts." The accepted theories should be critically revised. Far more important than the supposed links between the factions of the long since divided Social-Democratic party was the new common approach to current problems that had enabled Marxist and populist Defensists to work fruitfully together despite differences of principle. [27]

But the Revolutionary Defensists, who had worked hand in hand with the SRs during the "February" period of the revolution, were not prepared, for all that, to give up the idea of a united Social-Democratic party. Dan had begun his speech at the April Conference of Soviets with the announcement that he was speaking for "the Menshevik part of the RSDRP." In early May 1917, the "United" organization of Rostov-on-the-Don, in which Revolutionary Defensists of a rightist hue predominated, had declared that it had always aspired to "unification of all the Social-Democratic forces." Noting that "the CC [that is, the Bolsheviks] does not advocate unification of the S-D organizations, whereas the OC [that is, the Mensheviks] definitely takes that stand"—it had decided to link up with the OC, urging it to work for party unity. [28] Two weeks before the October overturn, B. S. Kibrik referred in the Moscow *Vpered* to the Menshevik "part of social democracy." Even after October, despite the obvious fictitiousness of the conception of a united RSDRP, the Menshevik CC preferred not to give it up as a goal, an "ideal." The masses were attached to it, and the CC probably feared that if the Mensheviks gave it up this would look like a surrender of the party banner to the Bolsheviks. Even this purely formal devotion to a party that existed only in fantasy must have weakened the Mensheviks in their struggle with the Bolsheviks.

2

The Mensheviks and the Provisional Government

The Views of Menshevik Defensists and Menshevik Internationalists on Participation in Government

The "bourgeois character" of the Russian revolution was a basic credo of all Russian Social-Democrats. According to the theory evolved by the founders of Russian Marxism, and in which the Mensheviks of 1917 had been reared, the RSDRP was to "instill more courage" in the bourgeois opponents of tsarism, "revolutionize" them, "push them on" to the seizure of power. But "Social democracy must not set itself the aim of seizing or sharing power" and should remain throughout this stage the party of "extreme opposition."[1]

Socialists should enter the government only when they could begin to carry out their "program-maximum," that is, build a socialist state. Until the bourgeois revolution had extirpated all remnants of feudalism and a broad capitalist economy had developed, the working class and its party would lack the cadres required to govern successfully. Moreover, with socialists in the government, the masses would expect radical reforms that could not be fitted into a capitalist order and for which the country was not ready. Enmity would develop between the disappointed masses and nonsocialist groups; possible allies would recoil from the working class and join the reactionary enemies of the revolution. M. I. Liber, who soon became one of the leaders of the

15

Revolutionary Defensists, expressed these ideas at the First Congress of Soviets, and counseled "moderating one's impulses," "falling in step with all of toiling democracy," not merely the proletariat of the capitals. At the Bund Conference in April 1917, he firmly opposed the idea of Mensheviks in government. [2]

Yet in May 1917, in the third month of the revolution, the Mensheviks felt *obliged* to enter the government; without socialists in it, it clearly lacked the authority to rule. I. G. Tsereteli and M. I. Skobelev became ministers in the new cabinet. Both were on the executive committee of the Petrograd Soviet and active members of the new bloc of Revolutionary Defensists. (Until February, both had been Internationalists.) As the Mensheviks kept pointing out, the Amsterdam Congress of the Socialist International in August 1904 had passed a resolution admitting socialist participation in bourgeois governments in exceptional cases. Nevertheless, the Revolutionary Defensists were uneasy about their decision and constantly felt compelled to explain and justify it. [3]

The Menshevik Internationalists remained opposed to participation in government. During the parleys that followed the resignation of Foreign Minister P. N. Miliukov and resulted in the first coalition government, they were not yet an important group. They could afford to repeat the old argument that pressure from the Soviets, not socialists in the government, would compel the provisional government to abandon Miliukov's policy and work for peace. By the time of the second ministerial crisis (which resulted on 8 July in the second coalition, with A. F. Kerensky as premier), they had realized that pressure from the Soviets was not enough. Refusal to participate in the government meant leaving the field to the Kadets (Constitutional-Democratic Party) and other representatives of the propertied classes—which clearly made no political sense. Yet by accepting the obligation to preserve the coalition, the socialist ministers and their supporters had in fact given the Kadets a veto over their own power to act. Thus the Menshevik Internationalists in turn came to revise the traditional stand, from their own point of view: since one could not leave the field to those who sabotaged every curative measure, the coalition must be abandoned—not by retiring from power but by taking it over entirely, forming a homogeneous, all-socialist government. The Menshevik Internationalists regarded the World War as a general crisis of capitalism and the beginning of *a new era*. This seemed to justify the revision of a theory evolved in a past, peaceful era.

An opportunity to form a noncoalition government seemed to present itself on 2 July, when the Kadet ministers resigned and Prince

G. E. Lvov left the post of premier, but it was lost because of the Bolshevik-led July demonstrations in Petrograd.[4] The historian N. A. Rozhkov, who in 1917 was a member of the Menshevik Central Committee, describes as follows the mood of the Menshevik Internationalists: "Much became clear after the break with the Kadets during the night of 2–3 July. The old illusions about possible collaboration between revolutionary democracy and the bourgeoisie seemed finished." The Bolsheviks were offering agreement, but there was much irritation against them, and their armed action of 3–5 July increased it. Most Mensheviks and SRs feared that agreement with the Bolsheviks would stimulate the growing reactionary movement. They also hoped for a turn in the masses' mood after the unsuccessful Bolshevik demonstration. As a result of all this, "the fear of being isolated prevailed once more, the lack of confidence in their own strength, the old prejudices." And the moment was critical. *"Perhaps for the last time* there was a chance to realize the revolutionary program of 6 May–8 July and thus save the revolution and assure the convocation and activity of the Constituent Assembly."[5]

Martov explained at the Unification Congress in August that the Internationalists' changed stand had been prompted mainly by the nonsocialist ministers' systematic opposition to all attempts to end the war and all proposals of agrarian and economic reform. No "pressure" from the Soviets had been able to overcome this opposition. The business classes were "gradually ranging themselves under the banner of counterrevolution," along with the landowners and the military caste. The Mensheviks had not expected the revolutionary role of the bourgeoisie to end so soon: within a few weeks, a counterrevolutionary bourgeoisie had "united around the motto of imperialist annexations." The past six months had convinced him, Martov stated, that the bourgeoisie was not interested in a democratic restructuring of the country. There had been no signs of the struggle between the liberal bourgeoisie and the landowner class that the labor movement was supposed to use for its own ends.

> At present we can observe certain segments of the bourgeoisie rapidly going over to the camp of reaction; this has happened...with Shul'gin's group, and Konovalov's, and others. At this stage of the revolution...the Russian bourgeoisie is no longer a revolutionary factor. The further conquests of the revolution will be made without it and against it.[6]

Martov maintained that the coalition government was "highly unstable" and would inevitably fall apart. The petty bourgeoisie in town and village leaned toward "union and agreement with the propertied classes in order to save the revolution and the country," but in fact the revolution could be saved only by fighting the propertied classes. Social-Democrats must make this clear to the petty bourgeoisie and convince it of the danger of its illusions. The governmental combination of socialists and Kadets hampered the political self-definition of the small urban and rural bourgeoisie. Martov put this very forcefully in his closing speech:

> We are being asked where our support is. The proletariat's task is to hasten the political maturation of the petty bourgeoisie and to free it from the influence of the bourgeoisie—and you are dragging back revolutionary democracy. *It is the task of the revolution to help the small bourgeoisie conquer power.* Otherwise everything will crash. This is the only Marxist tactic [italics added].

The Menshevik Internationalists thought there would be another chance to form a "homogeneous" government without Kadets and other capitalist groups when the "highly unstable" coalition collapsed once more. They did not intend to force events since conditions were not ripe for the kind of reorganization they had in mind. A resolution offered by Martov, however, made the point that prolonged stagnation under the coalition government was working in favor of the Bolsheviks: it was time to combat "the adventurist and anarchic tendencies in the labor movement" and to warn the masses against "anarchistic slogans and disruptive demonstrations."

To Potresov, who still believed that Russia's interests demanded continuation of the war, Martov threw a remark of uncanny prescience: "If a clique with the slogan of peace appeared today, it would *conquer the masses and put them in iron shackles*" (italics added).

Just before the Democratic Conference, Martov returned to the problem of achieving the aims of the bourgeois revolution without the bourgeoisie.[7] Marx, he said, had understood very early in the German revolution of 1848 that the big bourgeoisie had become reactionary, that the further development of the bourgeois revolution was possible only to the extent that social conditions encouraged all the democratic strata of society to combine into an independent political force—and then only if these strata had enough "Jacobin" will to fight side by side with the emerging proletariat against the propertied classes. These conditions had been lacking in the Germany of 1848. There were reasons to expect more favorable ones in the Russia of 1917. The defection of the "census elements"[8] and "the deep antagonism between all of the propertied classes and all of democracy over the treatment of the agrarian and other problems" *might* convince the petty bourgeoisie of town and village that only "a close alliance with the proletariat and a clean break with the capitalist bourgeoisie" could lead "to land, to a democratic republic, and save the country from the vise of the imperialist war." By breaking up the coalition, the Bolsheviks meant to bring about a socialist revolution or "at least a transitional one between the bourgeois-democratic and the proletarian socialist"; to the objective of state power "in the hands of all of democracy" they were substituting the seizure of power by "the proletarian minority of democracy" to "leap" beyond the historical limits of the bourgeois revolution.

Thus the Bolsheviks and the masses under their spell were putting a dangerously utopian content into the motto of democratic government. But the motto itself was sound, in line with the task of uniting the workers and the urban and rural petty bourgeoisie. Martov saw a parallel between the past relations of the S-D party with the SRs and its present relations with the Bolsheviks. The S-Ds had rejected the politically correct SR slogan "All the land to the people"—because the SRs connected it with the utopian concept of a nonbourgeois, semisocialist revolution—and had thereby scuttled their chances of "reaching an understanding with the peasantry and the peasant-minded part of the proletariat." It would be equally wrong to reject the now-correct slogan of political rupture with the bourgeoisie merely because the Bolsheviks related it to the utopian idea of rupture with the bourgeois revolution. With "all of democracy in power," a new bourgeoisie would emerge from the squalls of revolution. This had happened in England and France and would happen in Russia. Martov asked his readers to take a closer look at "the political figures among the urban and rural democracy that is now coming to the fore as the carrier of revolutionary development": they would see that a new bourgeoisie was in the making and that "all will go as it should if only we don't slip up."

"The danger of a maximalist, utopian understanding of political possibilities by the masses is undoubtedly very great at present," Martov admitted. "But one doesn't dive into the river to get out of the rain." The danger could not be averted by telling the masses that they must allow the capitalist classes to "stop the development of the revolution"—this too was a utopian idea, the "utopia of possibilism."

The novelty of Martov's stand and the imprecise formulation of its political inferences combined with fear of Bolshevik treachery to weaken his arguments. To be sure, on 7 July 1917 a conference of central bureaus and boards of trade unions and members of factory committees in Petrograd had unanimously adopted (with four abstentions) a resolution offered by the Mensheviks and (!) the Bolsheviks that was "Martovite" in spirit. It disapproved uncoordinated action at a time when "the organized bourgeoisie has left the ranks of the revolution" and "the workers' and peasants' democracy must henceforth *alone* lead the revolution to victory."[9] But a week later, an all-city conference of the Petrograd Menshevik organization, which usually followed Martov, passed a resolution offered by the Menshevik Organizational Committee, defeating Martov's—just barely, it is true (37 to 36 votes).

When the Unification Congress of the RSDRP opened (on 18 August 1917), it still appeared that the Bolsheviks would not be able to overcome—at any rate in the provinces—the effects of their July demonstration. The Kornilov uprising, which at once increased their chances, had not yet occurred. Most of the delegates at the congress still held on to the idea of "a government of the bourgeois revolution" modified by the coalition in which they had agreed to participate. Generally speaking, the delegates hoped that the provisional government would switch to a policy of peace and that the Western socialist parties would overcome "the resistance of imperialists of all countries, who are dragging out the war to the point of the peoples' complete exhaustion." The resolution adopted after Liber's report stated further that a separate peace would not end the war but, more likely, turn Russia into Germany's unwilling ally.

The congress demanded of the provisional government "decisive reforms" in the regulation of production, transport, distribution, finances, and in labor and agrarian policy. Only then could it "restore and increase the strength of revolutionary Russia, save the country from ruination and defeats, lead it to a democratic *international* peace, and draw into this work all the elements of the bourgeoisie *able to* [adopt] *the determined democratic policy* that *alone* can save the country and win the proletariat's firm support."[10]

Yet many Revolutionary Defensists had come to doubt that such elements existed in the bourgeois parties and that the coalition government would do much for peace and economic recovery. The workers and soldiers in the capitals were clearly succumbing to the Bolsheviks' radical agitation. Just before the congress, the Mensheviks had been badly defeated in the elections to the Petrograd City Duma. The army was falling apart, and there was no progress in the pursuit of peace. In the countryside the situation was becoming critical, yet the nonsocialist ministers continued to block all preparatory measures for the inevitable transfer of land to the peasants. Lacking the boldness to introduce economic reforms, the government simply issued more billions of paper rubles.

On 14 August, N. Chkheidze presented to the State Conference in Moscow a "Declaration of United Democracy" embodying the minimum of reforms that the Menshevik and SR supporters of the coalition government considered indispensable for "saving the country and the revolution" and still acceptable to the bourgeois members of the coalition. Many groups on the right socialist flank had endorsed the declaration, as well as more rightist groups such as cooperatives, the All-Russian Union of Zemstvos and Cities, most of the representatives of city self-governments, unions of government employees, and unions of crippled veterans. [11] The nonsocialist partners in the projected coalition opposed all these reforms—partly as "too complex" to be implemented in the short time remaining until the Constituent Assembly and partly because it was up to the Constituent Assembly to rule on them. [12]

In 1918, A. A. Bublikov (who had been a member of the provisional government and the representative of the Trade and Industry Group at the State Conference) would write that "much of what the Bolsheviks did later could and should have been done by the provisional government": the "basic and fatal characteristic" of this government had been its long resistance to "the creativity of the lower classes." [13]

On 27 August, a lead article in *Rabochaia Gazeta*, surveying the first six months of the revolution, sadly noted the masses' lack of discipline, the propertied classes' inability to make sacrifices and display any kind of statesmanship, the peasant disorders, the disintegration of the army, and the failure of the Russian revolution to affect Europe and "kill the war." The world proletariat was "moving too slowly." Now "we are facing a winter campaign, the threat of economic debacle, counterrevolutionary disorders, internal struggles and conspiracies."

And indeed, the next day, 28 August, the country learned of Kornilov's counterrevolutionary uprising. The danger of conspiracies and internal struggle became even more starkly apparent three days later, when the Petrograd Soviet of Workers' and Soldiers' Deputies, under the impact of the uprising, passed by a majority of 163 votes a resolution offered by Trotsky and became the main base of operations of the Bolsheviks.

The Kornilov Uprising. The Disintegration of the Defensist Bloc

The conspiracy of the commander-in-chief, General L. G. Kornilov, against the government that had appointed him raised unimaginable havoc in the army, effectively destroyed the masses' trust in the officer corps, and contributed to the success of Bolshevik propaganda. The Kadet party was clearly implicated in the plot although several of its members were in the government.

A good many Revolutionary Defensists had already lost faith in the efficacy of coalitions with the bourgeoisie. After the Kadet ministers' resignation, these Mensheviks definitively abandoned the idea of coalition. They were led by B. O. Bogdanov in Petrograd; elsewhere, by other members of the CC or important Revolutionary Defensists such as I. A. Isuv in Moscow and N. N. Zhordania in Tiflis. An influential group of Revolutionary Defensists, headed by I. G. Tsereteli, F. I. Dan, and M. I. Skobelev, did continue to favor a coalition government —as did, of course, Potresov's group of extreme Defensists. But the Central Committee of the RSDRP(0), just elected by the Unification Congress, declared on 31 August that *further participation of Kadets in the government was inadmissible.* [14]

In the small hours of 1 September, the Central Committee of the Party of Socialist Revolutionaries resolved to recall its official representatives in the cabinet if any Kadets remained in it and to notify Kerensky that he could not count on the support of the PSR if he formed a cabinet including Kadets. [15] That day, the SR *Delo Naroda* argued in a lead article that no one who cared for socialism and the revolution could work in a government together with Kadets: they had become spokesmen for the big bourgeoisie of industry and finance and their press campaign had tried to prepare a successful outcome for Kornilov's uprising. The author of the article, not bound by the Menshevik dogma of the bourgeois character of the revolution, went so far as to say that no one but workers, soldiers, and peasants should be represented in the government.

Kerensky had prepared a cabinet that included "Kadets not implicated in the Kornilov affair" but had to give it up in view of the opposition of the Central Committees of both socialist parties. Instead, a provisional five-member directory without Kadets was formed: Kerensky; A. M. Nikitin (a Menshevik Moscow lawyer) for the interior; M. I. Tereshchenko (a Kiev industrialist) for foreign affairs; General A. I. Verkhovskii; and Rear Admiral D. V. Verderevskii.

But there seemed to be no way of forming a complete government to replace the directory. The CC of the RSDRP(0) suggested calling a conference of the democratic organizations for this purpose. Even Martov was reconciled to the directory since it contained no Kadets and since Kerensky had agreed to proclaim a republic. Martov pointed out that the RSDRP(0) and the PSR had been successful when they finally confronted Kerensky with an ultimatum; he hoped that a noncoalition government could be formed under pressure from the projected conference. [16]

Bogdanov's group of Revolutionary Defensists also hoped that Kerensky would agree to a noncoalition government if the conference demanded it; and that such a government, free of ministers who sabotaged reforms and identified with the revolution in the eyes of the masses, would be able to handle the Bolshevik onslaught and immunize the masses against Bolshevik demagogy. The champions of coalition, on the other hand, hoped that the more realistic delegates from the provinces would convince the anticoalitionists that the bulk of the people would not accept a government in which no one but socialists was represented.

During the two weeks between the formation of the directory and the opening of the Democratic Conference on 14 September, both the pro- and the anticoalition groups defined their positions. It became evident that the CC's new anticoalition stand was widely approved by Mensheviks in the provinces. Bogdanov explained it on 31 August in a speech to the Central Executive Committee: the socialist ministers must remain; the posts vacated by the bourgeois ministers must stay vacant until the Democratic Conference, which would also include, along with representatives of Soviets, representatives of provincial dumas, zemstvos, and cooperatives and other public organizations. "Consequently the government established by this conference will have been organized by democracy itself." The new government without bourgeois parties (and apparently without Bolsheviks) would be accountable to the conference or to an organ the conference would elect, and thus to democracy at large.

The demand that the government be accountable to "democracy" was especially popular with anticoalitionists since the "census groups" maintained that the provisional government was the legal heir of the government originally established by the Duma and therefore not accountable to anyone.

Bogdanov observed that the new government would have to be firm in its policy, unafraid of radical reforms—but that it would be a "dictatorship of democracy" and not only of the proletariat and peasantry or of the Soviets (the latter formula was viable in Russia, if at all, only in Petrograd and a few other large cities). He was apparently looking for "correctives" to make the government more palatable to the urban and rural petty-bourgeois masses, while also reminding the proletariat that it had to remain a "government of the bourgeois revolution."

Bogdanov stated that until the Kornilov uprising he himself had been in favor of a coalition government, but since the Kadets had turned out to be the inspirers and ideologues of the uprising, a coalition of the old type had become impossible. There were no *parties* except the socialist that could be included in the government, but there were democratic nonsocialist elements, for example in the cooperatives and in organs of local self-government, which it would be foolish to alienate. The latter would become allies of the Kadets and of reaction if the Mensheviks took it into their heads to set up a government based exclusively on the proletariat and the poor peasant masses. These "democratic parties, whether they are called parties or not, will support us," Bogdanov said, "if we adopt a determined policy in the democratic spirit." [17]

Similar notes were sounded in the theses adopted on 1 September by the Menshevik Internationalists of the Petrograd organization [18] and in Martov's speech to the All-Russian CEC.

Boris Kibrik, a Revolutionary Defensist, explained in the Moscow Soviet of Workers' Deputies on 12 September that the Mensheviks had been in favor of coalition with the Kadet party and with organizations of the business bourgeoisie because these had agreed to carry out the general democratic program, and as long as it seemed likely that they would do so. Now, however, it was necessary to cast out those who had backed Kornilov or failed to make clear that they were against him. [19]

Most members of the Menshevik CC apparently visualized the "homogeneous" government of socialist parties that the Democratic Conference was to create as a government *without Bolsheviks.* Dan wrote in 1922 that in September 1917 a government including Bolsheviks, NSs, and right SRs was unthinkable; a government including Bolsheviks could come to power only against the will of "non-Soviet democracy"; *all* branches of menshevism were "fully aware" that such a government would lead to terror and civil war; "*none of us* [italics added] considered it possible to take responsibility for *that* kind of policy of a noncoalition government."

Bogdanov stressed that the new government must not become a "dictatorship of Soviets." Martov had backed the motto "All power to the Soviets" in late June, when the Bolsheviks were in the minority in most Soviets, but in September in his article in *Iskra*, no. 2, he offered instead the motto "All power to democracy." Apparently he, too, did not plan to include the Bolsheviks in the new government.

Dan recounts that in September the Bolsheviks tried to persuade the Defensist Presidium of the CEC to take power, but when they were asked whether they would support the government until the Constituent Assembly, the Bolsheviks replied that they would support it only for three to four weeks, until the Congress of Soviets. This would suggest that they had not been invited to *participate* in the noncoalition government. [20]

Tsereteli and Dan, the two Menshevik Soviet leaders best known to the country, and other members of the "Star Chamber," the inner circle that until the Kornilov uprising set the policy of the Central Executive Committee of the Soviets, found themselves in the minority in the Menshevik CC. They still believed that a coalition government including Kadets was the only realistic possibility under existing military, political, and economic conditions.[21] They knew that Kerensky did not want to, and in fact could not, form a cabinet without the only nonsocialist party, to which all the competent bourgeois statesmen belonged; and they feared that an all-socialist government would raise the masses' hopes for a socialist order. Lacking confidence in their own ability to govern, they found the theory of the bourgeois character of the Russian revolution a reassuring excuse for their mood.

Dan, Tsereteli, and Skobelev probably thought that a government of Mensheviks, SRs, and "non-Soviet democracy" would not be able to stay in power. Possibly they also foresaw that the Bolsheviks would soon dynamite a government into which they had been admitted and seize full power.[22]

On 1 September, at a joint meeting of the CEC and the executive committee of the Soviet of Peasants' Deputies, Tsereteli and Skobelev declared their dissent with the decision not to admit Kadets into the government, which the Menshevik CC had reached the day before. Tsereteli suggested a small change in the common resolution of the Menshevik and SR factions, formulated in accordance with the separate resolutions of the Central Committees of the two parties: he wanted to cut the phrase about excluding Kadets because they were in fact already excluded.[23] Skobelev said that certain bourgeois groups might well have participated in the Kornilov movement, but the majority probably had not. "Therefore we have *no right* to exclude them completely from the government." While Tsereteli's argument begged the question, Skobelev sounded more like a defense counsel in a criminal trial than a statesman looking for partners to share power.[24]

The discussion of Kadet participation in government really concerned the deeper question of whether to abandon the coalition policy altogether.

The Revolutionary Defensists who opposed coalition had concluded that the bourgeois leaders had already turned away from the revolution, that after the Kornilov affair the workers' and soldiers' mistrust of all nonsocialist groups had intensified and that collaboration with such groups would result in the ruin of the revolution.[25] This view clashed with the Marxist conception, Skobelev reproachfully pointed out on 1 September to his comrades in the CEC, the Revolutionary Defensists who had "undergone a mental revolution" in the past few days.

Bogdanov and the majority of the CC, who at first had proposed merely a "corrective" about the inadmissibility of Kadets, must have realized that the Kadets were the main, if not the only, nonsocialist party with any claim to participation in government. Thus the "corrective" brought them up against the necessity of abandoning the very idea of coalition and putting a purely socialist government at the head of the "bourgeois revolution."

The New Party Majority against Coalition. The Democratic Conference

On 7 September the Menshevik faction of the Central Executive Committee, which had always consisted mainly of Revolutionary Defensists, approved the stand of the Central Committee of the Party, rejected two resolutions offered by partisans of coalition (Potresov and Dan), and adopted Bogdanov's resolution, supported by the Internationalists and demanding a government "*directly* speaking for all the broad strata of the population, based on them, and *responsible* to them," which would organize simultaneously the country's defense and large-scale efforts for peace.[26]

A resolution adopted on the same day at a meeting of party workers of the Petrograd organization also attempted to satisfy both the Internationalists and those Revolutionary Defensists who had lost faith in coalition. It noted that although "the present revolution is a bourgeois revolution," continued coalition with the Kadets and other "census" groups would mean "further capitulation of democracy to the counter-revolutionary strata of the propertied classes." What was needed was a government accountable to "a permanent representation of democracy" (that is, the Democratic Conference or an organ it would create), a government willing to carry out "the program of revolutionary democracy" and, while "organizing firm resistance to enemy invasion," to "energetically struggle [?] with the Allied governments for peace." Coalition with "the already organized elements of census Russia" meant abandoning the "repeatedly declared program of reform" and feeding "the growth of anarchic, rebellious sentiments" in the masses. The coalition was actually "fostering the idea of proletarian dictatorship, unrealizable in economically backward Russia."[27]

On 10 September, the Moscow Menshevik Committee also came out for a socialist government to run the bourgeois revolution: the Kornilov affair had shown that there were no organized bourgeois elements able to share power with democracy and effect the needed reforms. Like the Petrograd Mensheviks, the Moscow Committee, which also included prominent Revolutionary Defensists, rejected coalition and stressed the government's accountability to "organized democracy."[28]

The Transcaucasia Regional Congress of the RSDRP(0) passed in September a similar resolution, offered by N. N. Zhordania: the Kornilov uprising had *completed* the withdrawal of the big bourgeoisie from the revolution, which could now develop only "against the interests and the will" of that class; both "extreme groups" were wrong—the one that insisted on coalition with the bourgeoisie (that is, the Tsereteli-Dan group) and the one that would give "all power to the Soviets" (that is, the Bolsheviks). Zhordania argued that it was not the abandonment of coalition but its continuance that would cause a rift between the proletariat and the petty bourgeoisie and increase the proletariat's pro-Bolshevik sentiments and "isolation." He hoped that it was not too late to "isolate the census bourgeoisie and unite revolutionary democracy and the proletariat."[29]

On 12 September, Tsereteli made an ardent speech in favor of coalition at a plenary session of the CEC; "*All* the census elements that could help Kornilov to victory have realized that he can bring nothing but ruin"; the Mensheviks' tactics of the past six months should not be lightly discarded. Tsereteli had not yet lost his prestige as a revolutionary leader, and his speech, according to *Vpered*, was enthusiastically applauded. The CEC nevertheless adopted Bogdanov's resolution against coalition with the Kadets, although both Bogdanov and Martov had taken care to point out that excluding them amounted to giving up the whole idea of coalition. Bogdanov also stated that adherence to "the principle of coalition" meant renouncing urgently needed reforms since these were unacceptable to the other partners in the coalition. "I am still in favor of coalition," he declared, adding ruefully, "[but] there is no one to coalesce with." So "the natural solution of the problem" was for democracy to take power into its own hands. Martov, too, ridiculed as naïve the hope of finding satisfactory partners.

At the same meeting of the CEC, the last before the Democratic Conference, the Potresovite Defensists, for the first time it would seem, officially spoke independently of the Menshevik faction, opposing the party line. They handed the Presidium a declaration in which they described themselves as "a group of Menshevik Defensists in the Soviets of Workers' and Soldiers' Deputies that considers [governmental coalition] between revolutionary democracy and the bourgeoisie *absolutely* necessary and believes that *only* such a government can save the country" (italics added). They were not satisfied with Tsereteli's stand that coalition was necessary in principle: for them, the necessity was "absolute." They were, however, prepared to support Tsereteli and Dan against Bogdanov, whose rejection of the Kadets "in fact destroys the possibility of agreement with the census elements."

This discussion took place after the Menshevik CC had adopted its resolution of 10 or 11 September, published in *Rabochaia Gazeta* only on the 14th but of course already known to the speakers. In it the CC had for the first time treated a noncoalition government as a concrete possibility—*if* it turned out that there really were no "census elements" willing to carry out the "program of united democracy," including the reorganization, that is, the reduction, of the army.[30] The final decision was left to the Democratic Conference. Discussions continued in its Menshevik faction, which comprised at least two hundred and fifty people from Petrograd and all over Russia. Their caliber made the meetings comparable to a well-prepared Party conference.[31]

The faction debates began on 13 September. Tsereteli thought it still possible to form a coalition that would put through a democratic program (the so-called Chkheidze Declaration); Potresov rejected the very idea of a noncoalition government. The Revolutionary Defensist Zhordania and the Internationalist Martynov rejected coalition with any bourgeois partners. Thanks to the Potresovites' support, Tsereteli's resolution, advocating coalition in general terms, was passed by a small majority (81 to 77). Immediately thereafter, however, it was decided by 86 votes to 51 that no Kadets were admissible. The coalitionists tried to have this revised—apparently on some technical grounds—but the result of their final effort was the opposite of what they wanted. Sukhanov tells us that "in the last battle, Tsereteli... reached the height of virtuosity. One could not but admire his lightning repartee and remarks as he unabashedly, in self-oblivion, interrupted the speakers. I had never yet seen him more brilliant."[32] Late at night on 15 September, with the debates finally over and the tallies checked and rechecked, it was found that *coalition with any census elements* had been rejected in principle, by 73 votes to 65. Martov became the official spokesman for the Menshevik faction. The new minority obtained two concessions: Tsereteli, too, would speak at the Democratic Conference, and individual members would be free to vote as they wished. Martov was also nominated spokesman for the Soviet faction of the conference; Dan, until then the leader of Soviet democracy, was to speak for the minority of the Soviet delegation.

At the very first meeting of the Democratic Conference, Bogdanov broadened his anti-Kadet stand: no coalition with any census groups; the power must pass "into the hands of democracy, the one that is gathered here today." One must "either forego power altogether or have the courage to assume full responsibility."[33]

The changed mood of the Mensheviks in the capital and the provinces was reflected in the nomination of candidates for the Presidium of the Conference. Dan, the Party's recognized leader, won over Bogdanov by only *one vote*.[34]

Much the same happened in the SR faction of the Democratic Conference. It approved coalition "in general" by 91 votes to 87 and immediately rejected coalition with the Kadets. [35]

Potresov's followers stingingly criticized in their paper *Den'* the new stand of the Menshevik CC. Stepan Ivanovich wrote on 7 September: "This is worse than bolshevism, this is absurdity." When the Menshevik faction of the Democratic Conference passed Bogdanov's resolution, *Den'* commented that "the levity of a handful of politicians, who have thought up the absurd formula of a coalition without the Kadets, has covered Russian democracy with shame." [36]

The Potresovites also tried to create a stronger opposition to the Central Committee—if need be, at the price of separation from the Party. They wanted to attract in the first place the right Defensists, who had been avoiding close contact with them as virtually an extra-party group. One item in this campaign was the appeal "Outside Coalition There Is No Salvation," signed by 82 "party workers, Menshevik Defensists," published in *Den'* on 7 September. It warned that "a purely socialist cabinet will be the signal for a hurried mobilization of the forces of counterrevolution, which will be joined by the masses of urban and rural petty bourgeoisie that have secretly or openly sympathized with the Kornilov adventure." The Kadets went unmentioned in order not to contradict point-blank the CC's resolution of 31 August. Coalition was advocated in general terms, and the authors avoided the usual sharp tone of *Den'*.[37]

The appeal was designed to set apart the right wing of the RSDRP(0). Rightist groups did defect in Moscow in mid-September and a little later in Kharkov and probably a few other places. They did not take root, however, and no Party schism ensued. Most of the prerevolutionary Defensists, even those who disagreed with Bogdanov and the new line of the CC, did not like to advertise their dissent outside the Party. The most prominent Revolutionary Defensists in the CC did not sign the appeal; also missing were the signatures of the members of the Presidium of the Soviet, of the leaders of the Printers' Union, and of the Mensheviks in the Ministry of Labor. Evidently they did not wish to identify themselves with Potresov's group, although many of them favored a coalition government and continuation of the war until a "general" and acceptable peace.[38]

Some Revolutionary Defensists opposed coalition in the hope that a homogeneous democratic government would be more likely to restore the army's fighting capacity. Shortly before the Democratic Conference, the "United Committee of Democratic Organizations for Defense," in which Bogdanov and M. I. Broido were active, had published, no doubt with their consent, an appeal to create local defense committees representing "all the cells of organized democracy—Soviets, trade unions, cooperatives, and land committees [*zemel'nye komitety*]," that is, the groups represented at the Democratic Conference. These committees were to "raise the entire people, young and old, to the defense of the country and of the conquests of freedom." The tsarist government had failed to defend the country, and this had been "one cause of its fall." The newly proclaimed Russian Democratic Republic would also be doomed if it failed to repulse "Austro-German monarchy." The long appeal did not so much as hint at ending the war. [39] It was in complete contradiction to the views of Martov's group. That there were different shadings in the approach to war and defense among the new majority was of course only natural.

The new majority turned out to be incomparably weaker than the bloc of Revolutionary Defensists that had just fallen apart. The Menshevik ministers and the most popular leaders of the Petrograd Soviets, far from supporting the CC's line, actively combated it. The Potresovites, not important in the Party but impressive enough in their influence over many non-Mensheviks at the Democratic Conference, now attacked the CC's stand with undisguised hostility ("worse than bolshevism"). The new majority proved unable to set the line of behavior of "democracy" as the old majority had done. The Mensheviks not only lost their leading role in the Soviets of the capitals (on 31 August in Petrograd and on 5 September in Moscow)—they failed to impose their viewpoint on the Democratic Conference convoked on their own initiative.

The conference closed without reaching a decision about the organization of government. Again a majority vote of the center and the right (766 to 688, with 38 abstentions) affirmed the principle of coalition, and again a majority of the center and the left rejected the Kadets. Finally, despite Martov's appeal, the conference rejected its own combined resolution (for coalition, without the Kadets) by an overwhelming majority (813 to 183). Among those who voted against the combined resolution were, on one hand, the Bolsheviks, the Left SRs, and the *Novaia Zhizn* group—because the resolution favored coalition "in principle"—and, on the other hand, the rightist part of the conference, but also Dan, Tsereteli, and Gots, because it barred the Kadets. [40]

The paralysis of the Democratic Conference made it impossible for the CC and the Menshevik party as an organized whole to influence the formation of the government and returned the initiative to Kerensky—and Tsereteli. The new government resulted from negotiations initiated during the conference and quickly completed after it between Kerensky, the CC of the Kadet party, and the right wing of the Democratic Conference, including the Menshevik advocates of coalition.

The Mensheviks and the Last Coalition Ministry

The new cabinet, the fourth since the outbreak of the revolution, was introduced to the country on 25 September 1917. The crisis had lasted a month. In another month, the Bolsheviks would unseat the provisional government.

The cabinet contained four Mensheviks. K. A. Gvozdev, formerly deputy minister, was now Minister of Labor, replacing another Menshevik, Skobelev, who had resigned. The other three, all from Moscow, were the Minister of Justice, P. N. Maliantovich; the Minister of the Interior, A. M. Nikitin; and the Minister of Food Supplies, S. N. Prokopovich. These three had not been active in the Party, especially in 1917.

Some key posts had gone to the Kadets, whom the Menshevik CC considered "inadmissible"—a position endorsed during the September debates by the majority of the Menshevik faction at the Democratic Conference and by the Menshevik organizations in the capitals and several provincial centers.

The immense majority of Mensheviks, including even partisans of coalition, held that the provisional government must be accountable to a representative "organ of democracy." A resolution to this effect, proposed in the name of the Menshevik CC by Liber, had been almost unanimously adopted by the Menshevik faction of the Democratic Conference.[41] The new government declared, however, that it would convoke a Provisional Council of the Republic but would *not* consider itself accountable to it—since it was itself the *sole*, that is, the sovereign, repository of state power.[42]

Consequently the Menshevik leaders looked askance at the new coalition, even though four Mensheviks were in the cabinet and four others[43] had taken part in the negotiations that had brought it into being.

Tsereteli and Dan had to tackle the difficulty of getting the Menshevik faction of the pre-Parliament to approve their conduct during the negotiations. The elections to the steering committee of the pre-Parliament at the first meeting of the Menshevik faction had already been a disappointment for Tsereteli: along with himself, two determined opponents of coalition, Martov and Bogdanov, had been elected.

Pleading for support for the new government, Tsereteli, Dan, and Skobelev again pointed to the weakness of democracy: if it rejected coalition, it would find itself isolated. The situation would be tragic,

Tsereteli said, if the leaders of the peasant movement, the zemstvos, the cooperatives, turned away from a democratic government and passively watched its struggle with the big bourgeoisie. Skobelev also spoke of "tragedy" for democracy at a time when the whole state was "dislocated." Dan spoke of the danger for democracy *"alone* to take the responsibility for the calamity that is in store for Russia." The majority of the faction, however, was clearly unwilling to accept the new cabinet, let alone support it. One proposed resolution (Martov's) demanded a homogeneous democratic government, predicting that the coalition would be unable to initiate an active policy for peace and put through important reforms. Another resolution insisted on the government's accountability to the pre-Parliament and postponed defining the attitude to be adopted toward it until this point was settled. Tsereteli had to agree to the vague compromise resolution offered by P. A. Garvi, F. I. Dan, and Ia. L. Rubinstein (a Defensist, mayor of Kharkov), welcoming the creation of the pre-Parliament and insisting on the government's "formal accountability" to it, yet finding "the agreement outlined by the delegation [about forming a government] acceptable in the present conditions" since "power can belong to a government the pre-Parliament trusts."

This resolution—later passed without changes at a plenary session of the pre-Parliament—polled only thirty votes in the seventy-member Menshevik faction. Twenty-five members voted for Martov's resolution, seven for postponing the decision until the government acknowledged its responsibility to the pre-Parliament, and eight abstained. [44]

The Menshevik faction of the pre-Parliament (seventy members and thirty alternates) probably reflected very closely the gamut of Menshevik sentiments at the end of the February Revolution—from F. Kon, N. N. Sukhanov, and O. A. Ermanskii on the left to A. N. Potresov, V. O. Levitskii, and I. N. Dement'ev-Kubikov on the right. In the Menshevik faction of the pre-Parliament—unlike the Central Committee and the Menshevik faction of the Central Executive Committee—the provincial Menshevik organizations were quite well represented. And the dominant mood was disappointment at the failure of the Democratic Conference and reluctance to accept the new coalition as "our own" government.

The Menshevik Internationalists were, of course, its most outspoken critics. Martynov insisted on declining "any responsibility for the experiment with another rotten coalition." The draft of a resolution offered in the CC by Menshevik Internationalists (it received only five or six votes) demanded that the Party retain "full freedom of action" vis-à-vis the new government and forbid Party members to hold posts in it. [45] The resolution actually adopted, on 25 September, emphasized the CC's reservations about the new cabinet: It had been formed on the basis of an agreement whose underlying assumptions were "not entirely satisfactory"; the CC "found it necessary to strive" for their revision; yet it considered that the agreement did establish the de facto, if not the formal, responsibility of the government to the pre-Parliament and was "the only way out of the existing situation that would make it possible to see the country through to the Constituent Assembly with the *least danger* of upheavals." This resolution admitted participation of Mensheviks in the government, but only with the CC's special permission "in each individual case." And Menshevik ministers who had this permission could remain in the government only so long as its policy "followed the announced line" and their presence in it was "compatible with the interests of the proletariat." An appendix stated that the CC found Gvozdev's appointment as Minister of Labor "desirable" since it assured "continuity" in the ministry closest to the Mensheviks. The other three Menshevik ministers were not mentioned at all. [46] They had not received the stipulated permission—whereby the Party underscored, as it were, that they did not officially represent it. The Internationalist *Iskra* (no. 2, 3 October) immediately demanded—with some justification—that the CC declare them "nonrepresentatives," "standing outside the Party."

Since all three were members of the Moscow organization, the Moscow committee undertook to lead the campaign against them. (The majority of the committee was anticoalitionist.) In a resolution of 27 September, published in *Vpered* on the 28th, the Moscow committee declared it inadmissible for Mensheviks to participate "in the present government." On the 29th, *Vpered* announced, in advance of the event, that the CC had asked Nikitin "to leave the ranks of the Party." Actually, no formal decision was taken until 2 October, when the CC notified Nikitin, and probably Prokopovich as well, that it did not consider them representatives of the Party and would not be responsible for their actions. Nikitin then tendered his resignation (on 5 October), which Kerensky ignored, probably with Nikitin's consent. On 8 October, *Vpered* announced his imminent retirement, giving as source an unnamed member of the CC who had "passed through Moscow." On 13 October, the Moscow committee stated in *Vpered* that it had decided to "inform" the ministers Nikitin, Prokopovich, and Maliantovich of its resolution that Party members could not hold posts in the government.

On 15 October, *Rabochaia Gazeta* told its readers about the CC's correspondence with Nikitin. On 21 October, the CC officially notified the three ministers that they must "immediately *leave the Party*" because their activity had been found contrary to the general Party program and tactics.[47] The organ of the right SR Defensists, *Volia Naroda*, reported on 22 October that the Menshevik CC had demanded that the three ministers immediately leave *the government*, but the bureau of the CC formally denied this in *Rabochaia Gazeta* on the 24th.

The CC's cautious attitude can be explained by the premonition of disaster that had seized the Menshevik leaders. While expecting nothing good of the new government, they saw no way of getting rid of it. Its forcible overthrow was the last thing they wanted. There was still the hope that it might see the country through to the elections to the Constituent Assembly "with the least danger of upheavals."

M. I. Skobelev, who had been the first Menshevik Minister of Labor and was an active partisan of coalition, felt compelled to demand the resignation of the Minister of Foreign Affairs, Tereshchenko, one of Kerensky's closest collaborators.[48] On the other flank of the Party, Martov blamed the government for popular discontent, yet argued that "at this moment one cannot reorganize the government, there is no time, the Germans are too close."[49] For all their opposition to the government, the Party leaders could not shake off the feeling that it was *the lesser evil*: they had realized with bitter disappointment the meagerness of the forces willing to defend a democratic order. Yet the Central Committee foresaw that the government would fail to organize the country's defense, end the war, steer the disorderly agrarian revolution into legal channels, and generally impose its authority and stop the growth of pro-Bolshevik sentiments in the masses.

For the Mensheviks, used to fitting all political events into the frame of class relations, the votes at the Democratic Conference had meant that "the greater part of the peasantry and the urban petty bourgeoisie are unable at this time to break with the census elements and turn toward...a purely democratic government." Along with this observation, the Moscow committee had noted increasing pro-bolshevism among the workers, especially in Petrograd and Moscow, and also in the garrisons of both capitals.[50] The Bolsheviks were getting ready to seize power, and there were no groups in sight that would actively resist their small but organized and enthusiastic forces.

The Bolshevik Challenge and the Threat of Counterrevolution

On 5 September the Moscow Soviet of Workers' and Soldiers' Deputies, following the example of the Petrograd Soviet, had declared its support of the Bolsheviks. By a majority of 355 to 254, it had voted to strive for a government "of representatives of the proletariat and the revolutionary peasantry."[51] The Menshevik faction had countered with a detailed declaration appraising the prospects, deeply pessimistic in tone. The Bolshevik resolution, it said, excluded from the government the entire middle stratum of the urban population and evidently most of the peasantry as well, since "revolutionary peasantry" in Bolshevik terminology applied only to the poorest hired-laborer type of peasants, just as "revolutionary army" applied only to the units that followed their slogans. What the Bolsheviks had in mind was a proletarian dictatorship. Therefore "we fighters for socialism, true to the principles of the class struggle...consider it our duty to say loud and clear: The Bolsheviks are leading the working class down the wrong path, toward isolation and inevitable defeat." Socialism and a proletarian dictatorship presupposed a highly developed capitalist order and the solidarity of large popular masses conscious of their interests. Backward Russia could not "pioneer" the social revolution, and the Russian proletariat could not lead the world proletariat. "The Russian working class is being drawn into an adventure in which seas of blood will be shed and the Russian revolution will perish."

This declaration already prefigured the analysis of events on which the Mensheviks would build their strategy after the overturn. It implied that the Bolsheviks' attempt to seize power would probably succeed; to stay in power, they would not stop even before the most bloody terror; they and their proletarian followers would earn the hatred of the petty-bourgeois peasants and townspeople, who would join the counter-revolution and thus ensure its victory. A massacre of the proletariat appeared to the Mensheviks almost as inevitable as the Bolshevik "adventure" itself, and they wanted no part in it. This reasoning led to fatalism. The declaration recognized that the Mensheviks had to "submit to the decisions of the Soviet" (even though they would "daily try to show the masses into what an abyss they are being led") and ended with the words:

> We Menshevik Social-Democrats shall not withdraw from the struggle of our class, we are prepared...to share its fate....It is our duty to fight and die together with the whole working class, but we cannot assume responsibility for the policy of the Soviet's majority, inspired by the Bolshevik faction.[52]

This mood intensified after the failure of the Democratic Conference to organize a government. The idea that the ultimate danger lay on the right was present in many minds, from hesitant Bolsheviks to the CC of the populist *Trudovaia Narodno-Sotsialisticheskaia Partiia* (NSs). According to one of its members, S. P. Mel'gunov, even this CC, although it had always been "national" in its orientation and "perhaps less infected than anyone else with the traditional prejudices of the democratic leaders," spoke of the "threat of counterrevolution" (even after the October overturn!)."[53]

The "traditional prejudices" affected Mel'gunov himself—the politician if not the historian. At the time, he wrote that there was only one possible outcome to "the illusory victory of the Bolsheviks and the Cossack suppression of the mass movement raised by ill-considered appeals"—the ultimate defeat of democracy. He warned of the "*inevitable triumph of the bourgeoisie* and, who knows, perhaps even the restoration of the tsarist regime." "With a kind of insane blindness," the Bolshevik leaders were creating a situation that the monarchists were already beginning to exploit. A counterrevolution could well succeed. Having trusted the Bolsheviks and been deceived in their expectations, the masses would "for a long time thereafter keep away from socialism."[54]

More rightist groups actually rejoiced at Lenin's "ephemeral" successes since these were bound to lead to a radical elimination of all "intermediate" democratic forces. They managed to discern a "salutary process" in the events, a promise of eventual restoration of "order." These ideas are reflected in the memoirs of the British ambassador to Russia, Sir George Buchanan. He, too, thought that General Kornilov would have been wiser to leave the initiative to the Bolsheviks and to crush them afterward.[55] Even nonreactionary officers (such as the chief of staff, General Dukhonin) doubted the wisdom of "defending" Kerensky from the Bolsheviks' "Pyrrhic victory."

It is scarcely possible to exaggerate the disastrous consequences of this political blindness. By sabotaging the revolution, by applying brakes to every initiative on the part of the government, these circles hoped to provoke quarrels among the "Soviet parties" and thus put an end to revolutionary "excesses." I. A. Isuv, a member of the Menshevik CC, had good reason to speak, on the very day of the overturn, of the forces of darkness that were basing their calculations on democracy's internal struggles and planning to pour "their own Black cadres into the breached front."[56]

We learn about the mood of the Moscow Mensheviks from an article by the Revolutionary Defensist B. S. Kibrik. It begins by saying that "...the Bolsheviks, after fairly prolonged wavering, have apparently decided to risk their all." Perhaps unknowingly, and perhaps even "with the best of intentions as to the interests of the working class," Bolshevik "hotheads and probably very honest souls" were in reality preparing the complete isolation of the proletariat by turning the rest of the people against it. This would naturally spell the doom of the revolution. "We are far from hoping," Kibrik remarked, "that our article may change the course of events. In the masses, attitudes have already *hardened* that prevent them from seeing the true correlation of forces between the struggling classes." In view of the "apparently" inevitable catastrophe, Kibrik tried to map out the future tasks of menshevism: "*It is not the aim of this article to arrest the course of events. Another important task* now confronts the vanguard of the working class." It must see to it that at the moment of rude awakening the masses "may remember that *a part of social democracy* warned them in good time that seizing power would be disastrous for the further struggle of the working class." This did not mean that the Mensheviks would now, Pilate-like, wash their hands. They must struggle and die with their class even when it is wrong. But they must combat the Bolshevik utopias to the end—and here the political meaning that Kibrik attached to this struggle becomes clear: events could not be arrested, but the struggle would rally all conscious, advanced workers for *the big task* of restoring "our" organization when the *masses*, disappointed in the Bolshevik promises, fell into apathy.[57]

This article reflects the specific Moscow atmosphere of the time. Elections to regional dumas had shown such enormous Bolshevik gains that they created a sensation even against the background of the Bolsheviks' other successes throughout the country. The large cadres of workers' intelligentsia in the Menshevik Moscow organization were unhappy about the masses' mood, so different from their own. And in the Bolshevik organization there were a good many "waverers," whom Kibrik probably hoped to influence.[58]

But Kibrik's mood was characteristic not only of Moscow and not only of Revolutionary Defensists. Similar notes resound, for instance, in Martov's speech two days later at a meeting of the All-Russian CEC. The provisional government's policies, Martov said, had "created a situation that *must* explode *spontaneously*." The Bolsheviks meant to use the explosion to seize power but would not be able to hold on to it, for at the moment one could not regard "the growth of the spontaneous movement as conducive to the creation of a *new stable government*." The Mensheviks must continue to combat "factors that impel to action," although "*we do not expect them* [the Bolsheviks] *to change their policy*" or hope to succeed in stopping them from embarking on their "adventure."[59]

The Eve of the Overturn

On 24 October, Kerensky finished an impassioned speech to the pre-Parliament with the plea "that this very day, at this...meeting, the provisional government receive your answer as to whether it can carry out its duty with confidence in your support." In the evening, a resolution was put through by Mensheviks, Menshevik Internationalists, SRs, and Left SRs, which Kerensky rightly interpreted as a vote of no confidence. It had been offered and reported on by Dan, until then one of the chief partisans of coalition. [60]

Dan (Tsereteli was not in Petrograd) and the SRs Gots and Avksent'ev personally informed Kerensky of the resolution in which the pre-Parliament blamed the successes of Bolshevik propaganda, "apart from the war and the havoc," on the government's inaction. It demanded the transfer of land to land committees, "decisive action on foreign policy," and the creation of a Committee of Public Safety comprising representatives of "city self-government organs and organs of revolutionary democracy [and] *acting in liaison with the provisional government.*"

Dan described the interview with Kerensky in an article published in 1923 in the Berlin *Letopis' Revoliutsii*. He recalled that he had wanted the government to post notices during the night that it had: 1) approached the Allies about immediately inviting all the warring nations to *stop military operations* and begin peace talks; 2) issued orders by telegraph about the transfer of landowners' estates to land committees; 3) decided to speed up the convocation of the Constituent Assembly.

The pre-Parliament's resolution spoke of "inviting" the Allies to "announce peace terms and begin peace negotiations." This formulation, also without the demand that the Allies immediately stop military operations, was repeated in a resolution offered by Dan later that night in the Central Executive Committee. Hastening the convocation of the Constituent Assembly was not mentioned in either of them.

It is not known whether the pre-Parliament's delegates brought Kerensky the program as formulated in Dan's resolution of 24 October or in his Berlin article. Be that as it may, Kerensky evidently did not realize that the eleventh hour had struck. According to Dan, the harried premier received the delegates haughtily and replied with some irritation that the government no longer needed admonishments and advice. It was clear that he would not change the policy that was pushing the masses into the Bolsheviks' arms and made it impossible for the Mensheviks to support the government any longer. The delegates left the palace and went to a joint meeting of the Central Executive Committees of the Soviets of Workers', Soldiers', and Peasants' Deputies. Dan spoke again, arguing that if the Petrograd Soviet actually seized power, this would "scuttle the Constituent Assembly and ultimately destroy all Soviets," and that "the method of terror by which the Bolsheviks will rule will only hasten the ruin of democracy."[61] The meeting passed a resolution, similar to the pre-Parliament's, about creating a "Committee of Public Safety with the participation of representatives of local self-governments, organs of revolutionary democracy, and the socialist parties."[62] The words "acting in liaison with the provisional government" had disappeared since the interview with Kerensky.

Kerensky and those Mensheviks and SRs who, despite their Central Committees, remained in favor of coalition and counted on the cooperatives, the zemstvos, the nonsocialist public figures, and the Kadet party, entirely failed to see that neither the presence of Kadets in the government nor its rejection of socialist support would ensure it any real support from the "census elements." In fact, by disdaining the unsolicited "admonishments and advice" of the pre-Parliament's socialist factions, Kerensky had deprived his government of its only broad support. He discovered at once that the government now stood isolated. Having lost the last vestiges of authority, it was like a motor running idle. The Kadets and the more rightist circles had no intention to rescue the "semi-Bolshevik" Kerensky. His hope that the army would defend the legal government also proved illusory.

A few hours after Kerensky's talk with Dan and Gots, the Right Menshevik V. V. Sher, a coalitionist and head of the political department of the Ministry of War, telephoned to Tiflis that the "effectives," that is, the troops stationed in Petrograd, would not suffice to defend the government.[63] General Levitskii, the army's representative with the government, reported to the Stavka that the troops guarding the Winter Palace were guarding it only nominally: "...they have decided not to take action." It looked almost as if the government were "in the capital of an enemy country."[64]

On the morning of 25 October, the chief of staff of the Petrograd Military District, General Bagratuni, reported to the commander-in-chief of the armies of the northern front, General Cheremisov, that "even the most obedient and disciplined units [cadets] are surrendering their sentry posts without resistance"; the government had lost all remnants of power, but there were no disorders, life was going on "normally."[65] Cheremisov decided that a government that had "lost all remnants of power" even before it was overthrown did not deserve support—and stopped the troops Kerensky had summoned from the front.

At 3 P.M. on 25 October, Captain I. I. Rengarten noted in his diary the news just received on the warships in the Baltic Sea: "It is true that in Petrograd cadets and some units are ready to fight and suppress the Bolshevik action, but that is all—no one wants to defend Kerensky and his govenment."[66] Mel'gunov mentions that officers came to Savinkov on the morning of the 25th to tell him that they would not defend the provisional government because they did not want to fight for Kerensky.[67] General Denikin also notes that the officers hated Kerensky;[68] and Miliukov, that officers "continued to view Kerensky as their enemy and the enemy of Russia."[69]

In a telephone conversation with Kiev, the Petrograd representative of the Soviet of Cossack armies sneered at the news that Cossacks intended to invite Kerensky to Rostov: "Of course he'll have to be taken in—as bait for a certain kind of fish."[70] For General Cheremisov, Kerensky represented the party "that had ruled Russia for some eight months and has *persecuted us commanding officers* as counterrevolutionaries." He spoke with contempt of the "notorious" Committee of (Public) Safety, in a telephone talk with his subordinate, the commander of the Twelfth army, on 4 November.[71]

Would some Petrograd troops have fought the Bolsheviks if it hadn't been for their unwillingness to defend Kerensky and "his government"? Or did the argument that Kerensky was a semi-Bolshevik merely serve as excuse for their apathy? The officers were still disoriented after the Kornilov uprising. The political directive they had liked in August— not to support the provisional government if the Bolsheviks rose against it—may have paralyzed them in October.[72]

The foremost Kadet, P. N. Miliukov, remarked that Kerensky seemed to have been in power too long. He expected the government to fall. A week before the Kornilov uprising, he had said in the CC of his party that a "surgical operation" was imminent: it could be brought about by hunger riots or by Bolshevik action.[73] Kerensky could no longer lean on the Mensheviks; the role of the moderate socialists was played out. It was "rather" to the Kadets' advantage to give the government a little more time: let "the inevitable repressions be undertaken...at the decision of the socialist government itself"; but the *country* "could only be harmed" by the policy of this regime. Miliukov found a legalistic excuse: "This process [an overturn by the right] will take place without us, but we...welcome it and sympathize with it to some extent...." (An omission follows in the source.) The main Kadet organ had said a month before the overturn: "The best way to get rid of bolshevism for years to come would be to entrust the country's fate to its leaders."[74] And just before the overturn, this time publicly, Miliukov had almost welcomed the radical temper of the masses and the Bolsheviks' success among them: the socialists had split, and the Kadets must make use of this. The Bolsheviks had managed to outbid the center in political promises. Having lost the support of the masses, the center would now seek rapprochement with the right. But Miliukov was against supporting it in its struggle with the left: the democratic center was "powerless and therefore useless. So why should we support...its false phraseology?"[75]

On the extreme right, the newspaper *Novaia Rus'* declared in early October that Kerensky's government no longer counted. "A second government is already openly forming in Moscow, where Russian people [*liudi*] are gathering and the People [*narod*] itself is oganizing its center, which the present Petrograd phantom of a government has proved so powerless to organize." The true government—Moscow— would summon Kornilov to its side. The Bolsheviks represented no lasting danger, for "Russia is advancing to salvation like a great flood, *she will step over any* [legal] *forms.*"[76]

Similar notions influenced the attitudes of big business. The Association of United Industry decided, in a strange aberration, that the time had come to fight the more orderly manifestations of the labor movement. When the Minister of Labor, Skobelev, managed to prevent a metalworkers' strike in Petrograd, and the Minister of Trade and Industry, Prokopovich, set wage rates with the consent of both sides, the association asked Kerensky to annul Prokopovich's decision and to notify the Main Committee of United Industry that he had done so. In late August, the same organization recommended that employers discharge members of factory committees who had not worked in their factory jobs for two weeks, "for only those who work can be considered workers and be members of workers' committees."[77] In early October, the Union of Printing Press Owners left the Petrograd Association of Factory Owners, which would not ratify a collective agreement between it and the printers' union and in fact preferred a strike. Yet the printers showed greater resistance to bolshevism than most other workers' groups![78]

Evgenia M. Ratner, a member of the Central Committee of the Party of Socialist Revolutionaries, told the Bolshevik tribunal at her trial a few years later that during those October events "behind the struggling parties, there stood the *tertius gaudens*, who perhaps rejoiced prematurely—the very bourgeoisie on which we were supposed to lean....Then the bourgeois parties openly declared that it was more advantageous for them to let the Bolsheviks triumph temporarily."[79]

Kerensky's government had been thinking unrealistically. The Minister of Foreign Affairs, M. I. Tereshchenko, while conceding that the military situation did not "permit one to count on complete victory," had thought it more profitable to postpone peace talks until the spring. The projected conference of the Allies could "by no means be regarded as direct preparation for peace." He had comforted himself and others with the notion that "despite all the difficulties," Russia had "enormous resources, in terms of human reserves as well as food."[80]

As Dan had assured Kerensky on 24 October, the Mensheviks did not want to precipitate a crisis: they would back the government if it "let democracy rally around it," told the country of its positive plans—all the people were awaiting its word.[81] That night, in his last speech before the overturn, Dan admitted that the policy of "Soviet democracy" had been built on mistaken premises and had played into the Bolsheviks' hands. The Revolutionary Defensists had wanted a happy peace "without losses for our country"—but, "as it *turns out*, the popular masses are too exhausted, have been driven to the last limits of despair, are *no longer able to wait*" for such a peace. So, "from now on" the unattainable goal must be abandoned and a quicker way to peace be found.[82]

Was it still possible, at that late date, to satisfy the masses' drives and impatience in the framework of a free, democratic order? Would it have changed the fortunes of Russia and the world if Kerensky had listened to Dan? If he had taken immediate measures about the country's urgent needs, agreed to collaborate with the Committee of Public Safety before handing over the reins to a more effectual democratic government? In retrospect, the pre-Parliament's last-minute attempt to prevent the Bolshevik overturn looks completely hopeless. To the actors, however, it did not seem so. We must remember that at the meeting held by the Bolshevik delegates to the Second Congress of Soviets, Stalin and others had been in favor of postponing the coup. Present Soviet historians speak of

> *the important matter that worried Lenin*: on 24 October the Mensheviks and SRs made a last attempt to disorganize the masses and scuttle the armed uprising. At their insistence, the pre-Parliament hurriedly decided to demand of the provisional government that it conclude peace and transfer the land to the peasants. Entreating Kerensky to agree to this step, the SR and Menshevik leaders tried to snatch from the Bolsheviks' hands the slogans under which they were leading the masses toward the uprising....Lenin's tactic...took account of *the danger of these maneuvers for the armed uprising.*[83]

The aim of Dan's strategy on the eve of the overturn was not confined to snatching their slogans away from the Bolsheviks. There also seemed to be a chance of snatching the Bolsheviks out of Lenin's hands.[84]

3

The First Days of Soviet Rule

The Stake on Bolshevik Isolation

On 24 October the Central Executive Committee of the Soviets of Workers' and Soldiers' Deputies and the Executive Committee of the All-Russian Soviet of Peasants' Deputies held an extraordinary joint meeting that lasted through the night. The SR leader A. R. Gots presided. Dan was the reporter. Realizing the imminence of the armed uprising planned by the Bolsheviks, he asserted that they did not command a majority even among the workers. The victory of an insignificant minority of the population was bound to result in a regime of terror that would "hasten the ruin of democracy." Dan appealed to the sense of responsibility of the Bolshevik "group of the democracy." After his speech and Trotsky's reply, two other members of the Menshevik CC, Liber and Martov, also spoke of the danger inherent in the Bolsheviks' plans.

To the masses, the Mensheviks could only address appeals to keep calm, not to participate in demonstrations, not to support conspiracies. Their "positive" demands were addressed to the government. They adjured it to respond, before it was too late, to the peasants' "land hunger" and the army's weariness. No demonstrations to support these demands were organized: this would have been grist to the Bolsheviks' mill. The Menshevik Central Committee asked the people of Petrograd: "Let not a single worker, not a single soldier, not one citizen, follow irresponsible, criminal appeals to come out into the streets, no matter by whom they are issued."[1]

The Menshevik Internationalists ended an appeal signed by Martov and six others with the "demand" that "every socialist worker, every revolutionary soldier, do his duty to the revolution at this critical moment and devote all his strength to the business of *calming* the elemental excitement of the masses, of repulsing all attempts by *provocateurs.*"[2]

The Potresovite Defensists had issued a sharper warning: "Anyone who in these frightful days for our motherland *calls for coming out into the streets* against the government is either a secret servant of tsarism, a *provocateur*, a thoughtless accomplice of the people's enemies, or Wilhelm's hired spy!"[3]

Dan's resolution, which the extraordinary meeting of the CEC adopted, also urged the Petrograd workers and soldiers "to preserve *complete calm* and not follow appeals to armed action, which can only lead to ruin."[4]

This was the resolution that also demanded immediate action on the part of the government for the transfer of land to land committees and for peace. Differing in spirit from the Potresovites' appeal, it said: "The present movement in Petrograd is rooted in the broad popular masses' feeling of *deep dissatisfaction* caused by the war, the economic havoc, *and the indecisive policy of the provisional government*" (italics added). Kerensky had refused to change his policy. An armed clash of his troops with the Petrograd garrison and Red Guards frenzied by Bolshevik propaganda would imperil the democratic order: many groups desired counterrevolution if not restoration.

R. A. Abramovich, a leader of the Internationalist wing of menshevism and the Bund, recalls his sentiments at the time:

> Our situation was especially difficult. Like the Bolsheviks, we were basically hostile to Kerensky's government. We felt that it was not doing anything to save the revolution, to conclude peace, to put through the land reform. Like the Bolsheviks, we wanted this government to cede its place to another, which would enact the urgently needed measures....But an *armed uprising* against Kerensky's government, an uprising that would trigger a fratricidal war among the partisans of the revolution, an uprising that would make it impossible for the socialist parties to agree and unite—this we regarded as a crime.[5]

Dan tried to convince both the Bolsheviks and Kerensky's partisans that "if the uprising is drowned in blood—no matter who wins, the provisional government or the Bolsheviks—this will mean the triumph of a third force, which will sweep away the Bolsheviks and the provisional government and all of democracy."[6] From the day of the overturn it was the Mensheviks' main objective to forestall—or to end with all possible speed—any armed clashes "inside democracy."

On the left flank of menshevism, A. Martynov demanded "utter haste" in stopping the civil war; at the center, the Revolutionary Defensists called for agreement "before it is too late," before the Germans made use of the internal strife to breach the front. Infinitely dangerous, *Rabochaia Gazeta* wrote, was "every extra hour of delay"; every day thousands of citizens were driven into the reactionary camp.[7]

It seemed to the Mensheviks that the way to achieve their aim was to isolate Lenin and Trotsky politically. By supporting those Bolsheviks who opposed the overturn, it might be possible to change the mood of the soldiers and workers who backed Lenin. With the provisional government removed, it was imperative to create some authoritative organ and counterpose it to the Soviet of People's Commissars.

On the morning of 25 October the Military-Revolutionary Committee announced that it had taken over the state power. Later in the day Lenin and Zinov'ev openly appeared at a meeting of the Petrograd Soviet. They welcomed "the victorious revolution of the proletariat and garrison of Petrograd" and "the social revolution that begins today." The Mensheviks immediately resigned from the Presidium and the executive committee of the Petrograd Soviet. All three Menshevik members of the executive committee—M. I. Broido, S. L. Weinstein, and M. I. Liber— signed the notice of resignation. They were Revolutionary Defensists (the former majority of the Menshevik CC), but they took care to say that they were resigning "in accord with the Central Committee of the RSDRP(0)": the entire Menshevik faction, *regardless of differences*, was opposed to the "criminal adventure" and would not be responsible for its consequences.[8]

The Second Congress of Soviets opened on the evening of 25 October. The provisional government was still in session at the Winter Palace, but the past twenty-four hours had shown its inability to counter even a single of the lawless acts of the Military-Revolutionary Committee. The Bolshevik delegates at the congress would undoubtedly side with Lenin. There was no reason to change the plans reflected in the declaration of the three members of the executive committee of the Petrograd Soviet. All Mensheviks left the congress, though not simultaneously. The declaration of the official Menshevik faction was read out by L. M. Khinchuk; those of the army groups, by the Mensheviks who played leading roles in them: Ia. A. Kharash for the Committee of the Twelfth army, and G. D. Kuchin for the front committees. R. Abramovich (Internationalist) and G. Erlich (Revolutionary Defensist), both of them members of the Menshevik CC, spoke for the Bund. The last to go—after the occupation of the Winter Palace—were Martov and the entire group of Menshevik Internationalists, some of whom would have preferred to stay. They made their last protest on 26 October. [9]

Others who left were the Socialist Revolutionaries, the United Jewish socialists, and the Jewish Social-Democratic Poalei Tsion. Remaining at the congress were the Left SRs, the United Internationalists grouped around the paper *Novaia Zhizn*, and representatives of the Polish socialist party Lewica, although the latter were personally close to Martov. Martov had tried to get all non-Bolshevik delegates to leave the congress in order to isolate the Bolsheviks as clearly as possible. He did not succeed, but all the non-Bolshevik groups voted against the creation of the Soviet of People's Commissars, and all, including even the Left SRs, remained in touch with the Menshevik Internationalists and tried to work together with them to prevent the consolidation of Lenin's one-party rule.

Trotsky's diatribes against the departing socialists ("trash barrel of history") probably impressed the Bolshevik delegates and the public, but many high Bolshevik leaders were appalled at the promises of socialism in a backward and bankrupt country. Their apprehensions were increased by the Bolsheviks' isolation from the other socialist groups. The notes of one such Bolshevik have been preserved. V. P. Nogin, member of the Bolshevik Central Committee, the first People's Commissar of Trade and Industry, leader of the Moscow Bolsheviks, had left Petrograd on 25 October, before the Congress of Soviets opened, to organize the seizure of power in Moscow. There he learned that the Mensheviks and SRs had left the congress. Nogin said at a closed meeting of the executive committee of the Moscow Soviet of Workers' Deputies: "I was sure that during the October Revolution all socialists would be in one camp, as they had been in February—that the other parties would not abandon us, betray us, leave us *alone to face the bullets.* I was sure that at the Congress of Soviets *all parties would do their best to unite,* to find a common language." In reply to indignant shouts from Mensheviks, Nogin explained that his "accusations were not directed at the entire faction." He repeated, "the time has come to close our ranks, otherwise all is lost," and added—whether in exultation or despair—"one cannot abandon the Petrograd proletariat at such a trying moment." [10]

Reminiscences of this kind seldom appear in Soviet publications. We do not know how widespread such feelings were among the Bolsheviks in the provinces. Let us, however, note the words of the Penza leader S. O. Savitskii in the local Soviet on 26 October, the day Nogin spoke in Moscow: "If the Mensheviks refuse to work with us, clearly democracy is finished and we shall probably not be able to save the situation. Instead of uniting, we are dividing."[11]

The Committee to Save the Revolution

The chief center of resistance to bolshevism immediately after the overturn was the Committee to Save the Country and the Revolution (*Komitet Spaseniia Rodiny i Revoliutsii*), created during the night of 25–26 October in the building of the Petrograd City Duma, on the initiative of the Central Committee of the RSDRP(0).[12]

The decision had been reached by the CC with the consent of Internationalists and Revolutionary Defensists before the meeting at the Duma. Disagreeing on this with Potresov's group, the overwhelming majority of Mensheviks did not want to combat the Bolsheviks under the flag of the provisional government, which had played into the Bolsheviks' hands both by its acts and its inaction and lost all authority even in the circles that sympathized with it.[13]

The Committee to Save the Country and the Revolution was intended to take over forthwith the power that the government had lost. The need to create such a committee had been agreed on in the pre-Parliament the day before. At first it was planned that a committee representing city self-government and organs of revolutionary democracy would *cooperate with the provisional government*, but later during the night, after Dan's abortive talk with Kerensky, the central organs of the Soviets formulated their wishes somewhat differently: the committee must be formed at once and must include representatives of the socialist parties. Collaboration with the government was not mentioned.

On the basis of the agreement reached in the pre-Parliament, the Mensheviks expected to oppose to the Bolsheviks the Committee to Save the Revolution as the generally recognized organ of government —but some groups had voted for the Menshevik resolution in the hope of preventing the overturn and went back to their old positions after it.

Present that night in the Duma building were the Mensheviks and SRs who had just left the Congress of Soviets; members of the City Duma; many members of Soviets; and many socialist party workers. News and rumors converged here, telephone contact was maintained with the ministers besieged in the Winter Palace. By no means all the assembled notables shared the Mensheviks' feeling that the revolution had run into an impasse. V. B. Stankevich, Chief Army Commissar, noted "many spirited, resolute words and confident faces."

A procession, impressive both for its size and the participants' earlier roles in the liberation movement, formed at the Duma and set out in orderly rows for the Winter Palace, which the Bolsheviks were preparing to attack. It did not get beyond Kazan Square, however, and returned to the Duma. There, at 3 A.M., with the palace already occupied and the ministers arrested, a more concrete discussion began. From two to three hundred people were present. [14] Many spoke, offering various proposals, but the decision to form a committee was reached at the very beginning of the meeting. The committee was to include three representatives each of the Petrograd Duma, the pre-Parliament, the Soviet of Peasants' Deputies, the All-Russian Central Executive Committee of the First Convocation (that is, the old CEC elected by the First Congress of Soviets), the Menshevik and SR factions that had left the congress, the organizations of the front, the Central Committees of Mensheviks and SRs, the trade unions of railroad workers (Vikzhel) and post-and-telegraph workers (Potel). [15] An executive committee was set up: representatives of the City Duma, of the two central organs of the Soviets (the Central Executive Committee and the Executive Committee of the Soviet of Peasants' Deputies), and of the Central Committees of the Mensheviks, the SRs, and the NSs. The Menshevik Revolutionary Defensists were represented by S. L. Weinstein, who became very active in the committee, and F. I. Dan; the Menshevik Internationalists, by R. A. Abramovich and Iu. O. Martov. [16]

The Mensheviks hoped that the committee—backed by the pre-Parliament, the democratically elected Duma, all socialist parties, the peasant and army organizations—would *immediately* open peace negotiations and be more readily accepted by the country than the one-party Soviet of People's Commissars. Popular sympathy was expected to turn so strongly in favor of the committee that the waverers among the soldiers, and the Bolsheviks wary of Lenin's plans, would be encouraged to insist on the self-liquidation of the organs of the overturn.

The Committee to Save the Country and the Revolution was to serve as the temporary central power badly needed by a country that had lost its political center and was offered no alternative to the Soviet of People's Commissars. The 26 October resolution of the Menshevik Central Committee advisedly limited the agenda to a few weeks and two tasks: to convoke the Constituent Assembly and begin peace talks. Only seventeen days remained until the elections to the Constituent Assembly, which would produce a new government. The provisional government was not mentioned in the resolution, nor in the lead article of *Rabochaia Gazeta* on the 27th, nor in the articles by the Revolutionary Defensists Erlich and G(arv)i on the first page of the same issue. [17]

In the provinces the resolution proposed the creation of local Committees to Save the Country and the Revolution, made up of representatives of City Dumas, Soviets of Workers', Soldiers', and Peasants' Deputies, and all other democratic organizations, political, trade union, and military. [18]

Many provincial centers adopted the line of the Menshevik CC, but in Petrograd a number of socialist and democratic groups resisted it. Some—in the first place, the Potresovites—balked at the very composition of the Committee to Save the Revolution: Did the CC mean to create a government of socialists alone? If so, the Defensists who in September had published the article "Outside Coalition There Is No Salvation" objected to the "homogeneous" committee's pretension to govern or to organize a government. The three Kadets elected to the committee from the Petrograd City Duma were quite lost in the mass of members. The Cooperatives Group in the pre-Parliament, ideologically close to Potresov, condemned attempts by "private, self-constituted organizations" to create a government "according to their own ideas and wishes." An appeal it issued on 1 November ended with "Long live the provisional government!" [19]

The Potresovites nevertheless established close contact with the Committee to Save the Revolution, especially with its military division, about whose activities many members of the committee did not even know. In the Potresovites' eyes, the function of the committee was to restore the Kerensky government: something concrete had to be opposed to the Sovnarkom, not a hypothetical government still to result from negotiations still to come. The provisional government was legal and it existed. The Potresovites were its champions longer than anyone else.[20] They issued their first appeal ("A Crime Has Been Committed") on 25 October, before the occupation of the Winter Palace. It called upon the soldiers and population of Petrograd to uphold and save the provisional government—otherwise the German army would trample the conquered freedoms and the "Black Hundreds" of reaction would set off a wave of pogroms. [21] The Potresovite leadership—the Petrograd Electoral Committee of Menshevik Defensists—published a formal protest against the policy of the Party's Central Committee. It was directed not so much at the Internationalists as at the Revolutionary Defensists in the CC, "unable to break out of the Internationalists' toils." An enormous part of the population, it said, supported the provisional government and regarded the creation of a purely socialist government as "an insane and disastrous step" that would alienate "broad democratic and *nondemocratic* strata . . . from the proletariat and its struggle" at a time when democracy "must rally *all the live forces of the nation* to the defense of the motherland and the revolution." [22]

Unlike the Menshevik Internationalists and many Revolutionary Defensists, the Potresovites did not worry about preventing a counterrevolution that would follow the Bolsheviks' downfall. For them, bolshevism was the counterrevolution. They did not merely say this polemically, as the Menshevik press sometimes did—they fully believed it. Potresov called bolshevism "the counterrevolution that has built itself a nest deep inside the labor movement."[23] "Nondemocratic strata," the propertied classes, the "creative strata of census Russia," all had to be mobilized to rescue the revolution and administer the country. It was not among these that counterrevolution lurked.

Potresov could not see—in late November 1917—any "organized counterrevolutionary forces anywhere *outside bolshevism*."[24] It was to the advantage of both the bourgeoisie and the proletariat that the country grow rich. For both urban classes, capitalist development and keeping Russia from becoming a German colony were "matters of life and death—which cannot be said to the same extent of the *peasantry*." Summing up the experience of 1917, Potresov said he hoped that "the city" would be able to take its revanche on the peasantry, "which had killed the Revolution of 1917" and threatened to "kill the future of this country" by Bolshevik "soldier-peasant anarchy."[25]

The idea of a sovereign Committee to Save the Country and the Revolution found no support among the socialist groups that were inflexibly loyal to the provisional government. There was a widespread feeling that for the sake of legal succession the new government that the committee was to create must receive its powers from the provisional government. Many held that it must "limit itself" to repressing the uprising and convoking the Constituent Assembly, which would then enact the land reform and other laws and take steps toward peace.[26]

Even the Central Committee of the Party of Socialist Revolutionaries, whose ideas came closest to the Menshevik center's, and which recognized the urgency of the agrarian reform and of an active policy for peace, believed in "legal succession." There was even a plan to exert pressure on Kerensky to compel him to "delegate" the power to the new government. In its appeal of 26 October, "You Have Been Basely and Criminally Deceived," the CC of the PSR urged workers, soldiers, sailors, and peasants to unite around the Committee to Save the Revolution, which, together with the socialist parties, would *create* "a new homogeneous revolutionary-democratic government" that would "immediately [that is, without waiting for the Constituent Assembly] transfer the land to peasant committees, propose to all the warring countries a general democratic peace, suppress both anarchy and counterrevolution, and see the country through to the Constituent Assembly."[27]

The first public declaration of the Committee to Save the Revolution was hammered out at a meeting that lasted until 9 P.M. on 26 October. Resulting as it did from mutual concessions and efforts to accomodate various groups, it could not satisfy the Mensheviks. Aside from determined appeals not to recognize the authority of and not to obey the Military-Revolutionary Committee, it gave only vague, elastic recommendations on the few issues it dealt with. [28]

The Failure of Armed Resistance

Meanwhile Kerensky was trying to organize armed resistance to the Bolsheviks. Upon leaving the Winter Palace on 25 October to meet the troops hurrying—so he thought—to the government's rescue, he drove more than three hundred kilometers without encountering them. At the Pskov headquarters he learned that General Cheremisov had stopped the troops that had been dispatched to Petrograd. By evening he was already in Ostrov, about four hundred kilometers from the capital, at the headquarters of General Krasnov, the commander of the Third Cossack corps.

Krasnov's detachment of less than one thousand men entrained in Ostrov on 26 October, arrived at Gatchina, some forty kilometers from Petrograd, at dawn on the 27th, and occupied that town without a fight. The troops of the Military-Revolutionary Committee either laid down their arms or went away to the north. The Gatchina garrison of fifteen thousand neither fought nor joined Krasnov. Urged on by Kerensky, he occupied Tsarkoe Selo on 28 October. Here, only fifteen kilometers from the capital, he decided to give his Cossacks a rest, although they were still putting to flight the large but not combatively disposed troops of the MRC.

It was like a film run in reverse: Bolshevik patrols had just taken over without any effort the government buildings of Petrograd; now Krasnov's tiny detachment had advanced four hundred kilometers in full sight of troops a hundredfold stronger and supposedly pro-Bolshevik. Krasnov's telegram, "Moving on to Petrograd tomorrow at eleven," did not sound farcical, for the garrison showed no fighting spirit. Sailors were the only organized force willing to fight for the Military-Revolutionary Committee.

Recalling these events six months later, Trotsky wrote of the "atmosphere of indecision" in the Petrograd garrison. Having begun by supporting the MRC, the soldiers imagined "that things would go on in the same way"—merely a change of the guard. Instead, they were being ordered out "against an enemy of unknown strength, to a battle of uncertain outcome.... Meanwhile the Cossacks' spearhead groups had advanced quite close to Petrograd, and we expected the main struggle to take place in the streets of the city."[29]

With Kerensky and Krasnov at the gates of Petrograd, the socialist parties had to reach some agreement. The CC of the PSR suggested setting up a socialist government without Bolsheviks and without Kerensky as soon as the Bolshevik uprising was brought under control.[30] The Menshevik CC also announced that it remained in favor of a homogeneous government without the Bolsheviks. The Committee to Save the Revolution was similarly inclined.[31] On 28 October, Skobelev and Zenzinov (a member of the CC of the PSR) referred to plans of forming a new government after Kerensky's return as if such plans already had been agreed upon. In a telegram on 30 October, Stankevich spoke of "complete accord of views and intentions," reached in personal talks, between Kerensky and the Committee to Save the Revolution on the subject of government and of "unifying all the forces of revolutionary democracy."[32]

SRs and Mensheviks—in Petrograd, especially the Menshevik members of the CEC of the First Convocation and the right wing of the Petrograd organization—conducted during those days an active propaganda campaign among factory workers and soldiers. Newspapers published by the First CEC specifically for soldiers (*Golos Soldata*, 26 October; *Soldatskii Golos*, 27 October; *Iskry*, 28 October; *Soldatskii Krik*, 29 October; and so on) were widely distributed.[33] Menshevik Defensist agitation in factories is mentioned in the protocols of the Bolshevik Petrograd Committee for 29 October.[34] The Mensheviks warned against civil war, pointed out that the Bolsheviks would not be able to negotiate a peace (the Germans would not talk with them), let alone a dignified peace in accord with Russia's interests. Along with exhortations "not to obey," "not to support," "not to recognize" the MRC, they and the SRs called for positive action: "throw off the Bolshevik tyranny," "wrest from the claws of the Bolshevik aggressors" the freedom they had stolen.[35]

The SRs and the Petrograd Organization of Menshevik-Defensists counted on an armed liquidation of the Bolshevik coup before, or simultaneously with, Kerensky's return. An attempt was made by a group of cadets on 29 October *under the flag of the Committee to Save the Country and the Revolution* and scored some initial successes. They occupied the telephone exchange, the so-called engineers' castle (which housed a part of the Nicholas I Military Engineering School), and the Hotel Astoria. But with no help forthcoming from the garrison, or from Krasnov's troops resting at Tsarkoe Selo, the cadets were savagely quashed on the same day. The Bolsheviks had learned of their plan of operations in advance.

The cadet uprising had been prepared, in liaison with the Stavka and Kerensky-Krasnov, by the secret "military group" operating under cover of the political meetings of the Committee to Save the Revolution, unbeknown to most committee members.[36] SRs and Potresovites had been in the plot. The military group worked hand in hand with Lieutenant Count Tolstoy, head of the political department of the Ministry of War, who managed to maintain telegraphic contact with the Stavka and the headquarters of the nearer fronts for several weeks.

The military group expected Kerensky's troops in Petrograd on 29 October. Even the hour was set: 11 A.M.[37] So the uprising was launched during the night of 28–29 October. The appearance of the newspaper *Za Rodinu i Revoliutsiiu*, the organ of the Committee to Save the Revolution, was timed to coincide with it. The paper urged the Petrograd garrison to fight "the insane adventure of the Bolshevik Military-Revolutionary Committee" and asked the soldiers to gather in front of the Military Engineering School, the headquarters of the uprising. Troops loyal to the revolution were approaching the city and "the leader of the Party of Socialist Revolutionaries and of the entire Russian peasantry, Comrade Chernov," was with them. The paper also featured an appeal of the electoral committee of Menshevik Defensists to "help the provisional government and Comrade Kerensky."[38] An order to the garrisons, in the same issue, was signed, among others, by a representative "of the military division of the Social-Democratic Labor Party of Mensheviks, Shakhverdov."[39] Other documents mention the Social-Democrat Sinani in this connection, but he really belonged to the *Edinstvo* group.

Among the non-Potresovite Mensheviks, M. Skobelev, S. Weinstein, and V. Voitinskii were probably informed of the projected uprising. Weinstein apparently had some doubts about the wisdom of the military group's plans. This may have been why he temporarily withdrew from work in the Committee to Save the Revolution.[40]

The cadets' failure predetermined the events of the next day, 30 October. When sailors resisted Krasnov near Pulkovo, he retreated to Gatchina. Peace talks began on 31 October. The Cossacks, in effect, surrendered. Kerensky went into hiding, and Front Commissar Voitinskii announced the end of hostilities.[41]

The political climate in Petrograd changed in favor of the Bolsheviks. Many workers' and soldiers' groups that had been watching from the sidelines now wanted to support them. The amateurishness of the cadet uprising, the total lack of support from the garrison, the instantly

suppressed attempts by "scions of the nobility" to overthrow a government of the poor—all this confirmed Lenin's contention that
the Bolsheviks could stay in power and pulled many waverers into
their camp.

The October overturn was going on in forms never foreseen by the
Bolsheviks or their opponents. There were no crowds in the streets,
whether angry or jubilant. Shops, factories, theaters, cinemas were
open, streetcars running as usual. Classes in schools began at the usual
hour. [42] The overturn had succeeded largely because tens of thousands
of soldiers had been, as it were, neutralized, no longer obeyed the
provisional government's orders, even adopted resolutions proposed by
agitators of the MRC. Some units were willing to carry out assignments
given them by the MRC and more or less directed against the provisional government, but only as long as this did not involve fighting
other soldiers or the cadets who were "guarding" buildings and bridges
but were equally nonbelligerent. Few were prepared to risk their lives
for the MRC. Menshevik and SR appeals not to obey its orders fell on
fertile ground.

N. I. Podvoiskii, one of the military leaders of the overturn, describes how soldiers, "used to making their own decisions," refused to
fight Krasnov's Cossacks. Krylenko, an experienced orator, made the
rounds of the barracks. "Everywhere his exhortations met with resistance." Hoping to turn the mood, Podvoiskii himself went to the
Volynskii regiment, which had been the first to rise against tsarism.
The regiment "unceremoniously replied" that it would not obey the
orders of the MRC. The same happened in several other regiments. [43]
Antonov-Ovseenko notes the "friendly but not very active sympathy"
of the garrison immediately after the overturn. [44] A. F. Il'in-Zhenevskii,
commissar of the MRC, recalls how he scurried from barracks to
barracks. On the morning of 31 October, a note from the secretary of
the Bolshevik group of a chemical warfare unit urgently summoned
him to a meeting " . . . as yesterday's meeting split in half and produced nothing. The resolution of the Defensists may pass." Il'in got his
own resolution passed, but while he was persuading the "chemists,"
the committee of the Grenadier regiment, of which he was also the
commissar, had expressed "discontent about the formation of a one-
party government," reversing its decision of the preceding day. [45]

S. P. Mel'gunov, having studied a vast body of Bolshevik memoir
literature, [46] concluded that the real force behind the MRC was the
sailors of the Baltic fleet (no more than two thousand), supported by
relatively small contingents of young factory workers organized in Red
Guard units. He writes that the huge Putilov plant, allegedly with
fifteen hundred registered Red Guards, provided a unit of only eighty

for the seizure of the Winter Palace. Materials published since Mel'
gunov's work give the same general picture. Typical, probably, is the
telegram sent from Petrograd on the day of the cadet uprising to
Tsentrobalt (the Bolshevik committee of sailors of the Baltic fleet) by one
of its members, Saltykov, asking it to dispatch to Petrograd "units of *fifteen to twenty men per day* until we say stop, but only militant ones."[47]

Abramovich recalls the quiet in Petrograd streets during the night of
24–25 October and the following days. Workers stayed at their factories or homes. There was nothing like the mass demonstrations of 18
June or 3 July, no spontaneous strikes, no excited crowds. The workers
watched developments with bated breath but did not come out for
either side.[48]

The picture changed when the cadet uprising fizzled out for lack of
response from the garrison and the citizenry. Now the Bolsheviks could
count on more active support from soldiers and workers in the event of
armed action. On 29 October, just before the cadet uprising, the lead
article in *Rabochaia Gazeta* had warned that if the Bolsheviks managed to mobilize Red Guard units, "the liquidation of the Bolshevik
crime could turn into the defeat of the revolution and the working
class." The lead article in the next issue already recorded active defense
of the overturn by a considerable part of the masses and foresaw "the
horror of endless carnage in the capital, especially in the working-class
quarters" and "the inevitable defeat of the revolution unless the civil war
is immediately liquidated."[49]

At the trial of the SRs, A. R. Gots would testify: "After the failure of
the movements on 29 October, we saw that we had *no more forces* at
our disposal for an immediate armed overthrow of the Bolsheviks, and
we *changed our tactics*."[50] The Revolutionary Defensist B. G(orev),
member of the Menshevik CC, wrote in *Rabochaia Gazeta* on 1
November that unless Kerensky was extremely careful, "the forces that
now oppose the Bolsheviks" would, despite themselves, end up in the
camp of reaction. Tsereteli felt that it was at the moment impossible to
organize a generally recognized people's government because most of
democracy was "in a state of passivity," while its "active part" supported the Bolsheviks.[51] At a closed meeting of members of the CEC of
the First Convocation he added that for him there was no doubt that
"liquidation of the Bolshevik uprising" meant "shooting the proletariat." Hence it was now "the main task of democracy to consolidate
its forces—*not in order to fight bolshevism* . . . but to increase its own
strength and save the revolution."[52]

Most Mensheviks and SRs shared these views. Overthrowing the Bolsheviks—impossible anyway because of "democracy's passive state"—was

also intolerable because it would mean "shooting the proletariat." On
30 October, the workers of the Sytin press in Moscow, after listening to
two eminent Bolsheviks, Bukharin and Skvortsov, passed a Menshevik
resolution by one thousand votes to thirty, denouncing the Bolsheviks
for isolating the working class and thereby putting all the gains of the
revolution in danger of being drowned in blood—but also declaring it
impossible to "go against" other workers and soldiers. [53]

There seemed to be only two possibilities left: negotiate with the
Bolsheviks about organizing a central government, or "ignore" the
Soviet of People's Commissars until its inevitable fiasco and the growth
of oppositional sentiments among the Bolsheviks and their sympathizers. The two strategies intermingled in the plans of all Menshevik groups
except Potresov's. (In 1918, his group formally seceded from the Party.)

With this exception, the disagreements within menshevism were now
blunted. On 8 November 1917, Defensists returned to the Central Committee, and they were included in the new one formed in May 1918.

To understand the feud between the Potresovites and the other
Mensheviks we must remember that all felt sure of the speedy collapse
of the Sovnarkom. As Richard Pipes has remarked, interest focused on
the *future* government: "The issue was not who rules but who will
rule." The Potresovites did not deny that there was some *danger* of
reaction. But unlike the Internationalists and those Revolutionary
Defensists who maintained (as did Tsereteli in the Caucasus, Isuv in
Moscow, Bogdanov in Petrograd) that the bourgeoisie had turned
against the revolution, the Potresovites continued to view the bourgeoisie and the proletariat as the two classes interested in a free and
"prosperous" capitalist development. For Potresov, a reactionary regime after the Bolsheviks' overthrow was not a foregone conclusion: it
seemed, on the contrary, less likely if the workers and their party
would fight the Bolshevik regime, clearly dissociate themselves from
the October overturn. Semirecognition, especially talks with the Bolsheviks about a coalition government with them, would greatly increase the danger of workers and socialists becoming identified with
the Bolsheviks and their crimes in the eyes of the Russian people.

When the Menshevik CC decided to open negotiations about an all-
socialist government "from NSs to Bolsheviks," the Potresovites accused
it of "betraying" the country and the revolution: instead of isolating
the Bolsheviks, it was creating the impression of close ties between the
advanced Menshevik workers and the Bolsheviks, "dealing a blow" to
the working class, "maligning the proletarian vanguard." By its action,
the CC had "deposed itself in the eyes of all Party members." The
Potresovites declared that they would not submit to the CC's decision,

and called again for the formation, " ... together with the other creative strata of democratic as well as census Russia, of a national government capable of saving the country from being destroyed by the Bolsheviks and the Germans." [54]

An article by Stepan Ivanovich, one of Potresov's most notable supporters, called the members of the CC "liberals of the revolution" who failed to understand that "the yoke of bolshevism can be thrown off, but negotiations with the Bolsheviks, a truce with them, strengthen that yoke." The liberals of the revolution would not influence Lenin any more than earlier liberals had influenced Nicholas II. "Lenin's new autocracy rests on the same ignorance, the same downtrodden state of the worker and soldier groups that are loyal to him. And just because a traitor to the revolution now stands at the head of these praetorians, are we to be afraid of applying methods other than useless and degrading attempts at persuasion?" [55]

The fear that the Germans might make use of a civil war to breach the Russian front and "trample the country" loomed large in the Potresovites' political theories. Even a brief rule by the Soviet of People's Commissars could offer the Germans unhoped-for opportunities. At a meeting of representatives of the Petrograd garrison on 11 November, Potresov argued before a hostile audience that the proposed separate peace talks between individual regiments and the enemy facing their trenches were "the greatest horror," "a nightmare": the "armistice decree" was destroying the army and nullifying the Bolsheviks' assurances that they would wage a "revolutionary war" if necessary. The army would simply disperse, go home, and "no force on earth would make the soldiers fight again." Russia would be at the mercy of its strong, disciplined enemy and suffer the fate of Persia or China. The final outcome would be "a long regime of terror and lawlessness in a destitute, famished land." [56]

4

Vikzhel

The Stand of the Internationalist Groups

As I have said, most Mensheviks wanted to liquidate the Bolshevik regime peacefully. This was especially true of the Internationalists, who blamed the masses' discontent mainly on the provisional government's inertia. Since the Bolsheviks had established a base and overcome armed resistance in Petrograd, democratic socialists must act peaceably in order not to exacerbate the country's counterrevolutionary mood, already fanned to a dangerous degree by Bolshevik excesses. The new regime appeared guilty of many crimes, but it had managed to identify itself with socialism and the proletariat. This in itself made the Menshevik Internationalists very cautious in dealing with anti-Bolshevik groups, lest they find themselves allied with reactionaries for whom deposing the Bolsheviks was merely the first step toward abolishing the democratic order achieved by the revolution.

The two Menshevik factions that had left the Congress of Soviets largely agreed in their estimates and prognoses. The declaration of the official Menshevik faction, read by Khinchuk, and that of the Menshevik Internationalists, read by Martov, both stressed, in almost identical words, that the overturn had been achieved by the Bolshevik party alone, by means of a military coup, and threatened to cause internal strife and "the triumph of counterrevolution." (Khinchuk's statement added "threat of catastrophe" in the war.) [1]

According to Khinchuk's statement, the one remaining peaceful solution was "negotiation with the provisional government about forming a government based on *all* strata of democracy." The declaration of the Menshevik Internationalists—their first since the overturn—already suggested "*agreement* between the part of democracy that has rebelled [that is, the Bolsheviks] and the rest of the democratic organizations," and the formation of a homogeneous government to which the provisional government "could painlessly transfer" the reins. Soon the Central Committee came to agree with this view.

Since their influence in the country was small, the Menshevik Internationalists probably never envisioned their own participation in government. The fact that they had opposed the coalition regime before October, plus their ties with the official leaders of "Soviet democracy," eminently qualified them, they thought, for the role of mediators. They were the most energetic champions of negotiating with the Bolsheviks. During the first session of the Congress of Soviets, Martov had proposed "designating a *delegation to negotiate* with other organs of democracy and all socialist parties" for "peaceful resolution of the present crisis" by forming a government of all democratic groups. After the congress, the Menshevik Internationalist faction and the Petrograd committee of the Party jointly published their reasons for leaving the congress: By rejecting Martov's proposal and voting for the one-party Bolshevik government, the congress had "challenged" the rest of organized democracy to accept the overturn or else submit to the tyranny of those who had seized power; Martov and his group could not assume responsibility for this act of civil war; they had left the congress to be able to work for "a peaceful resolution of the crisis" and to demand that "the Bolsheviks and all other parts of democracy" avoid civil war among the toiling people. [2] We find a similar wording in the Menshevik Internationalists' resolution of 28 October: it stressed the immediate *agreement* between "the Bolsheviks and other socialist parties and democratic organizations" about a homogeneous democratic government that would "*replace the Kerensky and the Bolshevik governments,*" convoke the Constituent Assembly, take steps to end the war, and give land committees control over land. [3]

The Left SRs and the United Internationalists grouped around *Novaia Zhizn*, who had remained at the congress, tried to prevent it from officially recognizing the overturn and establishing the Soviet of People's Commissars. They proposed that a *provisional* executive committee—that is, a provisional central executive committee—be elected instead, to negotiate the formation of a government based on all of revolutionary democracy organized in Soviets, including the peasants' Soviets. The Presidium of the Congress put their proposal to a vote after the resolution about establishing the Soviet of People's Commissars had passed. It nevertheless received about one hundred fifty votes. Some of the moderate Bolsheviks must have voted for it too. [4]

In the political spectrum of the time the Left SRs and the United Internationalists stood between the Bolsheviks and the Menshevik Internationalists. The latter naturally tried to keep these groups on their side, as well as the national socialist groups such as the Polish Lewica and the Jewish socialist parties. The Bund was linked to the Menshevik organization anyway.

The Left SRs were the most influential group in Petrograd, though the youngest in political experience. They had many followers in the Petrograd organization of the Party of Socialist Revolutionaries and to all intents and purposes supported the Military-Revolutionary Committee. During the Menshevik Internationalists' negotiations with them and other like-minded groups (enumerated below) a plan took shape for a joint campaign aimed at forming a government acceptable to both the Bolsheviks and "the rest of democracy." The talks resulted in an appeal, "The Revolution Is in Danger," [5] signed by five factions: Menshevik Internationalists, Left SRs, United Social-Democrat Internationalists, the Polish Lewica, and the Jewish Social-Democratic Poalei Tsion. The influence of Martov's group is evident from its contentions that the purely Bolshevik government lacked the support of "organized democracy" and therefore the necessary support of the country; a civil war would destroy the revolution; only a government "created and recognized" by all of organized democracy could meet the country's urgent needs. The appeal enjoined "both camps of democracy" to find a way to restore a united revolutionary front, "lest the revolution drown in the blood of soldiers, workers, and peasants." However, it made no mention of Bolshevik participation in the desired government. This is no doubt traceable to Martov's influence, which extended far beyond his own Internationalist group. Martov probably thought that if the Committee to Save the Country and the Revolution could be turned into a sovereign, authoritative, generally recognized government of the Russian republic, a socialist government without the Bolsheviks had a chance to become established. At this early stage he undoubtedly expected some armed action against the Bolsheviks from one quarter or another and hoped that Lenin's opponents among the Bolshevik leaders would have time to mobilize influential party circles and prevent a one-party dictatorship.

Even before the overturn, most members of the Menshevik CC had decided that an all-socialist government without the Bolsheviks was imperative. Martov feared that a demand to include the Bolsheviks, given Dan's opposition to it, might impel the Revolutionary Defensist members of the CC to join the partisans of coalition with the "bourgeoisie." He himself had long mistrusted Lenin and had clearly avoided any commitments about Bolshevik participation in government. The Menshevik Internationalists' appeal of 27 October spoke of agreement to form a government of all democratic groups; their resolution of 28 October demanded immediate agreement between Bolsheviks, socialists, and democratic organizations "on the transfer of all power to a homogeneous democratic government" without specifying its composition.

The Initiative of Vikzhel

Some members of the Bolshevik Olympus were alarmed by the growth of maximalist, Leninist aspirations in their party. They were prepared to relinquish the advantage gained in Petrograd if a way could be found to establish a radical regime "without civil war inside democracy." The joint declaration of the five Internationalist factions strengthened the hand of these moderate Bolsheviks. A real possibility of agreement seemed to emerge. But in Petrograd there was no forum where Bolsheviks and right socialists could thresh out their differences; even the Menshevik Internationalists were not represented in the Soviet organs, nor in the executive committee of the Petrograd Soviet, nor, of course, in the Central Executive Committee. In the Council of Trade Unions and the Central Bureau of Trade Unions, many Bolsheviks and Mensheviks favored a homogeneous government, but the SRs were not sufficiently represented, and the Left SRs not at all. In Moscow, however, there was an organization ideally suited to act as mediator: Vikzhel, the All-Russian Executive Committee of the Railroad Union, equally acceptable to the Bolsheviks and the right sector of "Soviet democracy."

All the parties interested in a purely socialist government were represented in Vikzhel. Its forty members included three Bolsheviks,[6] one Kadet, and two nonpartisans, but all the rest were members of socialist parties: eighteen SRs (several of them active adherents of the Left SRs), ten S-Ds, and six NSs. It was headed by the SR Malitskii and the NS Planson, both outspoken partisans of a homogeneous socialist government since the first days of the overturn and, in effect, supporters of the Internationalist stand. Six of the S-Ds were Defensists, four were Internationalists. The Mensheviks most actively involved in the negotiations were Seniushkin (sent by Vikzhel first to confer with Kerensky, then to the Stavka) and Antonevich (sent to the Stavka). According to Vompe, the members Dement'ev, Prianichnikov, Chukhmanskii, and Ukhanov were Mensheviks. [7]

Elected in July 1917 in the most democratic manner, Vikzhel truly represented the railroad workers' views and could count on their support. In the lower-level organs of the railroad union, the ratio of party membership approximately matched that of Vikzhel, even after the October and November elections.

Since railroads were the only means of transportation of goods and people in the enormous country, Vikzhel was a force that neither of the sides could ignore. It was an enthusiastic mediator, and the whole episode is known in the annals of the revolution as "the Vikzhel negotiations." Vikzhel had the unlimited use of railroad telegraph lines and became the country's chief source of information. On 25 October it moved from Moscow to Petrograd and its chairman, Malitskii, sent out telegrams all over the country with the first appeal of the Committee to Save the Country and the Revolution, "Do not Recognize the Government of Tyrants!" [8] The first of a series of telegrams from the bureau of Vikzhel, with a résumé of events, Vikzhel's comments on them, reports on its own activity, and instructions to railroad workers, went out on 26 October. It stated that in Petrograd the Military-Revolutionary Committee was "in effect in power," that the (old) Central Executive Committee and the socialist parties except the Bolsheviks *rejected the slogan "All power to the Soviets"* and were "almost unanimously" coming to see the need for a homogeneous socialist government. The bureau stressed its agreement with "the majority of the socialist parties" and instructed the railroads to "stop immediately" the transportation of Cossacks to Petrograd. Other troops could be moved if the special bureau of five Vikzhel members issued no instructions to the contrary. [9]

On 25 October, before leaving Moscow, Vikzhel had decided to support the Central Executive Committee that was to be elected by the Congress of Soviets. A telegram of 28 October countermanded this decision. Now Vikzhel asked all its member organizations to remain neutral in the struggle between the socialist parties and gave further instructions about transporting troops. [10] Notwithstanding the neutrality just proclaimed, Vikzhel promised to put its facilities at the disposal of "the group that will undertake to organize a homogeneous socialist government representing *all socialist parties from the Bolsheviks to the*

Narodnye Sotsialisty" (that is, matching its own political spectrum). The telegram ended with an appeal to all "organs of the union" to press for an armistice. [11] The slogan "a government from Bolsheviks to NSs" immediately became very popular. Many groups on the right socialist flank soon endorsed it—in some cases, overcoming strong doubts and a deep distaste.

The threat of a railroad strike unless "both camps of revolutionary democracy" sought agreement helped the Internationalists and the moderate Bolsheviks to get their more stubborn comrades to negotiate. A meeting took place on the evening of 29 October in the White Room of the Ministry of Transport, under the chairmanship of the lawyer V. A. Planson, an NS.

A correspondent who had visited Smolnyi Institute on 28 October described the preliminaries to this meeting in *Rabochaia Gazeta*, which still opposed negotiations:

> . . . a handful of Left SRs and United Internationalists . . . are dis-
> cussing the negotiations that *are going on* between the Bolsheviks
> and the rest of democracy. It seems that Kamenev has announced in
> the Bolsheviks' name that they are willing to agree to a homogeneous
> democratic cabinet, and the other side may also make some con-
> cessions. If an agreement is reached, the MRC and the CEC of the
> First Convocation will hand over their mandates to a new organ, to
> which the new government will be answerable. Kerensky will not be
> in the government. [12]

The Vikzhel member Vompe informed Moscow that the Bolsheviks had given in: "yesterday" (28 October) Kamenev had confirmed that their Central Committee had consented to negotiate. Vompe also reported that the five factions that had signed the appeal "The Revolution Is in Danger," as well as a part of the Bolshevik right and a part of the SR center, agreed with Vikzhel, but the Menshevik CC and the Committee to Save the Revolution did not; Vikzhel and its allies would present ultimata to the Bolsheviks and to Kerensky to stop the civil war and restore a united democratic front, or the railroads would strike. [13]

A telegram calling for a general railroad strike at midnight on 29–30 October was addressed to the offices of all railroad unions, to all Soviets, to the central committees of all parties, to trade unions, MRCs, army committees—and "all, all, all" (the stereotype formula). It re-peated the argument of the five factions, concluding that "a homo-geneous government formed with the participation of all socialist parties from Bolsheviks to NSs" was "the only means to secure internal peace." Vikzhel informed the country that "many organizations of Petrograd and Moscow" endorsed its stand and that the railroad union would declare anyone who persisted in armed struggle an enemy of democracy and a traitor to the country. [14]

The Vikzhel Negotiations

Vikzhel's initial success—the parties' consent to negotiate—had been virtually guaranteed in advance. The day before, the *Novaia Zhizn* group had received assurances to this effect from "members of the Bolshevik CC"; and the cadets' defeat had strengthened the advocates of a policy of agreement in the socialist camp. Negotiations began, and Vikzhel called off the strike.

The Potresovites at once dissociated themselves from the whole enterprise. The bureau of Menshevik Defensists announced that no representative of theirs had been at the Vikzhel meeting because "Menshevik Defensists categorically refuse to enter upon any negotiations with the Bolsheviks." [15] Plekhanov's *Edinstvo* and the SR *Volia Noroda* also condemned the negotiations, but these few protests merely underscored the success of Vikzhel's initiative. An impressive meeting took place. Represented were the Central Committees of the Bolsheviks, the Mensheviks (Dan and Erlich), and the SRs. The Menshevik Internationalists sent a four-member delegation (Martov, Martynov, Abramovich, Semkovskii). Also represented were the other Internationalist factions (Left SRs, the *Novaia Zhizn* group, Polish and Jewish socialists); the Petrograd City Duma; trade unions, including the more rightist ones such as the Union of Employees and Potel (post-and-telegraph workers); and even the Soviet of Peasants' Deputies, close to the extreme right of the SRs.

Differences of opinion did not seem to rule out agreement. The delegates of the Menshevik CC were the most belligerent. Dan may not have had time to weigh the implications of the cadets' defeat when he demanded that the MRC be dissolved, the Second Congress of Soviets be considered not to have taken place, and a new government without Bolsheviks be formed. (The same ideas had been expressed in a lead article in *Rabochaia Gazeta*. [16]) Weinstein, for the Committee to Save the Revolution, and Gendelman, for the Central Committee of the Party of Socialist Revolutionaries, also spoke against the inclusion of Bolsheviks in the new government. The Bolsheviks sounded far more conciliatory. Kamenev pressed for recognition "of the platform of the Second Congress of Soviets," for the new governement's accountability to the Central Executive Committee of the Soviets (which would include representatives of the factions that had left the Congress), and for agreement between all parties from NSs to Bolsheviks as to the composition of the new government: the Bolshevik CC recognized the need for "broadening the base of the government and possible changes in its composition."

Some of the non-Bolsheviks at the conference were probably aware that the Bolshevik CC had decided not to insist on definite candidates, not even Lenin and Trotsky. The best informed may even have known that four members of the CC, including its representatives at the Vikzhel meeting, had voted against adamant insistence (*ul'timativnoe trebovanie*) on Bolshevik participation in government. The CC's decision that "the foremost issue is the program of the government and its accountability, *by no means its personal composition*," convinced the knowledgeable mediators that their attempts to promote agreement had a chance to succeed.

More concrete proposals were put forward by Martov for the Menshevik Internationalists and Malkin for the Left SRs. Martov insisted that in the organ that would control the government not only Soviets be represented but also democratically elected city dumas and zemstvos. His group thought the inclusion of city dumas an indispensable corrective to the aspirations of the maximalist Bolshevik wing and an important safeguard for the Defensist Mensheviks and SRs.[17] Malkin proposed giving the Bolsheviks many of the portfolios, but not the majority, leaving the Defensists and the Bolsheviks the right to reject each other's ministerial candidates.

The large, unwieldy conference chose a commission of representatives of the main contending groups to conduct negotiations: Kamenev, Sokol'nikov, and Riazanov for the Bolsheviks; Dan (of the CC of the RSDRP(0)), Gendelman (of the CC of the PSR), and An-skii (of the Petrograd City Duma) for the right sector; and two representatives of the mediators: one a member of Vikzhel and the other Abramovich, who was taking a more active part than Martov in the negotiations and was more hopeful of their success.

After an all-night discussion, the commission had nothing definite to put before the plenary conference. The question of a truce had been shelved because all three representatives of the Bolsheviks had refused to commit themselves. They could not have committed the MRC in any case. And Kerensky was not represented: the delegation sent to him by Vikzhel (Planson, the Left SR Krushinskii, and the Menshevik Seniushkin) had brought back no concrete proposals. The two mediators and the three rightist members of the commission had voted for a truce, but with the Bolsheviks abstaining and Kerensky "missing," this was at best a "demonstration" of no practical import.

Furthermore, the new compromise proposals drawn up by the Menshevik Central Committee and offered by Dan had been seconded by Gendelman and An-skii but had failed to provide a basis for agreement. The Menshevik CC had suggested neutralizing the Petrograd garrison, giving it merely the task of preventing pogroms and violence, under the supervision of the City Duma, and not letting Kerensky's troops penetrate the working-class quarters. To be effective, the new government must contain no one "more rightist that the NSs"; its tasks must be limited: convening the Constituent Assembly, transferring the land to land committees, and arranging for a joint declaration by the Allies that they were willing to begin peace talks. Dan for his own part believed that a government "from the NSs to the Bolsheviks" was impossible "at the moment" because the inclusion of Bolsheviks would push "enormous parts of the nonpartisan democratic population" into the camp of reaction. [18] To sum up, the commission had agreed on only one thing: no bourgeois parties in the government.

The plenary conference made several decisions, in which the Bolshevik delegates apparently joined with the mediators and the right wing, contradicting the stand of Lenin and the MRC. Martov and the Bolshevik Lozovskii, representative of the All-Russian CEC, were entrusted with drafting a resolution against political terror. This resolution—directed against the MRC—was telegraphed to all parts of Russia. [19] The conference decided on an "immediate armistice," approved a message to this effect to the warring sides, and instructed a newly elected commission "definitely" to designate a government "from NSs to Bolsheviks," accountable to an organ to be created by the Central Executive Committees of the First and Second Convocation, the city dumas of the capitals (the Bolsheviks had not yet agreed to this), the trade unions, and the Peasants' Soviets. By this time the SRs had softened their stand: their delegate Rakitnikov was willing to accept individual Bolsheviks in the cabinet. The Menshevik CC and considerable groups in the Bolshevik party soon began to favor agreement—under the pressure of public opinion, especially of demands from factories and military units, which the Menshevik Internationalists and their allies had mobilized under the motto, "Demand agreement of all revolutionary parties and parts of democracy." [20]

In the Committee of the Petrograd Organization of the RSDRP(0), Internationalists predominated. In the Petrograd City Organization of the Party of Socialist Revolutionaries, Left SRs played a major role. *Rabochaia Gazeta* announced that, the Vikzhel negotiations having

run into an impasse, both the Menshevik Internationalists and the Left
SRs had made it their "mission" to convince the socialist parties of the
urgent need for agreement and were conducting intensive propaganda
for it. The Vikzhel slogan "from NSs to Bolsheviks" answered the mood
of the Petrograd masses and found wide support in circles that neither
the Revolutionary Defensists nor the Bolsheviks could ignore, especially since certain groups that only yesterday had backed the Bolsheviks now demanded agreement among the socialist parties and an
all-socialist government.

The Petrograd Council of Trade Unions had been under Bolshevik
influence for months. It had welcomed the overturn and on 27 October
had appealed to all Petrograd workers to support the new regime and
stop all strikes. Nevertheless, on 31 October, after a heated debate in
which Menshevik Internationalists spoke very sharply, the council
passed a resolution demanding "immediate agreement among all socialist parties" and a government including all of them. [21]

The Central Committee of the Trade Union of Sailors and River
Transport Workers on 29 October had also issued an appeal to support
"the new government," but on 30 October it demanded a socialist
cabinet "of all socialist parties and factions of revolutionary democracy." Similar demands appear in resolutions of other trade unions and
individual Petrograd factories. [22]

In the so-called Vyborg sector of Petrograd the Mensheviks had old
ties with the metalworkers' union, [23] yet the Bolsheviks had received the
absolute majority of votes in the elections to the sector duma in August
1917. On 29 October the Soviet of Workers' and Soldiers' Deputies of
the sector had condemned the "traitorous path" taken by Menshevik
Defensists and SRs. But on 1 November the same Soviet issued an
appeal signed by the Bolshevik, Menshevik, and SR factions (!) to "end
party squabbles and discord" and consolidate "all socialist forces." The
Vyborg sector duma with its absolute Bolshevik majority demanded on
31 October that the two camps of democracy immediately conclude an
armistice and organize a government from NSs to Bolsheviks. [24]

The great Obukhov metalworks provides a good illustration of the
impulsive changes of mood, the contradictory decisions, the political
waverings of the Petrograd workers at this time. At a meeting on 29
October, the Menshevik Internationalist Davin Dallin could not finish
his speech, and other Mensheviks could not even begin theirs, because
the workers objected to the least criticism of Bolsheviks. The audience
shouted for Dallin's arrest as counterrevolutionary, Kornilovite, traitor
to the people. On 30 October, the workers passed a resolution in the
spirit of the Vikzhel demands, and during the following night an

excited delegation from the plant burst in on a meeting of the Vikzhel commission, demanding peace among all socialist parties and—according to An-skii—the instant hanging of both Lenin and Chernov. [25]

Mel'gunov writes of a "wave" of resolutions demanding internal peace that swept the Petrograd factories. Abramovich reports that hundreds of telegrams came in daily from all over Russia in support of the Vikzhel stand. [26] The Army Committee (*Obshchearmeiskii Komitet*) at the Stavka in Mogilev was informed from Petrograd of "tremendous pressure exercised by the aroused masses on the organizational centers." [27] Even the Bolshevik sailors of the destroyer *Oleg*, which had been called out from Kronstadt, broadcast from their ship on 30 October the "glad tidings" of negotiations among "all socialist parties, who are trying to form a bloc." [28]

The Mensheviks' Stand in the Provinces

News came that Mensheviks in the provinces were also seeking to resolve the crisis through negotiations with the Bolsheviks.

The Georgian Mensheviks led by Zhordania had given up the idea of coalition with "census elements" before the overturn. In Moscow (where street fighting was going on) many favored agreement with the Bolsheviks as long as civil rights were preserved. The Committee of the Moscow Organization thought of creating in that city a joint democratic organ that would become, as it were, the nucleus of a homogeneous central government. [29]

In Kharkov, Mensheviks, Bolsheviks, and others were in a local organ of government that did not recognize the Sovnarkom. On 30 October, the Mensheviks and SRs, including the Left SRs, demanded the formation of a government on Vikzhel lines. [30] In Odessa, most members of the Menshevik organization were willing for Mensheviks to participate in a government including Bolsheviks if the latter desisted from "further adventures." [31] In Kiev, a local government (the Regional [*Kraevoi*] Committee to Defend the Revolution in the Ukraine) was formed as early as the night of 25–26 October. The Mensheviks were invited to take part in it but do not seem to have responded. The Bund, however, did join the regional committee (which soon delegated its functions to the General Secretariat, an organ of the Ukrainian People's Rada).

In Tula, a center of the metalworking industry, Mensheviks and SRs won a majority in the local Soviet after reelections in late October. At its first meeting, 30 October, the Soviet endorsed a united front. Five members of the Bolshevik faction voted with the Mensheviks, officially dissociating themselves from their party "on this issue." [32] In Orel, on 1 November, the Soviet of Workers' Deputies adopted by a majority of 56 votes to 39 Bolshevik votes a Menshevik resolution demanding a homogeneous government "of representatives of the three basic socialist parties" (that is, Bolsheviks, Mensheviks, and SRs), which would actively seek peace, transfer the land to land committees, control production and distribution of goods, tax the richer classes, and convoke the Constituent Assembly. [33] In the Ekaterinoslav City Duma the Mensheviks voted on 27 October in favor of organizing a homogeneous socialist government. [34]

In the Urals, the Perm Mensheviks opposed negotiations about a joint government with the Bolsheviks and even got the Soviet of Workers' Deputies to reject seizure of power by local Soviets, [35] but in Ufa Mensheviks did participate in local government organs together with Bolsheviks and SRs. [36] In Ekaterinburg, the center of the Ural region, Mensheviks, Bund members, Bolsheviks, SRs, and trade union representatives formed on 30 October a joint "People's Rule Committee," and on 31 October, a Military-Revolutionary Committee of all socialist parties. [37]

The Defensist-minded Menshevik organizations of Rostov-on-the-Don and nearby Taganrog and Novocherkassk had strong reservations about a joint government with the Bolsheviks. In this region the Bolsheviks did not get firmly established for a long time. [38] In a resolution passed on 3 November, a conference of the Don organization of the RSDRP(0) declared that it had "no ideological closeness with bolshevism" and would consider only "technical agreements with it." It condemned the "military conspiracy organized by the Petrograd Bolsheviks," yet stressed the need for "agreement of the socialist parties and central democratic organizations about creating a provisional government" that would "first of all" stop the civil war, and also restore civic rights, try to initiate as soon as possible peace negotiations "together with the Allies," and transfer the land to land committees "until the convocation of the Constituent Assembly." [39] This may have been cautiously worded (by this time, pro-Bolshevik sentiments were growing in the Rostov garrison and factories, while, on the other hand, Kaledin was already mustering his forces), but even so, the resolution was clearly not Potresovite in spirit. A few weeks later the armed struggle between the Novocherkassk Cossacks and the Rostov Bolsheviks began. The Mensheviks and SRs kept out of this struggle initiated by "adventurers of both camps" for aims that had nothing to do with the interests of soldiers, Cossacks, sailors, workers, or peasants—as an appeal pointed out. In late December, under Kaledin, workers' repre-

sentatives at a congress of the non-Cossack population of the Don
Region—most of them Mensheviks, according to Antonov-Ovseenko
—demanded the disarmament of the White army, nonrecognition
of the Sovnarkom, and a truce.[40] Martov approved the position of
the Rostov Mensheviks.[41]

Quite a few Defensist-minded organizations did conclude that a
government from NSs to Bolsheviks was the only solution. The slogan
was too popular—as the Bolsheviks, who disliked it, also admit.[42] It
was "the best way to satisfy the broad masses" and also "the only way
we can avoid bloodshed and civil war," as the chairman of the Mogilev
Province organization of the Mensheviks and the Bund, the Right
Defensist Braun, said as early as the evening of 26 October. "The
country couldn't manage" without it and without a program of "all the
land to the toiling people."[43]

Some of the most conservative organizations of "Democracy" also
issued their share of naïve resolutions in which abhorrence of Bolshevik
practices mingled with yearning for unity.[44] The Petrograd Office
Workers' Union protested against the persecution of Plekhanov and the
Sovnarkom's intention to arrest Kerensky, and decided to expel members who had disobeyed the union's resolution to sabotage government
offices—but at the same time it demanded "immediate formation of a
government of all socialist parties from NSs to Bolsheviks."[45]

An Annulled Agreement

On the morning of 31 October, the Menshevik CC resolved to
negotiate about organizing a government in which the Bolsheviks
would have a part. The decision was taken under pressure from
Petrograd workers and Party members after General Krasnov's retreat
to Gatchina. The short resolution read:

> Having discussed the situation and recognized that all other consid-
> erations must give way before the need at all costs to prevent con-
> tinued bloodshed, internal strife among workers, and the ruin of the
> labor movement, the CC of the RSDRP(0) resolves to take part in the
> attempt to organize a homogeneous government including the so-
> cialist parties from the NSs to the Bolsheviks.[46]

Internationalist members of the CC, in the first place Abramovich,
were already involved in the Vikzhel negotiations. The CC of the Party
of Socialist Revolutionaries was now also ready to reconcile itself to the
presence of Bolsheviks in the government. The Bolsheviks who represented the new All-Russian Executive Committee and the Bolshevik

CC in the special Vikzhel commission also favored agreement, and they hoped that the pleas of workers' representatives would help them to win the other Bolshevik leaders over to their views and away from Lenin's.

The contours of agreement were emerging—on relatively minor issues, it is true. The organ that would formally create the new government was to be planned—a "People's" or "Democratic Soviet" of representatives of Soviets of Workers' and Soldiers' Deputies as well as of the dumas of the two capitals, Peasants' Soviets, and trade unions, including Vikzhel and Potel. Now that even the Menshevik CC had issued a resolution in favor of agreement, Vikzhel at once relayed to its representatives at the army committee at the Stavka[47] the "glad, important news" about this statement.[48] From there it was widely and approvingly publicized through the army committee's bulletin.[49]

In an all-out effort, the Vikzhel commission managed to nominate mutually acceptable ministers: V. M. Chernov, premier; the Mensheviks Maliantovich and Gvozdev (who were in Kerensky's cabinet), and Professor N. A. Rozhkov, a Menshevik Internationalist; the most important posts went to Bolsheviks: Rykov for the Interior and Pokrovskii for Foreign Affairs. Lenin was not on the list, and Trotsky was removed from it.[50]

Abramovich copied out the list and gave his handwritten copy to Kamenev. He also composed (at the commission's wish) the proclamation that Kamenev intended to have printed and posted in the streets during the night. It announced an immediate truce, the release of arrested persons, and the creation of an all-socialist government. Abramovich recalls his joyful "bulletin" to the neighbors who were guarding the apartment house during those troubled nights: "At last! All is settled! Agreement reached, truce to be declared this morning. In a few hours, proclamation listing new government will be posted throughout city."[51]

But after Abramovich had gone home, the Military-Revolutionary Committee had refused safe-conduct to the delegation that was to inform Kerensky of the announced cease-fire. And on the morning of 2 November it emerged that the Bolshevik negotiators had been repudiated by their own Central Committee. Krasnov's retreat—the retreat of a few hundred Cossacks by a few miles—had further undermined the opposition to Lenin, already weakened by the cadets' defeat. Kerensky had fled, Lenin's line had prevailed in the Bolshevik CC. No proclamations were visible in the streets, and Abramovich vainly tried to reach Kamenev by telephone for an explanation.

Meanwhile the army committee reported in its bulletin (published on 2 November): "During all of yesterday, until late at night, negotiations about forming a government . . . went on simultaneously . . . in Petrograd, Gatchina, Pskov, and the Stavka." In Petrograd, the Central Committees of the socialist parties were in session. Vikzhel persisted in its efforts to promote agreement. So did the representatives of the army committee in Petrograd—and also the Committee to Save the Revolution (largely under the influence of the bad news from Gatchina). [52]

In Gatchina, Kerensky had conferred with his advisers and decided that his forces were not large enough or reliable enough to take Petrograd. He had telegraphed Vikzhel on 1 November:

> In accordance with the proposal *of the Committee to Save* [the Country and the Revolution] *and of all the democratic organizations* that have united around it, I have stopped operations against the insurgent troops and have sent a representative— . . . Stankevich— to open negotiations. Take measures to stop needless bloodshed [italics added].

Kerensky also telegraphed Dukhonin to take over the functions of commander in chief and informed him that he, Kerensky, had laid down the title of premier. "All the rights and duties of that office" were now at the disposal of the provisional government. [53]

From Pskov, V. M. Chernov, with another SR, A. Iu. Feit, and the Menshevik Defensist Ia. A. Kharash. a member of the CEC and head (together with G. D. Kuchin) of the Menshevik group of the Twelfth army, tried to hammer out an agreement with Duknonin about organizing a government without Kerensky, and vainly tried to get Dukhonin to remove General Cheremisov from the command of the northern front. [54]

At the Stavka, the army committee called upon all front organizations to support a new homogeneous government under Chernov, in the hope that it would prove possible to create such a government without, or with very little, Bolshevik participation. Under the circumstances one could no longer reject the Bolsheviks outright.

But the decisive events had taken place in the conference room of the Central Committee of the *Bolshevik* party. On 1 November, Lenin had finally obtained the CC's sanction of his own plans for the new government and the future course of his revolution.

5

The Consolidation of Bolshevik Rule

Lenin's Victory in the Bolshevik Central Committee

The decisive turn in the events we have recounted was, as we have seen, the refusal of the Bolshevik Central Committee to ratify the agreement Kamenev had reached. Vainly did Miliutin warn those who would "keep the power exclusively in our own hands" that the Bolsheviks could not withstand a prolonged civil war, [1] and Riazanov argue that having been left "alone, hopelessly alone," without even the Left SRs, "we have deceived the masses, after promising them a Soviet government." Vainly did Rykov prophesy that "even the groups that support us will recoil from us" and insist that Kamenev had been "perfectly right" in the way he had conducted the negotiations.

Trotsky and Lenin were strongly opposed to any kind of agreement. Lenin even resorted to the preposterous argument that Vikzhel "sides with the Kaledins and Kornilovs" and "cannot be let into the CEC." The negotiations, he said, had been "a diplomatic cover for military operations" and were no longer necessary. "Kamenev's policy must be discontinued at once." Nevertheless, the proposal to break off the talks received *only four* votes to ten. [2] Of the ten who did not want to break them off, only four liked the Kamenev agreement (Kamenev, Zinov'ev, Miliutin, Rykov). The rest, though loath to clash with Lenin, feared

73

the reaction of the masses of workers who had enthusiastically embraced the formula "from the NSs to the Bolsheviks."

Only the day before, at the 31 October meeting of the Petrograd Soviet, the Bolsheviks had argued that "all groups except the right SRs and the Mensheviks lean to agreement with the Soviet."[3] At the 1 November meeting of the Bolshevik CC, Sokol'nikov—an opponent of agreement—pointed out that "our situation has considerably worsened" since the resolution of the Menshevik CC; and another far from moderate member, Sverdlov, remarked: "*Everybody* is asking who is in the government besides Bolsheviks." He suggested, in passing, that "somebody in Vikzhel" should be arrested—presumably just to see what would happen.

The CC members who disliked Kamenev's agreement but feared an abrupt break in the negotiations would have voted for breaking them off if this could have been done on some pretext that would temporarily placate the groups that had to be taken into account. But neither the personal composition of the government nor, still less, the issue of terror and civil liberties, which the Mensheviks were stressing, would serve as an adequate pretext. Kamenev, facing his comrades' opposition yet anxious to avoid a formal break with Vikzhel, asked the CC to propose some other agreement. Naturally he favored the one he had made, he said, but "this does not mean that all the proposals [to which he had agreed] must be accepted."

The Bolshevik CC then proposed conditions that it knew to be unacceptable to the socialist parties: recognition of the Second Congress of Soviets as "the sole source of power"; accountability of the new government to the CEC; no representation in the CEC for organizations not included in the Soviets (that is, organs of local self-government). By Kamenev's agreement, the latter were entitled to one hundred seats, an equal number with the CEC, in the organ to which the government was to be responsible.[4] To please Lenin, the CC added a sharp instruction to its spokesmen "to take part *today* in a *last* attempt to form a new government, for the purpose of *final* disclosure of the unsoundness of this attempt and *final* discontinuance of further negotiations about a coalition [?] government." Only four "moderates" voted against a proposal to present the terms in the form of an ultimatum to be answered within two hours; on the other hand, only four "extreme" members voted in favor of the proposal. In the second round, one member who had abstained in the first round changed his mind, and the vote was five to four in favor of the two-hour ultimatum, with the rest of the CC abstaining.

The decision carried so little weight that Kamenev and the other "moderates" in the CC simply ignored it. So did the Bolshevik faction of the CEC. On 1 November it had unanimously endorsed the CC's proposals (causing the United Internationalists to leave the CEC), but on 2 November, after Kamenev's report, it reversed itself, resolving (with only six voting against) to ignore these and reopen negotiations. Vikzhel in turn was eager to keep up at least the appearances of continued negotiations for a peaceful agreement, even though the Central Committees of the socialist parties had "taken note" that the Bolsheviks had scuttled the attempt.

Kamenev and his followers persuaded the CEC (first its Bolshevik faction, then a plenary session) to accept a program of agreement that plainly contradicted the decisions of their CC, even the cut version published in *Pravda*. Kamenev, who had conducted the negotiations in the name of the Bolshevik CC, was to continue them as representative of the new CEC. So the Bolshevik delegation that had left the Vikzhel conference table on 1 November was back at it on 2 and 3 November.

The open revolt of the Bolshevik opposition against Lenin and the CC seemed to be just what the Mensheviks had hoped for when they banked on a peaceful liquidation of the overturn. Answering the members of the Menshevik CC who had opposed the decision to negotiate with the Bolsheviks, Dan argued that agreement was impossible "without a split in bolshevism," that the Leninists' rejection of it was costing the Bolsheviks "enormous masses of workers," and that "thanks to our tactics, the Bolsheviks are already splitting."[5]

The 2 November resolution of the Menshevik Central Committee stated that the decision of the Bolshevik CC "made agreement impossible" and that "the entire responsibility for the consequences" therefore fell on the Bolsheviks; nevertheless, the Menshevik Central Committee would continue its efforts to end the strife. The Mensheviks would resume negotiations if the Bolsheviks first complied with four basic conditions "guaranteeing the sincerity and efficacy of the agreement": 1) release political prisoners; 2) renounce political terror; 3) conclude a truce; and 4) put an armed force at the disposal of the Petrograd City Duma, to police the city and preserve order. All these were popular demands. The resolution stressed that successful government depended on the participation, on a coequal footing, of "all democratic strata and the parties and organizations that represent them"; a purely Bolshevik government, unrecognized by the other parts of democracy and most of the country, would lead to famine, military defeat, anarchy, civil war, and counterrevolution.[6] According to Abramovich, it was he and Martov who had suggested making the cessation of terror a condition for further negotiations with the Bolsheviks. [7] At the next meeting of the Vikzhel agreement commission, on 3 November, Martov and Abramovich represented the Menshevik CC and not merely its Internationalist faction, for which they usually spoke. [8] They announced the preliminary conditions, stressing in particular points 2 and 3: "abolition of political terror, restoration of freedom of the press, of speech, assembly, association, strikes, and the inviolability of persons in their homes," and "declaration of a truce wherever civil war is going on." The politically unsophisticated men of Vikzhel and the army committee in fact got the impression that the Mensheviks were absent and only the Menshevik Internationalists "on the whole endorsed the program of Vikzhel and the army committee." [9]

Two of the Bolshevik representatives at the Vikzhel conference of 3 November opposed any kind of agreement; four shared the Internationalists' misgivings about Lenin's terrorist tactics and hoped to reach agreement with the representatives of the parties of democratic socialism on a formulation that the extremist Bolsheviks, under pressure of revolutionary-democratic opinion, would not dare to reject.

However, the Menshevik and SR leaders in Petrograd felt increasingly sure that Lenin had subdued his Central Committee and would not accept any kind of agreement. Only a few members of the Menshevik CC continued to hope with Abramovich for a successful "pressure from the masses" and the creation of a new government by mutual consent.

The Ekaterinoslav Soviet published in its *Izvestiia* an interview with the left SR V. A. Karelin, chairman of the Kharkov Duma and a prominent figure in the negotiations. Karelin pointed out that the moderate Bolsheviks had been absent when the resolution of confidence in the Sovnarkom had been voted on. He hoped that "in a few days, the moderate Bolsheviks will be voting with us, forming a majority in the CEC. And then two outcomes will be possible: either Lenin and Trotsky will dare to establish their dictatorship, or the initiative will pass entirely to the moderate Bolsheviks, Left SRs, and Menshevik Internationalists." Karelin added that the Left SRs' current policy sought to isolate Lenin while preventing the isolation of bolshevism as a whole. [10]

Was this hope as illusory as it appears in the light of the data cited in the countless Soviet books on the October overturn? The workers had eagerly picked up both slogans—a government of all socialist parties and the abolition of terror. On 6 November, five days after Lenin's victory in the Bolshevik CC, the Bolsheviks still felt impelled to state in a new resolution of the CEC that they were willing to continue negotiations about an all-socialist government and were entrusting them to the men who had conducted them before (but who had since left the CC and the Sovnarkom!); the resolution added that 1) many arrested persons had already been released; 2) *all* socialist papers could appear freely; 3) no order to arrest the Committee to Save the Country and the Revolution had been issued; 4) the preservation of order in Petrograd was assured. [11] This looked like a "positive" response to the four Menshevik demands published in the same order in *Rabochaia Gazeta* on 5 November.

The revolt of the Bolshevik opposition on 4 November 1917—when five members of the Bolshevik CC (Kamenev, Rykov, Miliutin, Zinov'ev, and Nogin) and no less than eight other members of the new government resigned, publicly condemning Lenin's "destructive policy" carried out in defiance of the will of "an enormous part of the proletariat and soldiers"—encouraged the advocates of the policy of agreement in the camp of democratic socialism. The Bolshevik leaders had left the Central Committee and the Soviet of People's Commissars not in despair but to fight Lenin and work for an inclusive socialist government, since the only alternative was "the preservation of a purely Bolshevik government *by means of political terror.*" The former people's commissars declared for all to hear that the Soviet of People's Commissars had chosen the way of terror, which could only result in an "irresponsible regime," the loss by the proletarian mass organizations of their leading role in the country's political life, and the defeat of the revolution.

In a letter to the Bolshevik faction of the CEC, A. Lozovskii sharply protested against the terrorist bent of the Bolshevik summit: the workers were rumbling; they had been promised a Soviet regime, and it had unaccountably turned into a purely Bolshevik one; other circumstances, too, "imperiously demanded agreement with all socialist parties," on pain of ruin; he for one would not "indulge in a personality cult in the name of party discipline." [12]

The CC members who had publicly denounced the CC's decision had taken this step, very unusual in Bolshevik circles, because they felt that many Bolshevik party workers throughout the country were behind them and that even Lenin's supporters in the CC were wavering. The feud between Lenin and his Bolshevik antagonists, and the widespread rumbling against a purely Bolshevik government, did not abate until the Germans agreed to peace talks in mid-November, thus enabling Lenin to fulfill at least one of his promises—and the country's most eager hope—termination of the war, and to count on the continued support of millions of soldiers. Not only the Bolshevik opposition gave in to him then, but also the Left SRs and even Vikzhel.

The resistance to Lenin had been far stronger than Bolshevik historians would have it. In the CC's resolution of 2 November, Lenin had invited the opposition members of the CC to "take their discussion and their skepticism *to the press* and retire from practical work," but a few days later he "repeated" his ultimatum to the minority that they "adhere to the CC's policy in all their utterances."[13] On 3 November, planning for an extraordinary Party congress, Lenin threatened that if "the present opposition" were entrusted with forming a new government "together with their allies, for whose sake the opposition is now sabotaging our work," he and his followers would consider themselves *"absolutely free vis-à-vis that new government."*[14] He also said that his conflict with Kamenev and with the opposition in the CC "basically" repeated "our differences with the *Novaia Zhizn* group and Martov's."[15] This part of the resolution of 2 November and the ultimatum to the minority were not published at the time, but the news probably seeped through to the Menshevik leaders—their ties with the Bolshevik opposition were not yet completely cut.

Official Communist history refers to some "Kamenev" sentiments in provincial Bolshevik organizations but maintains that "the overwhelming majority" of them "supported the stand of the Central Committee. The Ivanovo-Voznesensk, Smolensk, Tula, Orel, western front, and other organizations categorically rejected agreement with the Mensheviks."[16] The listed cities do not suggest an "overwhelming majority," and even they did not reject agreement as categorically as all that. Let us take a look at some of them.

Tula: A. F. Il'in-Zhenevskii (brother of F. F. Raskol'nikov, the leader of the Kronstadt Soviet, later commander of the Baltic fleet) arrived in Tula on 10 November with a detachment of Red Guards and sailors. He found some "fear of Mensheviks and SRs," but "the arguments peacefully reposing in the muzzles of our cannon" bolstered the courage of those of his fellow party members who shared his views.[17] The local Bolshevik paper did indeed speak out against "advocates of agreement" only on 10 November. The role of the troops is even clearer if we remember that the Tula Soviet had refused to recognize the Sovnarkom and that in early November, according to Soviet historians, "a considerable part of the workers of the Tula armaments and cartridge plants and the railroad junction were still following the Mensheviks and SRs."[18] These plants and the railroad employed about 50,000 workers, over 90 percent of the Tula proletariat.

Orel: The Orel Bolsheviks began an open campaign against the SRs and Mensheviks who were still in the Soviet *only in January 1918*. Not until 10/23 January did the Soviet definitely recognize the CEC and the Sovnarkom.[19] The Bolshevik organization had been formed just before the overturn. I. I. Fokin, sent from Moscow by the Bolshevik regional bureau to work in Orel Province, had reported to the bureau on the situation in the city *in late September 1917*: In the Menshevik organization there were three hundred Defensists and Internationalists; the Bolshevik organization no longer existed—what Bolsheviks there were had merged with the Internationalists. [20] At a meeting of the Soviet held on 25 November it turned out that most of the workers' deputies sided with the Mensheviks, while most of the soldiers' joined the Bolsheviks. The workers' division of the Soviet elected to the executive committee nine Mensheviks, three SRs, three nonpartisans, and only five Bolsheviks; the soldiers' division, five Right SRs, one Polish socialist, one Left SR, twelve Bolsheviks and sympathizers, and one anarchist. [21]

I have not been able to check the references to Ivanovo-Voznesensk and Smolensk, but in the Bolshevik organizations of the western front some of the leaders undoubtedly sympathized at the time with the "capitulationists Zinov'ev and Kamenev." The Bolshevik Military-Revolutionary Committee of the western front sent a "capitulationist sympathizer," Gromashevskii (later People's Commissar for the Western Region), to organize the 2 November Congress of Soviets of the Third army. The congress not only failed to support Lenin against "capitulationists" but recommended a government of all socialist parties. [22]

During those days Lenin clearly doubted the reliability of his Central Committee. After attacking Kamenev in the Petrograd Committee, he went to a meeting of the CC, from which he sent the Petrograd Committee an urgent order: "The Moscow people are demanding agreement with Mensheviks and SRs. Must rebuff.... Immediately pass a resolution against agreement and bring it to the CC." [23]

The newly elected Central Executive Committee, too, seemed to be slipping out of Lenin's grasp, although it consisted of seventy Bolsheviks and only thirty members of other parties (mostly Left SRs). The 4 November resolution of confidence in the Soviet of People's Commissars received only twenty-five votes, with twenty-three against and two abstentions, although Lenin had taken the floor six times! [24]

Abramovich quotes V. Nevskii's statement that even in the Petrograd Bolshevik organization only the Vasil'ev-Ostrov sector and Latvian and Estonian Bolsheviks firmly opposed the Vikzhel plan. [25] In a number of provincial cities, Bolsheviks continued to seek peaceful agreement with the socialist parties even after Lenin had got the Petrograd Committee and the CC to condemn such attempts.

Partisans of an inclusive socialist government predominated, for example, in the Moscow Bolshevik organization, which was bigger than the Ivanovo-Voznesensk, Smolensk, Tula, and Orel ones combined. Contrary assertions in memoirs notwithstanding, both the right *and* the left members of the Moscow MRC invariably put forward the idea of a socialist coalition. Even after the CC had censured the opposition members who had left the CC, the Moscow Bolsheviks continued to insist that representatives of cities and zemstvos be given a share in organizing a government, and the Moscow Committee passed a resolution on the need to combine with the other socialist parties.[26]

To be sure, in Moscow and the provinces the atmosphere was not the same as in Petrograd. We can get an idea of the conditions under which the Mensheviks had to make their decisions outside the capital if we examine the moves of the Moscow Bolsheviks after the exit of the opposition from the Bolshevik Central Committee.

On 5 November, the (entirely Bolshevik) Moscow MRC decided to begin negotiations about local government. Mindful of their CC's resolution about "preliminary conditions," the Mensheviks did not wish to take part in them. The Bolsheviks then arranged a "private conference" with Left SRs and "Uniteds" (this group partly shared the views of *Novaia Zhizn*) and tried to enlist their help in bringing in the Mensheviks.[27] At the same time the MRC sent the Mensheviks an official written invitation to "take part in an interparty conference on the organization of government" at 3 P.M. on 6 November.[28]

The Menshevik *Vpered* of 5 November declared: "We demand of the Bolshevik government: 1) inviolability of person and abode; 2) abolition of censorship and full freedom of the press; 3) freedom of circulation in the streets and abolition of personal searches."[29] On 6 November the Mensheviks added a fourth demand: reinstatement of the City Duma.

The Bolsheviks reacted quite well. A meeting of the City Duma was allowed to take place at Shaniavskii University. On the issue of arrested cadets, the MRC invited a socialist group to visit the two prisons in which cadets were still kept. On the main demand—freedom of the press—the MRC resolved on 6 November that from 8 November all Moscow publications "regardless of orientation" could appear freely (that is, without being censored), because "the elections to the Constituent Assembly *presuppose freedom of agitation* for all parties and trends *without exception.*"[30] To appreciate this, one should keep in mind that two days *earlier* Lenin had argued in the CEC that "tolerating the existence of bourgeois papers means ceasing to be socialists."[31]

The Mensheviks nevertheless announced at the meeting of 6 November that they would negotiate with the MRC only after it had lifted its restrictions on "democratic freedoms" and restored a free City Duma. The representative of the United Social-Democrat Internationalists agreed with the Mensheviks but suggested that the organization of government could be discussed tentatively before the Mensheviks' conditions were met. The Menshevik A. A. Iugov replied: "As long as the Bolshevik terror lasts, there can be no negotiations with the Military-Revolutionary Committee"—whereupon the chairman, the Menshevik V. V. Mikhalevskii, laid down the gavel, and the conference ended. [32]

The next day, 7 November, a closed meeting of the executive committee of the Moscow Soviet tried to find a way out of the impasse. Isuv asked the Bolshevik opposition to state their intentions, and Rykov assured him that they planned to revitalize the army if it proved impossible to conclude a democratic peace; to guarantee "complete freedom in the elections to the Constituent Assembly" and to transfer all power to it as soon as it was convoked. Remembering the fruitless conference of the preceding day, Rykov demanded that the Mensheviks "either accept our plan of organizing a government *or present another plan on which we could agree.*" Isuv said that Rykov's views "could well provide a basis for agreement" but expressed doubt that the Bolshevik party really shared them. [33]

Simultaneously with Rykov's speech, the Moscow Bolsheviks requested that the Red Guards and sailors that had been sent from Petrograd leave Moscow—obviously wishing to protect their freedom of action from the armed pressure of Lenin's true followers. [34]

A Bolshevik journalist describes the atmosphere in Kharkov, a major labor center, as one of "mutual accomodation" between Bolsheviks and "petty-bourgeois parties." The Mensheviks and SRs feared a rupture with the Bolsheviks and their following of revolutionary soldiers and workers, and "the Bolsheviks in turn had to take into account that the Mensheviks and SRs still had the backward part of the masses with them." The great locomotive construction plant, for instance, "remained Menshevik for a long time." This situation led to a formal coalition between Bolsheviks and right socialists. In Petrograd "events were taking their course, but in Kharkov the political situation hardly changed until the October days *and even later.*" [35]

Another Bolshevik author and Menshevik defector, N. N. Popov, writes that the Menshevik-SR majority in the executive committee of the Kharkov Soviet "lacked the conviction and determination" either to support Kerensky or to recognize the Sovnarkom and favored "unity of revolutionary democracy." The Bolsheviks endorsed this, and "Kharkov came to stand aside from the struggle between revolutionary and counterrevolutionary forces, waiting for the blessed hour when a socialist coalition government would be formed in Petrograd."[36] A member of the Kharkov Bolshevik committee and of the executive committee of the Kharkov Soviet also considers that the Kharkov leaders were "not determined enough": some of them felt that the Ukraine would "develop separately and peacefully." He explains the situation by the fact that *after October* "the Mensheviks, the SRs, and the Ukrainian parties had the majority" in the Soviet, and the Bolshevik leaders needed "a push from outside" to change their conciliatory mood. The push was given by Sivers' military unit sent down from the north.[37] Somewhat later, again paralleling Moscow, "the conciliationists managed to get the executive committee to censure Antonov" (V. A. Antonov-Ovseenko, commander of the troops sent to the Ukraine); worse, the Bolsheviks summoned him to their meeting "to explain the activity of the troops arrived from the north."[38]

All this influenced the Moscow Mensheviks. In a lead article in their daily they tried to convince themselves and their readers that only "the extreme left Bolsheviks" continued blindly, insanely, to insist on a purely Soviet government. The democratic government "from NSs to *Bolsheviks*" that the country needed could be created "despite the Lenins and Trotskys" and their irreconcilable stand.[39]

Conflict in the Menshevik Central Committee

On 31 October, the Central Committee of the RSDRP(0) had decided to participate in the attempt to organize a government of socialist parties from NSs to Bolsheviks. The changed stand was explained by "the need *at all costs* [italics added] to prevent continued bloodshed, strife among the workers, and the ruin of the labor movement." The resolution appeared in *Rabochaia Gazeta* on 1 November.

Of the twenty-three members of the CC who had voted on the resolution, twelve had voted for it and eleven against. It had passed because several Revolutionary Defensists,[40] changing their stand in its favor, had voted with seven or eight Internationalists[41] against the majority of the Defensists. Dan had explained their new position: one could no longer count on the liquidation of the overturn in Petrograd itself; the approach of Kerensky's Cossacks had "made it the proletariat's business to defend Petrograd."

If Krasnov's approach had suggested "endless carnage" to the editors of *Rabochaia Gazeta*, his retreat dimmed their hopes for a voluntary surrender of power by the Sovnarkom. A bloody civil war in which workers would support the Bolsheviks seemed more and more inescapable. In defense of the CC's decision, Dan said that there were only two choices: a policy of agreement or else "participation in the repression of the working class." The members of the CC who had voted in favor of the resolution had "adopted the viewpoint of agreement, which the broad working masses demand."[42]

The resolution was hailed by all who still clung to the hope of uniting the hostile camps in a joint government.

Potresov's group, on the other hand, attacked it at once. They were determined to overthrow the Bolsheviks and considered any negotiations with them "a betrayal of the interests of the revolution and the proletariat."[43] It was imperative to break with a party organ capable of passing such resolutions. An earlier attempt to break with the Internationalist wing of menshevism promised no success. Only one member of the CC (K. A. Gvozdev) figured on the separate list of candidates for the Constituent Assembly the Potresovites had put forward in Petrograd in competition with the candidates of the official Party organization.[44] The reaction of their sympathizers in provincial Menshevik organizations had also been cool: only a few such groups had put up separate tickets. Even in Moscow, Potresov's followers had not done so, whether because they could not or would not.[45] Now the situation seemed to have changed. Many outstanding Mensheviks, most of the Revolutionary Defensists in the Central Committee, had voted against the resolution of 31 October.[46] Three days earlier, the so-called electoral committee of Menshevik Defensists had vainly appealed to the Revolutionary Defensists in the CC to "break out of the Internationalists' toils." Now it demanded that the "fatal decision" be rescinded or, if it was not, that the Revolutionary Defensists at once resign from the CC to combat its policy "both inside and outside the Party, without stopping before formal obstacles."[47] This time the electoral committee scored a brief success. During the day of 31 October, fourteen Defensists and Revolutionary Defensists, members or alternates of the CC, agreed on a joint protest. Late at night they presented it to the CC. The latter refused to revise its decision, and the group announced on 1 November that they were leaving the CC. *Rabochaia Gazeta* printed their notice of resignation on 2 November; and on 3 November, their "motivated explanation."[48]

Both documents were products of the short-lived compromise between Potresov's followers and those Revolutionary Defensists who had voted against the resolution of the CC. The former insisted on reinstating the coalition government and on an organizational split with the Menshevik Internationalists. The Revolutionary Defensists had lost faith in the coalition and greatly valued party unity. Any document encompassing such divergent views would naturally be hazy in form and substance. The Potresovites' categoric refusal to enter upon *any* negotiations with the Bolsheviks[49] was hedged about with qualifications: the resigning members were protesting against "negotiations with the Bolsheviks about *jointly forming a government*" and against "agreement with them about forming a government *together with them.*"[50] The wording was intended to satisfy everybody: those who hoped to reach an understanding with the Bolsheviks about a socialist government without Bolsheviks or merely without Bolsheviks "guilty of the overturn," and those who were against any agreement or negotiations with them; those who wanted a homogeneous government, and those who continued to insist on coalition.

The document printed in *Rabochaia Gazeta* on 3 November condemned "negotiations with the Bolsheviks about forming together with them a socialist cabinet" and "participating together with them in organizing a government on the basis of the overturn they have effected," thus "forming a socialist government jointly with the party that has dishonored itself by a bloody adventure." For Bogdanov and his circle, this formulation did not exclude a socialist government so long as it was not organized "on the basis of the overturn" and did not include the party that had "dishonored itself." The objections to a purely socialist government, also squeezed in, were much milder than the habitual utterances of the Potresovites. Referring to civil war, the document specified that "*under such conditions*" and "*in the present situation*" a socialist government would function in a climate of open hostility and organized rebellion and would be forced to resort to "limitless terror."

There is no question, however, that among the Revolutionary Defensists who had earlier discarded the idea of coalition with the bourgeoisie doubts began to arise about the possibility of an effective all-socialist government now that the Bolsheviks' excesses had "turned the petty bourgeoisie against the working class." This did not imply a revival of pro-coalition sentiments but, rather, a profoundly pessimistic expectation of another kind of homogeneous government— reactionary and antilabor.

Pessimism, and the absence of concrete slogans, in contrast to the Potresovites' clear aim of overthrowing the Bolsheviks and reinstating the provisional government, are very evident in the speech of Sofia M. Zaretskaia on 3 November in the name of the group that had left the Central Committee. "Since when does the Social-Democratic party have to be a governing party at all costs?" she asked. Why not be an *opposition party*? In tsarist times, the Mensheviks had seldom set themselves the direct aim of overthrowing the regime by armed force.

No more could they embark on military adventures now. Rather, it was the task of social democracy to "organize political opinion" through propaganda, through clarification.[51]

The departing members of the CC did not say in their statement—as Potresov would have wished—that working with the Menshevik Internationalists had become impossible, in the CC and in the Party generally. On the contrary, at a meeting of the Menshevik factions of the pre-Parliament and the Soviets on 3 November, Bogdanov put through a resolution asking the CC to reverse its decision, "whereupon the eleven members must rejoin the Central Committee."

At the same meeting, Dan defended the stand of the CC, quoting its resolution of the preceding day[52]: The decision of the Bolshevik CC makes agreement impossible; the Bolsheviks must first comply with the "preliminary conditions." In any case, Dan added, agreement was "impossible without a split in bolshevism." The Party must prepare the ground for agreement, relying on the mood of the masses that were not happy with the one-party regime. By a policy of agreement, by renouncing armed struggle against the Soviet regime, one might win back the support of the "healthier elements of the proletarian masses." Only by thus "separating bolshevism from the labor movement" could one hope to save the situation.[53]

In a long editorial on 7 November, *Rabochaia Gazeta* pleaded for abandonment of the "sectarian," all-out refusal to seek agreement with the Bolsheviks while their influence over the masses was strong: the masses would interpret it as a refusal to agree with *them*. The country had no government. Because of the Bolsheviks' stubbornness, no authoritative government had been formed; on the other hand, setting up a competing government would mean civil war, the ruin of the revolution, the victory of reaction. This in turn would prolong the influence of "the worst variety of bolshevism" over a large part of the proletariat. Giving up an irreconcilable "sectarian" attitude might *"accelerate the process of isolating* adventurist-conspiratorial bolshevism" and "convince the workers of the dreadful trap Lenin and Trotsky have prepared for them."[54]

Later, at the Extraordinary Party Congress, Dan specified in his speech of 30 November that the issue was not "agreement with the present leaders of bolshevism but with the people who march under the Bolshevik slogans." He visualized "a slow retreat of the masses from anarcho-syndicalist positions." He feared that the Russian labor movement would long remain under Bolshevik influence ("under the sign of syndicalism") and was far from sure that the masses' mood would change in time to prevent their bloody defeat. In that case it might take "ten to twenty years" before a genuine Social-Democratic labor party could come into being.[55]

Martov was not very optimistic either—about the issue itself or the time it would take for the masses' mood to turn. He thought that the question of agreement would come up in earnest only after the convocation of the Constituent Assembly. Even then, however, the Bolsheviks would not want to relinquish power. One had to hope for "the growth of the inevitable conflicts within bolshevism" and the results of Menshevik propaganda. So long as "we have no influence over the broad masses," the task of social democracy was reduced to trying to rally the proletariat around "our ideas." "It is not in our interest to provoke a crisis . . . on the contrary, our aims are best served by a gradual resolution of the crisis." The popularity of the slogan "a united revolutionary government from NSs to Bolsheviks" looked to Martov like "the one chance to save the revolution," but he remarked that by the time the Bolsheviks agreed to it, it might be too late. "A basis for agreement can appear only in the course of events—the masses' disappointment in bolshevism and their pressure on their leaders. So far there is no such basis. Perhaps there will be none."[56]

Evidently neither Martov, nor Dan, nor the editors of *Rabochaia Gazeta* viewed agreement as a concrete possibility. A resolution adopted by the Menshevik CC on 6 November (that is, before the members of the opposition rejoined it) launched the idea of creating, "as soon as possible," a "Committee of United Democracy" that would lay no claim to central government power, would continue to seek *a peaceful way out of the crisis through agreement with the Bolsheviks*, but which, "in view of the Bolsheviks' refusal," would try to become the rallying and guiding center for local governmental, public, Soviet, and army organizations and also ensure the performance of the limited functions necessary in taking elementary care of the people and the army and "saving the country and the revolution."[57]

The New Majority Consensus in the Party

The stand of the Central Committee's new majority was supported by such influential groups on the Party's periphery as the Caucasus Regional Committee and the Central Committee of the Bund. Formerly, rightist Defensist trends had predominated in the Bund, but the conference convoked by its Central Committee in Minsk on 7 November came to the conclusion that "the crisis of central power must be resolved by creating a homogeneous democratic government with the participation of all socialist parties, not excluding the Bolsheviks."[58]

The Caucasus Regional Committee together with the Tiflis Soviet of Workers' and Soldiers' Deputies sent the Central Committee of the RSDRP(0) a telegram supporting the resolution about a government from the NSs to the Bolsheviks and censuring the members who had left the CC.[59] N. Zhordania and E. Gegechkori confirmed this in a telephone conversation with S. Devdariani (San) in Kharkov.[60] The Mensheviks of the western front also welcomed in a telegram the decision of the Central Committee, calling the CC members who had voted against it "madmen and fanatics."[61]

Sentiments directly opposite to Potresov's were also growing outside the Party. On 2 November, the Central Executive Committee of the First Convocation, which actively opposed the Sovnarkom and consisted mainly of rightist Revolutionary Defensists, declared itself against the restoration of the coalition government.[62] On 4 November, the Committee to Save the Country and the Revolution, another anti-Bolshevik center, expressed willingness to accept a government that included Bolsheviks as long as the direct culprits for the overturn were not in it.[63]

The executive committee of the Soviet of Peasants' Deputies, which mirrored the views of the NSs and right SRs, had originally taken a very uncompromising stand, but after the 31 October resolution of the Menshevik CC it declared for "a homogeneous [that is, all-socialist] government without Bolsheviks"—adding that "if other public organizations should find it possible to participate in a government with Bolsheviks," it would not oppose such a government, "for the sake of stopping the fratricidal carnage." Thirty-three members of the executive committee of the Peasants' Soviet voted for this resolution; twenty-six even favored a government "from NSs to Bolsheviks."[64]

The chairman of the army committee at the Stavka, Perekrestov, who had just demanded that the Bolsheviks lay down their arms, now informed Petrograd that the government should consist of representatives of all socialist parties except the Bolsheviks, but if agreement with them was indispensable for creating a government immediately, "they can be included in the cabinet as a minority."[65] On 2 November the army committee sent a delegation to Petrograd to help in the Vikzhel negotiations.

Delo Naroda, the main organ of the Party of Socialist Revolutionaries, also came out in support of the new stand of the Menshevik CC. As early as 1 November, it endorsed the slogan "from NSs to Bolsheviks." On 3 November, it explained: "The PSR must not be a party of civil war with the Bolsheviks' government since it is not fighting the workers and soldiers who are temporarily following the Bolsheviks. It must overcome bolshevism by disclosing to democracy all the inner falseness of it." On 4 November, clarifying its position, *Delo Naroda* called for "fighting the Bolsheviks by . . . organization, and Kaledin by armed force."

In the conflict with its own minority, the Menshevik CC received the most effectual support from Tsereteli, who returned to Petrograd after having been absent during the first two weeks of the Bolshevik regime. He probably helped a great deal in resolving the intraparty crisis and persuading the opposition to return to the CC.

Tsereteli's estimate of the political situation, and the line of conduct he favored, were in many respects close to or identical with Dan's. He based his reasoning on the fact that the Bolsheviks had managed to consolidate their power to some degree, while the country had been unable to produce an organization that could be opposed to theirs. The country "has not and will not recognize" the Bolsheviks' regime, but they did have the support of "the active part of democracy," which believed their misleading slogans. Tsereteli insistently warned against armed action: it would only play into the hands of those who were watching for an opportunity to "drown all of democracy in blood."[66]

At a meeting of representatives of city and zemstvo self-governments, Tsereteli was asked whether he still favored a coalition government with the Kadets. He replied diplomatically that their presence would be desirable but that they would not agree: the overturn had placed them too far to the right.[67] He dotted the *i*'s at a closed meeting of members of the CEC of the First Convocation: a coalition was out of the question because "all the bourgeoisie of the Kadet party has united around the slogan of a bloody reckoning with the Bolsheviks." True, for the moment the bourgeoisie was silent, but the silence was dangerous, it portended blood. Democracy was split into two camps, the Bolshevik and the anti-Bolshevik. As long as the Bolsheviks were strong, they would not consider any agreement. On the other hand, no support had materialized for the Committee to Save the Revolution, which was to have united all socialists who opposed agreement with them. The attempt to create a socialist government without Bolsheviks had also failed. It seemed that the revolution could no longer be saved. However, the situation was not the same in all Russia. In the Caucasus, where the Bolsheviks were relatively weak, a plan of agreement with them had been put forward; in the Ukraine, where they were stronger, a viable government without them had been formed. In the capital, one had to wait until "the masses that are following the Bolsheviks realize the need for agreement." But what should "our position" be if the retreat took too long? If the regime began to falter, to disintegrate?

Its liquidation meant "shooting the proletariat." The socialist opponents of the Bolsheviks must prepare to help them retreat, must remember that they *could not remain irreconcilable* when the Bolsheviks' power waned and they were ready to fall.

Thus Tsereteli, while opposing agreement with the Bolsheviks, found it possible to work with the part of democracy that advocated agreement: counterrevolution apparently could not be avoided in any case; and the only acceptable way of combating bolshevism was the one that excluded "reprisals against the class of toilers." At the closed meeting, Tsereteli expressed deep pessimism: the situation was dreadful, and it was clearly impossible to organize a viable government. Given the popularity of the slogan of an inclusive socialist government and the conflict at the Communist summit, dropping the attempts at agreement would lose the democrats "many elements that could be extremely useful." He even doubted the wisdom of insisting on the "preliminary conditions." All he objected to was the policy of "agreement at any price." He had begun this speech with the words, "Right now the main task of democracy is to consolidate its forces—not in order to fight bolshevism . . . this could alienate many very useful elements." He stressed that democratic public opinion must be quite sure that the democratic forces were not "being rallied for reprisals against the Bolsheviks." [68]

Two basic issues marked the watershed in the menshevism of that time: whether or not to abandon the coalition with bourgeois parties and whether to participate in armed attempts to overthrow the Bolshevik regime. The new majority of the Central Committee and Potresov's group were poles apart on both. Tsereteli found himself in agreement on these crucial issues with the majority of the CC and closest to Dan.

Nothing came of the attempt to create a common front of Defensists and Revolutionary Defensists in opposition to the new line of the CC. To be sure, the Central Committee split on the issue of the possible entrance of Mensheviks into the Soviet of People's Commissars. But even as the eleven departing members were drafting their protest, it became apparent that only a few of them agreed with Potresov on the Kerensky government, on the proper method of liquidating the Bolshevik overturn, and on party unity.

With one exception, the members who had left the CC on 1 November returned to it on 10 November. *Rabochaia Gazeta* of that day carried an announcement that the CC was inviting all its members who had left "to return for common work." The answer, evidently agreed on in advance, appeared on 11 November: "Since at present the negotiations between the CC of our Party and the Bolsheviks have been broken off," these members were returning to the CC but would maintain their stand and oppose deviations toward so-called internationalism. P. Kolokol'nikov alone found it impossible to rejoin the Central Committee, "which by taking part in the negotiations . . . has helped to prolong the Bolshevik adventure . . . and still considers possible an agreement with the Bolsheviks on the question of government." His answer was printed in the same issue of *Rabochaia Gazeta.*

Kolokol'nikov was right that the CC had not changed its position since the resolution of 31 October, either on the question of agreement or on the admissibility of negotiations. Its resolution of 8 November, ending with the invitation to return, merely stated that *at present* there were no negotiations—and confirmed that the CC was *willing to resume them* if its demand to end terror was met. [69]

The Menshevik CC realized how futile it was to expect the Bolsheviks to refrain from terror and how little the slogan of an all-socialist government fitted the times. It was also sure that democracy could not undo the overturn by armed force—and equally sure that Mensheviks could not participate in any attempts involving bloodshed and strife within the working class. Kolokol'nikov could have pointed to another decision of the Central Committee: on the day it had invited the eleven members back, it had resolved to withdraw from active work in the Committee to Save the Revolution, which had refused to take "the only correct road in the interests of the revolution"—the road of agreement and a homogeneous democratic government. [70] If we decode the conventional terminology, it becomes clear that the Menshevik CC was in fact abandoning the idea of an all-socialist democratic central government in favor of the more modest task of creating a center of liaison for local self-government and other organizations that did not recognize the Sovnarkom and yet did not intend to "overthrow" it. The CC firmly dissociated itself from any attempts at organizing a government that might be initiated by the circles that set the tone in the Committee to Save the Revolution.

Potresov's arguments in favor of coalition with "census" elements and against liquidating the overturn by negotiating with the Bolsheviks were not accepted even by those Party circles that at first had been stunned by the resolution of 31 October. By and large, *Rabochaia Gazeta* had been right in predicting, as early as 1 November, that in the event of a split the Revolutionary Defensists would not join Potresov. The objections of the Moscow Revolutionary Defensists Kipen and Kibrik to Potresov's ideas in their speeches at the Extraordinary Party Congress on 30 November 1917 are characteristic: Kipen warned against "aiding in the destruction of the elements with which we ought to be linked," and Kibrik argued that another attempt at coalition would estrange the proletariat from its Menshevik vanguard, whereas the attempts to establish an all-socialist government were doing the opposite—dividing the Bolsheviks and "creating a group on which we can lean." [71]

In 1918, some Revolutionary Defensists would fight the Bolsheviks under the flag of the Constituent Assembly, but for the time being they all accepted the stand of the CC on armed conflict. A. E. Dubois, while admitting "the country's right" to overthrow the Bolsheviks, opposed armed action against them and against the proletariat drawn into their orbit "by the pull of the soldiers' movement." M. I. Liber protested against "compromises with counterrevolutionary bolshevism" but wanted to combat it "politically, not by military conspiracies and adventures." [72]

(New York, January 1966)

II. The Period of War Communism and the Civil War

David Dallin and *George Denicke*

Chronology of Events

(October 1917–January 1918; all dates in O.S.)

Gilbert Doctorow

23 October. The Central Committee of the Menshevik party decides to call an Extraordinary Party Congress.

25 October. The Bolsheviks initiate an armed uprising in Petrograd to overthrow the provisional government; they appeal to the convening Second Congress of Soviets to ratify their action.

The Internationalist faction of the Menshevik party at the Second Congress of Soviets declares itself opposed to the seizure of power as threatening a civil war; it advocates peaceful resolution of the conflict and the formation of a democratic government recognized by all "revolutionary democracy" to which the provisional government would surrender its power. The Defensist faction of the party issues an appeal for support of the provisional government, which it

This chronology of events is intended to assist the reader in following David Dallin's introductory remarks to the section of this volume that deals with the period from the October Revolution to the launching of the New Economic Policy. Dallin died before he had completed his contribution, and thus the crucial months from the Bolshevik seizure of power to the dissolution of the Constituent Assembly are treated only cursorily in his remarks. For a more detailed account of this period, the reader may turn to a brief monograph by the editor, presented as a companion volume to this work.

proposes be reorganized to rest on all strata of "democracy." Both factions leave the Congress of Soviets.

26 October. The Soviet government is formed. The Congress of Soviets approves the transfer of power.

28 October. The Central Committee of the Menshevik party states that accommodation with the Bolsheviks is impossible until their "adventure" is liquidated; it urges the working class to rally behind the All-Russian Committee to Save the Country and the Revolution as caretaker government until the Constituent Assembly meets.

29 October. Vikzhel threatens a general railroad strike unless an all-socialist government, "from the Bolsheviks to the People's Socialists," is formed. At Vikzhel's offices talks commence between spokesmen of the socialist parties.

31 October. The Revolutionary Defensist majority of the Menshevik Central Committee splits on the question of negotiations with the Bolsheviks for the formation of an all-socialist government. As Dan, Gorev, Cherevanin, and Erlich side with the Internationalist members, the Central Committee, by a vote of twelve to eleven, adopts a resolution in support of negotiations.

1 November. The Defensists M. I. Liber, B. S. Baturskii, L. I. Goldman, F. A. Iudin, K. A. Gvozdev, A. N. Smirnov, P. A. Garvi, K. M. Ermolaev, S. M. Zaretskaia, P. Kolokol'nikov, and B. N. Krokhmal resign from the Central Committee in protest against the resolution passed in favor of negotiations.

2 November. The schism in the Menshevik Central Committee is made public as *Rabochaia Gazeta* reports the resignations.

7 November. Vikzhel talks collapse.

8 November. The Central Committee declares that negotiations with the Bolsheviks will be resumed only when their policy of political terror is abandoned: it invites the eleven dissenters to rejoin the Central Committee for common work leading to the Extraordinary Congress.

10 November. Ten of the dissenting Defensist members return to the Central Committee.

12 November. Elections to the Constituent Assembly begin in Petrograd.

14 November. Electoral returns from Petrograd indicate a stunning defeat for the Mensheviks: the Bolsheviks receive 424,027 votes; the Kadets, 246,506; the Left SRs, 152,644; the Menshevik Defensists, 16,834; the Menshevik Internationalists, 10,531. Initial returns from the provinces are no more encouraging for Menshevik prospects.

19 November. R. Abramovich, I. Astrov, E. Broido, D. Dallin, V. Ezh-

ov, A. Krasnianskaia, Martov, A. Martynov, M. Rozhkov, S. Semkovskii, and A. Chernov issue a statement for the new Internationalist majority on the Central Committee condemning the Party's past policies and proposing the adoption of measures to influence the proletarian masses supporting the Bolsheviks and the petty bourgeoisie backing the SRs to facilitate an all-democratic coalition. The Internationalists call for a policy independent of the Party of Socialist Revolutionaries (PSR), which is blamed for the Party's electoral defeats and current paralysis.

23 November. Dan offers a rebuttal on behalf of the Revolutionary Defensists in the Party press. Dismissing differences of the past, he insists that the vast majority of the Party is no longer really divided over any major issue and appeals for the restoration of Party unity.

24 November. The electoral returns to the Constituent Assembly from Moscow again demonstrate Menshevik weakness as the Party receives an insignificant share of the 756,866 votes cast. The Bolsheviks claim 48 percent, the Kadets 36 percent, the PSR 8 percent of the ballots.

As of late November, early December, the returns of the elections to the Constituent Assembly show the PSR in the lead with some 16,000,000 votes, the Bolsheviks with 9,000,000, and the Mensheviks with 700,000.

(The final record would be PSR, 15,848,000; Bolsheviks, 9,844,000; Mensheviks, 1,364,826. The Menshevik vote was distributed as follows: Olonets Province, 127,000; Transcaucasia, 570,000; the Army of the Southwestern and Rumanian fronts, 114,000; the remaining provinces of European Russia and Siberia, 554,000.)

26 November. The Council of People's Commissars concludes a truce with the Central Powers on the Rumanian front.

28 November. The Extraordinary Congress of the RSDRP(O) convenes in Petrograd with some one hundred delegates present. Krokhmal, Abramovich, Devdariani, Romanov, Ermanskii, Dement'ev, and Glukhov are elected to the Presidium. The Congress agenda features reports on 1) "The current situation and the tasks of the Party in the Constituent Assembly"; 2) "Peace and the truce"; 3) "Participation in Soviets, revolutionary committees, organs of self-government and other organizations,"; 4) "Party unity"; 5) "Workers' control"; and 6)"National and regional autonomy."

2 December. At Brest, representatives of the Soviet government and the Central Powers sign a truce on all fronts, opening the way to a separate peace.

3 December. A demonstration in support of the Constituent Assembly, 150,000 strong, takes place in Moscow.

The Menshevik Party Congress approves a resolution "on the current situation" calling for agreement among all socialist and democratic parties, from the Bolsheviks to the People's Socialists, on the formation of a revolutionary government. The Party insists that this agreement be based on the following program: 1) all power to the Constituent Assembly; 2) the restoration of all political freedoms and an end to political terror, and the organization of a democratic republican order; 3) the immediate launching of negotiations for a general democratic peace; 4) the immediate transfer of the land to land committees and the immediate implementation of a democratic agrarian reform; 5) state control and regulation of industry and trade with the participation of labor organizations; 6) the issuance of legislation providing for an eight-hour work day, state unemployment insurance, and the organization of public works for the unemployed.

5 December. The Extraordinary Party Congress adopts a resolution "on Party unity" that maintains that while every minority must be granted full opportunity to defend its views in Party organizations and in the Social Democratic press, independent political statements opposing the decisions of competent Party organizations are absolutely impermissible outside the Party.

6 December. The Extraordinary Party Congress passes a resolution on "Peace and the truce" calling upon the Constituent Assembly to assume responsibility for the peace negotiations. These negotiations should be conducted in accord with the Allies, on the basis of the latter's recognition of Russia's imperative need for immediate peace; and accord with the Allies should be abandoned only if they prove the sole obstacle to the conclusion of a democratic peace. The Russian Social-Democratic Labor Party (United) (RSDRP[O]) is to take the initiative in convening an international socialist conference or congress to mobilize support among the proletarians of all countries for the achievement of peace: to this purpose, the Menshevik party drafts an appeal to the International and to all socialist parties.

7 December. The Extraordinary Congress elects to the Central Committee of the RSDRP (O) Axelrod, Abramovich, Astrov, Akhmatov, Ber, E. Broido, Gorev, Gogua, Dan, Ezhov, Martov, Martynov, Maiskii, Pinkevich, Semkovskii, Cherevanin, Erlich, and Iugov; it also provides that two elected members from Caucasian social democracy and one from the Bund are to be added to the committee. The Extraordinary Party Congress adjourns.

20 December. The Council of People's Commissars announces that the

Constituent Assembly will convene on 5 January with a quorum of four hundred.

21 December. The Council of People's Commissars sets 8 January as the opening date for the Third All-Russian Congress of Soviets.

30 December. A *Pravda* editorial warns that the Constituent Assembly will be dissolved if it opposes itself to the Soviets and to Soviet policy.

4 January A state of siege is declared in the capital, and Red Guard units are mobilized to prevent demonstrations.

5 January. The deputies of the PSR stage a march to the Tauride Palace, while a crowd of demonstrators in support of the Constituent Assembly clash with Red Guard units on Liteinyi.

The Constituent Assembly opens with some five hundred of its eight hundred elected deputies present. Sverdlov presents for its immediate approval a five-point declaration issued in the name of the Central Executive Committee of Workers', Soldiers', and Peasants' Deputies. The assembly is asked to ratify all the major Soviet legislation to date and to acknowledge the legitimacy of Soviet rule.

Tsereteli delivers an extemporaneous speech to the Constituent Assembly in which he excoriates the Bolshevik regime for failing to cope with the nation's economic dislocations and for entering upon peace negotiations while lacking the popular mandate necessary to avoid a shameful settlement. Tsereteli charges that splits within democracy engendered by the Bolshevik seizure of power threaten to destroy the achievements of the revolution by leading to a fratricidal civil war from which the bourgeoisie would emerge the victor. He urges restoration of unity within revolutionary democracy on the basis of a common recognition of the Constituent Assembly as national arbiter, and avoidance of maximalist strivings for socialist experiments. Tsereteli reads to the assembly the Declaration of the Social-Democratic delegation, proclaiming the RSDRP's fealty to the Constituent Assembly and setting forth the Party program: restoration of civic freedoms and the establishment of a democratic republic based on universal, equal, direct, and secret suffrage, without distinction of sex and with a system of proportional representation; creation by the assembly of a special organ staffed by assembly members to supervise the de facto armistice now in force on the Russian front and to propose to all belligerent countries immediate negotiations for a general democratic peace; enactment by the assembly of legislation providing for the transfer of church, monastic, and private lands to the peasantry, for the introduction of the eight-hour day for hired labor, for a comprehensive system of social insurance, and for public works for the unemployed; the adoption of measures to restore industrial production and the normal exchange of goods between cities and countryside; and the establishment of state organs to regulate and control the nation's economic life.

After the Constituent Assembly decides, by a vote of 237 to 146, to postpone discussion of the Declaration of the Rights of Toilers presented by Sverdlov and to proceed instead on the basis of the agenda proposed by the delegates of the PSR, the Bolsheviks denounce members of the assembly as fomenters of counterrevolution and withdraw their deputies. The Left SR deputies subsequently withdraw, ostensibly over the issue of a separate peace.

6 January. The Constituent Assembly adjourns at 4:40 A.M., having agreed to reconvene at 5 P.M. When the deputies arrive, in late afternoon, at the Tauride Palace, they find it locked and guarded by a detachment of the Red Guard. The Soviet government issues a decree announcing the dissolution of the Constituent Assembly.

Introduction

David Dallin

During the year following the October Revolution, the course of the Menshevik party was greatly, though not always consciously, influenced by three major psychological factors linked to the movement of events. One was the memory of the unexpected, unbelievable lack of resistance to the Bolshevik seizure of power—perhaps the strongest impression left by the events of October. In Petrograd, youthful cadets and women's battalions had fought briefly; that was about all. In a few provinces, local authorities had put up some resistance, nowhere for long. Kerensky had gone looking for help but found none. The enormous army at the front had accepted and virtually recognized the new regime. The country was rumbling, but months would pass before the formation of large White armies. At the same time everyone knew that the Bolsheviks were a minority party and that a great many of Lenin's own followers opposed his plans for a separate peace with Germany and considered Russia "unripe" for socialism.

The events belied not only orthodox Marxism but the blueprints of Leninism as well. The new government was no alliance of "labor" and "peasant" parties, no "dictatorship of the proletariat and peasantry." Up to 1917 the Bolsheviks had not planned on a government without the Mensheviks and Socialist Revolutionaries; in early 1917 the slogan "Soviet power" still had meant for them a coalition of the major revolutionary parties.

The Mensheviks had been closer than the other non-Bolshevik parties to the factory committees and trade unions; only recently they had had their "strongholds" on the industrial outskirts of cities. They tried to explain the "historical absurdity," the "paradox," of their defeat by the disintegration of the army at the front and in the rear, the wartime influx of peasants into the industrial labor force, the food shortages, and the general weariness. All this was true, but not a sufficient explanation.

In August 1917, two months before the overturn, the Menshevik party had had some 200,000 members, almost as many as the Bolsheviks. The weakness suddenly bared by the non-Bolshevik parties was all the more unnerving. Below I shall analyze the Mensheviks' ideological stance, but side by side with the ideology forbidding armed action against the Soviet government there always was that consciousness of physical weakness. An uprising could only too easily turn into *avantiura* (a word often used in contemporary polemics for foolhardy undertakings). The Socialist Revolutionaries developed similar notions —as always, with some delay.

Despite their lack of "activism" against Lenin's government, the Mensheviks made no ideological concessions as distinct from tactical retreats. On the contrary, the events of 1918—the dissolution of the Constituent Assembly, the Brest peace, the repressions and executions, the outlawing of the Menshevik party—intensified their antagonism to the Bolshevik regime.

In 1919, after Germany's defeat and the relative stabilization of the Soviet government, a sizable part of the Menshevik intelligentsia, including some leaders, would begin to defect to the Bolsheviks. But in 1918 few believed in the viability of the regime, even though the prognosis that it would last only "a few days" was extended to a few weeks, then a few months. It was known—not all personal contacts were severed as yet—that the possibility of defeat (which would leave the October Revolution merely a beacon for future revolutions) was often discussed in the Bolsheviks' inner councils. At the Third Congress of Soviets Lenin himself pointed out that the Soviet government had already been in existence "five days longer" than the Paris Commune.

The Mensheviks had lost hundreds of thousands of adherents who had cast their votes for them during the first half of 1917 in elections to Soviets, local dumas, and so forth; the 1,136,500 votes they polled in the elections to the Constituent Assembly (half of them in the Caucasus) were but a fraction of what they would have had if the elections had taken place in the spring of 1917. At first this ebb in popularity did not greatly affect the Menshevik organizations, still less the loyalty of leaders. The committees and editorial boards generally remained true to the Party; at the very top, the Central Committee (CC) and the central press of the Party maintained the established attitude toward bolshevism. The future defectors, Martynov, Semkovskii, Maiskii, Ermanskii, and Akhmatov, continued to sit in the Central Committee, and there was no shortage of writers for the many old and new publications. The conviction that the regime could not last lessened the shock that the lack of resistance to the October seizure had caused. These two psychological factors made for a certain political passivity on the Mensheviks' part during the first year of the new regime, notwithstanding their wholesale disapproval of the Bolsheviks' activities.

The outcome of the war was the third factor that came into play after the October Revolution. There had been the armistice and the treaty of Brest-Litovsk, a defeat that did not exactly endear the government to the population. The direst predictions were coming true: the western territories were split off, the Ukraine occupied, the Caucasus cut off. With the bulk of the German army now moved to the western front, Germany's victory over the Allies seemed assured. Russia would be at the victor's mercy. The hoped-for revolution in Germany had failed to materialize.

True, the United States had entered the war; but hardly anyone in Russia knew how much America could help Europe, while all were alive to the strength of the German divisions now free to fight the Allies. The only questions were, how much territory, goods, and people Germany would demand from Russia and whether the Allies would abandon Russia to her fate.

The situation was very different from the Second World War, whose critical point was passed in the winter of 1942–43. After that, Germany kept retreating, and her final defeat was only a question of time. In 1918 she seemed, on the contrary, to be gaining strength. Between February and July she launched several offensives, many of them successful. The belief in a German victory was so strong in Russia that, on 27 August, Lenin signed an unpublished addition to the Brest treaty, providing for Germany's help against an Allied intervention in Russia; and P. N. Miliukov went to Kiev in search of German help against Moscow.

The Menshevik Central Committee declared in a resolution of 22 February 1918 that by concluding the treaty of Brest-Litovsk the Soviet government was "sanctioning the triumph of German imperialism." A resolution offered by the Mensheviks on 20 March at the Fourth Congress of Soviets stated: "The peace treaty of Brest signed behind the people's back by the Soviet of People's Commissars . . . means the division of Russia, which must inevitably entail her further division among various imperialist predators." On this, all Mensheviks were agreed. But how much territory would Germany claim? Would she negotiate a compromise peace with the Allies, foregoing the acquisition of large territories from France in exchange for large acquisitions in the East? In other words, would the war end in a compact of "imperialists" among themselves? At the Menshevik Party Conference of May 1918 M. I. Liber submitted the following theses:

> The World War, unless it finally unleashes the spirit of revolution in the West, can be expected to have as its consequence the emergence of enormous imperialist formations (like those in Central Europe) and a further sharpening of their struggle for world hegemony and for the seizure of countries and peoples not yet divided among them. The main object of their appetites will be Russia with its enormous natural resources, [Russia] weakened by war and revolution. . . .
> As a result of its military victories, German imperialism has become the most formidable force among the many world imperialisms and has gained exceptionally favorable conditions for aggression on a worldwide scale. It has chosen [defeated] Russia as the next object of its predatory aims. [1]

With the unexpected surrender of Germany, a new era began for the Soviet government as well as for the other Russian political parties.

Since this seemed the only path to salvation from Russia's military defeat, Mensheviks of all shadings now hoped (in the spirit of the Zimmerwald program) that the World War would be the prologue to a major revolution in the West. Both Bolsheviks and Mensheviks expected this great European revolution to begin in Germany, the most industrialized country on the continent and the one with the strongest orthodox Marxist party. Large strikes and military insurrections broke out in Germany in 1918, and Russians tended to exaggerate their importance. In Lenin's entourage the hopes for an imminent German revolution ran high during the Brest negotiations; Lenin himself, though less sanguine than most, expected worldwide consequences from it. By accident, the role of leader of world socialism had fallen to backward Russia. More advanced nations would now take over, in the first place Germany. "The Russian has begun, the German, the Frenchman, the Englishman will finish," Lenin told the Congress of Soviets during the peace talks (paraphrasing Marx, whose prediction "the Frenchman will begin and the German will finish" he considered no longer viable). [2]

On the same grounds, the Mensheviks looked to the Socialist International. During 1917 they had tried to call an international socialist conference in Stockholm, in the hope that a meeting of French and

British socialists, members of their governments, with German socialists could result in a peace that would not be too damaging for Russia
and come closest to the formula "No winners, no losers." P. B. Axelrod
had been in Stockholm since August 1917 for this purpose.

The disagreements inside menshevism did not abate after October.
Factions continued to split into factions. The Congress of August 1917
had "united" the Party, but in November the Defensists formed
a separate group. Over the issue of civil war, the Central Committee would soon expel many members from the Party, and eventually
entire organizations.

Looking at the history of menshevism now, after many decades, we
are able to view it in perspective. Menshevism never had the monolithic quality of bolshevism (though "monolithic" fits the Bolsheviks of
1917–18 only in the sense that their leaders' disagreements did not
prevent them from seizing power and keeping it. Several times Lenin
had to confront the majority of his Central Committee with an ultimatum to make it vote for the actions he considered necessary). What
united the Menshevik leaders was, in the first place, a common historical experience. Almost all of them had participated in the Revolution
of 1905; together they had gone through the initial split with bolshevism; very few had joined the Party between 1905 and 1917. Second,
the Menshevik leaders shared certain basic attitudes and assumptions: a belief in broad political freedom; a rejection of all attempts to
restore the prerevolutionary order; the desire to keep Russia independent and undivided; and, until late 1918, the conviction that
the Russian revolution was bourgeois and that capitalism would
be Russia's economic system. Too general to determine concrete politics, these principles nonetheless held the Mensheviks together throughout their unions and their separations. Basically, these were "Western" principles, as against the Bolsheviks' growing belief in Russia's
unique destiny.

We must keep this common ground in mind as we examine the
Party's internal conflicts.

At the extreme left and the extreme right of menshevism there stood
men and groups rigidly devoted to once-accepted doctrines—religious
martyrs rather than practical politicians, more concerned with purity
of principle than with strategy, tactics and the expedient compromises
of political give-and-take.

One such man was the leader of the Defensists, Aleksandr Nikolae-
vich Potresov, the foremost representative of the movement that after

the war came to be called the Menshevik Right. He did not change his ideology by as much as a hair. For him the revolution remained bourgeois, and hence the government should be a coalition with the bourgeois parties. From these convictions he drew very logical inferences about foreign intervention, alliances with other parties against the Soviet regime, and much else. Soon after the October Revolution he wrote in the article "To Semi-Marxists," aimed at the leaders of the opposite tendency in menshevism:

> The central question for us as Social-Democrats must be the question of Russia's further capitalist development. . . .
> We want clarity from our opponents. We say to them, [it has to be] one or the other: either you believe together with the Bolsheviks that Russia is making a socialist revolution, the prologue to world revolution; then say so outright . . . and in that case you will be correct and consistent in rejecting all thought of joint action with the bourgeoisie, which this revolution dooms to annihilation. Or else your socialist conscience will not let you adopt this [view], and in that case you descend from the Bolshevik heaven to the sad, sinful earth of Russian reality, and the first thing you must recognize is that the trouble with Russia just now is not too much but on the contrary too little capitalist development. . . .
> If Russia is still capable of coming out of the present . . . impasse onto the highway of progress, clearly she must do so through the joint efforts of all her advanced classes, even if they are mutually antagonistic. [3]

In matters of foreign policy (of orientation, as it was called—toward the Allies or Germany) Potresov also held on to his wartime views, counting on the Allies' victory and their anti-Bolshevik intervention in Russia. In 1918–19 he was a member of the Petrograd *Soiuz Vozrozhdeniia Rossii* (it will be discussed later). Although he eventually admitted that "reactionary monarchist elements" gradually took over this organization and that his membership in it had been a mistake, Potresov maintained: "Was it admissible in principle to participate in the struggle against the despotism that was already becoming consolidated? Of course it was; of course it was admissible; of course it was legitimate." [4] Until the end of his life he never wavered in his belief that the Bolshevik regime was counterrevolutionary (differing in this from some members of his own group who viewed it as a phase of the revolution) and that any alliance was permissible when the object was to fight counterrevolution.

Plekhanov's group, *Edinstvo*, stood outside the Party organization and even farther to the right. Small and less influential than the others, it was sustained mainly by the personality of its founder. It combined the strictest orthodox Marxism with complete loyalty to the Allies and to the idea of a coalition with liberals. One of its main purposes was to fight "Zimmerwaldism." Several major revolutionary figures were among its leaders and sympathizers—Grigorii Aleksinskii, Fedor Dnevnitskii, for a time Petr Maslov, and such veterans of an earlier revolutionary era as Vera Zasulich and Lev Deich. Dnevnitskii wrote:

> What grounds have we for maintaining that both sides equally threaten Russia, Europe, and the whole world with imperialism? Absolutely none. The expansionist nature of German imperialism is obvious by now even to the deaf and the blind. . . .
> Against this . . . reaction are aligned the greatest democratic countries in the world—France, England, the United States. They strive to abolish the remnants of feudalism. . . . One side [represents] reaction, despotism; the other, the free development of peoples, democracy. Are they really alike for democrats, revolutionaries, socialists?[5]

Plekhanov's political activity ceased before the October Revolution. After an illness of several months (in Tsarskoe Selo, then in Finland) he died in May 1918. In Moscow there was a city committee of the *Edinstvo* group, and six sector committees. A congress and expanded publishing activities were planned for the spring of 1918, but repressions began against the organization; the weekly *Edinstvo*, which appeared on 1 May, folded. For a few more years Plekhanovites displayed some sporadic activity in the provinces, but by the end of the civil war the group no longer existed as an organization.

Among the Defensists active in 1918 within the Menshevik party, Mikhail Liber (earlier a member of the so-called bloc of Revolutionary Defensists) played a notable role. In time he accepted the line of the Central Committee. Other leaders of the right wing were Pavel Kolokol'nikov, Petr Garvi, Sofia Zaretskaia, Solomon Schwarz, Boris Baturin, and Mark Kamermacher-Kefali; many other prominent figures in the trade union movement also sympathized with the right.[6] Some leaders of the Menshevik party in 1917—Iraklii Tsereteli, Nikolai Chkheidze, and Vladimir Voitinskii among them—moved to Georgia, where Menshevik rule had been consolidated after the October Revolution.

Scanning the Party spectrum from right to left, we come now to the large group that turned leftward after October, breaking with the Defensists in favor of the "Internationalists." Its leading figures included Fedor Dan, Fedor Cherevanin, and Boris Gorev. No doctrinaires, they saw that under the new conditions a coalition with the bourgeoisie was impossible; together with the majority of the Party, they rejected both separate peace and the orientation toward the Allies; they (especially Dan) expected a crisis to develop among the Bolshevik leaders and were ready in that event for new political combinations. The majority of the Party had sided with Dan when he was the chief spokesman for the moderately socialist, pro-Allies tendency, and the majority followed him again in 1918 when he turned leftward and joined forces with Martov.

At the Party Congress and conferences it became clear that in the provinces menshevism had evolved in the same direction. The new realities seemed to dictate a new stand: formerly supporters of the provisional government, of the coalition with the Kadets and the alliance with France and England, most local leaders now favored a purely socialist government, "from the NSs [*Narodnye Sotsialisty*] to the Bolsheviks," and rejected the "Allied orientation." Once Dan and his group had broken with the right in November 1917, the leftists gained the upper hand. As this reflected a genuine evolution of the Party, few cared to question the leaders' right to adopt the new course.

On the left flank of the Party stood the Internationalists returned from abroad. In the spring of 1917, this group had been almost isolated. Martov had risked becoming as lonely a spokesman for outlived principles as Potresov was to be on the right flank after 1918. But the bulk of the Party had moved leftward, new men appeared in the Central Committee, the correlation of forces changed, and Martov found himself the Party's chief spokesman. This did not, however, turn menshevism into "Martov's party." He was an intellectual, not a single-minded commander. Able to weigh his opponents' arguments and partly accept them, he realized the dangers of his own course. His authority rested on intellect and devotion to the cause, but, unlike Lenin, he needed a leader at his side to direct the actual work and serve as a kind of "organizational bureau."

A convinced and congenital anti-Bolshevik, Martov nonetheless regarded bolshevism as "a branch of the working class," even if strongly deviating from the Marxian model. He could vibrate to the fighting spirit of the "Red battalions," but their savagery repelled him. The October Revolution was for him both a catastrophe and a "historical inevitability." He wanted "to be with the proletariat even when it is wrong" but could not bring himself to condone the new government's deliberate terrorism. Sometimes he told friends that he would like to retire. Three weeks after the Bolshevik overturn, he wrote Axelrod in Stockholm:

The time has come when conscience forbids us Marxists to do

what seems to be our duty—to stand by the proletariat even when it is wrong. After tormenting hesitations and doubts I have decided that the better course in the present situation is to "wash one's hands" and temporarily step aside rather than play the role of opposition in the camp where Lenin and Trotsky determine the fate of the revolution. . . .

This is the situation. It is tragic. For, after all, what is going on is a victorious uprising of the proletariat; that is, almost the entire proletariat stands behind Lenin and expects the overturn to result in social emancipation—realizing all the while that it has challenged all the antiproletarian forces. Under these conditions it is almost unbearable not to stand in the ranks of the proletariat, even if only in the role of opposition. But the demagogical forms in which the regime is decked out, and the praetorian underlay of Lenin's rule, deprive one of the courage to go there, especially at this time, when the new government is not yet firmly established and resorts to all kinds of violence to combat the passive resistance of the social organism. . . .

As you can guess, we are feeling very low. We are witnessing the ruin of the revolution and feel powerless to do anything [about it].[7]

Unlike most of the other leaders, Martov thought that the Bolshevik regime could endure:

Our Defensists have evolved the convenient theory that this is a purely "praetorian" overturn lacking the proletariat's support, which will burst like a soap bubble in a few days because it will be unable to cope with the economic crisis or to master the administrative apparatus and will choke on the blood of the pogroms it has unleashed. From the first, I had warned against excessive optimism: The coalition [with the Kadets] had been so full of dry rot, had turned the masses against the former leaders to such an extent, that the most paradoxical government of adventurers and utopians could stay in power "on credit" until the masses realize its inability to solve the internal and external political problems. . . .
. . . I don't think that Lenin's dictatorship is doomed to end in the near future. The army at the front is apparently going over to him for good, Germany and Austria have to all intents and purposes recognized him, and it is possible that the Allies will take a wait-and-see attitude.

Martov's own attitude swung from sympathy to revulsion. Intellectually, coming to terms with the Bolsheviks appealed to him, but in face of the arrests, the murders, the closing of newspapers, and the outlawing of political parties, the moralist in Martov overcame all intellectual arguments. With horror, he remarked that Lenin "signs a death sentence, goes to bed, and sleeps soundly until morning." A few days after the creation of the first Cheka, Martov explained to a friend in Switzerland why he opposed Lenin's government:

> Not only because of the deep conviction that trying to implant socialism in an economically and culturally backward country is senselessly utopian, but also because of my organic incapacity to reconcile myself to this Arakcheev idea of socialism and this Pugachev idea of the class struggle, which spring, of course, from trying to plant a European ideal in Asiatic soil. The result is such a reek that one can hardly stand it. To me, socialism has always meant, not negation of personal freedom and individuality, but on the contrary their supreme realization; I visualized the beginnings of collectivism as the very opposite of "herd-ness" and reduction to a common level. No one brought up on Marxism and on European history understands socialism in any other way. Here, however, there begins to flourish such a "barracks-and-trenches" quasi-socialism, based on "primitivizing" all of life—on a cult, not even of the "toil-hardened" fist but simply of the fist—that one feels somehow guilty vis-à-vis every cultured bourgeois. [8]

As an *idea*, coming to terms with the Bolsheviks retained its attraction for Martov for many years. It seemed a sound, democratic way out of a blind alley and was referred to as the "normative" way. For Martov, it did not mean the naïve plan of a Soviet government of Lenin and Martov that was sometimes suggested in the heat of polemics: he had no illusions about Lenin. But the Bolshevik party seemed about to split, and in that event many of its leaders might not be averse to a rapprochement with the other parties of the left. In the letter to Axelrod quoted above, Martov had written that at the time of the October Revolution there had been strong opposition to Lenin and Trotsky in their own party. Zinov'ev, Kamenev, Riazanov had tried to postpone the showdown. "Apparently Lenin saw the need for haste, and he cut the knot with a 'sword.'"

Many felt that the only solution was a government "from the NSs to the Bolsheviks." This became the official program of the Party. The Internationalists (who had opposed the coalition with the Kadets) accepted it fairly easily, but the Defensists left the organization in protest against the CC's new line. Some leaders who had formerly believed in coalition with the "bourgeoisie" now favored an SR-Menshevik government without Bolsheviks. This was obviously impossible, and the bulk of the Party followed Dan in accepting Martov's program—arguing for it, however, not out of hopes for a social revolution but in order to prevent fratricidal "civil war within the proletariat."

Pavel Borisovich Axelrod had returned to Russia from Switzerland in

May 1917, and in August the Central Committee sent him to Stockholm to prepare a socialist conference. Hence this ranking Internationalist, who closely agreed with Martov at the time, had little to do with the formulation of the new Party line. Before communication with the West was cut, Martov kept him informed about the Central Committee's decisions. For instance, he wrote on 30 December 1917 that the CC did not want to replace "Bolshevik anarchy" with another "inept coalition regime" but only with a "democratic bloc."

> Behind the praetorian and Lumpen side of bolshevism we are not ignoring its roots in the Russian proletariat. Therefore we refuse to organize a civil war against it; and we reject the Bolshevik "policy of peace" for the sake of international proletarian action for peace and not for the sake of "restoring accord with the Allies," that is, prolonging the war until the spring or later.

As the official representative of the Menshevik party in the West, Axelrod lectured in Sweden on Russian affairs and began publication of the *Écho de Russie* in January 1918 and, in June, of *Stimmen aus Russland*, the organ of the "delegation of the Russian Social-Democratic Labor Party and of the Party of Socialist Revolutionaries." Many official documents were printed in them. Axelrod worked together with the faction within the PSR (N. Rusanov, V. Sukhomlin, and others) that, like the Mensheviks, rejected the orientation toward the Allies and foreign intervention. In a programmatic article, Axelrod wrote:

> The members of the Russian delegation are unanimous in their firmly negative view of any military assistance from foreign powers, not only because of a natural and well-grounded fear of dangerous consequences from such an interference by other governments in Russian ... affairs, but also because overcoming bolshevism by armed force would in our opinion perpetuate the myth of the historic character of its reign—a stupendous falsification of history, of which the international proletariat will be the victim.[9]

Aleksandr Martynov, Semen Semkovskii, and Isaak Astrov—the other former members of the "Secretariat Abroad" (see p. 6)—played no particularly important roles in Martov's group. On the other hand, Rafail Abramovich was rising to a position comparable with Martov's and Dan's.

The "extreme left," to the left of the new Martov-Dan center, absorbed a good deal of Lenin's ideology; many eventually joined the Bolshevik party, for example Osip Ermanskii, coeditor of several Menshevik publications in 1917–18. The other groups, including Martov's, disliked and somewhat despised them as pro-Bolshevik and anticipated a break with them. [10] The Party generally came to share Martov's view that in the nature of Russian politics there could be no intermediate groups between bolshevism and menshevism: all would eventually have to join one or the other. This expectation was confirmed in respect to the *mezhraiontsy*, who went over to the Bolsheviks in 1917, the "Social-Democrat Internationalists" (Lozovskii's group), who did so in 1919, and similar groupings.

Among the important figures on the extreme left, besides Ermanskii, were Boris Bèr, the Kharkov leader; Ivan Akhmatov, also in the Ukraine, later in Siberia; and Andrei Vyshinsky, who, alert to the political weather, changed from right Menshevik Defensist to Internationalist, became a member of the extreme left in 1919, and eventually a Bolshevik.

The Party of Socialist Revolutionaries had been the Mensheviks' closest ally during the February Revolution. Their relations soured after October, mainly over international politics; still later, other issues came to divide them.

While the Mensheviks (except a minority of the right) rejected the orientation toward France and England as well as the Brest peace, the SRs (except the "Left SRs" and some individual leaders) remained loyal to the Allies and desired their help against both Germany and the Bolshevik government. An SR conference in Moscow in April 1918 declared itself in favor of continuing the war "on the side of the powers of the Entente, the alliance with which must be restored." The SRs welcomed the Allied military intervention, took part in uprisings and in anti-Bolshevik provincial governments—a policy rejected by the Menshevik party. [11] Some two years later, in connection with events in Siberia and the south, some SR groups changed their stand and a new rapprochement became possible. [12] On the whole, however, since the SRs were another persecuted socialist party, some cooperation with them in Soviets, trade unions, and other organizations continued all along, despite disagreements on basic issues.

6

From the Dissolution of the Constituent Assembly to the Outbreak of the Civil War

George Denicke

The dissolution of the Constituent Assembly was a dreadful blow for all democratically minded people in Russia, especially the so-called revolutionary democrats, who had had the majority in the assembly. At the time, outrage united them all, yet the reaction was not uniform even among the Mensheviks. It was largely determined by the expectations that had been pinned on the assembly. Its dissolution was not a complete surprise, but many had hoped that the government would not disband the people's representatives—at least not immediately. After all, the Bolsheviks had ostensibly seized power to represent the people. Martov apparently no longer considered the assembly a stable factor: he did not even mention it when he wrote N. S. Kristi on 30 December (O.S.), a week before its opening: "We are undoubtedly going, via anarchy, to some kind of Caesarism ... the whole people have lost faith in their ability to govern themselves."[1] In public Martov was less outspoken, but this private letter expresses sentiments that were not his alone, though in others they may have been less sharp. Tsereteli, on the other hand, was far from hopeless. Of all the Mensheviks elected in Georgia, he alone actually came to Petrograd to attend the assembly. According to Noah Zhordania,[2] the other Georgian delegates no longer believed that it could endure and prudently stayed home. A member of the Constituent Assembly, the right SR Boris Sokolov, quotes Tsereteli:

It is hard to believe that the Bolsheviks will dare to disband the C. A. Neither the people nor history would forgive this.... For decades, all the vanguard Russian intelligentsia have striven for the realization of [this] idea. It was the motto not only of our liberals but also in the first place of the revolutionaries. I am sure that the Bolsheviks only [want to] scare the opposition to make it more tractable. [3]

Martov and Tsereteli (if Tsereteli's words are accurately reported) represented the two extremes of a subtly graded scale. But judging by the contemporary press, the dominant feeling was fear that the Constituent Assembly would not survive its first encounter with the Soviet government.

By contrast, the right SRs were optimistic. As against the Mensheviks' 3 percent, they had received about 40 percent of the votes in the elections to the Constituent Assembly; counting those of the Ukrainian SRs, probably not less than half of the total vote. In combination with the national groups that were close to them, they could expect to have the majority. Even before the election results were tabulated, everyone thought of the assembly as "Socialist Revolutionary." The SRs found it hard to imagine that "their" Constituent Assembly could simply be dissolved, and they felt sure that such an attempt would provoke a storm of popular protest. Naming no names, Boris Sokolov quotes several prominent SRs whom he had questioned about defending the Constituent Assembly. All believed that the people would rise to its defense. One leader said: "Self-defense? How absurd.... We are the chosen [representatives] of the people. We are to give the people a new life, new laws. As for defending the Constituent Assembly, that is the business of the nation that has elected us." [4] He was mistaken. The Constituent Assembly was killed by a double blow—from above by the government and from below by the passivity of the masses. The people did not react.

Unlike the SRs, the Mensheviks could not hope anywhere but in Georgia for much support from the nonurban masses, and the results of the elections augured little success even among the industrial proletariat. In both Petrograd and Moscow the results had been nothing short of catastrophic: roughly 29,000 votes in Petrograd as against 424,000 for the Bolsheviks, and 21,500 in Moscow as against the Bolsheviks' 366,000. However, the Mensheviks were not quite as bankrupt as these figures suggest. They had pockets of support among workers, and the mood began to change in their favor even before the assembly was dissolved. The turn in the workers' mood received a new impetus from the violence done to the assembly and the violent quashing of a demonstration in its support. As we shall see, a new workers' movement arose in Petrograd under the Mensheviks' leadership that not only fulfilled but surpassed their hopes. In keeping with the stand of its majority and its Central Committee, the Menshevik party also assumed the role of opposition in Soviets, both provincial and central. For the next six months these were the two main lines of its activity.

There was no prepared, planned strategy. Not all Mensheviks felt sure that the government would refuse to tolerate elected popular representatives at its side, but no one discounted this possibility. The question of how to react to events that seemed inevitable to some and possible to others was not even posed, let alone discussed and answered. The future was too uncertain. That the Bolsheviks' attempt to introduce socialism in an underdeveloped country would fail was an axiom for all non-Bolsheviks, especially to Marxists of the Menshevik stamp. But about the time and manner of the collapse there were only guesses, on the basis of which various leaders variously defined the Party's tasks. No one doubted that the Bolsheviks would be unable to prevent economic chaos, cope with opposition from all quarters, organize the orderly administration of the country. But would they be overthrown, or would they come to realize the failure of their experiment, retreat, and seek agreement with the other social forces? The new Central Committee of the Menshevik party banked on the latter outcome, though far from all of its members believed in it. Martov did not, to judge by his letter of 30 December. ("We are undoubtedly going, via anarchy, to some kind of Caesarism.") No concrete plans were possible, and the Mensheviks' moves were largely improvisations in response to unexpected opportunities.

One such opportunity was the breakup of the demonstration in favor of the Constituent Assembly. Soviet soldiers fired at the crowd, and there were some workers among those killed. The session of the assembly lasted until after midnight. When it was forced to adjourn, the Menshevik paper *Novyi Luch* (6/19 January) had already come off the presses. Thus it happened that the issue was almost entirely given over to the breakup of the demonstration. The first page proclaimed in large print:

Infamy on the government for forcing workers to shed workers blood!

Men and women workers, protest against the culprits for the criminal carnage!

Glory to those who perished defending the conquests of the revolution from the aggressors!

Long live the sovereign [*polnovlastnoe*] Constituent Assembly!

Down with civil war!

The same slogans appeared in shorter form at the end of an unsigned article (probably Martov's), "A Crime Has Been Committed," which said:

> The worst has happened. Revolutionary workers and soldiers have shot at revolutionary soldiers and workers. Armed workers have shot down unarmed workers.... Whatever happens next, this infamous bloodbath will leave an indelible mark in the hearts of the popular masses of Petrograd. The thought that socialists shot down peaceable workers will cause a dreadful cleft in the people's soul, will pierce it with dreadful doubt: Was it for this that the people made so many sacrifices to the cause of its liberation?

The article admonished those who had "obeyed brutal orders and killed their brothers and sisters": "Only refusal to obey the instigators of civil war and bloody reprisals can erase the stigma of the crime and restore in the eyes of the international proletariat the honor of the Russian working class, besmirched by the fact that armed workers have fired at unarmed workers."

That night the press that printed *Novyi Luch* was demolished, and the next issue did not come out until 12/25 January. Thus the account of the Constituent Assembly's meeting was six days late, as were the slogans with which the Party reacted to its dispersal:

> Long live the all-nation Constituent Assembly!
> Long live the International!
> Long live freedom of the press!
> Long live the Russian Social-Democratic Labor party!
> Long live the Russian, long live the international revolution!

These slogans are somewhat cryptic. "Long live the International"— what International? The World War had destroyed the Second, and the Internationalists in the CC could not desire its restoration in the old form. What should the new International be like—with the Bolsheviks or without them? "Long live ... the international revolution"—did the CC consider that it had started? Did it merely hope that it would soon begin, as a consequence of the war? We must try to decipher these slogans to understand how the Mensheviks visualized the future and assessed the present. "International revolution" was explained very soon, in Martov's speech at the Third Congress of Soviets, which opened on 10/23 January. During the debates following Trotsky's report on the negotiations with Germany at Brest-Litovsk, Martov made a sharply critical speech, yet ended with the words: "Still, despite many mistakes, the steps taken toward concluding peace at the very height of an imperialist war are a strikingly audacious and revolutionary act on the part of the makers of worldwide international revolution."[5]

This utterly contradicted many statements of the new Internationalist majority formed at the Mensheviks' December Congress. For example, in an appeal "to the entire International, to all socialist parties of the warring and neutral countries," the Congress had said:

> After promising a general democratic peace . . . Lenin and Trotsky have begun negotiations with agents of German imperialism and Hindenburg's headquarters. Instead of a general democratic peace, they are getting ready to conclude a separate peace that will isolate Russia, strengthen German imperialism, put the nations of the Entente in an exceedingly difficult situation, and push the proletariat of all the warring countries into the arms of the imperialist classes.[6]

Clearly the Congress did not consider the Bolsheviks' initiative a *revolutionary* act. On 18 January, the last day of the Congress of Soviets, the lead article in *Novyi Luch* accused the Bolsheviks of senselessly playing at a socialist revolution, preparing an "obscene peace," and thus retarding the coming of socialism "in the entire civilized world by many long years."

How then were the Bolsheviks "makers of worldwide revolution"? These words clashed even with Martov's own letter to Kristi (see pp. 104 and 107), written only two weeks before this speech. Of course he spoke differently in public and in letters to close friends, but this hardly explains the striking contrast between the pessimism of the letter and the soaring conclusion of the speech. The letter ("unbearable reek," "cult of the fist," and so on) had breathed passionate indignation, profound repugnance. Yet one passage in it illumines these contradictions. What was going on, Martov had written, was "enough to make one fall into despair, even if one understands intellectually that history can lead to something good by the vilest crooked paths." These words point up the inner division that at the time, and for a long time to come, bedeviled most Mensheviks. They were not rational people calmly solving their problems. No one was consistent in those frightening days, not even the Bolsheviks. Judgments and decisions were often determined not by logic but by moral and emotional reactions. Martov and most others reacted with despair, even if they understood "intellectually"—or, rather, thought they understood—that things might not be so hopeless after all. It was too difficult, perhaps psychologically impossible, to abandon the struggle and give up trying to influence events. It was also impossible to keep track of the complex, contradictory events in Russia and abroad. Sometimes a single piece of brutal reality sufficed to bring on despair, at other times a few sparks rekindled hope.

In mid-January such a spark came from Germany, but Martov did not yet know of the German developments when he made his speech. As late as 18 January the lead article in *Novyi Luch* notes that "so far, the main strongholds of world imperialism—England, Germany, the United States of America—are standing firm"; there was no reason to expect revolutions in these countries before peace was concluded. "And if an obscene peace is concluded at Russia's expense, international imperialism ... will get enough fodder to sustain it for years." It seems most likely, therefore, that Martov appealed to the "makers of international revolution" in order to support in the Bolshevik camp the trend represented by Trotsky, who insisted, in defiance of Lenin, on rejecting the German peace terms. Whether Martov hoped for rapprochement with Trotsky and his followers on this basis remains an open question.

Within a few days, the hopes for world revolution revived at the news of strikes in Germany. The lead article in *Novyi Luch* of 20 January bore the title "The First Breach." Its author (almost certainly Martov) wrote:

> A mighty revolutionary wave has risen in Germany. We do not yet know all the details. . . . But we know already that the strike movement, undoubtedly initiated by the Independent Labor party, has spread to other large cities besides Berlin, and that the whole movement is united by the demand for a "democratic peace." This alone is reason enough for us to recognize this movement, whatever its future development and whatever its immediate results, as the greatest event of the World War since our February Revolution. . . .
> At last the great hopes that flowered in Europe after our February Revolution are beginning to come true.

The next passage seems to clarify the closing words of Martov's speech (and supports the assumption that the article too was his): "The new overturn, caused by the acute discontent and disappointment of the despairing masses, which has brought the country to a state of disintegration, famine, and anarchy, has raised anew the question of peace." Not because of the allegedly socialist dictatorship proclaimed in Petrograd but because "the revolutionary government has ventured to begin the most prosaic negotiations with imperialist governments, against which, according to 'theory,' it should have declared ruthless war." No matter how great the blunders of the new government, it had boldly put the question of peace on the order of the day and thus "brought about a new unrest in the European masses and a sharpening of their relations with the ruling classes. And if at present there glimmers the hope that the cause of revolution will gain its first victories in Europe, this awakens another hope—that Europe may save the Russian revolution from the catastrophe of self-exhaustion toward which it seems to have been moving in the last few months."

This was how the new hopes arose, but they were not to be fulfilled. The German strikes had no effect on the peace talks. The German delegation at Brest continued to insist on its onerous terms, and on 27 January/9 February[7] demanded their immediate acceptance. A decision had to be made. A fierce struggle had been going on among the Bolshevik leaders for several weeks. On 8/21 January, at a conference of the Bolshevik Central Committee and Bolshevik delegates to the Congress of Soviets, Lenin had spoken in favor of peace even on the harshest terms but had met with strong opposition, especially from Bukharin and Trotsky. On 27 January/9 February the majority of the CC still opposed Lenin. As head of the peace delegation, Trotsky rejected the German demands on 28 January, announcing at the same time the end of military operations on the part of the Soviets (his famous formula, "Neither peace nor war"). On 18 February (N.S.) a German offensive began along the entire front. It met with courageous but incompetent, improvised resistance. On the same day Lenin finally got the CC to agree to the German peace terms, but the Germans now presented additional demands. On 23 February Lenin persuaded the CC to agree even to these, and on 3 March the treaty was signed.

The Mensheviks had been against capitulation all along. When an extraordinary congress of Soviets met in Moscow on 14 March to ratify the peace treaty, they offered a sharp resolution against it: The treaty meant a division of Russia that would inevitably entail further division:

> Thus the Brest peace means a betrayal of the basic interests of the working class, a betrayal of the Russian revolution, which will be ruined by German political and economic tutelage; a betrayal of the international proletariat, whose entire movement will be dealt a fatal blow by the surrender of a revolutionary country to the worst enemy of socialism. . . . The Soviet of People's Commissars had no right to sign such a peace, and the Central Executive Committee had no right to ratify this signature.[8]

The Mensheviks asked the congress to reject the treaty, to express its lack of confidence in the Soviet government, raise a people's army, and convoke the Constituent Assembly. These demands seem fantastic, utterly oblivious of reality, but we must remember the climate of the times and the circumstances under which the Mensheviks had to chart their course. The resolution sounds like a cry of despair, and that is what it was. There were enough reasons to despair. The Left SRs followed a similar policy of desperation when they withdrew from the government after the signing of the peace treaty. Many Bolsheviks, including some of the most prominent, shared these feelings.

Later it became clear that the situation and the prospects had been wrongly assessed—not because of poor analytical judgment but because of sheer ignorance of what was going on in other countries. Once the Brest peace had freed Germany to concentrate on her other enemies, probably not one person in Russia expected a German defeat. Nor did anyone realize that Germany was unable by then to establish "political and economic tutelage" over Russia. To be sure, the final outcome of the war could not be predicted with certainty—but one had to be utterly ignorant of the actual correlation of forces, and of the Allies' determination, to imagine that peace with Russia assured a German victory. Where information was needed, there was nothing but surmise, unknown quantities evaluated on a basis of emotion or doctrine. One unknown quantity was the possible role of the United States. Hardly anyone gave it a thought. When peace with Germany was being debated, America had not yet made its weight felt on the battlefield (it would not really do so until the summer of 1918).

One misconception that strongly affected the thinking of all or most Menshevik Internationalists was the idea that the war would end in a peace "at Russia's expense" that would sustain "international imperialism" for years to come. This conception of the war as purely "imperialist" derived from a primitive understanding of the materialist view of history. Of all the many factors involved, only capitalist self-interest was taken into account. The war was a war between imperialists. They would make peace when the time came to divide the spoils.

The Menshevik Defensists, on the other hand, did not regard England and France as rapacious aggressors but as allies representing a more enlightened capitalism than Germany. A few months later these divergent views would strongly affect intraparty life, but at the time of Brest all were united in opposing the treaty.

Before the treaty was ratified, the hope that this opposition could influence events was not pure illusion. It had a tangible basis in the new anti-Soviet workers' movement that emerged after the dispersal of the Constituent Assembly and the shooting of workers during the demonstration. The projected "obscene peace" added fuel to this movement, which quickly assumed impressive proportions and a belligerent spirit. The Mensheviks, and then the SRs, exploited to the full in their propaganda the stunning fact that a government that called itself socialist had shot at workers. [9] Some of the victims were buried on 9/22 January. Scores of thousands marched in the funeral procession. For greater effect on a greater number of people, a distant cemetery had been chosen. The mourners had to walk about ten miles, the last stretch through the populous proletarian Neva sector. Crowds lined the route all along but especially in that sector. Workers of several factories came out with subversive banners. Two banners carried by workers of the Semiannikov plant (two Semiannikov workers had been killed) attracted special attention—a black one with the words "Memory Eternal to the victims of the violence of the Smolnyi autocrats," and a red one, "They are gone but their spirit is with us and calls to struggle for the Constituent Assembly." [10] A huge meeting of protest was held at the plant. The Bolsheviks sent a member of the Fourth Duma, Muranov, to pacify the workers, but they kept interrupting his speech with angry shouts and did not let him finish. The Menshevik speakers who followed were warmly received and a resolution they offered was passed overwhelmingly. [11]

Meetings were going on almost daily at one factory or another, and the Mensheviks always got their resolutions passed despite the Bolshevik speakers' efforts. It was clear that a strong anti-Bolshevik movement could be organized. In this way the "Assemblies of Factory Representatives" came into being, first in Petrograd and later in other cities.

The campaign had not been planned by any Party organ. A small group of Menshevik Defensists, at loose ends after the December Party Congress but, unlike Potresov's group, still members of the Party, on their own initiative began to attend these factory meetings, debate with the Bolsheviks, and offer resolutions critical of the government, which the workers invariably adopted. I have recounted elsewhere how this movement took shape. [12] On our way to a meeting at the Putilov plant, B. O. Bogdanov and I were discussing what to do next.

> Our successes did not satisfy either of us. We were overcoming the Bolsheviks at one meeting after another, but the matter ended there. We would get our resolution passed, but we could not speak again at the same factory for several weeks, and sometimes there was no second opportunity. We were thinking of how to consolidate our successes.

Bogdanov, used to thinking in organizational terms, came up with the idea of promoting "a new, independent, elective organization" (to counterbalance the Soviet, which had become a government organ). The mood at the Putilov plant was propitious, and Bogdanov, who spoke last, appealed to the workers to hold elections "to a new organization—the Assembly of Representatives of Petrograd Factories."

This was improvisation, the spark that could kindle a new movement. There remained the problem of holding elections at scores of factories despite the Bolsheviks' opposition. The German offensive provided a needed stimulus. A larger, more "official" founders' group was formed at a meeting in the Neva sector. *Novaia Zaria* printed an account of this new phase of the movement, which I am giving in paraphrase:

Under the impact of the harsh living conditions the Petrograd workers had been moving away from politics, concentrating on "belly" interests. But the war had resumed, the Germans were marching as conquerors through the Russian land, coming daily closer to Petrograd, meeting no resistance to speak of: the government was sending to pointless death untrained, ill-armed workers who had enlisted in the Red army. At the same time it was in a hurry to sign a peace that would be a triumph for German imperialism. During those critical days the Petrograd workers revived. Unable to express their will through the organizations controlled by the Bolsheviks, who did not allow reelections, most of them had welcomed the idea of the nonpartisan Extraordinary Assembly of Factory Representatives initiated by workers of the Neva sector. There had been doubts, the article continued. Having lost faith in their own strength, in elections of any kind, would the workers elect delegates? They had, and on 13 March the assembly met. All the largest factories were represented. Elections continued, and the assembly grew. [13]

It was difficult to organize these electoral meetings, partly because of the miserably functioning streetcars but mainly because they were not announced in the press or in leaflets in order not to alert the Bolsheviks and give them a chance to scuttle them. Possibly such caution was unnecessary: the Bolsheviks remained unexpectedly passive. No doubt they hesitated to antagonize the workers, whom they needed (or might need) to repulse the German offensive. Most of the work was still done by a small group of Mensheviks, but in keeping with their old tradition, they encouraged independent initiative and did not try to impose their own candidates. Many SRs were elected (including the worker Berg, chairman of the assembly) and an even greater number of nonpartisans. According to a count made soon after the assembly began to function, the total of 111 representatives was made up of thirty-five Mensheviks, thirty-three SRs, one NS, and forty-eight nonpartisans. [14] At the plenum on 27 March there were 170 delegates from fifty-six enterprises. [15] Their high caliber was especially striking. V. O. Levitskii (who had not been among the organizers) wrote P. B. Axelrod on 16 June:

All the live forces of the movement are grouped around this institution [the Assembly of Representatives]. In character, it is purely a workers' organization, and sad to say ... it took a whole year since the beginning of the revolution for a true *workers'* organization to emerge, one that really unites the best of the *workers' intelligentsia,* which is at present displaying maximal independent activity. [16]

The first plenum met on 13 March, too late to carry out the idea that had inspired the elections, namely, preventing surrender to Germany. There was no longer any doubt that the Congress of Soviets convoked for the next day would ratify the Brest treaty. The assembly would not take the course for which it had been enthusiastically created. It would deal with matters like the evacuation of Petrograd and the revival of independent workers' organizations. Nonetheless the plenum passed a resolution demanding that the Congress of Soviets refuse to ratify the treasonable peace. It also demanded the abolition of the Soviet of People's Commissars and immediate convocation of the Constituent Assembly, to which all power should be transferred. [17]

All this coincided with the demands of the Menshevik faction at the Congress of Soviets. There was perfect unanimity on these issues between the Party leadership and the Defensists who played leading roles in the Assembly of Representatives; in general, this was a period of rapprochement between the new majority (formed at the December Party Congress) and those Defensists who had refused participation in the CC but remained in the Party as a "loyal opposition," submitting to Party discipline despite differences of opinion.

Some of these differences concerned the Assembly of Representatives. Before the Menshevik CC moved to Moscow (along with the Soviet government), only Abramovich among the majority leaders spoke at a large meeting connected with the creation of the assembly. Martov and Dan refused to appear at such meetings since they viewed the new anti-Bolshevik movement as strife within the proletariat. But the Central Committee, which they controlled, did not try to arrest the movement. Its secretariat actually assisted the organizers who were not connected with either of the Petrograd committees (the Internationalists' and Potresov's). Yet if there was no hostility, neither was there any of the enthusiasm that fired the organizers of the assembly. The CC was not indifferent—an independent mass organization of workers had long been the Mensheviks' dream—but it had doubts that dictated a cautious attitude toward the movement and its spread to other cities.

The stand of the Party leadership—or, rather, of its majority—was not formulated in any official document until late May. But some oblique light is shed on the CC's stand by the April discussions of the

Soviets of Workers' Deputies. In May one of the "enthusiasts" of the new movement, G. D. Kuchin, would argue that "the most vital question confronting the labor movement at present is the question of *Soviets*." [18] Why? Because the Bolshevik dictatorship was identified as "Soviet power"? But all Mensheviks were already agreed that this was a fiction, that the Soviets were but subordinate organs of the Bolshevik party. Martov wrote in April:

> After all that the workers have gone through during the past six months, it should be clear to anyone that "Soviet power" is a fairy tale, and not a beautiful one at that. There is no Soviet power in Russia, and no proletarian power. Under this label reign armed members of one [the Bolshevik] party, who go against both workers and peasants when workers and peasants disagree with them. In reality, "Soviet power" has turned into an irresponsible, uncontrolled, unjust, tyrannical, and costly power of commissars, committees, staffs, and armed bands. [19]

Obviously the issue was not the Soviets' current role but their potential as elective organs of the working class. To understand why the question was so acute we must look at it both in historical perspective and in the actual political context in which it confronted the Mensheviks.

In March 1918, after the Brest peace, more was involved than the prospect of counterrevolution, which had alarmed many Mensheviks before October and alarmed the entire Party since the failure of negotiations with the Bolsheviks about a government "from NSs to Bolsheviks." The threat of counterrevolutionary reaction had been aggravated since the peace treaty by the possibility of Russia's transformation into a German colony or even into separate colonies of several countries. Because of this, the Menshevik party set itself the "national" goal of defending Russia's independence. But, being a labor party, it also had the specific duty to defend the working class. Should that defense be based on the Soviets of Workers' Deputies or the new organizations, independent of the government? On this point, opinions differed. For simplicity's sake, let us speak of "Soviet partisans" and "assembly partisans," since there was no clear-cut divide in this matter between the Party majority and the Defensists, although by and large the former favored the Soviets and the latter the assemblies.

The pressing question was: where to direct the Party's main efforts. Amid the gloomy general situation, the resurgent workers' movement was a ray of hope. The first issue, 22 April, of the periodical *Novaia Zaria*—an enterprise that for once united the Central Committee and the Party-member Defensists—reflected the whole range of sentiments dominant in the Party. After a survey of the grim state of affairs, the editors said in a programmatic declaration:

> Every extra day of this situation means the unhindered approach of further enslavement and of the final ruin of the revolution. All the blows of the future will fall on the proletariat. In the exceptionally difficult circumstances of today's troubles and tomorrow's predictable blows, the movement of the working masses is going on everywhere in the cities and townships of our region. [20] This *last* movement of the proletariat (the last for this period, since the working class is objectively, actually, making its last attempt to save the remnants of the revolutionary conquests) demands *intense* and *correct work* by all the leading conscious elements. [21]

But what was the best way to conduct this effort? The Party was not strong enough to act with equal energy in several directions (the Soviets, the Assembly of Representatives, the remnants of the organs of democratic local self-government). It was necessary to choose the object of the main thrust, and the CC chose the Soviets. Presumably, one reason for its wary view of the Petrograd Assembly of Representatives was the fear of diverting its forces from the aim of reforming the Soviets into independent organizations truly representing the workers. As we have seen, the Mensheviks nourished no illusions about the ability of the Soviets, such as they had become under Bolshevik rule, to defend the interests of the workers. But the Party leadership, and probably most of the Party, thought for a time that the Soviets could be transformed through reelections: new majorities would refuse to kowtow to the government. In this spirit the CC composed its "Letter No. 7," of which I shall speak later.

At the same time, the CC unequivocally rejected the idea of "Soviet power," even of reformed Soviets. Martov wrote (in his *Novaia Zaria* article, quoted above):

> The working class, at the head of the entire people, must begin the struggle for the creation of an all-nation state power, a democratic and republican power. And the way to this leads through the convocation of the nationally elected Constituent Assembly. . . .
> For the proletariat, renouncing "Soviet power" means renouncing *illusory* full power in order to win in a democratic republic the share of influence over state affairs that is commensurate with its abilities and that it can win through organization and consciousness.

This was self-evident for all Mensheviks, but Martov's next lines raised objections:

> Once deprived of illusory power, the Soviets can again become . . .
> organizations of the working class that, as free proletarian organiza-
> tions independent of the government, will be so strong and close-knit
> that any democratic government will reckon with their opinion. [22]

Those whom we call assembly partisans did not believe that the Soviets
could be transformed into "free proletarian organizations."

On 6 March, that is, before the first meeting of the Petrograd Assembly of Representatives, the regional bureau of the Central Region, with
a Defensist majority, had recommended in a special letter to its organizations that they elect nonpartisan workers' assemblies. Nevertheless,
at the plenum of the Committee of the Central Region on 13–15 April,
attended by delegates from many local organizations, the majority
supported the stand of the Party's Central Committee. I. A. Isuv, the
reporter on current problems, made out a strong case for the Soviets—
on the basis of the CC's "Letter No. 7," as he said in his account of the
meeting in *Novaia Zaria*. [23] The resolution adopted after his speech was
surprisingly optimistic:

> The Soviets, which played such an enormous role at the beginning
> of the revolution, are more than ever necessary to the working
> class today when the workers are even more disorganized. In the
> face of the imperialist bourgeoisie that is now raising its head,
> they will play the role of a citadel from which the proletariat
> must defend its political and economic rights. . . . Just now, when
> Bolshevik policy is destroying the last trade union and other workers'
> organizations, the Soviets remain the principal class weapon of
> the proletariat. To preserve the Soviets as organs of the proletariat's
> struggle, it is necessary to fight to return them to their role of
> class organizations, . . . to transfer their administrative functions
> to all-nation organs of government. This is *all the easier* to do
> since by now it is clear that the famous motto "Soviet power"
> is nothing but a joke hiding the uncontrolled power of the Bolshevik
> party over the Soviets.

All the easier! Yet in the same breath the resolution noted: "Undesirable Soviets of Workers' Deputies are just as easy to disband as
undesirable dumas and zemstvos." [24] The framers of the resolution did
not realize that this perfectly true observation nullified their, and the
CC's, idea of the role the Soviets could be made to play.

But was it still the Central Committee's idea in mid-April? This may
be doubted. We do not know the date of Letter No. 7. Isuv probably
rendered its contents correctly—but weren't the contents already ob-
solescent? Only a few days later, as we have seen, Martov wrote of the
Soviets' role far more cautiously—certainly without the fervor of Isuv's

resolution. The resolution said that the Soviets *will* play a role of a citadel, that they must "serve as points of support for restoring the trampled freedoms"; Martov wrote that they "can again become . . . organizations of the working class" with which any democratic government would have to reckon. A democratic, not a pseudo-Soviet government. Martov was speaking of a vague future, when a democratic government would be in power. Clearly his article denoted a revision of the CC's stand and was basically a corrective to Isuv's report and resolution. At the same time, it was not in the least polemical. Martov did not criticize the opinions of other Mensheviks, which was rather unusual for him.

Criticism of Isuv's stand came from another quarter—from M. Liber, the second reporter at the same plenum of the Committee of the Central Region. Neither report was published in full, but according to *Novaia Zaria* Liber defined the Party's main task as "taking the 'power' away from Soviets, restoring democratic organs of nationwide unity." "The proletariat will strengthen its position as a class only when it consolidates its political forces not in class organizations separated from the other strata [of society] but in all-nation centers (organs of self-government and so on)." Liber warned against too much enthusiasm for reelections to Soviets: "In certain cases they must be put to use, but it is necessary to go on to freer forms of the movement." The brief account gives no clear picture of Liber's position, in particular on the assemblies of representatives. Were they the "freer forms"? By and large, however, his stand was in accord with the formula "bypass the Soviets," which was then gaining currency.

Martov's article indicated a slight turn in favor of the assemblies since it did not mention reelections to Soviets as the Party's main field of action. (It did not mention reelections at all.) But in the Party the arguments about them continued. It was clear that a definite stand must be worked out. The issue of *Novaia Zaria* with Martov's article and the report on the plenum of the Committee of the Central Region also carried an announcement that the Central Committee was convoking a Party conference in Moscow for 20 May, whose agenda included the topic "The Soviets and Our Tactics in Them." The topic was heatedly discussed in Party organizations in preparation for the conference. Kuchin had not exaggerated: it was indeed the vital question since it concerned the Party's practical work. Some topics on the agenda such as the consequences of the Brest peace and the breakup of the Russian state could be debated, but the Party could not do anything about them. The Party's stand on the civil war, on the new anti-Soviet governments and foreign intervention would become practical—and tragic—problems, but only later. In contrast, the questions concerning Soviets demanded immediate answers and their immediate translation into action. Whether to stay in Soviets, to press for re-elections or not, to try to gain the majority in them or to remain even as an oppositional minority; in the event of staying, whether to partici-pate in the Soviets' commissions and committees, what to work for, what demands to put forward—all these were concrete "party work" questions. Underlying all of these was the basic issue: Was not any work connected with Soviets a waste of the Party's limited resources? Was it right to choose them as the main arena of struggle? Would it make better sense to "bypass the Soviets," create new workers' organi-zations? We must look at this problem in the setting of the time.

The Party was in trouble in all kinds of ways. It was not yet proscribed, but it was persecuted, even if the persecution may appear mild in comparison with the later terror. As can be seen from the quotations I have given, the Menshevik press criticized the government in no uncertain terms, and many publications were closed. If they managed to reappear under another name, contact with their readers was broken, which affected their finances. Many Mensheviks were arrested, though the top leaders were as yet immune. The rank and file were depressed, tired out by harsh living conditions and bitter dis-appointment. The Menshevik party, which had unquestionably been the most influential political body in Russia for a few months after the February Revolution, had become a defeated party—defeated both by the Bolshevik seizure of power and by its poor showing in the elections to the Constituent Assembly. The Central Region organization was one of the strongest, and it had among its leaders a remarkable organizer, its secretary L. N. Radchenko, a woman of superior intelligence and energy. Yet at the April plenum the Committee of the Central Region noted "along with the broader ideological influence of our organiza-tion . . . a decline in organizational building, weaker organizational work of our city and provincial committees: inadequate registration of members, irregular receipt of membership dues, inability to organize the work in such a way as to draw all the active forces of the organiza-tion into it."[25] But receipts were falling not only because of poor organization and falling membership: a good many members were unemployed and found it hard to keep up their dues. The financial report of the regional bureau, which received 10 percent of the dues collected by local organizations, dramatically illustrates the decline: in January its share had been 1,923 rubles; in February, 1,092; in March it rose again, to 1,870 rubles, but in April it plummeted to 490, and in May, to 112 rubles, 70 kopeks—seventeen times less than in January.[26]

Despite its waning strength, the Party put much energy into its campaign for reelections to Soviets, often successfully. In a number of Soviets the opposition became the majority. But, as Isuv had said, Soviets could be disbanded as easily as dumas and zemstvos. It was simply not possible to keep the Soviets in being and yet make them independent of the government. If the majority of the Party still clung to the CC's line, this can only be explained by a sentimental attachment to Soviets due to the role they had played early in the revolution. It was too depressing to admit that they had lost this role for good.

What reelections to Soviets did not accomplish, the assemblies of representatives could—or so it seemed in May. The Petrograd Assembly was a brilliant success. A really broad workers' movement emerged during the elections. My above-mentioned report on the Petrograd Assembly ended with the words: "Now it has become even clearer that the Bolshevik government is staying [in power] only thanks to armed force—that it has lost the workers' confidence completely and irretrievably, at any rate in Petrograd." This was a gross exaggeration, but it reflected the prevailing tendency to deny or minimize the workers' support of the government. Dan, too, had written that "Bolshevik Bonapartism now regards the working class as its chief enemy."[27] Yet for several months the government did not crush its "chief enemy." Only Soviet archives will some day disclose why it tolerated the openly hostile Petrograd Assembly so long. A few people were arrested, the assembly was viciously denigrated in the press, but it continued to function, though the government was undoubtedly strong enough to wipe it out. One cannot altogether dismiss the thought that the decision to disband a workers' organization came hard to the government because subjectively it considered itself a workers' government. At any rate it is a fact that in May, while the Mensheviks were discussing the problem of Soviets, the government was disbanding those it did not find to its taste, but the Petrograd Assembly survived, and new assemblies were forming in other cities. This strengthened the position of assembly partisans against Soviet partisans in the Menshevik party. Experience had shown that "regenerating" the Soviets in order to make them points of support for democracy was an insoluble problem. Why waste one's efforts in hopeless enterprises instead of creating new organizations that did not need "regeneration" and were more reliable supports for a democratic workers' movement?

However, this proved to be as much of an illusion as the hope of reforming the Soviets. If we do not know why the government tolerated the assembly even after the peace treaty was signed, we can easily guess why it was in a hurry to disband unruly Soviets. It needed obedient Soviets as the administrative organs on which the entire system rested. They were a necessity, while the independent organizations were merely a nuisance that could be removed any time. Failure to realize this could only lead to another disappointment, but it took a long time and many blows before the Party saw it. After the suppression of the Menshevik party and the labor movement in all its forms, it became very easy to criticize the Mensheviks' illusions, some of which now appear nothing short of fantastic. The hope of reforming the Soviets was an illusion, and so was the idea of being able to work in democratic organs of self-government and the belief that independent workers' organizations could endure under the Bolshevik regime. The biggest illusion of all was the conviction that only a bourgeois revolution was possible in Russia and that a government that tried to carry the revolution beyond that limit was bound to collapse. However, the historian's task is not to expose past illusions but to explain them.

In the first place, it was extremely difficult to evaluate the situation and the possibilities. To what extent was the economy disrupted, how much farther could the chaos go? Martov wrote in *Novaia Zaria* that the state of affairs threatened to "extinguish Russian industry, that is, extinguish the working class itself." If Russia remained much longer the economic and political vassal of German imperialism, the working class was headed for disaster. As it turned out, Martov was too pessimistic, although the future indeed brought great economic woes to the country and much suffering to the working class. There was no objective criterion by which to gauge possible developments. Martov also exaggerated the government's inability to cope with the disorder:

> We have no government able to lead [Russia] out of the impasse. . . .
> In the first place, because we have no *single* government. . . . Who
> is ruling in today's Russia, who gives orders backed by force? Alas!
> Anyone who . . . has a machine gun. Sector, city, *uezd*, provincial,
> regional Soviets are at loggerheads with one another. . . . In one
> place, there is an autocratic city Soviet . . . in another, the city
> Soviet is powerless, the provincial Soviet gives the orders. Here
> a provincial Soviet disbands a city Soviet, elsewhere a city Soviet
> deposes the provincial Soviet by force of arms!

All this was true, but it was not the whole truth. Amid the anarchy, a creative process of evolving new forms of government was going on. Martov could not see this, convinced as he was that the Bolsheviks were doomed because they had transgressed the objective possibilities of the revolution. About the consequences of the Brest peace, Dan wrote in the same issue of *Novaia Zaria*:

The longer the present situation lasts and the more ruthlessly the Austro-German coalition exploits the monstrous strategic, political, and economic advantages the Brest treaty has given it, the more will the countries of the other coalition strive to exploit the helplessness of revolutionary Russia to compensate themselves at her expense for their possible defeat in the World War and for the burdens imposed by it. If things continue as now, the partition of Russia begun by the Brest peace will inevitably continue....[28]

That this was completely unfounded would have been clear to the Mensheviks had they been better informed on the situation abroad. Errors of judgment were also caused by theoretical preconceptions, as I have mentioned.

In short, two months after the Brest peace there were still the same gloomy outlook and the same illusions. So much so that one cannot avoid repetition as one reexamines them against the data of May. In that turbulent period two months could bring great changes. The German occupation and the expanding civil war had torn off large chunks of Russia. The Allied intervention had begun. On 22 April Dan wrote in *Novaia Zaria* that the Germans and Austrians in the south and in Finland, the English and French on the Murman, the English and Japanese in the Far East, and the Turks in the Caucasus demonstrated "the fatal situation in which the so-called Brest peace had put Russia." It had not freed Russia "from the noose of the World War." And in unoccupied Russia, the Mensheviks thought, the government's incapacity to solve its stupendous problems was becoming daily more obvious. The resurgent activity of the working class, which the Mensheviks had been discerning since the beginning of the year, was meeting insuperable obstacles. Newly elected Soviets with antigovernment majorities were being closed or replaced with rigged Soviets, practically appointed from above. The proudest conquest, the Petrograd Assembly of Representatives, had no realistically achievable aim. Well aware that it could not aim at toppling the government, it did not even seek political power but attended to such matters as unemployment or the provisionment of starving Petrograd, taking comfort in the thought (as Solomon Schwarz said at one of its first meetings) that "in the course of struggling to realize practical tasks one can achieve some real gains, too. After all, a front can be breached in parts."[29] But even "practical" work had no practical effects. All the assembly could do was pass resolutions that nobody carried out.

Yet the Party literature that has come down to us does not give an impression of despair. In fact, some optimism can be detected. No doubt it came from the tenacious illusions. These preserved the Party from total discouragement, which would have meant passivity, political death. Without a ray of hope it was psychologically impossible to carry on any kind of struggle. If the hopes later turned out to be illusions, they did help the Party to go on living during that objectively hopeless time, and even to live intensely, displaying a rare fighting spirit and a unity it had not had since the beginning of the revolution. True, the number of active workers had declined, but in the narrowed circle there was no lack of energy and intellectual activity, and relations had become much more friendly. The differences between the majority and the Defensists who remained in the Party had not disappeared, but they had been largely smoothed out. The majority called this group "the loyal opposition" (in contrast to the Internationalists of the pre-October period). We can judge of the new intraparty harmony —temporary, as it turned out—from the periodical *Novaia Zaria*, to which I have already referred several times.

In principle, *Novaia Zaria* was the organ of the committee of the Central Region of the RSDRP, [30] in which Defensists predominated. Its editors were G. D. Kuchin and, from the second issue, myself—both Party member Defensists. Four issues came out, two of them double ones (3/4 and 5/6). Lack of funds prevented regular weekly publication. The first issue was dated 22 April, the last (no. 5/6), 10 June. The journal gives a comprehensive picture of the Party's ideological life during that period since it was not a one-sided organ of one "trend" but a general Party organ. Several members of the Central Committee not only gave their names for the list of contributors but really contributed. The four issues contained two articles by Dan and one each by Martov, Dallin, Gorev, Maiskii, and Troianovskii—all of them members of the CC. And these articles were not just "ornamentation" —they discussed important problems. Of all Mensheviks, only the Potresovite Defensists were not represented. That isolated group was really active only in Petrograd. Having left the Party, they could not participate in the May Party Conference or in the preliminary discussions. Yet this group cannot be deleted from the history of Menshevism. They were typical Mensheviks. Even during this period they did not as widely diverge from the rest as it seemed at the time.

On such fundamental issues as the Constituent Assembly and separate peace there were no disagreements in the Menshevik party. We have seen that both the CC and the Defensists insisted on the need to convoke the Constituent Assembly and to invest it with full powers. The distinction between Defensists and Internationalists had quite lost its former meaning. All Mensheviks, including the Internationalists, had become Defensists in that they protested against the separate peace, the acceptance of the German terms, and demobilization, calling instead for a people's army to repulse the German offensive. This made a rapprochement with the Party majority easier for the Defensists. Only the rift between Potresov's group and the Party remained and grew. This cannot be fully explained by the different political ideas that persisted even after the October overturn; other factors, psychological and moral ones, must be taken into account.

In Potresov's writings, moral outrage is especially apparent. The very title of an article, "Purification," which he wrote ten days after the overturn,[31] proclaims it. In this article Potresov accused "democracy" of being in some degree responsible for the sins of bolshevism because it had extended to the Bolsheviks the mantle of "comrades" instead of refusing to have anything to do with them and "declaring them enemies of Russia on a par with Wilhelm and Hindenburg." The negotiations with the Bolsheviks about forming a socialist government from NSs to Bolsheviks were not merely a political mistake, Potresov felt, but morally indefensible, a blot on the Party's honor. In another article he wrote that certain people in the ranks of democracy, "forgetting conscience and honor, have lent their subservient backs to prop up the *avantiura* of the enemies of the revolution and of freedom, under the illusion of stopping the civil war."[32] In Potresov's eyes, any contact with the Bolsheviks amounted to complicity in their crimes. This accusation was extended to all socialists who did not refuse contact or, like the new Menshevik majority, were even willing on certain conditions to come to terms with the Bolsheviks. Equally reprehensible from a moral standpoint was participation in Soviets, even in the role of opposition. These views created a chasm between Potresov's group and the Party majority that no considerations of political expediency could bridge. They precluded this group's return to the Party even when there was no longer any talk of coming to terms with the Bolsheviks and when the representatives of the Menshevik CC in the Central Executive Committee of the Soviets (mainly Martov and Dan) had taken a sharply oppositional stand.

To be sure, morality was not the only issue that ostensibly stood between Potresov's group and the Party majority. There were also the differing conceptions of the Russian bourgeois revolution. But these had existed for a long time without preventing their adherents from remaining in one party, even during such sharp conflicts as the one over coalition with nonsocialist parties. Actually, when the break came, the question of who would complete the bourgeois revolution had already become academic. It is difficult, I repeat, to explain the rift otherwise than by the Potresovites' moral revulsion at remaining in the same party as the new Menshevik leaders dishonored by their readiness to compromise with bolshevism. The other side in turn mistrusted the Potresovites: their view of the Bolshevik overturn as counterrevolution could lead to alliances with forces that the Social-Democrats had traditionally considered reactionary but that might now appear to the Potresovites a lesser evil than the Bolsheviks.

Ordinarily, neither side expatiated on this point. It was, however, aired in the press in February 1918. A remark about the Potresov movement had appeared in the central organ of the Party, *Novyi Luch*, to the effect that dreaming of "a single camp of all classes" meant either evading the issue or "going straight toward semi-Kaledinism."[33] In his reply, "To Semi-Marxists," Potresov interpreted this phrase to mean "going toward counterrevolutionary reaction."[34] A. Martynov answered that the phrase about "semi-Kaledinism" did indeed suggest that the striving for a common camp of all classes could well lead to the "camp" of real reaction.[35] Potresov indignantly denied this, sure that his position held no such danger. For him it was the only one consistent with Marxism: "There are only two logical answers, mutually exclusive—the Bolsheviks' and ours. No third answer exists. Even the *Luch* pundits cannot invent it." They were "dangling between the two.... And when we are consistent in our policy, this consistency scares [*Luch*] and it shouts about our counterrevolution," thereby "testifying to its own Marxist inadequacy, its dreadful spiritual impoverishment."

In this polemic between Potresov and Martynov, the two sides articulated their differing conceptions of the Russian bourgeois revolution. The Party had fought over these conceptions before October, but they had undergone some modifications since the overturn. Potresov could not understand whether the Internationalists and the new majority did consider the revolution bourgeois or "believed together with the Bolsheviks that Russia was making a socialist revolution, the prologue to world revolution" (see extensive quotation, p. 100). If the former, they must recognize that the proletariat, vitally interested in the growth of productive forces, was thereby "organically linked to its class antagonist, the bourgeoisie...." For both, it was a matter of life and death—which could not be said of peasant Russia. "The common interest of the proletariat and the bourgeoisie in the progressive development of capitalism predetermines their political alliance." Ultimately, the industrial and business city would "take its revanche on the peasantry that killed the revolution of 1917 and threatens to kill the future of the country as well, by its continuing soldier-peasant anarchy ... indifferent to the national destiny of the country." Thus Potresov in fact equated bolshevism with the peasantry who had "killed the revolution" and threatened to "kill the future." To counterbalance these forces of darkness, it was necessary to build a bridge between so-called revolutionary democracy and that progressive part of Russian bourgeois society that would be able to unite with it "in recognizing the sovereignty of an all-nation Constituent Assembly."

In his reply to this Martynov did not mention semi-Kaledinism again but accused Potresov of being no revolutionary Marxist but a "dry doctrinaire" incapable of understanding that "complex, contradictory reality cannot be fitted into a few flimsy formulas." Yes, he replied to Potresov's question, "our revolution is bourgeois: this means that [if it is] confined to national limits, it will not kill Russian capitalism in the event of victory but will further its development." It did not follow, however, that the bourgeoisie had to remain to the end the prime mover of the revolution. In fact, the Russian bourgeoisie had ceased to play a revolutionary role, had betrayed the "bourgeois revolution" and thus paved the way for anarchy. This was how the peasant anarchy had come about. Now, however, the peasantry "is already forming . . . a new, strong petty bourgeoisie, more viable than the 'progressive bourgeoisie' nurtured on the bounties of our tsarism." But this progress "by tortuous and roundabout paths" was taking too high a toll: "We shall pay for this 'progress' with a temporary decline in industry and the disintegration of the working class." This, Martynov concluded, "we are proposing to combat" by urging the proletariat "not to dissolve in the rowdy soldier-peasant element—not in order to restore 'national unity' with our impotent, myopic, and selfish bourgeoisie . . . but to preserve [the proletariat's] independence under any and all conditions and thus save the revolution as a democratic revolution."

The exchange ended with Potresov once more passionately insisting on the need for a "common national front."[36] But his response to Martynov's remark about the new petty bourgeoisie was notable:

Not the dirty-faced petty capitalist who is being produced by the present pseudosocialization of the country but all the riches accumulated in the past, all that is cultured in our economic and political life, should consolidate to bring about Russia's recovery . . . through pacifying the country within and organizing its outer defense.

Potresov reiterated these dark thoughts about the peasantry a month later, when after another closure his paper resumed publication:

In the ill-starred year 1917, the rustic boor in his best shoes trod on the industrial city, and the little, dirty-faced, latter-day "capitalism" in a soldier's uniform . . . suddenly began to rule the country

under the trademark of "workers' and peasants' government."
It is time for the city to take its revanche on these allegedly avant-
garde but in reality deeply reactionary rustics.... And the city
will get the better of these dirty-faced rustics if it will only understand that Russia's revival is the order of the day and that this
revival lies in the nationwide consolidation of all the forces of her
commercial and industrial development. [37]

It is easy to see the contradiction between Potresov's appeals for
"national unity" and his exclusion both of the "rustics," who after all
were the majority of the population, and of the pro-Bolshevik segments
of the working class and urban petty bourgeoisie. To these outcasts, as
we shall see, Potresov soon added a large part of the liberal bourgeoisie. What remained of the "nation" whose unity was to save Russia?
For Potresov himself this was a tragedy but not an intellectual contradiction, just as his socialist internationalism did not, in his view,
contradict his emphasis on national tasks. As a Social-Democrat, he
saw his party as the party of the working class and a part of international socialism; but at the same time he maintained that certain
national tasks transcended the interests of any one class. Ultimately,
national unity meant the union of all the "forces" involved in industrial
development. Russia needed a free development of productive forces,
in the first place intensive industrialization, of which no one at the
time conceived otherwise than in capitalist terms. The bourgeois revolution was to clear the way for the industrial development that
would benefit, among others, the proletariat. That was why the latter
must actively participate in a revolution that would put a hostile class
in power. The proletariat and its party must not only fight side by side
with the bourgeoisie but push the bourgeoisie onward to the comple-
tion of its revolution, trying at the same time to win as much democracy and as many rights as possible, and thereby also the best conditions for the next phase of the struggle. In its basic features this
conception was classical, and common to all Mensheviks. An analysis
of Potresov's ideas, for which there is no space in this essay, would
show, however, that his views on the dynamics of the revolution had
differed somewhat even before the war from those of the other Mensheviks. (For a brief discussion of Potresov's prewar views see Sapir's
essay in this volume, pp. 356–61.) With the war, the divergence had
become sharper. Potresov was disturbed by the Russian workers' primitive mentality, which kept them from becoming conscious of themselves as *citizens* of a unitary state with a share of responsibility for its
fortunes (which was what *national* consciousness meant). For him as
for the other pure Defensists (that is, those who were Defensists even

before 1917), defense of country became the paramount national task, in which the working class, too, must participate. Of course, not a single Menshevik was against defending the country—none preached nonresistance to evil and surrender to Germany. But for the Internationalists, including those who became "Revolutionary Defensists" in 1917, defense of country was, so to speak, someone else's job, in which the working class and its party should not take an active political part. Their task was to seek unification with the socialist parties of all the warring countries for the sake of the proletariat's common struggle for peace without winners or losers (and "without annexations and indemnities"). For Potresov's group, defense was a job into which the whole country—including the working class, vitally interested in preventing Russia's subjugation to German imperialism— should put its all. Potresov rejected the notion that the war was merely a struggle between various imperialisms, equally bad from the socialist point of view. He considered German imperialism reactionary and aggressive, a direct threat to Russia's development. To the Western Allies Russia should therefore remain faithful to the end: this was another national task. After the Brest peace, Potresov thought it imperative to restore the alliance the Bolsheviks had broken.

As we have seen from the polemics between Potresov and *Novyi Luch*, both sides continued to regard the revolution as bourgeois and a return to capitalism as inevitable—the Internationalists with the important qualification: as long as the revolution was "confined to national limits," that is, to Russia; as long as it was not accompanied by a socialist revolution in the West. But on the manner in which the return to capitalism would be effected and on the role of the proletariat and its party in this process there were differences of opinion basically similar to those over the question of defense. In the view of the Party majority, it was the task of social democracy to preserve the independence of the working class—let others restore capitalism. Martynov apparently assigned the main role in this restoration to the new peasant petty bourgeoisie. (This was not at the time, and certainly not later, the opinion of the entire Party majority.) In Potresov's view, on the other hand, the restoration of capitalism was a vital task of the working class. Not because he liked capitalism, of course, but because without capitalism it was impossible to revive the national economy, develop the country's productive forces (that is, overcome its backwardness), and open the way for democracy and the eventual transition to socialism. Further capitalist development would benefit not only the working class. The whole country needed it. Therefore it was a national task calling for the united effort of all the country's forces.

What were these forces? In the articles cited above Potresov had spoken of them only vaguely. His more explicit articles of February to April 1918 are somewhat surprising if one remembers his passionate advocacy of coalition in 1917. Now he wrote that the coalition had been doomed from the start because it was a coalition of the upper strata, not based on a fusion of national consciousness. At a lower level, a gigantic centrifugal process had been going on. Naturally the coalition was bound to fail, and it would be ludicrous to restore it. "The point . . . is not coalition in government but coalition in the country."[38] What were the forces that could be counted on for such a coalition? The liberal bourgeoisie, the Kadets? These Potresov now dismissed outright. In a polemic with the Kadet *Novyi Vek* he devastatingly criticized Russian bourgeois liberals:

> To be sure, revolutionary democracy is bad enough, it has taken many evil deeds on its conscience during the past revolutionary year. But you liberals are no better. . . . True, maximalism is not one of your sins. But you are guilty of something else—of that traditional liberal-bourgeois impotence, that incomprehensible minimalism, which is largely what [fostered] the maximalism of your antagonist, revolutionary democracy, especially those grouped around the working class. . . . One has only to remember the old tactics of the liberals, and of the Russian bourgeoisie generally, toward tsarism to understand the putrefaction that these tactics spread around them. This putrefaction became especially noticeable at the beginning of the war, when the bourgeoisie so unsuccessfully sought a symbiosis with autocracy.[40]

Potresov reminded the liberals that they had taken their idea of "national unification" to the tsarist government instead of taking it to the people (and telling the people that "the palm frond of national unity extended over the country presupposes a firm fist aimed at tsarism"). Now the bourgeoisie was trying to "get along with our so-called Communists just as it used to get along with autocratic tsarist officialdom." There was no patriotic bourgeoisie; but there was a great deal of the kind

> that is now casting a lusting eye on the foreigner: maybe cohabitation with him can be arranged? Such is the custom of our Russian bourgeoisie, its second nature—not to fight but to cohabit. It cohabited with autocracy and is trying to cohabit with the "Communist" government of Lenin and Trotsky. It will cohabit with the German—why not?

Outspoken about those whom he excluded from national unity, Potresov was vague about those he included: the "bourgeoisie" and the proletariat should reach an understanding with "progressive peasant elements"; the proletariat and "the advanced cultured elements" (for example, the organizers of cooperatives) should agree with "the progressive strata of the bourgeoisie." But where could such strata be found if Potresov excluded the liberal bourgeoisie? His conception remained somewhat unfinished. Obviously he expected some new social movement to put Russia, despite the October overturn, back on the road of the historically inevitable bourgeois revolution. In this respect, Potresov remained what may be termed an orthodox Menshevik.

No Menshevik regarded the overturn as a refutation of the theory of bourgeois revolution: it was a case of that premature seizure of power against which Engels had warned[41] and the results of which confirmed the traditional theory. The weekly *Novaia Zaria* during its short existence was valuable in that it permitted Menshevik writers to express their ideas more fully than in newspapers. In mid-May it printed an unsigned article, "The Hundredth Anniversary of K. Marx's Birth," written by me, a Defensist member of the "loyal opposition," but quite in keeping with the views of the Party majority. I shall therefore quote from it at some length. Having pointed out that the Marxist doctrine had been tested "by fire and sword" and come out victorious, I wrote:

> The application of Marxism to the study of Russian social relations had led to the well-known conclusion that Russia was headed for a bourgeois revolution ... [that] would not vault over the capitalist, bourgeois period of development but, on the contrary, clear the field for the luxuriant development of bourgeois relations ... by vigorously advancing the process of replacing some 500,000 landlords and some 80 million peasants (at present the figures are no longer the same) with a new class of landowners of the bourgeois type.

This, as Engels wrote in 1893, could not be done "without great suffering and effort." What was going on now?

> The turbulent anarchic current in our revolution proves to be at the same time a process of ... redistribution of property, a new "primitive accumulation," and the laying of foundations ... for a strong bourgeois-proprietory peasant economy. And side by side with this ... the effects of straight class instinct are more and more noticeable; a class struggle is ripening and developing in forms clearly determined by the changed economic "base" of society; and under our eyes ... the ideological "superstructure" atop this "base" is changing. We are witnessing the emergence of the need to bring legal and political relations, the philosophy of society, into accord with the tasks of industry, the acute needs ... of the national economy. Though disrupted and crippled, [the economy] is striving to straighten out—already seems in fact to be straighten-

ing out—along with the process of redistribution of property in rural areas, no matter how painful and ugly this process may be. The complex, painful, and contradictory process of the bourgeois revolution, further complicated by the effect of the German conquests, is nonetheless running its course, and this signifies a great victory for Marxist theory. [42]

This artificial reasoning was soon belied by events. At the time, however, apart from small variations of detail, all Mensheviks believed in the inevitable collapse of the Bolshevik experiment. "Back to capitalism," wrote Potresov; "forward to capitalism," said the Defensist Solomon Schwarz at a meeting of the Petrograd Assembly of Representatives. [43] This, too, was a notion that saved the Mensheviks from paralyzing hopelessness. There is an optimistic, if cautiously sounded, note in my article: the economy "seemed to be straightening out"—in other words, the return to capitalism was perhaps under way. In the same issue of *Novaia Zaria* Dan said virtually the same without any qualifications. His article "Bolshevik Bonapartism" was so critical of the Bolsheviks that it is a wonder the journal was not instantly closed:

> To us Social-Democrats it has been clear from the first that while it may have been possible [before the Brest peace] to speak of honest error, of fantastic delusions, of the Bolshevik government's ludicrous self-deception—after Brest, and in the conditions it has created, all the talk about establishing socialism is pure charlatanism, a conscious deception of the toiling masses.

This unjust accusation may baffle the reader and calls for explanation. The Mensheviks did not regard Lenin as a major historical figure. He had resorted to very dubious methods in the struggle against them. Most Mensheviks could no longer see his good and bad traits dispassionately. The Lenin with whom they had to contend since the schism was in their eyes an unscrupulous polemist, a master of petty intrigue, an adventurer thirsting for power. It is hard to say whether hatred or contempt was their prevailing emotion. They did not believe in the sincerity of his convictions, did not see his superior intellect or any other traits in him that befitted a great statesman. Dan wrote in the same article that Lenin was "clutching at power." In a sense, this was true: Lenin did all he could to stay in power, but not from personal ambition but to carry out what he believed to be his mission. Dan accused him of having defaulted his revolutionary obligations. "Socialism," "Soviet power," and other verbal frills were "mere bait for fools, a means of duping the popular masses"; Lenin had completed the cycle from communism to open Bonapartism, which led back to a capitalist society. Dan saw a confirmation of this in Lenin's new pronouncements that one must "organize industry, raise the productivity of labor, discipline it, regularize transport, put the state economy in order," and even "stop the 'Red-Guardist' attacks against capital." Moreover, Lenin had decided to "compromise" with experts "who know how to organize industry—to pay them twenty-five, fifty, a hundred thousand a year, and to put them in charge of the industrial mechanism." In short, his "communism" was a fiasco. The government was openly adopting a bourgeois-capitalist policy—which in itself would not be so bad for the workers, except that this return to capitalism was going on in forms that delivered the Russian proletariat "tied hand and foot" to capitalist exploitation and thus sustained "the outdated, parasitic, profiteering, predatory character of capitalism in Russia."

The Internationalist David Dallin, also a member of the Menshevik CC, filled out the picture: "Only one class in Russia has benefited and been strengthened by the external and domestic events—the well-to-do peasantry [krupnoe krest'ianstvo]. It will take the helm of Russia's government. It will be the state power." And "this new master of the Russian land represents a millions-strong, very impressive force whose established rule will be anything but paradise for the working class."[44]

But if such were the prospects, what should social democracy do as the party of the workers? It could not fight the process of turning over the proletariat "tied hand and foot" to capitalist exploitation because a return to capitalism was inevitable and necessary and neither workers nor Social-Democrats could influence the forms in which it took place. Potresov saw the matter differently: through "national unity," including the workers, the return to capitalism could be effected in forms beneficial to all. He was almost the only one to hold this view. Whether they were conscious of it or not, most other Mensheviks felt like helpless witnesses of a process managed by others. Their task was to take care of the future of the working class, preserve its independence, preserve or create independent organizations as strategic points from which to defend its rights. That was why the question of Soviets versus nonpartisan assemblies was crucial. Until the May conference, it remained the focal point—although by then another big problem had begun to trouble the Party: its stand on Allied intervention, which was to lead to far deeper dissent but was not yet openly discussed.

The Party could not subsist on debates and resolutions of no practical significance. So long as it felt alive, it had to seek areas of political activity. Reelections to Soviets, the organization of assemblies of representatives, produced results, whether good or bad. The question of assemblies had in effect been settled in the affirmative and their usefulness recognized by all, but the Soviets remained a problem, both in principle and as a practical matter of allocating the Party's dwindling forces. For the rank and file, as Kuchin had said, this was "the most vital" problem. The Central Committee had much else to worry about, organizationally and politically, and the top leaders did not campaign for elections to Soviets or assemblies of representatives and rarely spoke at mass meetings. (However, Dan did go to Tula for the May Day celebration.) They did represent the Party in the Central Executive Committee of the Soviets.

Originally, the Defensist minority had opposed Party representation in the highest organ of government, fearing that this might obscure the Party's uncompromisingly negative view of the Bolshevik dictatorship or even lead to attempts at finding a "common platform" with it. These fears were soon dispelled. The speeches of Martov, Dan, and Abramovich in the CEC stressed the differences rather than smoothed them out. To their own surprise, these Menshevik leaders were allowed to speak freely, to criticize the government in the sharpest way. Later this tolerance came to seem unbelievable. The chairman of the CEC, Sverdlov, was an unimpeachably "correct" parliamentarian. Once, it is true, he made Martov leave the hall (25 April), but then Martov had disregarded several calls to order, and Sverdlov did what any chairman of a democratic parliament would have done. Another time, when someone in the audience addressed disparaging remarks to Martov (they do not appear in the stenographic record) and Martov replied, "I am being threatened with lynching and I request that the scoundrel be stopped," Sverdlov did not censure him but tried to calm everyone down. For several months the Mensheviks were able to use the CEC as a tribune for their antigovernment views. This reassured the intraparty opposition, removing the main reason why the Defensists had refused to be represented in the Central Committee of the Party (in order not to share the responsibility for a possible compromise with the Soviet government). Relations with the government were in fact deteriorating. The Mensheviks' stand at the time was utterly uncompromising, both in the leaders' speeches and in the Party press. We have seen how far Dan had gone in his article "Bolshevik Bonapartism."

The CC devoted some of its time to drafting speeches and analyzing speeches already made, but this was not the main or the hardest of its tasks. The hardest was guiding the Party under inordinately adverse conditions. Tremendous changes had occurred since the December Party Congress. It was time for another congress, but contact with local organizations was difficult and sometimes impossible. The CC invented a new form, the "Party conference," with somewhat indefinite but lesser powers than a congress (it could not elect a new central

committee, for example). In an article about this "general Party conference" (I shall discuss its deliberations later), Kuchin wrote:

> Never yet had the Labor party been obliged to map out its path
> under such difficult conditions ... amid the debris of former
> Russia, at a cataclysmic time.... Two delegates [only two!] slipped
> through the cordon from occupied Ukraine and brought ...
> information about the "Belgian" conditions[45] in southern Russia....
> One citizen of Minsk also got through and told of enslaved Belo-
> russia. A delegate from Siberia came and informed the isolated
> center of the great events in the Russian east, of the westward
> advance, of the developing war.[46]

It was no exaggeration to speak of "debris of Russia," in the broadest
and in a narrower sense. The giant state known before the revolution
as the Russian Empire no longer existed. Between some of its parts
there was no communication at all. Of Russia in the narrower sense
(Great Russia) only one relatively compact part remained. Sometimes
it was actually called "Muscovy." The entire western part of the
empire (the Baltic countries, Poland, Belorussia, the Ukraine) were
German or Austrian colonies hypocritically called "states." This colos-
sal territory extended far to the south and also far into the heartland of
Great Russia, as far as Belgorod. Beyond Rostov-on-the-Don, which
the Germans occupied on 6 May, and almost to the Caucasus, there lay
a vast region with no formal frontiers, where tsarist generals and
Cossack atamans headed various "governments."

The breakup of Russia spelled breakup of the Party. One after
another, its organizations were torn off. Even in the part of Russia that
remained under Soviet rule, communication between the CC and local
organizations was very difficult. The mails, transport, all means of
communication, functioned badly or not at all. Contact with occupied
regions was even harder. For several months, local organs of government, Soviets of workers' deputies, and trade unions still continued to
operate, and there were Mensheviks in them, sometimes in the majority. As in central Russia, there were different tendencies among the
Mensheviks in these regions. Often local organizations had to make their
own decisions, which the Central Committee did not always approve.

Especially troublesome was the situation in the Ukraine. Besides
many specific problems, a general one of great importance arose.
Events forced the Mensheviks to declare themselves on the independence of the Ukraine. She had been a de facto independent state since
the October Revolution, but her status had not been legally established. It was expected to be settled after the restoration of a democratic order in Russia. The Ukraine was governed by the Central Rada,

formed after the February Revolution, mainly of socialists. But most of this socialist majority were SRs not connected with the Russian Social-Democratic parties as the Ukrainian S-Ds were. The Mensheviks and the Bund were but a small minority in the Rada's socialist sector. However, just as in Russia before October, the Mensheviks' influence was greater than could be expected from their numbers. In the elections to the Constituent Assembly the Mensheviks had received in the Ukraine only a little over 1 percent of the vote, but thanks to their influence in workers' Soviets, trade unions, organs of city government, and in the Rada itself, they represented a certain force in the de facto government. This did not involve them in problems of principle as long as Ukrainian independence was considered temporary and the questions of the Ukraine's relation to Russia and of its place among the other parts of the former empire were left in abeyance. The situation changed when nationalism began to prevail even in the socialist Ukrainian parties. When the Bolsheviks instigated an uprising in Kharkov in December, and Bolshevik troops invaded the Ukraine, separatism flared. On 9/22 January 1918 the Rada formally proclaimed the Ukraine a sovereign state. Only the representatives of the Mensheviks and the Bund had voted in the Rada against this decision. But the Mensheviks sided with the Rada against the Soviet Ukrainian government set up by the Bolsheviks in Kharkov. The Rada did not prove strong enough to repel the invasion that followed. The Bolsheviks occupied most of the country, including Kiev, where they moved their puppet government. The Rada fled to Zhitomir. Only a small piece of Ukrainian territory remained under its control. Nevertheless, it conducted peace negotiations with Germany and Austria and signed a peace treaty independently of the Soviet government. In February the Rada asked Germany for help, and German troops cleared the Bolsheviks out of the Ukraine. This, however, made the Ukraine an occupied colony of Germany and Austria. On 28 April the Germans engineered an overturn that put their protégé Skoropadskii, a former general of the tsarist army, at the head of the government, with the ancient title, Hetman.

This rough outline gives an idea of the conditions under which the Mensheviks had to tackle the problem of national self-determination. If it was hard to solve theoretically, it was nothing short of tragic when specific questions had to be answered with a definite yes or no. All Russian Social-Democrats, Mensheviks and Bolsheviks alike, recognized the right of nations to self-determination (the Bolsheviks even put special stress on "up to and including separation"). The Mensheviks could not deny the Ukrainians this right, but they considered separation extremely undesirable. For the industrial development of the entire country it seemed imperative to preserve the historical whole and the strong economic ties between its parts. The ties between Great Russia and the Ukraine were especially important—not only because Ukrainian agriculture helped to feed the less fertile regions of Russia and Ukrainian ore and coal were needed by Russian industry, but also because Russia had invested heavily in the industrialization of the Ukraine (which in turn had helped to make it the source of raw materials on which Russia depended) and had exported to it a great deal of manpower. In fact, in the eastern Ukraine only the rural population was purely Ukrainian in origin and language. The working class, especially in the Donets Basin, consisted mostly of Russians, among whom the Mensheviks enjoyed considerable influence. Valuable Party organizations would be torn off in the event of the Ukraine's separation. Apart from the Party's interests, there was the fact that the population of most cities and workers' settlements (except in the western Ukraine) was ethnically Russian and usually spoke only Russian, whereas the peasantry was Ukrainian. This augured great internal complications for the separate state. Although the Mensheviks did not in principle deny the right to self-determination, they could not help foreseeing dire consequences for the country as a whole.

The Mensheviks had held different views on the so-called national question, but by the time they began to discuss in concrete terms the structure of the future democratic state, a majority viewpoint had emerged: Since the Party recognized the right of ethnic groups to self-determination, it must resist attempts by any government to forcibly prevent separation if the people desired it; but while the popular will was still crystallizing, the Party could agitate against separation and for the preservation of a single state with broad autonomy for its parts; as a last resort, it could agitate for federation as against complete separation. [47] It had been fairly easy to agree on this formulation, but when it came to putting the principle into practice the Mensheviks found themselves in a predicament. From the ideological point of view, they had done the right thing in voting in the Rada against separation, but by so doing they had isolated themselves and lost what influence they had had on the government's policies. From then on they were obliged to struggle on several fronts without any allies: for reunification with Russia, but against the Soviet government and against surrender to Germany—which in effect meant struggling for the Ukraine's independence that they did not want; and later, against the Germans and the reactionary Ukrainian elements supported by the Germans. And as the reactionary elements gained the upper hand, the Mensheviks were increasingly persecuted—more than anyone else save the Bolsheviks. After the overturn that put Skoropadskii in power, they faced the added distress of being cut off from their party in Russia, not just by disrupted means of communication but by frontiers very effectively guarded by German troops.

In Russia the Ukrainian overturn made a strong impression. At the meeting of the CEC on 9 May, Martov noted that "all Russia, and in particular all Moscow, is deeply troubled over the counterrevolutionary overturn in the Ukraine and its consequences for Russia and the Russian revolution." With the excuse of "technical difficulties" in getting a full report from the Commissariat of Foreign Affairs, the Presidium proposed putting off the discussion of the event until the next meeting—to which Martov replied, "I can only marvel at this stoic sangfroid, this complacency . . . when in Petrograd, according to the papers, the working masses are in violent turmoil over these happenings." He insisted that the government's report on the political situation created by the Ukrainian overturn be the first item on the agenda. The majority of the CEC rejected this, as well as the proposal of other opposition groups to hold a special meeting the next day. [48] The Ukraine was not discussed until 14 May, after Lenin's report on current events (the second reporter was the Left SR Kamkov) at a joint meeting of the CEC, the Moscow Soviet of Workers' Deputies, and representatives of trade unions and factory committees. Toward the end of the tumultuous meeting, the Mensheviks offered a resolution "describing the situation in extremely gloomy terms and sharply criticizing the Soviet government." According to this resolution, "the abolition of the republic in the Ukraine and the overthrow of the government of Ukrainian chauvinists of the Rada . . . reinforce . . . the dismemberment of Russia and her transformation into a colony of German imperialism." The Soviet government, "having lost all moral authority in the eyes of the people" and unable to "instill in the popular masses the will to fight to regain freedom and independence," could not be counted on to save the situation. If all the democratic forces united, they alone could make

> a last attempt to revive in the popular masses faith in the revolution's power of resistance, save the country from . . . final enslavement, from a restored counterrevolutionary dictatorship of landlords and capitalists, from economic catastrophe. . . . And even if this attempt were to fail, the very defeat of free democracy by the superior forces of internal and foreign enemies would play an enormous revolutionary role, both for the future revival of the liberation

movement among the peoples of Russia and for the international proletarian movement.

Therefore it was necessary "to convoke immediately the Constituent Assembly dispersed on 5 January" to put all power in the hands of democracy until new elections were organized. In addition, the Mensheviks advanced the following demands:

1. Immediately restore city and village organs of self-government with all their rights.
2. Fully restore political and civil rights.
3. Decline the new German demands, which put new chains on Russia.
4. Arm the entire people.

Naturally the Bolshevik majority rejected this resolution. The stenographic record notes "noise among the members at the mention of the Constituent Assembly. Extraordinary amount of noise during almost the entire reading of the resolution."[49]

For all their appeals "not to panic," the Bolsheviks were well aware of the tragic seriousness of the moment. One of their speakers, Neibut, characterized Lenin's speech as "a report on the international situation, on our miserable situation." But in the country at large the Ukrainian overturn elicited quite different reactions as well. They are described in the unsigned (undoubtedly Kuchin's) article "Signal of Alarm" in *Novaia Zaria*, no. 3/4. In Kiev, the article said, not only had the dictatorship of "tillers of the soil" dealt a death blow to the revolution, its organs, laws, and relations—there had been another death, the death of the last remnants of the country's independence.

> In Kiev the final lash of the "master's" knout has struck the dishonored, enslaved country.... And how did Russia react to this? Some heaved a sigh of relief (crossed themselves in petty-bourgeois backwaters, smiled in "good families"); others ... shut their eyes tight, in agony: our turn next! Here is our shame, our impotence. Let us look around us at this ultimate hour. What is the prevailing mood, even in revolutionary circles? We are *waiting*. As if shackled, with no will, no strength, we are waiting, eyes closed, for something that seems unsurmountable. Let us not hide these moods. They reflect the country's situation.

This was written by a Menshevik who was relatively optimistic. The article appealed to all workers to heed "the signal of alarm," insist on special meetings of Soviets, convoke citywide conferences of delegates from all factories, trade unions, cooperatives; squarely demand the convocation of the Constituent Assembly and immediate reinstatement of self-government organs. In the same issue of *Novaia Zaria*, another unsigned article (mine), "Before the Final Struggle," ended with the words: "Russian social democracy, the party of the working class, must from now on be the most active party of national regeneration, of the struggle for Russia's reunification and independence." The authors of both articles were Defensists, but at the time almost the entire Party shared their stand.

True, the most extreme Internationalists still refused to recognize any "national" tasks—the very word was heresy to them—but the Internationalist majority did not agree. Martov himself said in the theses he prepared for the Party conference that combating the dismemberment of Russia was a basic task of social democracy and the proletariat and would be the basic task for future generations if the end of the World War brought no changes in the situation created by the Brest peace. This task of *national regeneration* and reunification was not in conflict with the class struggle or the proletariat's revolutionary mission. It was, on the contrary, closely bound up with them. [50]

Even Potresov could have signed this. But the controversy over the methods of struggle and the proletariat's desirable or possible allies continued and eventually led to a new division in menshevism. Just before the May conference, however, there was complete harmony, at least between Martov and the editors of *Novaia Zaria*. This period is interesting from the point of view of the evolution of Martov's thought. I shall draw on my own recollections to fill out the information found in the contemporary press.

Most Russian Marxists held on to the definition of the state as an instrument of class hegemony, although Marx and Engels themselves had been fully aware that apart from securing the political domination of the economically dominant class, the state also fulfilled functions needed by all of society. For the Russian Marxists it was obvious that in a capitalist society the state must be an instrument of capitalist hegemony. Even so, certain forms of government were more advantageous for the workers than others. Hence, while considering that only a bourgeois revolution was possible, they favored a democratic capitalist state. Even Potresov ridiculed the author of an article in the left socialist *Novaia Zhizn* for "inventing a new . . . formation that had not occurred to Europe": capitalism without the hegemony of capitalists. [51] My article in *Novaia Zaria*, no. 3/4, from which I have just quoted, referred as follows to a speech by Bebel demanding universal suffrage in Prussia: "Bebel's old prediction has come true that in the great struggle of peoples only that people will retain independence and national sovereignty that knows it has a homeland worth defending."

Of course the Internationalists, in particular Martov, were not against "independence and national sovereignty"—they simply did not think in these terms. Class was far more important. Martov had, however, sounded a new note in the article "Workers and State Power" (see n. 19), where he spoke of a single national state power—democratic, of course. Essentially, the article repeated what Barnave had said during the French Revolution: Peoples want freedom but cannot live without order, and if a people has to choose, it will choose order without freedom rather than freedom without order. Martov had written that a people could stand "economic chaos, bloody conflict, lawlessness, and personal insecurity" only so long. These were inevitable while an old order was being destroyed, but a revolution that kept them up became "hateful to the masses" and perished. Creating a viable and workable state power was therefore an essential task for the working class. This had been the reasoning of some partisans of coalition before October, but not Martov's or the other "moderate" Internationalists'. [52]

The German takeover in the Ukraine gave Martov's thought another impetus in the same direction. In the theses he prepared for the May conference he actually spoke of "the basic task of national regeneration"—a cardinal sin from the point of view of the extreme Internationalists. I can testify that this formula, as well as the theses generally, had been worked out by Martov and the editors of *Novaia Zaria* together. Not that we saw eye to eye on everything, but both sides wanted to reach agreement on the main issues. The differences that remained were wrapped in vague formulations (and will be discussed below in connection with the May conference). I should like to cite here one resolution of the conference that confirms my recollection that the Defensists and the Party majority followed a line jointly agreed on. Just before the conference, the Regional Committee of the Central Region held a plenum (19–21 May), which passed a resolution offered by me. Its Point 6 said: "While putting forward the all-nation task of fighting for the independence and unity of Russia ... the Party must at the same time vigorously combat any deviation of the national movement into chauvinism, national exclusiveness and hatred." Point 3 of the resolution adopted by the Party conference would say: "While striving for [reunification] of republican Russia ... and for the restoration of her independence, and regarding this task of national revival as consonant with, and closely linked to, the class interests of the proletariat ... the Party vigorously opposes any policy that inflames chauvinism and nationalistic quarrels among the peoples of Russia." Clearly the two resolutions were based on one text.

The Party conference in Moscow (21–27 May) marked in the Party's internal life the end of the period we have been discussing. The logical inferences were drawn from the increasing rapport between the majority and the opposition. The latter, which in December had refused to be represented in the Central Committee, now agreed to let Kuchin and Liber join it. On the other hand, the Potresovite Defensists left the Party, which made for a far more wholesome atmosphere within it. An amusing incident occurred at the conference: the rabid Internationalist Martynov made a speech praising the opposition for its loyalty, for observing discipline and not disrupting the Party's work as the earlier opposition had done. Somebody asked what earlier opposition he had in mind. Unabashed, Martynov replied, "us."[53]

The main point, of course, was not the opposition's good manners but the temporary disappearance of its sharp differences with the majority. No doubt this was partly due to the fact that, unlike Potresov's group, the Defensists who now remained in the Party did not formally set up an organization of their own within it. They had neither a directing center nor acknowledged leaders, nor did they hold separate meetings at which intraparty problems were discussed "over a cup of tea." Thanks to the predominance of Defensists of this type in the bureau of the regional committee of the Central Region, no one thought, as we have seen, of making the periodical *Novaia Zaria* the organ of a single trend. In short, the Defensists remaining in the Party did not form an organized opposition—and we know from the history of any political party that formally organized intraparty groupings tend to sharpen dissent since they stress what divides, not what there is in common.

The personal qualities of the Defensists who were particularly active during this period (beginning with the campaign that resulted in the Petrograd Assembly of Representatives) may have played a part in all this, but certain outside factors were even more important. For one thing, neither the majority nor the minority were as homogeneous as they had been before October. The sharp distinction between Internationalists and Defensists had disappeared. The new majority that emerged at the December Congress included Internationalists and Revolutionary Defensists—though by no means all of the latter but only the group headed by Dan. The rest joined the opposition. On the other hand, some prerevolutionary Defensists also joined the new majority and even defended its stand with especial zeal. At the April plenum of the regional committee the two reporters were the prerevolutionary Defensist Isuv for the majority and the Revolutionary Defensist Liber for the opposition. With the slight exaggeration almost inevitable in any generalization, it can be said that in 1918 the Mensheviks again became the individualists they had been before the revolution. During 1917 they had somewhat departed from their tradition of not recognizing any undisputed leaders except the dead Marx and Engels: the Revolutionary Defensists had fallen under the sway of Tsereteli's spellbinding personality; Potresov's intellect and lofty morality had made him the supreme authority among the extreme Defensists; and the same can be said of Martov among the Internationalists. By 1918, only Potresov retained absolute authority over his followers. Tsereteli had left for Georgia, and Martov, though greatly respected, was not even in full control of the Central Committee, now composed, as it was, of Internationalists and Revolutionary Defensists. The leadership of the Party majority was divided between him and Dan, and they did not always see eye to eye.

The Party drew together once the disruptive effect of formal struggling factions had disappeared. There is no trace of acerbic polemics or factional intrigues in the contemporary literature or in memoirs. However, the principal factor was the country's plight after the surrender to Germany and the separate peace. These events had erased the disagreements on war and peace that had so sharply divided Internationalists and Defensists, and created instead a far-reaching solidarity. The restoration of Russia's independence and unity had become the main task. Differences existed, but they were not always due to factional loyalties. To the extent that they were, both sides wanted to contain them, preserve peace, work out a common policy. This made for an impression of harmony, though the harmony was not as complete as it seemed. Some Defensists—and some others as well— gradually became profoundly dissatisfied: the Party policy seemed too passive, or, as Kuchin repeatedly wrote, "not revolutionary enough." On the other hand—and again not only among former Internationalists—there was an aversion to making national tasks the business of the working class and its party. The very word "national" was still taboo for a good many party workers. [54]

In his article summarizing the May conference, Kuchin recorded the objections to the statement in the resolutions adopted that struggling for Russia's independence and unity was the Party's task:

> The very fact that this question was posed evoked doubts and objections from a part of the Party. . . . The apprehensions about the "national" character of the task, the disagreements on the need to put this question in the center of our policy, in contrast to the "old" task of fighting counterrevolution . . . were traits of the conservative thinking of an insignificant part of our Party, which

impeded the live progress of the Party's consicousness by excluding from the Party's horizon the question of Russia's *ruin as an independent state.*"[55]

The last long sentence is rather nebulous—perhaps because Kuchin did not care to be too clear. If only "an insignificant part" of the Party suffered from conservatism, why should this impede the progress of the whole Party's thinking? Probably Kuchin felt that the leadership paid too much attention to the ideas of a small minority (shared by some of the leaders). But this had been so before the conference, Kuchin continued. Now the issue of Russia's ruin as a state "had arisen in all its fullness and clarity": Martov's theses had thoroughly explored it. This meant progress in Party thought, "of the greatest importance for the next period of struggle." Kuchin then quoted Martov's text on "the basic task of national regeneration." Clearly he agreed with it—which is hardly surprising since Martov had checked it with the editors of *Novaia Zaria* and accepted some formulations Kuchin and I had suggested. The theses were in fact a collective product. The starting point had been a draft prepared by Kuchin.[56] It is all the more significant that his account reveals some dissatisfaction with the decisions of the conference and its general character.[57] "It did not make a very forceful impression," he wrote, "and that is only natural. It had come together from a beaten movement, at a time of oppressive reaction." Of course it was only natural. "Not very forceful" was in fact a euphemism. The conference could only be a demonstration of weakness. It is easy enough to imagine the mood of the delegates as they traveled to Moscow, tired from overwork, dispirited by persecution—by the closing of newspapers, the proscription or scuttling of meetings, the arrests (and in some cases, not yet numerous, executions). The Party organizations often lacked funds for the most necessary expenses. At the plenum of the regional committee of the Central Region just before the conference, the bureau's secretary, L. N. Radchenko, had reported that "the financial situation of the bureau does not at all correspond to the extent of the work it must do, considering the many requests for agitators and speakers.... The cash box is often so [depleted] that there is no money for ... traveling expenses. Salaries are late, doled out in miserable sums."[58] The needy living conditions of most Party workers were too well known to be discussed at meetings. They could not be remedied in any case. No wonder the conference "sometimes worked sluggishly."

The liveliest debates concerned the Soviets of Workers' Deputies, almost the only area in which the Party could still engage in "practical work." They were also the most controversial issue since the other, deeper differences had not yet crystallized. The Soviets were the third point on the agenda, but I shall begin with it since it ties in with the discussions that preceded the conference. (On the first two points disagreements arose that were in time to destroy the unity reached before the conference.)

The differences on this issue, which appeared on the agenda under the heading "The Soviets and Our Tactics in Them," had been smoothed out in some respects but became accentuated in others. The doubts about organizing Assemblies of Representatives that some of the Party and its CC had entertained had been dispelled. Supporting and fostering this movement had become the Party's policy—with a proviso, it is true, that was included in the resolution but soon lost all practical relevance. The resolution recommended "appealing to the working masses to organize representative organs, independent of the government, of freely elected representatives of the working class"—but only where "the attempts . . . to change the composition and policy of the Soviets founder against the counterrevolutionary license of cliques that have got hold of the Soviets, so that this way of organizing the masses has become impossible." It was rapidly becoming impossible everywhere. The inclusion of this clause merely proves how difficult it was for the majority of the Party to give up the hope of turning the Soviets into instruments of struggle and "points of support" for the labor movement. Isuv, who had maintained in April that the Soviets were "the principal class weapon of the proletariat,"[59] still insisted at the plenum of the regional committee of 19–21 May that "the main line of struggle" should be "around the Soviets." At the April plenum the majority had agreed with him, but in May the votes were evenly divided and it proved impossible to draw up a resolution on which a majority could agree. On the other hand, the group that included the editors of *Novaia Zaria* had shifted to a sharply negative view of any struggle "around Soviets": Liber's stand had prevailed. In April he, too, had thought that in certain cases reelections to Soviets should be put to use, but he had gradually come to favor "bypassing the Soviets." Two weeks before the May conference, both editors of *Novaia Zaria* had urged the Party to take part in the reelection campaign. "The Soviets cannot be bypassed," I wrote, not naming Liber but obviously disputing his stand, and Kuchin wrote: "It is impossible for us not to participate in them [elections to Soviets]." But at the plenum of the regional committee Kuchin sided with Liber against Isuv in supporting the motto "bypass the Soviets."

At the Party conference, the two reporters on Point 3 were Abramovich for the CC and Liber "for the minority group," as Kuchin called the opposition since there was no organized opposition. We have no record of the debates, but comparison of the majority and minority resolutions illumines the two stands represented at the conference. The resolution that was passed by a majority vote had been divided into three parts, probably to circumscribe differences of opinion. The minority (eight votes) voted together with the majority in favor of the first part, which Kuchin described as "a well-rounded negative assessment of the present Soviets." On the tactics the Party should adopt there was no such unanimity. The resolution recommended organizing assemblies of representatives (with the proviso I have cited), but also struggling "for free reelections to Soviets" and their "transformation into independent organs of the working class." The resolution offered by Liber countered this with the following: "Participation in Soviets and their institutions, which by now have attracted almost universal hatred and disgust . . . demoralizes the working masses and isolates the working class from the other popular strata by making it responsible for the whole present regime." Therefore it would be better to recall Party members from all Soviets and appeal to the workers not to participate in them in any way. Nevertheless, the minority did not vote against the second part of the majority resolution, which spoke of free reelections and trying to transform the Soviets, but merely abstained. It was adamant only in its opposition to the third part, which recommended "remaining in the present Soviets in the role of irreconcilable opposition to the Bolshevik regime" and allowed participation in boards directing technical and cultural activities, though only if these boards were elected (not appointed by the government) and if participation was compatible with the Party's policy. The minority voted against this part. Kuchin noted with some satisfaction "a definite shift in the Party's stand on Soviets," although this shift did not "quite keep up with the changing conditions" and although the conference had failed to "chart the clear revolutionary line required at this juncture." Still, "the tactical directives of the resolution leave some scope for Party work." This was not the first appearance of the complaint that the majority was insufficiently "revolutionary." As yet it referred only to the issue of a clean break with Soviets. Later it would become clear that this criticism already contained the germ of the "activist" movement that was to employ methods of combating the regime that the Party majority would not brook.

The first two points on the agenda of the May conference were "War and Peace" and "The Disintegration of the Russian State." Dan reported on the first, Martov on the second. On both, Liber again spoke for the minority—a natural choice since he was well known to all Party members, having played an outstanding role during the "February" period of the revolution. He was an effective speaker, a temperamental man with a keenly logical mind—though his logic lacked subtlety and could lead him to too extreme conclusions, or so it sometimes seemed even to his closest followers. At any rate, no one else could have presented the differences between the majority and the minority more tellingly and without shrinking from certain conclusions that other members of his group had not yet reached.

Dan's and Martov's reports were debated together and resulted in a single resolution, "The Brest Peace and the Disintegration of Russia." Most of what it said was irrecusable; the one point on which there was any substantial dissent was the stand on the presence of Allied troops in Russia. The majority and the minority agreed that solving domestic problems with the aid of foreign intervention was an unmitigated evil and resolved to "avoid this calamity."[60] But what if it could not be avoided, if it were already a fact? Fighting for Russia's independence meant fighting against Germany and against the Soviet government that had surrendered to Germany. Such a struggle was clearly impossible and hopeless, not only for the weakened Menshevik party but even for all the opposition parties together. My article pointed out that things would be easier "if a period of time were granted us in which to restore our state by our own forces . . . and freely determine our foreign policy afterward. No such period of time is granted us. . . . The very process of establishing an independent state—independent in the first place of Germany, obviously—means fighting Germany. And at some point in this process a renewal of the former alliances is inevitable." This reasoning was undoubtedly correct, but under what circumstances would a renewal of the old alliances be admissible? Point 5 of the resolution answered in vague and even contradictory terms. The conference rejected "soliciting, in whatever form, the assistance of foreign powers in the task of overcoming Russia's internal political crisis," but also observed that "only if Russia's revival is accomplished by her own democratic forces and a democratic state is restored" would "military pacts with Germany's enemies" hold no danger of turning Russia into a passive instrument of some group of foreign powers. Obviously no revival could take place *before* the Germans were ousted—and once they were, no "military pacts with Germany's enemies" would be necessary. Thus it was absurd to speak of the revival of Russia—of *all of Russia*—before Germany's defeat. Clearly this point of the resolution was meant to convey something else. The key lies in its history, which unfortunately can be reconstructed only from memory. Point 5 had originally been one of the

theses drawn up by Martov and the editors of *Novaia Zaria*. The text
was revised several times to accommodate various political or tactical
objections. Further changes must have been made when it was discussed in the CC. This was perfectly natural, but the final text was a
compromise lacking in logic and clarity. It had no doubt been further
modified when the common resolution on Martov's and Dan's reports
was drafted. The original text did not refer to Russia as a whole. It said
that if the Soviet regime were overthrown in some *part* of Russia, it
would be permissible to form alliances with the old Allies and accept
their aid, provided the separation of this region from the Soviet state
was no ephemeral *avantiura*, nor a reactionary enterprise, and a
responsible democratic government had come to power in it. Quite
likely this formulation did not satisfy all the Party leaders, and Martov
himself may have had misgivings about it. In any case, the resolution
was open to several interpretations. Kuchin wrote:

> To be sure, Dan's theses and the adopted resolution indirectly
> recognize that at a certain point an agreement with the Allies may
> be possible, but the inadmissibility of the Anglo-French orientation
> is so stressed and elaborated, and the need to resist Allied inter-
> vention is posed so sharply . . . that the co-reporter Liber was
> obliged to point out, quite rightly, the *actual* situation in which
> intensified struggle against the Allies . . . would mean . . . strug-
> gling on the side of Germany, that is, a "German orientation"!

This passage foreshadows the differing attitudes toward armed action
on Russian soil, which everyone thought inevitable. The majority
hoped to preserve the Party's neutrality. The minority felt that the
Party's place was at the side of the Allies. These issues, however, were
not yet urgent: the minority did not vote against the resolution but
abstained from voting on the grounds that, although it "showed great
progress in the Party's united consciousness," it did not provide clear
political guidance. [61]

Despite the tragic situation of the country and the Party, the conference ended on a note of optimism insofar as intraparty relations were
concerned. Kuchin and even Liber, who had spoken for the opposition
with his usual trenchancy, agreed to become members of the Central
Committee. Apparently neither the majority nor the minority considered their differences important enough to preclude joint work in
the Party's leading organ. Neither side realized the full portent of the
dissent—probably because no concrete action on the controversial
issues was as yet required of the Party. It focused its energy on the
assemblies of representatives and the new workers' movement that was
spreading all over the country. The Petrograd Assembly had sent some

of its members first to Moscow, then to other industrial centers, to agitate for local assemblies. But while the government continued its cautious handling of the Petrograd Assembly, its reaction elsewhere was often brutal. From June on, there were occasional violent clashes. The assemblies were in principle nonpartisan, in the sense that several parties and trends were represented in them—usually Mensheviks, SRs and no-party people. Actually, the leadership was increasingly in the hands of Mensheviks. Some Menshevik party workers connected this movement with Axelrod's old idea of a workers' congress. [62] After the May conference, Kuchin devoted practically all his time to the preparation of an all-Russian conference of assemblies of representatives (or, as they were sometimes called, nonpartisan workers' conferences). Together with another member of the CC, Troianovskii, he set up in Moscow an organizational center, which held a meeting on 13 June with delegates from Petrograd, Moscow, Tula, and Briansk. All those present were arrested and imprisoned, including Kuchin, Troianovskii, and the foremost pioneers of local assemblies, the Menshevik Kamermacher-Kefali and a member of the Moscow committee of the Party, Malkin. In the small industrial town Ozery, delegates of the Petrograd Assembly were arrested, whereupon a crowd of workers, armed only with their tools, stormed the prison and freed them, then burned down the local Soviet. [63]

Preparations for an all-Russian conference went on despite the repressions. But the Petrograd Assembly decided to stage a general strike as a demonstration against the repressions. This time the government took preventive steps: not only were appeals to refrain from the strike distributed but machine guns were set up at strategic points. Debilitated by famine and other intolerable conditions, the workers lacked the spirit for a showdown with government troops. The wonder is not that no general strike took place but that several factories did strike. This partial success did not erase the depressing effect of the failure to mount a general strike. The intended demonstration of protest had turned into a demonstration of weakness.

This impression lasted until 20 July, when the All-Russian Conference of Factory Representatives met in Moscow. Outwardly it was a big success. Some one hundred fifty delegates came—from Petrograd, from several Moscow factories, from Tula, Viazma, Sormovo, Briansk, Kolomna, Iaroslavl, and other places. The first day was devoted to reports from local organizations, which on the whole revealed increasing discontent with the Soviet regime. Debates on future activities were scheduled for the next morning, but soon after the delegates had assembled, troops encircled the building; all were arrested and marched off to various prisons. As a member of the conference, I can testify that despite the encouraging reports from local organizations, the conference was in a rather depressed mood. Many of us felt that the movement that had raised such enthusiasm and so many hopes was coming to an end. And indeed the arrest of the conference members did signify the end of the last independent workers' movement in the country that was still called Russia but would soon become "the Soviet Union."

Meanwhile other events had taken place that made these arrests seem relatively unimportant. The May conference was still going on when a conflict flared up between the Soviet government and the Czechoslovak legion. The legion, incorporated in the Russian armed forces, consisted of former soldiers and officers of the Austrian army who had surrendered to the Russians rather than fight for Austria. They hoped for their country's independence after Austria's and Germany's defeat. After the Brest peace, the legion wanted to leave Russia by way of Vladivostok and join the Western Allies. France, too, insisted on this, and on 26 March the Soviet government signed in Penza an agreement with the Czechs and the French, allowing the legion to cross Siberia to Vladivostok—taking with it, however, only small arms. For about two months the agreement was carried out. Over ten thousand Czechs reached Vladivostok without a hitch. The origins of the conflict are still unclear, but there can be little doubt that Germany exerted pressure on the Soviet government to stop the evacuation, for she naturally did not like the idea of permitting reinforcements to join the armies she was fighting on the western front. The explanations of the Soviet government need not detain us here. What matters is who profited from the Czechs' departure for Europe and whom it could harm, and above all the Czechs' own attitude. On 21–22 May Trotsky's aide sent two telegrams ordering that the Czech units be stopped, disarmed, and disbanded. The Czech delegates in Moscow were arrested. Then Trotsky sent orders to all railroad stations on the legion's way: the Czechs were to be disarmed and interned, and those who resisted were to be shot. The legion reacted with lightning speed. Practically unarmed, a contingent near Penza occupied the city, seized an arsenal, then advanced eastward and took Syzran and Samara. Other Czech units, which were already in the east, occupied Cheliabinsk on 27 May. Soon all the towns along the railroad east of Irkutsk were in Czech hands. In Vladivostok the Czechs deposed the local Soviet and virtually took over the administration of the city.

The character of the civil war changed abruptly. No longer were reactionary generals the main adversaries of the government but democratically minded Czechs not in the least interested in restoring monarchy in Russia and whom the government itself had provoked. In Czech-occupied Samara the Committee of Members of the Constituent Assembly, secretly organized by the SRs, came to power on 8 June. The new conjuncture caused in the Menshevik party a clearer division than the one at the May conference, which had moreover been blurred by the wish for unity. An activist movement began to crystallize. At first it manifested itself mainly in Party members' departures for the eastern regions where (unlike the struggle in the south) a civil war was now going on without the participation of reactionary elements. In retrospect, it is clear that this activism, this readiness to join in armed struggle against the regime, and the orientation toward the Allies, had already been present, though not fully conscious, in the stand of the minority at the May conference. Although the minority had agreed that foreign armed forces must not be used to settle Russia's domestic affairs, its spokesman Liber had pointed out that under certain conditions "agreement with the Allies" would be inevitable. This could only mean agreement with Allied armed forces. To fight Germany and not to solve internal problems? But that was a purely theoretical distinction. War against Germany could not be separated from war against the regime that had submitted to Germany—in other words, from Russia's internal affairs. The minority sincerely considered foreign intervention a calamity that should be avoided if at all possible. But if intervention was not only inevitable but had become a fact, logic dictated its acceptance as the only salvation.

The Central Committee did not draw this conclusion. It remained adamantly opposed to intervention, to a forcible overthrow of the regime, to participation in the civil war. This stand, too, had its logic. It rested on the premise that an overturn achieved through armed force would result in the dominance of that force; and since reactionary generals were in control of it, the end result would be monarchist counterrevolution and restoration. This position, not clearly articulated in the CC's resolutions until later, was undoubtedly rooted in lack of confidence in the strength of democracy, in its ability to achieve an overturn on its own. Later events confirmed this pessimistic appraisal. But they also proved the illusoriness of the notion that the Menshevik party, backed by workers loyal to it, could play the role of a "third force" in the conflict between the two other forces, neither of which the Party leadership considered it possible to support. In order to be a third force one had to be a *force*, which the Party no longer was. The activists were especially loath to admit this. They still believed in the possibility of effective action in the east, where one region after another was being liberated from the Bolsheviks, thanks to the Czechs' eastward advance. And no doubt they found it hard to accept the idleness to which from June on the Party was condemned in Soviet Russia because of intensified repression.

We do not know why the government suddenly turned from relative toleration to harsh persecution of the opposition. The danger that the Czechs' successes presented may have impelled it to eliminate all groups likely to support uprisings. Almost all Menshevik publications were closed. On 13 June delegates at the meeting to discuss an all-Russian conference of assemblies of representatives were arrested. On 14 June the Mensheviks, the SRs, and other oppositionists were expelled from the Central Executive Committee, and soon also from most local Soviets. The Menshevik CC wrote in a letter it managed to send abroad: "Now, in connection with the expulsion, we expect terror to the limit.... Taking Martov, Dan, and others as 'hostages' has already been discussed at a meeting of the Central Executive Committee."[64] In the Soviet part of the country, the Mensheviks were tied hand and foot. Seldom was the CC able to publish anything. Its resolutions reached a very limited number of people, often not even all the provincial organizations. Later, referring to a declaration of the Moscow activist group, Martov wrote the old Menshevik émigré A. Stein in Berlin: "This has created in the Party a tactical schism, which isn't turning into a de jure schism simply because the terror is keeping all of us down, making polemics impossible, or even a conference or congress for a trial of the insurgent elements."[65] It can be shown fairly precisely when and why this de facto schism had become inevitable.

Within the CC itself, some members insisted on the need to find a way out of the Party's enforced inactivity. Maiskii offered a proposal to move the CC to the other, eastern side of the civil war front. It found no support. Answering Maiskii, Martynov agreed that the Party could do nothing in Soviet Russia and suggested that it and the CC temporarily give up all activity and, as he said, "lie low." Dan remarked ironically, "You personally, as A. S. Martynov, can lie low, but the Party cannot."[66] It is unlikely that Maiskii expected the CC to accept his proposal about moving to a region that, in the CC's conception, could become a hotbed of monarchist reaction.

In Soviet Russia the Menshevik organizations followed the CC and took no part in the uprisings that began in May. In Samara, when the Committee of the Constituent Assembly came to power, the Menshevik organization at first also adhered to the Party line. A special case, particularly important in its consequences for the Party, was the Iaroslavl uprising, in which many local Mensheviks, possibly the majority, took part despite their organization's disapproval. The uprising had been started by an outside group, the secret military organization *Soiuz zashchity rodiny i svobody* ("Union for the Defense of Motherland and Freedom"), but it caught on widely and was supported by considerable numbers of workers. Harsh repressions and very difficult living conditions had put most of the local inhabitants in an anti-Bolshevik mood. The military organization took over the city during the night of 5–6 July.

When the news of the Iaroslavl uprising reached Moscow, the Mensheviks had to take a stand on it, though no one as yet had any reliable information on its origin or nature. It should be stressed that both sides of the Party spoke out before they knew anything about the political coloring of the armed forces that had effected the coup. They had probably never heard of the organization *Soiuz zashchity rodiny i svobody* headed by the SR Boris Savinkov. Nothing was known except that a military overturn had taken place, that the population, including many workers, supported it, and that several prominent Mensheviks were in the government set up by the insurgents. The first reactions are more significant than their later rationalizations. They were not only characteristic of the two opposite trends in the Party—they showed for the first time how deep and irreconcilable the differences were. The Central Committee reiterated immediately and categorically that it was inadmissible for the Party to have anything to do with uprisings against the Soviet government. But for the minority grouped around the bureau of the Central Region the decisive factor was the working masses' participation in the uprising. They considered it the Party's duty to declare its solidarity with the workers engaged in mortal combat with the hated regime and to help them insofar as possible—the latter, however, on condition that the uprising was on the whole democratic in character, which seemed likely since Mensheviks were involved in it. That these prominent Mensheviks were taking part in the uprising without the local Party committee's sanction did not become known in Moscow until later. But even this did not make the minority change its stand. The first serious clash between the CC and the regional bureau occurred over this issue—namely, the attitude to take toward uprisings that were to some extent workers' uprisings, especially when they were organized by democratic elements. And beyond this issue loomed the larger one of participating in attempts to overthrow the Soviet government.

7

The Outbreak of the Civil War

David Dallin

The period from late May 1918 to the end of 1920 was the bloodiest of the civil war. Anti-Bolshevik armies were forming, Allied troops disembarking, new front lines crossing the country. In some regions the food shortage was reaching famine proportions, and mass epidemics broke out. Repression was becoming a systematic policy. An intensified civil war fitted in with Lenin's conception of a true revolution against all "urban and rural capitalist elements." On 11 June 1918, village Committees of the Poor (*Komitety bednoty*) were established. Within a few months, some 80,000 of them were set up, to implement the "social revolution" among the peasantry. Provisioning squads from the cities invaded the countryside.

V. Volodarskii was killed on 20 June; the German ambassador Mirbach on 6 July; the former tsar and his family on 16 July; M. Uritskii, the head of the Petrograd Cheka, on 30 August—the day an attempt on Lenin also was made, for which hundreds of innocent people were shot as "counterrevolutionaries." As the White armies formed in the southeast, new underground organizations sprang up such as *Soiuz Vozrozhdeniia Rodiny i Svobody* ("Union for the Regeneration of Motherland and Freedom") and the more rightist "National Center" (June 1918) and "Tactical Center" (April 1919).

One of the first acts of the new Supreme Revolutionary Tribunal was the death sentence of Captain Shchastnyi, executed within ten hours, 21 June 1918. Trotsky was a witness at the trial, and his testimony

156

sounded like orders to the judges. Viewing the case as the forerunner of a new wave of terror, the Menshevik Central Committee published a resolution about it and a strongly worded pamphlet by Martov. At the Second Congress of Soviets the Bolsheviks had passed a resolution to abolish capital punishment, and yet, wrote Martov,

As soon as they came to power, from the very first day, . . . they began to kill.

To kill prisoners taken after a battle in the civil war—as all savages do.

To kill enemies who had surrendered after the battle, on the promise, the word of honor, that their lives would be spared. . . .

. . . The abolition of capital punishment had been announced, but in every town, every *uezd*, all sorts of "extraordinary commissions" and "military-revolutionary committees" ordered the shooting of hundreds and hundreds of people. . . .

Human life has become cheap, cheaper than the paper on which the executioner writes the order to wipe it out. Cheaper than the extra bread ration for which the hired killer will dispatch a man to the beyond, on the order of the first scoundrel who seizes power. . . .

Having killed tens of thousands without trial, the Bolsheviks are now introducing executions by court order. . . .

Captain Shchastnyi denied his guilt.

He begged that witnesses be interrogated, including the Bolshevik commissars who were supposed to watch him. Who could know better than they whether he had indeed plotted against the Soviet government?

The tribunal refused [his request] . . . refused him the right that any court, except Stolypin court martials, grants even the worst offender.

Yet a man's life or death was at stake.

The life or death of a man who had earned the trust and love of his subordinates, the sailors of the Baltic fleet, who protested against his arrest . . .

Under Nicholas Romanov it was sometimes possible, by drawing attention to the monstrous harshness of a sentence, to stay its execution and snatch the victim from the hangman's hands.

Under Vladimir Lenin even this is impossible.

The beast has licked warm human blood. The machinery of [official] murder has been put in motion. . . .

The first example has been given, and now the Supreme Revolutionary Tribunal will be dispatching to the beyond all those whom the Bolshevik party may wish to obliterate. . . . [1]

After Uritskii's assassination and the attempt on Lenin, the Bolshevik press began to talk blood in a way never surpassed before or since. "Blood for Blood!" "To the Wall!" "No Mercy!"—under such titles

Zinov'ev's paper *Krasnaia Gazeta* printed the following, for instance:

We shall steel our hearts. We shall temper them in the fire of suffering, in the blood of fighters.

We shall make them cruel, hard, implacable.

So that no pity may enter them, so that they may not falter before the sea of enemy blood.

And we have undammed that sea.

Without mercy or pity, we shall strike down our enemies by the tens, the hundreds.

Let their numbers reach thousands.

Let them drown in their own blood....

... SRs and Mensheviks everywhere are carrying out the bloody orders of their masters.

In Iaroslavl, Samara, Baku, Petrograd, everywhere these Cains, the Menshevik-SR leaders, on the orders of the bourgeoisie, are striking down the staunch fighters for the revolution.

There shall be no mercy for them....

... let the blood of the bourgeoisie and its servants flow— more blood. [2]

In another short piece in the same issue we read: "Tomorrow we shall make thousands of their wives put on mourning. The bourgeois to the wall."

Krasnaia Gazeta of 1 September 1918 printed a telegram allegedly received "from the front" to the effect that there should be "no courts, no tribunals": "Let the workers' vengeance range freely. Let the blood of rightist SRs and White Guards flow. Destroy the enemies bodily."

The head of the Cheka, Peters, wrote that "in Petrograd there had been no executions before Uritskii's assassination, but after it there were too many, and often haphazardly—whereas Moscow replied to the attempt on Lenin merely by shooting a few tsarist ministers." About the arrested Mensheviks he said: "We divide them into active and passive ones. The latter will be freed, but there will be no mercy for the former." [3]

Throughout the country, the popularity of the Bolsheviks was waning. Having experienced the revolutions of February and October and been subjected to all kinds of programs, the people were ebbing away from political parties. They still voted in elections, though in lesser numbers; they voted for resolutions denouncing terror when they could, but they no longer "came out into the streets" and rarely engaged in "mass actions." The Petrograd paper *Rabochii Internatsional* (no. 11, 14 August) described a meeting of sixteen thousand workers at the Putilov plant that had somehow been permitted. Apparently none of the political leaders attended it. After some speeches, a muddled resolution combined Left SR, Menshevik, and also Bolshevik ideas. Still, it demanded that all newspapers be allowed to resume publication and all arrested socialists be freed, called for "immediate abolition of capital punishment," and concluded with "Long live the Soviets! Long live the dictatorship of the toiling people! Down with the dictatorship of individuals!"

The Expulsions from Soviets

The campaign against Mensheviks (and SRs) in the Soviets of 1918 can be divided into two phases. At first the Bolshevik authorities simply closed those local Soviets in which the opposition predominated, or else held new elections, often successfully. In other words, they were satisfied with keeping the Mensheviks and SRs in the minority.

In their role of opposition, the Mensheviks often displayed great energy. Entire plenary sessions were sometimes devoted to arguments with them. However, constitutional rights were becoming anachronistic. In a dictatorship there was no room for an active opposition, especially since the beginning of the civil war. In several cities the Bolshevik majority expelled all Mensheviks from Soviets to put an end to criticism and denunciations. These tactics, not yet sanctioned by the capital, seem to have begun in April. In Rzhev, Mensheviks were expelled from the workers' division of the Soviet. In Kaluga several Mensheviks were expelled on the grounds that legal action had been initiated against them (trials were a common method of combating them in 1918). In Vitebsk in late April, Red troops passed a resolution not to tolerate "conciliationists" (*soglashateli*) in Soviets: unless a new Soviet without a single conciliationist was elected within a week, they would "come out arms in hand against counterrevolutionaries, Mensheviks, and right SRs." A meeting of the Soviet followed, which all workers' deputies had to leave. In Kineshma, Mensheviks and SRs were forced to leave the Soviet. [4]

The campaign was especially violent in Saratov. Orenburg Cossacks, with whom the Saratov Bolsheviks were at war, camped near the city. The Red troops in the city refused to fight until they were paid. The Czechoslovak legion and the Committee of the Constituent Assembly were forming nearby. The local Bolsheviks demanded that Moscow expel the opposition from Soviets, but Moscow apparently hesitated. On 30 April, the local Bolshevik V. P. Antonov (Antonov-Saratovskii) reported to the Soviet:

The third important issue was that of the attitude toward pseudo-socialist parties—the Mensheviks, the right SRs, and so forth. On this our Soviet disagreed with the center, where they somehow put up with these people, while we could not tolerate [them]. We could not admit into the Soviet those parties that were organizing uprisings against the Soviet, organizing the Cossacks' attack on Saratov, organizing the most vicious sabotage, and so on.[5]

Although the Soviet, to quote Antonov, had "resolved that there was no room for these parties in a workers' and peasants' organ of government," Mensheviks must have remained in it, for on 24 May another Bolshevik, M. V. Vasil'ev (Vasil'ev-Iuzhin) proposed expelling the opposition because Mensheviks had taken part in the Saratov uprising of 16–19 May. The Mensheviks denied this. Again the Soviet resolved that there was no room for such parties in the Soviet and invited the workers of the factories that had sent SR and Menshevik deputies, or even nonpartisans "not standing on the platform of the Soviet government," to recall them within a week and elect new deputies "from among comrades incapable of basely betraying the workers' and peasants' interests."[6]

The second phase of the anti-Menshevik campaign began in early June. At a meeting of the executive committee of the Saratov Soviet on 5 June 1918, the press commissar, Venatovskii, reported that a copy of the *Nakaz* issued by the Petrograd Assembly of Representatives was displayed in the window of the Menshevik committee. The EC resolved to try the committee before a revolutionary tribunal on 9 June, to have the local Cheka arrest other Menshevik leaders, and to ask Moscow for permission to launch a "large-scale struggle against the counterrevolutionary actions of the Menshevik party and right Socialist Revolutionaries."[7] At the trial, the accusation proved to be unfounded, the public clearly sympathized with the accused, and the sentence was light: to declare them enemies of the revolution and "expel them from the ranks of the working class."[8]

It is not known what steps the Saratov Bolsheviks took in Moscow, but on 14 June the Central Executive Committee finally gave in, apparently after a "telephone conference" between Lenin, Sverdlov, and Avanesov held just before a meeting of the CEC, when its agenda was already prepared: Sverdlov proposed *adding* to it the issue of "anti-Soviet activities." Besides the stenographic (obviously edited) record of this meeting, I shall draw on a later description of it by E. Drabkina, who worked at the time in the CEC's secretariat, that is under Sverdlov:

> Sverdlov took the chairman's bell, squared his shoulders, and said, fixing the audience:
> "The Presidium proposes to include in the agenda . . . the ques-

tion of anti-Soviet activities by parties represented in Soviets."

Martov shot up:

"And I propose to add to the agenda the question of yesterday's arrests of Moscow workers."

Did he realize that this was the last session of the Central Executive Committee that he and his party would attend?

Surely, yes! An intelligent, experienced politician, he could not fail to sense that history had reached a new frontier beyond which the Mensheviks could not possibly remain in organs of the proletarian dictatorship. . . . . [9]

A second-rank Bolshevik, L. Sosnovskii, who "specialized in Mensheviks," offered a resolution to expel them. This was seconded by M. Pokrovskii, Iu. Steklov, and M. Latsis. The usual accusations were brought out: counterrevolutionary conspiracy, servants of foreign capital, and so on. Not only Martov and Dan objected, but also Karelin for the Left SRs and Lozovskii for the Internationalists. Martov said:

We are not preparing an armed uprising. We have no part in the Siberian, or any other, government formed in an *avantiura* involving foreign bayonets. Organizing the working masses is the only method we are using. . . . Behind every one of us, thousands will rise—and then woe unto you! [10]

Many delegates must have been against expulsion. When it came to voting, Sverdlov asked who was in favor of bringing the resolution to a vote. According to the official account, "a significant minority were against." Drabkina continues the story:

"The resolution is passed by an overwhelming majority," said Sverdlov. "I request the members of the counterrevolutionary parties expelled from the Soviets to leave the . . . meeting of the All-Russian Central Executive Committee of the Soviet of Workers', Peasants', and Red Army Deputies."

Martov, shouting curses against dictators and Bonapartist usurpers in his sickly, tubercular voice, grabbed his coat and tried to put it on, but his shaking hands could not find the sleeves.

Lenin, very pale, stood looking at Martov. What was he thinking at that moment? Was he remembering how, more than two decades ago, he and Martov—friends, comrades-in-arms, comrades in the struggle—had set out together on the road of revolution? Did he see in his mind's eye the Martov of the *Iskra* period, the talented publicist and speaker? . . .

. . . Pointing at Martov . . . a Left SR burst into loud laughter. . . .

"You have no reason to be so jolly, young man," croaked Martov, turning to him. "Before three months are out, you will follow us. . . . "

. . . With a trembling hand Martov opened the door and went out.

The resolution of the CEC declared that Mensheviks and SRs had been found guilty of

> organizing armed action against workers and peasants, in alliance with open counterrevolutionaries—Kaledin and Kornilov on the Don, Dutov in the Urals, Semenov, Khorvat, and Kolchak in Siberia, and finally, in the last few days, the Czechoslovaks and the Black Hundreds that have joined the latter.
>
> The All-Russian CEC resolves:
>
> To expel from its membership the representatives of the Party of SRs (right and center) and Mensheviks, and also to invite all Soviets of Workers', Soldiers', and Peasants' Deputies to remove representatives of these factions from their midst.

Without access to Soviet archives we cannot know to what extent this last instruction was carried out. In comments to Lenin's *Works* we read: "As a result of this decision, Mensheviks and right SRs were expelled from all local Soviets, and their publications closed."[11]

In the Moscow Soviet, the most important, the instructions were not obeyed: the Mensheviks remained; only the SRs had to go. A Menshevik member, B. Dvinov, explains this by disagreements among the top Bolsheviks in the Soviet.[12]

The Mensheviks in the Soviet protested against the SRs expulsion. Isuv made a long belligerent speech in the Party's name:

> We Social-Democrats strongly condemn terrorist acts, and we also condemn the murder of Volodarskii, for such murders, while useful to you, harm the workers, smother the young shoots of their autonomous class activity. Who put the knife in the assassin's hands? Who but you with your ... executions, you who exalt personal bloody reprisals into a Bolshevik credo? And what about the murder of our comrade Vasil'ev, an old S-D, one of the workers most devoted to the socialist cause? Wasn't this shameful murder committed by your agent, because of your gory delirium, your defamation of socialists? And the system has reached its peak in the execution of Admiral [sic] Shchastnyi, which will remain an indelible blot on our revolution. At the Second All-Russian Congress you solemnly abolished capital punishment for all time. And despite your own decrees, a legal murder of unparalleled baseness has been committed, on the order of the highest representative of your government. . . .
>
> Aren't we right? You demagogues promised to feed the people . . . but instead you have destroyed the organizations of provisionment, cut us off from the bread markets by your internal and foreign policy, and what remains of the Russia that you have ruined is

facing death from starvation; and to the deluded workers you are sending lead instead of bread, you sic the hungry workers on the peasantry, your crusade is preparing a bloodbath for the hungry workers. And you dare call yourselves a workers' and peasants' government! You are still calling your government a Soviet government, and when the workers wake up and leave you in catastrophic numbers, you adulterate the Soviets, you disband them, you kill. What other counterrevolution do you want—it is in you, inside you, in every step you take. . . .

Like all tyrants, you are afraid of the truth. You muzzle the socialists, throttle the hated press, making short shrift of it as Durnovo and Stolypin never dared. [13]

A Menshevik conference of the Moscow organization on 26 June discussed means of getting the electorate to react against the SRs' expulsion, to wit:

Suggest to the Moscow workers (a) to recall from the Moscow and sector Soviets those representatives of the government parties who voted for the expulsion and degraded themselves by violating the will of the worker electors, and immediately to elect new deputies in their stead; (b) to recognize all the expelled deputies as their representatives, disregarding the Moscow Soviet's decree about expulsion. [14]

The Mensheviks' situation remained unchanged for about six months. When Kolchak established his government in the east and the German revolution broke out, they and the SRs modified their stand, and Bolshevik policy toward them changed accordingly.

Uprisings against the Soviet Government

By the summer of 1918, with the spread of the civil war and Allied intervention, the stand on armed action against the government had become an urgent issue. There was disagreement about it not only among the different democratic parties but within menshevism itself. The Central Committee expressed its negative stand in numerous resolutions and through its leaders' articles and speeches. Uprisings and civil war, they all said, must in the nature of things lead to alliances with anti-revolutionary and pro-restoration elements, which were bound to gain dominance in an anti-Bolshevik camp during a civil war. Victory, therefore, would lead to reaction, the revival of many institutions of deposed regimes. A socialist party could not support such a course. And as the SRs were inclined (in 1918) to support it, close collaboration with them seemed impossible.

For Party members, this was formulated more "ideologically," in

Marxist terms: bolshevism and menshevism were two branches of the labor movement; even though bolshevism was a misguided, utopian socialist movement, a part of the working class was behind it; an armed struggle between Mensheviks and Bolsheviks would thus be an inadmissible "civil war within the working class."[15] By themselves, these scruples might not have outweighed the antagonism toward the regime, but most Party members were doubtful of success, conscious of the Party's inadequate strength and of the hazards involved in uprisings. The majority of rank-and-file members at conferences in Moscow and the provinces, and of "independent groups" at trade union congresses, favored the "conciliationist policy" of Martov and Dan—simply because any other seemed hopeless.

The Right Mensheviks, on the other hand, favored a policy close to the SRs'. They viewed the rule of bolshevism not as a utopian socialist experiment but as counterrevolution, not unlike the old regime in its suppression of democratic freedoms, which had to be overthrown through popular uprisings. "Coming to terms" with it was not only unthinkable in principle but also impractical: the regime was headed for disaster anyway; and when it fell, a democratic regime would replace it. Optimistic faith in the revolutionary democratic movements went hand in hand with disbelief in the Bolsheviks' capacity to mutate.

For the SRs the stand on uprisings was not much of a problem by this time (summer 1918)—all their factions considered them necessary and legitimate. The Left SRs tried to organize an uprising in Moscow after Mirbach's assassination.

Armed action required material help from the Allies—hence their aims had to be reckoned with and certain concessions had to be made. So long as Moscow was "oriented" toward Germany, collaboration with the Entente meant: (a) alliance with the Czechoslovaks on the Volga and in Siberia; (b) cooperation with the Americans and British in Murmansk and Archangel; (c) some compromise with the Japanese, who had disembarked in Vladivostok and were now beginning to move inland in pursuance of ambitious aims. After Germany's defeat, the interventionist programs assumed vaster proportions (French forces appeared in the south and in the Black Sea, renascent Poland coveted Belorussia and the Ukraine, Rumania wanted to annex Bessarabia permanently, and the Baltic countries wanted independence).

Of the civil war fronts of 1918, the eastern (Volga-Urals) and the southern (Don) were the most important. They differed in their political coloring, and hence the Mensheviks' tactics in relation to them also differed.

On the Volga an offensive of left-democratic elements (mainly SRs) was launched in the spring, after the insurrection of the Czechoslovak legion. [16] The anti-Soviet Czech corps happened to be the only important military force in the vast Volga-Urals territory. Local Soviets were deposed, and Russian democratic groups found themselves in power, with SRs predominating. A series of uprisings followed—in Samara, Kazan, Simbirsk, Ufa, leading to others in Iaroslavl, Murom, Rybinsk, and the formation of a "people's army" (*Narodnaia Armiia*). Oversimplifying a little, one might call this phase of the civil war a contest between bolshevism and populist democracy (the SRs).

For reasons indicated above, the Menshevik CC stood aloof from all this (its position was at first called neutrality, but the term raised objections and was soon dropped), while the Right Mensheviks favored collaboration with the SRs and expected great things from the Committee of the Constituent Assembly and the Ufa government.

Radically different from the Volga-Ufa, the southern front was a stronghold of monarchism. Here leaders like Kaledin, Krasnov, and Denikin came to the fore, and volunteers assembled to join the White armies. Hundreds of officers loyal to the old regime fled to the Cossack settlements from Soviet territories. To be sure, the Constituent Assembly was on all lips, but mainly for diplomatic and strategic purposes. Democrats were hated, including Kerensky and the "terrorist" SRs. So long as Germany occupied large sections of the south, the White movement developed rather sluggishly. Its time came in 1919, when Kolchak had defeated SR democracy, and help from the Allies enabled Denikin to approach the Moscow region.

Dissatisfied with the role of neutral "third force," most of the Menshevik party would now favor support of the Red army against "counterrevolution." This inimical view of the White armies caused friction with the right-wing Mensheviks.

The secret organizations formed in 1918 in Soviet-held parts of Russia to support anti-Soviet fronts were mostly unions of SR, Kadet, and NS party centers, with an admixture of the military. Among them were the *Soiuz Zashchity Rodiny i Svobody* ("Union for the Defense of Motherland and Freedom"), the *Soiuz Vozrozhdeniia Rossii* ("Union for the Regeneration of Russia"), the tactical center, and a few others, differing politically (more "left" or more "right") in the presence or absence in them of SRs and NSs and in their ties with the former allies (Czechoslovaks, French, English, and Americans). The Menshevik party forbade its members to belong to these organizations. When a few leaders nevertheless joined them, intraparty conflicts arose.

The Iaroslavl Uprising of July, 1918

This was the first reasonably well organized anti-Soviet uprising led by political figures of consequence.

The Mensheviks were influential among the Iaroslavl workers and virtually controlled the local trade union movement. When the Soviet was disbanded (9 April 1918), forty-seven of its members were Mensheviks (plus thirteen SRs), while only thirty-eight represented the bloc of Bolsheviks and Left SRs. The newly created Cheka was not doing its job properly, as even Bolsheviks admit. [17] "Rightist" Mensheviks reasoned that with the Soviet dissolved, the newspapers closed, and famine threatening, an uprising could succeed. Was it sensible to renounce victory and freedom for the sake of Party discipline? Perhaps the Moscow center did not fully understand the situation.

The uprising was planned and organized by Boris Savinkov, formerly a member of the SR Fighting Organization, a Defensist during the World War, Kerensky's closest collaborator in 1917, and now a member (or initiator) of several of the anti-Soviet political unions that maintained contact with representatives of Western powers in Russia and with Russian generals in the south. The first of these unions was the *Donskoi Grazhdanskii Sovet* ("Don Citizens' Council"), in which Generals Alekseev and Kornilov, and Peter Struve, played leading roles. Savinkov joined it. In January 1918 he went to Moscow and Petrograd to promote movements under the banner of the Constituent Assembly. In February he organized in Moscow the *Soiuz Zashchity Rodiny i Svobody* (called *Narodnyi* [People's] *Soiuz Zashchity Rodiny i Svobody* during its brief revival in the spring of 1921). It consisted mainly of officers. [18]

G. V. Plekhanov was one of the people Savinkov tried to enlist in this union. Later, at his trial, Savinkov said: "The main purpose of my trip to Petrograd was to see Plekhanov, whose opinion I valued highly. But Plekhanov was already dying, I did not get to see him, and left for Moscow." [19]

The Supreme Court was very interested in Plekhanov's role in the affair:

The Presiding Judge: Whose idea was it to invite Plekhanov? General Kaledin's?
Savinkov: Mine, of course. . . .
Presiding Judge: And [it] was approved?

Savinkov: Yes. On paper, of course.

Presiding Judge: There were no objections?

Savinkov: There was a great deal of talk, of course, but I have already told you that I won a certain paper victory—that's it, a paper [victory]. [20]

Plekhanov's widow published a "Letter to the Editors" in the Moscow press (on 4 September 1924):

> I am extremely surprised at the forgetfulness and irresponsibility of this repentant leader of the White Guard movement.
>
> In January 1918 he came to Petrograd as a delegate to Plekhanov from the *Donskoi Grazhdanskii Sovet*—yet on 3 November 1917, that is, two-and-a-half months earlier, in reply to his invitation to form a cabinet "when victorious Cossacks, after a battle at Pulkovo, enter Petrograd," Plekhanov had clearly and definitely told Savinkov: "I have devoted forty years of my life to the proletariat, and I will not be the one to shoot it, even if it does follow the wrong road."
>
> . . . .
>
> Georgii Valentinovich's friends were so well informed about his attitude toward Savinkov and his schemes that when the latter, upon his arrival in Petrograd in the winter of 1918, tried . . . to obtain an interview with the gravely ill Plekhanov, they had no compunction about refusing outright. [21]

Besides Plekhanovites, Savinkov tried to enlist Menshevik Defensists. The Menshevik party as such took no part in the conspiracy. [22] A Plekhanovite, the cavalry officer "M," headed the "mobilization department"; a former Social-Democratic Duma deputy, "N. N.," the "agitation department." The Plekhanovite Dr. Nikolai Grigor'ev ("Dr. Aksenov") was in charge of contacts with other cities, virtually directing the entire underground work. His nursing home (on Ostozhenka, Molochnyi pereulok, No. 2, apt. 7) served as Savinkov's headquarters. [23]

In Iaroslavl, Savinkov's right hand and the de facto leader was Colonel Aleksandr Perkhurov, a monarchist loyal to the republican Savinkov. The city seemed a promising place for an uprising—the workers' support could be expected, and possibly that of the socialist parties. [24] Once begun, the uprising was likely to spread to other cities—Rybinsk, Murom, Kaluga. Savinkov had apparently drawn his plans in agreement with the French: Noulens informed him by telegram from Vologda that the Allies would land in the north between 3–8 July. Savinkov decided to act in Iaroslavl and Rybinsk on 5–6 July. [25]

The Iaroslavl uprising began on 6 July, soon after the Soviets had been overthrown with the Czechs' help in several places in the Volga region, and it was successful at first. The Rybinsk and Murom risings were soon put down, but in Iaroslavl Soviet laws were abolished and a new army was to be formed. *Izvestiia* reported on 21 August: "The entire guard of the Soviet turned out to be on the side of the White Guards, for the commissars of the militia were among the important conspirators of the overturn." The paper mentioned the commanding officers who had "joined the Whites." "The city exulted, everyone was issued three pounds of bread." Rumor had it that the Kremlin was besieged and about to surrender.

Meanwhile tanks were rolling from Moscow to quash the "riot."[26] Help from the Czechs and the Allies did not materialize. The uprising began to lose momentum. Within two weeks, on 21 July, it was over. Mass executions followed (the official figure exceeds 350).

Before the uprising, Perkhurov had managed to enlist several Mensheviks, for instance I. T. Savinov, a railroad employee who promised the support of two thousand workers if arms were issued; E. Diushen, who had been the provisional government's commissar for the province in 1917 and at one time a member of the local Menshevik committee; Bogdanov-Khoroshev, secretary of the Iaroslavl printers' union; and the sailor Abramov. Soviet sources also name the Mensheviks Musatov and Meshkovskii as active participants in the uprising.[27]

When Savinov reported to the Iaroslavl Menshevik committee that he was helping to organize an uprising, the committee resolved to dissociate itself firmly from the affair, "preserving its neutrality ... and retaining freedom of action." A member of the Moscow regional committee, Rybal'skii, who was then in Iaroslavl, approved. Diushen, Savinov, and other Mensheviks were told to resign from Perkhurov's staff. Diushen and Savinov refused and were expelled from the Menshevik organization.[28] The committee also wanted to issue an "appeal to the workers" but was not allowed to; neither did its attempt to organize a rally succeed.[29]

A few days later Bogdanov-Khoroshev had to flee the city. In Moscow he reported to Martov,[30] who called a meeting of the Central Committee for 17 July 1918. The CC endorsed the Iaroslavl committee's decision, confirmed the expulsion of Savinov and Diushen, and stated in a resolution:

> The ongoing armed clashes in Iaroslavl with the Bolshevik government are not an uprising of broad workers' and democratic masses but a military undertaking guided by politically ambiguous groups leaning on the country's antidemocratic strata and merely utilizing the masses' legitimate discontent and outrage at the regime of violence, unemployment, and savage dictatorship.
>
> Hence, whatever the outcome of this encounter, it gives the proletariat and democracy no guarantees that the ignoble regime of Bolshevik dictatorship will not be replaced with a regime, more

or less concealed at first, of counterrevolution.

Therefore, confirming its resolutions of 1 July and 8 July, the Central Committee once more points out to Party comrades that they absolutely must not join uprisings of this kind or serve as tools of the groups that direct them. The Party's task in events of this kind is to organize the workers into an independent third force, seeking above all

1. To restore democratic organs of local self-government . . .
2. To arm the workers.
3. To put an end to bloodshed and violence. [31]

Since this resolution annoyed the right-wing Mensheviks who were more favorably disposed toward uprisings, the CC called a special conference of the Moscow region organizations in the latter part of July. It approved the CC's and the Iaroslavl committee's line by a substantial majority: "In the present political circumstances any armed action against the Bolshevik government is *avantiurizm* benefiting only the counterrevolution." [32]

The Uprisings on the Volga, in the Urals, and in the North

The Party's policy in the Iaroslavl uprising impelled the right wing to declare its differing stand and thus helped the rightist trend in menshevism to assume its distinct form. The Party's position was dictated by the extremely complex problems raised by the civil war. The Iaroslavl uprising was but the first major event of its type. The Volga-Ural movement in the summer of 1918 was much broader and potentially more important. Instead of one isolated city, a vast region with a population of millions rose against Moscow. The Volga peasants had traditionally supported the party of Socialist Revolutionaries; now, bedeviled by "provisioning squads" and Committees of the Poor, they were more than ever willing to support the movement. The prospect of returning to the conditions and slogans of 1917, this time with SRs heading the government, appealed to many, including some Mensheviks. The new Samara government, the Ufa conference, the new directory were the main attempts of democracy to overthrow Soviet rule. The history of the civil war records other offensives against Moscow, but the Volga-Ural movement remains the most important effort to restore democracy in Russia. The Menshevik party, as we have seen, did not believe that it could succeed. Local organizations, however, quite often resisted the Central Committee's instructions.

On 27 July, the CC explained its stand in a resolution that it sent to all its organizations. It ended with the words: "So long as objective conditions remain unchanged, social democracy does not deem it possible to make the organization of uprisings aimed at overthrowing the Bolshevik government an immediate task of the working class."[33]

A few days later, having discussed the problem anew in response to inquiries, the CC categorically forbade Mensheviks to take part in uprisings:

> In view of proposals advanced in some organizations that individual members of local organizations be allowed freedom of action if local uprisings occur in connection with the advance of Allied and Czechoslovak troops—the Central Committee informs local organizations that such a solution is absolutely inadmissible; that the meaning of the Party's decisions is not only that organizations as such cannot take part in the preparation and execution of similar *avantiury*, but that those organizations granting freedom of action to individual members will be held responsible for the actions [of those members].[34]

This already reflected the news from Samara, the seat of the hurriedly organized "Committee of the Constituent Assembly" (*Komitet Uchreditel'nogo Sobraniia*, or KOMUCH). When the Czech legion, moving westward, had reached a line running from Syzran to Samara to Simbirsk to Kazan, it became possible to set up the new government in Samara, headed at first by five members of the Constituent Assembly. The Czechs and the SRs found it easy to agree on the main points of a program that was both anti-Soviet and anti-German. Claiming that the Czechs were a military force under the command of the Allies, and KOMUCH a Russian government allied with them, both the Czechs and the SRs denounced the Brest peace and viewed their encounters with Soviet troops as a continuing war with Germany, a new Russian-German front inside Russia, with Moscow caught in the middle.[35] The Czechoslovak advance had begun from Penza in late May. Samara was occupied on 8 June and Kazan on 6 August. Soon the "Territory of the Constituent Assembly" embraced Simbirsk, Orenburg, and other cities, extending into the Urals. August was the month of greatest successes. In September the Ufa conference drew up the formal constitution of the new government (the directory). In November, Kolchak unseated the directory. It had been in existence five months.

At first the Samara Mensheviks turned a cold shoulder on KOMUCH, but the mood soon changed. A conference in early August of eleven Menshevik organizations in the territory of the Constituent Assembly decided to support KOMUCH and empowered the regional committee elected at this conference to carry out the new policy. With the front line west of Samara, and communications with the Central Committee cut off, the regional committee was the highest Menshevik authority within reach.

Leaders from all over Russia and Siberia converged on Samara to help their comrades with the great new tasks—including the SRs Chernov, Zenzinov, Avksent'ev, Breshko-Breshkovskaia, and the Mensheviks I. Maiskii, K. Ermolaev, and A. Dubois. About one hundred former members of the Constituent Assembly congregated in the territory.

The Mensheviks' participation in the Samara government and the Ufa conference is sometimes referred to as "the Maiskii affair," but this episode was far more important for the history of menshevism than any individual "affair." Maiskii merely attracted special attention. Samara had to act secretly in enlisting the cooperation of sympathizing leaders —doubly so in the Mensheviks' case, for they concealed the names of departing members not only from the Soviet police but also from their own Central Committee. Maiskii was actually a member of the CC. Having lately been active in the trade union movement, he asked the CC's secretary, E. Broido, to obtain for him a pass to Perm "on cooperatives' business." He needed it to cross the front line, and it was issued. [36] Maiskii promised not to appear publicly as representative of the CC. He arrived in Samara in early August and was offered the post of Minister of Labor. (Maiskii maintains that this came as a surprise.) He accepted, with the regional committee's sanction; but since he had not been a member of the Constituent Assembly, his title was merely "director of the Department of Labor."

A resolution of the regional committee published in the Menshevik *Vecherniaia Zaria* of 16 August stated that "the restoration of normal economic and administrative life" required "free development of productive forces as well as maximal protection of the workers' interests" through broad social reforms achievable within the framework of a capitalist society—and "under such conditions it is the duty and obligation of social democracy to extend the fullest support to the Committee of Members of the All-Russian Constituent Assembly in its great task of creative statesmanship." [37]

Needing experts in social legislation and the trade union movement, Maiskii made several attempts to enlist S. Schwarz as deputy minister, but the latter, though a rightist Menshevik at the time, "disapproved of such undertakings." [38]

Some other Menshevik groups on the Volga shared the views of the Samara group. The Kazan committee published on 6 September a resolution stating that "all its forces, physical and spiritual, are at the disposal of the Committee of Members of the Constituent Assembly and its military arm, to be used against the enemies of the country, the enemies of the working class." [39] The Ufa *Golos Rabochego* (4/17 July 1918) expressed similar views. The Orenburg *Rabochee Utro* (2/15

August), commenting on the decisions of the Social-Democratic regional committee for the territory, declared it unthinkable "to stand aside, to fence oneself off from the work of government."[40]

The Samara Mensheviks appealed:

> The fate of Russian democracy is inseparably bound up with the fate of Samara. All those who are struggling not only in words but in fact for democracy, for a better future for the laboring [people], must give their all to the People's army. The fall of Samara would mean the defeat of democracy. . . . Everyone to the defense of Samara![41]

The Samara Soviet with its Bolshevik majority was disbanded and new elections produced a Menshevik majority. In the elections to the City Duma about half the vote went to the Menshevik-SR bloc (and in Orenburg even more).[42]

Yet there was no unanimity in the Social-Democratic organizations of the KOMUCH region. Some members sympathized with the stand of the Central Committee. It is difficult to gauge the extent of these sympathies, but they were quite manifest at times, irritating the SRs and especially the parties of the right, which tended to regard the Mensheviks (the extreme legal left) as "semi-Bolsheviks" anyway. Partisans of the CC often called themselves "Menshevik Internationalists," to delimit themselves from official local menshevism.[43] In their public appearances they supported neither KOMUCH nor the Soviet government and called for immediate termination of the civil war. "Enough blood" was their slogan. In Samara, the capital of KOMUCH, they launched a weekly paper, *Svobodnoe Slovo*, but it was closed after the second issue.[44]

The Kazan Soviet was replaced with a Non-Partisan Workers' Conference (*Bespartiinaia Robochaia Konferentsiia*) of 384 members elected by 32,256 workers and employees, an impressive number by local standards. It was entirely pro-Menshevik—its chairman was the Menshevik S. Efimov, and among its leaders were V. Ivanov and the "Menshevik Internationalist" Rudelson.

In a Soviet report, published later, we read:

> The stand of the non-*uchredilovtsy* [those who did not support KOMUCH] amounted merely to a proposal to end the carnage between Whites and Reds. Comrade Chistiakov offered a proposal to elect a delegation to send to Moscow, for the purpose of finding ways to end the civil war. A thunder of applause greeted this proposal. Comrade Rudelson (Internationalist) spoke in approximately the same vein. His speech, too, was several times interrupted by applause.[45]

"Enough blood" was also the leitmotiv of a series of articles by Bruk, the editor of the Kazan Menshevik paper. He noted that the commission on the affairs of arrested persons included a member of the Menshevik organization, V. N. Ivanov, whose intercession saved the lives of many Bolsheviks. [46]

When the Central Committee learned of Maiskii's government post (before reports from the local organizations had come in), it announced in *Utro Moskvy* of 9 September that "according to official newspapers, I. A. Maiskii, former member of the CC of the Russian Social-Democratic Labor party," had accepted a responsible post in the Samara government; that he had done so without the CC's knowledge; and that "henceforth" he was no longer a member of the CC.

The Menshevik regional committee in Samara, having learned of Maiskii's expulsion from the CC, resolved on 28 September "to request the Central Committee to revise its decision." Meanwhile the Ufa conference had taken place—and reconciliation was out of the question. The Ufa conference, which opened on 8 September, included various groups, with SRs predominating and Kadets well represented. Altogether some one hundred to one hundred seventy people attended it. There were deputies from Siberian governments and from national minority groups; among the Social-Democrats, besides Maiskii, there were Kibrik and Lepskii (all three listed at first as "members of the Central Committee of the RSDRP"); from Plekhanov's *Edinstvo* group, A. Matov (A. Stepnoi) and V. Fomin (V. Ol'gin). [47] Maiskii delivered the Menshevik declaration forecasting "capitalist development" for Russia and rejecting the orientation toward Germany. At later sessions Kibrik spoke for the Mensheviks (Maiskii had returned to Samara).

It took about two weeks to hammer out the new government's structure, composition, program, and powers. *Edinstvo* proposed to include in the government the well-known Menshevik economist P. Maslov. Maiskii's nomination was opposed by Siberian antisocialist deputies. [48] On 23 September a five-member directory (the "all-Russian provisional government") was announced: two SRs, one Kadet, one NS, and General V. Boldyrev of the *Soiuz Vozrozhdeniia*. The SR N. Avksent'ev was elected chairman.

By then, however, military reverses had already begun. Kazan fell to the Red army on 14 September, Simbirsk on 21 September, Samara on 7 October. Admiral Kolchak was appointed the directory's Minister of the Army and Navy on 4 November, but on 18 November his coup d'état overthrew the directory. A number of SRs were arrested, others left for the Far East.

The Menshevik CC in Moscow felt that its stand had been vindicated, not only by the outcome but by the entire course of the "experiment." On 18 October it had sent out a "letter to Party organizations,"[49] analyzing the Ufa decrees and noting a shift to the right on the agrarian problem, the absence of any mention of an eight-hour working day or of a republic ("state" was used instead), and so on. The Party's view of the Ufa "Statute of the Formation of a Supreme Authority" (*Akt ob obrazovanii Verkhovnoi Vlasti*), the letter continued, was therefore "totally negative." The Constituent Assembly no longer stood for "popular revolution." The Party must retain its "political independence."[50] The CC also stated that "political conditions" rendered it powerless to insist that the policy of its eastern organizations conform to its own.

Maiskii was expelled from the Party.[51]

In the north, events followed on a smaller scale much the same pattern as on the Volga. American and British troops landed in Archangel on 2 August 1918. A "Provisional Administration of the Northern Region" (*Vremennoe Upravlenie Severnoi Oblasti*, or VUSO) headed by the old populist (later NS) N. V. Chaikovskii was set up. Chaikovskii eventually recognized the Ufa directory. The administration's policies gradually shifted to the right.

This government combined SRs, NSs, and Kadets. The available data are insufficient for a rounded evaluation of the local Mensheviks' stand. From their paper *Severnyi Luch* the Soviet literature cites material favorable to the new regime, ignoring unfavorable statements and articles. According to Soviet sources, the Archangel Menshevik committee nominated a local Menshevik leader, A. N. Viacheslavov, for deputy director of the Department of Trade.[52] *Severnyi Luch* wrote on 1 September 1918, that the government

> has already begun the restoration of local democratic institutions (city *upravy*, zemstvos, and so on). Its goal is the reunification and revival of democratic Russia. This is indeed the program that is needed and is acceptable to all of democracy, for unless it is put into practice, the proletariat can neither develop nor carry on a successful struggle. Consequently the proletariat must fully support the High Administration of the Northern Region, and this support must be real, not merely expressed in resolutions. Proletarians must join the volunteer People's army, for the army is the force on which the government rests.[53]

But the same *Severnyi Luch* wrote at about the same time (the date is not given):

It is our impression that the attitude of the working class in face of the events can be described as wait-and-see, and its mood as disoriented. Obviously such an attitude and mood are not consistent with the importance of the present events nor with the interests of democracy as a whole and of the working class in particular. True, the restored labor press is calling for the workers' full support of VUSO, but we . . . observe neither a united response nor the enthusiasm needed for rehabilitating Russia and preserving the conquests of the February Revolution. [54]

There were the inevitable conflicts betwen rightists and leftists in the government. While Mensheviks, trade union leaders, and workers protested against certain "infractions of the workers' basic rights," the government continued to move rightward. This created a tragic dilemma for those Menshevik groups that felt it necessary to support the new regime. *Severnyi Luch* wrote in a lead article (no date):

There is no doubt that in may cases . . . the workers' indignation is justified. . . . But the present situation calls for extreme circumspection on the part of the proletariat. If it turns away in resentment from the democratic government intent on restoring the people's rule and causes its fall, it will only play into the hands of reactionary forces, facilitate the restoration of their regime—the Bolshevik regime of the right.

The working class must remonstrate with the democratic government . . . about all infractions of its rights, all repressive measures against it; it must insist that its true revolutionary conquests be retained and safeguarded. But it must support this government to give it the strength . . . to work toward the people's rule, toward a democratic order in Russia. [55]

When the Kadet N. A. Startsev was made chief of civilian affairs (*nachal'nik grazhdanskoi chasti*), he ordered the arrest of the Mensheviks A. N. Viacheslavov and S. S. Gal'perin, along with a few SRs. The Menshevik bureau in Archangel was sealed. [56] In January 1919 General E. Miller became head of the government, and in April he recognized Kolchak.

Foreign Intervention

The problem of "orientation," much discussed in the spring and summer of 1918, did not become really pressing until August. To be sure, small Japanese contingents had landed in Vladivostok in April, but the significance of this had been unclear (even to Japan's allies); and the Czechs' activities, though more "interventionist," were a relatively minor operation of former prisoners of war, without the support of foreign troops. The first British forces had landed in Murmansk in March, but the Soviet press tended to soft-pedal this, for reasons discussed below. Only in July/August did new French and British troops begin to arrive in the White Sea ports, mainly in Archangel. Soon afterward, Americans landed in the north and in Vladivostok, and the period of serious military intervention began. It was to last for two years.

Officially, the Allies were in Russia to keep the supplies furnished by them and stored in Russian ports from falling into German hands. Scarcely convincing from the start, this explanation became even flimsier after the end of the war. The real objective was to bring down the Soviet regime.

The Allied intervention differed substantially from the German, and the population was far less hostile to it. Both, of course, involved the presence of foreign troops and considerable interference in Russian affairs, but the Allies had no territorial ambitions at Russia's expense, nor did they export foodstuffs and raw materials from the starving country. Even the Japanese in Vladivostok and the Rumanians in Bessarabia could not compare with the Germans in the Ukraine or Belorussia. The Bolsheviks themselves were at first not unfriendly to the Allies in some cases—for instance, toward the British in Murmansk and the Americans in the Far East. The Menshevik Central Committee, in an article probably written by Martov, conceded that

> the Allied occupation involves neither the pillage nor the danger of the feudal landlords' return to power that went with the German occupation.... Still, recognizing the difference between the two imperialisms is a far cry from "inviting the Varangians" of Anglo-French imperialism. [57]

We must bear these differing feelings in mind, especially if we want to understand the right-wing Mensheviks. And we must remember that the first Allied intervention (on the Murman coast in March 1918) had the Bolsheviks' blessing. The Murmansk Soviet had asked Moscow for instructions since it seemed likely that Germany would refuse to sign the Brest treaty. Trotsky replied:

> To the Murmansk Sovdep. 1 March, 20:25. Top priority. Peace talks apparently broken off. Petrograd in danger.... You must accept every aid from Allied missions.... Bandits are attacking. It is our duty to save country and revolution. No. 252, People's Commissar Trotsky. [58]

On the strength of this, the Murmansk Soviet concluded a "verbal agreement" for joint defense of the Murman coast by the British, the French, and the Russians, which stated, in part:

> Under the supreme authority of the Sovdep, the high command of all armed forces in the region belongs to the Murmansk military council of three members—one appointed by the Soviet government and one each from the English and the French. [59]

British soldiers landed at once, and British and French ships appeared in the port. [60]

Such was the emotional underlay, so to speak, of Russia's reactions to intervention. The Defensist parties and trends that had favored the "Western orientation" during the war—that is, the Kadets, the SRs, and some elements of the rightist parties—usually welcomed the Allies. The extreme, pro-German right hated them. Ultimately, however, all who wished to unseat the Soviets had to turn to the Allies—without their help they could not hope to win the civil war. This became very plain in the fall of 1918 when the right's expectations of German help against Moscow collapsed. In short, reactions to foreign intervention were predetermined by attitudes toward anti-Soviet uprisings.

The Menshevik CC was unanimously against intervention. True, its right-wing members did not attend its meetings in the summer and fall of 1918 (Liber was in the Ukraine and Kuchin in prison). But among the remaining members, the differences that usually divided them (for example, on economic issues or the Constituent Assembly) disappeared whenever intervention was discussed, and this unanimity prevailed in the following years.

On the very day the CC learned of the Archangel landing, it passed a resolution condemning both Allied intervention and the Soviet orientation toward Germany. In this strongly worded document the CC protested against "the occupation [*sic*] of northern and eastern Russia by Allied troops" and declared that

> the agitation now going on in Western Europe in favor of armed intervention has nothing to do with the socialist Russian proletariat. Regardless of the horrors of the Bolshevik regime . . . of the repressions and executions daily inflicted on it by a handful of Bolshevik usurpers, the socialist working class of Russia rejects any intervention by capitalist governments aimed at rescuing it from the bloody Bolshevik dictatorship and relies solely on its own strength, the strength of the democratic masses, and the assistance of the international proletariat, to eliminate this regime. [61]

Criticizing Soviet foreign policy, the CC added:

The CC protests anew against the policy of subservience to imperialist Germany, with which the Soviet of People's Commissars is in fact acting in complete alliance, thus furnishing desirable arguments to the partisans of intervention in the Allied countries.

The CC asked P. Axelrod, who was soon to leave for Stockholm, to "bring this protest to the notice of the working class of the Allied countries."

Different sentiments were, however, growing in the "right current" of menshevism, especially in the regions that had come under the influence of some foreign power—the Volga region, the south, the east. Many rightist leaders who disagreed with the CC moved to these parts in 1918. Liber went to the Ukraine (after the May Party conference), where he spoke at Menshevik meetings. [62] P. A. Garvi was active in Odessa as editor and political leader. Stepan Ivanovich also worked in the south. I have already mentioned Maiskii's activities in Samara and Ufa.

Conditions were less stifling in these parts of the country than in Soviet Russia, at least in the early days. Bolsheviks were repressed, but Mensheviks and SRs had the right—within limits—to have publications, meetings, organizations. The trade unions, a traditional Menshevik stronghold, enjoyed relative freedom. We must also remember the far better food situation in the outlying regions, and the mood of the population that had suffered so much from Soviet Extraordinary Commissions. If we add to all this the traditional pro-Entente sentiments of the former Defensists and their approval of uprisings against Moscow (which could not succeed without foreign aid), we shall understand the rightists' stand on intervention as well as the conflicts that divided menshevism during that period.

In Odessa, Rostov, Samara, Kazan, Archangel, and other cities, the Menshevik press supported intervention until reactionaries took over in the new Russian governments and repealed the "freedoms." It goes without saying that in all these places there also existed more leftist Menshevik groups, but since they could not act openly the Central Committee had no way of gauging their size and potential. The line dividing the legal from the illegal cut across menshevism, so to speak. Only those whom the governments tolerated remained on the surface of political life.

The Odessa Menshevik organization, headed by P. A. Garvi, was not in favor of intervention when the French landed there in the fall of 1918. However (as Garvi explained years later, when Moscow was gathering compromising material in preparation for the Mensheviks' trial):

We had to reckon with the immutable *fact* of Allied occupation, just as we had to reckon earlier with the fact of German
occupation.... With the intervention of a cruel fact of military-
political reality, some comrades, including myself, conceived for a
time the hope that the interventionists would adopt a more democratic policy thanks to the pressure upon their governments of
democratic elements in the Allied countries, in the first place the
socialist parties. [63]

Garvi was referring to the French socialists and British Labourites
who, as members of their governments, could have been expected to
ensure a "democratic" attitude toward Russia. When a congress of
French socialists protested against the French intervention in Russia,
Garvi was sorely disappointed. He wrote in *Iuzhnyi Rabochii*, the
paper of the Odessa Social-Democratic Committee that he edited: [64]

> The last congress of the French Socialist party, at which Lon-
> guists [left socialists] had the majority, has passed a sharp resolution
> protesting against Allied interference in Russian affairs. No doubt
> this was prompted by goodwill toward Russia and profound respect
> for the principle of national sovereignty. Nonetheless we must state
> categorically that the decision of the French socialist congress
> profoundly contradicts the interests and duties of international
> democracy generally and socialist democracy especially.
>
> Either the French socialists are blind and deaf to what is going
> on in Russia and consider the Soviet state [*sovdepiia*] a normal
> form of human community life—and if so, their decision is reaction-
> ary since it directly or indirectly supports a tyranny perhaps un-
> equaled in the history of modern times. Or else the French socialists
> know what is going on in Russia, know that there reigns a reaction
> the like of which has not been seen in Europe for a long time, but
> refuse to interfere, postulating the principle of national self-
> determination—and if so, their decision also is reactionary, for
> even the best formula for progress and liberalism easily turns into
> Pilate's formula if the reality to which one applies it is disregarded. [65]

Socialists should support intervention more actively than nonsocialists, Garvi insisted. Noninterventionism was a product of bourgeois hypocrisy.

> Until now we used to think that the unconcern of diplomats and
> ruling cliques with horrors perpetrated in "allied" countries was a
> feature of bourgeois politics, which has sanctified the motto of non-
> intervention and even built a serious liberal tradition around it.
> How could this false and hypocritical ideology have seeped into the
> socialist milieu? Marx and the Marxism of his time were strangers to
> this reverence for the fetishes of international politics. Whether Marx

was correct or not in that particular case, he had the moral right to demand a military campaign against Russia to demolish the Cossackry.[66]

When the CC's decisions on the issue of intervention reached Odessa, Garvi said at a meeting of the local Social-Democratic organization on 9 January 1919:

> The Allies did not come here because they were invited—they were drawn here by definite interests of their own. It would be madness and *avantiurizm* to fight them. Democracy must mobilize its forces and get together with the democracy of the countries of the Entente to try to bring about a rupture between the Allies and the reactionary Russian circles and a democratic orientation of their policy toward Russia.[67]

Priboi, organ of the Sebastopol and Tauris [Crimea] regional committees of the RSDRP (the French zone), addressed the French and British socialists:

> You are against military intervention, you want to disarm those who are fighting bolshevism? Very well. But begin by disarming the Bolsheviks. Force them ... to relinquish power to the Constituent Assembly, and let the elections take place under your control. Save the Russian people from lawless executions by Chekas made up of criminals and psychopaths, and from the criminal experiments in socialization that are destroying the national economy.
> It is time to be done with the illusions that the democracy and the working class of Western Europe nourish about the Russian Bolsheviks.[68]

The Ufa *Golos Rabochego* said during the Czech occupation:

> A military agreement between the central government of renascent Russia and the Allies for a resolute struggle against German imperialism operating under the Soviet flag, and the working masses' active participation in this struggle, can ensure both the restoration of Russia's unity and independence and genuine noninterference of outside powers in internal affairs.[69]

In western Siberia the Menshevik *Zaria* demanded the creation of a new Russian army that would "coordinate its operations with those of the Allies."[70]

If Soviet archives were opened, the picture would be more complete but essentially the same: In the outlying regions, many Menshevik voices in favor of intervention, and vain attempts by many local leaders and groups to oppose it; the hope that intervention would not turn into interference and that the SR-Kadet coalition would endure and succeed in overthrowing the Soviets with the help of the Allies.

Under less restrictive conditions, the dissident Menshevik groups that crystallized over the issues of intervention and civil war would have formed new socialist parties. As it was, they declared their dissent without leaving the RSDRP.

In the summer of 1918 *Kievskaia Mysl'* printed a "Declaration of the Right Movement," which stressed fidelity to traditional Marxism and at the same time approved anti-Soviet uprisings with "Allied aid." (Reprinting this declaration in *Izvestiia* on 12 September, Iu. Steklov ascribed it to "a group of Mensheviks headed by Liber, Potresov, and Levitskii." More plausible data point to a group of Moscow rightists—Kolokol'nikov, Kipen, and others.) Their goal, the authors said, was "a return to the democratic order established by the February/March Revolution"; Bolshevik rule was "a dictatorship of the dregs of a disintegrating country"; it should be replaced with a "bourgeois-democratic order" combining "all economically progressive classes"; social democracy must reach an agreement with bourgeois democracy to fight counterrevolution, whether Bolshevik or monarchist. After criticizing the Menshevik central organs' "neutrality" in the fight against bolshevism, the declaration announced:

> Therefore we, a group of old and responsible [party] workers of the RSDRP, are forming within the Party the autonomous "Group of Struggle for Russia's Independence and a Democratic Order."
> The name itself defines the aims that our group pursues. . . . In forming a separate group within the Party, we are not predetermining the organizational forms our activity will assume.

Naturally no names were given. The group stressed its ambition to centralize the resistance to the Party's leading organs:

> Our group is setting itself nationwide tasks and therefore considers itself the all-Russian center around which it will strive to organize all the Social-Democratic partisans of an active policy in the direction indicated above and to unify and guide their local activities.

On 26 August, before *Izvestiia* reprinted this document, the Menshevik CC had discussed and condemned it, mainly for "demanding an alliance with Anglo-French imperialism" and political pacts with "all economically progressive classes," not with revolutionary democracy alone. "The 'Group of Struggle for Russia's Independence and a Democratic Order' threatens to involve the Party . . . in political activities running counter to its intentions." The CC made it clear that it would not brook such a policy within the Party framework.

The CC was also in conflict with Potresov's group in Petrograd, which had issued a declaration signed "The Petrograd S-D Group, December 1918," breaking with the policy, ideology, and organization of the RSDRP more decisively than the earlier declaration of the Moscow right:

> The last resolution of the Central Committee of the RSDRP, despite certain adverse statements about the Soviet government, in fact recognizes this government and, worse, openly offers its services to those who during the year of their rule have brought Russia nothing but the destruction of all her material and moral resources. [Therefore] we, a group of members of the RSDRP, who already have repeatedly declared our disapproval of the CC's official policy in the past few years, feel impelled to ... protest against this attempt to impose on the entire Party a tactic that turns it into a passive executor of the Bolsheviks' designs and plans, and to disclaim any responsibility for this stand, which is fatal to the interests of the proletariat. [71]

The Revision of Party Policy

The Menshevik Central Committee began revising certain basic policies and principles in the summer of 1918 and published the results first in its October "theses," then in resolutions of the Party conference in late December. The issues turned mainly on so-called formal democracy: universal or limited suffrage, the rights of self-governments or Soviets, the Constituent Assembly as the crowning realization of the democratic idea. Since the inception of the RSDRP, a constituent assembly had been one of its foremost demands; after the February Revolution of 1917 it was invariably thought of as the long-awaited means to solve a multitude of constitutional and political problems. The disbandment of the Constituent Assembly in January 1918 aroused new enthusiasm for it as the antidote to dictatorship and terror. Little by little, however, it began to symbolize for the Mensheviks the coalition of "unreliable" democrats with the parties of the right, the evolution of the new governments into military dictatorships, and the ideas of intervention and civil war.

Doubts developed as to the need to cling to the Constituent Assembly as an *immediate* objective. Did it indeed represent the essence of democracy, or was democracy possible without it? What, in fact, did "democracy" mean? Martov expounded the view (mainly in private conversations) that democracy meant civic rights—the right to criticize the government openly, freedom of assembly, a free press; in sum, the rule of law (*zakonnost'*) instead of license and police dictatorship. Granted that the Constituent Assembly, as well as city and other organs of self-government elected by universal suffrage, represented abstract perfection; he, Martov, and the CC would for the time being accept a less formally perfect democracy in order to establish the principles of political freedom and legality. Much intraparty friction arose over this demarcation of the Party's democratic demands from "formal democracy." From October 1918 onward, the CC passed a number of resolutions on the subject and sent out many letters to Party organizations (usually written by Martov). The letter of 16 October explained the CC's change of heart about the Constituent Assembly as a Party motto:

The Constituent Assembly elected in November [1917] was an expression of the progressive revolutionary development begun in February. The fact that [the assembly] was facing the Bolshevik government created by the October overturn naturally shifted its position to the right, from where it tried to halt the country's disintegration and keep it from plunging into utopian experiments. But even in this more rightist position it still remained a product of the popular revolution and the carrier of its spirit. It set itself the goals of solving the agrarian and the national [minorities] problems in a revolutionary way; of radically democratizing the country according to republican principles; of giving the proletariat all the social reforms compatible with a capitalist order; and of achieving a genuinely democratic peace, with neither of the adversaries destroyed. *This* kind of Constituent Assembly social democracy did support and was obliged to support, even against the part of the laboring masses that was carried away by the utopia of immediate communism and pseudo-class dictatorship. Social democracy was prepared to continue supporting such a Constituent Assembly. But a government that, under the flag of the Constituent Assembly, represents in fact a seizure of power by social groups not standing on the plane of democratic revolution or having left that plane; a screen behind which the party that won the elections refuses to govern, compromising instead with counterrevolutionary forces of capitalism and militarism outside the Constituent Assembly —such a government naturally cannot claim the support of the socialist proletariat. [72]

On the left flank of the Party, a group consisting of O. Ermanskii, A. Vyshinsky, O. Domanevskaia, B. Bèr, and a few others pressed for drastic "organizational measures" against the right and for further steps toward bolshevism—believing that these concessions could buy the prerogative for a socialist opposition to exist legally.

In the resolutions of that period—the fall of 1918—Martov deliberately accented his disagreements with both the right and the left. He castigated the SRs and their allies among the Social-Democrats who, he felt, were disrupting Party unity and compromising the Party in the eyes of Western socialists. He was especially trenchant in the "theses" of October 1918, accepted by the CC:

> The Bolshevik overturn of October 1917 was historically necessary, for in breaking the ties between labor and capital it expressed the urge of the laboring masses to subordinate the course of the revolution entirely to their own interests. Without this, it was impossible to retrieve Russia from the vise of Allied imperialism, conduct a consistent policy of peace, put through a radical agrarian reform, and ... regulate the entire economy to the best interests of the popular masses. This stage of the revolution also tended to increase the impact of the revolution on the course of world events. [73]

In keeping with this view of the October overturn and the Soviet regime, the CC rejected governmental combinations based on coalitions of democracy with the capitalist bourgeoisie or relying on "foreign capital and militarism." Nor did it countenance seeking foreign aid for the revolution. Any pact with capitalist classes, any use of foreign arms in the struggle for power would deprive democracy of independence and "turn it into the tool of these classes and imperialist coalitions."

On the issue of intervention, the Menshevik party declared its "political solidarity" with the Soviet government insofar as the latter "strives to liberate Russian territory from foreign ... occupation and combats the attempts of nonproletarian democracy to extend or preserve this occupation." However, the CC stressed that these concessions were temporary and tactical and that it remained faithful to democratic principles. In particular, it demanded "abolition of special organs of police repression and extraordinary tribunals, and termination of political and economic terror."

K. Radek discussed the Mensheviks' decisions in *Pravda* of 15 October 1918 under the heading "A Voice from the Tomb." (He was trying to be witty about "the Central Committee of the Party of the Dead.") The paper *Utro Moskvy* interviewed Martov. The first question was:

> "Are the rumors about some rapprochement between the Mensheviks and the Soviet government correct?"
> "Evidently you are referring to Radek's article 'A Voice from the Tomb' in *Pravda* [replied Martov]. He interprets our resolution, in which we do not mention the Constituent Assembly but merely demand 'a radical change in the government's policy,' as an attempt

at rapprochement. That is nonsense, of course. A radical change in Soviet policy is necessary at this critical time so that the popular masses of Siberia, the Ural, the Ukraine, and so on should not fear reunion with Great Russia and not hang on for dear life to the foreign occupation, which we consider pernicious."

"Then you are willing to reconcile yourselves to the Soviet government?"

"Not at all. We remain convinced that only in the people's rule, in a democratic republic, will the laboring classes find the lever for their liberation and for saving the revolution threatened on all sides."

"Still, you are giving up the Constituent Assembly?"

"Why? Even under tsarism we always put forward demands whose realization would create more favorable conditions for gaining a republic and a constituent assembly. This did not mean abandoning the motto of a constituent assembly, although friends of Citizen Radek accused us of it at the time. We are doing the same now."

"Then your party will remain in the opposition even if the policy of the Soviet government changes in the way you demand?"

"Of course. The part of the proletariat that is with us cannot suddenly come to believe in instant socialism and in the salutary effects of the methods by which it is being implanted."

"How far is it true that the masses that used to follow the Mensheviks are drawing away from them?"

"There is not a single fact that I know of to support this. The only arguments used in combating us consist in filling the prisons with our Party members, closing all our newspapers and organizations, and outlawing our Party. The level of development of the Russian working class is not such that arguments of this kind can convince it that the people who use them are right."

"But Radek avers that you can see from your membership lists that the masses are leaving you?"

"Oh no! The extraordinary commissions have most of these lists—and they do indeed use them to reduce the cadres of our Party by moving some into cellars and others directly to the beyond, as in Rybinsk."[74]

(From then on, the Constituent Assembly was no longer mentioned in the CC's resolutions.)

Opportunities to send letters abroad were rare: the mails did not work, and the Menshevik leaders were closely watched. Martov smuggled out a letter to A. N. Stein in Berlin, describing his troubles with the SRs on one hand and with the intraparty opposition on the other:

It has become clear that petty-bourgeois democracy, being so flaccid, is incapable of merging its struggle against the Bolsheviks with the mainstream of the struggle for the revolution. In the east and the north it is hopelessly pulling toward "all-nation" unity, toward coalitions with the plainly counterrevolutionary bourgeoisie, and hence it invariably loses the confidence of the working masses the very next day after the Bolsheviks are ousted with the approval, if not the help, of these same masses. This largely explains the Bolsheviks' quick success in reconquering Simbirsk, Kazan, and Samara. And this is getting worse and worse, since an ever greater role in the anti-Bolshevik struggle is being played by all sorts of units made up of officers and cadets with at best Kornilovite and at worst monarchist sympathies, which are becoming a more decisive factor in the "all-nation" coalition than the Committee of the Constituent Assembly and similar elements.

Martov went on to describe the intraparty difficulties with the right and the new, increasingly strong, left:

All this has created a lot of turmoil in the Party. First . . . our right elements, trying to adapt to the . . . situation, took a further step by openly announcing their solidarity with the foreign occupation and the "coalition" line of struggle against the Bolsheviks, for the sake of the "all-nation task" of restoring the capitalist order. With Liber et al. at their head, they have come out as a "committee of active struggle for Russia's regeneration." This has created in the Party a tactical schism, which isn't turning into a de jure schism simply because the terror is keeping all of us down, making polemics impossible, or even a conference or congress for a trial of the insurgent elements. But as a result of this same situation, another part of the Party, by way of reaction against this activism, has begun to "wobble," especially under the influence of reports of the Bolsheviks' growing popularity in Europe. There is talk that the socialist world revolution is evidently "bypassing democracy" and taking the Bolshevik road, and that it is dangerously doctrinaire to oppose this process—one must look for some kind of "bridge" with bolshevism. Actually, of course, no bridge is possible except outright surrender, since bolshevism does not admit the idea of an opposition party, even if it is ultraloyal and accepts the Soviet principle. The only "reconciliation" they admit is for members of this or that opposition party to join them as "individual guests."

Martov then related the defection of many Mensheviks to bolshevism, for ideological or careerist reasons:

In this impasse, the wobblers naturally think of forming a new group, and the more determined or more unscrupulous among them go over to the Bolsheviks *avec âmes et bagages*. We haven't had so many defections in the entire history of menshevism. You will see from our resolutions how the CC is reacting to this process—

how it tries to reformulate the Party's general attitude to the problems of the revolution, to eliminate the former haziness and contradictions that came from having to reckon with our right [wing] and to preserve internal unity. By dotting the *i*'s, by formulating our position more precisely, we hope to calm down our people somewhat. [75]

The theses of October 1918, written before the German revolution but taking into account the political strikes and riots in Central Europe that marked the last months of the war, described the Russian revolution as a "ferment" affecting the whole world. "All the proletarian masses now rising against the war and its instigator, capitalism," had a stake in its success. Everywhere the proletariat's outrage was leading to a full-blown struggle between it and capitalist society—that is, toward "social revolution."

With the World War ending in Germany's defeat and a new era beginning for Russia and Europe, the Menshevik party felt the need to revise its stand. Questions were pouring in to the Central Committee about the meaning of the revolution (was it "bourgeois" or not?), the attitude to be taken toward traditional ideological tenets, the "socialist" reforms of the Soviet government, the possibility of a "transition period" before socialism won the day. The theory of bourgeois versus socialist revolution once more became a burning topic. (Its revision would continue for several years.)

More than ideology was involved: industry had been nationalized in June 1918; almost all foreign trade was in the hands of the state that called itself socialist; in every city, trade union leaders had a voice in managing industry, which seemed to confirm the "proletarian" character of the new order. Under such conditions, what did "bourgeois revolution" mean? Some Menshevik publicists, especially in the rightist faction, demanded "return to capitalism." How? Return the nationalized concerns to their old owners, invite them back? The idea was unpopular in Menshevik circles, especially in trade unions. Barring a return to capitalism, what kind of social structure should be established in Russia as a result of the revolution? We have seen that in October 1918 (that is, before Germany's surrender and the revolution in Berlin), Martov, Dan, and the majority of the Central Committee began a revision of the old ideology. It was difficult and painful.

The New Conception of the Revolution

The theory of bourgeois revolution was giving way to a theory of a "transition period," which was elaborated and refined in resolutions, platforms, and programs from late 1918 to the middle 1920s. The

Mensheviks still considered Russia unripe for socialism, but the transition was now seen as an evolutionary process, not an explosion after a long interval following the bourgeois revolution. With its program-minimum discarded, Russian social democracy came closer to the Western socialist parties.

Before discussing the revision in detail, let me state the basic points of the new theory:

1. A "government of the laboring classes" was a requisite for the gradual transition to socialism. This government was understood as a coalition of all socialist parties and groups on a democratic basis.

2. Nationalization was necessary in certain branches of industry with key roles in the economy such as mining and metalworks. It was undesirable where a healthy economy could be restored more efficiently through collaboration of state and private capital. Various forms of such collaboration were proposed. The Party went so far as to demand denationalization of enterprises that it was unprofitable for the state to keep; they should be leased or given back to their old owners or to new ones.

3. The Party rejected Lenin's "socialization" of peasants. All the resolutions and programs of that period demanded private or voluntary collective peasant ownership of landlords' and state lands acquired by the peasants during the revolution. The Committees of the Poor should be scrapped as well as all attempts at coercive agricultural communes.

4. Neither then nor later did the Party consider the new regime a socialist one. It must be noted that even the Bolsheviks seldom defined it as such. In the new name of the state (R.S.F.S.R.) the word "socialist" stood for the goal, the ideal to be reached at some future time. The Mensheviks, with their view of political freedom as an inalienable part of socialism, were even less inclined to bestow the label on the conditions of 1918–20. Their leaders' speeches and articles (insofar as they could appear) teemed with sarcastic references to the "socialism" of the period.

5. All Russian Marxists believed in the interdependence of Russian and Western socialism. Even the Bolsheviks did not envisage an independent Russian socialism—still less the Mensheviks, who represented the Western strand in Russian Marxism. Only Stalin would tear the tie. Trotsky never relinquished the idea of interdependence. For the Mensheviks, the success of Russian socialism hinged on that of the Western socialist movement. A requisite no less important than the "toilers' rule" was a transformed West and political, economic, technological, and cultural help from the West. When

the lack of these requisites became clear in the middle twenties, another crisis developed in the Menshevik party.

Martov outlined the new conception in a letter to Axelrod:

The world has entered a phase of major social upheavals that will result in the transition from capitalism to socialism, in different forms and at a different pace in different countries. In some countries the rule of the proletariat and the transition to collectivism may come about through catastrophes and civil war, in others— gradually, partially, through a series of intermediate forms; essentially, however, it will be the same historical process.... [As] capitalism disintegrates and evolves toward socialism in advanced countries, the development of backward countries also changes direction, insofar as they are affected by the general revolutionary process.... If the revolution in Russia is quashed, economic development will probably take the direction of state capitalism on a basis of small private ownership in the rural areas. If the state power remains in the hands of the toiling classes, there will be a possibility of that gradual "permeation" of the national economy with collective principles (*im Anschluss* to the communization of economy in advanced countries), which we thought utopian in Bernstein's constructs about the "organic" era of capitalism, but which can become reality in an era of worldwide revolution and of ... state power in the hands of the toiling classes.[76]

The right faction did not accept the CC's new stand. I have quoted (p. 182) from the declaration of Potresov's group that amounted to a break with the RSDRP. Potresov wrote the Swedish socialist Branting on 2 December 1918:

It distresses me that all of Western European democracy is apparently on the verge of making an enormous mistake. I have in mind, of course, the protests against the Entente's projected intervention in our internal affairs. Nothing could be a greater mistake than these protests. If they are made for domestic political reasons, I am unfortunately unable to comment since, among other conquests of the Communist era, we have a Bolshevik monopoly of the press that leaves us in complete ignorance about Western European life. If, however, the comrades mean to render service to my poor fatherland, they are totally in error....

Now is the time for swift, energetic intervention. The last drops of blood are being sucked out of our country and our people; to the extent that intervention is postponed, Bolshevik arrogance daily grows worse, and friends of the Entente grieve that the promised intervention is merely turning into another Salonika expedition.

In the name of his Petrograd group, Potresov wrote Branting that the crisis of world capitalism had not yet begun:

> There is not the slightest reason to expect a breach in the capitalist front in these countries [America, England, France] in the near future. And there is, on the contrary, every reason to think that capitalism will find a way to adapt to the problems of the complex international and internal conjuncture and create the necessary apparatus for such adaptation. . . .
>
> The present international intervention of the "Allies" in the affairs of eastern Europe, aimed at destroying the Soviet regime and reconstituting Russia, is, as it were, the first experiment with such a function of an alliance of nations. The victor-states are achieving two aims at one blow: they are establishing the spheres of their future political and economic influence, and at the same time preserving international order by liquidating the Bolshevik dictatorship—which cannot be fitted into any state order anyway—and by uniting the broken pieces of former Russia into a new state organism on a bourgeois-democratic basis. [77]

The new conception of bourgeois and socialist revolution was not unanimously adopted even by those members of the CC who otherwise supported the Martov-Dan line. To some (Dallin and Troianovskii) this turn toward a "transition period" and acceptance of nationalization looked like an unwarranted concession to Bolshevik ideology. They did not, however, publicly voice their opposition. The leftist stand was represented in the CC by Ermanskii and Akhmatov, who later broke with the Party. The left was becoming more and more noisy and insistent, especially in the south.

The atmosphere was stifling, no one entertained rosy hopes about the near future, life was hard. But all this had begun to change, or so it seemed, when the World War was over, the Germans had left Russia, and the dissolution of the state was about to end. However, the hopes for a quick recovery proved to be vain.

8

Between the World War and the NEP

David Dallin

The last months of 1918 brought many changes in the Soviet government's affairs. The defeat of Germany, which the Bolsheviks had not foreseen, eliminated the worst consequence of the Brest peace by clearing most of the south of its German occupants. Their protégé Hetman Skoropadskii fled to Western Europe. The Ukrainian nationalist troops were less of a menace than the German army had been. On the other hand, the Allied intervention was in full swing—a British fleet appeared in the Baltic, and French and British fleets in the Black Sea; the French occupied Odessa, Kherson, Sebastopol, and Novorossiisk; British ships stood in the ports of Poti and Batum. But London and especially Washington were not averse to coming to terms with Lenin. Soon President Woodrow Wilson sent William Bullitt to Moscow, and for a moment the proposed conference of the Red and White Russian governments on Prinkipo Island appeared feasible. The outlook for Soviet Russia seemed to be rapidly improving.

There were also great internal changes. When Admiral Kolchak overthrew the directory in November 1918, the "democratic" phase of the civil war, with SRs, KOMUCH, and the Ufa conference in leading roles, came to an end. The Party of SRs was falling apart. N. Avksent'ev and V. Zenzinov, members of the directory, escaped from Kolchak's officers to the Far East and later left for abroad. Other SR leaders—for example, the KOMUCH president V. Vol'skii, and M. Vedianiapin—

191

were negotiating with the Soviet government about ceasing armed resistance in exchange for amnesty for the combatants. On 26 February 1919 the CEC revoked its decree of 14 June 1918 in respect to the SR groups that had given up armed struggle. Its policy toward the Mensheviks had changed long before this decision concerning the SRs. The decree of 14 June about the expulsion of Mensheviks from Soviets had been revoked on 1 December 1918 on the grounds that the Menshevik party had "given up its alliance with bourgeois parties and groups." However—

> Since the CC of the RSDRP cannot effectively be responsible for the conduct of all the groups and members of its Party, the CEC . . . points out that the present decision does not apply to those Menshevik groups that maintain their alliance with Russian and foreign bourgeoisie against the Soviet government.

The expelled Mensheviks were not automatically reinstated: the new decision merely allowed Mensheviks to run for election. In the provinces this was often ignored and they were still barred from Soviets.

The top Bolshevik leaders were divided on the questions of how far a dictatorship should go, whether all socialist parties should be suppressed, how much power to give the Cheka. The slight thaw took place to the accompaniment of discussions and articles about "revolutionary legality" versus "socialist legality." Most of the imprisoned socialists were released. Lenin wrote in *Pravda* of 21 November 1918:

> The period of sharp divergence between our proletarian revolution and Menshevik and SR democracy was a historical necessity. There was no avoiding the intense struggle against this kind of democrats when they swung toward the camp of our enemies and tried to restore a *bourgeois and imperialist* democratic republic. At present [however] many slogans of this struggle have congealed and ossified, hampering correct understanding and expedient utilization of the new juncture, when this democracy is beginning to make a new turn, a turn toward us, and a turn that is not accidental but rooted in the deepest conditions of the entire international situation. . . .
>
> It would be preposterous to insist solely on tactics of repression and terror toward petty-bourgeois democracy when the course of events is forcing it to turn toward us.

On 8 December the Menshevik organization held a large and successful public meeting at the Polytechnical Museum in Moscow. Martov, Dan, and Abramovich spoke, making it clear that the Central Committee's stand did not mean surrender: the Party remained in opposition to the government. Members of the audience, evidently Bolsheviks, asked when the Mensheviks would recant. The Menshevik leaders replied that they never would.

Making use of the new semilegal status, the CC convened a Party conference in late December.

The Party Conference

The Party conference of 27 December 1918 to 1 January 1919 was representative but incomplete. Because of snowbound trains and other transport problems, and an inaccurate report in Ukrainian papers that the conference had been postponed for two weeks, only thirty-two delegates with a vote turned up, plus a number of visitors. Martov and Dan were the chief reporters, and P. Kolokol'nikov presented divergent views on the two main topics, "The Party's Policy in Soviet Russia" and "The Economic Policy." Kolokol'nikov's presence bespoke dissent among the right: Potresov and his followers had broken with the official Party and set up their own centers; Kolokol'nikov's group, although disagreeing with the Martov-Dan line, was willing to work within the Party.

Noting that during the months of Red terror several Mensheviks— Krakovskii in Sestroretsk, Ridnik in Sormovo, Levin and Romanov in Rybinsk, Sokolov in Tambov, and Smyshkin in Vitebsk—had been executed without trial and "for no apparent reason" other than "courageously expressing their views," the conference resolved to demand an investigation and to "publish the fact of these executions in the socialist press of all countries."

Then Martov surveyed the international situation and outlined a far-reaching policy based on the expectation of a socialist revolution in the West, with Germany the chief ally of revolutionary Russia[1] and all factions of the Socialist International (including the Bolsheviks) united against "imperialist counterrevolution." A long resolution written by him set forth the main points of the Menshevik stand: The collapse of capitalism in the advanced countries was bound to affect the backward countries; when the former were in the throes of revolution, the proletariat should:
1. try to broaden the arena of revolution by drawing other countries into it;
2. counteract the plans of the victors' imperialist coalition to isolate the proletariat of Germany and Austria from the revolutions going on in other countries.

For successful socialist reform, the new regimes had to be democratic, "elected by the majority of the population, functioning as such, and based on the broadest self-government of citizens, political freedom, and independent activity by the masses." The conference resolved to support the German revolution "as the spearhead of world socialist revolution" and to express its solidarity with the policy of the German Independent Socialists.

Martov denounced the idea of a separate Communist International, hoping instead for collaboration between right and left socialism. The conference resolved "to promote the convocation of an International Socialist and Workers' Conference to unite the forces of the international proletariat for the defense of the socialist revolution from the threat of imperialist counterrevolution." [2]

Dan spoke of the Party's work in Russia and proposed altering its stand on the Constituent Assembly. The conference declared that the Party would continue to promote the ideal of true democracy but, accepting the Soviet regime as a fact, give up "the slogan of the Constituent Assembly." A separate resolution explained that it was impossible to reinstate the old Constituent Assembly or even to elect a new one, since elections under existing conditions threatened to make it "not an organ of revolution but an organ of counterrevolution." [3]

Although little scope was left for Mensheviks in the Soviets, Dan called for increased participation in them and in elections to them as the only activity still open to a party deprived of the right to issue publications and hold meetings. Only eight months earlier, at the May conference, several delegates had proposed that the Party turn its back on Soviets and focus on "genuinely democratic institutions" such as the Assemblies of Representatives and city dumas. Realities had made this impossible. Dan offered a proposal, which the conference accepted, to demand "free elections and reelections of Soviets with full freedom of oral and printed agitation for all parties" and also "true subordination of the government and local authorities to the Soviets." This was part of that "struggle on the basis of Soviet legality" that was to be the Party's policy for the next few years. The conference noted that in most places the resolution of the CEC restoring Social-Democrats' participation in Soviets went unheeded: pressure and terror were used during elections and most Soviets remained subsidiaries of the Communist party.

While stressing the need "to concentrate all state power in the hands of the toiling classes" and foreseeing a "transition from a capitalist to a socialist order," Dan's resolution stated that the RSDRP remained in opposition to the regime

> since [the RSDRP] rejects in principle, as utopian, the striving for immediate socialization of the whole economy, and considers that establishing a government of the laboring [classes] through party

dictatorship and forcible repression of the freedom of most of the laboring masses is fatal to the interests of the working class, to the revolution, and to economic development. [4]

The conference devoted much time to the intraparty conflicts, the expulsions and defections. It approved the Central Committee's stand on KOMUCH and the Ufa conference:

> The Party organizations of the Volga-Ural region, in open defiance of the Party's will and the CC's directives, systematically supported the policy of the committee of the Ufa conference, [a policy] that in the struggle against bolshevism inevitably resulted in alliances with counterrevolutionary elements; these organizations approved the entrance of the former member of the CC Maiskii into a government leaning on foreign bayonets, [an act] committed by this former member of the CC in open defiance of the latter's will; and a Party organization took part in creating a coalition government (the Directory) at the Ufa Conference.

Displeased with a zemstvos' and cities' convention in Simferopol for having approved a policy of "coalitions and interventions," the Menshevik conference stated that the responsibility fell on the All-Ukrainian Regional Center and the Don and Crimea centers, "whose duty it was to control the activities of the factions at the Simferopol convention."

On the controversial subject of Georgia's independence, the conference declared: "The policy of Georgian social democracy, which is trying to save the democratic order and the self-government of Georgia at the cost of orientation toward foreign help and separation from Russia, has put [Georgian social democracy] in conflict with the tasks of the Party as a whole."

Yet the conference demanded that the government refrain "from military repression—on whatever pretext—of the . . . parts of Russia where democratic governments are in power." Instead, it should "conclude temporary agreements with such governments as a transitional measure toward restoring the unity of the Russian state on a revolutionary democratic basis." [5]

The resolution also demanded that the "group of active struggle" in the Party (the extreme right) "dissolve immediately and not reconstitute itself as a distinct organization." It also condemned the deviations toward communism of Mensheviks in government service. In view of the unusual conditions, the CC was to have the right to declare expelled from the Party, "until a Party congress or the next general Party conference," the groups or individuals found guilty of such deviations—"upon careful investigation duly observing all safeguards for the comrades concerned."

The Central Committee felt that the conference by a substantial majority had endorsed its new line against both the right and the left. In the foreword, probably written by Martov, to a pamphlet about the conference, the CC explained why it was imperative to revise

> certain elements of the political ideology advocated by the Party during the past year that have been outdistanced by life and proven erroneous. No revolutionary party can lay claim to infallibility, especially in an era of profound revolutions that make absurdity out of sense and evil out of good, from one day to the next. Ruthless self-criticism is the first duty of a socialist party of the proletariat. Hence it is no wonder that our Party at present is not prepared to defend in full the political prognosis of events it made a year ago, or to propagandize without any changes the tactics it recommended to the proletariat last spring.[6]

After the Bolshevik overturn, the revolution could have taken two courses, and the Party had had to be prepared for either. The war between the Bolsheviks and the democratic parties might have intensified, or a part of the Bolshevik party might have evolved toward "restored class unity and voluntary abandonment of maximalist utopias and minority-dictatorship methods." Either of these developments was still possible. Armed action against the government had been rejected, but, the foreword continued, the conference had also rejected

> all attempts to shift [the party line] too far to the left . . . blurring the Party's stand on democratic principles and blurring or toning down the basic postulate of its socioeconomic policy—to wit, that the historical task of the Russian revolution can only be a reconstruction of the economy that preserves its foundation of independent individual units in agriculture, no matter what elements of collectivism and state planning are introduced.[7]

The conference passed no separate resolution on economic policy, but it approved F. A. Cherevanin-Lipkin's speech advocating extensive state planning, and it directed the CC to form a "permanent economic commission to guide the Party." This commission of notable economists (Cherevanin, Groman, Khinchuk, and others) worked out a programmatic declaration, "What Is To Be Done?" (see pp. 212–13).

The December conference marked the beginning of a revision of ideology and policy that was to absorb the Party's best minds until Martov's death several years later.

The Thaw—and Renewed Repression

On 22 January 1919 the Menshevik party's Central Committee resumed publication of a newspaper, *Vsegda Vpered*, under Martov's editorship. No doubt Lenin had authorized this anti-Bolshevik paper in order to impress European opinion, especially the left socialists. His and Zinov'ev's efforts to attract them into a new International often ran into protests against the persecution of socialists in Russia.[8] The Moscow radio broadcast to the world the appearance of the new Menshevik paper. Mensheviks were readmitted into the CEC and allowed to open clubs, organize public lectures, and so on. The thaw lasted until the end of March.

Vsegda Vpered was spectacularly successful. It was printed in 100,000 copies, although the government tried to cut its ration of newsprint. Beginning with its issue no. 4, the paper came out daily. Both its content and its success must have annoyed the Bolshevik leaders. On 22 February, Lenin drafted a resolution about closing the paper because of A. Pleskov's article "Stop the Civil War!" The draft read:

> The CEC resolves:
> a) to close the newspaper *Vsegda Vpered* until the Mensheviks prove by their deeds their resolve to make a clean break with Kolchak and firmly defend and support the Soviet government;
> b) to take all preliminary measures toward deporting into the area of Kolchak's democracy those Mensheviks who interfere with the workers' and peasants' victory over Kolchak.[9]

The paper was closed on 26 February, ostensibly for publishing Pleskov's article. The CC was notified, however, that the closure was not "unconditional": permission to resume publication might be granted if the Party promised not to "undermine the strength of Soviet Russia's resistance to her enemies" (the CC's proclamation of April 1919). And indeed, the weekly paper *Rabochii Internatsional* came out on 11 March—but its first issue remained the only one. The Cheka forbade the government presses to print anything "of Menshevik character," even the pro-Menshevik *Gazeta Pechatnikov*. But the SRs were allowed to publish the paper *Delo Naroda* (V. Chernov, editor), which lasted until late March. By that time the government was less worried about its "image" abroad: the support of the European socialist parties had become questionable in any case. The hopes raised by the revolution in Germany had been deceived. Thanks to the victory of the Majority Socialists, Germany had become a parliamentary democracy, not a Soviet state. In the elections of 19 January to the German Constituent Assembly, the Majority Socialists had polled 11.5 million votes and the Independents 2.3 million. The two socialist parties together had received 45 percent of the votes cast and did not have a majority in the Constituent Assembly. The Independents refused coalition with the nationalist parties, and a coalition government of Majority Socialists, Democrats, and the Catholic Center party was formed. In January an uprising led by the Spartacus Bund (which later became the German Communist party) was put down. Moscow now began an open offensive against the democratic socialist parties and created the "Third" Communist International, whose first congress took place in Moscow on 4 March 1919. The changed policy was reflected in the Soviet government's treatment of the Mensheviks.

For a time, Lenin had apparently been satisfied with the Mensheviks' acceptance of the Soviet constitution as the basis for collaboration with the government. Though never inclined to compromise with the opposition and regarding his regime as the unlimited dictatorship of one party, Lenin sometimes spoke of the Mensheviks like a constitutional premier. Thus, referring to the Mensheviks' "neutralism" and their disapproval of foreign intervention, he had said at a meeting of Moscow Bolsheviks on 27 November 1918:

> At present this neutralism, this good-neighbor attitude on the part of petty-bourgeois democracy is not alarming but welcome. Therefore we say, looking at the matter as representatives of the class that is putting dictatorship into effect: we do not expect anything more from petty-bourgeois democracy. This is enough for us. You will have good-neighbor relations with us, but we shall have the state power. After your declaration about the "Allies" we shall gladly legalize you Mensheviks. This will be done by the Central Committee of our Party. [10]

As we have seen, the thaw did not last. Soon new repressions began. The Mensheviks' activity was in effect put under the heavy hand of the Cheka. Three months after the above speech, at the Eighth Party Congress, Lenin sounded a new note. In answer to questions from delegates, he expounded, not very convincingly or logically, the rationale of his new "police" line toward Mensheviks and SRs:

> We shall often be obliged to change our line of conduct, which may seem strange and incomprehensible to the casual observer. "How come?" he may ask. "Yesterday you made promises to the petty bourgeoisie, and today Dzerzhinskii announces that Left SRs and Mensheviks will be put to the wall. What a contradiction!" Yes, a contradiction. But just as contradictory is the conduct of petty-bourgeois democracy, which does not know where to settle, tries to sit between two stools, hopping from one to the other and falling in turn to the right and the left. We have changed our tactics toward it, and every time it turns in our direction, we say, "Welcome!" [11]

As we have seen, the Menshevik paper was closed in February and the SR paper in March 1919. Again there were individual and mass arrests. On 20 March the Cheka invaded a conference of the Central and the Moscow committees of the RSDRP and took all those present to Cheka headquarters (Martov and Dan among them). This was the signal for similar operations in the provinces. The Party's premises on Miasnitskaia were sealed. A list of all the arrested persons was made, for future use. Most were released the next day, but Dan, Gorev, and a few others were kept a little longer. The Cheka explained that it had been looking for deserters. Ia. Latsis, speaking for the Cheka, announced that Dan was accused of being a deserter, whereupon Dan announced in the SR paper that he was suing Latsis and the editor of *Izvestiia* for libel. [12]

The Menshevik CC protested the sealing of its premises to the chairman of the Moscow Soviet, L. Kamenev. (According to the Constitution, the Cheka was subordinated to the Soviets.) On 22 March, the Presidium of the Moscow Soviet sent the Mensheviks a copy of its verdict on the matter—a unique document of the short-lived Bolshevik liberalism:

> To the Central Committee of the RSDRP(Menshevik)
> Forwarded to you herewith for information,
> Excerpt
> from the ruling of the Presidium of the Moscow Soviet of Workers' and Red Army Deputies of 21 March, current year.
> Resolved:
> Having heard the statement of the representative of the Central Committee of the RSDRP, the Presidium of the Soviet of Workers' and Red Army Deputies finds:
> 1) That the decree of the CEC of 1 December 1918 concerning the legalization of the Menshevik party remains in force in relation to this Party (until annulled through proper procedure).
> 2) The Presidium invites the MChK to explain its actions toward the party in question, which took place during the night of the 20th to the 21st, and to indicate the reasons for the detention and the individual guilt of every arrested person.
> 3) The Presidium deems it necessary to order that the premises of the CC of the RSDRP be immediately unsealed. [13]

In April 1919 the Menshevik Central Committee issued a leaflet about the reasons for the new wave of terror: The ruling party, nine-tenths of which in the provinces consisted of new people, refused to understand the principle of legal opposition—why give anyone the means to criticize Bolshevik policies? The leaflet said:

> Six months of terror have so corrupted the ruling party that it

is unable to tolerate in its vicinity any force independent of it. Despite their multibillion budget, their monopoly of education, their hundreds of publications, their monopoly of printing presses, newsprint, premises suitable for meetings, they have become mortally afraid because for three weeks the masses could read a two-page oppositional socialist paper barely managing to come out and because Mensheviks could appear at meetings in Moscow factories and agitate for Party candidates during elections to the boards. Realizing its complete helplessness in the ideological struggle with—in its own words—"a negligible group of Mensheviks," the ruling party has decided to put an end to the legality of socialist parties and to return to ... terror.

The leaflet also answered Lenin's accusations that the Mensheviks were disorganizing the Red army:

One has to be insane or a liar to assume that the RSDRP can regard the *disorganization* of the Red army, its insurrections, refusals to go to the front, and so on, as something on which it can build political expectations or with which it can sympathize. From the day the Red army was formed, social democracy has welcomed everything that contributed to its transformation into a genuine people's militia, everything that contributed to ... strict democratic discipline and the eradication of those habits of sloth and parasitism that the party which is now in power had been sowing so shamelessly in the old army for a whole year for demagogic ends.

... All their [the accusers'] actions and utterances against the RSDRP bear this stamp of patent nonsense and inconsistency. Our paper is closed, and then we are told that the closure is not unconditional and that we may obtain permission once more if we promise not to "undermine the strength of Soviet Russia's resistance to her enemies." Our premises are sealed, then unsealed, then resealed. We are arrested on the pretext of checking our identity papers, and the press announces forthwith that five deserters have been found among us. We are released with apologies and rearrested a week later. In the interim, the Presidium of the Moscow Soviet declares that we are a legal party and can exercise all the rights of a legal party, and a few days later the same Moscow Soviet declares us enemies of the working class, and its resolution consecrates the arrests of Mensheviks and the persecution initiated against us by official newspapers. [14]

Of course these protests had no effect. Terror continued and grew. More Mensheviks were arrested, more publications closed. Soon there was not a single Menshevik organ in the entire country. During elections Menshevik leaders and candidates were imprisoned, often to be released as soon as the elections were over. On 3 June 1919 Martov was put under house arrest for five days—a "liberal" gesture on Dzerzhin-skii's part toward an old leader of social democracy, Lenin's former friend, and the founder of Zimmerwald. [15] On 1 September Potresov was arrested in Petrograd and taken to Moscow. Friends obtained his release by the end of the year, but he came out of prison a broken man, gravely ill.

A New Phase of the Civil War

In 1919 the nature of the civil war changed. The armed struggle between the democratic forces (principally SRs) and the Bolsheviks had ended in November 1918 when Kolchak took over in the east. Some of the leaders of the Constituent Assembly gave up the struggle and concluded an agreement with the Soviet government. Kolchak's war, which lasted until his defeat and execution in February 1920, was antidemocratic and, despite the support of Western European govern-ments, gradually lost its support among the population. In April 1919 the Red army, though still small and weak, launched an offensive against Kolchak.

In the southeastern part of European Russia, the limited White movement of 1918 developed into a major campaign. When the Ger-mans evacuated the Ukraine, all of southern Russia became a battle-field. The Allies' modest help in money and supplies enabled Denikin to launch a vast offensive in the direction of Orel and Tula, with Moscow as the target. By the end of the summer, the White armies had occupied the Donets Basin, the northern Caucasus, and the Ukraine; in early October they took Orel and approached Tula. Simultaneously—that is, in the fall of 1919—General Iudenich was nearing Petrograd from the west and General Miller was fighting the Bolsheviks in the north. The year 1919 was mainly a period of war betwen Red and White armies. And since tsarist generals and officers dominated the latter, antidemocratic elements were sure to prevail in Russian politics if they won.

In 1918 the Menshevik party, as we have seen, had not taken sides in the civil war and had tried to get the Bolsheviks and the SRs to make peace. In 1919 such a policy was not only unrealistic—neither of the adversaries would have considered peace—but also contrary to the general policy of menshevism. Having been for decades a part of the Russian revolutionary movement, Mensheviks regarded the White movement as a revival of everything they had fought. Long before the CC's resolution on the subject, local Menshevik organizations in the areas under Kolchak and Denikin had had to decide how to act in this new phase of the civil war. The new White governments consisted of political antagonists of the socialist parties (Menshevik organizations were, however, allowed to exist here and there, and the Mensheviks still wielded a strong influence in trade unions). The Central Committee formulated the dilemma: either fight the White regimes or, for the sake of reunification with the Soviet part of the country, ask Party members to join the White armies, ask the press to support the White campaigns—and end up with a reunited, "national," but antirevolutionary Russia.

Not all Menshevik factions agreed that there were no other choices, nor did all those Mensheviks who saw the "dilemma" agree that the first of the proposed solutions was the better one. Certain rightist leaders and groups, in their hatred of Bolshevik terror, were inclined to join the White movement. The majority of the right wing did not go quite so far but wanted the Party to stay out of the conflict—in other words, to apply the tactics evolved in 1918 during the war between Bolsheviks and SRs.

The official Party, that is, the CC and local committees, and the newspapers and leaflets they issued where these could still appear, promoted support of the Soviets against Kolchak, Denikin, Iudenich, and Miller. The CC called a Party conference (18 May 1919) to work out a general policy. Because of the repressive conditions, only a limited number of members were convoked and no resolutions were passed. On 26 May the CC reported on the work of the conference in a letter to Party organizations:

> The Party's opinion is, on the whole, that wherever the Party is not altogether deprived of the possibility of engaging in organizational work, it must actively participate in the organization of armed resistance to counterrevolution; participation in the defense of the revolution must go hand in hand with propaganda for such changes in the political course as will make this defense successful by [drawing] the working masses and especially the peasant masses into it. From this point of view, it is inadmissible for organizations to [demand]—as has been done in a few places—that the government change its policies first, as a condition for their taking part in the armed struggle against counterrevolution. At present this would mean neutrality in the struggle between bolshevism and counterrevolution. But it is also inadmissible ... to give up the struggle against those aspects of the government's policy that make for the success of counterrevolution. Their elimination through pressure from the working masses for the first time will put the defense of the revolution on a solid basis. [16]

In late summer 1918, the CC had sent B. I. Nicolaevsky to the eastern provinces to coordinate the policies of the local Mensheviks with its own. At the time of the Volga uprisings, the committee of the Constituent Assembly in Samara, and the state conference in Ufa, Nicolaevsky, under the name B. Golosov, visited a number of cities from Samara to Vladivostok. During his trip the directory was overthrown and Kolchak became "supreme ruler." Thus, when Nicolaevsky established new contacts with the SRs, the new government was already persecuting them and the democratic movements. Upon his return to Moscow, the CC organized a large public meeting at the Polytechnical Museum on 3 July 1919. Dan presided. The Bolshevik press reported that Nicolaevsky had said, after describing White terror in the Kolchak regions: "All Siberia awaits the Bolsheviks. The Red army's march through Siberia will be a triumphal procession. The Bolsheviks will be met in Siberia as saviors, with bread and salt, with the ringing of church bells."[17] But they would fare no better than Kolchak if they introduced their methods of government, their Committees of the Poor and provisioning squads. The same issue of *Pravda* quoted Nicolaevsky as having said: "We are for a united revolutionary front. Without merging with the Bolsheviks politically, we are ready to clobber Kolchak together with them. This has been our stand for a long time." Martov and Dan spoke, supporting Nicolaevsky. Then the Bolsheviks L. Sosnovskii and I. Mgeladze "unmasked" Nicolaevsky and his party as Kolchak's helpers, but these standard accusations probably failed to impress the audience.

The next day, at a meeting of the CEC and the Moscow Soviet, Lenin misrepresented Nicolaevsky's mission (according to Lenin, he had gone east in the belief that he would find a Constituent Assembly, democracy, and universal suffrage) and said that judging by the experiences "of these people," Kolchak had alienated not only workers and peasants but even kulak peasants:

> Even kulaks are rising against Kolchak! . . . Now we are told that uprisings are going on in the Urals, and we are entering a period of genuine workers' uprisings, and we say again that there is every chance and every reason to expect within the next few months that a victory in the Urals will be the turning point to complete victory of the entire mass of the Siberian population over Kolchakism.[18]

Meanwhile, however, Denikin was advancing in the south, taking one city after another and hoping to reach Moscow by fall. In August 1919, at the height of these battles, the Central Committee called another Party conference (to which many Menshevik organizations were unable to send delegates). The conference passed the following resolution about Party policy in the areas under Denikin's and Kolchak's dictatorships:

> At present the basic objective of the Party in these regions is the revolutionary overthrow of Denikin-Kolchak regimes and reunification with Soviet Russia as the organized government center of the Russian revolution as a whole. For the sake of this overthrow, the Party supports emerging revolutionary movements against the military-and-police regimes and does not decline participation also in partial uprisings if these appear advisable under the circumstances, taking care at the same time that this policy does not degenerate into rebel *avantiury* . . . .
>
> Viewing these forms of government as something extraneous and transient, and therefore not attempting to reform them, the Party rejects any so-called organic work in central and local representative institutions created by the Kolchak and similar governments of military dictatorship. At the same time, the Party uses elections to these institutions, and participation in them, and any other opportunities for legal activity, to agitate for consistent democracy and complete freedom and to combat terror and violence in the firmest way. It subordinates all its legal activity to the task of organizing the proletariat for the revolutionary overthrow.[19]

In comparison with the CC's earlier decisions, this resolution shows that the CC was becoming less particular and more enterprising as the White armies advanced and the danger grew that the Soviet regime might be overthrown.

After the conference, the CC sent an explanatory letter to local organizations:

> Of the two regimes locked in implacable struggle we must choose the one that, in our opinion, can serve as starting point for a development that is desirable in the interests of the proletariat and the revolution. You, comrades, having chosen together with us the Soviet and not the Kolchak-Denikin regime as the "point of transition," have already declared thereby that it alone holds a possibility of developing into democracy, a possibility of saving the revolution and protecting the interests of toilers. And if so, can one really say that the Soviet-Bolshevik government, with all its "outrages" (often perhaps no less horrible than the monstrous Kolchak-Denikin outrages) is objectively as "deeply reactionary" as the counterrevolutionary governments? And can one refuse to defend—arms in hand if necessary—a regime that, despite everything, still contains some possibilities of revolutionary development against a regime whose victory would spell the ruin of the revolution, and in future perhaps the revival of the idea of bolshevism in the working masses, with all its "outrages"? For in that event Bolshevism would surely

go down in a halo as the *only* defender of the revolution. . . .
It is a plebeian and revolutionary regime, whereas the Kolchak-
Denikin regimes, which have absorbed elements of the regime
toppled by the revolution, are aristocratic and counterrevolutionary. That is why the transformation of the Soviet regime is at least
conceivable, no matter how small the actual chances of reforming
it from within. [ABN]

Where would such a policy lead the Party? Martov (who had written
the letter) foresaw several possibilities, but he was vague on the
subject of coming to terms with the Bolshevik regime:

A tactic of agreement with the ruling party is dictated by the
fact, if nothing else, that in the present situation, as we have just
agreed, our Party cannot adopt a tactic aimed at overthrowing
[the ruling party] without opening the door to patent counterrevolution. The only chance of saving the revolution lies in the
reformation of the Bolshevik regime from within. [20]

However, the CC warned against certain expectations entertained in
the left wing of the Party:

Of course one must not imagine this regeneration as an immediate
radical change in the entire ruling [party], a change in its beliefs
and its habitual methods that will enable it to come to an
agreement [with us] on the platform we are proposing. . . . The
dedicated elements among the Bolsheviks will have to undergo a
serious evolution, and bolshevism itself will have to go through
a gruelling internal crisis, a sharp inner struggle. That such tendencies exist in the depths of bolshevism no one is likely to deny.
Whether these tendencies will become clear-cut and strong enough
to induce a beneficial crisis—this is something no one can tell,
for it depends on many internal and international factors. [21]

In the absence of a Party press, the CC wrote its organizations even
about tactical questions that raised no dissent at the top but had to be
clarified to provincial leaders. Thus, some local pro-Bolshevik groups
favored putsches against Kolchak and Denikin, and the CC on 30
August 1919 sent out a resolution of a Party conference warning
against such *avantiury*. Elsewhere the Party's decision to adhere to the
Soviet constitution was interpreted to mean that "All Power to the
Soviets" (the Bolsheviks' battle cry in 1917) could become the Party
slogan. In its letter of 2 December 1919, the CC explained:

One of the local Party organizations has taken part in the official
October celebrations, marching in a procession with a banner
inscribed "All Power to the Soviets."

The comrades meant this inscription to draw a contrast between Soviet power and the present travesty of it, the dictatorship of commissars and Communist cells.

The CC cannot but regard this fact with the sternest disapproval. . . .

Coming out with the slogan "All Power to the Soviets" is nothing short of hiding the true views and aims of the Party behind an ambiguous formula. "All Power to the Soviets" in its original sense, as it was understood by the masses that made the October Revolution, means anarcho-federalist chaos, which is incompatible with the needs of the national economy, as the first months of the Soviet republic proved. As the official formula, this slogan has since come to cover up the bureaucratic party dictatorship based on complete suppression of self-government and of the masses' independent activity—the dictatorship under which Russia is living now. [ABN]

As Denikin's armies approached central Russia, "defense of the revolution" increasingly became a slogan the CC recommended to the Party. On 1 October the CC decided to send two of its members and several other Moscow Mensheviks to Tula and Briansk, the most important cities "from the point of view of defense," to guide the local organizations and the mass movement in "repulsing counterrevolution." Discarding the considerations that had earlier prevented it from "mobilizing" the Party, the CC instructed local organizations to invite their members "to work most actively at giving service to the Red army and agitate among the proletariat for the most active participation in defense."[22] The delegation to Tula included A. Vyshinsky, several Moscow workers, and D. Dallin of the CC. They stayed in Tula 11–28 October. From CC documents published later, we can judge of the attitude of the population in regions adjoining the front. Public meetings with Menshevik speakers were a surprise after almost two years of consistent repression of Mensheviks. The military authorities in Tula were doubtful about permitting them. After reflecting for three days and consulting Moscow, they did—and then reflected for three more days whether to provide premises for the meetings. Finally the Moscow Mensheviks were allowed to proceed, though not as "Mensheviks" but as the "Tula Commission of the RSDRP for Implementing a Resolution of the CC." The delegation reported to the CC:

We managed to achieve a great deal, but the mass of workers, debilitated by hunger and indignant about the repressions, could not be expected to become enthusiastic on the spot and rush into battle at a word from a Social-Democratic orator.[23]

Meetings were held at the local SWD, at a conference of trade unions, and at various factories. The Mensheviks did not conceal their opposition to the Soviet government and made it plain that supporting the Red army against Denikin did not mean surrendering to the Communists. A leaflet they issued explained the Party's stand ("Citizens of Russia, you are very forgetful! Barely three years ago you deposed the old regime. Now General Denikin ... "). Vyshinsky, the future Soviet diplomat and brilliant orator in the United Nations, was the least impressive of the Menshevik speakers. His fast, indistinct delivery carried no conviction, and no Tula group invited him a second time.

The four-member delegation to Briansk, headed by A. Pleskov, also embarrassed the authorities: forbidding their public appearances was ridiculous—had they not come to encourage support of the Red army? —but permitting them might increase Menshevik influence. In the end, they were permitted. However, at the very first meeting, at the arsenal, with an attendance of about four hundred, it became plain that "the decline in political feelings and interests of the broad working masses is far greater than could have been expected." The workers reacted listlessly to both Menshevik and Communist speakers.

> Clearly the masses had lost faith and were utterly tired of the food shortages and the political confusion. Besides, the governing party displayed no intention to democratize its policy. This was one of the main reasons that largely paralyzed all appeals to active struggle against the Denikin counterrevolution, which at the time was ... within a few scores of miles of Briansk....
>
> The workers' reaction to both our and Communist speakers differed according to local conditions. Thus, in Liudinovo (Mal'tsov district), where the Cheka had strongly repressed individual workers, the masses were clearly hostile to the Communists, and no appeals to fight Denikin could soften this mood.
>
> In Bezhitsa, on the other hand, where the police were less obtrusive and the Bolsheviks acted very "correctly," the workers were less discouraged.... The same is true of the meeting at the workshops of the Moscow-Kiev-Voronezh railroad. [24]

Menshevik party workers went to other cities as well. O. Ermanskii was sent to Tver. A report to the CC reads:

> There is much antisocial passivity; the "bread" mood predominates, especially among women workers. The local Communist authorities were tolerant toward Comrade Ermanskii and did not prevent his appearances at meetings, but decided that these inconveniently popularized Social-Democratic tactics. In the end,

this was summed up . . . as "five kopeks worth of help to the cause and a ruble's loss to us."[25]

The Moscow organization discussed the CC's appeal on 21 October and approved it overwhelmingly. A "mobilization commission" was elected, which approached Kh. Rakovskii, head of the political department of the Revolutionary Military Council of the Soviet Republic. He authorized representatives of the RSDRP to go to the front and make speeches, but apart from mentioning that they disagreed with the Communists on some points, they were not to expound their program in order not to provoke "undesirable" polemics. Local authorities were merely informed that the Menshevik delegates were "carrying out directives of the Central Committee of the RSDRP." Moscow mobilized twenty-four delegates, some of whom went to the Turkestan and some to the southern front.

The Seventh Congress of Soviets

In late 1919 Iudenich and Denikin retreated, and in the east the Red army took Omsk, the capital of Kolchak's government. The danger of the Bolsheviks' defeat was past. The relations between Moscow and the Entente once more became an important topic. England seemed the most ready to negotiate. Foreign policy began increasingly to preoccupy the Menshevik party.

The Seventh Congress of Soviets met in early December, 1919. Naturally, there were no Menshevik delegates: where Mensheviks still belonged to Soviets, they were in the minority and were not elected, and from most they were barred altogether. However, the Presidium of the CEC invited the RSDRP and a few other parties to send delegates to the congress in an advisory capacity. The Menshevik CC sent Martov and Dan. Dan made a speech saluting the congress and celebrating the victories in the civil war. Martov spoke on foreign affairs, outlined a vast anti-Bolshevik program, and read a declaration on internal policy. Here are excerpts from Dan's address:

All of you are well aware of the reasons why our Party [cannot represent] at this congress . . . the working masses that stand behind it. But at this momentous time we decided to accept even the kind of invitation extended to us by the Presidium, so that . . . in the presence of friends and enemies of the Russian revolution we might once more address to all workers and peasants our fervent appeal to unite in a single revolutionary front to repulse the attacks of counterrevolution [and] the predators of international imperialism.

After reminding the audience of the Bolsheviks' policy during the war with Denikin and Kolchak, Dan continued:

> Now that our common foe has been weakened, we shall try all the harder to achieve the main requisite for the permanent, definitive victory of the revolution—the unity of all the working masses of Russia, their renewed revolutionary alliance with the peasantry, [and] the close interaction, the mutual support, of the Russian and the international revolution, the Russian proletariat and the proletariat of the advanced countries. . . . And we should wish to see this Seventh Congress of Soviets break the ground for creating the conditions, totally lacking so far, for a united front of the toilers. [26]

Izvestiia of 6 December remarked that the audience attentively listened to Dan's appeal "to close ranks around the Soviet government for the defense of the revolution" and loudly applauded it. "Lenin, Zinov'ev, Kamenev, and others also applauded."

The first part of Martov's speech, on foreign policy, was essentially anti-Bolshevik but couched in academic terms and calmly delivered. The second part, however, was a belligerent denunciation of the government's internal policy. In violation of the constitution, Martov said, no congress of Soviets had been convoked in over a year; nor the All-Russian executive committee; hardly a single decree had been discussed by the CEC—the small Presidium had replaced it. Contrary to the constitution, People's commissars were appointed and shifted without the CEC's approval. The same was going on in the provinces —all the actual power was in the hands of uncontrolled Ispolkoms. Reelections to Soviets were more and more of a rarity. Non-Communist parties were being expelled from Soviets. A large part of the workers and peasants were not represented since electoral rights had been curtailed. Freedom of the press applied only to Communists. Government was degenerating into bureaucracy. The organs of repression and police terror were turning into autonomous powers. The Cheka, originally intended as a temporary organ, had grown to gigantic proportions. The RSDRP believed that "to secure the conquests of the revolution and assure economic recovery" the following were necessary:

> 1. Renewed observance of the Soviet constitution and its further democratization. . . . Responsibility of all organs of government to the working and peasant masses and accountability [of these organs] to their representatives. Correctly functioning regular reelections to Soviets.
> 2. Equal rights for all toilers in city and countryside.
> 3. Freedom of the press, unions, and assembly.
> 4. Inviolability of the person, assured by the jurisdiction over all

citizens of the same People's courts acting in accordance with precise laws.

5. Cessation of lawless reprisals, administrative arrests, and government terror. [27]

When Martov was speaking of the Cheka, L. Sosnovskii interrupted: "This is a declaration for last year, Comrade!" Martov replied, "For last year and forever."

S. Lozovskii spoke for the Internationalists and V. Vol'skii for the SRs, but only the Mensheviks injected some life into the debates, which otherwise turned mostly on administrative matters. Lenin devoted much of his closing speech (on 6 December) to Martov's address: "When we hear such statements from people who had announced that they were on our side, we say to ourselves: No, terror and the Cheka are absolutely needed." Without the Cheka it would have been impossible to defeat Denikin, Kolchak, and Iudenich; the Soviet Union was not a bureaucracy but a "proletarian democracy"; the constitution was observed to an extent unequalled anywhere in the world. Lenin's speech may not have been very convincing, but it was, of course, deafeningly applauded.

The Menshevik Party toward the End of the Civil War

During the first years of Soviet rule, a vast new stratum of "Soviet employees" came into being. It comprised people of different political beliefs who worked for a living and were not involved in politics. Often they retained their old beliefs without doing very much about them. Despite its increasing passivity and submissiveness, this new class harbored a great deal of discontent, which manifested itself only sporadically in the rare free elections to Soviets.

While trying to attract members of various parties by offering "privileged" salaries and rations, the government was never willing to make the slightest concession to the political convictions of its employees, though often entrusting them with important tasks. Less perspicacious Soviet leaders occasionally tried to enlist Mensheviks. The idea always was to let them work in the economic field without reaching political agreement—to tap the brainpower of menshevism in order to refine and implement the plans engendered in Lenin's entourage. In the summer of 1919 Iu. Larin[28] offered to introduce Dan into the Supreme Council for the National Economy as deputy chairman under G. Piatakov; K. Radek[29] approached Martov through P. Lapinskii with a similar scheme for "agreement." Both offers were turned down without being discussed. The "agreement" that figured since the October overturn in the Mensheviks' program presupposed a change in the government's methods. Neither Larin nor Radek were in a position to offer political agreement. They merely proposed to absorb individual Mensheviks into the new bureaucracy, where they would enjoy the privileges connected with government service and perhaps follow the same path as certain leaders of other parties, for example the Internationalist Lozovskii. Several Mensheviks did choose this path: Khinchuk, Martynov, Chirkin, and, later, a number of others.

Rumors of a coming reconciliation between the Menshevik party and the Soviet government emanated from two sources: Litvinov was dropping hints calculated to improve foreign relations and impress European socialists, and Western groups sympathetic to the Russian right tried to discredit the Mensheviks as conciliationists ready to compromise with the Soviet regime. These rumors were unfounded. At that time no Menshevik leader as much as envisioned immediate agreement with Lenin. Axelrod, who was abroad, was asked to refute these stories. Martov wrote him:

> Just in case: naturally all the rumors that I, Fedor Il'ich [Dan], and others were to enter the government are pure balderdash, evidently spread by the Asiatic diplomat Litvinov. *Never* have there been any negotiations about this, or even a hint at negotiations. [30]

In the same letter, Martov described the intraparty situation:

> Since the closure of our last paper in March 1919, and the subsequent breakup of the Petrograd committee and the Moscow committee, we have no means for broad open work among the masses. Our Party's influence began to drop uncontrollably, with no little contribution from the *Seitensprünge* of our comrades in Siberia, on the Volga, in the Caucasus, the Crimea, and so on, which enabled the Bolsheviks to represent us as allies of the Allies, of Kolchak, and so forth. Illegal agitation is infinitely more difficult under a regime like the Bolshevik, which after all had its roots in the masses, than under tsarism—as not only our own experience but that of the right and left SRs has shown. . . .
>
> Insofar as we nevertheless did act, we ran into the lamentable situation in which any party finds itself during an intense civil war if it propounds "moderate ideas" against fanatics and sectarians. We had a sympathetic audience, but it always turned out to be much more rightist than we. Following a healthy instinct, all those who feel crushed by bolshevism gladly supported us as the boldest fighters against it. But they . . . took in only what they needed— only the critical exposure of bolshevism. So long as we branded bolshevism, we were applauded; as soon as we went on to say that a changed regime was needed to fight Denikin successfully, . . .

to eliminate speculation and facilitate the victory of the international proletariat over reaction, our audience turned cold or even hostile. We did not have our *own* masses of the proletariat and revolutionary intelligentsia. That is, we had only their old decimated cadres. The new, younger elements, who have come to politics only now, are either irresistibly drawn into the Communist camp—which, with the aid of a huge state apparatus, put hundreds of tentacles around the life of the young, the women, the non-partisan workers—or, despite their proletarian origin, [these younger elements are drawn] into the camp of reaction, which rejects, along with bolshevism, all socialism. . . .

In the south—in the intervals between the invasions of reaction—the situation is much more favorable (besides, industry is less eroded there, so that old cadres of proletarians still remain). Before Denikin came the last time, the Bolsheviks in Kharkov "tolerated" our paper, our journal, and several trade union and cooperative organs for a long while (in the north, none of this is tolerated). They closed our paper only at the very end, both in Kiev and in Kharkov. Down there our Party therefore retains everywhere its old ties with the masses even now, is influential in trade unions, and so on. At present (as long as it lasts!) we are also publishing a paper in Kharkov.

Under these conditions [the Party] has for the past year been playing essentially the role of a "propaganda society" maintaining contact among its members and trying through resolutions and declarations to give its appraisal of current events and answer the most important topical questions. Active intervention in events has been an exception. . . .

The many Party conferences of 1919–20 devoted much time to the Party program and "platform." Menshevik theorists tried to find their way through the maze of foreign and domestic problems and to reconcile Marxist ideology with the policies the Party recommended in the given situation. With mails and railroads functioning erratically, it was hard to convoke conferences. Provincial Menshevik leaders sometimes came to Moscow to congresses of trade unions, cooperatives, teachers, and so on, and these occasions were used to discuss with them their local problems and the Party line. Most of the CC usually attended these meetings. Among the Party conferences, the one of December 1918, which I have already mentioned, and the one of April 1920, attended by eighty-six delegates (thirty-six of them in an advisory capacity), most notably affected the history of menshevism.

The CC carefully prepared for all meetings, big and small. The proposed resolutions were fruits of collective labor, in most cases carefully edited before they were brought before the meetings. Especially important were the declaration "What Is To Be Done?" published on 12 July 1919, and a resolution of the April 1920 Party conference in Moscow.

The former, a popularized exposition of the revised stand adopted by the Party during the civil war, spoke of the "political rule of toilers in the state," explained in simple terms the program of partial nationalization of industry, with some of it left in private hands or leased to individuals or cooperatives, rejected the idea of nationalizing small retail businesses, and demanded abolition of Committees of the Poor and provisioning squads. The provisioning system, it said, should be put on a new basis, more profitable for the peasants; trade unions should remain primarily representatives of the workers' interests vis-à-vis the government and private industry. The declaration further demanded restoration of Soviets, freedom of the press, assembly, and organization; termination of the civil war on a basis of broad self-government, especially for the Cossack territories; regional self-government for Siberia; and recognition of Finland's and Poland's independence.

The Party conference of April 1920 discussed ideology in more theoretical terms.[31] Martov in a speech on "World Social Revolution and the Tasks of Social Democracy" outlined a new set of views that he and the leading organs of the Party considered correct for the period. The preconditions for the social revolution that would precede the era of socialism were on hand on a worldwide scale. It was "objectively impossible to restore a national economy exhausted by war" while retaining capitalism. A "revolutionary crisis" was present even in backward countries because the state apparatus was bankrupt and disorganized. Hence even in these countries the social revolution would create the conditions for an accelerated progress to socialism. But a social revolution was a long and complex process of gradual socialization of the economy. Its pace could not be the same in all countries. "The readiness and ability of a powerless majority to overthrow a minority in power is a precondition for social revolution." While faithfully retaining the term "dictatorship of the proletariat," which had been in the Party program since 1903, Martov stressed in his speech and in the resolution he offered:

> Under no circumstances is the class dictatorship of the proletariat ... directed against other strata of the toiling masses, whose active and willing participation in the process of social reform is a necessity, for only then can the proletariat solve the problem of reorganizing the economic forms through further development of the productive forces.... Based on the interests of the overwhelming majority of toilers and ... their growing awareness of their real interests, the socialist dictatorship of the proletariat thus does

not involve foisting its will on the majority of the people but
[rather] the organized implementation by the proletariat, the
revolutionary vanguard of the toiling majority, of the latter's will.
    ... Revolutionary social democracy will most energetically
resist the strivings of the minority, which contradict socialism's basic
tenet that the liberation of the working class can be achieved only
by the working class itself, and which reduce the toiling masses
to the status of a passive subject for social experimenters. Social
democracy sees the gravest danger for both the revolutionary
development of the working class and the success of the social
overturn in the tendencies to establish in open or hidden form the
dictatorship of a minority. [32]

In these statements Martov for the first time presented his new
conception of democracy—a limited democracy in the framework of
"proletarian dictatorship." Earlier, he had already expressed the
opinion that almost any democracy was circumscribed:

> Thus, the free republic of America emerged as a democracy
> of the white race. Similarly, the new workers' democracy arising
> on the ruins of capitalist society is a democracy of those who share
> in society's productive labor. In principle, therefore, there is no
> contradiction between the democratic essence of a class dictatorship
> and the denial or curtailment of the civic rights of social groups
> that stand outside this democracy, that is, outside society's pro-
> ductive labor. Consequently, denying the laboring classes' *right* to
> [practice] such exclusion or restriction, and appealing to the absolute
> democratic ideal against this, does not stand up under criticism. [33]

Dan reported on foreign policy, with A. Dubois and B. Bèr as
coreporters for the right and left factions. The rout of Kolchak, Denikin, and Iudenich, said Dan, had put an end to the counterrevolution
that wanted to restore the old social order with foreign aid. However,
a different and still greater threat of counterrevolution lurked inside
the country, in the social relations created by the revolution. The very
masses that had made the revolution were profoundly dissatisfied with
the new socioeconomic conditions. [34] This counterrevolution might not
only establish an openly capitalist regime and prevent Russia for years
from sharing in the world revolution—it might establish a capitalist
regime crushingly indebted to foreign capital and ruthlessly exploiting
the proletariat, which was now hated by the entire bourgeoisie without exception—big and small, urban and rural. [35] The government's
policy was not calculated to prevent counterrevolution. Terror must
stop. The measures initiated for the peasants' voluntary transition from
petty-bourgeois to socialist economy must be scrapped. The majority of

the conference approved the CC's stand and the proposed resolution.

Then Martov and Pleskov spoke on the ideological and political disagreements within the Party, which the repressive conditions accentuated. The conference expelled from the Party the right faction of the Kharkov organization, putting certain conditions upon its return to the fold. It roundly condemned the policy of the Odessa organization during the Allied occupation and under Denikin: "[It] has placed itself outside the Party politically and has made it impossible for the Party to be responsible for it." The conference resolved to reorganize the Odessa organization on a new basis or, if this proved impossible, to disband it and set up a new one.

At the April conference certain disagreements among the Menshevik leaders came to the fore. The right and left tendencies were no longer the same as during the earlier period—there were, rather, shadings of opinion within the left wing. Some of Martov's ideas about the international revolution, especially about the progress toward socialism of backward Russia (the "transition period"), evoked bafflement and protests. To many leaders, the notion that Russia could move on to socialism, especially in the absence of a revolution in the West, seemed un-Marxist and smacking of Bolshevik theories. Martov had incorporated his idea of "international revolution" in the resolution on organizational questions—oddly enough, in the part of it that concerned the government of Siberia. Linking Siberia to the socialist revolution seemed a paradoxical deviation from traditional Marxism. The resolutions submitted by Martov were passed, but the turmoil over his ideology continued. The left, especially the main committee for the Ukraine, headed by Bèr, insisted that Martov's theories be incorporated into a well-defined, binding program. (However, the ideological differences within the CC did not yet affect its stand on the big political questions such as resistance to the White armies.)

The arguments continued after Martov's departure for abroad. The CC often returned to these questions because of pressure from the left. Dan and Abramovich considered it necessary to make the thesis about social revolution a binding point of the Party program; Ermanskii, Iugov, and others supported them; Troianovskii, Nicolaevsky, Dallin, and others disagreed. In November–December 1920, the CC reached the decision to draft a new platform in order to "codify" the Party line that had emerged at the recent conferences.[36] A five-member commission was elected for this purpose. At a meeting of the CC in late December, Dan proposed that Martov's theses—the so-called April theses—be declared binding on the Party. Many members objected. Troianovskii went so far as to say that he disagreed with the theses so completely that if their acceptance were to become obligatory it would be impossible for him to remain in the Central Committee and probably even in the Party. [37] It was decided to consult the absent Martov and Abramovich. Martov replied that he had talked with the Western Marxist theorists Kautsky and Hilferding. The latter, wrote Martov, "frankly admitted" that he was not sure that capitalism was in the last phase of decline. Rather, he foresaw a lengthy period of further capitalist development, paralleled by "revival of reformism" among the workers. If Kautsky and Hilferding harbored such doubts, one had better be cautious about basing the Party's political program on fundamental tendencies of economic development. He, Martov, had come to the conclusion "that it would be most dangerous at this point to work out a Party program or a document that would be its surrogate." [38]

At about the same time, Martov wrote Axelrod:

For a whole year the left ... has been campaigning for the acceptance by the Party of some Party document supplanting or supplementing the program of 1903, which would be binding on everyone who wishes to remain a Party member. I have firmly opposed this plan all along, arguing that during the present transition period in both international and Russian socialism it is impossible to try to "codify" the Party credo, to make a genuine program of the more or less utopian generalizations that we are obliged to work out rather hastily in order to shed some light on the road we are traveling. At such a time we can work out only programs of action that impose but one obligation, namely, not to disrupt the Party's activity; but we must not try to write a new program that may well be refuted by facts within a year, and we cannot make the acceptance of such a program the basis for separating from the Party those who disagree.

My opposition wasn't very successful even while I was still in Russia. Not only the left but also a goodly part of the center and, most important, locally influential workers, although agreeing that I was right "theoretically," kept demanding some "binding document" of such a kind that refusal to sign it would suffice to "eliminate" our rightists.

After my departure ... the situation worsened even further. Under pressure from local organizations and for fear that the left wing, in which there are valuable workers, would leave the Party and join the Communists, the CC has in principle decided to give in ... and to adopt at the next conference (in March) a "binding document," whether in the form of last year's theses (about dictatorship and so on) or in a briefer, more or less concrete formulation of the same ideas. Both Abramovich and Fedor Il'ich [Dan] consider that in the present situation this is unavoidable.

I remain strongly opposed. F. I. [Dan], Nicolaevsky, and others insist that I return for the conference, to cool the "division ardor" somewhat.

I don't know what to do. Am very much afraid that my presence will be of little help and am inclined to think that, on the contrary, my absence could be used to insist on shelving the question. And gaining time in such cases means gaining everything. [39]

The February arrests put an end to these discussions. The conference scheduled for March 1921 did not take place. But the differences in Martov's and Dan's views left their mark and were to crop up again in the twenties and thirties.

When Martov and Abramovich left Russia in the fall of 1920, the Central Committee was replenished. I. Rubin, I. Iudin, and B. Nicolaevsky were its new members. Nicolaevsky, S. Ezhov, and A. Iugov were elected to the executive bureau of the CC; K. Zakharova-Ezhova was the secretary. In this form the CC existed until the mass arrests of 25 February 1921.

The Moscow group of leftists, which had been fairly active in 1918–19, fell apart in late 1919. Its leader was N. Sukhanov. Among its members were Ermanskii, Vyshinskii, O. Domanevskaia, Prushinskii, and others. L. Pistrak relates that after an agitated meeting in late 1919 (the group usually met at Sukhanov's home) it was decided to break with the Party. This was, of course, not mandatory, but almost all did resign (the exceptions were Pistrak and Kurkin). Sukhanov's resignation attracted the most attention, although the Party did not consider him a major leader but rather a gifted journalist and memoirist. Martov commented: "He suddenly discovered that it was we who were breaking up the mass parties by preventing them from joining the Third International, which everyone should join in order to reform it from within.'" [40]

A few more leftists defected in 1921 (Domanevskaia [?], Kapelinskii, Petrashkevich, and Strumilin, according to *Pravda* of 23 April).

Foreign Policy and the War with Poland

A revolutionary party such as menshevism was until 1917 cannot as a rule have a comprehensive foreign policy. Foreign policy was mentioned in connection with fighting "militarism" and "imperialism," certain demands were advanced concerning the Japanese war and the First World War, the Franco-Russian alliance, the friendship between the monarchs of Germany and Russia. The attitude toward diplomacy was ironical, the tsarist government and all its works were viewed with distaste. None of the revolutionary parties paid much attention to the Balkans, Austro-Hungary, the Far East, and so on.

During the early years of the war and in 1917, problems of foreign policy moved to the forefront: issues such as Defensism, the Bolsheviks' "defeatism," and the attitude to be taken toward the Allies were heatedly discussed. But only in 1918–19 did the Mensheviks' ideas on foreign policy evolve into a coherent system, despite the muzzling of the press and the difficulty of discussing anything under police conditions. This side of menshevism is less known to historians and researchers than are other aspects of its ideology and tactics.

The starting point for the work on foreign policy was the Brest peace with Germany. The Mensheviks' view of it had differed from that of the SRs from the beginning. While the latter did not "recognize" the treaty, demanding continuation of the war in alliance with the Entente, the Mensheviks refused to take this extreme stand, for many reasons. One of them was Russia's military weakness. With the defeat of Germany this issue disappeared, but that of the German revolution, on which Russian and Western socialists were banking, assumed greater importance. Then it, too, became less acute as the German government's political color faded. Other problems arose, more difficult for the Mensheviks to solve.

In December 1919 Martov spoke on foreign policy at the Seventh Congress of Soviets. To most of his audience the purport of the issues he raised was still unclear. Four of the problems discussed were to preoccupy the Soviet government for years. Even now they are, in part, among the "sick issues" of international relations:

1. (Straddling internal and foreign policy.) Some of the regions cut off from Soviet Russia during the civil war—for instance, the Cossack territories and Siberia—were integral parts of old Russia that could not have separated without foreign aid. In the Mensheviks' view, they should return to Russia, with a measure of autonomous self-government.

2. Other parts of the former empire were inhabited by non-Russians, and their existence as separate states was considered practical—the three Baltic and three Caucasian countries, Finland, and, of course, Poland. (The Ukraine remained a moot subject.) The Bolsheviks' attitude to the new states was unclear; there was no little dissent about them among top leaders. The idea of the Red army carrying communism to the West was strong in Bolshevik circles, but almost as strong was the desire for peace after so many years of foreign and civil war. After the defeat of Iudenich, Trotsky insisted on a march on Estonia; the sovietization of Latvia was all planned;

in the event of victory over Poland, Lenin envisaged in 1920 a big campaign into Germany and beyond. On the other hand, the Finnish Bolsheviks had been forced to lay down arms when Lenin's government had had to withdraw its support of them after the Brest peace. The Mensheviks demanded complete independence for all these ethnically non-Russian countries. At the Seventh Congress, Martov reminded Lenin that at the time of Brest

> the Revolution found it possible to tell the Finnish proletariat that for the sake of higher, even if more remote, interests, it [the Revolution] considered that it had the right to leave its ally to his own devices—[an ally] already engaged in a bloody struggle, locked in mortal combat with a mortal enemy. The situation was tragic for both sides. Now Soviet Russia has a much greater right and many more reasons, especially from the point of view of the program and ideology of the governing party, to tell herself, and in the first place herself, that in the interests of the common revolutionary struggle she can leave it to the natural development of local revolutions to free the proletariat of various small countries, and concentrate on creating . . . tolerable conditions . . . in revolutionary Russia herself.[41]

Referring mainly to the Baltic states, Martov spoke with approval of the appeal the congress had voted to address to small countries:

> We know that the Soviet government . . . is extending a hand of peace also to the nations and states established in the territories of the former Russian empire, expressing its readiness to make important concessions for the sake of protecting itself and the frontiers of Soviet Russia from constant threat and danger. We, the party of the opposition, can only welcome and support this line of the Soviet government's foreign policy.

3. Peaceful cooperation of the new Russia with all other countries was stressed. This was in fact the theory of "coexistence" that Lenin is supposed to have invented several years later. For the long-range interests of the revolution and the proletariat, said Martov, good relations should indeed be maintained with the non-Russian border states, "no matter what we may think of their temporary or permanent separation from Russia proper."

4. With the end of foreign intervention, the relations with the Western powers would have to be settled. (It seemed at the time that wars and interventions were coming to an end; actually, they continued for another year.) There were the questions of lifting the blockade, of de facto and de jure recognition, of trade agreements, of diplomatic immunity. The Mensheviks thought that de jure recognition

of the Soviet government by the Western powers was most likely to ensure peace. Martov said:

> If these attempts at peace are stymied or delayed, I should wish all the guilt, all the responsibility, to be the other side's—not only in our own minds but in the consciousness of all the nations of the world. Speaking of peace as of something possible, and of the perspectives it would open for the further development of the Russian revolution, we must of course remember that this peace is important for the revolution not only because it will at once halt the flow of English and American gold and arms to the Russian hotbeds of counterrevolution and thus facilitate the task of ending the civil war and the complete victory of the revolution. It is also, and mainly, important as a way out of the impasse, out of the destitution brought on by many years of imperialist and civil war. It will allow free economic relations with the outer world, without which Soviet Russia cannot recover to any great extent.

Referring to Lenin's speech of the day before, Martov said that Soviet terror was a "moral and psychological factor" in foreign relations:

> The chairman of the Soviet of People's Commissars himself recognized this when he addressed Europe over our heads and for the first time, I believe, tried to justify himself, or the Soviet government, in the matter that provokes the most venomous attacks . . . on the part of Soviet Russia's enemies—[that is] when he tried to explain that the terror of the Russian revolution . . . was forced upon [us] by the terror of our enemies, the White Guard counterrevolution, and that as soon as this pressure of European imperialist reaction ceases . . . there will be . . . no reason for terror.

Answering the Menshevik declaration, Lenin said that Martov's views "would not hold out for one year." He was mistaken. Martov maintained them until the end of his life.

Martov's principles were applied by the Mensheviks sooner than anyone had anticipated. In 1920 the war with Poland broke out. It would soon develop into a Bolshevik campaign against Western Europe, but when Polish troops first crossed the border in late April and began their rapid advance on Kiev, there was no question in anyone's mind that for Russia this was a defensive war. The SRs wrote the Presidium of the Moscow Soviet in this sense; General Brusilov and other officers of the old regime offered their services to the Red army; the Mensheviks announced a mobilization of Party members.

A joint meeting of the Moscow Soviet, the CEC, factory committees, and trade union boards to discuss the war with Poland was scheduled for 5 May. The Menshevik CC met on 4 May to prepare Martov's speech. No one disputed the "defense" stand, but many members were surprised at Martov's warning: from chance remarks, scattered phrases in Lenin's and other Communists' speeches, he had concluded that if the Red army did repulse the Poles it would be ordered to continue westward, occupy Warsaw, penetrate Germany, and renew the struggle with the Entente. It was important to specify from the first that the Mensheviks supported true defense but no more. Difficult as it was to announce such a stand at this time, said Martov, the Party must make it clear that it would not support military aggression. The stand was indeed difficult and dangerous. The Poles were advancing. Any criticism from the opposition would be interpreted as treason. Martov was nevertheless authorized to make the declaration. Needless to say, this required great personal courage.

Martov divided his speech into two parts, the war and the Menshevik party's declaration. First he spoke in favor of defense and expressed his certainty of a victorious outcome. Then, in carefully chosen words, he said:

> We hope that in this war that has been forced upon it, the Soviet government will be able to avoid injecting any elements that would give this defensive war a nationalistic character and thus enable the Polish propertied classes to represent it to the Polish masses as a continuation of the old quarrel with tsarist Russia. . . . Our Party . . . will support every step of the Soviet government that is aimed at ending this war as quickly as possible and concluding a peace acceptable to both sides, which will enable our revolutionary country to engage in peaceful construction. [42]

The government must take "a more stable course, continue negotiations with the border countries," and rectify "all the harm that has been done lately." The Bolsheviks understood. Martov's speech was cut short, its offensive parts were not reported in the newspapers or were jumbled in such a way as to make them unintelligible. *Izvestiia* of 6 May remarked: "Martov began a tedious and poorly documented criticism of some of the government's diplomatic steps. . . . Shouts of 'Enough!' were heard. Martov had to curtail his speech." *Pravda* of the same date said that Martov had promised support but "could not resist the temptation of recalling all the 'mortal sins' of the Soviet government; the indignant audience deprived him of this pleasure."

The Menshevik declaration was still more outspoken. *Izvestiia* printed it on 7 May, omitting a part (the CC protested against the omission, but of course to no avail). The cut part concerned the conditions under which, in the Mensheviks' view, the Soviet Republic could "easily cope" with the Polish aggression: The government's policy should be consistently aimed at peace everywhere (this was a warning against "revolutionary war"); anything that could turn the Ukrainian peasantry against the Russian revolution should be eliminated (this was aimed at the Soviet treatment of peasants); the laboring masses must be reassured that "the preservation and development of the revolutionary regime" meant their "political freedom and full political equality."

Many members of the Menshevik party enlisted in the Red army and left for the front, S. Schwarz and G. Kuchin among them as well as several Kiev Mensheviks who had been convicted in the trial of the Menshevik party in Kiev.

In June the Red army began its counteroffensive. As it was nearing the Polish border, the British government on 12 July suggested an armistice on fairly good terms for Russia. Lenin declined and telegraphed Stalin at the front: "Please expedite the order for a furiously increased offensive," and on 30 July there "emerged" in Belostok the Polish Revolutionary Committee, under the chairmanship of Marchlewski. This committee consisted of Polish Communists newly arrived from Moscow and was to be the nucleus of a puppet government. It issued an appeal to the Polish people to chase out the capitalists and proclaim a Polish Soviet Socialist Republic. (In 1939 Stalin would resort to the same method of combining revolutionary war with "nonintervention" when he set up O. Kuusinen's government in Finland.) The plans that were taking shape at the Bolshevik summit did not become known until much later. Martov had been right: Lenin wanted to invade Poland and Germany and was gradually winning his circle over to the idea. He had overcome Stalin's, Rykov's, and Radek's objections. Trotsky says in his memoirs that he himself never agreed to this plan; however, it remains somewhat unclear what his stand on "revolutionary war" had been.

Before the Red army's advance on Warsaw, Martov wrote A. Stein in Berlin:

> But now the time is near when peace, it would seem, will become an actual possibility: Poland can be expected to sue for peace, and England seems to be coming around. And yet I am almost sure that this time the Bolsheviks themselves will scuttle this outcome. In that event we shall have to alter our policy considerably, center our agitation on the demand to renounce *avantiury* in foreign policy (to renounce bringing to the Poles [and the Germans!] a Soviet

system at the tips of our bayonets; to renounce *avantiury* in the east, renounce compromising with English capitalism). I think the European comrades, too, will soon find it impossible to overlook this very influential "temporary" tendency in Russian bolshevism. [43]

The next day Martov developed these thoughts in a letter to Kautsky:

Now, with the change of government in Poland and Lloyd George's increasing willingness to make peace with Russia, it is becoming an acute question which policy will prevail—the realistic-opportunistic one, or Communist *avantiurizm*. As the head of a state that rests on the peasantry and cannot escape economic debacle without "Western" industry, Lenin inclines toward the realistic policy, but as the "pope" of the Third International, the same Lenin is departing more and more from the correct road to peace and is taking the road of highly dubious adventures. The same ambiguity can be observed in Trotsky the candidate for "economic dictator" and Trotsky the Minister of War obliged to reckon with the Bolshevik military. I fear that the adventurous tendency will soon prevail and that in the negotiations with England and Poland a rather Asiatic diplomacy will be used, to drag things out until some new internal or external factor brings about another change of mood in the Entente countries. And all this in the hope of forcing a revolution in Germany through "total victory over Poland." Radek is already promising that by autumn Germany will be quite ripe for a Communist revolution. [44]

The CC drew up some foreign policy theses for the planned Party conference:

The task of actively assisting the development of a proletarian revolution in capitalist countries through material and military aid ... must take second place whenever it conflicts with the task of concluding peace....

Aggressive revolutionary war as a method of carrying social revolution into foreign countries is unacceptable to social democracy in principle since the aim [of such a war] is to force artificially the development of class contradictions in countries where the proletariat is not yet able to seize state power and its movement has not yet assumed the character of civil war....

Insisting on genuine observance of the principle of national self-determination with respect to Azerbaidzhan, and on sincere, responsible ... peace negotiations with the border countries (Georgia, Lithuania, Latvia, Estonia), the RSDRP ... also recommends a policy of compromise negotiations between the Soviet and the present Polish government, if Poland renounces expansionist tendencies and interference in the internal affairs of revolutionary Russia. [This policy] will facilitate the conclusion of peace with both Poland and the Entente. [45]

The Red army was repulsed before it reached Warsaw. Soon after, Lenin revealed the ambitious plans he had formed:

> If Poland had become Soviet, if the Warsaw workers had received from Soviet Russia the help they expected and [would have] welcomed, the Versailles peace would have been demolished and the whole international system achieved through the victory over Germany would have collapsed. France would not have the buffer that protects Germany from Soviet Russia. It would not have the battering ram against the Soviet Republic.... A few more days of the Red army's victorious advance, and not only would Warsaw have been taken (this wasn't all that important), but the Versailles peace would have been demolished: this was the issue.... [46]
>
> Our army's approach to Warsaw had conclusively shown that the hub of the whole system of world imperialism based on the Versailles treaty lies somewhere in the vicinity [of Warsaw]. Poland, controlled by the Entente, is such a mighty factor in this system that the whole system began to wobble when the Red army threatened that bastion.... When our army approached Warsaw, all of Germany began to boil. [47]

Martov described the same events very differently at the congress of the German Independent Socialists in Halle:

> The Russian Red army was nearing the gates of Warsaw; the organized workers of England and other countries, remembering the Soviet government's repeated solemn promises to conclude peace with Poland as soon as Poland gave up its expansionist plans, were doing their best to force the Entente to withhold aid from Poland and thus compel it to sue for peace. [And] this was achieved!
>
> But the Red army continued to advance on Warsaw, it crossed the Vistula, occupied Soldau, and Soviet diplomacy obviously tried to delay negotiations; and when they finally began, it presented demands tantamount to [a call for the Polish] government's resignation, that is, calculated on its inability to accept them. And all this was done after a solemn conference of the Petersburg Soviet (whose chairman is Zinov'ev), which passed and published the following resolution: No peace with Poland—until the bourgeoisie is deposed and a Soviet Republic established!...
>
> Zinov'ev has said here that the Bolsheviks did not try to involve Germany in a war with the Entente. That is not true! Trotsky himself said in one of his speeches at the height of the Russian victories: "We shall fight the Entente on the Rhine." In Soldau, officers and commissars of the Red army told demonstrating German nationalists ... that Russia was restoring Western Prussia to the German fatherland.

Martov ended his speech at Halle thus:

Nothing could hurt my pride in the Russian revolution more than the constant questions of German comrades: Won't it affect your fate when you return to Russia if you engage in polemics with Zinov'ev here? I am filled with shame for my fatherland when I think that the Russian proletariat has gone through twenty years of heroic struggle and three revolutions only to give foreign comrades the right—every right—to ask such a question, and the only thing I can reply is that *even before I return to Russia, the Bolshevik rulers corrupted by systematic terror will undoubtedly revenge themselves in some way on my Party comrades, hundreds of whom are languishing in Bolshevik prisons,* for every word I publicly say here against the Bolshevik party and its policy.[48]

The war with Poland was short and intraparty conflicts about it did not have time to develop. The right wing had not been enthusiastic about defense;[49] and the "extreme left"—especially some Bund leaders —were not averse to a revolutionary invasion of Central Europe in alliance with Poland and Germany.[50] The Soviet defeat and the armistice eliminated these problems.

The British Delegation and the Printers' Union

In May 1920 a seven-member delegation from the British Labour Party and trade unions plus two delegates from the Independent Labour Party came to Russia to see for themselves what Soviet conditions were like. The Labour Party was in favor of peaceful relations with Soviet Russia and did not quite believe the reports of Cheka atrocities, repression of free trade unions, and so on. Anti-Marxist and antirevolutionary, it stood on the right flank of the Second International and was ideologically more opposed to bolshevism than were the Russian Mensheviks; but for reasons of foreign policy its line was in a sense more pro-Soviet.

On 10 May the delegates arrived in Petrograd, and on 16 May in Moscow, where they were quartered at Delovoi Dvor, one of the better hotels. They spent several weeks in Russia, were taken to the Polish front and to several provincial cities, welcomed with orchestras, fêted at banquets. One of the delegation's secretaries got in touch with the Menshevik CC (Axelrod had given him Dan's address). The CC showed the British a memorandum about conditions in Russia it had prepared for a delegation from the Socialist International, which never came. Several members of the CC visited the Britishers at their hotel, and the latter attended two meetings of the CC. (One delegate refused to see any members of the CC.) The government kept the delegates under close surveillance, through the official interpreters and by other means. Their mail was opened and sometimes destroyed. Cheka agents watched their rooms and "checked" everyone who went in or out. "Independent visits to factories were out of the question."[51]

Among other Soviet officials, the English saw I. Ksenofontov, deputy chairman of the Cheka, who assured them that it had come out at the trial of the Tactical Center that the Mensheviks belonged to a bloc of counterrevolutionary organizations. When the English told Martov about this, he gave them a written statement that Ksenofontov was lying.

On 18 May a big meeting in honor of the delegation was held at the Bolshoi Theater. It was organized by the CEC, the Moscow Soviet, factory committees, and other Soviet institutions. The Menshevik CC was invited, and Abramovich welcomed the delegates in the name of the opposition party. He said that the Mensheviks favored world social revolution and dictatorship of the proletariat but understood the latter as dictatorship "of the majority of toilers." Abramovich finished his speech with the words, "Long live the fighting fellowship of proletarians of all countries!"

Another big meeting was organized by the Moscow printers on 21 May. The estimates of attendance vary from three to six thousand. The printers' union had not only managed to preserve its independence of the government but was very active in the trade union movement. Its Moscow board included M. Kefali, A. Deviatkin, N. Chistov, I. Buksin, and A. Romanov. Though right-wing Mensheviks, they all followed the CC's line on important political issues. They even gave the English delegation a copy of the CC's resolution on trade unions, which spoke of "the beginning international socialist revolution," "transition from capitalist to socialist methods of production," and fighting counterrevolution as one of the tasks of trade unions. These were Martov's theses endorsed by the CC on 31 March; the leaders of the printers' union disagreed with them in the privacy of the Party but remained loyal to the party line. In the name of the board, Kefali wrote on the copy of the resolution he gave the Britishers: "The Moscow board of the printers' union fully shares the principles . . . of the Central Committee's resolution of 31 March 1920." The board and the CC jointly drew up a resolution to be brought before the meeting at which the board was to honor the delegates.[52]

At the mass meeting, which was chaired by Deviatkin, Kefali was the main speaker. He said that the printers had pioneered in the Russian trade union movement and had stood in the front ranks of the

Revolution of 1905; they could not possibly be called counterrevolutionaries; no other trade union would be able to bring together a free meeting of this size; the visitors might be shown bogus meetings of committees and deputies that no one had elected—the VTsSPS among them; but the Bolsheviks would not be able to convoke a free meeting of workers with a Communist majority. [53]

Dan, for the Central Committee, spoke of the Menshevik conception of democratic socialism and the need to end foreign intervention. Several Bolshevik speakers followed. The meeting was drawing to a close when a man with a long beard mounted the steps to the platform and approached the chairman. The latter announced that a representative of the Party of Socialist Revolutionaries had the floor. Dan writes:

> Only when the orator began to speak did I recognize Chernov, to my great surprise—the long beard changed his appearance so much. For Chernov to show himself at this meeting was a tremendous risk since the Cheka was hot on his traces.... When the speaker had finished, the Bolsheviks began to shout, What is the name? Let him tell his name! Chernov stepped forward and identified himself. The result was not what the Bolsheviks had expected. To their bloodhound zeal, to their cries, "Arrest him!" the audience responded with a loud ovation for the quarry, which made the Bolsheviks lose their heads. In the confusion, Chernov disappeared as unnoticeably as he had come. [54]

This meeting, wrote Dan, was a bitter pill for the Bolsheviks. It showed the extent of the opposition among workers. The government took steps to prevent such demonstrations from ever occurring again. First the Bolshevik Moscow committee laid the ideological basis for the coming repressions, publishing "theses" that read, in part:

> By having, in the name of a workers' meeting, libelously denounced the Soviet government to Lloyd George and company, the Mensheviks have made the blockade and war against Soviet Russia [appear] justified—in other words, they have helped the world's capitalist predators, and White Guard Poland in its aggression against us. [55]

Dan was soon exiled to Ekaterinburg. Abramovich was recalled from the Soviet by his constituents, who had been threatened with a reduction of their food rations. Eleven members of the board of the printers' union were arrested during the night of 17–18 June, as well as twenty-nine representatives and members of factory committees. Among those arrested were eleven members of the Moscow Soviet. On 18 June the premises of the printers' union were seized. The printers' meeting was the last big oppositional meeting in the history of the revolution.

Axelrod and the Socialist International

When the CC sent Axelrod to Sweden in August 1917, a coalition government that included Mensheviks had been in power. All Mensheviks were eager to "revive the International." Helping to bring this about was Axelrod's mission abroad. Although he belonged to the Party's Internationalist wing, he represented the Party as a whole. The struggle with the Bolsheviks was not yet a major issue—they came to power two months later. Lenin's break with the Allies, the civil war, and the persecution of political opponents in Russia confronted Western socialists with new problems. This made Axelrod's mission more difficult and more important.

Approval of Lenin's regime was quite strong in Western socialist parties. Some factions and a few entire parties were disposed to join the new International for which Lenin began to lay the groundwork in 1918. Axelrod's role was complicated by the fact that, as a Zimmerwald socialist, he rejected the "defensist" stand and had been criticizing the right socialists; and the left socialists were largely oriented toward Moscow. As I have mentioned (pp. 104–5), Axelrod and some SRs in 1918 declared themselves against foreign intervention. He carried on a vast correspondence, gave lectures, and generally prepared for the postwar revival of the Socialist International, in which he hoped that his party would have its due place. The International, paralyzed until late 1918, indeed began to revive in early 1919. However, it could not encompass all the socialist factions. Conspicuously absent were the Russian Bolsheviks, on whom the world's attention was focused. The active Zimmerwald parties such as the Italian, the French, and the German Independent maintained their reserve and soon responded to Moscow's overtures. In 1919–20 they agreed to participate in a congress for the purpose of creating a new International.

Axelrod attended the first postwar conferences of the Socialist International as the official representative of the RSDRP. He did not want to break with the old, for the most part "social-patriotic," International—largely because he hoped for support of his anti-Bolshevik policy from its main parties, even though he disagreed with some of the political steps they had taken. He saw the situation as a dilemma: either all the non-Bolshevik parties would unite, or Lenin's International would prevail. His plan—to which he held on for a long time—was to send to Russia a "commission of inquiry," elected by the

Socialist International, to study and evaluate the Bolshevik methods of achieving socialism. He hoped that such a commission would include the greatest figures of European socialism and that their verdict would influence Lenin, whose policy had not yet jelled at the time, and also influence the Western socialist parties, which he believed to be sadly astray in their gropings for the right way to the socialist revolution. To be sure, Axelrod foresaw many difficulties. His letters of the period (for instance, to Chkhenkeli) discuss some of them: Moscow would refuse entry to such a commission; some of the delegates might be hoodwinked; they would be kept away from the socialist opposition in Russia; attempts to discredit them might be made; the Russian socialists might not help much, and some assistance from Caucasus and Ukrainian socialists might be needed. But none of these problems made Axelrod change his mind. He wrote:

> Only an open, internationally organized act (an "intervention") by the Western labor parties against the Asiatically savage and medievally anarchic Bolshevik regime can save the nations and the democracy of former tsarist Russia both from the threat of ruin that Bolshevik dominance holds for them and from the dangers connected with military intervention. But such an "intervention" by the Western proletariat is unthinkable as long as the latter remains under the spell of those illusions and fables about the character of our "Soviet power" that are still being vigorously promoted and kept up among [its members] by innumerable mercenary and disinterested agents of that power. [56]

For a while it seemed that Axelrod's plan would materialize. Delegates to the Lucerne conference of the Socialist International in August 1919 decided to send a "commission of inquiry" to Russia and nominated several participants.

Meanwhile the Mensheviks in Russia were less and less favorably disposed toward the old International. Most of the leaders, including former Revolutionary Defensists, disapproved the policies of the large Western socialist parties. The participation of these rightist, "reformist" parties in Western European governments (Germany, France) increased the antagonism of Russian social democracy toward an international organization that supported these policies and was therefore answerable for them.

Other factors came into play in late 1918 with the revision of the Menshevik party's ideology, the expectation of a social revolution in the west, the civil war, and the general leftward trend among Russian socialists. During that period Axelrod was acting abroad as the emissary of Russian menshevism. Whenever the Soviet press attacked him, the Central Committee rose to his defense—in the press if possible, or in letters to Party organizations. Here is one of the CC's statements:

> In his appearances *before Western European socialists*, Comrade P. B. Axelrod, as representative of the CC of the RSDRP, naturally lays bare all the untruths that Bolshevik agents disseminate abroad about the state of affairs in Soviet Russia and explains the true situation—in particular, the Communists' terrorist policy toward socialists who think differently and toward workers' and peasants' organizations. . . .
> But at the same time Comrade Axelrod, in strict accord with the CC's directives, publicly protests—and has been doing so for a long time wherever he can—against all forms of imperialist intervention in Russia, explains to the socialists how deeply harmful it is to the entire Russian revolution, and declares that our Party accepts only intervention by proletarian European parties in moral support of those socialists who are fighting in Soviet Russia for a policy of proletarian unity and a single revolutionary front. [57]

What with the civil war, the blockade, the absence of postal service between Russia and the west, the CC had trouble keeping in touch with Axelrod. The Soviet press printed only tendentious reports on the Socialist International. On 26 May 1919 the CC resolved to restrict its association with the International to informational purposes. This amounted to giving up membership, although Axelrod still had the right—and made use of it—to offer proposals and speak on Russian affairs at international conferences. The CC's resolution stated that the Party could be bound only by decisions of international conferences and congresses that in principle and practice stood for "an independent revolutionary class policy, consistent internationalism, and scientific socialism." This statement prefigured the platform of the future Vienna International: "revolutionary class policy" meant rejection of coalitions with bourgeois partners; "consistent internationalism" was set against "social-patriotism"; and "scientific socialism" meant Marxism and class struggle.

Axelrod got the impression that the CC was "indifferent" to what was going on abroad. As he wrote S. Shchupak, he thought of ceasing to represent the Party officially.[58] Actually, the trouble was not indifference on the CC's part but dissatisfaction with the International. And the CC was far less hopeful than Axelrod about the proposed investigation by the International, though it did approve the idea and even prepared some material to give the delegates. In the spring of 1920, when postal service was partially restored, Axelrod informed the CC that he was laying down his mandate.

Delegates from Western socialist parties came to Moscow for the Second Congress of the Comintern in the spring and summer of 1920. Many of them were Lenin's partisans. Among his opponents were some leaders of the German Independents, some Frenchmen, and others, but even they disapproved of the old Socialist International. The Mensheviks discussed the creation of a new international organization with the foreign delegates and at their own two Party conferences, in March and April. The March conference approved the idea: "It is indispensable to create a new center uniting the revolutionary elements of the working class of Europe, equally free of opportunism and sectarianism." In the CC, opinion was divided. Martov and Dan were skeptical but remained in the minority. Martov wrote Axelrod:

> I personally do not hope to build a durable edifice on the German-French "center." On this issue Fedor Il'ich and I stand somewhat apart from the other members of the CC, who, independently of their degree of leftism, seem optimistic about the possibility of building an International on the present middle parties. I rather incline toward F. Adler's skeptical view that the time is not yet ripe for the organizational political recreation of the International and that just as after 1870–89 there is need for a period of *Uberwindung* of the ideological chaos and crystallization of the political ideology before an International can be created that will be at all effective and authoritative. [59]

The letter went on the explain the CC's motives in agreeing to the idea of a new International:

> We had to give in to the comrades who are justifiably afraid that the center parties' lack of organizational activity, plus the bourgeois quality—which is obvious to us—of the right International, will make Moscow the center of attraction for all the anticoalition parties, despite all the reservations about it.

Axelrod had tendered his resignation partly because he disagreed with the plans of the German and French socialists for a new International, and now even the Russians were for it. The March conference resolved to appoint someone else to represent the Party abroad. In April the CC accepted Axelrod's resignation, "taking into consideration that because of our complete segregation from Europe Comrade P. B. Axelrod has for two years been unable to maintain contact with the CC and, as he himself has often pointed out, to keep abreast of the actual stand of the Party on the most topical questions—and that the Party therefore is not really represented abroad." In the summer the CC decided to delegate Martov and Abramovich to Europe. Martov intended to return to Russia for the next Party conference toward the end of the year. When he applied to Narkomindel for a passport, he did not conceal that he was planning to attend the congress of the German Independents in Halle, where Zinov'ev was to represent the Comintern. Passports were issued, first to Martov, then to Abramovich, and later to several other members of the CC. As Litvinov explained to one of them, Lenin felt they were harmful in Russia, whereas abroad their propaganda against intervention and in favor of recognizing the Soviet Union might do some good. [60]

Martov left on 21 September 1920 and after a stopover in Reval arrived in Halle in good time for the congress. He would never see Russia again.

Announcing his resignation as representative of the Mensheviks in the International, Axelrod had written its secretary, C. Huysmans (on 22 May) that he had received the first letters in two years from his Moscow comrades (dated 23 and 30 January 1920), informing him that they had decided to withdraw from the Second International ("evidently under the influence of the German Independents," Axelrod added). In his official capacity he, Axelrod, was relaying this to Huysmans, but he had written to Moscow that he disapproved. He also remarked, "If a few of the Russian Menshevik leaders could come to Europe, they would see that this stand is wrong."

Huysmans tried to persuade Axelrod to stay on,[61] but meanwhile Axelrod had received Dan's letter of 28 May accepting his resignation: "We are constantly forced to confront you with facts with which you do not always agree and which you can defend only *a contre-coeur.*" On 4 July, Axelrod wrote Huysmans:

> Imagine my situation.... I had been totally cut off from my Party for a long time, and now it turns out that my views about the revival of the International are the direct opposite [of the Party's]. Moreover, I am also isolated in the anti-Bolshevik camp of our Western comrades, in respect to the methods of combating bolshevism. I am isolated mainly because even [the anti-Bolshevik comrades] fail to realize the need for an *internationally organized* struggle against the poisonous influence of the hotbed of Moscow bolshevism on the international proletariat. They greatly underrate the importance of this influence and think they can cope with the Bolshevik tendencies by their own local means, in their corner, in their country. [62]

Axelrod wrote a friend that he differed with the CC's "evaluation of the so-called center of the International—the French reconstructionists and the German Independents. I call both of them 'the bog.'"[63] But there were other issues that had come between Axelrod and his old comrades, and he discussed them, too, in his correspondence. This was a difficult time for Axelrod. At seventy and in poor health, he was losing his status as a universally recognized Menshevik leader. He hoped to bring Martov around to his views when the latter finally came to Europe—after all, they had stood side by side for seventeen years, through 1905, Zimmerwald, and the Bolshevik seizure of power, losing many friends but not each other. But his meeting with Martov in late 1920 did nothing to smooth out their differences, though personal friendship was renewed. Axelrod was not on the editorial board of *Sotsialisticheskii Vestnik* (*SV*) when Martov began publishing it in Berlin. So far as is known, he had not been invited.

During the last eight years of his life Axelrod did not belong to any organization. He corresponded with many friends in the West; Mensheviks of all shadings visited him when they came to Berlin, but they tried in vain to enlist his support. A long letter he had written the CC the previous summer but that never reached its destination was published with Axelrod's consent in *SV* of 20 April and 4 May 1921. I regret that I cannot quote this remarkable letter in full. Axelrod criticized the European Marxists, especially Otto Bauer and others who, he felt, "sanctioned" bolshevism for Russia while rejecting it for the West. The constant comparisons with the French Revolution and the Paris Commune incensed him:

> To all these references, this obstrusive pointing to the great French Revolution, I replied: no doubt there are superficial similarities in the Jacobin and the Bolshevik regimes, but the similarity is about the same as between a clever parody and the original, or between a skillful *imitation* of a great spontaneous event and the event itself.

Axelrod agreed with Kautsky that the Jacobins had come to power because their aims and policies did not clash with their ideology, which could not be said of the Bolsheviks. As one of the founders of Russian Marxism whom Lenin and Trotsky had earlier considered their teacher, Axelrod referred to the "Liberation of Labor" credo that socialism could not be installed in backward Russia at a time when capitalism still reigned in the economically advanced countries of Europe:

> I need not remind you that from the day of its appearance on Russian soil, Marxism began to combat every Russian variety of the utopian socialism that proclaimed Russia the land historically destined to leap from feudalism and semiprimitive capitalism straight to ... socialism. In this struggle Lenin and his literary collaborators took an active part. Hence, when they made their

overturn in October, they betrayed their principles and embarked on a criminal Herostratic adventure, which is inseparably linked, as cause and effect, to their terrorist regime and all their other crimes.

If the Bolsheviks, like the Jacobins in their time, were fulfilling a historical mission, "our struggle against them [would be] basically counterrevolutionary"—the right thing to do would be to join them and, if necessary, criticize them in a friendly spirit. Axelrod stressed, however, that he shared the CC's disapproval of uprisings against the Bolsheviks—not as a matter of principle but merely from the point of view of expediency. He referred to an article he had written to this effect in 1918 when the Volga front was forming.

At the end of his letter Axelrod analyzed the issue of "international socialist intervention" and a simultaneous "*broad, internationally united, and energetic campaign* among the Western proletarian masses against Bolshevik barbarism"; this movement, he said, must demand of the Soviet government "concessions to the socialist opposition that will enable [the opposition] legally to defend the interests of the Russian revolution and the laboring masses."

Martov replied in *SV* of 20 May 1921 that the supposed differences on the issue of uprisings stemmed from a misunderstanding: he, too, rejected them for reasons of expediency, not principle. He opposed "reconciliation with bolshevism" while admitting that the Soviet regime had some achievements to its credit:

> It seems to him [Axelrod] that the admission that the Bolsheviks have to any degree fulfilled a historically necessary task, have pulled Russia out of the World War, advanced the lagging agrarian revolution, purged the administration—insufficiently purged by Kerensky—of elements that were still clutching at the past, and so on—that [any such admission] necessarily reflects an *apologetic* attitude toward bolshevism....

Only where bolshevism defends "the true conquests of the revolution" against counterrevolution "do we unreservedly align ourselves on the side of bolshevism."

The End of War Communism

In late 1920 the political picture began to change rapidly. In October the armistice with Poland was signed; in November, the last White armies evacuated the Crimea. England and France had not recognized the Soviet government or resumed trade with Russia, but they had given up military intervention. Moscow's relations with the Baltic countries had eased and, with Finland, stabilized. But in Central Asia minor military clashes were still going on, and Stalin thundered in the Caucasus that Menshevik Georgia was "in its last days." Kautsky, Vandervelde, and Ramsay MacDonald had visited Tiflis and were advising Moscow to emulate the socialist policy of the Georgian government. Several Russian Mensheviks, V. Voitinskii among them, worked in Georgian organs of government. The local Menshevik press (in the Russian language) criticized the Soviet regime, though not in a challenging tone. The Menshevik CC in Moscow was aware that the situation in Georgia was explosive.

With the food crisis reaching awesome proportions, economic problems were crowding to the forefront. The Bolshevik party tried out various remedies. First, electrification, for which Lenin tried to work up some enthusiasm; but even under the best of conditions it would take years to implement. Next, departing from integral socialism, Lenin signed a decree about granting concessions to foreign capitalists. Finally, in 1921, the New Economic Policy replaced War communism. (Lenin's "War communism" had served to justify the Committees of the Poor, the labor armies, the repressions. Bolsheviks and Mensheviks were now agreed that it had in fact been an attempt to install socialism, that it had failed, and that the government would have to retreat from many of its positions.)

In November-December 1920, the grant of economic concessions to foreigners was animatedly discussed in Bolshevik councils. Lenin clearly pinned greater hopes on them than they deserved. A pamphlet was issued, and then also distributed abroad, describing the three kinds of proposed concessions—in lumber, food supplies, and mining. At conferences Lenin was sometimes asked (usually in writing) if the Mensheviks had not foretold a return to capitalism and the inability of the government to solve its economic problems. Lenin assured his party that these concessions were state capitalism of a new type; the government would have full control over both concessions and concessionaires.

Anti-Bolshevik circles in Russia and abroad objected to concessions, accusing the government of "selling Russia in bits and pieces"; on the other hand, they maintained that it made no sense for capitalists to invest in a Communist country. The Mensheviks were ready to support Lenin's plan if trade unions were allowed to act independently of the government, both in the concessions and in state industry. Dan spoke of this in detail at the Eighth Congress of Soviets. (I shall return to his speech.)

But the new plan, too, would take a long time to bear fruit, and meanwhile the economy was near famine. Lenin had given up the Committees of the Poor somewhat earlier, but the harsh use of anti-profiteering detachments, the repression of the "free market" and "speculators," continued. Later it became known that Lenin had been ready to abandon these practices, too, in his policy toward the peasantry, but other Bolsheviks had objected: The concessions already seemed to imply that the Mensheviks had been right in opposing "instant socialism"; they and the peasant parties would now be vindicated on many more points. During War Communism it may have been necessary to repress the socialist parties because they advocated private peasant economy and held that in the cities a compromise with capitalism was unavoidable—but perhaps it was time to legalize these parties, time for a new kind of "Soviet democracy"?

Some opposition parties, including the Mensheviks, were invited in December 1920 to the Eighth Congress of Soviets—the last they were to attend. At Communist caucuses—closed, consequently, even to nonpartisan deputies—Lenin spoke mainly of the international situation and of concessions; Dzerzhinskii maintained that "Now that peaceful building has begun, malicious criticism of the Soviet authorities is more inadmissible than ever," and Trotsky agreed: "Now that the civil war is over, the Mensheviks and SRs are especially dangerous and must be fought with particular ruthlessness." As yet no new policy toward the peasantry was discussed.

At the congress, the Mensheviks propounded their program, including some points on which the Bolshevik leaders were still keeping silent. Dan said:

> I was very astonished when the chairman of the Soviet of People's Commissars in yesterday's speech gave a long list of countries with which peace pacts have been signed and friendly relations are being established—and omitted one country, the country with which rapport and cooperation are very important for the whole policy of peace in the east. That country is Georgia.

Dan also spoke in detail about the degenerating "Soviet system." Local Soviets had ceased to meet; their executive committees and presidiums were acting in their stead. Laws were being applied independently of the Central Executive Committee. Its decree of amnesty on the occasion of the third anniversary of the October Revolution was not enforced for political prisoners. Yet it had not been the CEC's decision to exclude them—the Cheka had in effect changed the law. Dan showed and read a letter of the Cheka to support his point. Lenin's closing speech was largely a reply to Dan. All he could say to justify the arbitrary disregard of laws by the political police was that the head of the latter was a member of the CC of the Communist party and of the CEC.

Dan pointed out that the decree about concessions nullified the earlier emphasis on a fully nationalized economy. It was

> a public admission that Russia's productive forces cannot be restored through a Communist nationalized economy alone—that the assistance of private capital is necessary.... Calling in private initiative and capital in certain forms and within certain limits under the regulating guidance of the state ... is the very idea for which we Mensheviks have been branded servants of capitalism. Now the Soviet government is adopting this idea ... because concessions are one way of drawing in private capital to restore Russia's productive forces.

The trade unions had not been given a chance to say what they thought about the concessions before the decree was passed—on the grounds that the state represented the workers' interests anyway:

> Will the workers who work for capitalists have the right to defend their interests, to fight for lowering the share of surplus value, for better pay? Or will they be denied the right of trade union struggle against capitalists as well?... Will the minimal wage rate ... be mandatory? Or will there be two kinds of trade unions? So that if woodland concessions are arranged, as Trotsky says, in a checkerboard pattern, alternating with Soviet enterprises ... there will be trade unions deprived of the right to economic struggle in one [area]—the Soviet—while next to it, in ... concessions, there will be trade unions that do have the right to defend the interests of the working class against capitalists?

D. Dallin also spoke at the Congress. He discussed the food problem and offered a resolution of the Menshevik CC that in effect would allow the peasants to sell their produce in the open market—the basic idea of the NEP decrees, which would be introduced only in March 1921. The main reform proposed by the Mensheviks was this: "Building the food policy on such a basis that after fulfilling strictly defined obligations to the state, all surplus could be sold by the peasants on a basis of voluntary exchange of goods or at prices set in agreement with them." Voices from the audience exclaimed that Dallin was speaking in favor of free trade, of speculators (the delegates had not yet been let in on the projects ripening in the Kremlin), and a loyal resolution in the spirit of War Communism was passed. On 17 January the Central Administration of Military Schools (GUVUZ) dismissed Dallin from his post of history teacher at one of its schools. The reason: "an oral directive from the chief of the Political Department, Comrade Abramov." Martov commented that it would be interesting to know what punishment was meted out to Comrade Abramov for opposing the economic policy that the Central Committee of the Communist party adopted soon thereafter. "According to our information, Dallin was going to be arrested," wrote Martov. "This did not happen only because by that time he was already beyond the Cheka's reach."[64]

The Communists and their opponents both felt that a new era of the revolution was beginning. The civil war was over, and with it the attempts at a quick transformation of the economy on pseudosocialist lines. No social revolution in the West was in sight. Would the political system change along with the economic? There was much unrest— even within the ruling party—but there were no great popular movements. The strong police state refused to make any concessions to the opposition. On the contrary, the group that ruled Russia from the Kremlin would go to any lengths rather than give up a particle of its power.

The Menshevik party worked "in a makeshift, sporadic way, snatching at favorable occasions like trade union congresses or elections to Soviets"[65] and hoping for a change when the panic fear of another war had dissipated. Martov wrote:

> When the respite comes, I believe we can still snap back. The very fact that even amid the foulest terror and the universal toadying to the Bolsheviks, there are people all over the world (right now, only us), often simple workers, who openly and firmly set their own credo against the Bolsheviks—this very fact, even if it irritates the masses already used to meekly following the dictators, nevertheless builds up a reputation for us ... that will count at the critical moment.[66]

Everything seemed to depend on peace with the West. But—

> aside from the Entente, a great deal depends on the Bolsheviks. More and more they are following blind impulses (including "himself") [the reference is to Lenin]—impelled today to fight Poland until a Soviet revolution has taken place there, and tomorrow to raise the Islamic East against England.[67]

This bent for risky operations abroad remained a trait of Lenin's (and later Stalin's) policy. Martov wrote in 1921 that the tendency to "carry a Communist revolution into Europe on the bayonets of forcibly conscripted anti-Communist Russian peasants" was a constant threat to Soviet Russia in her foreign relations:

> We warned the Russian proletariat of the possible dangers of such a foolhardy policy at the very beginning of the Russo-Polish war, when the Bolshevik government, supported not only by the pro-

letariat and peasantry but also by some of the bourgeois intelligentsia, advanced a program of purely defensive war. We most resolutely protested against . . . this tendency when Lenin's government, enticed by the military successes that had brought Russian troops to the gates of Warsaw, attempted a forcible "sovietization" of Poland and received a well-deserved lesson in the subsequent defeats that forced it to sign a peace surrendering to Polish imperialism a number of non-Polish territories, against the interests of the Russian laboring classes. [68]

Later the Soviets attempted to form an alliance with the German military against Poland, intrigued in Afghanistan and Persia against England, and in the middle twenties engaged in dubious operations in China. Lenin's death did nothing to change this tendency. The "peaceful coexistence" he had proclaimed was to remain a hollow formula.

III. The Mensheviks under the NEP and in Emigration

Simon Wolin

9

The Opposition to the NEP

A new chapter of the revolution opened with the introduction of the New Economic Policy (NEP) in the spring of 1921. Wars and interventions were over, the time of building had come. This meant, in the first place, rebuilding the utterly disorganized economy and easing the famine. On the other hand, the government could no longer explain away the one-party dictatorship, the terror and hunger, by the need to fight internal and imported counterrevolution. Omens of a blowup had appeared in late 1920. In February 1921, a month before the Kronstadt uprising, the first issue of *Sotsialisticheskii Vestnik* (*SV*)[1] noted that Russia was going through a "critical period." Discontent was rampant in all strata of the population and even in the Communist party itself. Both the ruling party and the opposition had to reexamine their stands.

Reviving an old tradition, the Petrograd workers in early 1921 began to hold meetings in the streets, for the first time since 1918. Factories went on strike. In Moscow, Kiev, Tula, and other cities, workers also clamored for food, free trade, the abolition of Communist cells in factories, which were in effect organs of the police. In some cases, the demands included freedom of assembly and speech. The Mensheviks supported most of these demands but took a wary view of the unorganized movement as a whole: the defeated but not yet destroyed reactionary forces might make use of it. Similar fears had dictated Menshevik policy over the past three years. In the words of F. Dan, head of the Petrograd committee of the RSDRP at the time, our organization decided not to inflate the movement . . . to counsel the workers to be content with partial concessions—but at the same time to use the events to clarify to the masses that there was a connection between the present disasters and the general policy of bolshevism, stressing especially the need to renounce wholesale nationalization, to accept small peasant proprietorship, and to end party dictatorship. [2]

The Petrograd committee issued a proclamation in this vein "To the Starving and Freezing Workers of Petrograd" (in one thousand copies).

When the Kronstadt uprising forced Lenin to retreat from his extreme positions and institute the NEP, the idea of uprisings appeared in a new light. Earlier, the RSDRP had condemned any armed action against the government. (This stand had been the main cause of its break with the SRs and with the Mensheviks who had left the Party or been expelled.) But the Kronstadt uprising was not counterrevolutionary: the rebels were peasants and workers, many of them Communists, and their slogans were the old Menshevik slogans: free Soviets and trade unions, free trade, abolition of dictatorship. The uprising was a result of the government's failure to cope with economic problems; it was also a natural reaction against the corrupt bureaucracy, whose privileges shockingly contrasted with the masses' privations, and against terrorist dictators, big and small. In its very first article on the uprising, SV tied it to the workers' unrest: factory meetings, their repression, and the mass demonstrations against repression were bringing forth a distinctly political mass movement of the kind "everyone of us has seen in Russia so many times." What was needed was "an immediate and final break with the regime of terrorist dictatorship, an appeal to the workers' independent activity . . . renunciation of the utopian economic policy," and agreement with the other socialist parties to establish a "toilers' rule [vlast' trudiashchikhsia]." [3]

In the next issue of the journal, an unsigned article (undoubtedly Martov's) spoke of the uprising with sympathy, pointing out that the Cheka's version (that Mensheviks, SRs, agents of the Entente, and so forth were involved) was untrue: the insurgents had advanced the old Menshevik demands on their own initiative. "This proves that a united proletarian front . . . is possible. . . . This is a fact of enormous importance. And this fact fully confirms the correctness of our Party's policy during 1919 and 1920." The government had committed a crime in quashing the uprising by armed force. Marching on Kronstadt, Trotsky was marching to destroy "perhaps the most dependable fighting force on which the revolution can rely at the critical moment of counterrevolutionary danger."

The Menshevik Central Committee (CC) had been depleted by

arrests, and its remaining members disagreed on Kronstadt.[4] After two meetings to discuss it, the CC issued on 7 March a joint leaflet with the Moscow committee of the RSDRP, which restated in hackneyed terms demands for a more democratic regime and a changed peasant and provisionment policy (demands to be advanced "loudly, without fear of persecution") but was on the whole very cool toward the uprising: "We are not urging the working class to overthrow the Soviet government but to press for changes in its wrong policy, which is ruining the revolution. We advise the workers to act, not through disorderly strikes, but through organized promotion of their demands in Soviet organs."

On the same day the Petrograd Committee (PC) said in a leaflet:

> The workers' government should have found out the real causes of the Kronstadt events. [It] should have openly, in full sight of the working class, reached an agreement with the workers and sailors of Kronstadt. Instead, it declared a state of siege, presented an ultimatum about surrender, and began to shoot workers and sailors.
>
> Comrades! We cannot, we must not, listen calmly to the roar of cannon. Each shot may cost scores of precious lives.
>
> We must step in and put an end to the bloodshed.
>
> Demand that military action against the workers and sailors of Kronstadt be stopped at once.
>
> Demand that the government immediately begin negotiations with them, with the assistance of delegates from factories and plants.
>
> Immediately elect delegates to take part in these negotiations. Stop the murders!

Thus, while the CC advised the workers to calm down, the Petrograd committee encouraged them to support the insurgents and protest against terror. Abroad, the CC's representatives Iu. Martov and R. Abramovich judged the CC's appeal "very poor."[5] In Martov's opinion, it showed that the CC did not understand the nature of the uprising. SV (no. 5) printed only excerpts from this colorless appeal but gave that of the PC in full.

The Mensheviks realized that the Kronstadt uprising was a major event in the history of Soviet Russia and counted on its beneficial effects. They demanded economic reforms because the state was unable to cope with the gigantic task of administering the economy of backward Russia. Whether from the conviction that the revolution was bourgeois (the right) or that Russia was gradually becoming socialist (the left), both wings of menshevism considered the wholesale nationalization of industry, transport, and banks harmfully utopian. The majority held that the state should retain control of the more important branches of industry (as a step toward future collectivization) but let private enterprise handle the other branches; and that foreign capital should be brought in, by way of concessions and loans, in view of the Russian bourgeoisie's weakness. Just before the NEP, Martov had written: "I am defending [the idea of] concessions from the attacks of the left Bolsheviks and I consider it demagogy when the SRs and Kadets write that concessions mean selling Russia in bits. If we or the SRs were in power, we would compromise with capitalism, especially foreign capitalism."[6] The Mensheviks also protested against the Soviet repudiation of foreign debts—not from a legal standpoint but because they rightly foresaw that this would impair Russia's economic relations with the West for a long time.[7]

On the other hand, the RSDRP warned against bondage to foreign capital. A resolution of the CC in January 1921 said that the concessions should furnish the necessary guarantees to investors but no excuses for meddling in Russia's political or economic affairs—a double aim that could be attained only by a state based on law and popular self-government. The idea was expressed more distinctly toward the end of the year, in the demand for a system "enabling the various strata of the differentiating new society [that is, becoming differentiated under the NEP] to defend their special interests openly and fully."[8] This was a change from the earlier period, when the RSDRP had stressed the right of a revolutionary government engaged in building socialism to limit the political freedom of nonproletarian groups.[9] Now the Party accented the right of these groups to freedom.

Martov did not see any contradiction between granting civil rights to the bourgeoisie—whose role was bound to increase under the NEP because of partial denationalization—and the principle of "toilers' rule" that he advocated at the time. During the early NEP period, the Mensheviks overestimated the possibilities of capitalist development under the Soviet regime. They considered such a development necessary for the economic recovery of the country and wanted to create conditions that would facilitate it, yet leave the workers in power. Martov thought that a democratic government of the laboring classes "should leave enough latitude to the propertied classes for peaceful struggle for influence over the course of events in the state and over the popular masses."[10] For this, broad democracy was necessary.

The Mensheviks began to take more interest in the peasantry, with which they had hardly any links. The peasants were the majority of the population, they alone could provide relief from the famine, and they had to be the workers' partners if a true "toilers' rule" was to be achieved. The lead article of SV, no. 6, "Agreement with the Peasantry," maintained that the peasants would accept the revolution and work for economic recovery only when the so-called dictatorship of the proletariat was abolished. "The dictatorship of commissars over an almost rightless peasantry" should be replaced by "a *division of power* between the proletariat and the peasantry."

When the NEP was introduced, the Mensheviks decided that it was their urgent task to create the preconditions for agreement between the two classes. But they understood "agreement" more democratically, more realistically, and, from the Marxist point of view, more consistently than Lenin. They rejected the division of the rural population into poor, middle, and kulak peasants—the basis of Lenin's policy toward the peasantry—and believed that the peasants needed individual farming and a market economy rather than socialism. Accord between the "petty-bourgeois" peasantry and the "socialist" proletariat seemed imperative and possible at this stage of the revolution: having received land, the peasants were vitally interested in keeping the "conquests of the revolution" and would be willing to submit to the guidance of the more advanced and organized proletariat. Unlike Lenin, the Mensheviks stressed the workers' "guidance," not "hegemony," in this alliance. Soviet policy threatened to turn the peasants against the revolution. *SV* remarked that at present "the peasantry automatically 'generates' SRs. This is not only a 'chemical law' but also a very lucky circumstance for the Russian proletariat"—but in time the peasantry might begin to generate conservatives as in some other countries. [11] Therefore the Mensheviks demanded abolition of the surplus-appropriation system and antiprofiteering squads, an open market for agricultural produce, and civic rights for the peasants to enable them to defend their interests.

At the Eighth Congress of Soviets in December 1920—the last before the NEP—the Mensheviks had again demanded the economic reforms they had been seeking throughout the period of War communism, and Lenin had again rejected them. After Kronstadt, he incorporated some of them in the New Economic Policy. In practice, however, the NEP had little in common with the Menshevik proposals. The changeover from War communism had been forced and insincere, some local authorities sabotaged it, and progress was slow. Faced with discontent in his own party, Lenin made contradictory announcements: the NEP had been introduced "in all seriousness and for a long time"; the NEP was nearing its end. Gradually the Mensheviks came to see that the NEP, though an improvement over War communism, was "half-hearted, timorous, and insufficient," not a radical renunciation of utopia and state control, and of little value without political reform. Martov thought Lenin's policy "purely Zubatovite: economic concessions while retaining political dictatorship."[12] And *SV* wrote that under the old political system the NEP was "a lifeless thing."

The absence of workers' organizations and the people's lack of rights, especially that of free speech, were more intolerable than ever now that the bourgeoisie was bound to grow. Besides the industrial bourgeoisie, whose growth the Mensheviks considered necessary, a new one of black market operators was beginning to flourish—potential supporters of "Bonapartism" and "Thermidor." These terms constantly figured in Menshevik speech. The French and the Russian revolutions were both considered "bourgeois" and therefore much alike—as if the nineteenth century had not intervened between them and their causes and development had not been totally different. "Bonapartism," it was felt, could also come from the Soviet military and civil bureaucracy if it managed to seize power and become a supra-class government thanks to the citizens' lack of rights.

To balance the bourgeoisie, the trade union movement had to be revived. The trade union crisis, which even the Communists did not deny, appeared to the Mensheviks as "the inevitable result of the policy of party dictatorship, of excluding all parties except the Communist from the movement's leading organs, the policy of obligatory membership, extraneous tasks, demolition of unions, and terrorist management of the economy."

The RSDRP rejected all the remedies proposed by various Communist party groups during the "trade union debates" of 1921: Trotsky's plan of "militarized labor" was an attempt of Communist bureaucracy to save itself by virtually abolishing trade unions. "It radically denies that defending the workers' interests is one of the functions of trade unions today." Not much better was the position of the more moderate Lenin-Tomskii group: ready to grant purely verbal concessions, it represented the "halfhearted, irresolute, most conservative and quite ineffectual" trend that was mainly responsible for the trade unions' collapse. Finally, the Workers' Opposition was wavering between equal rights for all workers or only for Communists, and its economic notions were viewed as even more utopian than anyone else's. In view of all this, the RSDRP must maintain its old stand on the independence of trade unions: "We strongly warn our comrades against unconditionally supporting any of the Communist factions in the present struggle [in trade unions]."[13]

The Central Committee's theses, accepted by the Party conference of August 1921,[14] blamed the economic debacle on the ruling party's policy as well as the war and the blockade: "The political bankruptcy of bolshevism is especially clear from the fact that, while having seen the need for a sharp turn in economic policies in the direction long advocated by social democracy, the Communist party ... has proven unable to satisfy the essential social demands of the popular masses." Moreover, the regime was not cut out to encourage foreign or Russian investments in industry; Soviet officialdom was corrupt; farsighted bourgeois groups (for example, Miliukov's) were already harboring new ambitions, trying to get closer to the peasantry through alliances with populist groups (Avksent'ev's and others) that had forsaken socialism. "To this end they feature the motto of the Constituent Assembly, which under present conditions is a cover for bourgeois counterrevolution." The RSDRP must endeavor to change the situation through

a) democratization of the present regime by replacing party dictatorship and terror with a regime of workers' democracy based on a solid alliance of the proletariat and the peasantry; and b) reorganization of the government on the principle of agreement among all socialist parties that reject coalition with the bourgeoisie and are prepared to defend the conquests of the revolution.

Since the Party majority accepted as necessary the elements of capitalism contained in the NEP, a rapprochement between it and the right wing became possible. [15] The remaining disagreements concerned mainly the democratization of the regime. The right rejected the principle of "toilers' rule," wanted the Party to promote the "old truth" of parliamentary democracy, and considered the methods by which democratic freedom was to be attained a matter of tactics, not principle. [16]

10

The Party's Activities in Russia

Organization

When the political émigrés returned to Russia after the revolution, their days of exile seemed to be over for good. Barely four years later, however, a new exodus of Menshevik leaders began. This, and the conditions in Soviet Russia, made it necessary to reorganize the Party and to set up two centers, one in Russia and one abroad.

Martov arrived in Berlin in late September 1920 and Abramovich in early November. The People's Commissariat of Foreign Affairs had granted them visas on the order of the Central Committee of the Communist party—a liberal gesture calculated to make a good impression abroad: the Bolsheviks were preparing for their appearance at the congress of the German Independents. As Martov remarked, they felt the need to wash up so as to look respectable to the West.

Together with Eva Broido (another member of the CC) and David Dallin, who arrived a little later, Martov and Abramovich formed in Berlin the Delegation of the RSDRP Abroad. On 1 February 1921 they began publication of its organ, *Sotsialisticheskii Vestnik*. In January 1922 several other Menshevik leaders were permitted to leave Russia (after a hunger strike in prison), among them the CC members F. Dan, B. Nicolaevsky, and I. Iudin. (They were given a week to get ready, and the time was used to convoke the last plenum of the CC in Moscow. More about this below.) In Berlin they became members of the delegation abroad, and Dan also one of the editors of *SV*. Soon the CC member A. Iugov joined the delegation. Other Menshevik leaders were co-opted later—G. Aronson in 1922, B. Dvinov in 1923, M. Kefali in 1924, and S. Schwarz in 1926.

Meanwhile, repressions forced a reorganization of the Party center in Russia. Since no all-Russian congress could be convoked, the CC, though replenished by co-optation, had not been reelected since 1917. It kept in touch with its provincial organizations mainly through letters transmitted by hand when opportunity offered. Sometimes a member of the CC toured the committees, or the latter sent someone to Moscow for information and instructions. Local committees used to be elected at general meetings of Party members. When these became impossible, some cities introduced two-stage elections; others chose their commit- tees upon agreement among the local Party factions. The names of committee members were not divulged even to Party members. Arrests kept the composition of the committees fluid. Most organizations maintained Red Cross groups to help the imprisoned and deported. The Social-Democratic Bund, which had its own Central Committee and local committees, was part of the RSDRP. One member of its CC was also a member of the CC of the RSDRP. The two organizations worked well together, without serious friction. [1]

After the arrests of early 1921, only four members of the Menshevik CC remained at large (Rubin, Iugov, Troianovskii, and Iudin). To help them, four advisors were invited to the meetings of the CC from March on (V. Groman, B. Dvinov, S. Kats, and A. Malkin). Because of the abnormal situation, many Party members, especially in the main committee for the Ukraine, came to feel that the CC should be reor- ganized and its functions curtailed, even though this had disadvan- tages for a party claiming to be legal. Moscow and Berlin discussed the plan in letters. The CC members imprisoned in Butyrki (Dan, Ezhov, Nicolaevsky, and Pleskov) opposed it. On 12 August they wrote the CC that an authoritative center was more than ever necessary: Now that the Mensheviks' economic program had been accepted almost en- tirely, the Party must work for political reforms, or the NEP would develop "not a socialist but a rapacious bourgeois character."

We would be neglecting our duty if we did not impress upon the working masses, especially on [their] socialist elements, to whichever party they may belong, that the conditions we have indicated must be fulfilled *as soon as possible*—in the first place, *honest* agreement among all socialist parties.... No matter how much we have been weakened lately, we all think that given full consciousness of the task's importance and the necessary energy, it will be possible in

Moscow, Petrograd, and a few other places to gather and consolidate around the CC the needed forces and material and technical means [i.e., people, funds, and printing facilities].

In a situation on the whole so favorable for the RSDRP, the CC should step up its work, not curtail it.

Outside the prison walls, this optimism was not shared. Martov wrote to Moscow in August that instead of the CC, whose status and composition were abnormal, a bureau of the CC should be created in Russia to fulfill technical rather than political functions. The majority of the CC approved this plan, with one amendment: a bureau not instead of, but in addition to the CC, whose abolition would have a demoralizing effect. The delegation abroad did not object, and a bureau was set up, but the CC remained the top organ. (Soon, however, the bureau became not only the organizational but also the de facto political center in Russia.)[2] These changes in the Party constitution were approved by the Party conference of August 1921 in Moscow.

It was a major blow for the Party when two members of its Central Committee, Troianovskii and Ermanskii, defected in the spring of 1921. Troianovskii, an ex-Bolshevik, had been a member of the right and critical of the CC's line as too soft toward the Communists. His decision was a complete surprise. Yet only a month later he was making important speeches on behalf of the Communists. Eventually he became ambassador to England. Ermanskii had stood on the extreme left of the Party, but his defection, too, was unexpected. Soon he was given a professorial appointment, and in time he became a member of the Communist Academy.

In October 1922 the delegation abroad, apparently in agreement with the bureau, ratified the new constitution: 1) the CC would consist of the bureau and the delegation abroad; 2) in addition to its present members, the delegation would include any member of the CC who emigrated with the CC's consent, but it could not increase its membership in any other way; 3) the bureau of the CC would be confirmed by the CC and replenished through co-optation in agreement with the delegation abroad.[3] Thus the overall leadership would be in the hands of the CC, which would consist of two coequal parts, the bureau of the CC in Moscow and the Delegation of the RSDRP Abroad. Important decisions published over the CC's signature would require the sanction of both. Lesser questions could be settled by either of them alone.

The bureau and the delegation corresponded in code. For instance,

"Mira met Irene at Nadia's" meant that Liber had conferred with Petrenko (a Rostov Menshevik) in Petrograd. Their conspiratorial skills having become somewhat rusty, the writers occasionally blundered.

The two centers usually agreed on important matters, but certain lesser ones irritated the bureau—for instance, the departures of Party leaders, which local organizations resented. The problem was discussed at the last plenum of the CC just before Dan and others left Russia in January 1922. Each case was considered separately. In the end, permission to leave was granted all who had asked for it (and only two, Cherevanin and Ezhov, did not make use of it), but during the debates their "flight" or "escape" (*begstvo*) was severely criticized. Later, when more Party members had left, the bureau passed a resolution on the need to check the wave of departures.[4] The "departants" themselves took the lighter view that they were leaving for a year or two, no more. All had done long stretches in prison; for some, foreign visas were alternatives to "deportation" within Russia.

Points of prestige were another source of trouble. With the top leaders gone, the bureau consisted of second-rankers not at all inclined, however, to play second fiddle to the delegation abroad: it was they who lived in constant danger and carried on the work. On 9 June 1921 the bureau asked the delegation, "Hasn't your perspective become warped?" Later the bickering increased. The bureau accused the émigrés of "self-conceit": they imagined it was their mission to save the party's reserves by sitting abroad—an attitude that people working in Russia regarded as a sign of weakness. "We find these overtones in your attitude extremely unpleasant. They indicate a great psychological estrangement from us."[5] The bureau was sensitive to the delegation's apparent unwillingness to treat it as a political equal and to trust its judgment. "We carried on an intensive correspondence with the delegation abroad. Its answers did not satisfy us. We felt all the time that there was no real *correspondence*, no exchange of opinions."[6]

In Russia, as I have mentioned, the NEP led to a rapprochement between the Party majority and the right (the extreme left was negligible), but abroad the factional struggles did not abate. The delegation did not approve when the Party conference of October 1922, which confirmed the composition of the bureau, decided to add to it a representative of the right. It should be noted that even in Russia some dissent remained, in particualr over the rightists' ideological closeness to the extraparty Mensheviks, with whom the majority did not want to have any dealings. However, with the majority's shift to the right, factional conflict had become less acute and there was a political and psychological basis for collaboration. Besides, the local organizations were eager to consolidate their remaining forces. The decision to include in the bureau a representative of the right proved to be a good one. Joint work tended to smooth out dissent. [7]

The bureau delegated Kuchin and Rubin to negotiate with the right, represented by Liber, Bogdanov, and Buksin. The main purpose of the talks was to clarify the positions of the right. The bureau stressed that there were to be no organized separate factions within the party. It welcomed "live initiative aimed at ideological and organizational unity." If the comrades of the right agreed, it would nominate one of them for membership in the bureau and advise the delegation abroad of his candidacy. And it reiterated the need for free expression of ideas within the Party but also for *"obligatory concerted action along the party line."* [8]

Liber, the chief spokesman for the right, had left the Party in 1918 in disagreement with some of its policies but had been readmitted, at his own request, in May 1922, despite remaining differences. During the talks he defended the standpoint of the right but declared his willingness to work loyally with the majority. As before, the rightists did not believe in a democratic evolution of the regime. For them, a democratic republic was not a topic of theoretical discussion and propaganda but of immediate concern. They were against a common front with the Comintern, and consequently against the Vienna International, and admitted agreement with Western Communists only on specific practical issues. [9]

At first the rightists advanced big demands. Bogdanov suggested reorganizing the Central Committee: in his opinion, the right now constituted the majority of the Party. Liber wanted reunification with the extraparty right. The bureau rejected these demands, but the rightists did obtain recognition as a distinct ideological group, and an agreement was reached. Local organizations welcomed it, but the first meetings of the bureau in which the opposition was represented were far from harmonious. "There was much wrangling, altercation, mutual criticism, but on the whole the new organizational policy paid off. It brought a number of active, responsible forces into party work. This can be stated with certainty." [10] The bureau had defined the basic principles of agreement (applicable to the left wing as well): distinct ideological groups were allowed within the Party, but not formally organized factions; if a member of such a group was elected to a Party organ, his status was the same as everyone else's: he was not to represent a faction but only an ideological trend. [11]

The agreement had to be endorsed by the delegation abroad—and the delegation did not like it, especially Leber's inclusion in the CC. A long correspondence followed. In December Abramovich and Aronson voted to accept Liber, but first to question the bureau on the current stand of the right in Russia; the other members of the delegation were opposed to the whole idea. The bureau replied in a letter signed by all its members that rejecting Liber would be "extremely harmful to the cause." In February the delegation decided that the right's membership in the CC was desirable, on condition of adherence to the party line; in March it finally approved Liber's inclusion, by five votes to four. The bureau wrote that the delegation's handling of the matter was "entirely out of tune with the present atmosphere in the Party" and was "reviving old complications" and hampering agreement. [12]

By this time all but a handful of Mensheviks were in jail or in exile. The bureau of the CC nevertheless drew up new rules for local organizations and "top secret" rules for "sympathizing groups." [13] Having become practically illegal, the Party should concentrate on issuing leaflets "summing up Soviet policy in all areas, baring the substance of existing political conditions, and formulating the present tasks of the proletariat." These leaflets should be aimed mainly at factory workers but also at "Soviet employees" with their cultural, psychological, and environmental peculiarities. The peasantry and other groups were not mentioned. Circles should study the Social-Democratic program and tactics and pay special attention "at this critical time" to ideological problems. The rules for sympathizing groups stated that any sympathizer recommended by a Party member could enroll in them. Every member must "strictly conform to underground rules" and render "minor services." Participation in "fighting work" (organizing escapes, printing, pasting up appeals, and so on) was optional.

Political Work

During the dreadful famine that hit Russia in the spring of 1921, millions died of starvation, cases of cannibalism were officially recorded, and there was no hope of relief until the next harvest, months away. In June and July the Central Committee of the RSDRP asked Western labor organizations to help the starving population; on 5 August a similar appeal was broadcast from Moscow in the name of the CC. The Delegation of the RSDRP Abroad appealed to the Vienna and Amsterdam Internationals, which relayed the requests to their member organizations. Its attempt to form an international relief committee fell through because of disagreements among the socialist parties. In Russia, the RSDRP encouraged workers' self-help committees attached to trade unions, cooperatives, and so forth, but it refused to join the All-Russian Civic Committee to Aid the Starving (*Vserossiiskii Obshchestvennyi Komitet Pomoshchi Golodaiushchim*) set up by Prokopovich, Kuskova, Kishkin, and other members of the radical (but non-Communist) intelligentsia on the grounds that the committee had been formed without the participation of broad democratic circles and depended on the government's sponsorship. [14]

The Petrograd Committee's leaflet of 7 March 1921, printed in SV (no. 5), blamed the famine not on agents of the Entente and White generals, as the Communists did, but on the government's treatment of peasants as class enemies. "What is needed is not a policy of coercion but a policy of reconciliation with the peasantry."

The trial of the SRs inspired another Menshevik campaign. In February 1922, forty-seven SRs, including prominent leaders, were arrested and accused of being agents of the Entente, plotting to assassinate Soviet officials, and so on. This first major political trial in Soviet Russia began in June and lasted about two months. The nature of the indictment, the uproar in the Soviet press, and the presence among the accused of two obvious agents of the GPU left no doubt that death sentences were to be expected. The Mensheviks conducted their campaign by every means open to them in Russia and abroad but avoided anything that might be construed as endorsement of SR policies. They denounced the trial as an illegal way of getting rid of the opposition, an instance of the terror that was killing the revolution. On 18 March the CC declared in a leaflet that the trial was an attempt to legalize terror.

The SRs asked the CC of the RSDRP to have its representatives appear as defense witnesses at the trial. Ber and Pleskov, for the Menshevik left, demanded that the RSDRP dissociate itself politically from the SRs. The right demanded an unqualified defense, holding that a common cause was involved, and threatened to appear at the trial even without the CC's permission. After sharp debates, the bureau of the CC decided to take part in the defense without concealing its differences with the accused. Three defense witnesses were chosen: S. Weinstein from the right, I. Rubin from the center, and B. Ber from the left. As a concession to the left, a statement was sent to *Pravda* and *Izvestiia*—which, however, did not print it but gave it to the GPU. The CC notified the military tribunal of its wish to take part in the trial. Permission was refused on the grounds that the occasion would be used for counterrevolutionary propaganda. The CC protested in a second note to the tribunal, on 1 June. [15]

A mass demonstration to demand death sentences for the accused was scheduled in Moscow for 20 June. Two days before the demonstration, the CC appealed to the workers not to take part in it: "You are being asked to demonstrate under mottoes unheard-of in the history of the labor movement, monstrously disgracing the cause of socialism." [16]

When the Western socialists E. Vandervelde, T. Liebknecht, and K. Rosenfeld arrived in Moscow to appear as defense witnesses, the CC gave them a memorandum on the true state of affairs, which it also distributed among workers. Altogether the CC put out seven leaflets about the trial of the SRs. [17]

Like the bureau of the CC, the delegation abroad did not wish to give an impression of political solidarity with the PSR—the profound disagreements of the past four years were not settled. Yet it was important to register a strong protest against the trial and the methods employed. SV and the representatives of the RSDRP in the International began a concerted campaign. The stress they laid on their disagreements with the SRs lent all the more weight to their protest. SV printed reports from Moscow about the trial and a series of articles on the true sense of the indictments. Martov burned to go to Moscow himself to defend the accused. [18] On 14 March the delegation sent telegrams to the executive committees of the Second and the Vienna Internationals, which read, in part: "By bringing up long forgotten episodes of the civil war, the Bolsheviks wish to launch a new wave of terror. There will be new executions. We demand the most energetic immediate intervention by all international organizations and affiliated parties, to prevent the crime that is being prepared." On 12 June, the Delegations Abroad of the RSDRP, the Bund, the PSR, and the Left SRs appealed to the "socialist parties and labor organizations" of the West to support the accused.

When representatives of the three Internationals had met in Berlin in April to discuss the "common front," the Comintern delegates had promised that the trial of the SRs would be open to the public, that there would be no death sentences, and that the accused would be allowed to select their defenders. The Soviet government broke these promises. The foreign socialists who had come to Russia to defend the accused were treated so badly that they left in the middle of the trial. Fourteen of the accused were given conditional death sentences—not to be carried out if the PSR refrained from "counterrevolutionary activities." The Menshevik Central Committee on 9 August issued a leaflet protesting against the concept of "hostages" that the verdict introduced into Soviet legal practice.

The conditions of the first years of the NEP tended to isolate the Menshevik party more and more. All its attempts to "penetrate the masses" were thwarted and its contacts with the workers were dwindling.

There was no way to escape the Communist cell's espionage and its dictatorial power in the factories. If at some factory there still remained a compact group of opposition-minded workers (S-Ds or sympathizers), and this group managed to elect a factory committee or a deputy to the Soviet, the Bolsheviks stopped at nothing to destroy it. A new, Communist factory director was appointed, Communist agitators were brought in.... Workers were not issued enough food and pay, production wasn't increased; it was promised that ... conditions would improve when there was a Communist factory committee or deputy.[19]

The Party had almost no means of support. It lacked funds even for such basic needs as maintaining a small salaried staff, printing leaflets, assisting imprisoned comrades. In late 1921 the Petrograd Committee still had some bonds with the workers and occasionally issued leaflets. Unlike the Moscow Committee, it was dominated by the right. Despite arrests, party work somewhat revived in Moscow toward the end of 1921. It was decided to elect a new Moscow committee and to bring Party membership rolls up to date. (Three hundred registered.[20]) These last elections to the MC took place secretly, at small gatherings in factory neighborhoods, at which the first reporter presented the views of the Central Committee and the second those of the right. Usually the majority agreed with the CC.

Livelier work was going on in the Ukraine. In late 1921 the main committee for the Ukraine drew up theses on the trade union movement, cooperatives, and the common front. On the first two, there was no dissent; and on the resolution favoring a common front only three members disagreed. The committee kept in touch with twelve local organizations. Kiev was backsliding. In Poltava and Kremenchug the Mensheviks refused to participate in elections to Soviets. In Kharkov a few issues of a newspaper, *Sotsialdemokrat*, printed on a hand press, came out; in the balloting on the common front resolution, fifty-one votes were cast for the CC's line and fifty for the opposition's, and the local committee was made up in the ratio of five to four. There were old Mensheviks among the skilled workers of Kharkov, and their enterprising spirit contrasted with the masses' apathy. In September 1921 the main committee protested in a circular against the idea of reducing the Party's activity, which was favored by many in Kiev, Odessa, Ekaterinoslav, and other cities, even in Moscow, though nowhere by the majority. The delegation abroad heard from Moscow in early 1922 that there was no "broad activity" in the Ukrainian organization, that it had largely gone underground, but was "inwardly strong."[21] During that year, new Party organizations were formed in Berdichev, Belaia Tserkov, Kremenchug, and Rostov, with considerable help from the youth league (*Soiuz Molodezhi*).[22]

Despite the complications that beset the Party during its retreat to the underground, the CC in Moscow ranged beyond organizational matters. According to B. Dvinov, in February and March 1922 it discussed the following topics: the character of *SV*; Menshevik speeches abroad; the activity of the committee of the Constituent Assembly in Paris; the Russian question at the Genoa conference; how Mensheviks should behave when questioned by the GPU; the common front; the Party platform; various matters connected with trade unions; and the Soviet government's foreign policy.

SV helped to keep local organizations alive. Its distribution was so well managed that it reached them almost regularly and not a single shipment was seized. The number of copies increased from fifty to eight hundred by the end of 1922. During the winter of 1921–22, *SV* was sent out from Moscow to seventeen cities and the Far Eastern Republic. The demand for it always exceeded the supply. [23]

The printed word was the only remaining means of "penetrating the masses." In the absence of printing presses, money, and personnel, periodicals were out of the question, but leaflets and bulletins did appear. The CC wrote:

> At present the Party's central task is the organization of a Party press. In this period of cruel crisis, when the results of the Russian revolution are becoming apparent, when the urge for self-defense is tempestuously growing in the working class, and its mood is one of disappointment, questioning, searching for a way out—today is the time for the Social-Democratic word to be spread among the workers as widely as possible, providing clear and fruitful material for their political and class consciousness. [24]

The last legal Menshevik paper had been closed in 1919. In 1921 illegal leaflets began to appear frequently. In Moscow, for instance, printed or hectographed leaflets discussing the Genoa conference, the famine, the common front, repressions against the RSDRP, hunger strikes in prisons, the trial of the SRs. The Petrograd Committee put out three leaflets during October and November 1921: on reelections to the Soviet, the Communists' "victory" in them, and the fourth anniversary of the October Revolution.

G. Kuchin's report to the delegation abroad summarized the results of Party work for 1922–23 as follows: 1)Nonpartisans and even some Communists, especially young people, were displaying interest in the RSDRP, but there was no way to organize them. 2) Great psychological changes had taken place in the Party. There was more enterprise and devotion, especially among young members; the more the situation deteriorated, the stronger these feelings became. New members, including students, had joined the Party. 3) The Party organizations were going underground. They maintained contact with the points of distribution of illegal literature.

Legality or the Underground?

There were now two main reasons for the persecution of Mensheviks. First, a socialist, democratic opposition could be especially dangerous once the primitive notions of instant socialism and world revolution had been abandoned in favor of NEP capitalism. Lenin said that "petty-bourgeois counterrevolution" (the Mensheviks were included under this term) was now more of a danger than Denikin. Second, an organized opposition was intolerable to a regime already developing totalitarian traits. Repression was the means of destroying the Mensheviks politically and bodily. Lenin declared that "for public profession of menshevism our courts must order execution, otherwise they will not be our courts but heaven knows what." [25]

The Mensheviks found themselves in a strange situation. Early in the NEP period, some were still in local Soviets while others were in prison. The Party was "legal," but nothing could be legally printed; public appearances at meetings and work in trade unions were virtually impossible; an outsider could land in jail for contact with Mensheviks known to the police. Administrative exile for "political criminals" was reintroduced.

Although the Party could not work openly, the retreat to the underground was slow, mainly because of its implications. Vis-à-vis the regime, the RSDRP was "reformist" and as such committed to keep its activity legal. Once it went underground, it would be a more radical, not to say a revolutionary, party. The right did not object to this, but the majority and the leaders were unready for it. In 1917 they had come out of the tsarist underground as victors. They had become used to open activity and were reluctant to give it up. Many were somewhat dispirited by defeats and persecution. There was a general feeling that in the twenty-five years of its existence the Party had never been in worse straits. Only the basic cadres and the young displayed initiative, at times even optimism: "This cannot last long."

The CC wrote local organizations in late 1921 that the capitalist tendencies of the NEP, the weakening of the proletariat, and the proscription of workers' organizations could end in destroying the revolution. Therefore, "the party that has gone through so much persecution and survived in the struggle of the past four years of incredible terror must at this time of transition, on the eve, perhaps, of decisive events, use every means to consolidate and strengthen its apparatus." The prospect of "decisive events" made legality doubly desirable. The Party must be preserved for better days. The CC emphasized that the RSDRP was still a party of the masses, not a secret circle. [26]

But by 1922 the Party remained visible, "aboveground," only in

Moscow. Elsewhere it was virtually in hiding, especially in Petrograd and the Ukraine. Local organizations pressured the CC for permission to abandon legality. Moscow wrote the delegation abroad: "Our situation is becoming absolutely unbearable. No matter how great one's self-control, sometimes it seems that the only way is to pick up a red flag and go out into the streets." The main committee for the Ukraine suggested creating a "passport bureau" and other appurtenances of conspiratorial organizations. But in the CC only Drabkin favored illegality. The extreme leftist Pleskov (he soon left the Party) insisted on conforming to every rule of strict legality. [27]

Principle and realities were growing farther and farther apart. A compromise was found: the Party remained formally legal but its apparatus "went illegal." The problem sharpened when the GPU on 3 July 1922 raided a meeting of the bureau of the CC. (Its members escaped arrest thanks to the raiders' stupidity.) The bureau still insisted on preserving the Party's legal status. In August it sent local organizations another letter to this effect, and the Moscow committee expelled members who had denied their membership in the RSDRP when questioned by the GPU. This point was repeatedly discussed in the CC. On 23 February 1922 the CC resolved that Party members interrogated by the GPU must admit their membership but answer other questions only in court. [28]

The Party conference of October 1922 confirmed the principle of legality, but with a substantial qualification: "It is suggested to all local organizations that they conceal their major branches of work and their active forces [that is, the names of their active members] but hold on to the old principle ... of struggling for the right of the working class to open opposition." [29]

By the end of 1922, not only the apparatus but the whole Party, or what remained of it outside prisons, had gone underground. This clarified the situation, reduced personal risk, and made for increased activity. The bureau wrote the delegation abroad:

A crisis in party work is definitely at hand. There is nowhere to turn. In many places, organization members are completely exposed, as if under a bell jar, and the main forces are long since in exile. The famine that has hit the cities of the southern Ukraine is creating a climate of death in which all aspirations wilt. In many places there is no way of getting into factories (this isn't the tsarist regime for you!). . . . This process is bound to continue, and under prolonged terror the organizations [are bound] to fall apart. [30]

The bureau of the CC came to see the need for conspiratorial methods—for instance, that leaders should be selected, not elected;

that liaison between local groups and the center should be maintained through individual secret contacts, not "representatives"; that local organizations must be given greater autonomy along with their greater responsibilities; that the best way to build Party organizations was to have many small cells grouped around individuals. [31]

The stand on Soviets also was determined by considerations of legality. The more activity was restricted, the more important it seemed to figure in Soviets and especially in elections to them—the only area in which the Party could still work legally. In April 1921 eighteen Mensheviks were elected to the Moscow Soviet as against forty-five in the previous election. The CC protested to the Executive Committee of the Soviet against artificial methods influencing elections:

> Reelections are scheduled when over one hundred members of the RSDRP, arrested without any charges against them, are kept at Butyrki, Taganka, and Novinskii prisons and the Lubianka.... Thousands [of workers] will be unable to express their will freely by casting their votes for those whom they trust. [32]

With no hope of success, the Moscow committee nonetheless conducted an active campaign. Mensheviks spoke at meetings whenever possible. A leaflet urged voters to insist on free elections and civil rights. At the first meeting of the new Soviet the few elected Mensheviks spoke about terror, rigged elections, the food problem. Several hundred nonpartisans voted for their resolutions. At the meeting of 14 May, Menshevik members of the Soviet denounced the beating of political prisoners in Butyrki on 25 April and succeeded in getting an investigation commission appointed. But since the commission consisted entirely of Bolsheviks (nonpartisan deputies had asked to be represented but had been turned down), it brought no results. On 31 May, B. Dvinov, representing the RSDRP in the Soviet, offered a proposal that immunity for deputies be guaranteed. The nonpartisans seconded this motion and it was passed—but it was in fact annulled by the Communists' amendment that a deputy could be arrested with the sanction of the Presidium rather than that of the Soviet as a whole. [33]

In the provinces things were no better. When reelections were due, the GPU often arrested all Mensheviks known to it. At electoral meetings Menshevik candidates and all who voted for them were threatened; the tallies were tampered with; and local Soviets sometimes expelled Mensheviks. Still, the Mensheviks scored a few relative successes. Twenty-four were elected in Odessa in May 1921—but twelve of them were disqualified and two were already in prison. In Kharkov in the fall of 1921 the Mensheviks issued a leaflet demanding free elections and a more democratic regime. On the eve of election day three hundred searches and one hundred and twenty arrests were made. Not one Menshevik was elected.

More and more Party members came to doubt the usefulness of participating in such elections and such Soviets. Yet a letter of the CC in late 1921 still urged Party organizations to take part in them wherever possible since the RSDRP remained "a broad mass party of the working class." Also, "by all means, work in trade unions, cooperatives, workers' committees for famine relief, in all proletarian organizations. Special attention should be paid to young people."[34]

The CC considered nonparticipation in January 1922, on the eve of elections to the Moscow Soviet. Advocates of boycott pointed out that reelections produced no results and led to more arrests; and the Mensheviks' presence gave the illusion of free elections, which enabled the Bolsheviks to claim "victory." However, the majority of the CC wanted to preserve every form of legal activity. The Party did participate in the elections and got five deputies elected. These were the last elections to a Soviet in which it took part.

The mood changed as the pointlessness of persisting became more obvious. Yet the Party gave in reluctantly, for there was a general feeling, especially among second-rank leaders, that a change in the regime was imminent and the Party must hold on to its rights. The CC decided on boycott only in the summer of 1922—explaining that this was a protest against terror, not against the Soviets as a political institution:

> Everywhere the last legal opportunities have been destroyed. The deterioration of Soviets has reached its limit . . . . Nonparticipation in elections is the obvious form [of protest]. Many localities report that comrades have lately been suggesting this themselves. Under existing conditions, nonparticipation has the advantages of being a clear protest and of sharply exposing the specific nature of the elections— there is no trace of glossing-over. Of course, a tactic of active boycott would contradict our tactical and political stand vis-à-vis the regime. Therefore the bureau of the CC is not putting forward the motto of "scuttling" the elections, or any motto based on unleashing the movement.[35]

A leaflet explained to the workers that they were helpless against the reviving capitalism of the NEP and that elections to Soviets were "a pitiful farce." "The specters of prison, exile, loss of job stand at the gates of electoral meetings." The Party advised the workers, "Do not give your votes to Communist candidates. Let them be elected by the votes of Communist cells."[36]

The delegation abroad approved the bureau's decision.[37] A part of the right had been against participation in Soviets since 1918. This had also been the invariable stand of *Zaria* (Potresov's group), which had accused the Mensheviks of inconsistency during the years they were taking part in elections while regarding them as a farce—especially as the Soviets were not legislative organs but organs of government, and their members represented the regime, not the people.[38]

The Youth League

The Social-Democratic Youth League had grown from a group of a few young people formed in Moscow in May 1920. Its spirited opposition to communism caused some concern to the mother party, bent as it was on maintaining legality. The league established contacts in factories and organized informal discussions. In August 1920 it was broken up by the Cheka, but within six months it was active again. At the time it was still possible to speak occasionally at youth meetings, and the league sharply debated with the Komsomol. Nonpartisans often responded to its speakers, but it was difficult to get the floor, and sometimes league speakers were beaten up and expelled from meetings. They were most successful in the strongly Menshevik printers' union.

In the fall of 1920, locals of the youth league opened in several major cities. Communication with the center in Moscow was difficult. In December the Moscow organization adopted a statute making the league an autonomous organization that merely accepted the RSDRP program. By and large, the league followed the Party's guidance, suffered the same repressions, and supported *SV*. Its members discussed political, economic, and literary topics in educational circles. Outside activities included organizing circles for young workers and *intelligenty* in factory neighborhoods. Many leaders were arrested in 1921, but this did not kill the league. Released toward the end of the year, they resumed work and created new organizations in Kharkov, Kiev, and Odessa. The league published hectographed leaflets and some short-lived periodicals: in Moscow, *Iunyi Proletarii* in December 1920 and three issues of a bulletin in 1921; in Kiev, *Molodoe Delo* in 1923; in Odessa, eight issues of a bulletin in 1921–22; in Petrograd, *Klich Molodezhi;* in Kharkov, *Iunyi Sotsialdemokrat* in 1922;[39] and others.

The end of 1921 was a period of lively activity. In Moscow the league took part in elections to a nonpartisan printers' conference, at which it formed a faction of twelve members and offered a resolution that polled about one-quarter of the vote. The influx of new members was cut short by arrests. The league published leaflets on the terror, the Komsomol, and so on. On 1 May, following the custom of tsarist times, it organized an out-of-town celebration. By summer it had to go underground. During the two years that the league's Moscow organization was active, thirty-three of its members had been arrested a total of fifty-two times and had spent the equivalent of thirteen years in prisons. [40]

In the fall of 1922 a group of escaped deportees organized in Kiev a Central Organizational Bureau to conduct the affairs of the league. While nominally a separate organization dedicated to youth, the league was to all practical purposes a part of the RSDRP. Many of its young members were already veterans of the underground. People matured quickly under those conditions. In some ways they resembled the young Social-Democrats of the Party's first years. The Party apparatus, which did all the work and ran all the attendant risks, included a good many league members, some of whom rose to prominence in the Party. Thus, the secretary of the Central Organizational Bureau, A. Kranikhfeld, was attached to the bureau of the CC; in 1922, L. Lande became secretary of the main committee for the Ukraine; B. Sapir was one of the leaders in the Kharkov organization of the Party. However, the Party did not escape the "fathers and sons" problem. The older generation, while giving its due to the idealism of the young, found them too expansive and radical:

> Youth groups in effect took over the Party work in many places. Here and there, conflicts with grown-ups arose. The youths were impulsive and not inclined to observe secrecy. But they brought much animation into the work....All these youths displayed an astounding penchant for the outward forms of broad organizational sweep: more groups, more publications.... All had a terrific drive. At the same time they all struck us as "brain people," with a tendency toward all sorts of revisionism.... Among themselves, they argued to the point of madness. [41]

The youth league consisted largely of *intelligenty*, with a strong admixture of skilled workers, mainly printers. Like the Party, it viewed "penetrating the masses" as its main goal, tried to establish links with workers, and succeeded to some degree, especially in the Ukraine. Apart from intervals due to arrests, the league continued its activity through 1923.

11

The Evolution of Ideology

The Need for Reorientation

Barely a year after the "April theses" of 1920, the Mensheviks began to feel the need to revise their platform. Complex problems had arisen with the NEP and the "Thermidorian" mutation of bolshevism. Should the Party remain "reformist" and legal? As we have seen, local organizations clamored for revision. The extreme left wanted the April theses confirmed, in the hope that this would force the rightist Mensheviks to accept them or else leave the Party. As Martov said, "centrifugal" tendencies had increased with the end of the civil war.[1] Moscow wanted Martov to return to Russia to take charge of the revision. Dan wrote him to this effect, but Martov thought it unwise to announce firm principles in a transition period. Within the Party, however, debates on reorientation began. They lasted through 1922–23 and resulted in a new platform in 1924.

The focal issue was, of course, the attitude to be taken toward the Soviet regime. The Communist party was unquestionably turning into a state bureacracy less and less concerned with the workers' well-being. The Mensheviks' opposition had become more pronounced, as we have seen, when the defensive war with Poland had turned into aggressive war. The Minsk Mensheviks, whom the Party had "mobilized" into the Red army, had raised the question of "demobilizing" the Party. (The idea was abandoned because of the Red army's defeat and Wrangel's offensive.) [2] Dan had contrasted the Red army's enthusiasm in the civil war with its reluctance to fight aggressive wars: this was the most telling proof that "in all the civil wars of the Bolshevik period the Russian muzhik and he alone was the real victor." Martov had written that war "sustains not only Boshevik terror and the Bolsheviks' international prestige but also bolshevism itself as an unnatural economic system and an equally unnatural Asiatic system of government"—hence "Bolshevism is vitally interested in permanent war and instinctively shies away from . . . peace." [3]

But for all its criticism of "degenerating" bolshevism, the CC did not agree with the right that there was no hope of democratizing the regime and coming to terms with it. As we have seen, an exchange between Martov and Axelrod on this subject was published in *SV* in early 1921. [4] In his private correspondence with Axelrod, Martov further tried to clarify, and at least partly to minimize, their differences. He noted that Axelrod had criticized the Mensheviks for their estimate of the Bolshevik revolution, their rejection of uprisings, and their motto of legal struggle on the basis of the Soviet constitution. Yet on the subject of uprisings there was no basic disagreement: Martov himself rejected them because they were inexpedient, not as a matter of principle. "Of course we do not hold the sentimental view that uprisings against a government consisting of socialists and revolutionaries are always inadmissible" (although many members of the Party majority in fact held this view). But a considerable part of the population did support the Bolsheviks; and any unprising carried the danger of counterrevolution. On the Soviets, too, the differences were "not so great" since "for us, tactical considerations play the decisive role," not recognition of Soviets as the highest form of democracy. The motto of the Constituent Assembly should be temporarily dropped, for it had become thoroughly discredited in the eyes of the masses thanks to the activities of the SRs. The main difference was about the character of the Bolshevik revolution. He, Martov, considered it petty-bourgeois and anachronistic—the kind of revolution that belonged in the eighteenth century—but still historically progressive since it had radically destroyed the old order and cleared the way for further development. Its methods, however, were inadmissible. There was no inconsistency about holding a positive view of the revolution and opposing those who had distorted the revolution. [5]

In Russia, too, the Party felt the need to revise its program. The Central Committee discussed this in the summer of 1921 and decided to call an all-Russian Party conference. The agenda was ambitious: the CC's theses on the political and economic situation, on the International, and on trade unions; reports on the activity of the CC and the delegation abroad, on *SV*, and on organizational problems. The CC was already meeting secretly. Some of its members were in prison. The conference opened illegally in Moscow on 25 August 1921 and lasted only two days. Few people attended it: besides the incomplete CC, two delegates each from Moscow, Kiev, and Kharkov; one each from Petrograd, Minsk, and Kherson; and one from the Far Eastern Republic, where the Mensheviks were still represented in a coalition government with Communists.

The political theses of the conference were debated at length. As the CC wrote the delegation abroad, a "deviation to the right" was noticeable in the delegates' views (as compared with those of the CC); the compromise resolutions adopted by the conference caused some dissent in the CC itself. The extreme left, headed by Bèr, insisted on the old line: a government of all socialist parties, including the Communists. The right rejected any coalition with the Communists. Never settled since Vikzhel, this controversy had become more concrete: the left thought that it would suffice to democratize the Soviet regime to achieve a democratic order; the right argued that no such order could be established without first removing the antidemocratic Soviet government—only after that would the question of organizing a new government arise. The compromise resolution evaded the question of whether Russia was or was not going through a "transition period" to socialism. And instead of agreement between parties it spoke of agreement between classes—the peasantry and the proletariat—which no one opposed anyway.[6]

Dan has smuggled out from prison a set of his own theses. The strengthening of the bourgeoisie under the NEP, he stated, called for a strengthening of the proletariat. This could be achieved only through "freedom for the toiling classes," rather than freedom for all. Broad democracy could be introduced later, when the political situation had stabilized. Dan favored a government by all socialist parties and rejected as feeble and unclear the formula about agreement between classes, not parties. He refused even to pose the question of which should come first, a change of government or democratization: the two should be parallel and concurrent. Since conditions made it impossible to work with the masses, Dan suggested organizing for the time being only the upper crust of workers. Finally, he thought that counterrevolution had become a more serious threat since the inception of the NEP, and was strongly in favor of dropping the motto of the Constituent Assembly.[7] The conference rejected Dan's theses. Among the CC members still at large only Bèr sided with him. The majority agreed to minor amendments, for example about the threat of counterrevolution. Dan was not satisfied, but the CC accepted the amended resolution, and it was published in *SV*, no. 21.

Martov wrote the CC that he and Abramovich agreed with the resolution. In this way the Party learned that Martov and Dan diverged on the basic points of the platform—on democracy, the toilers' rule, a government of all socialist parties, and the Party as a mass organization. [8] These differences were to affect the revision of the Party program.

The Common Front and the Toilers' Rule

The dissent between the top leaders reflected the changing mood of the Party. The drift to the left that began in late 1918 had resulted in the theses of April 1920. Since then, a movement to the right had set in, in reaction to the government's ineptitude and terrorism. But the majority was still far from agreement with the extreme right; its retreat from the April theses took several years and, unlike the right, it considered that the "liberal" line had been correct under the different conditions of the past.

It was the majority that mainly worked on revising the platform. The right saw nothing in the social relations of the NEP period to warrant a change in its old stand, and the left did not consider the new developments important enough for a radical reorientation. Martov's shift to the right, already evident in his exchanges with Axelrod, became more pronounced. Other leaders of the center followed suit. In May 1921 David Dallin argued in *SV*, no. 8, in the article "Away with Illusions," that it was time to scrap the idea of an imminent social revolution—along with the conclusions that the Mensheviks and some Western socialists drew from it. Western capitalism had proven its ability to restore ruined economies. The temporary economic difficulties that arose were capitalist crises but not a "crisis of capitalism." The labor movement was weakened by apathy and division, largely thanks to the Communists. In Russia the idea that a social revolution was at hand played "a positive role, in a sense"—it had inspired the Red army during the civil war. "In Russia, this was a grand illusion . . . but in Western Europe this illusion can only do harm." One should forget about the "transition period to socialism," concentrate on democracy, "and along with criticizing capitalism, *defend . . . the democratic order against monarchist restoration, and at the same time struggle for a maximally full realization of democracy.*"

Dallin's article, challenging one of Martov's basic premises, provoked lively discussions. Martov replied in *SV*, no. 16, that capitalism might still be able to function, but could not surmount the postwar difficulties. In particular, it could not create social stability: the proletariat was too deprived, the decay of the middle classes had gone too far. Consequently, a "revolutionary situation" was indeed present and the era of social revolution opening. The proletariat's apathy should not be taken too seriously: the phenomonon had been observed before; it quite often preceded a revolution. In short, Martov held on to his concept of a transition period. But he now interpreted democracy more broadly than in the past, demanding civil rights not only for "toilers" but for all—including the well-off bourgeois and peasants. The dispute intensified during the latter half of 1922. Another prominent member of the majority, Cherevanin, wrote from a Russian prison:

> It seems to me the time has come to ruthlessly extirpate this point [a governmental coalition with the Communists] from our platform as not in the least consistent with the present situation. At present it puts us in a downright ludicrous, pathetic, humiliating position. Who is offering a common front to whom? A destroyed, crushed party, cut off from the working class by artificial means, unable at present to speak for the working class or any significant part of it, is offering this common front to the party that rules the country, is in command of it—all right, through coercion and not by the country's free choice, but even so, history has never seen a stranger spectacle. . . . Therefore, down with the common front . . . an irrelevant and inherently contradictory formula (a *socialist* front with *non-socialists*). [9]

But Cherevanin, too, put his hopes in "the evolution, not the forcible overthrow" of the regime, for uprisings were likely to end in the triumph of reaction. The same considerations led him to insist on keeping the Party legal.

A secret Party conference met in Moscow in October 1922. With great difficulty, a room had been found for the meetings and places for the provincial delegates to stay overnight. Raids were expected at any minute. *SV* commented: "It takes enormous reserves of enthusiasm, heroism, and spiritual fortitude not to lay down arms after five years of the revolution amid terrorist orgies and the NEP, which have turned so many [others] into corrupted, spiritually eviscerated renegades and cowards." *SV* (no. 21) published only the theses and resolutions of the conference and a short report on it from Moscow, but not the place, the date, or the participating organizations. There had been few delegates: one S-D each from Petrograd, Kharkov, Ekaterinoslav, Odessa, and the Far Eastern Republic, and two from Moscow; one

Bund member each from Moscow, Kharkov, and Gomel; and three representatives of the bureau of the CC—Kuchin, Rubin, and Drabkin (the members had drawn lots, and the rest did not attend in order not to risk having the entire bureau arrested). A representative of the right had been invited in an advisory capacity, "in view of the emerging tendencies toward rapprochement in the Party and the need to consolidate social democracy," but he was unable to appear. [10]

The conference had been carefully prepared. The bureau's agent I. Rashkovskii had toured local organizations to glean information and strengthen Party bonds. The bureau had drawn up theses on the issues to be discussed. It had been unanimous on internal policy, but on the question of the International Drabkin had spoken against the Vienna Union. The conference agreed with Drabkin but compromised in passing no resolution on the International and merely mentioning in a general resolution the need for contact between the Russian and the international movements.

The political theses adopted by the conference were based on the premise that "an antiproletarian psychology and a Bonapartist antidemocratic philosophy" were developing in the Communist party, which was "becoming more and more a contradictory conglomerate of different social forces." Hence coalition with it was untimely:

> A democratic "content" for the country's political life, the restoration to the popular masses, including the proletariat, of civil and political rights and free independent activity are the cardinal requirements of the moment; they remove the question of the form and composition of the government to a farther perspective.

Political freedom "is now being put forward as the central demand and is becoming objectively a proletarian motto"—but freedom could be won only through the masses' orderly pressure, not through haphazard uprisings.

Letters from Moscow to the delegation abroad praised the good morale in the half-stifled local organizations and at the conference itself. G. Kuchin, who was inclined to overoptimism but was well informed on what was going on in the Party, wrote the delegation:

> Comrades who had attended previous conferences said that there had never been such a fresh, enterprising spirit. . . . All had brought with them *a sense of change and of new prospects for the Party*. The debates on the political report [I was the reporter] were most meaningful. The theses were adopted unanimously. All were at one in realizing the impossibility of putting forward, as before, the slogan of socialist coalition. All (including all the members of the bureau of the CC) were at one on the need to concentrate Party activity on the

essential political relations in the country, that is, on a democratic regime and political freedom. In this respect the evolution in Party thinking was very apparent at the conference—the shift of position that at your end found expression in Iu. O.'s [Martov's] article.

This evolution in Party thinking was a movement away from some of the old illusions and toward greater insistence on democracy. Martov had set the example, but the conference went farther than he had done. As at the previous conference, provincial delegates stood farther to the right than the CC. Kuchin, just back from exile and full of energy, was made a member of the bureau of the CC and became its leader. He wrote: "There were no group, or factional, speeches; the old positions were mixed up. Some former proponents of the official stand displayed such impetuousness in their evolution that on a number of points I for one had to stand up for our theses, so to speak, 'from the left.' " For Kuchin this was not a new situation. Without belonging to the right, he was close to it, yet on some specific points he was closer to the majority. Thanks, as he put it, to "shifted positions and convergence of trends," the organizational problems were settled unanimously. A new bureau of the CC was elected: G. Kuchin, I. Rubin, V. Drabkin, and a representative of the Bund, Zorokhovich. One place was kept open for a representative of the right because of "the need to concentrate the S-D party forces, enhance the personal authority of the bureau of the CC, and broaden its base." As we have seen in the preceding chapter, this decision led to a long correspondence between the bureau and the delegation abroad.

Since the conference wished to step up Party activity, it disapproved of emigration as well as of the tendency of some local organizations to reduce activity in order to keep Party members alive for better times. It recommended that departures for abroad be allowed only in special cases, with the consent of the bureau of the CC, and it also rejected the idea of moving the Party center abroad. But since legal work in Russia was impossible, the Central Committee in Moscow was disbanded, leaving only the bureau of the CC. *SV* was made "the central organ of the RSDRP" (instead of the organ of the Delegation of the RSDRP Abroad) from its issue no. 20, in October 1922.

These debates and resolutions stimulated intraparty discussion. Abroad it was carried on in *SV*. In a programmatic article in no. 19, Martov argued that the old policy had been correct, but conditions had changed—that was why everyone felt the need to revise the line of 1918–20. It had become clear that economic recovery would have to proceed along capitalist lines. "Under the given historical conditions this is the most rational way." Since the country was evolving toward state capitalism, the Party should for the time being struggle merely for the *preconditions* for socialization and for free workers' organizations. The Communist party was losing its revolutionary character and its closeness to the masses:

> This situation . . . narrows the area in which we must act as a party supporting the government brought forth by the revolution. Cases of counterrevolutionary activity, of uprisings or invasions that may confront us with that old task are possible even now. . . . But at present they can only be exceptions. . . . Supporting the Soviet government against internal and foreign counterrevolution . . . has ceased to be one of the main lines of our policy.

Martov proceeded cautiously. He tried to differentiate between the government and the Communist party, or at least the best elements in it. Although he had abandoned the idea of a common front with the regime except in special cases, he remarked: "Even now, we are not rejecting a general agreement among all socialists, including Communists"—that is, the few remaining "ideological" ones, who could help in forestalling a reactionary epilogue to bolshevism. He concluded: "The basic political task of the moment can be formulated in our program as a struggle by all the means at the disposal of an organized mass movement for transition to the *normal regime of a democratic republic*" (italics added). Such a regime was necessary to prevent Bonapartism and also to make a true toilers' rule possible. CC members in Russia found Martov's article an important contribution to the work of revising the Party platform.

Two members of the editorial board of SV, Abramovich and Dan, held that conditions had indeed changed and some revision of the Party platform was necessary, but not basic reversals. Like Martov, Abramovich wrote that the old line had been correct—noting in support of this that the members of the right who were "implacably opposed" to the Soviet government had always found themselves in difficulties when asked to formulate their *positive* program of action. They had concentrated on "external manifestations" of the regime, on its antidemocratic and utopian measures, overlooking its "revolutionary content." The situation had changed with the growth of a sturdy class of peasant landholders, a new rapacious bourgeoisie, and a new Communist bureacracy—all of them typical elements of a postrevolutionary society. In SV, no. 22, Abramovich cautiously formulated his conclusions on the basic issue of agreement with the regime: "The changed political conditions have made the motto of the 'common front,' *at least in its old form*, anachronistic" (italics added).

Thus, Martov and Abramovich, in agreement with the Party majority, both rejected the common front, but with differences in shading. Unlike the right, they did not reject it in principle: abandoning it was merely a tactical step dictated by circumstances. Two facts bear out this contention. One, they considered that the old policy had been right in its time; consequently, a return to it was possible if conditions changed. Two, in the negotiations about recreating the Socialist International, of which we shall speak later, they sided with those European socialists who urged an international common front including Communists.

Dan held that the common front policy must be preserved. He wrote in *SV*, no. 23/24, that Abramovich was "sinning against the evolution of the Russian CP in demanding that the tactic of agreement be definitely abandoned." (Dan promised a special article on agreement with the Communist party but never wrote it.)

Kuchin argued in an interesting article in *SV* in 1923 (no. 1) that the old policy had been wrong and that the current ideas did not represent its further evolution, as Martov maintained, but a complete break. The April theses had been "an unforgivable surrender to the fact of Bolshevik rule" and were becoming more and more of an anachronism. However, the situation in Russia was so complex that the platform should not be changed too sharply. The apathetic population would not respond to drastic demands. Kuchin was not only against uprisings: he insisted that the motto of a democratic republic, though necessary, should not be presented as a "straight and simple" task but in the more cautious guise of partial demands. On this point he was closer to Dan than to the right.

G. Aronson expounded the views of the right flank of the Party. His sharp criticism of the old policy caused some trouble between him and the delegation abroad, which preferred not to publish in *SV* any "criticism of past trends." Old disagreements could be brought up only "insofar as necessary for the basic task."[11] Aronson wrote in *SV* (no. 22, 1923) that the revision undertaken by the majority revealed no intention of breaking with the Soviet regime in principle—it was "an uncertain repetition of the stillborn and already discredited idea of agreement." The Party had been retreating before bolshevism, step by step, since 1918: it had watered down its freedom slogans, renounced the role of the third force between bolshevism and reaction, given up the Constituent Assembly; even in its fight against terrorism there was a "Tolstoyan nuance." In not quite giving up the idea of agreement, it was still harboring some diehard illusions. With whom did the Party propose to agree? With the decayed elements of the CP or with its left groups that dreamed of a return to "October"?

Another persistent illusion was the hope of democratizing the Soviets; they had never been anything but a screen for dictatorship. On these premises Aronson built his main point—concerning uprisings. "We must reject conspiratorial adventures as we always have," and of course a peaceful, bloodless end to the dictatorship would be best, but all this would turn out to be "empty and pitiful ratiocination" if the dictatorship did not agree to reforms. Suppose there was a vast popular movement? Suppose the organized pressure of the masses turned into a victorious uprising against the hated regime? "Should Social Democracy evade a consistent revolutionary tactic? No."

Martov answered Aronson and Kuchin in the last article he wrote before he died (SV, no. 2, 1923). He considered the post-October divergence between the CC and the right deeper than that between Internationalists and Defensists before October. The root cause, in his opinion, was not the CC's acceptance of the concept of a "transition period" but the different attitudes toward the regime—liberal on the part of the CC, revolutionary on the part of the right. The CC had chosen the liberal line because menshevism and bolshevism both represented the working class. This had determined the CC's stand on civil war, on the Constituent Assembly, and on agreement with the Russian Communist party. Martov contended that the CC never renounced "consistent democracy." The question was, what did it mean? In his opinion, the criterion was not universal suffrage but "the possibility of effectively bringing out the will of the popular majority"—a condition absent in capitalist democracies. The Party had accepted the idea of "toilers' rule." He hoped that the Party would keep this slogan in the new platform—that is, would "urge the peasantry, the decisive force in Russia, to unite in a democratic republic not with the capitalist bourgeoisie but with the proletariat."

To return to Aronson's article: his "consistent revolutionary tactic" referred to the main point of dissent between the right and the rest of the Party, whereas his remark about "conspiratorial adventures" was evidently aimed at the extraparty right. The latter's extreme views, especially on uprisings, sometimes disrupted the affinity, the ideological closeness, that undoubtedly existed between the two rightist groups and, of course, irritated the Party majority.

The extraparty Right Mensheviks, who considered themselves followers of Plekhanov and Potresov, had their center in Berlin, where, between April 1922 and February 1925, they put out thirty-four issues of the journal Zaria. They also maintained organizations in Moscow, Petrograd, New York, London and Paris.[12] Their leader until Potresov's arrival was Stepan Ivanovich (Portugeis), the editor of Zaria. The journal's first issue formulated the group's position as follows:

We are Social-Democrats. This means that socialism as the economic order and democracy as the political order are our double goal, the two parts of which are organically merged.... Therefore, struggling for freedom and equality against all forms of oppression, against the dictatorship of nation over nation, class over class, and man over man, is our supreme law.... In the struggle with Red autocracy, Social Democracy has the right and the duty to apply the same principles and methods that were considered good in the struggle against Black autocracy.

The goals of universal suffrage and a constituent assembly remained in full force. Bolshevism was not a stage of the revolution but its catastrophic breakdown. The soft line of the Menshevik CC, its policy of seeking agreement, was "silly in practice; and in principle, dampening the spirit of revolutionary protest against despotism." St. Ivanovich held that there was nothing left for Russia but revolution; the RSDRP's obsessive fear of counterrevolution was unfounded since the last bulwark of reaction, the landowner class, had disappeared. Trotting out the bogey of reaction was "unintelligent mystification."[13]

The Moscow group of *Zaria* expressed similar ideas:

We are not Mensheviks, we are Social-Democrats....Without reservations and hesitations, decisively, categorically, we reject the Soviet regime, Soviet power, bolshevism, semibolshevism, and anything that runs counter to the idea of a democratic mass movement.

Relations between the *Zaria* group and the delegation abroad were extremely strained. Party members were forbidden to write in *Zaria*. St. Ivanovich was refused membership in the Berlin group of the RSDRP because he allegedly had been a member of the Union for Regeneration in Odessa during the civil war and had recruited volunteers for Denikin's army.[14] In this connection, *Zaria* (no. 4) announced that "none of the contributors to our journal has been a member of a recruiting commission for General Denikin's army," and that St. Ivanovich, when he had called for resistance to the Red army, had been supporting the independent military unit of the Union for Regeneration but had not recruited anyone.

Martov disagreed with St. Ivanovich so strongly that he found "even a Miliukov straining to develop some militant democratic spirit more congenial than a St. Ivanovich, organically unable by now to fight in any direction except against the left."[15] He felt insulted by the latter's accusation that the RSDRP with its idea of toilers' rule was covering up the government's persecution of nonsocialists, and replied in *SV*, no. 17:

The RSDRP, itself subjected to Bolshevik terror, has loudly protested against the violence done by the Moscow dictators to representatives of the propertied classes—for example, when the Kadet party was outlawed in 1917; when the bourgeois press was closed in 1918; when the officer Shchastnyi was sentenced to death; when the former grand dukes were shot in Petrograd in early 1919 and only one protest was heard in all of disorganized, terrorized Russia—that of the central organ of our Party, *Vsegda Vpered*, which told the killers the truth about this senseless cruelty. [16]

In *SV*, no. 1, 1923, Martov accused St. Ivanovich of nourishing "democratic illusions" at a time when Western democratic institutions ought to be used for the proletarian class struggle and prevented from becoming "a fig leaf for capitalist dictatorship." In the face of fascism, military cliques, secret diplomacy, and so on, it was naive to believe, like Kautsky, in a "peaceful, painless development via democracy to socialism." St. Ivanovich replied in *Zaria*, no. 3:

> One cannot, as Martov does, separate and counterpose the class struggle and democracy.... The conception of class struggle as direct frontal combat—that is what underlies Martov's reply.... It had its historical justification in an era when the proletariat was a depressed minority, politically rightless and culturally very undeveloped.... This time is past. [Now] the proletariat occupies a completely different social position in the framework of democracy, and hence the class struggle has naturally assumed an entirely new character, far removed from frontal combat.

Martov rightly regarded the extraparty Mensheviks as the kind of "reformists" he had fought all his life, while they looked upon the RSDRP leaders as old-fashioned "orthodox Marxists" who had outlasted their time. Some of St. Ivanovich's ideas—for example, that the transition period to socialism had not yet begun, that class struggle must not conflict with democracy, that socialism resulted from organic development not revolution—reflected the ideology that had emerged in Western socialism early in the century and become dominant in it after the war.

After Martov's death the conflict between the two trends abated for a while. The obituary in *Zaria* (no. 4, 1923) testifies to Martov's prestige in all Menshevik circles:

> Of Martov as of no one else it can be said: He gave his all to it [the Party]. And he had a very great deal to give.... To the cause of Russian social democracy he gave all he could give: the brilliance of his spoken and printed word, all of his fragile health, the passion and talent that pervaded everything that emanated from him, the ever young.

Martov's life, the article concluded, had replayed the tragedy of all great historical movements, which in their early stages devour their most selfless members.

The Common Front in the International

The Mensheviks attached great importance to the recreation of the international socialist organization destroyed by the war. Although the RSDRP had cooled to the idea of a common front in Russia, it continued to promote it in the West. One argument in favor of including the Communists in the International rested on Axelrod's idea of "socialist intervention" in Russia by the Western labor parties—which, however, the Central Committee of the RSDRP understood otherwise than did Axelrod, who had in mind a common front against the Communists, not with them. The Mensheviks hoped that pressure from the international labor movement, in which Communists would be in the minority, would induce the Soviet government to agree to basic political reforms and thus create the conditions for a common front in Russia as well.

On the international scene, a common front of a dynamic socialist working class seemed necessary to repulse the capitalist reaction that the Menshevik leaders thought they saw approaching. The role that the International was to play was at first tied to the idea that the transition period to socialism had begun (a view that, as we have seen, caused dissent within the party). To achieve unity, agreement had to be reached with the biggest socialist organization, the Second International. For most Mensheviks this was a loveless marriage: the Second International represented the socialist groups that the Menshevik leaders found least congenial—the diehard reformists and "patriots" (during the First World War). Like the centrist parties of the West, the RSDRP held that nationalists could not recreate an International and that the main socialist organization could not be led by parties that in their home countries formed governmental coalitions with the bourgeoisie. On the other hand, the centrists could not see how the Comintern could be excluded since it did represent a part of the Russian proletariat and some Western labor groups.

In early 1920 two opposite plans had emerged in the West: for a revived Second International, and for a union of the centrist socialist parties with the Comintern. The RSDRP had rejected both and promoted instead "ideological and political rapprochement between Marxist parties and elements" (i.e., including leftist circles in the Second International), which would eventually lead to an International as free of the "illusions of Bolshevik communism" as of "nationalist opportunism." Therefore the RSDRP decided in April 1920 to take part in an international conference in Bern later in the year, though only as observer. As a first step toward "socialist intervention," the Mensheviks proposed that a delegation from Western labor parties be sent to Russia—but a delegation "completely independent of the Bolshevik authorities" and therefore trustworthy in the eyes of the Russian and European proletariat. [17]

The centrist parties met in Bern in December. Martov represented the RSDRP (the Swiss had refused a visa to the second delegate, Abramovich). The Mensheviks still believed that the centrist parties would play the leading role in the future union, and when the French proposed that over and above the three international groupings a general council of all three be created, Martov voted against it, because "a general council from Scheidemann to Lenin would only provoke laughter on both sides." Soon this ambitious goal had to be abandoned.

Martov was pleased with the Bern conference and its leftist manifesto. He noted that "the attitude toward us—to the Party and to me personally"—was most friendly. On his way back he saw Axelrod, who found the manifesto "less unacceptable than I [Martov] had expected, and his view of the conference itself is quite tolerant"—even though Axelrod still favored the Second International. [18]

The conference that founded the International Union of Socialist Parties took place in Vienna in February 1921. The RSDRP expressed its views on the new organization in the first issue of *SV*:

> The bankruptcy of the Second and the unsoundness of the Third International as ralliers of the proletariat's forces for revolutionary activity have necessitated the temporary union of the so-called center parties that has been initiated at Bern. Its object is to prepare— through ideological clarification and political action—the conditions for recreating a true International. For the uniting parties [are convinced] that so long as no class unity of proletarians has been achieved on a national and international scale, the working class cannot make full use of its weight in today's society to excercise revolutionary pressure on the policies of bourgeois governments, let alone to wrest the power from them.

In other words, the International Union was not another International along with the Second and the Third but a provisional organ for the purpose of creating a single International combining all the parties that believed in the class struggle and wanted to overcome capitalism through the united efforts of an international working class. The union's immediate tasks were the defense of the Russian revolution from foreign imperialism, the abolition of the Treaty of Versailles, and the liberation of colonial peoples.

The Mensheviks held that instead of the coordinating center it had become after the war, the International should be an organ truly directing the labor movement and to which member parties would be subordinate. The Communists could not accept such a organization; neither could the socialist parties that participated in the government of their home countries.

The outlook for unification was not good. The parties of the Second International wanted a common front not with the communists but only with the centrist parties, hoping that the current drift to the right would ensure their dominance in such a union. The Communists, in Dan's opinion, were taking part in the negotiations merely in order to use the international labor movement for their struggle against intervention, the blockade, and so on. Their representatives behaved insolently, threatening to "rip off the masks of the flunkeys of the bourgeoisie" sent to the conference by imperialists. The Mensheviks nevertheless persisted in their efforts to create a common front with the Communists. Sometimes this was painful. At the April 1922 conference of the three Internationals, a delegate of the Second suggested attaching certain conditions to the Comintern's continued participation in the talks—for instance, release of political prisoners in Russia. Such a move on the part of an international body must have warmed the Mensheviks' hearts, especially as it was made mainly in response to their own public protests against Soviet terror (and also to the impending trial of the SRs). Yet they opposed any kind of ultimatum to the Comintern since this could abort the negotiations. Their devotion to the common front was so strong that they sacrificed themselves. The unanimous declaration of the conference included the slogans "For the Russian Revolution, For Starving Russia, For the Resumption of Political and Economic Relations with Russia," but made no mention of terror. Martov had written earlier, in a private letter, that he wanted to avoid complicating and embarrassing the negotiations "by bringing up the persecution of Russian, Georgian, Armenian, and other socialists"; yet

> we feel very sure that at the conference this question cannot be ignored without harm to the cause and to the prestige of the International Union of Socialist Parties. . . . We therefore consider that [it must] be touched upon. . . . In such a way, of course, as not to give anyone a welcome pretext for scuttling or spoiling the work of the conference. [19]

A commission of nine (three from each International) was charged with the preparations for union, mainly the convocation of a congress of all three Internationals, on which the Comintern particularly insisted. But relations with the Comintern were deteriorating. After the diplomatic conferences in Genoa and The Hague, and the Rapallo pact of 1922, the Comintern no longer felt so much in need of a common front. And the price for it came high: parleys with socialists compromised Lenin's reputation as a rockhard Bolshevik and confused the Western Communists trained to regard the socialist leaders as traitors. On 23 May 1922, the Comintern recalled its delegates from the nine-man commission, on the pretext that the commission was delaying the planned congress. This left the centrist parties in a quandary. With one of the three partners gone, the union itself was, so to speak, suspended in the air. Still the RSDRP did not give up: "What now? Instead of 'complete union,' an 'incomplete' one? Instead of a common front of three, a union of two Internationals? Yes, if it is a step toward general union. No, if this makes it objectively impossible or impedes it."[20]

For another year, until the utter hopelessness of the project became clear, the Mensheviks and the Western centrist parties continued their propaganda for a united international movement dedicated to the class struggle. The stabler political situation in Europe and the Second International's growing influence made union without the Comintern appear more feasible. It was discussed at the meetings of the Vienna Union and the Second International in Frankfurt on 8 December 1922 and in Cologne on 5 January 1923. But the Mensheviks were loath to give up the common front in its original form. In Frankfurt, their delegate suggested keeping the Second and the Vienna Internationals separate and merely setting up a committee to coordinate their activities. This proposal was rejected. At these conferences and at the one of the Amsterdam International of Trade Unions in December, Abramovich criticized the "traitorous tactics" of the Communists, yet appealed to them to honestly accept unification. At the Amsterdam meeting, he said:

> To take the measure of the insincerity of their [the Communists'] statements one has only to ask them a single question: Are you offering a common front in Russia too? A common front of victim and hangman, of prisoner and jailer?... We are ready even now to forget all the blood you have shed, your crimes and mistakes, and to take your proffered hand—on one condition: In your Communist state, give the working class at least the freedom it has in the capitalist countries of Europe.[21]

The various conferences closely listened to Abramovich, and both the delegation abroad and the bureau of the CC approved his speeches. Neither of the Party centers was happy about a union of Vienna and London without Moscow. The bureau conceded that the

Communists had made such a union inevitable "for a time" but added that it must not lead to absorption of revolutionary elements by reformist groups; the decisions of the International must be made binding on all member parties; and the International must remain the highest instance in the event of international conflict. [22]

The impossibility of merging the three Internationals was becoming evident. At its last meeting, 20 May 1923, the executive committee of the Vienna Union decided on a merger with the Second International—which took place at the Hamburg congress of the two organizations, 21–26 May. The Mensheviks continued to criticize the Soviet government. A report by Abramovich on conditions in Russia was coldly received: international tensions had developed, and some Western parties did not want to exacerbate relations with the Soviets.

The RSDRP's reaction to the merger was ambivalent. *SV* (no. 11) stated that the "great historical significance" of the Hamburg congress must be admitted and its results "joyfully welcomed": it had "swept away the scum of old quarrels [with the Second International] that have lost all meaning." But the same article expressed regret that the Communists remained apart at a time when the postwar demoralization of Europe encouraged both extremes in the working class, the rebelliously Communist and the reformist. Moreover, Hamburg had not been "a congress of a really united international organization but rather a forum for talking out and coordinating the national viewpoints of various parties." An International with purely coordinative functions did not satisfy the RSDRP.

Inside the Party, the idea of an international common front met with objections from several quarters. The right did not strenuously oppose it because it had little interest in the matter, but any cooperation with Communists was contrary to its views. Axelrod was against the Vienna Union and for the Second International. There had been some friction between him and the CC about the Second International as far back as 1918. [23] In early 1922 the French socialist paper *Le Populaire* (no. 346) printed an interview with him. There were two prerequisites for a common front, Axelrod said: a common understanding of goals and means, and a sincere desire to work together. These existed in the parties of the Second and the Vienna Internationals despite their differences. Hence their merger was feasible.

> As for the Third International, it consists of two disparate elements, which must be examined separately: on one hand, the parties of Western Europe which call themselves Communists; on the other, Russian bolshevism.
> The European Communist parties are workers' organizations.

However difficult it may be to achieve closeness with these parties infected with utopian ideas, demagogical in their work, corrupted by the putrefying influence of Moscow, we shall never forget that they are our brothers in the great class struggle.

Russian bolshevism is something else again. It is not a workers' party but a government organization practicing power through terror.

The Comintern was an organ of this regime, and there was no hope that the regime would evolve. "The Moscow government must be forced to give its subjects at least the freedom that the subjects of the German Kaiser had before the revolution." To assure peace, one must try to get the Soviet government recognized by other governments, but there was no need for socialist parties to recognize it.

Axelrod had been asked to join the delegation of the RSDRP to the Vienna conference in February 1921. Martov wrote him:

> We realize that you are fundamentally against...leaving the Second International and concentrating [our] forces on opposing not only the Third but now also the Second [International]. But since this is already a fact, would you consider accepting it and joining the delegation?[24]

Axelrod declined this offer, as well as a similar one in 1923 from the Moscow organization of *Zaria*, which wanted to send a delegation to the Hamburg congress. *Zaria* had always favored the Second International; it called the common front with Communists "a crazy idea" of uniting "representatives of the proletariat struggling for the liberation of mankind with representatives of the most reactionary regime in the civilized world." Axelrod wrote that he was deeply touched by the "Moscow comrades'" offer but could not accept it since he knew nothing about the members and activities of *Zaria*; besides, though opposed to the Vienna union and wanting it to merge with the Second International, he disapproved separatism within the Party.[25] His choice of words—"within the Party" and "comrades"—indicates that, unlike the delegation abroad, he considered *Zaria* an ideological trend within menshevism, even though separate organizationally.

The delegation abroad not only refused that group's request to include its representative in the delegation of the RSDRP but also resolved not to assist *Zaria* in gaining separate admission to the Hamburg congress—on the grounds that only the official Russian parties, that is, the RSDRP and the PSR had the right to be represented. At the same time it was unwilling to act together with the SRs.[26] The delegation to Hamburg consisted solely of members of the RSDRP, including representatives of its right wing.

Yet there were doubts about the common front even within the majority in control of the delegation abroad. In June 1922 Dallin wrote in *SV* (no. 10): "Experience with the common front has clearly shown that this tactic had only one fault: it could not work." Russian Social-Democrats must no longer put international socialist unity above all else: "At present the complete, final liquidation of the terrorist regime becomes the basic, central, cardinal issue." The Zimmerwald struggle against the Second International had been a wartime affair. Only "a poor, a very poor politician would keep repeating the old songs about social-patriots." The Second International was backed by 70 percent of the politically organized workers of Europe as well as by the International of Trade Unions. "Old schisms should not be preserved, they should be buried." Vienna and London must unite without Moscow.

Martov replied to Dallin (and to Kautsky, who had also said that it was foolish to wait "for the Moscow wolves to become vegetarians") in *SV* (no. 21, 1922), arguing that the drift to the right in the Western labor movement was temporary, the Second International was not constituted to dictate basic tactics to the national parties, as the Vienna International was; and without this kind of centralization the International would be no more effective than it had been in 1914.

In Russia there also arose opposition to the common front, more symptomatic perhaps of a general shift in Party thinking. In the spring of 1922, most local organizations had agreed with the CC, hoping that a socialist center would influence Western Communists and through them the Russian Communist party. The Vienna Union seemed best suited to play this role, whereas the Second International with its ultimata to the Comintern threatened to wipe out the efforts of the RSDRP.[27] But later in the year the Party's mood must have changed. When the bureau of the CC had discussed the common front in preparation for the October Party conference, all but one of its members had voted for continuing the "Vienna" line. The conference itself did not have time to debate this point in detail, but a tentative ballot produced only four votes for the CC's proposal and six against, with one abstention. Evidently the majority of the Party now felt that the Vienna line was unrealistic and that it was time to intensify the struggle against communism.[28]

Georgia; Diplomatic Recognition of Soviet Russia; the Ruhr

The Mensheviks had opposed foreign intervention during the civil war. They took the same stand on Russia's intervention in Georgia in

1921—all the more so since the "uprising" of Georgian Bolsheviks had been fomented, financed, and armed by Moscow. The Soviet diplomatic mission in Tiflis had a staff of four hundred, most of whom had nothing to do with diplomacy. Yet the uprising did not quite succeed in overthrowing the Georgian government, and the Red army had to be brought in to help. It occupied Tiflis on 25 February 1921 and installed a Soviet government. This open military aggression against a small independent state dealt a blow to the common front policy, to which the Mensheviks still fully adhered at the time. The delegation abroad declared in a resolution on 3 March:

> The solution by armed force of problems dividing two countries ruled by socialists is the greatest disgrace for socialism, undermines the foundations of international class solidarity in forcing Russian socialist workers to shoot at Georgian workers, and causes enormous harm to the Russian and the world revolutions. [29]

When the news of the invasion reached the February 1921 conference of the Vienna International, the Mensheviks tried to put through a sharp resolution of censure. Martov wrote that the conference, fearful of annoying Moscow, wished to slur over the matter. "The protest came out far less firm and pungent than we wanted. Abramovich and I shouted ourselves hoarse, presented ultimata, heaped abuse on the [pro-Soviet] Germans, but did not get all we wanted." [30]

At later conferences of the International, the Mensheviks seized every opportunity to defend Georgia's independence. [31] This is all the more remarkable since they did not at all sympathize with the deposed Georgian government. Its British "orientation," its hostility to the Soviet government precluding a common front, its nationalism, the very declaration of independence that was part of the "dismemberment of Russia" that the Menshevik had always resisted—all this ran directly counter to the policies of the RSDRP. Relations between Russian and Georgian Mensheviks were glacial. The bureau of the CC in Moscow was even less tolerant than the delegation abroad. In December 1922 it reproved SV for publishing articles by Georgian leaders: this might give the impression that Martov and Zhordania were working hand in hand. The bureau would prefer "Georgian articles and documents to be printed in a way that would make it clear that this isn't our Party but another"—perhaps in the form of letters to the editor. When the bureau wanted to set up a printing press in Moscow and the Georgian Social-Democrats offered to help with this difficult undertaking, the bureau declined—partly because it thought such closeness between the two parties undesirable. [32]

Diplomatic recognition by other countries was the one point on which the RSDRP fully supported the Soviet government—not in order to strengthen it but to save Russia from new wars and ease her economic distress. As Martov had said, "We came to the conclusion that this was necessary...when we realized that without political agreement (which presupposes recognition or leads to it) the European governments would not consider ... resuming trade."[33] For the RSDRP, recognition did not imply moral approval. It was merely a diplomatic act safeguarding Russia from foreign military interference. For similar reasons, the RSDRP, had not protested against the Riga treaty with Poland, although many émigré groups, especially the Kadets, had accused it of sanctioning Russia's dismemberment. In the press and at socialist congresses, the RSDRP campaigned for recognition and for aid to starving Russia. Before the Genoa conference, the CC of the RSDRP and the CC of the Bund (S-D) jointly addressed the European socialist parties and labor organizations:

> It is not just recognition that is important, but also its conditions. ... Recognition must not entail turning Russia into a colony of Western European capital but ... economic help.... The interests of the Russian revolution and the international proletariat are the same. For their sake, and for the sake of ... the dying ... we appeal to you: come to Russia's aid! [34]

Martov thought this appeal too leftist and wrote the bureau of the CC that it could give a wrong impression of the Party's stand since it contained no criticism of the regime; now that the luster of the Russian revolution had faded, one should be more circumspect in calling upon the international proletariat to support the Soviet government.[35] On 16 February 1922, the Menshevik CC published a protest against an appeal *not* to recognize the Soviet government or make peace with it, issued by the executive commission of members of the Constituent Assembly. The CC wrote: "In Russia there is not a single at all significant group of toiling democrats that—regardless of its attitude to the Soviet regime—would oppose its international recognition." The commission of the Constituent Assembly had no right to speak in the name of Russian democracy.

As the party cooled toward the common front, its campaign for recognition also became less fervent; and it took care to formulate this demand in a way that could not possibly be interpreted as support of the Soviet government's methods. The RSDRP displayed little enthusiasm about the diplomatic negotiations in which Russia was involved with the Western powers in the spring of 1922. In April and June of that year, Soviet Russia took part in the Genoa and Hague conferences, and on 16 April the Russo-German treaty of Rapallo was signed. The results of the two conferences were negligible, but they implied de facto recognition of the Soviet government by several European powers; and the Rapallo treaty included de jure recognition. The Soviets had breached the diplomatic blockade. The CC of the RSDRP had hoped that the Genoa conference could be used to obtain recognition and economic aid for Soviet Russia, on certain conditions, and had urged the European workers to exert pressure to this effect. Of the conference itself, however, the Mensheviks took a very dim view. It looked to them like an attempt by Western colonizers to work their way into Russia and an attempt by the Soviet government to get foreign loans for its army and police, not for the country's needs. Only the abolition of the Versailles treaty and democratization of the Russian regime could create proper conditions for normal economic relations, beneficial to the West and badly needed by Russia. The workers of Russia and the West should try to do what the diplomats could not. Dan wrote: "Genoa speaks to the world proletariat of the need to raise the Versailles question by their own efforts and in its full scope. It speaks to the Russian worker of the need to put an end to the regime that is devastating Russia."[36]

In international affairs the Mensheviks were generally pro-German and anti-Entente. France and England, the victors in the World War and the chief interventionists in Russia, appeared to them as the embodiments of imperialism and reaction bent on turning both Russia and Germany into colonies, and hence as possible sources of new armed interventions. Germany presented no military threat. It was itself a victim of imperialist plunder, the Mensheviks thought, and its socialist and trade union traditions could make it the battering ram that would open the way to great social reforms in the West. Abolishing the Versailles treaty seemed to the Mensheviks one of the urgent tasks of the proletariat. In the International, their representatives insisted on a concerted campaign against the Entente, especially France with its extreme anti-German policy, particularly after the French occupation of the Ruhr in January 1923. The loss of this coal-producing region was a heavy blow for Germany and a threat to the living standards of the German workers. A leaflet issued in Moscow by the bureau of the CC stated:

> The Versailles peace, intended to end the World War, contained from the first innumerable sources of new clashes and conflicts.... It strangled the German people like a noose, forcing the starving German worker and the bankrupt small folk to pay countless billions

of marks and supply tens of thousands of tons of coal. . . . The question put in the Ruhr cannot be answered in terms of the struggle between the German and the French nations. It is a question of the united international struggle of the world proletariat against the imperialist appetites of the bourgeoisie, against the Versailles peace. [37]

The lead article in *SV*, no. 3, maintained that France was in the "honeymoon of imperialism," and that Germany, despite her defeat, was still economically strong—a situation that could lead to new armed clashes and the growth of facism in Germany. "Only the growing influence of the working class, only the pressure of the socialist parties, can dampen the fervor of the civilized barbarians in Western Europe and tame the terrorist dictators in the east."

12

Two Party Centers

Berlin: The Delegation of the RSDRP Abroad

After Martov's death, Dan became the acknowledged leader of the Party majority, which had begun to call itself "the Martov movement." David Dallin replaced Martov on the editorial board of *Sotsialisticheskii Vestnik*. A. Iugov was elected secretary of the delegation abroad.

SV was not just another émigré publication: its editors kept in mind their readers in Russia. On the other hand, the reliable and extensive information about Russia impressed even the journal's enemies. *SV* was the first periodical in the world to publish the contents of Lenin's "political testament," which Stalin had concealed. Thirty years were to pass before the existence of that document was admitted, at its Twentieth Congress, by the CPSU. For the benefit of Western socialists, the delegation abroad published from March 1924 to November 1932 a bulletin in German, *RSD. Mitteilungsblatt der Russischen Sozialdemokratie.* Four hundred and forty-eight issues of it came out.

Martov had been increasingly anti-Soviet during his last years. Under Dan, there was a turn back toward the "April theses."[1] The Party was facing many problems. In Russia, the NEP was still seeking its final form. Postwar Europe had not stabilized politically or economically. Certain signs suggested that the crisis of capitalism and perhaps the awaited transition to socialism were at hand: in England and Denmark the first labor governments had come to power; fascism had triumphed in Italy; Germany was in the grip of monstrous inflation and developing a spirit of revanche. The RSDRP closely observed the interplay of all these developments, in Russia, in the West, and in the Socialist International.

The NEP in its third year seemed to confirm the Mensheviks' gloomy predictions. What was wholesome in it had failed to overcome the corrupting effects of dictatorship. The weakness of the government-controlled major industries made the Soviet economy depend on the denationalized small enterprises. Now the Mensheviks criticized the Soviet economy no longer as a harmful "socialist experiment" but as state capitalism—of the worst kind, since it denied the workers the right to defend their interests through trade unions, strikes, and the like. "The NEP has played itself out," wrote *SV*. "All the young shoots of economic development brought forth by it are being smothered under the iron cloche of Bolshevik dictatorship." The rightist leader P. Garvi even wrote that the NEP was "a transitional stage not to socialism but to capitalism. . . . Under our eyes, the social-Bonapartist oligarchy is turning bourgeois-Bonapartist."[2] Menshevik criticism of the NEP was increasingly sharp, but their demands remained the same as in its early period: restoration of civic rights; abolition of dictatorship; keeping only those industries nationalized that the government was able to run.

Nevertheless, the idea of a common front with the Communists, to which Martov had cooled in his last days,[3] remained strong in the Party majority led by Dan. Abramovich wrote in a pamphlet (published in German to acquaint Western socialists with the situation in Russia) that it was the Party's current "historical task," in a united proletarian effort, "to push the policy of the present government in the desired direction and, in the struggle for the vital interests of the proletariat, to attract the class-conscious elements of the RCP [Russian Communist party].[4] "Pushing" a government meant reforming, not overthrowing, it; and if the pushing was successful, collaboration would become possible. This conception was obviously contradictory. The Mensheviks were fully aware of the material and moral decline of the Russian working class, aggravated by the influx of nonproletarian, mostly peasant, elements. Yet the Party majority, true to the theory of class struggle, continued to view the Russian workers as a force able not only to overcome dictatorship through skillful, organized pressure but even to establish the first democratic regime in Russia.

A continuous dispute went on between the majority and the right opposition. In the spring of 1923 a group of Party rightists in Russia drew up theses on the political situation.[5] They agreed that capitalism was unable to cope with the economic havoc left by the war; but, unlike the majority, they felt that the workers' cultural and organizational level precluded "successful struggle . . . for immediate transition to a socialist order." The main obstacle to Russia's recovery was the reactionary Communist dictatorship, which social democracy must ruthlessly combat. The basic point of the theses was that the Party must fully adhere to "consistent democracy," that is, struggle for political rights and freedom without class distinctions. This was incompatible with the common front, with the idea of agreement with the opposition in the RCP, and with the view of the RCP as a utopian and misguided but still a socialist party. The right proposed:

> The Party will expose the true nature of the [Bolshevik] dictatorship as an oligarchic dictatorship of declassed elements over the entire people. . . . The RSDRP sets itself the goal of organizing the broad masses of the working class for comprehensive struggle against the regime. In choosing the means of struggle, the Party will be guided, besides general principles, solely by its estimate of the correlation of forces, rejecting both the tactics of passive waiting and appeals to light-headed, premature, and unorganized action.

On the basic issues—democracy, the nature of the Soviet regime, the methods of its liquidation—the right agreed with Axelrod, who wanted the Party to steer a course toward overthrowing the regime, not coming to terms with it. Axelrod had written Karl Kautsky, whose stand was sharply anti-Soviet:

> Your criticism of the Bolshevik dictatorship should be specially noted as a major service to the international proletariat. A radical victory over bolshevism, the destruction of the myth of its worldwide historical mission is one of the most important, not to say the most important, conditions for completely resolving the ideological and political crisis that our international movement is still undergoing. [6]

The bureau of the CC in Moscow kept insisting that the majority and the right reach agreement, and the delegation abroad also discussed this. In the spring of 1923, Dan began negotiations with representatives of the right—P. Garvi, M. Kefali, and V. Voitinskii. The two sides had lately come somewhat closer to each other, but the right wanted a more active role in directing the Party, with representatives in the delegation abroad and on the editorial board of SV. Dan insisted that they must first sever their contacts with the extraparty right and submit to the line of the majority. [7] No agreement was reached.

In the fall of 1923, the delegation decided that it did not in principle object to co-opting a member of the right (though a rightist on the editorial board was still unacceptable), but that since the right had "more than once ostentatiously stressed that joint positive work in accord with the general party line was unacceptable to it," new talks and a clear formulation of the conditions were necessary. The question was not settled until the summer of 1924, when the delegation coopted Kefali as a voting member.[8] Aronson, who had been a member in an advisory capacity since 1922, was given the vote in 1927.

The bureau of the CC was against attaching conditions to the inclusion of rightists in the delegation. Kuchin wrote to Berlin that the bureau disapproved any kind of "treaties." Some statement by the right was desirable, "but not as a condition." The bureau had found its own collaboration with the right very satisfactory.[9]

Agreement with the other socialist parties was even more difficult. Since the quarrel over the civil war, there had been only a formal truce with the SRs during their trial in 1922. As a rule, the Mensheviks avoided public disputes with them, but collaboration was precluded because the SRs opposed diplomatic recognition of the USSR and readily cooperated with the Kadets. Except for its right wing, the delegation rejected union with the SRs, who had twice raised the question in the International.[10] It informed the executive committee of the International that it did not "consider it possible even to discuss the question"—mainly because Mensheviks could not unite with a party that formed alliances with bourgeois groups to overthrow the Soviet government.[11] The bureau of the CC thought that the PSR had lost all roots in Russia.

Usually the delegation spoke out on foreign policy only in cases of international conflict. Most of its members viewed the newly formed League of Nations as an organ intended to preserve the status quo and unable to rise to the postwar problems: it had not prevented clashes between imperialists, had not done away with secret diplomacy or reduced the danger of war; it was a league of governments, not peoples. However, some Mensheviks held that with all its faults the league represented the democratic principle in international relations and should be improved, not rejected. Later this view came to predominate in the Party.

The Mensheviks extended their hatred of imperialism to the new Soviet imperialism. Besides, they felt that the USSR's pretension to act as a world power despite its military and economic weakness was unrealistic. They condemned in particular the Soviet attempts to penetrate the Near East—via the Turkestan to Persia and Afghanistan—based, in their view, on Lenin's theory that the Soviet revolution would reach Europe through the Asian colonial countries. "There is no excuse for this policy of revolutionary *avantiurizm.*"[12] But the RSDRP backed the Soviet government in its conflict with Romania, which had annexed Bessarabia in 1918. The Soviets had proposed a plebiscite, and the RSDRP supported this, with two reservations: it would not join the bloc of Russian liberals and conservatives who also approved the proposal; the plebiscite should not be conducted by the Soviet government, which had resorted to plain coercion in Georgia, Azerbaidzhan, Bokhara, and Khiva—just as Romania had in Bessarabia.[13]

Lenin's death did not strike the delegation abroad as a very important event, despite the deep impression it made in Russia, even in circles not at all friendly to the Communists. The International sent the Soviet government a message of condolence. ("Incomprehensible, fantastic," commented Stephan Ivanovich.) *SV* printed only two articles on Lenin's death. One of them said that it was not the political opponent or the dictator one remembered at such a time but the man who together with Martov had created the party in which the Mensheviks remained but which he had left. Lenin and Martov had stood side by side at the source of a movement that combined

> Marxist Eurpoeanism and elemental semi-Asiatic peasantry . . . all the tangle of contradictions that characterizes the history . . . of the Russian proletariat and of all of Russian society. . . . Throughout his oscillations and waverings, sometimes amazingly unprincipled and morally indiscriminate, through all the zigzags of his . . . activity over thirty years, there runs like a red thread the unshakable guiding principle: I am the Party, I am the State. . . .

As the selfless leader of a sect, the article concluded, Lenin had shown traits of genius.[14]

The International and *SV* absorbed most of the delegation's energies. This work was not very extensive, but it was very taxing. Life was much harder for the new émigrés than it had been for the old. Problems of historical scope arose at every turn. Instead of one clear enemy on the right, there was also an enemy on the left, sometimes a hidden enemy, harder to combat because he infiltrated the milieu closest to Social-Democrats. Instead of fairly stable contact with Russia and faith in the growing influence of the Party, there was the growing realization that the Party's life was flickering out. In the International, the RSDRP had been an equal among equals; now it was a minor group of internal opposition among parties that played important roles in their countries. To the Moscow bureau's critical remarks about *SV*, the delegation replied on 28 October 1923 that *SV* was, after all, written by only a few people:

> Why aren't the others writing? Some, because they cannot. Others, for the same reason of spiritual searchings, doubts, about which you write us from Russia. Don't you see that getting away

from the GPU does not always mean psychic and spiritual equilib-
rium? That being cut off from their country, from public activity,
plus the crisis in the movement to which they have given their life,
only aggravates for many their searchings and doubts and distracts
from creative work.... Many lack the strength for it. Surely it is no
accident, this paucity of theoretical thought not only among us but
in all of socialism.

The living conditions of most émigrés were miserable, yet

we, a small, group of people, devote all our time to Party affairs: we travel to all bureaus and congresses, write aritcles for *SV*,
gather news for it, draft and compose documents and appeals,
collects money for *SV*, provide services for foreign groups, correspond with you— are these the proper conditions for serious theoretical work? Of course not.... Insofar as we can, we try to give
general analyses, to outline prospects. That is, problems are discerned and posed, not solved. These are some of the reasons that
explain the defects in theoretical work, ours and yours.

Yet it was the theoretical work of completing a new platform that was
now the most pressing task confronting the Party.

The RSDRP and International Socialism

The new International, in which the Vienna and the Second had
merged, included all the more important socialist parties of Europe,
with a membership of seven million, but organizational unity did not
mean ideological harmony. As in the RSDRP, there was a constant
tug-of-war between the right and the left, with the difference that in
the International the right was the stronger. The secretary of the
International, Friedrich Adler, complained in 1925 that orthodox
Marxists were in the minority. The predominance of reformists,
headed by the non-Marxist British Labour party, greatly disappointed
the Mensheviks. Within six months of the merger, the Delegation of the
RSDRP Abroad wrote the bureau of the CC:

We all think that if the objective conditions were right, another
"Vienna" should be convoked. But these conditions are lacking....
The basic reason, of course, is not the leaders' treachery but the postwar weariness of the masses and the cleavage in the labor movement.... We have a growing wish to renew the campaign for a
"common front," that is, to call a joint congress of the Hamburg and
the Moscow Internationals. The onslaught of reaction, the situation
in Germany, Bulgaria, Russia, urgently demands this. So does the
situation in the international trade union movement. [15]

Dan wrote that the International had deceived even the modest hopes that had been put in it, since it continues the traditional policy of "social-patriotic Burgfrieden," while the Communists were doing their disruptive work outside it.[16] Abramovich, the chief representative of the RSDRP in the International, complained in early 1924 that membership in an organization largely controlled by elements "openly reformist, nationalistic, and in general far from Marxism theoretically" presented great "political and psychological difficulties." A year later, Abramovich (unlike Dan) would reluctantly concede that the labor movement had become integrated with national life and that under such conditions "each section of the International must *willy-nilly* have very great autonomy" (italics added) and the International should be not so much a directing organ as a forum for member parties to thresh things out and make joint decisions.[17]

Axelrod had foreseen, as the delegation abroad had not, that in the merger the Second International would in effect swallow the Vienna Union. He had welcomed the merger but was still dissatisfied with the International's stand on communism. He wrote Adler:

Bolshevism is nothing else than the realization—on a titanic scale, in barbarously violent form—of the precepts of Bakunin and Nechaev, those spiritual fathers of bolshevism. Marx and Engels, Bebel and Liebknecht clearly saw the danger that anarchism and Bakuninism held for the international labor movement and combated it fiercely.

. . . In its conduct toward the Bolshevik progeny of Bakuninists the Socialist International should long since have been guided by the same irreconcilable spirit as . . . our great socialist precursors in their struggle with the [Bakuninists].[18]

The delegation campaigned against Bolshevik terror in the International, the Western socialist press, and at conferences in Europe and America—with increasing success as the Western parties learned more about the Soviet Union and cooled toward communism. Abramovich and Tsereteli reported, respectively, on the situation in Russia and in Georgia at conferences of the executive committee of the International on 16–17 February and 28–30 September 1924; in the summer a report by Kuchin (who had come from Moscow illegally) strongly impressed the executive committee. It adopted a resolution condemning Soviet terror but welcoming the recognition of Soviet Russia by England and Italy and inviting other countries to follow suit. These were the principles the RSDRP had long been promoting. In its resolution on Georgia, the executive committee invited the parties of the International to campaign for "freeing Georgia from Soviet troops." It also sent a message to political prisoners in Russia, saluting their "fidelity to socialist principles despite unparalleled persecution"; suggested that every member party set up a committee to aid socialists in Russian prisons; and resolved to publish in three languages a pamphlet about Soviet terror. The British and the Lithuanian parties published protests against the terror. On 30 January 1924 a congress of the French party resolved to demand amnesty for political prisoners in Russia, in particular SRs. A "Society to Defend Imprisoned Revolutionaries in Russia" was formed in France. In November 1923, at a meeting in Paris organized by the French Socialist Youth League, a representative of the Russian Youth League spoke on Soviet terror and warned that the USSR was one of the powers that were pushing the world toward a new war. In all this, Menshevik initiative or assistance played a substantial part.

On issues unconnected with Russia the Mensheviks were less successful. They vainly insisted in the International on active measures against the "imperialist policies" of the victor nations, especially England and France, criticizing the socialists of these countries whose policy they considered nationalistic rather than proletarian. In the International as in SV, the Mensheviks accused Western imperialism of causing the chaos in Germany, which was a threat for all Europe. At the 3 October 1923 meeting of the executive committee of the International, Abramovich advocated mass demonstrations, especially in France and Belgium, in defense of the German working class and the German revolution. He offered a resolution to this effect, but it was rejected.

Abiding by the principles of internationalism as defined at Zimmerwald and Vienna, the RSDRP did not break with the Western parties but maintained alliances with their oppositional groups. Opposing internationalism to nationalism and revolution to evolution, it disapproved of socialist governments where there was no revolutionary situation and deplored the tendency of socialist parties to enter the government of their countries.[19] The Mensheviks accused German social democracy of having developed "a large section that is standing with both feet on the ground of extraclass democracy, social peace, and national unity" and condemned it for participating in a coalition government: as a result of this reformist policy "a revolutionary situation without revolutionary prospects" was building up in Germany.[20]

The Mensheviks supported the International's protest against the savage suppression of the anti-Soviet uprising in Georgia in 1924. They demanded that the principle of self-determination be applied to Georgia and sharply criticized both the British Labourites, who had tried to soften the protest, and the German socialists of the extreme left, who disapproved of the Soviet action but saw no reason to protest against it more strongly than against England's colonial policy in India or Africa. To the Mensheviks it seemed grossly wrong to equate British colonialism and Soviet imperialism. At the same time, they censured Georgian social democracy for cooperating with bourgeois parties in a "national bloc" and thereby recognizing the primacy of national unity over class unity—which led to the subordination of the proletarian party to the petty and middle bourgeoisie.[21]

The delegation abroad drafted two basic resolutions before the congress of the new International in Marseille (22–27 August 1925). One of them outlined the general policy of the RSDRP: for all its opposition to the Soviet government, it favored a common front with communism in view of the growth of reaction in the West; since the Comintern was the main obstacle to the common front, its organizational and financial dependence on Moscow must be terminated and democratic principles applied within the Communist parties.[22] Most of the delegation abroad actually believed that this was realizable, at least in the Western Communist parties.

The other resolution dealt with the threat of war in Eastern Europe. The point was on the agenda of the Marseille congress. There were the conflicts between Lithuania and Poland over Vilno, Poland and Germany over Danzig and the "corridor," Russia and Romania over Bessarabia. The Baltic countries were in a state of constant tension over possible Communist uprisings and Soviet intervention. The resolution pointed out that this tension was caused, on one hand, by the chauvinism of the new states and the Entente's wish to make them anti-Soviet and anti-German bulwarks and, on the other hand, by the annexationist plans of the Soviet Union. "These two sources of the war threat complement and nourish each other." To remove the threat, one must "fight for the revision of the Versailles and other treaties . . . the rights of national minorities . . . and expose the militaristic and annexationist character of Soviet dictatorship."[23]

At the Marseille congress the RSDRP and the PSR had six delegates each. Abramovich was elected to the permanent bureau of the executive committee. The "Russian question" was discussed in the "Eastern commission" of the Congress, set up to examine the situation in Eastern Europe, which worried the International. Two clashing views emerged. The Austrian leader Otto Bauer blamed the explosive situation partly on the Soviet Union's wish to lead the colonial peoples in a war against capitalist countries, but mainly on England's wish to weaken the USSR in Eastern Europe in order to divert it from the Far East. Bauer wanted the International to support the liberation movement of colonial peoples and to state that the war threat emanated mainly from the Western powers, not the USSR, although the latter also displayed aggressive tendencies. Dan (deviating from the resolution of the delegation abroad) expressed his "complete solidarity" with Bauer: "As a socialist party of the working class, we do not for a moment forget, despite all our dislike of bolshevism, that our main enemy and the main source of the war threat is world capitalism." V. Chernov for the SRs and I. Tsereteli for the Georgian S-Ds argued that Soviet aggressiveness was the main culprit. The congress adopted a weak resolution:

> On one hand, these [eastern] states are in danger of uprisings organized under the leadership of the Comintern, which would prepare for them the fate of Georgia and Armenia; on the other hand, the imperialist powers are in a position to exploit them for their own ends as outposts in the struggle against Soviet Russia.

The resolution welcomed the Soviet Union's improved international status, asked the socialist parties to combat their countries' aggressive policies toward the USSR, but noted that the danger of war would diminish if Russia had a democratic government. "Therefore the International most decisively supports the efforts of the socialist parties in the USSR to democratize the regime . . . and to establish political freedom."

The Mensheviks were displeased with the words "socialist parties in the USSR," which lumped them together with the SRs and the Georgians. The International's resolutions on Russia were often vague since it tried to find formulas acceptable to several dissenting parties. The British delegation had announced that it would not vote for a resolution attacking the Soviet government. The rightists were in the majority but wanted no conflict with the British and agreed to compromise. The "threat of war" resolution was passed unanimously, the SRs alone abstaining.

With its "on one hand" and "on the other hand," this resolution basically agreed with that of the delegation abroad, which also referred to two sources of the war threat, but it did not correspond to Dan's views. He and Bauer had objected to a formula that gave equal weight to an evil and a relative good. The other representatives of the RSDRP in the "Eastern commission," Abramovich and Garvi, did not speak on the subject because the Mensheviks avoided airing their differences in public. From that time on there were in menshevism two divergent views on the function of the International. Dan wanted it to be a directing center, not a parliament, and Abramovich no longer did. They also disagreed on the influence of the "Vienna precepts."

Dan believed it to be increasing—he saw signs of this at the Marseille, and later at the Brussels, congress. But actually the International was moving in another direction. To give both sides a chance to express themselves, the delegation decided to have two permanent representatives in the International—Dan and Abramovich. They were to take turns in attending the meetings of its bureau and executive committee.

Moscow: The Bureau of the CC

Lenin said that Mensheviks should be "carefully kept in prison during the NEP." The GPU overfulfilled the assignment. The bureau of the CC constantly heard from local organizations about arrests, deportations, clashes between inmates and jailers in prisons and concentration camps. Some organizations continued to work, on a reduced scale. Periods of relative animation alternated with almost complete quiescence.

During 1923–25, much of the Party's strength was taken up by a kind of private war with the GPU. For two months in early 1923 the GPU conducted a major campaign against Mensheviks, especially in Moscow. The Bolsheviks were preparing for a congress of Mensheviks who had left the Party.[24] Prison inmates were "taken care of," deportees moved to still more distant places. A member of the Social-Democratic Youth League, Aronovich, hanged himself in prison on the way to Solovki concentration camp. He was eighteen years old and had been shifted from prison to prison for two years. In Solovki, a young SR, Sandomir, committed suicide by cutting a vein, and an old S-D, Egorov-Lyzlov, by jumping out of a window. In late 1923, over a trifling matter, a conflict flared up between the administration of the camp and the inmates. According to official sources, six prisoners were killed and two were wounded. A particularly harsh regime, on the model of the Inner prison on the Lubianka, was introduced at the Suzdal camp, which housed many prominent socialists, among them the S-Ds M. Liber, I. Rubin, V. Levitskii, and the SRs Vysotskii and Rikhter, the Georgian S-Ds Lordkipanidze and Gogua. Upon his release from camp, Liber was deported to Semipalatinsk, where he remained under GPU surveillance. Except those sentenced in the trial of the SRs, all had been sentenced by the GPU without any court procedure. During these years almost every issue of *SV* contained information of this kind, received from the bureau of the CC.

In the fall of 1923 the GPU launched another large-scale persecution of Mensheviks. The bureau wrote the delegation abroad:

The first period of terror this year left us in changed, weakened circumstances, with great losses, great gaps, but we still retained some forces, their unity of spirit, the momentum of their collective existence. Now a second period of aggression is beginning. Our Party will have to go through the exceptional conditions created by the terror. Today the combat begins. What shall we have when we emerge from this second spell? No one can tell. One thing must be kept in mind: intensification of the Party's ideological life, cohesion of all its parts, organizational energy, and all the things you often mention when you write about us—"heroism," "self-sacrifice," and so on—all these are imperatives of the moment. [25]

Leaflets put out by the bureau's illegal press were the only means of protest. Two came out in March 1923: "To the Pillory," and "25 Years." On the twenty-fifth anniversary of the RSDRP, the GPU conducted mass raids. "This police orgy ... puts an indelible mark of ignominy on the Soviet government....It has not stopped the work of social democracy and it shall not." The "jubilee" leaflet outlined the development of menshevism and its role in 1905 and 1917. "And now the working class, robbed of freedom and civil rights, has been thrown back from [where it was] in 1917 and even in 1905." The May Day leaflet of the same year proclaimed: "The working class celebrates May Day this year deprived of its organizations, enslaved as never before. And the old demands, the old slogans rise before us in their full stature." In July 1923 the bureau printed an address to the International welcoming the resolution of the Hamburg Congress against Soviet terror: "More than ever the fate of the Russian proletariat depends on the European labor movement, the unity of the international proletariat, the growth of its fighting solidarity. In our difficult struggle, the awareness of this tie does not for a moment leave us." In September, a leaflet addressed the intelligentsia as well as the workers:

> The universities have been turned into barracks of stereotyped thinking and brazen privilege. They have never known a more reactionary regime. You are given Marx to read but the whip whistles at your shoulder and you swear allegiance on your knees to Bukharin's "ABC."...The best of your comrades are going through a harsh revolutionary school in the wastes of Siberia and Archangel. [26]

This was probably inspired by the successful work of the youth league among students.

The Communists knew from their own illegal past that to destroy an underground organization one had to cut it off from its sympathizers—

its sources of contacts, money, hiding places. As one means to this, the GPU organized a peculiar "movement of former Mensheviks," who publicly, in letters to newspapers, disowned their past allegiance and declared that they had gone over to the government's side. Most had long since drifted away from the Party. A few had been known as active Mensheviks. Through arrests and threats of deportation, the GPU obtained "confessions" in which the signers villified their own past. Some of these were honorable, even brave, men who succumbed from disorientation, apathy, the feeling that no political work was possible anyway. Their letters to the press were usually larded with fictitious facts supplied by the GPU and discreditable to the Mensheviks, who had no way of refuting them. In 1924 the GPU organized congresses of ex-Mensheviks in Moscow, Rostov, Tiflis, and other cities; and in Kharkov, even an all-Russian conference.

Underground work was stimulated by Kuchin's return to it. Kuchin had made his mark as a party worker before 1914. After military service in the war, he worked for the Party in Moscow, then in Kiev, where he was tried, along with the other Mensheviks, when the Soviets occupied the city. The verdict was imprisonment until the end of the civil war. Released during the war with Poland, Kuchin enlisted in the Red army—the war was still a defensive war. Later he went underground, was caught and deported to the Turkestan, ran away, and returned to illegal work as a member and the de facto leader of the bureau of the CC. After his secret trip to Berlin in 1924, Kuchin was "administratively" sentenced to ten years in prison, although at that time administrative punishments usually did not exceed three years. He spent three months in the Inner prison in Moscow, was moved to Cheliabinsk jail, then to a solitary cell at the Saratov concentration camp, where he staged a fifteen-day hunger strike, demanding to be moved to a common cell. Instead, he was returned to the Inner prison. The GPU threatened to press a new charge, liaison with Menshevik émigrés. Having learned of this, the executive committee of the International, which Kuchin had addressed during his trip, sent a telegram to "Inmate Georgii Kuchin," care of the GPU: "The executive committee of the LSI, gathered in Zurich, remembers the common work at one of the previous sessions and sends fraternal greetings to our tried-and-true fellow fighter."[27]

Party work was somewhat easier in Petrograd than in Moscow. Kuchin found it almost restful and "even went to the theater" when he stayed there in the spring of 1923. With great difficulty, some type had been obtained and a primitive printing press set up in an apartment rented by three Party members posing as a family. All possible precautions surrounded the press and it worked steadily. Kuchin describes it:

> A small dirty yard, narrow stairs; from the yard, you first look at the signal in the window. On the stairs, you ring the doorbell to the flat for a long time (they don't open right away, they are busy, everything has to be hidden). A two-room flat, cozy, commonplace furniture, everything so quiet. In the second, almost dark room, the electric light is on all the time. The whole flat is rather dark, you really seem to enter a mysterious "underground." The type and hand press are on the sofa. Behind a screen, on a bed, freshly printed galleys. A pair of wooden typecases—all as it should be, all the equipment. They live quietly, do not see anybody.... The atmosphere ... is downright idyllic ... instant calm envelops you.... It was always so pleasant to spend an hour or two in that perfect commune. They could not bear not to work. The appearance of an issue [of *Sotsialdemokrat*] was always a joy. [28]

Kuchin was so favorably impressed because his own life was even grimmer, but reality was far from idyllic. The police were combing the city for the commune. In true conspiratorial fashion, its members left the flat only when absolutely necessary. The monotony was enervating. But the work went on and improved when seven more poods of type were procured, which the members, at great risk, carried to the flat under their coats. In November 1923 they noticed that the house was being watched. The next day they carried out ten poods of type and disappeared. "During those days the few available people were practically run off their feet, they kept going on their last nerves." It took two months to set up a press in other quarters. There was no money. False passports manufactured in the south were a big help.[29] The GPU found the press only in 1925.

In Moscow it was difficult to find a place for an illegal person to spend the night, or a room for a few members of the bureau to hold a conference. In summer they met in the woods. The financial situation of all the illegals was ghastly. Nevertheless, in the summer of 1923 the bureau arranged a conference with representatives of the Menshevik right and of the Bund. The topics: organizing a youth conference; elections to Soviets; the next leaflets; the journal *Sotsialdemokrat;* the ex-Mensheviks; and the situation in the Party. At this conference the idea of curtailing party work was first put before the bureau and voted down. The raid on the youth league had been a heavy blow. The Odessa and Kiev organizations were cut off from the center, but the latter was still in contact with Kharkov, the Donbas, Rostov, and Sormovo. In view of the police difficulties in Moscow, it was decided to leave only the organizational apparatus there and to move the political center to Petrograd. [30]

What impelled these lonely people to go on with the hopeless struggle? They were sustained by faith in the rightness of their ideas and the conviction that their work "answered a tremendous historical need," as the bureau put it in a letter to Party members in the summer of 1923. There would be more resistance to a Bonapartist reaction, and a better chance of saving the revolution, if the Social-Democratic party left a strong imprint on the workers' minds. The letter continued:

> The task of Russian social democracy is this: continue our work for all we are worth, despite the exceptionally unfavorable conditions, despite the nightmare of terror and social disintegration, despite the total absence of organized political life—continue our work, over-coming all these conditions. [31]

But the conditions could not be overcome. By the fall of 1923, formal Party organizations survived in only eight centers. Elsewhere only literature was distributed. The young generation alone displayed energy. Why party work was grinding to a standstill can be seen from the bureau's report to the delegation abroad:

> The fall [1923] months were extremely hard. . . . Politically we sank deeper and deeper into the underground, and the surrounding milieu was becoming more and more alien and demoralized. The membership of the Party groups had shrunk and changed because of the continuous struggle against arrests all summer long: almost every-where some comrades were already illegal, the groups had with-drawn even from the former weak contacts with "public life"; the severed liaison with the center and the general state of affairs reduced their active work still more, and a halfway normal ideologi-cal life became almost impossible. This life, which had surged so high in 1922–23, is now almost extinct. In these dreadful conditions, every-thing boils down to bare struggle for the survival of the Party collec-tive . . . enormous efforts on a puny scale. [32]

Trying to keep the moribund organism alive, the bureau of the CC was less concerned than the delegation abroad with intraparty dif-ferences. It co-opted a leader of the right and it always invited a representative of it to its "enlarged" meetings, well aware that common work tended to smooth out ideological dissent. A letter to Party members in early 1923 pointed out that unity was the foremost "requirement of the moment"; the changed socioeconomic conditions created by the NEP

> partly remove and partly reduce the significance of the disagreements over principles and tactics that . . . divided the Party into two camps during the past few years. Gradually the groundwork is being laid for fertile interaction of the various ideological trends . . . for working out a single party line and putting it into practice. [33]

The sharp divisions of the civil war era had indeed noticeably abated. Only the extraparty group *Zaria* was still anathema to the bureau: "This movement is becoming more and more insufferable and of course a clear-cut demarcation from them is necessary."[34] In Russia even the Party right was against *Zaria*, differing in this from the émigré right.

After Liber's arrest the bureau coopted the rightist B. Vasil'ev. The delegation agreed that a Party member of his caliber should not be wasted, but reminded the bureau that the party line and "ideological closeness to the stand of *SV*" must be preserved. In 1924 Vasil'ev was sentenced to three years in the Suzdal camp. In 1925, the delegation approved the inclusion in the bureau of V. Kononenko, who was close to the Party center.[35]

Much work went into leaflets and other illegal publications—the only remaining means of public protest.[36] The collection of the delegation abroad, not necessarily exhaustive, contained sixty-four such organs, published between 1922 and 1924: twenty-nine of them in Moscow, twenty-one in Petrograd, and from one to five each in Kharkov, Kiev, Odessa, the Volga region, Ekaterinoslav, and Tula.[37] These publications were produced not by strong organizations but by small isolated groups.

The more the Party was hemmed in, the more incongruous it seemed to act as if it were still an important party, to address the masses, seek their support, speak in their name. Members began to feel that their sacrifices were useless: it would be more sensible to lie low, to preserve the Party cadres so that they might emerge as soon as the dictatorship was overthrown and perhaps play a decisive role in the democratic finale of the revolution. Such ideas arose not only in the deep underground of local organizations but even in the bureau and the delegation abroad. They did not prevail, for the majority considered them symptomatic of decline and discouragement—yet in many cases they stemmed from sober assessment of reality or even from the optimistic conceptions of the "Martov movement." At an enlarged meeting of the bureau in the summer of 1923 the opinion was expressed that with its present pretensions the Party looked like "a naked man in a top hat."

In a long letter for which he had obtained special permission from the delegation abroad,[38] Dallin wrote the bureau that the Party's survival depended on ideological unity and a strong organizational apparatus. In Russia, the first had been more or less achieved, but the second was gone. The situation was much worse than in the reactionary years 1908–12, when there had been Party organizations, the Duma, lectures, and so on; it was more like that of the Liberation of Labor group, which had worked for years laying the ground for a party without being able to become one itself. What should the RSDRP do in these conditions? For the present, Dallin wrote, it should remain merely a collective of like-minded people, which might play a considerable role in the future—if it stayed within its possibilities:

> With the organizational apparatus demolished, and as yet no sign of new life in the popular masses, we have to concentrate on developing that solidarity, that political cohesion, which welds us into a single collective and which the steel hammer of terror is unable to crush.

When the dictator is abolished and political life revives,

> our advantage will lie not in our numbers and not in the "apparatus," but in the enormous superiority of our sociopolitical ideology over the muddled, ephemeral theories of the heroes of Bolshevik decadence.

Side by side with the Party, the youth league continued its fight for survival. In late 1923 it even managed to convoke an all-Russian conference, which approved the political line of the CC and the work of the league's organizational bureau. The conference found that work among the masses should be confined to distribution of literature; the league should pay special attention in its propaganda to the workers' economic needs; work among the young intelligentsia had autonomous significance; under the prevailing conditions, organizational centralism was imperative and also stricter observance of secrecy—with democratic principles honored as far as possible. It was unanimously decided to join the Socialist Youth International. For "police reasons" the conference had to close in a hurry and did not deal with all the points on its agenda. [39]

The underground route by which the bureau and the delegation communicated was still functioning in the middle twenties, though less reliably. Sometimes the police discovered a link in the chain and contact was broken for some time. A package with fifty copies of *SV* disappeared in the spring of 1924, probably intercepted by the GPU. The bureau wrote the delegation about its work, the situation in the USSR, the fate of arrested comrades; discussed ideological problems such as the attitude to be taken toward the intelligentsia, the peasantry, or the latest government decrees; and asked many questions about events in the West, which the Soviet press distorted. In May 1924 it asked the delegation to appoint one or two of its members "special correspondents" about the West.

When Kuchin returned from his trip abroad and learned that the Party had undergone a new assault, he wrote that the Communists seemed to be in a state of "mad rage" against Mensheviks and that the GPU was "beside itself over the continuing work of the RSDRP." He wanted to tell Party members about his trip, but this was difficult to arrange: "Scattered, isolated individuals . . . We are thinking of a few meetings of small groups with informational political reports. Will form a youth group, too. . . . All this is small, laborious work." But it was all the more necessary since "the isolation is so great here, and so many minds are unhinged." Summaries of foreign news were smuggled into prison camps. If the Party had to rely on its old cadres, it would have to fold up. Luckily, "as a result of our work, we have a new generation. . . . We shall have to rely on them when work resumes. They want activity, their energy is astounding, and there is a new phenomenon: their spontaneous wish to work among the proletariat. Thus new contacts with workers are established."[40]

With the help of students going home for vacations, the bureau was able to renew contact with several provincial organizations and to send them some Party literature. "Unfortunately there was hardly anything to send."[41] While noting hopeful developments, the leaders were not blind to the undesirable tendencies among workers. The number of "conscious workers" was shrinking.

> Right now two extremes can be observed among workers, two kinds of "bolshevism": one is the Communists armed with all the weapons of the state, the other is the unarmed, weakened mass, ready to claw the former to bits. Between them, a thin, a transparently thin, layer of workers' intelligentsia thinking in Marxist terms. Both bolshevisms lead to ruin; the middle is weak, sickly, small.[42]

The party must provide ideological and practical leadership for this thin layer. But leading the labor movement out of the blind alley was a "thankless and difficult task. History has assigned it to you"—the émigrés. The bureau's critical view of them had given way to recognition of the significance of their role. "If anything can rally the socialist forces of Russia, it is the monolithic organization and ideology of Social-Democrats abroad."[43] In Russia, party work had become impossible, a new policy could originate only abroad. The center of gravity had shifted ideology and leadership to the émigrés.

The bureau's gloomy view of the tendencies among the workers did not keep it from thinking of the traditional Menshevik goal, a mass movement. Currently there was none, but the Party must be ready for its revival. In a letter apparently written by Kuchin, the bureau informed the delegation abroad that party workers everywhere were asking questions that could be summed up in one: what to do to become part of a mass movement again.[44] Concrete guidelines were needed—for example, how to act in the event of strikes, whether to belong to factory committees, clubs, and so on. Nonparticipation meant giving up "mass activity" even where it was still possible; yet the work could not produce useful results. Since the Party program gave no answers to such questions, the bureau suggested adding to it a document "on methods."

In practice, of course, such problems rarely arose. As before, the bureau and local organizations were mainly concerned with keeping up old contacts, establishing new ones where possible, and distributing *SV* and their own publications. For its daily work the bureau found it necessary to maintain at least three members in the underground and a legal one for technical work; only minor jobs could be given to sympathizers. Lack of money was a great handicap. In 1925 the bureau wrote the delegation, "We have lost six [party] workers in the past few months"—because of inability to provide bare subsistence pay. Underground safety rules had to be broken; sometimes this led to arrests. Once a group of deportees collected fifty rubles among themselves and sent them to the bureau. One bureau member lived on ten rubles a month.

The Party published leaflets in Moscow and the provinces. In 1926, after a long interval, the bureau put out its informational bulletin *Iz Partii*. In March 1927 a *Biulleten' TsK RSDRP* appeared in Moscow. During November and December, 1927, a leaflet, "To All Workers of the Soviet Union," was distributed in factories. It stated that the terror against the opposition in the Communist party bespoke the "death throes" of the dictatorship; workers must have a share in deciding the form of government that would replace it. "It is time to break the silence. Unite, draft political demands." Reaction was threatening, and it was useless to count on the Communist party, even on its opposition elements, to combat it. Peaceful liquidation of the dictatorship was the thing to strive for. Begin with demanding freedom of assembly, free elections, amnesty, abolition of the GPU. In March 1928 a Menshevik leaflet scattered at the gates of two Kharkov factories created a sensation—among the workers and in the GPU—less by its contents than by the mere fact of its appearance. In April an appeal "To All Workers and Employees of the Soviet Union" signed by the Central Committee of the RSDRP, in connection with a campaign for new collective agreements, pointed out the growing unemployment and the workers' deteriorating situation: nothing but independent trade unions really defending workers and employees could save them.

SV was a more regular means of disseminating Menshevik ideas. Because of transmission difficulties, the bureau wrote the delegation abroad in May 1924 to reduce the number of copies sent to Russia to twenty-five or thirty, but in the following August it requested regular shipments of three hundred. The bureau asked the editors of *SV* to give more space to theory, less to intraparty controversies; to include more information about the Western labor movement, and popular articles geared to a broad readership. By 1926 the distribution improved, the issues were "read and reread, torn to tatters. . . . *Vestnik* must remain first and foremost a militant political organ. Turning it into a 'discussion sheet' is out of the question."[45]

A new field of activity opened for the bureau with the visits to Russia of foreign "labor delegations." These usually consisted of fellow-travelers or uninformed people easily blinded by the artful "hospitality" of the Soviet government. The delegates were influential in their organizations at home, and their glowing reports of what they had seen in the mysterious land of socialism largely shaped Western public opinion. The bureau, the delegation abroad, and *SV* tried to correct the picture. In late 1925, a German and a Czechoslovak delegations published enthusiastic accounts. Once, in early 1926, the Cheka removed all political prisoners from the Kharkov preliminary detention prison before it was shown to a group of Western young people—and they reported that despite rumors there were no "politicals" in the prison. A second German delegation, in the summer of 1926, included several Social-Democrats who had joined it against the wishes of their organizations. The bureaus of the CC and of the Moscow and Petrograd committees of the RSDRP sent the German Social-Democratic party a joint memorandum giving details on the terror and the true situation of the workers in the USSR and denying that the RSDRP was counterrevolutionary—a Bolshevik accusation that most delegates believed. The memorandum also pointed out to the German party that all the visitors so far had been "conscious or unconscious tools of Communist propaganda and policy."[46]

While the delegation abroad remained almost unchanged, the bureau of the CC often lost members through arrests and coopted new ones—in most cases prominent Party workers who had escaped from their places of exile. Strictly following the Party rules, the bureau always asked the delegation's approval, but after the conflict over Liber[47] the delegation never again rejected the bureau's nominees.

The changes in personnel did not greatly affect the bureau's work but they did influence its political orientation. The bureau had stood on the right flank of the Party's center, had wanted to cooperate with rightists in the Party and had coopted their representative. After 1925 it apparently shifted to the left. It advocated a common front with the Communists, accepted "limited democracy," that is, struggling for democracy through partial demands, and became hostile to the Party right.[48] It ascribed the rightists' activities abroad to their having lost contact with Russia and failing to understand the situation. Just when the workers' apathy was "giving way to increased interest in politics," the rightists' stand threatened a schism in the RSDRP.[49] The bureau was also displeased with the émigré right for participating in Potresov's and Stepan Ivanovich's *Biblioteka Demokraticheskogo Sotsializma* and for its nonclass approach to problems involving democracy.

A very hostile view of the right émigrés emerged in 1928 in the Leningrad organization, which blamed their activity on Potresov's arrival abroad: "The news. . . about the *fronde* initiated by certain comrades against the directing organs of our Party cannot but alarm us [Party] workers in Russia."[50]

That summer, the Leningrad organization was wiped out. As the bureau wrote the delegation abroad, the GPU razed it to the ground—nothing was left but "an empty spot."

The last mention of the bureau of the CC appears in the minutes of a meeting of the delegation abroad on 5 April 1931, about a month after the Mensheviks' trial (see Appendix C).

The other Party center in the USSR, the main committee for the Ukraine, which sometimes called itself the bureau of the CC for the Ukraine and which supported the line of the delegation abroad, survived until at least March 1928.

Correspondence between individual Party figures in Russia and the Delegation of the RSDRP Abroad continued for some years, though no longer regularly.

13

The Platform of 1924

The New Platform and the Theses of 1920

It took the Party a full two years to work out its new platform, which had to include a thorough analysis of the political situation in the West, had to be agreed on by the delegation abroad and the bureau of the Central Committee, and gave rise to long disputes. The discussions began with Martov's article in *SV* in October 1922 and at the simultaneous Party conference in Moscow. The bureau and a group of Moscow rightists then drew up their respective theses. [1]

The feeling that the old platform was obsolete was keener in Russia than abroad. If only to guide them in running underground publications and maintaining their tenuous contact with the masses, the "illegal" Party leaders needed a line adapted to the new conditions. The bureau of the CC was aware of the Party's growing need "to look back, sum up the results of six years, and objectively take stock of the present situation." [2]

The delegation abroad prepared a draft of the new platform in June 1923. The bureau found it "not a very successful literary document. . . . Objections of principle intermingle with editorial objections." In particular, "the conception of the democratic movement is presented . . . too abstractly." [3] Except for Kuchin, the bureau held that the time was not ripe for a broad and detailed definition of principles. The platform should be more concrete, answer current political questions rather

than questions of principle: for example, was the attainment of democracy an immediate demand or a long-range goal? Although the
bureau's attitude toward the Soviet government was more militant
than the delegation's, on this basic question it tended to be cautious.
Somewhat earlier, Kuchin and a few other members of the bureau had
come to feel that the demand for an immediate democratic republic
was too abstract and unrealistic to inspire the population at large. The
bureau stated that its criticism of the draft was not due to basic dissent
but concerned formulation, approach, argumentation. The Party
should try to penetrate the masses instead of concentrating, as Dan had
advocated in the early period of the NEP, on the thin layer of "conscious" workers.

In February 1924 the delegation prepared a second draft, which was
discussed and accepted in Berlin in May at an enlarged plenum of the
CC: eighteen people, including the Delegations Abroad of the RSDRP
and of the Bund, and invited representatives of the main trends in the
Party and Kuchin as representative of the bureau. (He had come from
Moscow illegally to take part in these discussions.)

The platform of 1924[4] was more comprehensive than Martov's "April
theses" of 1920, which it supplanted. It was neither a far-ranging
statement of ideology nor brief, compact theses, but in the full sense a
"platform" defining the considered policy for the given juncture.
Clearly, however, its framers also meant it to provide the ideological
basis for the common front of international labor. More than a quarter
of it was given over to analysis of postwar conditions in the West.

The foreword stated that the platform differed from the theses
mainly in that it reflected the changes in the labor movement in the
intervening four years, during which the proletariat's frontal attacks
on capitalism had ceased and the development of the movement had
come to a temporary standstill. Martov's head-on strategy must give
way to a strategy of defense and a turning movement, "in the general
context of the era of social revolution."

Both documents were based on the premise that a socialist revolution
was now possible. But the theses had taken it for granted that the
advanced countries were ready for it and that in the backward countries transitional forms could be introduced, on condition that "the
state power depend on the toilers." The platform, on the other hand,
recognized that the revolution had been delayed by the "temporary"
stabilization of capitalism and the "inner unreadiness, the divergent
political ideas, the organizational divisions of the proletariat." The
inference to be drawn was not formulated but it was obvious: to
achieve a socialist overturn, it was necessary—and sufficient—to
overcome the negative phenomena in the labor movement. It was this

inference that determined the Party's stand in the International, on the common front issue, and largely in Russia. Ultimately, this conception, combined with the conception of "bourgeois democracy" as class dominance of the bourgeoisie, underlay the "leftism" of the Party majority that the platform reflected.

The struggle of the working class for political power would be "the content of the next historical era." Several countries already had labor or coalition governments. To be sure, these were "transitional and halfhearted," and the slow progress toward power was further braked by "reformist opportunism" bent on reducing class antagonisms and promoting class cooperation—this on the very eve of the revolution. Communism, too, was causing harm with its "utopianism alien to the interests of the working class." However, the main criticism was aimed at the right. The International should adopt a policy of internationalism and rally the revolutionary Marxist elements against reformers and "nationalists."

It was this part of the platform that differed most from the theses of 1920. Three factors explain the difference: the "drawn-out" revolutionary process in the West, the far from drawn-out growth of totalitarianism in the USSR, and the ceaseless intraparty dissent. The platform did not mention dictatorship of the proletariat, which the theses had stressed as "concentration of all power" in the proletariat's hands in advanced countries, where the working class formed the majority of the population. In backward countries, including Russia, the theses had postulated "division of power between the proletariat and the other toiling classes" as a preparatory stage to dictatorship of the proletariat. The notion of a dictatorship of the majority was replaced in the platform with a demand for the abolition of the Soviet dictatorship and for the establishment of

> a democratic republic headed by a government leaning on the broad proletarian and peasant masses and based on universal, equal, direct, and secret suffrage, the broadest political freedom, an elected and accountable administration, a militia replacing the abolished regular army. . . . The RSDRP considers the proletariat the basic force able to steer the liquidation of the Bolshevik dictatorship into the channel of democracy.

Unlike the April theses, the platform clearly spelled out the democratic nature of the government that was to replace the Bolshevik dictatorship. Yet at the same time it insisted that this government keep the NEP from leading to a restoration of capitalism. The only form of government that could meet these requirements was the "toilers' rule" —a rule in which all toilers would have a stake, "without distinction of the socialist, or even Communist, factional and party groups to which they may belong."

The RSDRP is advancing these demands, on the basis of which the further development of democracy is possible, as a *platform of agreement* for all groups, parties, and their parts, that are able in this developmental process to stand firmly on the ground of the revolution, to defend the interests of toilers, and to recognize the need to form a government willing to work for a democratic reorganization of the state and prevent the Bonapartist degeneration of the revolution.

On the thorny question of a common front with the Communists there could be no compromise between the majority, the right, and the extreme left. Kuchin vainly tried to effect a rapprochement. During the final discussion of the draft before the conference, he wrote that the whole platform was "tactically leftist":

You have to agree that this is so. Given this premise, certain formulations could well be softened [as a concession to the right].... As a compensation to the left, I consider it quite possible to sharpen the point about agreement (for it is the most important, which unites us all) if a satisfactory formulation can be found (you will recall that the commission could not find one).[5]

Since the Mensheviks wanted to reform, not overthrow, the regime, the platform demanded observance of the Soviet constitution. Not because it was good but because it was available: its genuine implementation would be a first step away from dictatorship.

The wish for agreement did not stop the Mensheviks from criticizing the regime. Apart from rejecting in principle the dictatorship of a minority, the platform stated that it had turned into the dictatorship of a clique, a party apparatus; the NEP had been due exclusively "to the Bolsheviks' wish to preserve their shaken power" and therefore was not working efficiently; the regime had spawned an irresponsible bureaucracy and created a basis for Bonapartism.

Among the social forces that the NEP had brought to the fore, the intelligentsia and the peasantry seemed predestined to play important roles in straightening out the revolution. The Mensheviks now paid more attention to these groups than they had before. The theses of 1920 had included technicians and "the proletariat of intellectual labor" in the concept of "toilers." The platform accorded the intelligentsia autonomous significance—on condition that it overcome the passivity into which it had fallen:

A relatively small segment of the intelligentsia has cottoned up to the present regime, has become part of the ruling layer or its supporter and apologist (turncoatism), but the mass of the intelligentsia suffers from the surrounding cultural decline, the ideological coercion, the exceptionally hard struggle for survival, the economic dependence on the government. But the deep moral and intellectual crisis it has lived through ... has somewhat unfitted it for its traditional role of pioneer and guiding spirit of the democratic movement. It is itself in need of an impulse from such a mass movement in order to overcome its disarray and passivity and again become a consequential factor in the country's political and economic democratization.

It was regrettable that specialists in various fields were "under the orders and supervision of spies and agents of the dictatorship" who owed their power merely to their membership in the ruling party.

Equally dangerous processes were going on in the peasantry. The platform demanded changes in agrarian policy—the earlier reform had been insufficient. SV commented on the economic plank of the platform:

> A change in the industrial system is necessary mainly in the interests of the millions-strong peasant mass, which in the final count can decide the fate of the revolution. An attentive attitude toward [the peasantry] is the most important demand of the moment. Therefore Social Democracy is putting the agrarian program in the forefront. [6]

The reallotment of land had been far from satisfactory, but the main thing now was to "secure and guarantee possession." It did not greatly matter whether the system was private or state capitalism or long-term leases as in England. What counted was to give the peasants, especially the middle peasants on whom Russia's agricultural progress depended, enough incentive to farm the land and security in their possession of it. The existing allotments should be legalized; land exploitation organized in such a way that a peasant could leave the commune if he wished; voluntary cooperation encouraged; and the *sovkhozes* abolished, except a few model ones.

Foreseeing that "Bolshevik management" would strengthen capitalist elements, the platform demanded that the state retain control over heavy industry and over enterprises of a monopolistic nature, such as railroads and postal service, while letting organs of local self-government manage the production of consumer goods. Trade should be decentralized, and private trade allowed.

The platform was adopted at an enlarged plenum of the CC by thirteen votes, with five rightists abstaining, and thus became the basic document of the Party. Despite this solid majority, the disputes over it continued.

The five rightists explained in a memorandum why they had abstained: They could not accept the limitation of democratic principles inherent in the "utopian idea of toilers' rule"; they rejected agreement with the Communist party and the demand to observe the Soviet constitution, which "perverted the character of the struggle for a democratic republic." They agreed with the platform insofar as it supported the idea of a democratic republic, especially important "in face of the Bonapartist danger." They also agreed with the realistic prognosis that Russia's economic development would strengthen capitalist elements. Although the points of dissent outweighed those of agreement, they had abstained from voting out of loyalty to the Party and also because the delegation had promised to coopt their representative if they did not weaken the impact of the platform by voting against it.[7] The right did not object to the thesis about imminent social revolution in the West but disagreed with it as far as Russia was concerned. [8]

Criticism of the Platform

Neither the right nor the left opposition was satisfied with the compromise formulations of some of the articles. The rightists insisted on their right to criticize the new platform in print. The delegation abroad refused to let them do it in *SV*, since it tried to keep the Party's fighting organ free of internal polemics, but agreed in 1925 to publish a collection of polemical articles in book form. A series of such volumes was planned, but only one came out,[9] with articles by a rightist (P. Garvi), an extreme leftist (M. Valerianov), and a reply to both by a member of the majority (F. Dan). This book is of interest, for the views of the two flanks of Menshevism are not expressed in comparable detail anywhere else.

Garvi was a product of the old tsarist underground, deeply devoted to the Menshevik cause. He had always been one of the anti-Bolsheviks in the Party. In 1905 he had taken part in the Moscow uprising; in 1907 he had been nominated candidate to the Central Committee; later he had become a "Liquidationist," and during the First World War a "moderate Internationalist." Life in the West as an émigré and his personal friendship with Kautsky had strengthened Garvi's rightist convictions. Although he continued to consider himself a true Marxist, the Party majority justly accused him of a reformist streak.

In the volume on the platform, Garvi recognized that the ideological differences between the majority and the Menshevik right had become less pronounced since the launching of the NEP. Both sides now discerned the partial revival of capitalism, the impending collapse of the Soviet regime, and the danger of "Bonapartism." But from these common premises the two sides drew different tactical conclusions: while the leaders of the Party majority advocated "oppositional reformist" tactics, the right doubted their practicality: "Together with Axelrod and Kautsky, we prefer peaceful evolution but, unlike them, we doubt that it is realistically possible." The more effective way for the Party to try and avert counterrevolution was not "half struggle, half conciliation" on the basis of the Soviet constitution, but implacable struggle against any kind of dictatorship. Garvi rejected "the obsessive idea of 'toilers' rule'" not only as contrary in principle to democracy, to "the people's rule," but also as impractical, without foundations in Soviet reality. The peasants were bound to play a big role in the shaping of postrevolutionary society, and it was important to gain their sympathy, especially that of the peasant poor. But thanks to the government's policies, the peasants had already become anti-revolutionary and antilabor. A sincere struggle for democracy and a lawful government might still attract them, but not the prospect of sharing power with the proletariat. Under the NEP, the influence of the old and new bourgeoisie was also growing, and it had also developed reactionary tendencies. But unlike the landowning gentry, the bourgeoisie had a future in Russia; therefore the existing "little particles of bourgeois liberalism and democratic spirit" should not be disdained.

Here we come to the weakest part of Garvi's argument. "The people's rule" would seem to imply some form of alliance with sincere democratic forces. That some right-wing Mensheviks thought such an alliance desirable is borne out by their public appearances in the company of Kerensky and even Miliukov.[10] But Garvi only wrote obscurely that after the fall of the Soviet regime the party of the working class "may be faced with the necessity to participate temporarily in some governmental coalition." This formula, stressing the forced and temporary nature of such a coalition, did not rise above the level of the 1905 formulations on the same subject. Among the potential supporters of the democratic movement, Garvi also ignored the intelligentsia, which had played an important role in the revolution and whose significance the platform recognized.

On the other hand, he rejected the allies on which the platform counted—the common front in the International and the opposition in the Communist party. Like Potresov and Axelrod, he held that the democratization of the Communist party was a vain hope since "Leninism is essentially an attempt to divorce democracy from socialism." Hence it was necessary to fight this party and all its factions rather than seek agreement. Garvi rejected the idea that the conflict between socialism and communism was a temporary conflict within the labor movement. He insisted that the International take an uncompromising stand against communism, as Axelrod and Kautsky demanded, instead of playing with harmful, utopian, "common front" notions. The RSDRP had done a great deal to dispel illusions about bolshevism in the International, but its championship of the common front was undoing this work.

When the volume of polemical articles was being planned, M. Kefali had objected to the inclusion among its editors of Valerianov since the small group on the extreme left differed little from the majority.[11] Dan had agreed with Kefali: "[Valerianov] fully accepts the tactical orientation of the Party. . . . He merely holds that the Party does not apply its principles . . . consistently enough." Nevertheless, he was included among the editors of the volume, along with a representative of the right and the editors of SV.[12]

Valerianov argued the necessity of a common front and of agreement with the Soviet government. Russia needed agreement among all socialist and Communist elements for the sake of fighting Bonapartism "and for the gradual democratization of the Soviet regime, with the aim of creating a democratic order, the social content of which will be the toilers' rule." In the International, the common front and the defeat of reformists should be the main tasks, but the RSDRP was not attending to them—it was, in fact, sharpening the struggle against communism and promoting a common front with reformists. There was a great difference between necessary criticism of the Communists and "one-sided reformist antibolshevism." The Party should take its orientation from the will to true unity "already ripening in the Communist labor movement." Valerianov did not mention the kind of "unity" between socialism and communism that the Soviet regime had established in Russia.

Despite their pro-Soviet tendencies, the extreme leftists did not secede from the Party. In 1929 the delegation sent Valerianov to Russia for illegal work, in particular to improve the channels of communication between Russia and the delegation.[13] He was arrested and disappeared without a trace.

Dan's reply dealt almost exclusively with Garvi's article and was relatively short since the stand of the majority was already expressed in the platform. The key to his position is to be found in something he wrote two years after the adoption of the platform:

> The program is based on the same principles of revolutionary Marxism and the same tactical lines as have guided the Party throughout the Bolshevik phase of the revolution.... Conflicts between the toiling classes must be resolved through agreement, not through highly dangerous armed struggle. [14]

In Dan's opinion it was not the shifted views of the majority that explained its diminished disagreements with the right but the right's retreat from its old positions. While repeating its old slogans of adamant opposition to bolshevism, it had in fact become much more moderate. The toilers' (proletarian-peasant) rule was interpreted by Dan as a temporary principle, to be applied only during the first period following the dictatorship. This interpretation was not consonant with the platform's spirit or with Dan's own later declarations.

The extraparty right led by Potresov largely shared the views of the Party right. Potresov left Russia in 1925, studied the émigré Menshevik literature and the trends in the Party, and had several talks with Dan, which Axelrod had arranged in the hope of bringing them together. Dan gladly met the old leader, but friendly feelings could not overcome ideological differences. Afterward, Potresov wrote Dan:

> I took my differences with my old comrades very hard, both during the war and still more in 1917–20. At present it is in some ways even more painful for me to feel some sort of "barrier" between me and the Menshevik party milieu, which despite everything is the only one I really feel close to and whose fate worries me like a personal concern.... SV, despite some softening retouches, is still keeping to the traditions of 1920 and therefore coming more and more in conflict with the ripening processes of postrevolutionary Russian reality. [15]

According to Potresov, the Party majority suffered from "a split psyche" making for a split ideology and fuzzy thinking, "so unlike the logical consistency of the late Martov." The source of the trouble was the idea that communism was a branch of the labor movement and could be criticized but not fought with uprisings—an idea that had forced "many of us old Social-Democrats to leave the Party organization, in outrage and pain." [16]

Till the end of his life Potresov considered himself a Marxist, though he broke the rules of orthodox Marxism by calling bolshevism a plebeian revolution that did not fit into the framework of class struggle.

He argued that "without a doubt, dictatorship of the proletariat is a term of Marxist literature that has completely outlived its time"; menshevism with its idea of toilers' rule denied the inalienable rights of citizens in favor of "a sober, moderate, tidy utopia (even utopias can be that)." The bourgeoisie was a class enemy but not a criminal and parasite who could be denied his rights without violating the first principles of Social Democracy.

The Soviet regime, Potresov said, had all the bad traits of capitalism without the attendant growth of the labor movement. Criticizing the 1924 platform, he wrote that before trying to rescue the proletariat from bolshevism "Social Democracy itself must break out of the vicious circle of paralyzing notions" that made it incapable of leading the masses. Unlike the Party right, Potresov did not fear even the victory of Bonapartism because "'Bonaparte' has already been despoiled by the Bolsheviks." Under a different, even a Bonapartist, dictatorship the situation would be simpler and clearer, for the enemy facing the masses would not have the demagogic advantages of bolshevism. With his vizor raised, he would be easier to defeat.

Dan criticized Potresov as sharply as Potresov criticized the Party majority. Tsereteli, a close friend of Potresov's, approved the latter's strong formulations but thought that he was wrong in linking his current stand to the Defensism of the World War.[17] (Tsereteli had then been an Internationalist.) The Party right on the whole agreed with Potresov except in certain details; for example, they took more seriously the threat of Bonapartism. Indeed, they would have consolidated their ties with Potresov but for the fact that this would have meant breaking with the Party organization.

The discussion of the 1924 platform was a landmark in Menshevik ideology. It reinforced, though not for long, the Party's basic position and brought out the various views prevalent in it at that stage. In one respect the discussions were a failure: no one seems to have changed his mind. The conflicting views had taken deep roots during the six-and-a-half years of Soviet rule. The differences were determined not so much by principles—these the contestants often shared—as by political intuition and the kind of perception that cannot be fitted into logical schemata and yet plays a large role in the formation of political views. So the controversies continued, and flared up with new intensity when the "general line" replaced the NEP.

14
The Party in Emigration

During the second emigration, the RSDRP had three centers outside Russia. One was the delegation abroad, which together with the bureau of the CC in Moscow constituted the Central Committee of the Party. The delegation became increasingly autonomous as the situation of the bureau grew more precarious. After the delegation had coopted M. Kefali and given the vote to G. Aronson and S. Schwarz, and E. Broido had left on an underground mission in 1927, its membership of ten remained almost unchanged until the Second World War.[1] In 1926, Boris Sapir, just out of Solovki concentration camp, was appointed representative of the Menshevik Youth League in the executive committee of the Socialist Youth International.

The second center was the editorial board of *SV*, which met regularly to discuss the contents of its issues. In important cases, joint meetings with the delegation abroad and specially invited guests were called.

The third and largest center was the conference of the Berlin organization of the RSDRP. Often attended by as many as a hundred members, it discussed current ideological and political problems. Its resolutions were not binding on the delegation abroad. The majority of this group agreed with the delegation's policies. Other Menshevik groups existed in Geneva, Liège, Paris, Bern, and New York.[2]

Apart from a few of the émigrés' own offspring, no new members joined the Menshevik party abroad. An émigré party could not engage in direct propaganda and there was no milieu from which it could draw adherents. Nor did the leaders wish to introduce untried, perhaps dubious, new members into the Party. On the other hand, not one Menshevik defected to another party abroad, and only one broke with the RSDRP to return to Russia—G. Gonikberg, an old Menshevik married to a Communist.[3] In this connection, the delegation resolved: "Members of the RSDRP who intend to return to Russia must inform the delegation abroad of all steps taken in this direction and must act [only] with its knowledge and consent."[4]

Publishing in non-Menshevik organs was restricted. Members of the RSDRP could not write for political publications of the Russian Communist party even if they had the opportunity; they were allowed to contribute to technical, economic, or historical publications that did not polemize with the RSDRP, but of course such organs were few.[5] Similar rules applied to the émigré press. After the appearance of an article by Aronson in Kerensky's paper *Dni* in 1926, it was decided that members of the delegation could write in non-Menshevik émigré papers only in exceptional cases and then not on politics and not in papers that campaigned against the RSDRP.[6]

In 1927 there appeared in the Party majority the first signs of a rift that was to deepen in the following years. Some members came to disagree with Dan's increasingly leftist stand and moved closer to the right without merging with it. This new center group consisted of Abramovich, Dallin, Nicolaevsky, and a few followers who were not members of the delegation. In the early thirties this group's disagreement with Dan became quite profound.

Of the three main groups (Dan's left, the new center, and the right—the extreme left hardly counted) Dan's following was the most numerous, and also the most cohesive, thanks to Dan's gift for leadership. The schism in the majority often caused complications: when the center voted with the right, the votes were split five to five and no decision could be reached.

Partly because they had new allies, and partly because of events in Russia, the activity of the rightists increased. Their representatives often spoke in the delegation, offering proposals and protesting the Party's stand. They felt that ten years of Soviet rule had proven the majority wrong: the Bolshevik regime was not evolving toward democracy but toward a one-man dictatorship; the NEP had turned out to be a temporary maneuver; in the West, the Communists increasingly divided the labor movement. All this seemed to vindicate the stand the rightists had taken as long ago as 1917. Even within the right, however, there was no unanimity. Its radical wing, whose views came close to Potresov's, often disagreed with the rest, who were more inclined to compromise with the majority for the sake of Party unity. But one strong bond that united all the rightists was their unalterable hostility to the Soviet regime through all its transformations. [7]

On 22 February 1932, *Pravda* published a decree depriving thirty-seven political émigrés, among them several Mensheviks and Trotsky, of Russian citizenship and even forbidding them to enter the country as aliens, because of their "counterrevolutionary activities." It is not known on what basis the selection was made. The intent, obviously, was to discredit the people named, but the decree made no impression abroad.

In view of the growth of Nazism, the delegation resolved in the summer of 1932 to move the Party center from Berlin to Paris if the democratic German regime fell. This was done as soon as Hitler came to power.

The long and often sharp polemics of the majority with the intraparty, extraparty, and foreign right gave way to warm expressions of friendship on "personal occasions." Thus, a special issue of *SV* in honor of Axelrod's seventy-fifth birthday printed, besides articles about him, an official greeting from the CC of the RSDRP, which said, with blatant exaggeration, "Now as before, you are the most irreplaceable participant in Social-Democratic work in Russia."[8] When Axelrod died on 17 April 1928, *SV* expressed similar sentiments, without minimizing its differences with him.

On the tenth anniversary of Plekhanov's death, *SV* spoke of him with respect rather than affection: Plekhanov had been "a master in the realm of ideology," but politics had not been his forte: he had made no firm choice between menshevism and bolshevism in the early years of the century. Obviously referring to Plekhanov's stand during the First World War, *SV* criticized him for having, unlike Axelrod, sometimes given precedence to national goals over class goals.[9] During Plekhanov's last years his relations with the leaders of the Party majority had been far from friendly. (Toward Axelrod, the Mensheviks' devotion did not diminish.) A blend of personal sympathy and ideological antagonism can be observed also in the Mensheviks' relations with foreign socialist leaders. The delegation sent greetings to Eduard Bernstein, the theoretician of revisionism, on his seventy-fifth birthday, and a member of the right wrote in *SV*: "Today we Russian Social-Democrats are at one with the entire international labor movement in feelings of love and respect for the old Bernstein, saying with pride, 'he is ours.'" [10]

New polemics with Kautsky, mild in tone but sharp in content, arose when he published *The International and Soviet Russia* in 1925 and *Bolshevism in a Blind Alley* in 1930. Dan translated the latter into Russian and added an analytical appendix, arguing mainly against the following theses: that the Soviet regime would be overthrown by a peasant uprising; that there was no need to fear the reactionary regime that might follow it, for it would be no worse, and probably better, than bolshevism; and that Russian social democracy should cooperate with other Russian democratic groups against dictatorship, whether of the left or the right. Dan felt that these views violated the class principle, though he did not deny that Kautsky remained a sincere Marxist. On Kautsky's seventy-fifth birthday, Dan wrote: "If Marx and Engels can be called Kautsky's spiritual forebears, Kautsky ... can be called the spiritual father of the proletarian generations that are destined to realize socialism."[11]

Potresov, on the other hand, was criticized for deviation from Marxism, especially after publication of his book *V plenu u illiuzii* (In Bondage to Illusions). Dan wrote that Potresov was making a fetish of democracy and failing to realize that in the Western working class the enthusiasm for democracy had given way to enthusiasm for socialism. *SV* printed Potresov's reply, in which he in turn accused official menshevism of failing to understand the counterrevolutionary nature of bolshevism and the fact that in the working class the urges for democracy and for socialism were no longer compartmentalized—the two had been fused into a "twofold passion" befitting the higher— statesmanlike—level of labor in the West.[12] This was the only article by Potresov to appear in *SV*. Twice the right wing had vainly asked the delegation to invite him to contribute to *SV*. Potresov himself realized that his participation in the official Party organ would have made no sense.[13]

After Potresov's death, Dan wrote an obituary noting his "enormous, unforgettable" role in the Party in the 1890s. Later, Dan said, Potresov had done more than Lenin for the victory of *Iskra* over Economism. The disagreements of the last years had been caused by the "basic peculiarities of his political thinking and political biography, so like Plekhanov's": both had stood "at the apex of the intelligentsia's revolutionary thought." (Coming from Dan, this meant deviation from "proletarian revolutionary thought.") Garvi described Potresov as an aristocrat of the spirit but also a democrat to the marrow of his bones, and stressed that Potresov had stood in the front ranks of menshevism against Lenin in 1903 and that during the World War the majority of the Party had sided with him.[14]

15

Socialism and Stalinism

The "General Line"

The changes that occurred in the 1920s in the attitudes of the working class in Russia and the West impelled Mensheviks and Western socialists alike to seek a more concrete definition of socialism. There was also the novelty of state capitalism to be taken into account. Was it a more progressive system than private capitalism? Could it be a stepping-stone to socialism?

The old idea that state ownership of the means of production at once made a society socialist was giving way to the idea that the transition to socialism might be a lengthy process, in which cooperatives, especially agricultural ones, might play an important role even in advanced countries. *SV* wrote: "We deny outright that a nationalized industry is a socialist industry"—for collective ownership and planning did not yet make socialism: both could also be found under capitalism. Besides, "the transition to socialism of small industries, trade, farming, must be gradual," starting from cooperatives that would prove the superiority of a socialized economy and stimulate its voluntary acceptance.[1]

The Western socialist left shared this view. Otto Bauer said that "to realize socialism it does not suffice to concentrate the means of production in the hands of the state."[2]

This reasoning originally shaped the Mensheviks' view of Stalin's superindustrialization. The "general line" of forced-draft industrializa-

324

tion and collectivization that replaced the NEP looked to them like a return to the utopias of War communism. The collectivization of agriculture, they thought, would ruin that branch of the economy as well as drive another wedge between the peasants and the proletariat. On these points there was at first little disagreement among the Mensehviks. Even the extreme left was convinced that the five-year plan announced in 1929 was "doomed to fail."[3] In Dan's group this opinion persisted until it became obvious that the plan would indeed be fulfilled. Iugov wrote that thanks to the general line "signs of a return to the methods of War communism are growing and multiplying; like a gangrene, the economic crisis born of the utopian policy is spreading to transport, fuel, trade, finances, farming, and creeping up even to industrial production."[4] Another prominent member of Dan's group argued that "in the post-NEP era, the historical prospects of the working class are becoming more and more menacing. . . . The chances for organic development are decreasing."[5] Dan himself wrote in 1931 of "a rift all along the line between the government and all classes of postrevolutionary society. The road of the general line leads not to the sunny heights of socialism but to the abysses of counterrevolution."[6]

During the third year of the general line Dan's group modified its stand, partly because of the success of the five-year plan and partly under the influence of the Western movement whose spokesman was Otto Bauer, the noted theoretician of the International and its expert on the USSR.

The early period of the general line coincided with a revival of pro-Soviet sentiments in the Western labor movement. These had been quite strong in the Socialist International during the civil war, had considerably cooled, though not disappeared, in the twenties, and emerged with renewed force after 1929, under the stimulus of the worldwide economic crisis and the Nazi menace in Germany. Capitalism seemed unable to cope. In the West, the socialist parties saw idle factories, ruined families, six million unemployed in Germany—a reservoir of willing recruits for communism and Nazism. The demilitarization of the Rhine zone was causing international tensions. In the USSR, by contrast, the West could observe a rapidly developing industry and a stable government under a socialist banner. The left socialists were not the only ones to be impressed. After visiting Russia in 1931, George Bernard Shaw told of the enthusiasm with which the people of that country were building socialism. Otto Bauer, long an advocate of the common front, discerned some good in the Soviet regime and the general line

For many years Bauer had had close political and personal ties with the left Menshevik leaders, especially Dan. In 1925, he had written:

In October 1917 we were all under its [bolshevism's] influence. . . .
Martov was the first to teach European social democracy to criticize
bolshevism not from the bourgeois but from the proletarian standpoint, from the point of view not of counterrevolution but of revolution. *Vestnik* continues what Martov began.[7]

But in his book on capitalism and socialism, published in 1931, Bauer
wrote that the successful five-year plan had convinced him that it was
leading to socialism; the sacrifices it demanded were therefore justified.
The seeds of the general line would yield a rich harvest within a few
years: as soon as heavy industry was sufficiently developed, the government would be able to expand light industry; the population, its basic
needs satisfied, would cease to resist the government. Dictatorship
would become unnecessary, a labor democracy would replace it, state
capitalism would turn into socialism.[8] For a few years, the backward
country needed dictatorship: nothing else could force 150 million people
to put up with the inevitable temporary hardships. When sacrifices were
no longer required, the Soviet government would "gradually, step by
step" abolish dictatorship. Bauer was not in principle an advocate of
dictatorship, let alone of terror. He condemned the persecution of the
intelligentsia in Russia and the "dekulakization" of peasants, and hoped
that the industrialized West would reach socialism by another road,
peaceful and democratic, if only the bourgeoisie did not become fascist.
But in Russia "the fall of the Soviet dictatorship would plunge the Soviet
Union into civil war," which in turn would lead to the victory of
reaction in Russia and the West, the breakup of Russia, and a European
war.[9] Consequently, whoever worked for the fall of the Soviet government was doing harm.

The Mensheviks launched a campaign to dispel the illusions Bauer
was planting in the minds of Western socialists. They also protested
against the implication that they should discontinue their opposition to
the Soviet regime.[10]

Although Dan had for years argued together with Bauer that revolutionary elements were present in the Soviet regime, Bauer's new opinions struck him as nothing short of an apologia of bolshevism. Even in
1932, when he had adopted many of Bauer's views and his own party
accused him of having capitulated to bolshevism, Dan firmly disagreed
with Bauer's stand on dictatorship. The idea that socialism could
precede democracy seemed to him profoundly wrong. Meanwhile,
another leader of the left, Friedrich Adler, was already recommending
"toleration" of the Bolsheviks. Like all Mensheviks, Dan refused to
accept Bauer's discrimination between advanced countries, which
would reach socialism democratically, and backward Russia, which

needed dictatorship. Bauer's views did, however, rub off on the left Mensheviks to some extent. Dan admitted that although he polemized with Bauer they saw eye to eye on a good many things.[11]

The left Mensheviks revised their stand on the general line and the questions connected with it when it became clear that the first five-year plan would not only be fulfilled but fulfilled ahead of time, and that the collectivization of agriculture also was proceeding faster than planned. If the first step was spectacularly successful, would not the next be even more so? In that case the regime might well be an instrument of social progress. The left Mensheviks could not bear to think that menshevism might find itself in the role of critic and spectator, on the sidelines and not in the fighting ranks, when the social revolution finally came. To avoid this, old mistaken theories should be given up and reality accepted. Economic recovery was proceeding apace. "In monstruously brutal forms, at a dreadfully high price," said Dan, but industry was growing.[12] This was the old leftist idea: the methods were dreadful, but the revolution was going on and bringing socialism closer.

The left believed that the general line was fostering the advance of technology in industry and agriculture; supplanting private capitalism with more progressive state capitalism; helping the workers to break free of their peasant origins and mentality, thus raising their cultural and political level; and weakening the bourgeoisie—though it put a new class of managers in its place.

What was this new system, state capitalism? It was more than a kind of appendage to the private economy, wrote S. Schwarz; it was a new system, born in the USSR in almost pure state:

> The preponderance of state-capitalist features in the Russian economic system will prove to be an economically progressive fact, which will benefit the broad toiling masses.... A state-capitalist society also is a society divided into classes, but its sociology is a sociology sui generis, and the dominant class is a new bureaucracy, not a new bourgeoisie.[13]

From this point of view, the general line was not utopian, and the Soviet regime was still a labor and socialist regime, though in need of major reforms. With this image, the RSDRP was impelled to move back to the April theses of 1920.[14] Dan was moving closer to Bauer, but he lacked Bauer's consistency. He accepted the general line but not the dictatorship without which it could not be carried out. Himself a member of a persecuted party, Dan continued to view dictatorship as an evil. He even thought that it hampered the implementation of the general line.

The right and the center were united in their implacable opposition to the general line as economically impossible, socially harmful, and politically totalitarian. The views of the left seemed to them incompatible with Menshevik ideology—in fact, an adaptation to Stalinism. They accused the left of making a fetish of technology and confusing a successful economic plan with the building of a new social order, whereas the general line was merely a further development of those traits of bolshevism to which the Mensheviks had always objected. In fact, Stalin's new policy had destroyed the hope that the Soviet regime might little by little veer toward democracy. Therefore the center group demanded a revision of the Menshevik party line.

The disputes took on an acid tone. Abramovich called Dan's views "a historical rehabilitation of the general line and Stalinism," and Dallin called them "inordinately schematic, abstract, and factually unsound," a kind of "Left SR Menshevism," something midway between an orientation toward the NEP and approval of the five-year plan. Nicolaevsky said that the general line, "designed in the name of the utopian objectives of integral socialism," played not a progressive but a reactionary role; and Aronson: "Dan advocates a return to the illusions of the civil war era." Aronson also put the question in a broader context: The Party's orientation toward reform of the regime, toward agreement with the Communists, had been proven wrong; menshevism must have the courage to evolve a new line on a new basis. "It is time to break free of the Martovite tradition." [15]

In the eyes of the center and the right, the theories of Bauer and Adler, which were gaining converts in the International, were undermining the very foundations of socialism and ignoring the fact that even major capitalist crises like the one of 1929 did not necessarily lead to socialism but, on the contrary, often weakened the labor movement. Moreover, they fostered the mistaken and dangerous notion that the bourgeoisie was turning fascist en masse, and the working class, dictatorial—which in turn implied that democracy could legitimately be discarded in order to achieve socialism.

The left realized that its stand was incompatible with the Party platform of 1924 and asked in 1931 for a revision of the platform—not of separate planks but a general revision. The right and the center protested—not because the platform was good but because they thought a revision would make it worse. No revision took place because the votes for and against it were evenly divided.

The Peasantry and Collectivization

The second part of the general line, collectivization, introduced new economic, political, and social factors into the agrarian problem, for which the Mensheviks had never worked out a satisfactory solution. The Soviet government needed collectivization to broaden the food and raw materials base of its program of superindustrialization, and also to destroy those hotbeds of proprietary psychology, the twenty-five million individual peasant households. The view is now generally accepted that it was at this time that the Soviet regime definitely became totalitarian. Its war with the peasantry demanded total terror. Yet the peasantry proved to be one of the very few social forces that the regime did not succeed in subjugating completely. The Mensheviks closely observed all these processes and took them into account.

Before the revolution, they had approached the class differences between the proletariat and the "inherently bourgeois" peasantry more theoretically and less politically than the Bolsheviks. They had tended to regard the peasantry as a doubtful and temporary ally.[16] It is no accident that the number of Party members of peasant origin had always been negligible. After the October Revolution, this attitude changed. The Mensheviks realized that the Soviet government had won the civil war mainly because it had made itself the champion of the agrarian revolution. Later it became clear that neither the White movement, nor the bourgeoisie, nor foreign intervention, but the unorganized, diffuse, powerful pressure of the peasantry had compelled Lenin to shift from War communism to the NEP.

Agreement with the peasantry and even a sharing of power with it in the "toilers' rule," with the proletariat as leader, became basic Menshevik policy. One of the accusations they leveled at the government was that it talked of agreement with the peasants and broke it in practice. The wish for agreement grew during the NEP, when peasant unrest subsided. In actual fact, however, Menshevik collaboration with the peasantry was impossible. An underground party could do some illegal work in cities but not in the countryside. Like the Western socialists, the Mensheviks came to believe that the relationship between proletariat and peasantry was "one of the most important problems for the proletarian class movement of our era," whose solution was facilitated in backward countries by the common need to abolish remnants of feudalism, and in advanced countries, by the hostility of a petty-bourgeois peasantry toward big capitalism.

Even the Menshevik circles most wary of the peasantry came to see the need for cooperation between the two classes, or, as Dan put it, for "honest compromise," that is, concessions. The peasantry had been conservative in the French Revolution and the European revolutions of 1848, but since then new, democratic tendencies had appeared in it. The RSDRP held that peasant movements could no longer develop independently—they would perforce be linked with either reactionary or democratic urban elements. To assure their ties with democratic ones was the Party's task. But the Party had no clear idea of how to go about it. It did not recognize the SRs as spokesmen for the peasantry, and there was no one else. Agreement remained an abstraction. The principle was held in common by all Menshevik factions, but they assigned different meanings to it.

At first the entire RSDRP, including its extreme left, condemned forced collectivization,[17] for three main reasons. As *SV* said in a lead article, the "monstrous violence" of its methods beat all previous records of Bolshevik terror; economically, it was a utopian scheme that would ruin, not increase, productivity; politically, it fostered enmity between workers and peasants and dashed the hopes for democratization of the regime. The RSDRP set forth its views in 1930 in a memorandum to the Socialist International on the situation in Russia:

> Collectivization could be carried out to any considerable extent only by means of the most cruel coercion, reminiscent of the worst times of the civil war. . . . Under such conditions, the peasant masses have every right to view the policy of "dekulakization" and "collectivization" as a policy of. . .expropriation and. . .state corvée, and above all as an attempt upon their land. . . . The peasants, shouldered out of village Soviets by henchmen of the dictatorial government and thus deprived of the last legal means of self-defense, are resorting to desperate methods of resistance such as arson, destruction, beatings and murder of the dictatorship's agents, and open revolt, savagely suppressed.

Collectivization was making counterrevolutionaries not only of peasants but also of workers who had ties with their home villages, and of Red army soldiers, most of whom were peasants. Instead of collectives, voluntary cooperatives should be encouraged.

The memorandum impressed the International. Although its executive committee avoided the ticklish "Russian question," it published on 13 May 1930 an appeal to the workers of the USSR, expressing the fear that continued terror would "put a chasm between the two classes upon which the Russian revolution rests." Collectivization should be abandoned, a free rural economy restored, and the peasants given the right to dispose of their produce as they saw fit.[18]

The seeming success of collectivization broke the Party's unanimity on this matter. Dan's group revised its stand on kolkhozes at the same time as its stand on industrialization. Although the most doctrinaire of the Menshevik groups of this period, it claimed to base its views on a realistic appraisal of facts: machinery and improved methods were raising production; the large collective farms were helping to break up patriarchal traditions. The group's economic expert, Iugov, believed that the rural "productive forces" were rising to a "higher technical level," even if in distorted, ugly ways. He also discerned other than economic advantages in collective farming: along with machines and scientific techniques, it had brought into the villages a new way of life and higher material and cultural aspirations.[19] Dan saw in the kolkhozes yet another advantage, which he found it hard to explain logically, let alone "realistically": although horrified at the terror and well aware of the peasants' hatred of kolkhozes, he felt sure that eventually the good traits of the system would outweigh the bad and the peasants come to like it; and once the idea of collective work was accepted, voluntary cooperatives would replace kolkhozes.

In the heat of Party arguments, the left was often accused of having swallowed the idea of collectivization wholesale and capitulated to Stalinism. This was unfair. The group not only condemned the brutal methods but remained faithful to the old Menshevik view that some elements of capitalism had to be preserved in the USSR—in particular, that those peasants who did not wish to join collectives should be free to continue private farming. The future, however, appeared to Dan as follows: Once dictatorship was gone,

> peasant cooperatives will become no less important a form than small private households, perhaps even the basic form of post-revolutionary agriculture. [Social Democracy must] adapt its agrarian program to this historical fact. Along with the demand of full freedom for the...peasant...it must put forward the task of all-out support of peasant cooperatives and the transformation of kolkhozes into free agricultural collectives, not simply their abolition; for such support, full use [must be made] of the means accumulated in the government's hands (machine-tractor stations and so forth).[20]

Dan's abstract approach to the most sensitive question of the day, his emphasis on the "progressive" side of collectivization, displeased both opposition groups. Nicolaevsky wrote that these views reflected Dan's "old phobia of peasants." The center group wanted agreement with the peasants on the basis of their interests and their rejection of kolkhozes.

Nicolaevsky gave the first comprehensive exposition of the center's views on these matters at a meeting of the Berlin organization on 26 March 1931. In every revolution, he said, there were periods of upsurge and of decline; and not all revolutions were good. Thus, the Communist uprising in Austria in 1919, put down by the government with the help of Social-Democrats, had been harmful. Stalinism in Russia also was a harmful revolution. The history of the NEP was basically a story of the peasantry's struggle for political influence. The

Soviet regime had been faced with the dilemma of giving in to the peasants or crushing them. Stalin had chosen the second course. "Liquidating the general line in the rural areas" was the basic task of "the progressive forces of the country." The general line was reactionary. The forces that abolished it would play a positive role.[21] It was not enough to give the peasants the right to leave kolkhozes; kolkhozes must be abolished. If this was done by democratic forces, Russia would have democracy; if not, it would have reaction.

Abramovich expressed, more cautiously, the same views. His main argument was that the kolkhoz system was leading to ruin and driving the peasants toward counterrevolution.[22] Most peasants were petty-bourgeois in outlook, yet the regime was carrying out or trying to carry out utopian plans, "against which we must protest in defense of workers' and peasants' interests.... I think that...the motto of renouncing forced collectivization has every chance to be a success."[23] Abramovich remarked, however, that some of Nicolaevsky's views reflected the Menshevik tendency to make hasty prognoses "while the lava is flowing but has not yet hardened."

Dan had said in the speech from which I have just quoted that kolkhozes should not simply be abolished. The center group replied that this was, on the contrary, the "basic task," from which political inferences were to be drawn. Inasmuch as the political developments of the general-line period were strengthening the police state, the RSDRP's reformism was obsolete. "It is time to stop being afraid of the word 'revolution,'" Nicolaevsky said—especially as in a police state any strike or demonstration could turn into revolution. A solid, lasting alliance of labor and peasantry was the foremost requirement, for the sake of which the workers would have to make major concessions: they must atone to the peasants for the general line, for the twenty-five thousand Communists sent to enforce it in the villages, and for much else.

These pro-peasant dispositions did not mean that the center was getting converted to the populist creed. Nicolaevsky said, on the contrary, that along with a reoriented RSDRP, a new party representing the peasants was needed in order to create a firm basis for collaboration with them. "We must begin right away to lay the first foundation stones of a pro-peasant policy of the workers' party so that a pro-worker peasant democratic party may come into being in the future."[24]

The right on the whole agreed with the center's views on kolkhozes.[25] The draft of a letter to the International offered by the right in 1930 referred to the Soviet government's "insane antipeasant policy" and the need for the proletariat to "join forces with the peasant movement" since only the peasants were actively resisting the regime, even if in a chaotic, politically formless way. In October 1933 the right composed a draft of a Party platform that pointed out that despite industrialization the peasantry would still be the main class in the USSR. The draft rejected kolkhozes and criticized the left for linking them with free cooperatives, now or in the future:

> The orientation toward preserving sovkhozes and kolkhozes, even in a modified shape, as the main form of Russia's agricultural economy ignores the private-property bent of the peasantry and threatens to exacerbate the relations between village and city, peasants and workers. Socialist propaganda for agricultural cooperatives must not be related to the painful legacy of forced collectivization, which the peasants have come to regard as a new kind of serfdom. [26]

The right objected to the general line mainly because only a harsh antiworker and antipeasant dictatorship could carry it out. This fact added fuel to the right's hatred of the regime. The rift between the two flanks of the Party deepened, and the right was more and more displeased with the compromise policy of the International.

The Road from Dictatorship to Democracy

While opposing the reformism and revisionism of Western socialism, the RSDRP itself had been "reformist" with respect to Russia, counting on a change through evolution rather than revolution. The tighter dictatorship that went with the general line showed that this had been wishful thinking. The need for reorientation was most keenly felt by the Mensheviks' new center group. Nicolaevsky reminded the Party that the Marxist ideal was the liberation of mankind, not of one class. Where democracy existed, Social-Democrats must try to fill it with social content; where it did not exist, they must struggle for parliamentary democracy above all else. Nicolaevsky took up the idea Martov had expressed early in the NEP period and pursued it further:

> In the light of the present Bolshevik experiment...it becomes especially necessary to emphasize the general human aspects of socialism. Bolshevism in Russia is an attempt to ply the proletariat with "social advantages" without political freedom. It is all the more necessary that Russian social democracy restore the balance between "politics" and "economics" by putting the problem of political democracy in the forefront. [27]

Throughout the thirties, the issue of "democracy" was widely debated in the Party. Dan's group held on to the views evolved in civil war times that the Soviet government was revolutionary and proletarian and that the situation in the West precluded peaceful democratic development. The growth of fascism reinforced the idea, not new in left-wing circles, that the bourgeoisie was turning fascist and that the old "simple" interpretation of democracy was outdated. Now there could be only a "workers' democracy" or else fascism. Proletarian unity must be restored. Therefore a common front with the Communists, on condition of major concessions on their part, was still desirable. According to Dan,

> the time of organic development of bourgeois parliamentarism is past and cannot return.... Everywhere the struggle for democracy is also a struggle for the rule of the working class.... Democracy will either be a good, a workers', democracy or there will be none—there will be fascism.[28]

The rest of the Party opposed these views so strongly that a split might have ensued if the RSDRP had not been an émigré party.[29] The right saw no need to revise its stand—it had always wanted to fight for democracy in the USSR. The program it drafted in 1933 offered the following formula:"The RSDRP rejects...a mere dosed-out attenuation of terror and dictatorship. Any wavering on the question of dictatorship versus democracy would definitely weaken the ideological and political positions of the RSDRP."

All Mensheviks knew that the regime could be democratized only at the cost of intense struggle. Was the confused, destitute proletariat able to take its place at the head of the democratic forces of the country? And who would be the allies of the workers' party?

During the twenties, the delegation abroad had rejected alliances with émigré organizations. When the League of Eastern Nations, which concentrated on national-minorities problems, had asked the RSDRP to allow its members to join the league, the delegation had replied that it disapproved of "all blocs, joint organizations, and political combinations abroad."[30] This was partly due to the wish to stay aloof from the "national question," which often involved separatism, but the delegation was equally adamant about Russian democratic groups. After some Paris Mensheviks had attended a banquet in honor of Miliukov, the delegation ruled:

> Groups [of the RSDRP] abroad can take part in demonstrations of a political nature, even in the form of jubilees, banquets, and so on,

only in agreement with the delegation abroad. Individual comrades may participate in such demonstrations only if so instructed by the groups of which they are members or with their consent.[31]

The right and the center disagreed with this "isolationist" line. The entire philosophy of the right demanded collaboration with democrats in order to overthrow the Soviet regime and prevent counterrevolution. Its above-mentioned draft of a program in 1933 made it the Party's task

> to activate and unite *the working class and the urban and rural classes adjacent to it* for the struggle for a democratic republic as the system under which it is possible to retain, strengthen, and broaden the sociopolitical and agrarian conquests of the revolution to a maximal degree and carry on a successful, organized struggle for the realization of genuine socialism.... The RSDRP appeals to the interests and the political intelligence of the classes that have made the revolution—*the proletariat, the peasants, and the broad urban democratic strata* [italics added].

More concrete, and therefore more difficult, was the problem of collaboration with oppositional groups in the Communist party. Such groups had appeared before the NEP, and Lenin had unsuccessfully tried to eliminate them with his resolution "On Party Unity," which the Tenth Congress of the RCP had adopted in 1921. In the later twenties Stalin set out to demolish first the left opposition, then the right. Since both groups undermined the regime, collaboration with them became for the Mensheviks an immediate practical question.

The left Communist opposition wanted to stop the "retreat toward capitalism that the NEP represented and to wipe out all its remnants in city and village. It wanted intensive industrialization of a nationalized, not state-capitalist, economy. The enormous capital required was to come from even greater taxation of the peasantry. E. Preobrazhenskii, a theorist of the left, called this method "primitive socialist accumulation."

The right opposition, led by Bukharin, Rykov, and Tomskii, wanted a more "organic" industrialization at a slower pace. Their program was basically pro-peasant: lower taxes, more freedom for individual farming, the right to lease land, even toleration of kulaks. The peasants' increased purchasing power would stimulate production of consumer goods. The program thus included two important Menshevik principles: "sincere agreement" with the peasantry and better living conditions for all.

The left opposition was demolished at the Fifteenth Congress of the RCP in 1927, and the right two years later. Positions, combatants, alignments shifted in the course of the struggle. Finding themselves among the victims, both the right and the left demanded freedom of debate, voting, and elections. Parroting the Mensheviks, Trotsky spoke of "Thermidor," and Bukharin of bureaucratism. But, as *SV* noted, both groups demanded freedom for Communist party members, not for the entire people; and neither was against dictatorship—each wanted to be the dictator. To the Mensheviks both seemed to be looking back, not ahead: the left, to War communim, and the right, to the early form of the NEP, that illegitimate offspring of economic realism and political dictatorship. The Mensheviks therefore thought of these groups only as potential future allies—if their sounder principles evolved in the proper direction.

As far back as 1923 David Dallin had written that "inside the huge womb of bolshevism" groups were maturing that represented the interests of different classes and might eventually produce a new workers' party with which the RSDRP could collaborate.[32] The idea had not been taken up at the time. *SV* had declared in 1925 that it would be a "fatal mistake" to let the left Communists influence the RSDRP, and that on the other hand, Bukharin's "saccharine speeches" were no better than Molotov's "myopic police philosophy."[33]

In 1928, after the defeat of the Communist left, Dallin concluded that the right opposition could become the Mensheviks' ally since it found support outside the RCP, among the intelligentsia, the peasants, and the workers, thus "reflecting the entire nation in its struggle against the outdated regime." Only its dictatorial bias was still unacceptable. This appraisal of the right Bolshevik opposition largely shaped the stand of the center group of the RSDRP. It proved to be a mistaken appraisal under Soviet conditions, but a quarter-century later the uprisings in Hungary and Poland, led by local Communist groups, would suggest that there had been a grain of political realism in it.

Stalin's turn toward the left in 1928–29 reinforced the Menshevik center's preference for Bukharinism. Dallin wrote:

> The right opposition represents an enormous step forward from Stalin's relapse into violently terrorist communism.... Only within the right opposition can there form more or less significant cadres of Communist workers who might renounce utopianism and thus come closer to Social Democracy.

For the time being, however, the antidemocratic spirit, the incompetence and cowardice of the Communist right inspired "great mistrust" toward all its works.[34] In other words, Bukharin's group merely contained some tendencies that might later transform it into a desirable ally.

Nicolaevsky, who knew Bukharin well, was the main advocate of agreement with the Communist right. He was aware of its defects and he, too, considered it no more than a possible future ally, convinced that it represented the forces that had fought in the civil war and were grounded in the "positive period" of the revolution. Given the "political silence reigning in Russia," the right opposition was the spokesman for these forces. "I am not blind to the half-and-half, or even quite undetermined, quality of its position. I need it not as it is today but for its underlying tendencies."[35] The chief of these was the will to agree with the peasantry. Bukharin's defeat did not disturb Nicolaevsky. He may have viewed it as an incentive for increased anti-Stalinism in the remnants of the opposition.

Although the Trotsky-Zinov'ev group seemed to have nothing in common with menshevism, there was some sympathy for it among the Menshevik left. During the early period of the general line Dan had thought that the revolution could no longer be redeemed—the abandonment of the NEP and the tightened dictatorship spelled its end. He saw "Thermidor" approaching as a result of a spontaneous mass movement that would destroy all political organizations and find itself leaderless. If the revolution was to perish, Dan wanted social democracy to live in history as a party that had combated the Soviet regime not on the side of capitalism and parliamentarism but "from the left," from the positions of orthodox Marxism. A "common front" with the left Communists still imbued with the dynamism of the civil war could help Russian social democracy take its proper place in history.[36]

In 1929 Dan had criticized the right opposition for its "national," as against class, goals as well as for evading the issue of dictatorship, vitally important to the proletariat, while promoting a pro-peasant policy that was taking on "an anti-worker character." He had criticized Trotsky as well for his dictatorial attitude and utopian economic ideas, though he considered the latter "harmlessly romantic" and remarked that "in a sense" *Pravda* was right in saying that Trotsky's group in effect "played the same role as the Menshevik party had played in the USSR in its time."[37] Dan's view precluded merging with Trotskyism, but future collaboration might be possible. This view could also facilitate for the left Mensheviks the acceptance of the general line, which was based on Trotskyite ideas.

At the opposite pole, the Menshevik right rejected cooperation with any Communist group, orthodox or oppositional, now or in future: "Any policy of our Party oriented toward agreement with any part, group, or elements of the ruling party seems to us completely hopeless and incompatible with the interests of the country and the working class." The only correct way was to promote the activity and organization of workers and an anti-Bolshevik democratic movement in town and country.[38] Alliances were needed with enemies of the regime, not with its own oppositional groups. In the Berlin organization, Garvi and Kefali argued in many speeches that the opposition were still Communists, proponents of dictatorship. This alone made them impossible allies, and there was little hope that they would evolve away from dictatorship, the keystone of Leninism. G. Aronson wrote in *SV* in April 1932: "At every stage of Bolshevism, and especially in the general-line period, it is imperative to eradicate from our tactical line the slightest trace of any connection with the socioeconomic and political regime that the Bolsheviks are still trying to pass off as the revolution."

Like Dan, the right was concerned with the historical image of social democracy, but it wanted to keep the record free of compromises with any part of the regime. Alliance with the Communist opposition looked like a new variant of the common front. But this old idea had a new meaning: Nazism victorious in Germany, infiltrating even the working class, and fascist tendencies in France and elsewhere had alarmed the socialist parties and made them strive for unity. After Hitler's accession to power, the Comintern, too, proposed agreement between parties (as against its former tactics of a "united front" from below, with the socialist masses against their leaders.) On the initiative of the French, the common front again became a topical issue in the International. In the RSDRP it was discussed at great length. Since these debates brought out the ideas of the Party's main groups, it may be useful to examine them here, although they took place in a period that my discussion does not cover.

After a fascist demonstration in Paris in February 1934, the French socialists and Communists joined forces. Having learned of this, three Menshevik exiles in Kazan—S. Ezhov, K. Zakharov, and B. Bèr—sent a telegram to the French socialist paper *Le Populaire*, "joyfully hailing" the alliance and hoping for similar agreements throughout the world. This telegram elated the Menshevik émigrés: it proved that persecution had not broken the Party, that the senders saw eye to eye with the delegation abroad, from which they had been cut off for years, and that the Soviet government attached great importance to the common front since it had permitted deportees to contact foreign socialists. With a meeting of the executive committee of the International in the offing, the delegation decided to clarify its own stand on the common front. Each of the three main groups presented theses for discussion. All agreed on the need for socialists and Communists to unite against fascism, but motives and proposed methods differed substantially.

The left held that the wish for a common front of all socialist forces was part of a "movement for unity, dictated by the entire course of world events, as an indispensable condition for increasing the revolutionary-socialist activity and the fighting capacity of the working class"—and this front must include Soviet Russia because of the leading role it played in the Comintern and "the decisive importance that the. . . fortunes of the gigantic revolutionary country inevitably have for the fortunes of the international proletariat." Accordingly, one should "in every way contribute to the success of the 'united action' movement" and try to get the Socialist International to lead it. To insure success, the Comintern must not be confronted with "preliminary conditions"— that is, the Soviet government's internal policy should not be mentioned. Not mentioning terror was for the Mensheviks a great sacrifice, to be paid only because of the growing threat of fascism and war.

The center group, agreeing that extraordinary measures were needed, pointed out that the Comintern had changed its stand on the common front because the Communists had lost ground. Their new stand was therefore sincere and should be taken seriously. However, the center did not envisage collaboration hopefully, as the left did; it merely accepted it under the pressure of circumstances, and only under certain conditions: in fascist countries a common front was useless—in fact, in the absence of a free press, it could confuse people as to the difference between socialism and communism; in stably democratic countries, it was unnecessary; only in countries like France, where fascism threatened, was united action useful. In any case, "the socialist parties realize that this temporary and conditional union cannot be a substitute for the organic unity" that could result only from agreement between the two Internationals, not from local pacts. Where common action was truly imperative, the center, like the left, would desist from confronting the Communists with "preliminary conditions." This was, however, qualified by the remark that genuine proletarian unity was impossible so long as lawlessness and violence prevailed in Russia.

The tension in Europe was so great that even the rightist Mensheviks admitted, for the first time since 1917, that "unity of the labor movement and a common front" were urgent objectives of the international socialist movement. But unity required harmonious basic aims, and these were lacking so long as socialists fought for democracy and Communists for replacing fascist dictatorship with their own. Joint action was therefore admissible only in extreme cases. Moreover, the right drew a distinction, as Axelrod had done, between the Western and the Russian Communist parties. The first were genuine branches of the labor movement; the second was an instrument of government.

And the contrast between the terror in the USSR and the Communists' conciliatory tactics in the West "cannot but shake the workers' faith in the sincerity of the Communist maneuver of the common front. . . . Keeping silent about this contrast would lead to false idealization of the Soviet regime, to ideological and political capitulation to bolshevism, and to Communist seizure of leadership in the common front." The right was not willing to forego the "preliminary conditions"—and the Soviet government could not accept them without relinquishing power.

In short, the theses of the left proposed unity between the Socialist International and the Comintern; those of the center, collaboration in certain countries; and those of the right, only occasional joint action. The theses were discussed at a meeting of the delegation abroad that included members of the editorial board of *SV*. The balloting resulted in five votes for the left, three for the center, and two for the right. In the balloting on the theses that had received the most votes, the right joined the center and the vote was five to five. The center's efforts to reach a compromise with the left failed, and no decision was taken.[39]

The Problem of Nationalities

The platform of 1924 had not touched on the so-called national question. It had been discussed at the conference that drew up the platform, but no decision had been reached. A special commission had been appointed to draft a resolution on the subject, to be added to the platform. This resolution was not published until 1929.[40]

The discussion took so long because the Mensheviks had given this matter little thought in the past. The program of 1903 had recognized in principle "the right to self-determination for all the nations composing the state" and their right to conduct school instruction in their own languages. Beyond that, the Mensheviks had no use for nationalist movements—they ran counter to proletarian internationalism and put national unity before class unity. The matter was not further elaborated until 1917, although several national parties, among them the Jewish Bund and the Social-Democratic parties of Poland and Lithuania, had joined the RSDRP. The Mensheviks' relations with the small party of Ukrainian S-Ds were not close.

After the February Revolution it became clear that self-determination required a more precise definition. The independence of Finland and Poland, autonomy for the Ukraine, Georgia, Armenia, and Azerbaidzhan were the order of the day.[41] A resolution of the "Unification" Congress of 1917 stated that "the national struggle generated by the course of capitalist development" (this peculiar wording must have been a compromise) created unfavorable conditions for democracy and the class struggle. To stop it, nationalities should be given complete equality and territorial and cultural autonomy. However, Russia's development tended toward "ever closer economic, political, and cultural ties between all parts of the country," not toward breakup along ethnic lines into independent or federated autonomous regions.[42] "Separatist-federalist aspirations" were harming the revolution. They could be overcome by recognizing national freedom—so long as it was left to the Constituent Assembly to decide each particular case. The very term "separatist-federalist," lumping together two different concepts, reveals an equally negative view of both. The platform adopted by the congress for the elections to the Constituent Assembly enunciated the same principles as this resolution, adding that Social-Democracy would defend Russia's integrity because it assured "the most favorable conditions for her economic and political development."[43]

Nor did anything new appear in the resolution of the Party's December Congress of 1917. It repeated that decisions about autonomy must be left to the Constituent Assembly, and said nothing about federation, which was becoming a sharp issue. The reporter of the national question, S. Semkovskii, probably expressed the opinion of most members of the congress when he said that federation was good if it combined formerly separate parts into a whole but not if it divided an existing whole, and that in Russia's case the demand for federation sometimes assumed a distinctly reactionary character.[44]

Yet the Mensheviks could not object to a federated state in principle. They had gone much farther in recognizing the right to self-determination "up to separation." Indeed, they supported the independence of Finland, Poland, and the Baltic countries, although viewing these as special cases. But movements for "self-determination" were springing up all over Russia, and demands for a federative order easily turned into separatist demands inspired by chauvinists and reactionaries and having little to do with the people's will. Accordingly, all Mensheviks —Defensists as well as Internationalists—rejected separatism and defended Russia's integrity; only the Constituent Assembly had the right to tamper with it. Though expressed in the habitual class-struggle terminology, these views came close to Potresov's idea that the working class now had state as well as class functions. The Mensheviks' stand was further articulated in their unanimous opposition to the Brest treaty and Ukrainian independence.

The resolutions of 1917 soon proved unsatisfactory. Strong nationalist movements arose in Georgia, Uzbekistan, the Ukraine, and lesser parts of the former empire, sometimes partly out of hostility to the

"Russian" Soviet regime. They had to be taken into account—the example of Austria had shown that nationalist movements could break up a multinational state.

The Party platform of 1929 recognized some positive elements in such movements: they raised the cultural level of the masses, they could enhance the workers' class consciousness by freeing them of national oppression, which blurred class contradictions, uniting bourgeoisie and proletariat against the oppressor nation. In Russia, the liberation of nationalities from tsarist oppression had been "one of the greatest conquests of the revolution." But new problems had arisen: entire states had been cut out of Russia; the Soviet government had quashed national movements; Soviet troops had occupied Georgia. The platform stated that the RSDRP recognized the sovereignty and existing frontiers of Finland, Estonia, Latvia, Lithuania, and Poland and the right of all nationalitites of the USSR to free democratic self-determination

> in the form of autonomy, federation, and even independent statehood for peoples constituting a compact territorial whole, and in the form of cultural . . . autonomy for territorially dispersed nations and national minorities. The RSDRP rejects most decisively any forcible suppression, on whatever pretext, of national self-determination based on the democratically expressed will of the popular masses themselves. [45]

This was a precaution against the pressure of chauvinistic or Communist minorities. The platform also urged workers to use the right to self-determination not for parochial ends but in a manner benefiting all nations of the USSR, and to resist separatist propaganda, which could lead to another civil war. Finally, it repeated the demand that Soviet troops leave Georgia.

Émigré spokesmen for national minorities criticized the platform for demanding Georgia's independence under its former Social-Democratic government while not demanding independence for the Ukraine and Armenia, which had had no such governments. The platform did indeed make this distinction—not because the Georgian government had been socialist, however, but because the population had overwhelmingly supported Georgia's democratic constitution when it had become an independent state in 1918. In 1921 that state had been conquered by the Red army. In the Mensheviks' eyes, the question of independence appeared in a different light in regions where no such things had happened. Actually, as we have seen, the relations between Georgian and Russian Social-Democrats were far from cordial. Their ways had parted in late 1917, largely over the national question.

N. Zhordania, president of the Georgian government-in-exile, described their relations as armed truce, notwithstanding the Mensheviks' public protests against the occupation of Georgia and the suppression of the anti-Bolshevik uprising in 1924. In 1927, *SV* (no. 16/17) printed a polemic between Zhordania and Abramovich. Abramovich disputed Zhordania's view of the Soviet regime as counterrevolutionary despotism that should be forcibly overthrown, and his advocacy of a war by England and France against the USSR and the division of the USSR along ethnic lines. His arguments convinced neither Zhordania's group nor the more leftist Georgian group headed by Tsereteli, which rejected war and division but not uprisings, accusing the Mensheviks of a "dogmatism" that made them too tolerant of Communism. [46]

The Mensheviks laid the growth of anti-Semitism in Russia at the door of the government: it was the Soviet system, not "survivals of tsarism," as the Communists claimed, that fostered it. On the other hand, in all socialist parties, including the Bund, there was strong opposition to Zionism as a utopian movement whose nationalistic aims blurred class distinctions. In the twenties, when even non-Jews in the socialist parties, especially in England, began to regard Zionism with approval, Abramovich argued in *SV* and in the International that it weakened the unity of the labor movement: in eastern Europe, with its numerous Jewish workers, Zionism actually was "an antisocialist, antiproletarian factor against which the Jewish workers have to conduct a life-and-death struggle." [47]

In 1929, *SV* (no. 18) printed an article by Kautsky presenting the case against Zionism from the European point of view. The war had shown, Kautsky said, that the Jews had become part of the nations in which they lived. "Only narrow local patriotism can depict the Jews of Europe as aliens. But European Jews will always be aliens in the Islamic world." Unfortunately, Zionism had become dependent on the countries of the Entente and found itself pitted against Arab nationalism, which was sure to gain the upper hand. In Europe, Jews were at home, whereas their claim to Palestine had lapsed—after two thousand years. (*SV* rarely printed foreign authors. The appearance of Kautsky's article meant that the editors agreed with it.)

The "Russian Question" in the International

The Congress of the Socialist International in Brussels in August 1928 issued a manifesto to all workers, which included an appeal to Russian workers "to unite with us on the basis of the world policy of the proletariat, built on...the need to defend democracy where it is in danger and restore it where it has been abolished." The Mensheviks regarded this wording as their victory: the extreme left had objected to it in the political commission of the Congress which had drafted the text. The delegates of the British Labour Party had said that the International had developed an anti-Bolshevik mania under the influence of Russian émigrés, and that the manifesto gave more space to bolshevism than to fascism.

On its third day, the congress discussed dictatorship and terror in fascist countries and in Russia. As a gesture toward the parties that worked under terror, the congress elected Abramovich, Turati (Italy), and Rusanov (an SR) to its Presidium. Abramovich said:

> However much fascism and bolshevism may differ in their social ideals and class content, they are alike as blood brothers in their methods and ways. Fascism and bolshevism are the two great dangers threatening the working class from opposite sides but equally strongly. It is imperative that the Socialist International fight them, in different fashion but with all the energy and strength it can muster.

Disliking this approach, Dan also took the floor. He did not directly contradict Abramovich or deny that Bolshevik and fascist methods were alike, but pointed out a major difference between the two dictatorships: fascism had abolished democracy in order to destroy the labor movement, whereas the Bolshevik dictatorship reflected the instincts of immature revolutionary masses. "It is the pride of Russian social democracy that even under a hail of atrocious persecution it followed the rule given by our unforgettable Martov...not to lose sight of our common proletarian basis and our common final aim."

There are no data on how the other Menshevik delegates felt about Dan's reference to Martov, who had never taken a coldly dogmatic view of terror but had protested against it with all the fire of his temperament even when the victims had nothing to do with social democracy. De Brouckère, chairman of the commission to aid political prisoners, was closer to the truth when he referred to Martov in proposing a resolution against capital punishment. He saluted the Mehsheviks and SRs as "equally deserving the gratitude of the socialist world" for remembering that socialism required freedom. The congress unanimously passed the capital-punishment resolution and protested Trotsky's deportation.

The Mensheviks' policy of presenting a united front paid off in the International. Their differences paled before their prestige as the only socialist party actively working against communism in their home country, under terror. And their stand was more in harmony than that of the SRs with the International's own moderate stand on communism. Closing the Brussels Congress, E. Vandervelde paid tribute to the dead veterans of socialism:

> The last on this long roll of mourning is our Axelrod. Together with Plekhanov, he was the father of Russian socialism. At this meeting we see brilliant pupils of his who show us by word and deed that even now Russian socialism and the Russian workers are adequately represented.

In July 1929 a congress of the Socialist Youth International discussed the threat of war on the Russian borders. The small but active British Independent Labour party, following its usual pro-Soviet line, complained that the Socialist International was supporting the capitalist countries whose preparations for attacking Russia caused the threat of war. Boris Sapir answered in the name of the Russian Youth League that the threat came, on the contrary, from the militaristic Soviet policy, and that the International had always been against foreign intervention in Russia. The congress protested against terror in the fascist countries and the USSR. This point never raised many objections.

Terror was discussed at most of the congresses and conferences of the International, usually on the Mensheviks' initiative. Upon reports by Abramovich and Tsereteli, the executive committee of the International resolved in February 1927 to appoint a commission to study the situation of political prisoners in various countries. A resolution of the executive committee condemned fascism in Italy, fascist tendencies in Hungary, Rumania, and Lithuania, and, most sharply, "the barbarous and senseless system of terror" in the USSR. The International's May Day proclamation of 1927 called for "Restoration of Political Freedom and Democracy! Amnesty for Political Prisoners!" In 1928, the Brussels Congress examined the problem of terror. In 1929, the International's commission of political persecution published a bulletin that gave much space to the USSR. In November 1929 the bureau of the International passed a resolution condemning "the crimes of the Bolshevik dictatorship, committed allegedly in the name of the proletariat." None of these resolutions had any results, but the Mensheviks never slackened in their campaign against terror.

Soon after the Brussels Congress, a wave of illusions about the USSR swept the West. Various socialist groups began to think that the International's policy might need revision—that in the light of new developments in Russia certain things that had formerly been condemned should perhaps be accepted. The Mensheviks tried to combat the spreading misinformation. Much of it came from English sources. One example: In the early thirties, the Fabians Sidney and Beatrice

Webb visited Russia, collected a great deal of material, and published a two-volume work, *Soviet Communism: A New Civilization?* They had found that a new high culture was in the making in the USSR; the inhabitants liked the ruling party, and this had been achieved by persuasion; Stalin had less power than the president of the United States; he did not want to be a dictator, and could not be one in any case since he was neither prime minister nor president but merely the general secretary of his party, appointed and paid by its Central Committee. The Mensheviks were assigned one short paragraph in connection with the 1931 "trial of Menshevik professors"[48] (see Appendix C). The Webbs' reputation and the plethora of material—no doubt supplied by the government—gave their book great weight. After their deaths, a leader of the opposite, left wing of British socialism, Harold Laski, wrote:

> They are, I am sure, right in insisting that neither Lenin nor Stalin ever played the part of dictator. . . . I am confident that they are right in arguing that no nation since the time of the ancient Greeks has done so much to put culture, including science, so profoundly into the very foundation of its daily life.[49]

Still later, a noted British historian of the labor movement G. D. H. Cole, declared:

> To regard what has happened in the Soviet Union as having nothing to do with socialism, as so many Western socialists seem now ready to believe, is I am sure, bad thinking; Stalin's misdeeds can no more destroy the essential legacy of 1917 than Napoleon could destroy that of 1789.[50]

The changed atmosphere could not but affect the Mensheviks' tactics in the International. They had always been aware of the danger of finding themselves in the position of a purely émigré party. This may explain certain compromises and inconsistencies in the resolutions of the delegation abroad on problems discussed in the International. But the Mensheviks managed to remain the only émigré party enjoying respect and influence in the International. The memory of the role that the émigrés Axelrod and Plekhanov had played in the labor movement undoubtedly contributed to this.

In their campaign against illusions about the USSR, the Mensheviks, including their left wing, used two specific arguments to stiffen opposition to the Soviet government. First, that the sacrifices made by their comrades in Russia benefited all of socialism. Dan said at the Brussels Congress that if the Russian Social-Democrats continued to work, it was because "they are inspired by the proud knowledge that their work in their supremely dangerous and responsible post serves not only the cause of the Russian revolution and the Russian proletariat but also that of the entire international labor movement." Therefore the Mensheviks demanded that the International support them on the "Russian question" instead of merely protesting against terror generally, as it had been doing of late.

Second, they objected to the view promoted by Bauer and Laski that Bolshevik methods, inadmissible in the West, might be suitable for Russia because three centuries of autocracy had conditioned the Russian masses to the knout—Russians were not interested in the political forms that were elementary needs for the civilized West. According to Laski, Russian socialism had inherited many of its traits from Ivan the Terrible and Peter the Great; Russian culture stemmed from Byzantium, not Rome; in Russia, historical conditions made bolshevism realistic and menshevism utopian.[51] The Mensheviks rejected this theory as historically unsound and politically harmful, driving a wedge between Russia and the West. They pointed to the history of the Russian liberation movement, to nineteenth-century Russian literature, and so on.

The growing discontent of the peasants and the threat of a new civil war impelled the delegation abroad in 1930 to present to the International a memorandum on conditions in the USSR. The executive committee of the International appointed an "Eastern European commission" to examine the situation. Representatives of Eastern European parties, including the RSDRP, were invited in an advisory capacity. The British refused to serve, fearing to stimulate separatist tendencies by discussing the problem of nationalities. Under the influence of the Mensheviks' memorandum and speeches, the International for the first time addressed a separate appeal to Soviet workers. Expressing the "deep concern" of the socialist workers of all countries about "the fate of the Russian revolution," it invited Soviet workers to unite with socialists to save the revolution and exert pressure on the government "to force it to take the proper road."

Shortly before its next congress was due, the International received a message of greetings from exiled and interned Mensheviks, signed "Conference of the organizations of the RSDRP in the Soviet Union." It is difficult to ascertain whether such a conference had in fact taken place and whether the message really came from a group of deportees. It briefly described the tense situation in the USSR, adding: "Now as never before the interests of the Russian revolution require even greater support of our Party by the international labor movement in the struggle against the despotic dictatorship of the VKP."[52]

The congress of the International opened in Vienna on 25 July 1931. A pamphlet on conditions in the USSR, prepared by the delegation abroad and printed in three languages, was distributed to the delegates. Mensheviks were included in the political, economic, organizational, and disarmament commissions.

In the disarmament commission, Garvi spoke about the League of Nations: the socialists' attitude toward it should be neither subservient nor nihilistic; the Soviet proposal of total disarmament could not be sincere since the government depended on military force for its existence, but partial disarmament should be carefully considered; furthermore, the International should support Russia's admission to the League.

The congress was less concerned with Soviet affairs than with Hitler. It discussed antidotes to Nazism, such as annulment of war debts, economic aid to Germany. The Mensheviks did not insist on discussing communism. As Abramovich said, in the current mood of the International this might do more harm than good. The Mensheviks did, however, get some satisfaction at the plenary session of 31 July, chaired by Abramovich and the Swiss delegate R. Grimm. Referring no doubt to the recent trial of Mensheviks (see Appendix C), Grimm in the name of the International saluted Abramovich as a victim of despicable slander and a representative of a party that for a quarter of a century had been a notable member of the international labor organization. "Our sympathies," said Grimm (as reported in *SV*), "lie with the Social-Democrats persecuted in the USSR—to those who languish in prison we send our greeting." Abramovich replied:

> I know that it is not easy for foreign comrades to define their attitude to what is happening in Russia. Even for us, for each of us individually, the attitude to the Russian events represents the outcome of a painful inner struggle, I may say, an inner tragedy. It is so easy to become disoriented, so easy to confuse "left" and "right," "revolution" and "counterrevolution," "socialism" and "capitalism." And it is so hard to find the correct, truly revolutionary tactic that combines socialist principles with concern for the future of the Russian working class.

IV. Notes and Reflections on the History of Menshevism

Boris Sapir

To the memory of Vasilii Semenovich Kononenko
and Ivan Grigor'evich Rashkovskii

Introduction

The party about which this book has been written no longer exists. All of its leaders are gone; indeed, any surviving Russian Social-Democrats are hard to find. The history of the party that bore the proud name of RSDRP ended under Soviet rule. Strange as it may seem, academic interest in it surged up when almost nothing of it remained.

Whatever the breath of the Russian Revolution has touched has become a subject of study. Menshevism has acquired citizenship rights in the academic world because no complete history of bolshevism can be written apart from it. Probably it never occurred to Axelrod, Martov, or Potresov that their life work would escape oblivion thanks to Lenin's success. To be sure, there is the additional reason that such leaders as Dan, Liber, Tsereteli, and Chkheidze came to the fore during the "February" period of the revolution and did their share in directing its course.

A close study of menshevism should have begun in the thirties or forties at the latest, when its ablest representatives were alive to recount the events of 1905 and 1917. Great credit is due the Inter-University Project on the History of the Menshevik Movement for collecting, at the last minute, so to speak, the personal reminiscences and historical accounts of scattered remaining Social-Democrats. The task was indeed urgent: of the five major contributors to this volume, two—Dallin and Denicke—are dead; and so are six of the fourteen other original associates of the project: R. A. Abramovich, V. A. Aleksandrova, E. A. Anan'in, L. O. Dan, B. I. Nicolaevsky, and M. D. Shishkin.

The editor of this volume has asked me to present reflections on the history of the Menshevik party in its post-October period and to fill in, as far as possible, some factual lacunae in the works of the other contributors that may hinder the understanding of the events they describe.

Although all the contributors to this book except the editor are Mensheviks, it is not intended to be an apologia of menshevism. The decades that have passed have brought such seismic changes that the Revolution of 1917 seems an epoch away. Supposedly immutable values have been radically revised. The Menshevik contributors to this volume have sought to view the past with detachment. They have tried to place the ideology, tactics, and activity of their party in historical perspective by using all available sources as well as their own memories. They have tried to give a comprehensive picture of the life, the struggle, the hopes and the faith—and the death throes—of Russian social democracy in the most tragic period of its existence.

New York, 1966

16

The Mensheviks before the Revolution of 1917

Between the Two Revolutions

Menshevism and bolshevism separated during the low tide of revolutionary activity after the defeat of the Revolution of 1905. The division was complete by the time of the First World War, even though Martov spoke of "our part of the Party" in 1916, [1] and so-called United Organizations of the RSDRP existed in many cities until after October 1917 (see Appendix A). A struggle had been going on ever since Martov and Lenin clashed at the Second Party Congress in 1903, when the RSDRP was still a single party. The roots of dissent reach back even earlier, almost to the origins of the Russian revolutionary movement, to the populism of the seventies, but it is only after the suppression of the 1905 Revolution that menshevism and bolshevism developed into widely differing political entities. For bolshevism, as Dan wrote in his appendix to the German edition of Martov's *History of Russian Social Democracy*, the crucial period was 1907 to 1913: "During that time the tactics began to take shape that a decade later became the hallmark of communism." [2] And: "During those years took shape the characteristic traits of the Bolshevik organization that manifested themselves so sharply in its later activity." [3] B. Nicolaevsky draws the same conclusion in his as yet unpublished work on the Bolshevik center. That the same period was equally important for the evolution of menshevism has not been noted by anyone so far as I know, if we discount polemical outbursts such as Iu. Kamenev's *Dve partii*. The Mensheviks themselves were not always aware of the important changes that the evolution of their party implied. To outsiders this was even less apparent. In the Party press, in the leaders' speeches, debates were carried on in the Marxist style familiar to the eye and the ear, with references to standard authorities and dogmas popular in Party circles. But the content of the old formulas was changing, and they were used in a new context.

In the light of the events of 1905 the significance of the separation becomes clear. During Russia's First Revolution, despite factional conflict and differing ideological constructs, the actual work of Mensheviks and Bolsheviks ran more or less along the same groove. Trotsky was not far wrong in saying that "the differences of opinion between our factions are so insignificant, so uncertain, so minute, that they seem like chance wrinkles on the great brow of the revolution."[4] In 1906 Axelrod said in his well-known speech about the Duma at the Unification Congress in Stockholm: "on the whole, the Menshevik tactics have hardly differed from the Bolshevik. I am not even sure that they differed from them at all."[5]

In his aforementioned appendix to Martov's book, Dan describes how the Social-Democrats, both *intelligenty* and workers, reacted to the fiasco of the Revolution of 1905. The experience was all the more unnerving as everything in Russia had changed. The labor movement found itself in a new setting; the whole atmosphere in which social democracy had to work was new. (I am advisedly not saying "the Party," for the Party as an organized whole did not exist at the time. This applies to both Bolsheviks and Mensheviks, though the less centralized Menshevik apparatus was the more disorganized.) There were scattered groups around different leaders, not properly linked together, feeling their way amid the disappointment and apathy pervading Russian society. Gradually it became plain that some new way would have to replace the tried ways of the 1890s and early 1900s. The illegal organization, much criticized before, was now thoroughly discredited in the eyes of many thoughtful leaders. At best, they wanted it to be radically reformed. Besides, underground work appeared to have lost much of its point now that labor could struggle openly and achieve certain gains despite persecution and censorship. The great objective, the overthrow of autocracy, had not been attained, but the government had retreated; and although it seemed firmly ensconced in its new positions, the principles of public control (the Duma) and independent initiative (organizations, newspapers, clubs, trade unions, and so on) were gaining wide public acceptance despite obstacles and setbacks. Civil liberties, of course, were a thing of the past. Axelrod, Martov, Dan, Martynov, and other conpromised party workers had had to leave Russia. (Martov and Dan would return in 1913.) Potresov remained—and became the magnet for the Mensheviks who had not been swept away by the tide of reaction and continued to take part in the labor movement and the political struggle. This was true not only for Petersburg but for all Russia, especially after Potresov founded *Nasha Zaria* in 1910. It is no exaggeration to say that this journal played no less a role than *Iskra* had until 1905. Potresov's focal importance is also evidenced by the fact that he was one of the editors of the symposium *Obshchestvennoe dvizhenie v Rosii v nachale XX veka* (The Social Movement in Russia at the Beginning of the Twentieth Century).

If we disregard formal hierarchy, of no great moment in any case, the leaders of menshevism from 1907 or 1908 to 1914, insofar as one can speak of central leadership, were Dan, Martov, and Potresov, supported by Axelrod.

This is not the place to dwell on Pavel Borisovich Axelrod. Suffice it to say that menshevism with all its good and bad traits as a political system, and its specific moral approach to the Russian labor movement, was the creation of this remarkable man. Poor health prevented him from attending to details of "practical work" or writing much in the Party press. He influenced the Party mainly through personal talks and correspondence. Dan, Potresov, and Martynov were his disciples. They undertook no important steps without his approval. One had to read the letters to Axelrod of the lesser luminaries of menshevism, such as B. S. Vasil'ev, P. A. Garvi, V. O. Levitskii, E. Maiskii, and, *horrible dictu*, I. M. Maiskii (preserved at the International Institute of Social History, Amsterdam) to get an idea of the affection, esteem, and authority Axelrod enjoyed in the Party. I remember B. O. Bogdanov's stories at the Solovki camp about the Petersburg Mensheviks' visits to Axelrod when he lived in Finland in 1906. Bogdanov felt that the so-called legal labor movement that developed after the Revolution of 1905 owed much of its form and substance to Axelrod's talks with the young men from Petersburg who came to him for counsel and guidance.

The assumption that Plekhanov was the spiritual father of menshevism is mistaken. He was no forebear of menshevism nor a Menshevik by temperament. He was the father of Russian Marxism, siding now with the Mensheviks, now with the Bolsheviks, only to become estranged from both. In 1917 he would find himself completely isolated from the party that owed him its Marxist philosophy.

As I have said, the actual leaders of menshevism between the First

Revolution and the First World War were Dan, Martov, and Potresov, mainly by way of letters between him and Martov.[6] As Martov often wrote in Dan's name as well (his usual formula was "F. I. [that is Fedor Il'ich Dan] and I"), the Correspondence reflects the thoughts of all three.[7]

The "triumvirate" held that the revolution was over (the question whether Russia was still in a state of revolution was much debated at the time). They agreed on the need to use legal means to develop workers' organizations and a labor press, and they favored "partial slogans" to draw workers into the movement and above all to create a workers' intelligentsia that could eventually head a true labor party. In other words, they were all Axelrodists. An especially close relationship developed between Axelrod and Potresov.[8] The latter wrote Axelrod's biography[9] — an undertaking Dan had attempted but had been unable to carry out.[10] On practical issues there were no disagreements between Dan, Martov, and Potresov.

Less harmonious were their estimates of the future course of factional struggles and ideological searchings. Potresov had written off the restoration of a united RSDRP. Dan and Martov tried to mend the rift and to seize the Party banner by exposing the cancre of Bolshevik "revolutionism" (for example, "expropriation") that was disrupting the Party and the labor movement. Therefore they participated in the common Party organs whose lineage went back to the London Congress of 1907. Potresov merely shrugged his shoulders—for him, the Bolsheviks had ceased to be a intraparty issue, and he was now more influential than Dan and Martov. The center of gravity had shifted to Russia; the émigrés had to reckon with Potresov more than Potresov with them. The new balance of power was demonstrated after the plenary meetings of the Central Committee of the RSDRP in Paris in 1910. Dan and Martov thought they had carried off a signal success: Lenin had been brought to his knees, and the factions seemed to have reached an agreement. But their careful plans, which had cost them great efforts and nervous strain,[11] were scotched by the refusal of P. Garvi, K. Ermolaev, and I. Isuv ("Iurii," "Roman," and "Mikhail") to sit in the CC together with Bolsheviks.

A basic reason for the refusal was the distaste of Potresov's group for illegal work. The immense majority of Mensheviks in Russia were enthusiastically engrossed in founding and serving workers' organizations. They preferred to shelve underground activites even if they felt that this "corrective" to the legal movement might in the long run prove necessary. Theoretically they probably agreed with Martov that the Party in Russia should be "an illegal organization of Social-Democratic elements fighting for an *open* labor movement, that is, among other things, for its own open existence." [12] In practice, however, little was done in this direction, and when the workers recovered from their post-1905 apathy, it was the Bolshevik underground apparatus that caught up most of the new cadres in the legal organizations that the Mensheviks had created. This began, roughly, after the Lena shootings (April 1912). Then the Dan-Martov line became more popular among the Mensheviks, but a crucial moment had been missed.

Ideologically, the main issue on which Dan and Martov had diverged from Potresov was this: Would Russia follow the road of revolution or that of the so-called Prussian development, that is, amalgamation of the bourgeoisie with a tsarist regime that would finally do something about the country's political, economic, and cultural needs? Dan wrote in 1909: "No, our train will not run like the German train!" [13] It was mainly Dan who analyzed for the Party the social meaning of the Stolypin regime and the role of the bourgeoisie. As early as 1907 he had written (presenting his views in a somewhat simplified but incisive way):

> On the ruins of the October-December revolution...the shabbiest, most parasitic class of old Russia has erected its throne. The feudal gentry...has climbed to the heights of power....All the forces of bourgeois society are sure to rebel against the "dictatorship" of the feudal gentry....The gentry's "dictatorship" is bound to propel even the big bourgeoisie into the opposition. [14]

Two years later, in his above-mentioned article, Dan described the regime in almost the same words and explained the political implications of his analysis in Marxist terms:

> The...bourgeois transformation of Russia's social structure, as well as the approaching clash between the progressive evolution of this structure and the regressive movement of the political "super-structure," is a historical fact that cannot be headed off....The so-called leftening of the bourgeoisie is one manifestation of this complex historical process and at the same time its powerful motor force. Only its clash with the feudalists will budge Russia's stagnant political life. Of course this does not mean that at some stage of its development the Russian capitalist bourgeoisie will unfurl red flags and lead the masses to the barricades. But it does mean that its growing "oppositionism" will create favorable conditions for the proletariat's revolutionary initiative and for drawing into the

movement the urban and rural petty bourgeoisie, as well as for solving the problems that were not and could not be solved by the Revolution of 1905. [15]

Martov agreed with this. In the same issue he referred approvingly to Dan's article.

Potresov took a different stand. In a number of letters to Martov (for example, those of 7/20 April 1908, and 25 December/7 January 1908–1909) he criticized Dan's theories in passing; and when Martov on 4/17 April 1909 wrote of his basic agreement with Dan, Potresov replied, on 15/28 April:

> For a long time I've been watching with some perplexity the development into what looks to me like an *idée fixe*, among you people abroad, of the correct but not novel idea that the big business bourgeoisie cannot long remain as reactionary as the gentry, reactionary *sans phrases*—that it needs a better ordered and more-cultured regime, a regime more adapted to the development of the country's productive forces than the present regime, and so on. At first it seemed to me that this was mainly F. I.'s [Dan's] idea, but now it is apparently shared by the entire group abroad [that is, the editors of *Golos Sotsial'demokrata*]....All right, let us suppose for a moment that you are correct, that the big bourgeoisie is destined in the near future to play the role that the liberal zemstvos played in the past era. What comes after that? What...innovations can we expect from this "liberalization" of the bourgeoisie? Does this "leftening" shed any light on the most basic question that awaits our answer and solution,...whether the present crisis will bring forth a new social movement, a revolutionary finale, or..."Austrian" concessions by the government, its gradual Europeanization. I could understand you if you firmly adhered to the latter version—like, for example, Cherevanin....But apparently you consider this version the least likely; apparently you presume that a repetition of the populist movement is possible....But precisely in the *latter case* I consider it impossible for the big bourgeoisie to play a significant role as a liberal force....If a "bourgeois" revolution is conceivable in our country, it is conceivable, of course, [only] with the dominant participation—independently of the proletariat's participation—of the other elements of bourgeois society, the middle and petty bourgeoisie, with the peasantry in their wake. These are the very elements we usually call bourgeois democracy and to which we assigned the mission of guarding the interest of the bourgeois development as a whole. I continue to hold this conviction and I think that *precisely this combination of bourgeois elements—again, together with the proletariat—will pull Russia out of the impasse, if Russia is still going to have a revolution* [italics added]....But a quite

different prospect is also conceivable, I think—that of partial, non-revolutionary changes reforming Russia. In that case we shall go through an era of governmental adaptation to the bourgeois development and to the interests of the big bourgeoisie. But even in that case there will be no era of...liberalism, for the industrial bourgeoisie of the Austro-Prussian type, and in that case the line of development of the liberal-democratic movement may well lie farther to the left and be antagonistic to the political representation of the big bourgeoisie.

This long but interesting excerpt expressed Potresov's stand not only before but also during and after the First World War. While Martov's and especially Dan's ideas were close to the traditional schema of Russian Marxism about bourgeois and socialist revolution, Potresov sought new ways—without, of course, abandoning Marxism. To the end of his life he considered himself an orthodox follower of Marx and Engles, even though he increasingly stressed evolution rather than revolution, the proletariat's national rather than class tasks. His dissent with Martov and Dan was purely theoretical and did not prevent the triumvirate from working together. (Under Stolypin's regime Social-Democratic work was narrowly circumscribed: differing estimates of the bourgeoisie's future role did not interfere with joint work in founding labor organizations.)

Potresov drew far-reaching conclusions from the defeat of 1905. Despite his pseudonym Starover ("Old Believer"), he took the initiative in revising certain postulates of the *Iskra* period. Nor did he shrink from critically examining the tactics recommended by the Liberation of Labor Group, that is, by Plekhanov, aiming his sharpest darts at the idea of the proletariat's "hegemony." Launched by *Iskra*, the term was understood as leadership of the working class in the coming revolution. Referring to Martynov's article "The Motor Force of the Russian Revolution" in *Golos Sotsial'demokrata*, no. 1, Potresov wrote Martov on 7/20 April 1908:

I conclude from it that for Martynov nothing has changed in the conception that the Liberation of Labor Group used to promote of the Russian revolution and the forces active in it. Alas, I do not share his views on this point and I think that here, too, corrections are needed, on the basis of [the experiences of] the past few years. Unfortunately the "hegemony" of the proletariat that the Liberation of Labor Group envisioned also proved impossible and is unlikely ever to become possible in the Russian *bourgeois* revolution.

And on 18 November/1 December:

Plekhanov alone is responsible for the [idea of] hegemony; I could demonstrate that his old conception of the early nineties can very easily lead to Parvus's viewpoint [that is, the theory of permanent revolution]. He has never been able to reconcile the question of hegemony with that of the attitude [to be adopted] toward the other oppositional and revolutionary elements. There always was the dual picture of extreme amiability toward possible liberal allies and actually what can only be called dictatorship of social democracy in the Russian revolution.

Dan and Martov showed no great zeal in defending the proletariat's hegemony. Whether under Potresov's influence or on his own, Dan had long since decided that "the proletariat is no longer in a position to play the brilliant but hardly profitable role of monopolist in the political struggle."[16] And Martov did not care to argue an issue that had just lost its relevance. "Your letters are again raising the question of 'liquidating' the idea of hegemony," he wrote Potresov on 4/17 April 1910. "I think that what you write about liquidating the Party exactly applies here: there is nothing left to liquidate. Almost no hope remains, even among the Bolsheviks, that the 'hegemonic' position in democracy will be ours again." Potresov replied on 26 April/9 May: "It seems to me you are badly mistaken that in this matter we have nothing to 'liquidate'....I often hear...that for a great many people the wreck of the idea of hegemony means the wreck of all hope, loss of the Social-Democratic position, the opening of doors to a restored *narodopravchestvo*." (*Narodnoe Pravo* was an organization founded by M. A. Nathanson in 1891 and soon wiped out by the police. It tried to unite socialists and democrats exclusively on the basis of struggling for political freedom.)

Dissent about "hegemony" also underlay Plekhanov's conflict with Potresov and the editors of *Golos Sotsial'demokrata* over Potresov's article in Volume 1 of *Obschestvennoe dvizhenie v Rossii v nachale XX veka*. Plekhanov had vetoed the article. Having received no support from the other editors of the series (Martov and Maslov) or from the editors of *Golos Sotsial'demokrata* (Axelrod, Dan, Martov, and Martynov), he refused to collaborate in the series, resigned from the paper's editorial board,[17] began an anti-Menshevik campaign, and sought rapprochement with the Bolsheviks. Many found his reaction unreasonable and ascribed it to hurt pride: Potresov had failed to give him his due as the propagator of Marxism in Russia. That Plekhanov could react violently when he felt affronted was well known from the *Iskra* experience. In this case, however, hurt feelings were not the main cause, though they cannot be discounted. Dan wrote Axelrod[18] that Plekhanov had found Potresov's article "Philistine." Knowing Potresov's views from his correspondence with Martov, we can decode the word: Plekhanov had sensed in Potresov's writing a tone unusual for Russian Social-Democrats—and the revolutionary of bygone days had awakened in him. Forgetting his own pronouncements of 1905–06, far more rightist than Potresov's, he attacked the latter and the Mensheviks who sided with him for traducing the pre-1905 S-D policy. Dan, Martov, and the Mensheviks grouped around Potresov in Russia had indeed deviated from that policy. They were evolving in the same direction as all the socialist parties of the Second International, and that is why they did not perceive the new spirit in Potresov's "Philistine" article. L. O. Dan has an entry in her reminiscences under the heading "Iu. O. Martov": "1908...conflict with Plekhanov over Potresov's article, and Plekhanov's departure from the editorial board of *Golos Sotsial'demokrata*. Incidentally, by now it is clear that basically Plekhanov was right." I feel sure that here Mrs. Dan echoes her husband's later ideas. In the late thirties he, too, forgot the role he had played before and during 1917, suddenly recaptured the revolutionary ardor of his youth—and realized that Potresov's article had reflected the retreat of Russian Social-Democracy from "revolutionism." Moreover, Dan wanted to link Potresov's policy after October 1917 to the "deviations" he had begun to manifest long before the February Revolution.

The wish to present a political biography as a straight line can easily lead to false conclusions, for it usually consists of zigzags. Thus, Plekhanov, a Social-Democrat of the extreme right in 1906, supported Lenin in 1910, only to become a rabid anti-Bolshevik in 1917. Dan, a Menshevik leader for almost forty years, the man for whom "Bolsheviks of all shadings have...a kind of visceral hatred,"[19] descried a socialist element in Stalinism in 1946. Martynov, a *Rabochedelets* until 1903, an orthodox contributor to *Iskra* after the Second Congress, published "permanent revolution" articles in *Nachalo* in 1905, then became one of Axelrod's most devoted disciples, and ended as a leader in the Comintern. No doubt there are explanations for these shifts—but that is the realm of psychology, not politics. By 1917, menshevism had largely outgrown the radicalism of the *Iskra* period. It had absorbed all the novelties brought into Russian life by the so-called pseudo-constitutionalism that pervaded the empire after 1905. And it had lived through the First World War.

The War

Martov had had a kind of foreknowledge about the coming storm. In late 1908 he wrote Potresov:

The world is undergoing, or beginning to undergo, a crisis the like of which has probably not been seen since the period of '48-'71,

which ended in the emergence of the German and Italian monarch-
ies. All politics and all ideological development in Russia will now be
increasingly influenced by approaching violent events of a worldwide nature. [20]

A few months later, he returned to this theme:

The ground [on which "the working class is destined to move"] has
from the beginning been mined throughout its length and breadth
by those contradictions of an international nature that can always—
regardless of the pace of Russia's internal development—lend a sud-
den urgency to all the problems the people has to face and draw the
country into...revolutionary events earlier than now appears likely. [21]

This was premonition, no more. In 1914 Martov like everyone else
was shocked by the disintegration of the International and the patriotic position taken by most workers of the belligerent countries,
especially Germany.

The war also destroyed the triumvirate that effectively had led the
Menshevik party. In the summer of 1914 Martov was abroad to attend
a conference that the International had convoked for the purpose of
healing the split in Russian Social Democracy. He did not return to
Russia until 1917. Dan was arrested even before the Duma meeting of
26 July 1914, at which war credits were voted, and was deported for
three years to Enisei Province. Only Potresov remained in Petersburg
throughout the war. He became the ideologue of Defensism, whereas
both Dan and Martov took the Internationalist stand. It is hard to say
whom the majority of Mensheviks followed. Levitskii wrote Martov
that Defensism was popular with the Liquidationists, especially among
the workers' intelligentsia. [22] Ezhov thought that Defensists were in the
minority even among the regular contributors to *Nasha Zaria*. [23] Be
that as it may, the war caused a split in menshevism—or, rather,
brought it into the open.

For all his opposition to defensism, Martov appreciated the subtlety
and pithiness of Potresov's argumentation. [24] Potresov had indeed per-
ceived and formulated the very core of the dissent. Today, decades
later, one can hardly doubt that the Defensists were basically right in
stressing the organic ties between labor and country. The whole development of the socialist parties from the foundation of the Second
International until 1914 could in fact be described as a gradual inte-
gration of labor organizations into the fabric of state. By 1914, workers
were no longer pariahs but citizens of their countries. Their growing
representation in parliaments, the new labor laws, the rising levels of
income and education had largely cured the industrial workers' aliena-
tion from society and the pauperism caused by "primitive accumu-

lation." These were no longer determining factors in the policies of socialist parties and trade unions, whose revolutionary spirit now found an outlet in trying to improve the existing order. Potresov and his followers had early sensed this trend. What they were saying, in effect, was that workers were being integrated into their respective national societies and that the alliance between national units of the international labor army must now rest on this basis. The color red gradually faded from Potresov's palette. This was his strength—and also his weakness, for the period ushered in by the Sarajevo shots was anything but propitious for organic development.

The great changes in Europe and the world, the shifted frontiers, the emergence of nations awakened from long slumber or never before independent, the obsolete economic forms of so-called *Hochkapitalismus*, crying out for renovation; the increasing participation in politics of great masses that heretofore had been merely the objects of policies; finally, the proliferation of the so-called technical intelligentsia and various intermediate groups shaken out of their secure niches and fearful of becoming mere hired help—all this made for an accumulation of dynamite that a single spark could explode. But the organized labor movement, becoming integrated in the existing order, was losing the sense of the revolutionary nature of the era. Socialists were faced with the paradoxical task, on one hand, of conducting a policy oriented toward taking over the leadership of the state of which they had become a part and, on the other, of pressing for urgent radical reforms.

Martov's vocabulary included the words "nation" and "reform" (see George Denicke's part of this book), but he concentrated on the new ideas generated by the war and stressed the revolutionary character of the period. The elements that played such a large role in Potresov's Defensist ideology seemed in comparison unimportant. The proletariat's collaboration with other classes in defense of country was as unthinkable for Martov as was for Potresov the admission that the war was an imperialist war for which all the belligerents were equally responsible. For a time, Martov and Potresov were still united by the idea that the Russian revolution, should it take place, would be a bourgeois revolution, but by 1917 they diverged even on this. From 1914, there were thus two trends in menshevism, each partly correct: the Defensists, who saw the national tasks of socialists in their true light; and the Internationalists, who understood the revolutionary character of the era.[25] This divergence, and whatever had been learned from the period 1905–14 and from the defeat of the February Revolution, lurked in the wings of the stage on which the curtain rose in October 1917.

17

The Conception of the Bourgeois Revolution

Russian social democracy, born as a party of revolution par excellence, rose on the yeast of the self-restrictive theory of the bourgeois character of the coming Russian revolution.

Unlike the populists, most Russian Marxists—until 1917, even the Bolsheviks—refused to attempt to combine the overthrow of autocracy with a socialist reorganization of the country. Economically and culturally retarded, Russia must pass through a stage of capitalist development to become ripe for the superior economic form. Autocracy obstructed the growth of productive forces; by removing this hindrance, the revolution would clear the way for the bourgeoisie, already strong enough to become the basis of the regime that would replace the Romanov dynasty; the proletariat was vitally interested in a maximally democratic outcome of the bourgeois revolution, which would create favorable conditions for the labor movement; the latter would grow strong and healthy in the climate of political freedom; eventually it would carry out its own socialist revolution.

In a nutshell, this was the theory of bourgeois revolution, discussed in this book by George Denicke and Leo Lande. It is not my aim to analyze the sociological merits of this theory or the question whether it really followed from Marx's and Engels' teachings. Scientifically demonstrable or not, truly Marxist or artificially grafted on, it was an article of faith for generations of Russian Social-Democrats. I shall deal only with this fact and try to answer two questions: How did this conception come to be regarded in Russia as almost the fundamental tenet of Marxism? What was its effect on the political activity of the Social-Democrats?

Many remarks by friends and foes of Russian Marxism seem to point to a close relationship between this conception and the general drift of the RSDRP's political decisions. For example, Kerensky tells us that during the first days of the February Revolution the Executive Committee of the Petrograd Soviet of Workers' Deputies "refused to participate in the Provisional Government because in the opinion of the Committee, which was led by Mensheviks, the revolution was a bourgeois revolution." [1] Chernov says much the same:

> It was easy and joyful to march shoulder-to-shoulder and in step with them [Tsereteli, Dan, Weinstein-Zvezdin—that is, Menshevik leaders]. But over all of them hung an old and in my opinion obsolete dogma, which often rendered their work futile. It proclaimed that the Russian revolution had to be a purely bourgeois revolution and that any attempt to overstep these natural and inevitable bounds would be a harmful adventure. [2]

Tsereteli confirms these observations:

> Russia's situation at the time imperatively demanded a coalition. In the conception of all classes, a purely socialist government is inseparable from a socialist revolution; the presence in the government of representatives of the bourgeoisie reassured the bourgeois elements of the population and reminded the socialist masses of the actual importance of the bourgeoisie for the country's economy. [3]

Dan blamed the S-D's inability to end the war in 1917 mainly on the ideological traditions of Russian socialists—that is, on the same conception of bourgeois revolution. [4]

Pace these authorities, it is doubtful that the theory dictated the Mensheviks' decisions. Usually these were made under the pressure of circumstances. The conception was featured in debates to reinforce arguments because the leaders were accustomed to think in traditional categories, but it was filled with different content at various times, and the inferences drawn from it were of one kind in 1905, of another after February 1917, of yet another after the German revolution of 1918, only to sound in the NEP period exactly as they had originally. Analyzed, these transformations suggest that the conception exerted its main influence on a different plane from the one the above writers had in mind. It only slightly affected the S-D's tactics, but it largely determined the atmosphere in which the Party was steeped. It was the intellectual prism through which the Russian S-Ds viewed the struggling social forces of their country.

What is most striking about the formula is that it was so emotionally charged—as if it were the holy of holies or, in more mundane terms, the very foundation of Social-Democratic philosophy. This is largely traceable to the circumstances under which it had emerged. In the early eighties a sharp conflict developed between a small group of former *Chernoperedel'tsy* and the dying *Narodnaia Volia* with its aura of heroism and its still powerful hold on the revolutionary intelligentsia. Plekhanov, who laid the foundations of Russian Marxism, took for his basic postulate—his fulcrum, so to speak—the idea that Russia was growing into a capitalist economy. *Narodnaia Volia*, he said, had run into an impasse because it had ignored this fact. Not the peasantry but the industrial proletariat, that inevitable satellite of capitalism, was the socialists' best hope, the mainspring of the movement that would kill autocracy. With the defeat of *Narodnaia Volia* the revolutionary intelligentsia had lost its *narod*, its "people" (an observation we owe to Potresov). Plekhanov gave it a new "people," the industrial proletariat, and thus revived its hopes for Russia's future. More, Plekhanov's Marxism *guaranteed* victory. Potresov in his article in Volume 1 of *Obshchestvennoe dvizhenie v Rossii v nachale XX veka* excellently describes the revolution that took place in the thinking of the intelligentsia as soon as they felt the support of the urban proletarian masses, a new factor in Russia's development. This was just what Marxism had promised and what the strikes of the nineties had confirmed. For the new converts to Marxism, the doctrine of Russia's capitalist development (and of the bourgeois character of the Russian revolution) was not tainted with "minimalism." On the contrary, it "scientifically" demonstrated that a socialist revolution must follow the capitalist stage; it seemed to insure a realistic approach to Russia's political problems, to give a firm basis to the ideas inherited from Herzen, Belinskii, Chernyshevskii, and Dobroliubov. Moreover it aligned Russia with Western Europe, especially Germany, where strong socialist parties had arisen under the influence of Marxism and were training the workers to fight for power. To sum up, the doctrine sounded like an appeal to rally the conscious workers under the socialist banner. ("Conscious workers" meant those who knew what they wanted and how to bring it about.) Any deviation from it looked almost like intellectual dishonesty and was branded "utopianism" or "Blanquism": Plekhanov's disciples had before them the lessons of 1848 and the Paris Commune. His interpretation of Marxism seemed to promise that the Russian proletariat would avoid the old mistakes and refuse to serve merely as cannon fodder for the bourgeois revolution. Knowing the historical limitations of the given stage of development, the conscious workers would manage to entrench themselves in their new positions after the overthrow of autocracy and would fight the last "decisive battle" only when the time was ripe. Armed with the knowledge of what was possible and what was not, the proletariat would form the right alliances. It would crush the monarchy in a common assault with the bourgeoisie, but simultaneously develop into an independent force with its own socialist aims.

All this gave the doctrine of bourgeois revolution a philosophical flavor. It was a view of the world rather than a guide in concrete problems. Yet it had to be adapted to changing circumstances, and so it was variously interpreted in the RSDRP before the split and, within menshevism, after it. Everyone subscriberd to the doctrine, but it became an elastic credo, stretched to fit Lenin's plan of a worker-peasant provisional government, the "permanent revolution" of Parvus and Trotsky, Martov's motto "always in the minority," and so on.

The Mensheviks proved to be the most steadfast adherents of the doctrine in its original conception—the only one, I should say, that made political sense even if it was far removed from reality. But among the Mensheviks, too, it was variously interpreted. Denicke has good reason to speak of two Menshevik conceptions of the bourgeois revolution (pp. 127 ff. of this book). In its unadulterated form the conception presupposed the existence of some objective yardstick by which to measure where the bourgeois revolution would end and the socialist revolution begin. It also presupposed that the Russian bourgeoisie would carry out the bourgeois revolution, and that social democracy would play the role of opposition, taking no part in the government that would succeed autocracy: participation in a bourgeois government would cause conflict between social democracy and the working masses.

For all their remoteness from the practical aspects of life, the Russian revolutionaries realized that some of the above preconditions might be lacking. Like their comrades in other countries, they did not at first give much thought to the borderline between capitalism and socialism, but they could not fail to see that social democracy would probably lead the revolution. The Menshevik Conference of May 1905—the first separate gathering of the emerging Menshevik party—resolved that if social democracy were carried to power, the Party would be obliged, even at the risk of sharing the fate of the Paris Commune, to proceed with its program-maximum, that is, the socialist reorganization of the country. (Martov had already expressed this idea before the conference. [5]) There is something desperate about this resolution: Social democracy knows that it is objectively impossible to reorganize Russian society and economy along socialist lines; it wants to avoid such a necessity; but if it is forced into power, it would rather perish honorably than stoop to the bourgeois reforms that alone are possible in Russia.

In November of the same year the legal Menshevik paper *Nachalo*, strongly influenced by Parvus and Trotsky but with Dan, Martov, Martynov, and Potresov among its contributors, began to promote a different idea. *Nachalo* saw nothing wrong with adandoning the bourgeois character of the revolution. It expected the Russian revolution to spark a European revolution. The proletariat of industrialized Europe would seize power and come to the aid of backward Russia, thus facilitating the "growing over" of the bourgeois into a socialist revolution. The editors' programmatic statement in *Nachalo*, no. 1, ended with the ringing declaration:

> The further successes of the Russian proletariat toward realizing a workers' democracy—which will already be successes of the world proletariat—can provide the impetus for the decisive struggle between the proletariat's sociorevolutionary organizations and state power in Western Europe.... Then we shall face the task of expanding our revolutionary program beyond a workers' democracy. The revolution in Russia is only beginning to develop. In its course it will arouse the peoples and shake the foundations of the whole capitalist world. Hail to the Russian revolution! Hail to socialism!

After the defeat of 1905, the Mensheviks reverted to the old conception of the bourgeois character of the Russian revolution, but the latter failed to withstand the test of 1917. The traditional scheme was revised by the Defensists, on one hand, and the Internationalists, on the other. Both wanted social democracy to take part in governing the country—the former, in coalition with the bourgeoisie, and the latter, in a purely socialist government. Neither intended to carry out the program-maximum but only to secure the gains of the democratic revolution, which in their eyes was a bourgeois revolution.

When the German revolution broke out in 1918, the Menshevik party majority, blithely resurrecting some ideas of *Nachalo*, began to theorize about the interaction of Russia and Europe. This theory is most fully expressed in Martov's April theses of 1920.

Emptied of meaning after so many metamorphoses, the dogma of the bourgeois character of the Russian revolution might have been expected to lose its magic. Yet it continued to fascinate the Mensheviks and even enjoyed a resurgence after the introduction of the NEP. In his indictment of bolshevism in the middle twenties, Dan accused

Lenin of betraying the dogma inherited from the Liberation of Labor Group:

> In 1917, as we know, Lenin cut the knot..., sacrificing the basic postulates of the Social-Democratic program of 1903, according to which capitalism was an unavoidable stage of Russia's economic development, and a bourgeois-democratic republic the next goal of the revolution. Lenin thereby jettisoned those postulates that had put social democracy since its beginnings in strong opposition to the traditions of Bakuninist "populism." He proclaimed socialism the *immediate* goal of the revolutionary overturn in backward Russia. This was the decisive moment that completed the evolution of bolshevism and marked its final break with social democracy and its transition to so-called communism. [6]

A very intelligent man, Dan did not appeal to the traditional conception in its pristine purity. Too many holes had been punched in it by the Mensheviks' own amendments, adjustments, and explanations of 1905 and 1917. He censured Lenin, that is, bolshevism, merely for wanting to introduce socialism in Russia *immediately.* In other words, he amended the dogma by saying that the socialist reorganization of Russia could not be achieved through frontal attack—admitting by implication that it could be achieved through a turning movement. This left very little of the theory of bourgeois revolution. The rightist opposition within the party had some grounds for accusing Dan of the very sin of which he accused Lenin. Dan himself understood how much he was contracting the traditional scheme, yet he was sincere in accusing Lenin of betraying the basic Social-Democratic policy. Despite all its transformations, the scheme continued to seem to him perfectly realistic. Its extensive, varied influence over the remnants of the Party in Russia and abroad can be observed throughout the post-October history of menshevism, up to the disappearance of Russian social democracy

Along Untrodden Paths

During the period of legal Marxism, the Social-Democrats, using "Aesopian language," sometimes hid behind the word "pupils" to identify themselves. This was an apt designation since the newly converted followers of the Liberation of Labor Group considered themselves disciples not only of Marx and Engels but also of the Western European Social-Democrats, mainly the Germans, who seemed to them a model worthy of imitation. The Revolution of 1905 did not change this state of affairs, but the First World War dimmed the admiration for Germany and after the October overturn of 1917 the roles were reversed: the Germans, the French, the Italians, and so on, now looked to their eastern comrades for guidance in understanding the intricacies of the Russian revolution and applying its lessons in their own countries. The Mensheviks were the first members of the International who had to deal with a Communist party in power in their homeland.

The Mensheviks knew that the Bolshevik regime was descended from the same Social-Democratic party as they, and connected with the same socialist proletariat. It was dedicated to the socialist ideal and hated by the propertied classes in Russia and abroad. Moreover, it was a regime bursting with energy and daring, and it had superseded a provisional government entangled in a coalition and therefore incapable of creative reforms that would have united the masses into a compact army willing to make sacrifices to defend the February conquests.

On the other side of the ledger was the view that the Soviet government had been carried to power mainly by armed soldiers and had established a dictatorship of a small minority, ignoring the will of the overwhelming majority of the population (as witness the disbandment of the Constituent Assembly and of organs of local self-government, Soviets, and labor organizations that remained true to the socialist parties). Breaking its promises, Lenin's government had concluded a separate peace with Germany, revoked the civil rights gained in the February Revolution, and plunged the country into civil war and political and economic chaos. To top it all, the successful overturn did not fit the Marxist scheme and must have troubled the Mensheviks' Marxist conscience. According to the canons absorbed since their earliest days, Russia was not ready for the integral socialism that the regime tried to establish during the period of so-called War communism.

I. M. Maiskii, expelled from the Menshevik party for accepting a post in the government of the Committee of Members of the Constituent Assembly, or KOMUCH,[7] published a book intended to blacken his former party and promote his career as a Communist. In it he quotes a letter he sent to the Central Committee of the RSDRP in late October 1918, defining the choice that, in his opinion, the Mensheviks had to make:

> When, in October 1917 . . . the Bolsheviks seized power and openly set their course toward a social revolution, the S-D party was faced with the question of what to do. Clearly, three positions were conceivable: supporting the Bolsheviks, fighting the Bolsheviks, or, finally, neutrality. Having rejected the first and the third after some

initial wavering, our party officially declared itself in favor of fighting the "Communist" dictatorship as [a regime] leading the country to civil war, political freedom to its death, and the national economy to ruin. [8]

Maiskii is insincere in trying to make out that his participation in KOMUCH was consistent with the stand of the RSDRP's Central Committee. It is true that the Mensheviks had from the beginning decided to combat the Bolsheviks—and they never abandoned this decision—but they admitted certain forms of struggle and rejected others as inconsistent with their aims. They rejected armed struggle against the Bolshevik government (unlike their recent allies, the SRs, who came to agree with them after a few disastrous years of civil war). But they tried to stimulate the pressure of the laboring masses on the government, in the hope of dividing the Bolsheviks and thus bringing about a democratic evolution of the regime, that is, a socialist government that would abandon Lenin's vagaries, adopt a realistic economic program, and restore civil rights.

Gradually the question of participating in government became academic. The prospect was nebulous at best. Its continued discussion merely denoted the Mensheviks' interest in big politics, so to speak. Their policy was aimed at peaceful liquidation of the regime. Everything else was secondary.

The Mensheviks needed to preserve their Party's legal status in order not to lose contact with the masses. Mindful of their experiences of 1905–14, they temporarily watered down some of their slogans (for instance, about the Constituent Assembly), hoping to rally the workers around reduced demands. Their compromises or, rather, tactical adaptations to Soviet reality, which their detractors (and the intraparty opposition) sometimes described as capitulation, were not always limited to tactics. Certain points of Martov's April theses came close to the Bolsheviks' theories. There were several reasons for this: the elation of the Martov group over the sharpening revolutionary situation in Germany and other countries, their reappraisal of the crisis of capitalism brought on by the war, and their belief that socialist reforms would spread from the West to Russia, taking her out of the impasse created by the policies of War communism. Be that as it may, the ideological zigzags of official menshevism during War communism did not change the basic party line. As before, the Party banked on the liberalization of the regime under mass pressure.

Almost from the first, the official majority of the Party had foreseen that all attempts by democratic elements at armed action against the Soviet regime would fail—either because they would be defeated or because they would turn into counterrevolution. In the clash between the regime and the democratic groups (the Committee of Members of the Constituent Assembly) the Menshevik CC had maintained the neutral position of a "third force," but in the war with the Whites its sympathies were on the side of the Red army. (The Party even "mobilized" its members into the Red army.) In both instances, however, the CC's political line remained the same: opposition to the government in order to build up the workers' pressure on it and thus force its evolution toward democracy.

Naturally the Bolsheviks' success in seizing power and hanging on to it unsettled the Mensheviks. Their Marxist conscience rebelled against socialist experiments and their Marxist reason against the fact that a government engaging in such experiments stood undefeated. Did not the level of development of productive forces fit the country only for a bourgeois revolution? Yet it would be a mistake to think that the Mensheviks lost faith in the seemingly disproved theory. On the contrary, they were convinced that the scheme still applied to Russian reality. They drew moral and political support from it, and a feeling that the class-conscious proletariat was intellectually superior to the Bolshevik simplifiers who, in Marxist terminology, represented "petty-bourgeois elements." Until the German revolution of 1918 the Mensheviks made no ideological concessions to the maximalistic mood that pervaded the country. They looked down on what they considered a lunatic attempt to implant integral socialism in a backward land. Here it may be apropos to record a recollection of my own: At a meeting in the spring or summer of 1918 at the Party club *Iskra* in the Zamoskvorech'e section of Moscow, in an argument with N.N. Sukhanov, who represented the Party left, Martov described the post-October Mensheviks as "an intelligent superfluity" and read a letter received by the CC from one of the provincial organizations consisting entirely of workers. The letter said that it was difficult to maintain a Marxist stand amid the raging revolutionary passions and ended with an appeal to the CC that can be paraphrased as "Make things easier for us, give us permission to become less intelligent."

Even after the German revolution, when the Party, in the person of its CC, began to admit the possibility of far-reaching changes in Russia far exceeding the limits of the orthodox bourgeois revoluiton, it clung to some irreducible minimum of the traditional conception. This minimum was hard to formulate logically, and the right intraparty opposition (which rejected the orientation to a European socialist revolution that would pull Russia into the mainstream of socialist transformation) easily found crushing arguments to prove that the

Party majority was betraying the doctrine of bourgeois revolution. Yet Martov and his group, far from feeling like traitors, based their constructs on traditional Russian Marxism—adapted to the circumstances, to be sure, less adamantly insistent on the impossibility of socialism, but not therefore the less "scientific" or less in the spirit if not the letter of the inherited doctrine. Even at the height of Larin's reckless projects, Bukharin's and Preobrazhenskii's "ABC of Communism," and the ruling party's naïve raptures over Lenin's discovery that communism was the Soviet regime plus electrification, the Mensheviks kept their sober, realistic approach to economic problems, as witness their platform, "What to Do" adopted by the CC in July 1919 and "since then forming the basis of the Party's economic policy." [9] It repudiated the surplus-appropriation system and wholesale nationalization and outlined a plan of mixed economic forms. "This was the program that is now accepted by almost all socialist and Communist labor parties," writes Abramovich; at the time, the Party wanted to chart a way "along which the revolution could be carried to its *historically possible limits* without . . . clashing with the interests and wishes of the immense majority of the nation." [10] The conception of the "historically possible limits" of the bourgeois revolution remained alive among the Mensheviks—admittedly an elastic conception but one that nevertheless set definite bounds to even the wildest fantasies, and thus effectively divided the conscious or unconscious believers in the principle "anything goes" from the determinists who rejected the wild leaps in a country's economy. All Mensheviks were in the latter class.

The belief in the primacy of economics over politics and in the validity for Russia of the general laws of historical development firmly bound the Mensheviks to traditional Russian Marxism, gave a quasi-scientific tenor to their arguments, and nurtured their conviction that in the long run their stand would prove right since it was based on objective analysis of all economic and political factors. "The Future Is Ours," the motto of the Menshevik Youth League, was no empty boast. It had deep roots in the Mensheviks' philosophy. It expressed their faith in the deathless, ultimately invincible quality of Social Democracy.

Still, the Bolsheviks' success called for an explanation. It was found in the theory of social substitution developed by Axelrod as far back as 1904. Bolshevism was, so to speak, a stand-in for the bourgeoisie, playing the role the Russian bourgeoisie had failed to play. With the Bolsheviks the working class would not build a socialist society but only serve as the battering ram for that historically determined stage of Russia's development, the bourgeois revolution. Fascinated by the new vistas opened by the German revolution, official menshevism had temporarily lost sight of Axelrod's theory. But many readers of Dallin's article "The Coming Era"[11] in 1919 must have recalled it. The article made a strong impression. Dallin, a member of the Menshevik CC endorsed the CC's tactics, yet argued that in Russia all socialist measures were bound to fail and that the revolution would end in a bourgeois-capitalist order. In 1919, Dallin was a lonely figure among the Party's official majority. Only A. A. Troianovskii, another member of the CC, agreed with him.

In 1919-20 Martov, the chief ideologue of official menshevism after October, published a series of essays on "world bolshevism," in which he tried to give a Marxist explanation of the growing Bolshevik influence in Russia and the West since 1917. The cause, he said, lay in the depletion of the conscious proletariat by the draft, and the influx of new elements, in particular women, untrained in the class struggle and highly susceptible to demagogic and maximalistic slogans.

We need not analyze whether Dallin's viewpoint was right and whether Martov's theory fully explained the changes in the labor movement after 1917. Correct or not, far-fetched or realistic, these theories were part and parcel of the intellectual baggage of Mensheviks, who drew from them their conviction of being right and therefore ultimately invincible, and used them in trying to help Western socialists get their bearings in the Russian revolution. They also used them to combat the Comintern's propaganda.

Axelrod's efforts to clarify Russian affairs for the parties of the Second International are described in Dallin's part of this book (pp. 228 ff.). Once Martov and a number of other notable Mensheviks had left Russia, the Delegation of the RSDRP Abroad became the central organ for propagating Menshevik influence in the Second International.[12]

In principle, the delegation consisted of members of the CC who found themselves abroad. Until 1922, they were Martov, Abramovich, Dallin, and also E. L. Broido, who had left Russia on her own. The group that arrived in Berlin together with Dan included the members of the CC of the Bund Iudin (Eisenstadt) and Aronson; and Nicolaevsky, who had been coopted into the CC of the Party before he left Russia. Later Iugov, a member of the CC, and Gurevich-Dvinov, a coopted member of the bureau of the CC, were able to leave Russia legally. All these became members of the delegation abroad. It also coopted S. M. Schwarz; and, after the conference of 1924, M. S. Kefali, as representatives of the right intraparty opposition. Everyone had expected P. Garvi to represent the right in the delegation, but Garvi felt that precedence should be given Kefali, the former head of the Printers' Union and the only Menshevik labor leader abroad. There was, however, another angle to this: having been a member of all the successive Central Committees, Garvi counted on being included anyway, but Dan was too astute a politician to weaken his majority by admitting one more member of the opposition. Garvi was not included—and he harbored resentment against Dan almost to the end of his life.

Martov died in 1923, and the leadership naturally passed to Dan, who had been, as it were, the Party's "chief of staff" from its beginnings. A strong-willed personality, an effective speaker and publicist, Dan would in normal times have made an ideal parliamentarian. Used to working hand in hand with the top leaders, he could not but feel superior to the rest of the delegation abroad: besides him, only Eva Broido and I. Iudin belonged to the old guard, and they were not otherwise remarkable. Abramovich was an outstanding figure—adept at handling mass meetings and, until Dan's arrival, Martov's alter ego; but he had matured in the Bund and was a relative newcomer among Russian political leaders. Dallin, a gifted younger member, was "the hope of the Party." Nicolaevsky was engrossed until the late thirties in the history of Russian social movements; later he did plunge into the thick of politics and became one of the best-known members of the delegation. Iugov was the economic expert. S. M. Schwarz, a highly educated man of a scholarly bent, concentrated on social problems and also took an interest in problems of economic development. Gurevich-Dvinov was the *praktik* and organizer par excellence. Kefali, Aronson, and Garvi (the last was not admitted to the delegation, as we have seen, but was an authoritative ideologue of the right opposition) formulated the views of the right on all questions discussed in the delegation. All the above-named were experienced leaders and highly regarded in their respective fields. Despite inner controversies, the delegation until the late thirties stood out against the émigré background as an unusually cohesive group. It also had a "periphery," from which it drew contributors for its journal, *Sotsialisticheskii Vestnik*, founded in 1921, when Martov was still alive. Thanks to the boundless, selfless devotion of its editors—in the first place, Dan and Abramovich, and after the latter's death, Schwarz—the journal continued to appear regularly until the end of 1962. (In 1964 and 1965, four issues came out.)

In 1933 the delegation moved to Paris; and after the German occupation of France in 1940, to New York. Until his death in 1928, it kept in close touch with Axelrod, who stood apart from the factions but often served as arbiter in their disputes. Toward the end of the Paris period the delegation suffered a heavy blow—its rupture with Dan, who had begun the reappraisal of the Menshevik positions that eventually led to the new conception of social democracy expounded in his book *The Origins of Bolshevism.* [13] Dan formally resigned from the delegation in 1942, together with Iugov. (After Dan's death in New York in 1947, Iugov in effect went over to the Communists.) In the United States, the delegation coopted P. Garvi, Iu. Denicke, and myself. In 1951, it dissolved because of disagreements over postwar Russian émigrés (Vlasovites and "solidarists").

The delegation's influence on the European and American labor movements can hardly be overestimated. Not that it contributed new ideas, but it helped these movements in their fight with the Comintern by keeping them informed of what was really happening in Soviet Russia and interpreting the Russian revolution from the socialist viewpoint.

Actually, this work began even before Martov left Russia. Arthur Crispien, a representative, together with Dittmann, of the German Independent Social-Democratic party at the Second Congress of the Comintern, relates in *SV* how both of them in the summer of 1920, in Moscow, had sought out the Mensheviks, in particular Martov, and had heard in the Menshevik CC an analysis of the situation in Russia that had helped them to understand the true nature of the Bolshevik regime. [14] This was by no means the only meeting of Mensheviks with foreign labor delegates who visited Russia. Dallin gives a detailed account of the famous visit of an English group in the same year (pp. 225 ff. of this book). The next major event in the struggle against Bolshevik influence over the Western proletariat was Martov's speech at the congress of the Independent Social-Democratic party in October 1920 in Halle, which was to decide on the merger of the Independents with the Comintern. The Comintern had delegated its chairman, G. E. Zinov'ev, an eloquent demagogue who spoke German. Martov was no orator, at any rate not in German, and he was already suffering from the throat disease that was to kill him. The contest was clearly unequal: on one hand, Zinov'ev, self-assured, at the height of his powers, skillfully playing up the glamor of the Russian revolution; on the other, Martov, physically unprepossessing and hoarse. Zinov'ev's speech made a strong impression, but the mere presence of Martov, his speech (read by Alexander Stein; Martov himself said only a few words), and his talks with the other delegates prevented the Comintern from gaining control of an important segment of the German labor movement. Nearly 40 percent of the delegates voted against joining the Comintern. Hilferding felt that the Zinov'ev-Martov encounter had ended in a victory of social democracy. In his article dedicated to Martov's memory he wrote: "In Halle was won the great battle between bolshevism and European socialism; it was there that bolshevism suffered its decisive defeat in the European labor movement." [15]

In November 1920 Abramovich came to Berlin. Forty years old, healthy, resilient, fluent in German and generally gifted for languages, an orator sensitive to his audiences and good at handling them, Abramovich wholeheartedly joined in the campaign Martov had begun. Until Dan's arrival in January 1922, he shouldered all the Menshevik public speaking abroad. Martov, a publicist par excellence, relied mainly on his pen and on personal contacts with European socialist leaders. Menshevism attracted these leaders because it rejected foreign intervention in Russia, demanded recognition of the Soviet government, and yet attacked bolshevism from the standpoint of the labor movement's interests. The moderate Social-Democratic parties, obliged to reckon with their conservative opponents' horror of the Russian revolution, needed a line that was critical of the Communists yet different from the line of the Kremlin's bourgeois enemies. The very concessions, tactical and ideological, that official menshevism made to Lenin's party and that the right S-Ds in Russia so severely criticized, made Martov and his group precious allies for the Western socialists who wanted to resist the Comintern while retaining their workers' following. The prestige of the Comintern stood high in the early thirties. "Revolutionized" by the war, the working masses were looking with hope to the east and mistrusted disclosures about Soviet Russia as stemming from Russian counterrevolutionaries or from re-actionaries in their own countries. It was endlessly difficult to breach this wall of mistrust. Menshevism was fortunate in having such pol-itically unimpeachable and personally charming spokesmen as Martov and Abramovich. The arrival of Dan with a group of other exiles and, earlier, that of Dallin, ensured continued work after Martov's death, on 4 April 1923. This work would have been impossible without the support of Western socialist leaders and the Menshevik "periphery" in various countries. [16]

The Kuchin Era

History has a way of repeating itself. In Soviet times as under the last Romanovs, the émigrés were the standard-bearers of the opposition. The delegation abroad became to all intents and purposes an indepen-dent organ. Its tenuous contacts with Russia ceased entirely in the mid-thirties, but even in the twenties, while the illegal S-D groups in Russia still had a central organization, only the émigrés, out of reach of the GPU, could systematically formulate the Party's views and speak in its name. The Party in Russia depended on the émigrés, not vice versa. The secretary of the bureau of the CC (the illegal Menshevik center) wrote the delegation abroad on 7 November 1926: "We await with great impatience what the next mail will bring. Again nothing? You may be able to live without us, but *we are barely alive without you*" (italics added).

Subjectively, the delegation did not consider itself an émigré group. Dan insisted that *SV* was a journal for Russia. He despised émigré politics and would not hear of recruiting members among Russian exiles. It was his goal to preserve the collective of which the delegation and its periphery were a part and to take it back to Russia ideologically intact. The collapse of these hopes must have played a role in his slow change of heart, which began in the late thirties. There was, however, a fairly long period—from 1922 to about 1925 or 1926—when Dan's position did not seem unrealistic. This was the period during which Georgii Dmitrievich Kuchin, an unforgettable figure in the post-October history of Russian social democracy, was at the height of his activity.

After the departure of Martov, Abramovich, Dallin, Dan, and others, a decline began in the Menshevik leadership in Russia, partly because of increasingly frequent arrests. Many prominent members withdrew from political work or went over to the victors; for example, M. S. Balabanov, F. A. Bulkin, V. Galuzin, K. A. Gvozdev, B. I. Gorev, V. G. Groman, D. Zaslavskii, O. A. Ermanskii, V. M. Korobkov, I. M. Maiskii, A. S. Martynov, A. M. Naumov-Ginzburg, A. A. Pleskov, I. I Rubin, S. Iu. Semkovskii, A. A. Troianovskii, A. M. Fishgendler, L. M. Khinchuk, A. B. Stern—*intelligenty* and workers, of the Menshevik right and left. All these, and all the other old S-Ds who left the Party, must be taken into account in assessing the loss in potential replacements for disappearing leaders. Far from all of these defected out of fear. Some were honestly disappointed with menshevism, and the best were attracted by the seemingly limitless opportunities for applying their talents to the reconstruction of the state.

On the other hand, the Party leaders who remained at their posts were too visible, too exposed, too easy targets. The following were soon "taken out of circulation": B. N. Bèr, B. O. Bogdanov, B. S. Vasil'ev, S. O. Ezhov, K. I. Zakharova, the brothers Aleksei and Boris Malkin, F. A. Cherevanin—to name only those who lived in Moscow in 1921–22.

Party activities suffered not only from a shortage of people. Another difficulty was the illegal nature of the work. Legal opposition to the

Communist dictatorship became impossible from about 1923, but during the first year of the NEP the Mensheviks were still extremely reluctant to go underground. Banking on the evolution of the regime, they wanted to preserve their status of legal opposition. To be sure, some of the more temperamental Party members, whatever their political bent, were eager to fight repression by the traditional methods of Russian revolutionaries. The Youth League in Moscow, disregarding the scruples of their elders, distributed in 1922 the illegally manufactured *Iunyi Proletarii*. In the provinces underground publications had appeared even earlier. It is probably no exaggeration to say that from the spring of 1921 almost all Menshevik meetings took place secretly. The Party organization was going through a transition period and its status was not clear. [17]

Social democracy had been tolerated on a semilegal basis during the years of War communism, but the NEP brought systematic persecution. Lenin himself gave the signal in his pamphlet on tax in kind, published in May 1921: "We shall keep Mensheviks and SRs, whether open or dyed into 'nonpartisans,' in prison." [18] The government reinstated administrative exile, set up special concentration camps in the north (Kholmogory, Pertominsk, Solovki) and a network of forced-labor prisons styled "political isolators." The dry guillotine went to work in earnest. Yet at this very time, despite the heavy losses and throttled activity—despite common sense, one might say—the Mensheviks' mood suddenly became euphoric.

Everything in the world is relative, and the first years of the NEP were a happy time for Russian social democracy. Happy only in the sense of the leaders' mood: objectively, there was little cause for rejoicing. But when the Tenth Congress of the Communist party, in March 1921, replaced the surplus-appropriation system with tax in kind, thus repudiating War communism and inaugurating the NEP, the RSDRP felt that the Marxist law of historical development had triumphed. The bourgeois revolution, which the Bolsheviks had chased out the door, was breaking in through the window. Official menshevism was vindicated, was confirmed in its belief that Russia needed cooperation between city and country, a mixed economic order, abandonment of wholesale nationalization (the platform "What to Do"). The right Menshevik opposition saw in the NEP a confirmation of the traditional conception of bourgeois revolution, undiluted by speculations about a European revolution. Both official menshevism and the right found Marxist arguments to prove that the new social forces already consolidating in the postrevolutionary society would erode the Communist dictatorship. The words "Bonapartism" and "Thermidor" appeared more and more often in Party documents. Intraparty disputes subsided. A wave of enthusiasm swept the RSDRP and its peripheries. It was no longer an "intelligent superfluity," it had a useful function: to defend the interests of the proletariat sure to be exploited in a market economy—a proletariat opposed to the regime, threatened by grasping nouveaux riches who would make fortunes on its sweat. The new conjuncture brought new forces into the Party, though in modest numbers: on one hand, young people, and on the other, "reactivated" S-Ds who had been confused by the post-October events that did not fit the Marxist scheme of historical development. Now everything seemed to fall back into place. The mood is best described by a phrase Martov used—in another context, at another time—in a letter to Axelrod: "Our history proceeds along 'incredible paths,' but when all is said and done—so far as the Party and the working class are concerned—it still proceeds according to Axelrod."[19] Nicolaevsky reported to Axelrod on the situation in Russia as soon as he arrived abroad in January 1922. The worst was behind, he wrote; the Party was alive and active despite sustained blows. Most important, it was attracting the young.[20]

Thus the ideology was formed and the human material sifted that permitted the party to negotiate the transition from legality to the underground, to build up a relatively widespread secret organization and continue its struggle against bolshevism. Today, from the distance of forty-five years, it is easy to discern the flaws in the pseudoscientific Marxist propositions—and to see that the enterprise was doomed. Yet the Party's activity was not merely quixotic. In the light of later events its assumes historical significance. Without fully realizing it, menshevism was the champion of democratic socialism against the totalitarianism into which bolshevism was degenerating. If menshevism was bound to succumb in the unequal contest, the breath of tragedy was upon the Bolshevik leaders, too. Had they been more farsighted, they would have realized where their own policies were leading. Eight or ten years later most of them, too, would perish in prisons, concentration camps, the cellars of the Cheka, or, worse, undergo the mockery of Stalin's show trials.

The period of transition to the underground ended for the Mensheviks with the arrival in Moscow of Georgii Dmitrievich Kuchin in early August 1922.

Kuchin, a lawyer, had attracted the Party's notice before the revolution. In 1912, an article of his, "An Old Question," signed "K. Oranskii," appeared in *Nasha Zaria*. It took a new approach to the problem of Liquidationism. "Who is Oranskii?" Martov asked Dan, who was then in Petersburg. "Heavy writing, but makes sense."[21] In 1915 Kuchin became a member of the so-called Organizational Committee (OC), that is, the Menshevik central committee in Russia. He was drafted and fought in the war as artillery officer. After the revolution he was elected chairman of the committere of the Twelfth army, later of the entire northern front, and became a member of the All-Russian Executive Committee of the Soviets of the First Convocation. The rebuff he administered to General Kornilov in the name of the army committees at the state conference in Moscow in August 1917 made him nationally famous. As one of the leaders of the army delegation at the Second Congress of Soviets in October 1917, he left the congress together with all the other Mensheviks. It was he who read the declaration of the Twelfth army committee (see p. 45).

Coopted at the May conference of 1918, together with Liber, into the Party's Central Committee as representative of the right opposition, Kuchin was one of the initiators of the movement of Assemblies of Factory Representatives.[22] He was also the "vital nerve" of the Menshevik committee of the Central Region and *Nasha Zaria* His colleague George Denicke elaborates in his part of this book on Kuchin's role during that period. Especially noteworthy was Kuchin's ability to get disparate Party elements to collaborate on concrete tasks. As Denicke says, the committee of the Central Region and *Nasha Zaria* became the center of a broad united front, from Martov and Dan to Liubov' Nikolaevna Radchenko. No fanatic, Kuchin was not shackled by the dogmas of any one faction. Unabashed by reproaches of "factional patriots" who accused him of inconsistency, Kuchin, an opponent of the official party line, could still give their due to Dan and Martov, thanks to whom the Party had defended the revolution against the Whites during the civil war, and still reject the ideology of the April theses of 1920. He wrote that if in the past period of the revolution the Party had "fulfilled the task assigned to it by history," it had done so *despite* many blunders in its orientation.[23]

As chairman of the Central Council of Trade Unions in Kiev in 1919, Kuchin tried to strengthen workers' organizations and keep them independent of the Denikin regime. He has recorded his experiences of this period in the book *Dobrovol'cheskaia zubatovshchina*, published in Berlin in 1924. When the Red army took Kiev, he and other Mensheviks were tried before a revolutionary tribunal, mainly for their memorandum to Western socialists describing the plight of the labor movement under White and Red terror. With the outbreak of the war with Poland, Kuchin, in accordance with the decision of the RSDRP, joined the Red army as a volunteer. After that war he returned to party work in Kiev and Kharkov and was arrested together with many other Mensheviks active in southern Russia. In 1922, during the GPU's offensive against Mensheviks all over Russia, he was "administratively" deported to the Turkestan. Among the other victims were the active members of the youth league in Moscow, Kiev, Kharkov, Orsha, and Kremenchug.

Kuchin realized that the legal status of social democracy had come to an end. To serve the labor movement, the Party had to reorganize to fit the NEP conditions. He observed that in the Party a new orientation was emerging which synthesized the ideas of the official majority and the opposition:

> However just and necessary were the opposition's objections to the many aspects of the sociopolitical ideas of the Party's official stand [the April theses], the Party center's [that is, the CC's, led by Martov and Dan] resolute rejection of armed struggle against the Soviet government and its recognition of the revolutionary situation in Russia and of its implications not only showed a correct assessment of the active forces... but, above all, helped to unite the Party forces and keep the Party on the positions that correspond to the interests of the revolution and the proletariat of today and tomorrow. [24]

Kuchin concluded: "Never yet have we been as close as we are now to the organic unity of an ideological position worked out by life itself.... Our youth leagues are a very significant fact."

In this mood Kuchin decided to flee from the Turkestan to engage in illegal work. Probably he hoped to share it with like-minded comrades—but when he reached Moscow he turned out to be the central figure, towering head and shoulders over the Party members he found in the capital. His strength lay in knowing what he wanted. He wanted the Party to switch to illegal work, to devise a new policy adapted to the NEP conditions, jettisoning the outdated disputes between right and left. Reared in Marxist menshevism, Kuchin could not know— and did not suspect—that the NEP was not the definitive Bolshevik policy. (Very few Mensheviks suspected that Russian history would not necessarily run "according to Axelrod." I can remember only two— Rafail Grigor'ev and G. O. Bienstock—who at this time had begun to doubt the theory about the primacy of economics; more by intuition than by anything else, they knew that political coercion was a factor of prime importance and refused to rely on the so-called laws of historical development that made the collapse of the Bolshevik regime inevitable.) Perhaps it was this unawareness that gave Kuchin the strength to work in the infernal conditions of the underground, which he described during his short stay abroad in 1924.[25] Kuchin was convinced that the NEP was winding up the revolution and that no Bolshevik stratagems could obviate Russia's bourgeois-capitalist development and its preordained consequences. As a Marxist, he thought he knew the role that the proletariat would play in the new society, and he believed in social democracy's mission to defend in it the interests of the exploited working class. The new people he drew into this work as well as those he had found in Moscow fell under his sway, and so a whole new movement came into being, differing from the stand of the majority of the delegation abroad as well as from that of the so-called right.[26]

Kuchin did not fit into either the right or the left. He always was an individualist, especially during the time he headed the illegal organization (1922–25). Under War communism, not sharing the ideological extremism of the Party majority, he had sided with the right oppostion and had entered the CC as its representative. During the civil war, his agreement with the CC's line must have estranged him from the so-called right. From 1922, he was no longer connected with it even organizationally. This is borne out by his conduct at the 1924 Berlin conference to discuss the new Party theses. Speaking for the illegal organizations in Russia, Kuchin tried to mediate between the left majority led by Dan and the Menshevik right, while leaning rather toward the former. The right itself did not claim any ideological, let alone organizational, closeness to Kuchin.

Incidentally, the intraparty right was not the monolith it is often assumed to have been. This was true to some extent, and then with reservations, only of the émigré group headed by Garvi. The rightists who remained in Russia are well described by B. S. Vasil'ev, chairman of the Party's Don committee and a leader of the opposition, in a letter he wrote Axelrod from Butyrki jail: "...alas, it is an equally indisputable fact that the opposition confronting the CC 'on the right' is discordant and mixed."[27]

Kuchin's appearance at the helm broke the Party center's direct descent from the Central Committee elected by the December conference of 1917. The CC was replaced with the bureau of the CC, appointed by the October conference of 1922, which had been prepared and primed by Kuchin and which laid the foundations for all Social-Democratic activity in Russia during the following years, up to the Party's complete disappearance.

The bureau consisted of Drabkin, Kuchin, Rubin, and Svetitskii, and maintained a "travelling agent," M. Egorov-Lyzlov. Rubin took almost no part in the bureau's work. Frustrated in his desire to go abroad, he immersed himself in scholarly work in Riazanov's wing at the Marx-Engels Institute until 1931, when he was one of the accused in the "Menshevik trial" [see Appendix A] and was coerced to lie about Abramovich's mythical visit to Russia and to slander his benefactor Riazanov. Egorov-Lyzlov was soon deported to the Solovetskii Islands and went out of his mind. The Party also lost an alternate member of the bureau, L.M. Zorokhovich, formerly permanent secretary of the Kharkov committee of the Party. He, too, had escaped from the Turkestan, but a day or two after reaching Moscow had the bad luck of meeting in the street a Turkestan Chekist, who recognized him. This time he was sent to Solovki. Thus the bureau was reduced to Kuchin and the Bund members Drabkin and Svetitskii. Its composition changed over the years. In Kuchin's time, B. S. Vasil'ev and M. I. Liber were added, but as both were soon arrested, their participation left little trace. Greater "longevity" was the lot of A. F. Deviatkin, a well-known leader of the printers' union, and V. S. Kononenko, a gifted young native of southern Russia.[28] Deviatkin was arrested in 1924, Kononenko in 1926; both died in exile.[29] Unfortunately, it is impossible to ascertain the names of all the Mensheviks active in the work of the bureau in its various capacities. Only the early period, when Kuchin was in control, is relatively well documented.

Kuchin had escaped from the Turkestan together with a few comrades: Èmil Kantorovich, of the Kharkov Youth League; the Kievian Iakov Bernstein; and Shmois, a Bund member from Kharkov. These and the helpers he found in Moscow, became the nucleus of the new underground apparatus. M. S. Kononenko (brother of V. Kononenko), I. G. Rashkovskii, and I. S. Iakubson toured the larger organizations to prepare the October conference. Iakubson had an additional assignment: to get in touch with exiled members of the youth league (in Malo-Arkhangel'sk and Korocha) and organize their escape. He succeeded, and thus the Party organizations of Petrograd, Kharkov, Rostov, and Kiev gained a number of new workers. A central bureau of youth leagues was set up, which managed to establish liaison with S-D youth groups in the provinces, especially in the south, and even to convene an all-Russian conference in September 1923. (It met at Irpen', a suburb of Kiev.) Unfortunately, the GPU got wind of the conference, and all the delegates ended up in Solovki. Svetitskii, of the bureau of the CC was caught at the same time.

Not only did Kuchin organize the underground apparatus—he created a new trend in the Party, which I shall call Kuchinism. His group expressed its stand in the theses adopted by the October conference and published in SV, no. 21, in 1922. The theses took a pessimistic view of the Russian proletariat's situation and accordingly set forth very modest objectives, noting that under the NEP conditions *"proprietary interests"* were in the ascendancy and *"capitalistic relations"* were quickly becoming established. (Here and below I italicize the words that are emphasized in *SV*.) "In its present situation, the *proletariat* is exceptionally isolated from the intermediate social strata." The authors of the theses—the main author, if not the only one, was Kuchin—viewed the NEP as "Thermidor" and concluded that Bonapartism was a very real threat. To prevent such an outcome, it was necessary to implant democratic principles in Russian society. The theses supported the majority's line predicated on a democratic evolution of the Soviet regime—but not with the objective of forming a socialist government:

> As before, the Party draws attention to the political dangers of striving to unseat the Soviet government, as well as [the dangers] of the tendencies imbued with bourgeois-coalition illusions. The Party considers that the proper method to acheive the above goal [save the democratic conquests of the revolution] is to increase the *independent activity of the proletarian masses* and their organized *pressure* on the government in order to induce it to democratize the political system.

For stronger ties with the workers, the theses recommended that the Party "stand close to the current spontaneous *economic struggle of the proletariat.*" Finally, there was a nationalistic note: "As before, the Party considers it its duty to defend the *independence* of the revolutionary country against all attempts on it by counterrevolution and imperialism."

In other words, Kuchin and the October Conference approached the tasks of social democracy pragmatically. Aware of the workers' passivity and the Menshevik party's consequent weakness, they deliberately sacrificed broader political tasks. They wanted to focus on organizing the workers, to protect their immediate interests as sellers of manpower. Never mind the frills as long as we can keep body and soul together, the theses seemed to say in their stress on the elementary freedoms of speech, the press, unions, and so forth, *"relegating the question of the form and composition of the government to a farther perspective* and naturally [making] it depend on . . . the correlation of social forces, in particular the degree of the proletariat's pressure" (my emphasis).

Martov and Dan responded to the theses as well as to the fact that the conference had been convened. By welcoming it as a necessary step in the Party's reorganization, they in effect sanctioned the transition to the underground. Both approved certain points of the theses but neither agreed that the proletariat was isolated; and both criticized the theses' "minimalism," their conscious evasion of "big" politics, their failure to discuss the government that would supersede the Sovnarkom, and the Social-Democrats' participation in it.

Martov asked: "This pessimistic view of the future, predicting complete isolation for the Russian proletariat, doesn't it have something to do with 'The wish is father of the thought'? The wish to come out as soon as possible on a narrow little path, far from national objectives— to attend quietly to one's purely-class business?" He concluded: "In a revolutionary epoch there is no escape onto narrow little paths. One has to walk the big roads laid by history."[30] Dan objected to the same parts of the theses and drew similar conclusions: If the proletariat is really so isolated, "all it can do...having reconciled itself to the *inevitability* of Bonapartism, is to prepare at some distance from the main road for renewing the struggle on a new...basis, engaging for the time being in so-called purely labor politics....The theses do not draw this direct conclusion of returning to a peculiar 'Economism.' " Nevertheless, Dan observed, they "consider it necessary to relegate 'to a farther perspective' *'the question of the form and composition of the government.'* "[31]

The sentiments expressed in the theses of the October conference were widely shared in the Party's illegal aparatus. In May 1925, when Kuchin had already been arrested, the bureau of the CC forwarded to the delegation abroad a long letter, dated 29 May, from Vasilii Kononenko, who was perplexed by the 1924 platform. (On the platform, see chapter 13 in Simon Wolin's part of this book.) In his opinion, the drift toward capitalist relations came from the peasantry—and this was leading up to an alliance of the peasantry with the city bourgeoisie and foreign capital, not with the proletariat. "How then is it possible to recommend, side by side with the platform, a political alliance of the proletarian party with the peasantry against the Bonapartist danger?" The proletarian party should put in the forefront "the *tasks of defending* the proletariat against all the forces of bourgeois reaction and seek to fulfil these tasks through an *independent class policy*. Yet the platform, contradicting the analysis given in it, calls upon the proletariat to play the role of 'gatherer of the Russian land,' the role of defender and leader of a broad democratic movement aimed at liquidating the present regime." And further on: "The tasks of the struggle for democracy [must be fulfilled] by way of independent political organization and activity, by way of *class self-defense.*" This was not just his personal opinion, Kononenko wrote, but also that of other Party members , in particular a rather large conference of southerners he had recently attended. The head of the bureau of the CC who forwarded the letter ("Evsei"—his identity remains a mystery) added in his own letter, dated 31 May, that he agreed with Kononenko on many points. It is safe to assume that "Kuchinist" sentiments prevailed among the Mensheviks who worked under Kuchin and his immediate successors.

Why then did Kuchin vote at the 1924 conference in favor of the platform that in many ways disagreed with "Kuchinism"? We have no grounds for assuming that Dan persuaded him to revise his views (Martov was already dead). More likely, Kuchin simply did not attach much importance to the parts that dealt with "big politics," concentrating rather on what seemed attainable. Shortly before the Berlin conference he had unequivocally stated his views on the Party's tasks:

> *Prospectively* [italics added], social democracy faces the task of organizing a broad democratic movement headed by the proletariat. But on the road to this goal, amid the flood of public reaction and the complete ruin of public life, Social Democracy has to put forward as its first, closest task merely the *preparation* of this movement, the accumulation of its concrete forces—and consolidation of the *vanguard* battalions of the concious proletariat. [32]

The platform of 1924 did include this first task and was oriented to organizing the spontaneous labor movements that were springing up here and there—a matter close to Kuchin's heart. He did agree with the basic political stand—a democratic republic, a return to the unadulterated conception of the bourgeois character of the Russian revolution. All the rest may have seemed secondary. Given his choice, he probably would have omitted the parts about organizing a government as irrelevant while the proletariat was fragmented and disorganized.

If Kuchin accepted the points he disagreed with, it was not only because the platform incorporated his basic views but also because he had come to Berlin on a mission of peace, to unify the Party as far as possible; in particular, to draw the Menshevik right into party work. In this he succeeded. The delegation abroad coopted M.S. Kefali and agreed to publish a collection of polemical articles under the editorship of representatives of all the trends in the Party. Kuchin did not give up anything essential in voting for the platform, and his concessions helped to cement together the Menshevik groups abroad. These continued their work for at least thirty years after Kuchin himself and all of illegal social democracy in Russia had disappeared.

Neither Kuchin nor Dan, Abramovich, and Garvi could know that the NEP would soon be superseded by the collectivization of agriculture, the general line, and so on. Least of all could these Russian Marxists foresee that the state power would eradicate entire ideological movements by killing off their proponents, as happened under Stalin. And it surely never crossed their minds that under certain conditions economics does not determine political development but politics transforms the economy—in other words, that the "foundation" and the "superstructure" could be turned upside down.

It may be argued that menshevism failed the test of history in this regard. Yet the victory of Leninism in its Stalin hypostasy does not prove the permanent ideological defeat of menshevism any more than the victory of fascism in Italy or of Nazism in Germany signified the end of democratic ideas in these countries. The evolution now going on in Soviet Russia, however difficult it may be to forecast its final forms, is already showing up the precariousness of the social order built on the dictatorship of the Communist party. As a political doctrine, the theory of the bourgeois character of the Russian revolution has been disproved. But the Mensheviks' dedication to it was the pivot of the libertarian, humanitarian strivings of Russian social democracy, making it part of an international "third force" equally opposed to totalitarianism and to self-seeking bourgeois capitalism indifferent to the material and cultural needs of the great majority of people.

Unable to replenish its ranks, and subject to the biological laws that govern all living things, émigré social democracy died out without producing a new doctrine to replace the one inherited from the Liberation of Labor Group. Underground menshevism was physically annihiliated much earlier. But, unless the world is destroyed by an atomic explosion, the time will come when Russia will "awaken from sleep" (Pushkin). In their quest for a way to overcome the effects of the Communist dictatorship, the new generations will turn to the ideological legacy of democratic socialism, of which menshevism was one of the battalions. The martyrdom of Kuchin and his comrades and the superhuman efforts of Menshevik émigrés in keeping *Sotsialisticheskii Vestnik* alive and fighting bolshevism in Europe and America will not have been pointless.

Appendix A

Some Statistics of the Unification Congress, August 1917

Leo Lande

The Unification Congress of the RSDRP sat in Petrograd from 19 to 25 August 1917. Its 222 delegates from 195 organizations represented about 200,000 members. About fifty of the organizations were provincial or regional bodies, each including several lesser ones.[1] At the Party conference of 7-12 May in Petrograd, only fifty-two organizations, with a total membership of a little over 40,000, had been represented. Even granting that twenty-two organizations, which by May had aligned themselves with the Menshevik organizational committee, may have been unable to send delegates to the conference, the figures show that the number of members and organizations had considerably increased between May and August. Some organizations, even predominantly Menshevik ones, had desisted in May from identifying themselves with one "faction" of the Party. Among the ones that in May were not yet attached to the OC were those of Kursk, Orel, Tver, and Tula.

The "Extraordinary" Party Congress in Petrograd (30 November to 7 December 1917—already under Bolshevik rule) also was less "representative" than the Unification Congress. It was attended by 120 delegates representing about 125,000 members.[2] Some border lands were already cut off from Russia, railroads were not operating properly, and a number of major organizations—in some cases, entire regions—were unable to send delegates. None of the well-known Georgian Mensheviks—Tsereteli, Chkheidze, Zhordania, and others—were present. (It is not clear whether Zurabov, who did attend, had arrived from the Caucasus or from somewhere else.) Devdariani (San), representing the Kharkov organization, was one of the few delegates from the south and the Ukraine,[3] where a regional Menshevik conference was going on at the same time (Kiev, 2-5 December) to prepare the elections to the Ukrainian Constituent Assembly.[4] It was in these regions, outside Russia's heartland, that the Mensheviks were relatively strong, as the following breakdown of the Party membership at the earlier Unification Congress shows (in thousands):

Transcaucasia (Georgia) 43.0
Donets Basin (28.6), Southern Region (10.5),
    Northern Caucasus (1.7) 40.8
The Bund (18.3), Latvians (1.6), Baltic
    States (1.2), Northwestern Region (7.8),
    Southwestern Region (10.6) 39.5
Central (Moscow) Region 30.0
Volga Region (8.2), Ural (10.5) 18.7
Northern Region, including Petrograd 13.1
Others: Asian Russia (4.4), the Front (3.7) 8.1
                                                                   193.2

Over 60 percent of the Party members were residents of Georgia, the Donets Basin and the rest of the Eastern Ukraine, and the Western Regions—less than one-third came from the rest of European Russia. The above list particularly shows the Party's weakness in Petrograd and the north.

The ballots of the August Unification Congress also give a picture of the Party's factional makeup two months before the overturn. Five percent of the delegates sided with Potresov's group; 55 percent supported the platform of the Revolutionary Defensists; 30 percent were Menshevik Internationalists. Of the latter, 17 percent sided with Abramovich, Dallin, Ezhov, and others who were prepared to submit to Party discipline; 13 percent supported Martov's independent stand. Finally, 10 percent were United S-D Internationalists.

The Central Committee elected at the Congress consisted of sixteen Defensists and eight Internationalists. The twenty-fifth seat, for all practical purposes merely honorary, was reserved for P. B. Axelrod, the nominee of all the Party groups without exception, who had left for Stockholm, and, as it happened, never again returned to Russia.

Two of the sixteen Defensists in the CC (P. N. Kolokol'nikov and F.A. Iudin) stood quite close to the Potresovites. Of the eight Internationalists, three (R. A. Abramovich, E. L. Broido, and S. O. Ezhov) disagreed with Martov's independent stand on Party discipline; two (N. A.

Rozhkov and V. I. Iakhontov) represented the Moscow United Inter-nationalists; and the last three were Martov and his supporters A. S. Martynov and S. Iu. Semkovskii. [5]

Immediately after the August congress, when the Kornilov affair and another crisis in the provisional government raised anew the question of Social-Democratic participation in government, the Revolutionary Defensists lost their majority in the CC. But the Party's, and some of the Soviet, apparatus remained largely in their hands. Even in Petrograd, where the local committee often supported Martov's stand, the Menshevik faction of the Soviet continued to side with the Defensists.

Appendix B

The Social-Democratic Press of 1918

(incomplete list)

George Denicke

Partiinye Isvestiia, organ of the CC of the RSDRP, Moscow

Novyi Luch, organ of the CC of the RSDRP, Moscow

Rabochii Internatsional, organ of the CC of the RSDRP, Moscow

Vpered, organ of the CC and the Moscow committee of the RSDRP, Moscow

Iskra, organ of the CC and the Moscow committee of the RSDRP, Moscow

Novaia Zaria, organ of the Committee of the Central Region of the RSDRP, Moscow

Proletarii, organ of the Moscow committee of the RSDRP, Moscow

Edinstvo, organ of the Plekhanovites, Moscow

Partiinye Isvestiia, organ of the Petrograd committee of the RSDRP, Petrograd

Rabochii Internatsional, organ of the Petrograd committee of the RSDRP, Petrograd

Delo, organ of the bloc of Plekhanovites and Menshevik-Defensists, Petrograd-Moscow

Nachalo, organ of Plekhanovites and Defensists, Petrograd

Nashe Edinstvo, organ of Plekhanovites, Petrograd

Bor'ba, organ of the Transcaucasus and the Tiflis committees of the RSDRP, Tiflis, and after the separation of Georgia also of the CC of the Georgian party

Priboi, organ of the Sebastopol and Crimea regional committees of the RSDRP, Sebastopol

Severnyi Luch, organ of the Archangel committee of the RSDRP, Archangel

Iskra, organ of the RSDRP, Baku

Severnaia Zaria, organ of the Vologda committee of the *Edinstvo* group, Vologda

Rabochee Delo, organ of the Kazan Province committee of the RSDRP, Kazan

Iuzhnyi Rabochii, organ of the Odessa committee of the RSDRP, Odessa

Rabochee Utro, organ of the Orenburg committee of the RSDRP, Orenburg

Vecherniaia Zaria, organ of the Samara committee of the RSDRP, Samara

Proletarii Povolzh'ia, organ of the Saratov committee of the RSDRP, Saratov

Rabochaia Zhizn, organ of the Tiumen committee of the RSDRP, Tiumen

Golos Rabochego, organ of the Ufa Province bureau of the RSDRP, Ufa

Appendix C
The "Menshevik" Trial of 1931

Simon Wolin

The NEP had been abandoned in December 1927, at the Fifteenth Congress of the Russian Communist party, in favor of the "general line." The following period brought a decline in living standards, which had somewhat improved under the NEP, a campaign against the intelligentsia, more terror, and a sharp struggle within the ruling party. The persecution of the intelligentsia reflected the Bolsheviks' old mistrust of it as bourgeois-minded and also their wish to make the intelligentsia appear responsible for the bad economic consequences of superindustrialization. In the Shakhty trial of engineers in 1928, in the trial of the "Industrial party" (*Prompartiia*) in December 1930, the "confessions" of the accused and their mutual denunciations were calculated to convince the world that the implausable indictments were true.[1] These show trials were connected with Stalin's leftward turn against his recent supporters, the right Communist opposition.

In 1930 the government decided to stage a trial of Mensheviks. During the second half of that year and the first months of 1931, fourteen people in responsible posts in the highest economic organs—the State Planning Commission, the Council of National Economy, the Commissariat of Trade, the All-Russian Union of Consumers' Cooperatives (*Tsentrosoiuz*), the State Bank—were arrested and charged with sabotage, espionage, and so on. The "trial of the fourteen" differed from the others in that "economic" accusations played an auxiliary role to its political purpose. This became abundantly clear during the trial.

394

N. Shvernik, a trade union and party worker who had never had any connection with the law, presided over the special sessions of the Supreme Court. The other members of the court were V. Antonov-Saratovskii and M. Muranov. N. Krylenko and G. Rozhinskii prosecuted. Two defense counsel, Kommodov and Braude, represented the accused Volkov, Finn-Enotaevskii, and Teitelbaum. The rest had refused such aid. [2]

The trial lasted from 1 to 9 March 1931. The accused were alleged to have been members of a mythical "Union Bureau (Soiuznoe Biuro) of the Central Committee of the RSDRP" or closely associated with it. According to the indictment, the bureau had consisted in 1928 of V. Groman, V. Sher, A. Ginzburg, L. Zalkind, K. Petunin, M. Iakubovich, A. B. Stern, A. Sokolovskii, I. Volkov, and A. Finn-Enotaevskii (in 1929, N. Sukhanov had allegedly become a member; in 1930, Stern had died). Four people were put on trial as their collaborators: V. Ikov, I. Rubin, B. Berlatskii, and M. Teitelbaum. The bureau had allegedly been financed by the Delegation of the RSDRP Abroad and had carried out its instructions, to wit: to try to overthrow the Soviet government and restore capitalism with the help of foreign military intervention; to sabotage the economy; and to arrange organizational and financial contacts with the Western bourgeoisie and the Socialist International. The prosecution contended that these activities logically followed from the Menshevik platform of 1924. The platform's demand for denationalization was construed as intent to restore capitalism; and the demand for a democratic republic, as intent to overthrow the government. By 1928, the indictment read, the government's successes and the switch to immediate socialist construction had impelled the RSDRP to abandon its policy of peaceful opposition in favor of sabotage and foreign intervention. To this end the bureau had been created in February 1928. To keep in touch with it, the delegation had allegedly sent Abramovich to Russia in the summer of 1928 and M. Brounstein in the spring of 1929.

Before the trial, the Soviet press launched a vicious campaign against the RSDRP and the accused. The delegation abroad countered with a campaign of its own. Abramovich and Dan were instructed to study all materials connected with the trial, call a press conference, and set up a special commission for unexpected announcements or other urgent action during the trial. [3] Articles about the affair were published in the foreign press. Dan's articles in the German Social-Democratic *Vorwarts* (28 February) and *Abend* (3 March) denounced the indictment as pure invention and the confessions as forced lies. On 2 March Abramovich spoke on the trial at the Berlin Sports Palace before and audience of 20,000. His and Dan's press conference took place on 5 March. The delegation issued an announcement of 28 February that no "Union Bureau of the CC of the RSDRP" had ever existed; the bureau of the CC, as could easily be ascertained from foriegn and from illegal Menshevik newspapers, had been founded in 1922 and was still in existence; only one of the accused, Ikov, belonged to the Menshevik party; eleven had left it ten years earlier; no reorientation of policy had taken place in 1928, and Abramovich had not gone to Russia that year. The police and witnesses confirmed Abramovich's presence abroad at the time when, according to the accused, he had been conferring with them in Russia: from 26 June to 26 July he had been in Germany, and from 1 to 12 August at the Brussels Congress of the International, where hundreds of people had seen him. The delegation also declared that it had received no subsidies from the German Social-Democratic party. The CC of the German party officially confirmed this.

The International spoke out too. On 22 February Vandervelde told the Sovnarkom in a telegram that he was familiar with the views and activities of the RSDRP and that the accusations were "a scandalous misuse of force....I have been empowered by the executive committee of the Labor and Socialist International to register the most decisive protest against this misuse."[4]

At a meeting of the delegation abroad on 24 February Dan and Abramovich volunteered to go to Russia to testify at the trial. The delegation decided against it: the government would not let them see the necessary people or speak freely at the trial, and might not let them out of the country afterward.[5] On 9 March the delegation considered the case of the only Party member among the accused, V. Ikov. A member since 1901 and a delegate to the Stockholm (1906) and London (1907) congresses, he had later been a Liquidationist, a Defensist, and a rightist Menshevik. Upon his return from exile in 1929, Ikov had accepted the Party platform, worked in the underground, and become a member of the bureau of the CC. If his testimony was correctly reported, it was a mixture of outright lies and underground facts— which should not be divulged. Therefore the delegation decided that he should be expelled from the Party if the official reports of his conduct turned out to be correct.[6]

The prosecution built its case entirely on the self-accusations of the fourteen and gave no concrete instances of their attempts to sabotage planning, transport, the circulation of goods and money, and so forth. No credible witnesses and no documents were produced except three letters from the delegation abroad and the bureau of the CC, found in Ikov's home, and one letter form Ikov to the delegation, intercepted by the GPU. (It had been typed on onionskin paper and inserted in an issue of *Pravda* addressed abroad.) The delegation's letters concerned Brounstein's fate, told of the protest organized abroad against recent arrests in the USSR, and did not discuss sabotage. Ikov had written, on 9 January 1931, two months before the trial: "We must be prepared for the worst. Krylenko and the GPU, relying on reports of secret and open agents and combining voluntary testimonies with madmen's notes, will manage to cook up an affair on the scale of the Shakhty and Ramzin ones." This letter did prove the connection, which no one denied, between the delegation abroad and the bureau of the CC, of which Ikov was a member, but not with any "Union Bureau." The failure to produce other documents is significant. The GPU undoubtedly had many more in its possession. The numerous searches had certainly yielded a great many letters, copies of letters, and so on. They could not be used because they would have revealed facts directly contradicting the accusations.

SV noted another singularity—the absense of real Mensheviks who were in the hands of the GPU. Brounstein, for example, had entered Russia illegally in the spring of 1929 and had been in touch with the bureau of the CC. A few months later he had been caught and sentenced to five years of solitary confinement. After serving a stretch in Suzdal and another in Verkhneural'sk, he had been brought to Moscow before the trial, obviously for the purpose of using his testimony. His name kept cropping up during the trial but he did not appear. Nor did E. Broido, a member of the delegation abroad, sent to Russia in November 1927. She had been arrested in April 1928 and sentenced to three years in the Suzdal "isolator." These two Mensheviks recently active in the underground would have made priceless witnesses or accused. Apparently the GPU did not succeed in breaking their spirit and turning them into obedient tools of the prosecution.

On the very first day of the trial all the accused pleaded guilty and confirmed the activity of the RSDRP as described in the indictment. Yet it should have been clear from the Mensheviks' printed and oral statements and their legal and illegal work that neither they nor, still less, the accused could have been guilty of the intentions imputed to them. Sher, a Party member from the 1900s until the NEP, testified that the "Union Bureau" had been organized in 1928 in accordance with instructions from the delegation abroad; that Dan had informed the bureau that the delegation would finance its sabotage activities; and that during the bureau's existence "there had been three plenums . . . in 1928, 1929, and 1930," the first of which had decided to make contact with the right opposition in the Russian Communist party. This was strange in more ways than one. A group that met once a year could not direct underground work and keep in touch with numerous organizations. Yet, according to Sher, it had been in touch with economic organs in the provinces and with RSDRP groups in the upper and lower Volga regions, Kharkov, the Northern Caucasus, and Leningrad. All these, Sher said, were largely intelligentsia groups engaging in sabotage.

The functions of the bureau were described by Groman, a Social-Democrat since the 1890s who had left the Party in 1922. A noted economist, "father of Soviet planning," member of the Presidium of the State Planning Commission, and director of planning in the Council of National Economy, Groman had always courageously defended his views. When collectivization was introduced, he had sent the Sovnarkom a written protest "from a socialist who does not share the views of the Communist party." A friend of Groman's has expressed the opinion that the GPU got the better of him because he suffered from angina pectoris plus addiction to alcohol—of which he was deprived in prison—and because he saw that his own creation, state planning, was serving purposes directly opposed to the ideals to which he had dedicated his life.[7] Groman testified that the bureau was to bring about a counterrevolutionary uprising, through sabotage and with the aid of foreign intervention, and to put in power a provisional government of representatives of the RSDRP, the *Prompartiia*,[8] the peasant *Trudovaia Partiia*, and Bolsheviks who had left the RCP. Sokolovskii said that to this end the bureau distributed literature printed abroad and in Russia—but not one specimen was shown in court. Ikov was accused of trying to set up a new Menshevik center after the bureau's arrest. This was the one point he denied.[9]

Sher said that in 1928 the bureau had recieved 120,000 rubles; in 1929, 200,000 rubles; in 1930, 160,000 rubles. Out of the total, 200,000 had come from *Prompartiia*. All had been received through the delegation abroad,"which in turn, as I heard from Groman as well as from Abramovich and Broustein, received considerable sums from circles close to German social democracy and the Second International." Money had allegedly been sent to the conspirators in Russia through a foreign consulate (unspecified). Groman, Zalkind, and Finn-Enotaevskii confirmed Sher's deposition.

The trial was conducted in an atmosphere bordering on lunacy. Malevolent shouts from the audience interrupted the accused. In the street outside, thousands of people in organized demonstrations waved banners with the Krylenko slogans, "Death to Counterrevolutionaries," "No Mercy for the Servants of Capital." The accused, facing death sentences per Article 58 of the Code of Laws, gave long lectures rather than relevant testimony. They described their views of the NEP period truthfully but added fantastic stories about their party work: the NEP had seemed to them a realistic policy with great potential, leading away from communism to limited state capitalism and a strong national economy; this had induced them to serve the government loyally, even devotedly, since it was putting into practice their own ideas, and they had turned away from menshevism; actually, they had been against it throughout the twenties. Now they allegedly realized that their old ideas about the NEP had been wrong and their activity in the bureau criminal. They begged the court to give them a chance to serve communism, the general line, the USSR. Some of them analyzed the history, the ideology, even the psychology of menshevism, asserting that the Menshevik left always gave in to the right. None produced any proofs of this. Sukhanov said: "What is today's menshevism? [It] is the foundation of today's bourgeois-capitalist society." Groman: "We represent those who serve the interests and aims of the bourgeoisie....Our social democracy isn't opposition, it is counterrevolution....Sabotage is an enormous part of our organization's activity." And Rubin, who had joined the Bund in 1904 and had been a member of its Central Committee, and from 1921 to his resignation from the RSDRP a member of the CC of the Party and of the bureau of the CC, said that "this trial lays bare the decay of social democracy during the last few years...its complete conversion to counterrevolutionary ideas."

Groman declared that in 1925 and 1927 he had seen Dan and Abramovich in Berlin and made arrangements for the transfer of money, which he had also discussed with Abramovich when the latter had come to Russia. Ginzburg said that he had gone abroad in the fall of 1927 and seen Dan and Garvi, who had approved the plan of organizing the bureau. Iakubovich told the court that the late Stern used to go abroad every year for his health and during these trips attended meetings of the delegation abroad and also saw Kautsky, Bernstein, and Hilferding.

Petunin spoke of a letter from Dan and Abramovich in 1929:

> The letter said that as a result of the struggle in the CC of the Bolshevik party, the stand of the Trotskyites was essentially the same as that of social democracy; [and] that...one could expect the right deviationists to take the same stand. The harder the struggle, the more surely this would happen.

The incongruity of this with the views of any group of the RSDRP is obvious. The stories of the accused about meetings with Western socialists (which the latter denied) and with the delegation were designed to prove the ties of the "bureau" with the Menshevik center abroad. However, the prosecution relied most heavily on the supposed visit of Abramovich to Russia. The accused recounted what he had said, where he had stayed, what trips he had taken. The script had been carefully written and rehearsed.

Sher reported that he had arranged a conference at the secluded villa he occupied in Alabino, near Moscow, where Abramovich had explained that the main work must now be entrusted to high Soviet employees and "the work of disorganization stepped up." Then Abramovich had left for the provinces to renew lost contacts.

According to Zalkind, Abramovich had told the bureau that the new policy of the Soviet Communist party threatened world social democracy. Nothing could save it but the destruction of the Soviet Communist party and the Soviet government—the bases of world communism. One way to do this was to sabotage Soviet economy; another was foreign military intervention. The delegation abroad supported intervention, and so did the International, although "for internal reasons" it was obliged to speak against it. (Actually, of course, both the RSDRP and the International had consistently opposed intervention since 1918.) Groman confirmed Zalkind's story, adding that a letter from Abramovich, received in November 1928, "emphasized that the situation was coming to a head, that intervention was close, and that it was imperative to intensify the work of disorganization."

Groman, Sher, and Ikov testified that Brounstein had brought similar instructions. Ikov told of a conversation in which Brounstein had remarked on the difference between present times and 1924, when the Menshevik party in the USSR "had its own legal press, published its own legal paper," and maintained a whole net of organizations. This absurd statement was intended to draw a contrast between the NEP times and the present, when such things were impossible.

After all the lies, the fourteen had to submit to one more humiliation. In slightly differing words, all stated that they were confessing of their own free will. Sher took the opportunity to mention that in 1905, after taking part in the Moscow uprising, he had been in prison awaiting execution and had not feared death, "but now I no longer have the same courage." This seemingly innocuous statement may have been his way of explaining his conduct, over the judges' heads, to his old comrades.

Defense counsel Braude also stressed the voluntary nature of the confessions. "Abroad they do not believe these confessions, they do not believe in this remorse"—"they" ascribe them to fear. "To say this, one has to be either hypocritical or unintelligent." Counsel in fact did not defend the accused, made no effort to disprove the accusations or to challenge the prosecution's estimate of them. Kommodov said: "The undeniable facts and undeniable arguments of the prosecution limit the task of the defense." The only plea was for indulgence in view of the sincere repentance of "these far from ordinary and highly qualified people," whose confessions, moreover, had "dealt a death blow to Russian menshevism and world menshevism."[10]

The prosecution demanded death sentences for five of the accused.[11] Krylenko asked the court to treat all those with maximum severity. The stenographic record notes "loud applause."

Capital punishment was not yet as common in Soviet practice as it was to become later. None of the fourteen was sentenced to death. All got prison terms with loss of civil rights: Ginzburg, Groman, Sukhanov, Sher, Iakubovich, Finn-Enotaevskii, and Petunin, ten years; Ikov, Sokolovskii, Zalkind, and Berlatskii, eight years; Rubin, Volkov, and Teitelbaum, five.

Why did the Bolsheviks stage this trial, which agitated public opinion abroad and cost them invaluable specialists? One clue is their placing the story in 1928, the first year of the general line. The population had to be convinced that the building of socialism justified terror—that the frightened "world bourgeoisie" and its "servants" were preparing counterrevolution and foreign intervention, just as they had during the civil war. Most important, the Communist party had to be convinced that its monolithic unity was more than ever necessary. The right Communists had to be shown the fate that awaited them if they did not conform. (A few years later they did suffer the same fate as the Mensheviks.) Hence the constant references to the right opposition in the Soviet Communist party, and in the "letter from Dan to Abramovich" and in Ginzburg's testimony that "many Mensheviks regarded the right deviation as a kind of undeveloped menshevism." The trial could help the regime to survive the "Third Revolution," as this period is sometimes called, and it could help the Comintern, too. Its Sixth Congress in 1928 had discarded the line of semipeaceful coexistence with foreign socialist parties and declared open war on them. The German Communists helped the Nazis to overthrow the Social-Democratic Prussian government. The socialist parties had to be represented as antilabor, espionage organizations. Ikov and Groman accordingly testified that the International, in particular Hilferding and Breitscheid, had supported sabotage and intervention. The preamble to the stenographic record of the trial states that the court had established the existence of "close ties of the Russian Mensheviks with foreign Mensheviks and through them with the Second International. . . . To have the broadest masses of the Western European working class realize the political consequences of this fact—this is the aim that the publication of this stenogram is to serve."

Abramovich had been given a star role in the script because he was a conspicuous figure in both the International and the RSDRP and thus well suited to link them with the nonexistent "bureau." [12]

The Menshevik trial was an important chapter in the consolidation of Stalinism.

Notes

Introduction

1. *Revoliutsiia 1917 goda* (*Khronika sobytii*) 5 (Moscow-Leningrad: Istpart pri TsK VKP, 1926): 169, 177.

2. From the Moscow Mensheviks' declaration of 7 November 1917. S. Piontkovskii, *Sovety v oktiabre. Sbornik dokumentov* (Moscow: Izd-vo Kom. Akad., 1928), pp. 38-39.

3. The "O" stood for *Ob'edinennaia* ("United"), a title adopted by the Menshevik party after its "Unification" Congress in August 1917; it was soon dropped. See chap. 1, pp. 11-12.

4. *Rabochaia Gazeta*, no. 199, 29 October 1917 (italics added).

5. Restoring the Kerensky government was contemplated only by Potresov's group and by individual Party members who had remained in the government after the Party as a whole had dissociated itself from it. I shall return to this.

1. The Basic Currents in Menshevism

1. The members of the Secretariat were P. B. Axelrod, Iu. O. Martov, A. S. Martynov, I. S. Astrov, and S. Iu. Semkovskii.

2. The ten members elected in late 1915 to the Workers' Group of the Central War Industries Committee were all Mensheviks. The group's chairman was K. A. Gvozdev, later minister of labor in the last

cabinet of the provisional government. Its secretary was B. O. Bogdanov, a leader of the Petrograd Soviet during the "February" period.

3. In its last leaflet before the revolution, on 23 January 1917, the Workers' Group (consisting entirely of Defensists) of the Central War Industries Committee declared that ending the war would not ease the people's plight unless "the people itself, and not the present autocratic government, liquidates the war." *Overthrow* ("decisive elimination") of the regime was now "a question of life and death for the working class and democracy." "Only by establishing a provisional government leaning on the people, which is getting organized in the course of the struggle," could the country be saved and peace attained "on terms acceptable to the Russian proletariat as well as to the proletariat of other countries." A. Shliapnikov, *Semnadtsatyi god* 1 (Petrograd: Gosizdat, 1923): 280.

Possibly this leaflet was a reply to one issued earlier by the relatively unimportant "Initiative Group" of Menshevik Internationalists in Petrograd, which had also said that only "a peace achieved by the will of the people" would "save the people from ruin and degeneration." The Initiative Group nevertheless reacted adversely to the leaflet of the Workers' Group, warning the Petrograd workers against "all sorts of anonymous leaflets" in which "certain groups of workers" were calling "for action" (ibid., pp. 265, 290).

Let me note here that B. Dvinov disagrees with me in his detailed documented analysis of Menshevik controversies. In his opinion, the differences between Internationalists and Defensists remained unresolved, and by 1916 actually sharpened. B. Dvinov, "Pervaia Mirovaia Voina i Rossiiskaia Sotsialdemokratiia," Inter-University Project on the History of the Menshevik Movement, Paper No. 10.

4. In Bolshevik jargon, the Soviets during this period were "liberdaning"—from the names of two Mensheviks prominent in their leadership, M. Liber, who had been a Defensist since the beginning of the war, and F. Dan, an Internationalist turned Revolutionary Defensist after February. Martov wrote in May 1917: "The situation is worse than we expected. The *majority* of influential Mensheviks who were anti-Defensists before the revolution have become Revolutionary Defensists (Dan, Tsereteli, Chkheidze, Skobelev, Ezhov, and many others)." Letter to Ol'berg, 22 May 1917. Archives of B. Nicolaevsky (ABN in future references; italics added). Dan wrote that only "some individual leaders on the right flank of menshevism, like A. Potresov," had taken a stand close to Plekhanov's, while "the *vast majority* agree on the Zimmerwald program." Dan's appendix to J. Martow, *Ge-*

schicte der russischen Sozialdemokratie (Berlin: Dietz, 1926), p. 294 (italics added). And Potresov complained that "almost from the first days of the revolution, the Defensists fell into the arms of 'Zimmerwaldism.'" A. N. Potresov, *Posmertnyi sbornik proizvedenii* (Paris: Dom knigi, 1937), p. 244.

5. *Rabochaia Gazeta*, no. 139, 22 August 1917.

6. The Menshevik Internationalist *Iskra*, no. 12, 4 December 1917, reported that in November about two hundred "extreme Defensists" had announced their withdrawal from the Moscow Menshevik organization. The protest of the Moscow Bureau of Menshevik Defensists (V. Grinevich, G. M. Lunts, P. P. Maslov, and V. G. Epifanov) was supported (in letters to the editors of the right socialist *Vlast' Naroda*) by over fifty Mensheviks, some of them well known, although a few of these had drifted away from the Party several years earlier.

7. *Rabochaia Gazeta*, no. 192, 21 October 1917.

8. The question of *Edinstvo's* representation was raised and voted down several times in the executive committee. See *Petrogradskii Sovet rabochikh i soldatskikh deputatov. Protokoly zasedanii ispolnitel'nogo komiteta i biuro I.K. 1917 g.* (Moscow: Giz, 1925), pp. 107, 262, 175, 142, 181. To the commission to conduct negotiations about the first coalition government, three NSs were elected along with five Mensheviks (Bogdanov, Voitinskii, Dan, Tsereteli, and Chkheidze).

9. *Rabochaia Gazeta*, 4 and 14 July 1917.

10. G. O. Bienstock, Kapelinskii, Feliks Ia. Kon, A. Grinevich (Shekhter), and E. Uspenskaia. *Rabochaia Gazeta* no. 111, 20 July 1917.

11. Indifferent organizers, the Menshevik Internationalists took four months to start their own Petrograd organ, *Iskra*, on 26 September. Between then and 4 December, twelve issues appeared.

12. A. Ermanskii, *Iz perezhitogo* (1887-1921), (Moscow: Giz, 1927), pp. 163, 171. A somewhat different version is in *Rabochaia Gazeta*, no. 86, 21 June 1917.

13. Among the Menshevik Internationalists who did not follow Martov's example and continued to write in *Rabochaia Gazeta* were R. A. Abramovich, E. L. Broido, D. Iu. Dallin, S. O. Ezhov, B. I. Nicolaevsky, and N. A. Rozhkov. At the Unification Congress only a minority of the Menshevik Internationalist faction had supported Martov on nonsubmission to the Party's Central Committee, but at the Democratic Conference his followers apparently predominated in the faction and designated the twenty candidates to the preParliament allotted to the Menshevik Internationalist faction. Of the six members and alternates (Abramovich, Broido, Ezhov, Rozhkov,

Dallin, and Krasnianskaia) elected to the CC in September from among the Internationalists who had disagreed with Martov at the Congress, only Abramovich was sent to the pre-Parliament, and even his name was omitted from the first list of members of the independent faction of Menshevik Internationalists. *Iskra*, no. 4, 17 October 1917.

14. Lindov (delegate from Tula) was its chairman and Sagirashvili (from Tsaritsyn) its treasurer. It included three members of the editorial board of *Novaia Zhizn* (Avilov, Bazarov, and Stroev) and N. A. Rozhkov from the so-called Moscow Uniteds (or, more precisely, the Moscow United Social-Democratic Organization). *Novaia Zhizn*, 20 and 27 June 1917.

15. *Vpered*, 29 August, and *Rabochaia Gazeta*, no. 143, 26 August 1917.

16. Compare the figures given by the credentials committee in *Rabochaia Gazeta* of 22 and 27 August (that is, before and after the *Novaia Zhizn* group refused to join the Party): 207,398 versus 193,172 members.

17. A report on the 8 September conference is in *Vpered*, no. 154, 10 September 1917; Rozhkov's statement and the decision of the CC, in *Rabochaia Gazeta*, no. 163, 17 September, and *Vpered*, no. 159, 17 September; reports on the October conference, in *Rabochaia Gazeta*, no. 183, 11 October, and *Vpered*, no. 179, 11 October 1917.

A letter from Iakhontov and the fourteen others to the Menshevik Moscow Committee is in *Vpered*, no. 184, 17 October. The group wrote that since a union of Bolsheviks and Mensheviks appeared impossible "in the near future," they felt that the existence of a separate Internationalist organization only hampered unification by strengthening the "extreme flanks" of the Bolshevik and the Menshevik organizations; on the whole, they agreed with the Menshevik Internationalists and would have enough freedom in the RSDRP(O) to defend their own conception of an "indepdendent class policy of the proletariat under the banner of the International."

18. *Partiinye Izvestiia*, no. 1, 15 July 1917. The conference lasted from 6 to 12 May.

19. Ibid. The list, published in the same issue, is incomplete: it does not include the *Izvestiia* and other organs of Soviets, trade unions, workers' insurance, or even governmental organs under Menshevik influence.

20. For Odessa see *V bor'be za oktiabr'. Sbornik dokumentov i materialov ob uchastii trudiashchikhsia Odessy v bor'be za ustanovlenie Sovetskoi vlasti* (Odessa: Odesskoe Oblastnoe Izd-vo, 1957), p. 159; and *Shestoi s"ezd RSDRP (bol'shevikov) avgust 1917 goda;*

protokoly (Moscow: Giz, 1958), p. 36. For Riazan see *Velikaia Oktiabr'skaia sotsialisticheskaia revoliutsiia. Khronika sobytii* 4(12 September to 25 October) (Moscow: Izd. Akad. Nauk, 1961), p. 313. For Penza see V. F. Morozov, *Penzenskaia organizatsiia bol'shevikov v period podgotovki i provedeniia Velikoi Oktiabr'skoi Sotsialisticheskoi Revoliutsii* (Penza: Penzenskoe knizhnoe izd-vo, 1959), pp. 34, 38. For Pskov see *Rabochaia Gazeta*, no. 185, 13 October 1917.

21. For Vologda see M. Vetoshkin, *Revoliutsiia i grazhdanskaia voina na Severe* (Vologda, 1927), p. 126 (reviewed in *Proletarskaia Revoliutsiia* 73, no. 2 [February 1928]: 172-78). For Mogilev see G. Lelevich *Oktiabr' v stavke* (Ist part, Gomel: Gomel'skii rabochii, 1922), p. 15, and E. Bugaev, *Vozniknovenie bol'shevistskoi organizatsii i obrazovanie kompartii Belorussii* (Moscow: Gos. izdat. polit. literatury, 1959), pp. 104, 171.

22. The Moscow Internationalists who, with Iakhontov at their head, had joined the United (Menshevik) organization, argued that all groups of Russian social democracy had been invited to the congress. True, most delegates had adopted the Revolutionary Defensists' stand, but there had been "no irregularities in the convocation of the congress"; one should therefore remain in the "United party formed at the congress" and fight "opportunistic tendencies" within it. *Vpered*, no. 184, 17 October 1917.

23. *Vpered*, no. 310, 16 April 1918.

24. Document no. 83 in D. A. Chugaev (ed.), *Revoliutsionnoe dvizhenie v Rossii v mae-iiune 1917 g. Iiun'skaia demonstratsiia* (Moscow: Izd-vo AN SSSR, 1959). In series *Velikaia Oktiabr'skaia Sotsialisticheskaia Revoliutsiia—Dokumenty i materialy*.

25. Ermanskii, *Iz perezhitogo*, p. 178.

26. Potresov, *Posmertnyi sbornik proizvedenii*, pp. 230-42.

27. Ibid., pp. 252-54 ("K voprosu ob ob"edinenii partii") and p. 265.

28. *Rabochee Delo* (Rostov-on-the Don), no. 4, May 7, 1917.

2. The Mensheviks and the Provisional Government

1. From a resolution of the Menshevik Geneva Conference of 1905, quoted in F. I. Dan, *Proiskhozhdenie bol'shevizma* (New York: Novaia Demokratiia, 1946), p. 371.

2. D. Zaslavskii and V. Kantorovich, *Khronika fevral'skoi revoliutsii* (Petrograd: Byloe 1924), p. 213.

3. Tsereteli said at the Party conference on 7 May 1917 that their presence in the government would help to "kill the war." Dan repeated

on 14 May that the Mensheviks had entered the government for this purpose. In August, in the draft of a platform for the elections to the Constituent Assembly, the Mensheviks were still arguing that they had been obliged to join the government *"when it turned out* that despite the bourgeois character of our revolution, the purely bourgois government did not try to meet the demands of democracy and did not have the confidence of the people and the army." *Golos Bunda*, 8 August 1917.

4. See the joint declaration of the committee of the Petrograd organization, which was under Martov's influence, and the Menshevik Internationalist faction in the Central Executive Committee, in *Rabochaia Gazeta*, no. 104, 12 July 1917, with critical comments by the editors.

5. From Rozhkov's introduction, written in January or February 1918 to A. L. Popov, *Oktiabr'skii perevorot* (Petrograd: Novaia èpokha, 1918), pp 21-22. The dates in our text refer to the program of the first coalition government, published on 6 May, and that of the second coalition, published on 8 July.

6. Martov's report at the meeting of 19 August is in *Rabochaia Gazeta*, no. 139, 22 August; his closing speech on 20 August in no. 140; the resolution he offered, in no. 145, 28 August. The congress adopted Tsereteli's resolution.

7. Iu. Martov, "Kak byt' s burzhuaznoi revoliutsiei," *Vpered*, no. 159, 17 September 1917.

8. This term was originally used in prerevolutionary Russia to refer to those privileged groups in society that, by satisfying certain property and other "census" requirements, exercised exclusive or preponderant weight in various elected institutions, both at the national and local levels. In 1917, the term was applied more loosely to those groups that were presumed to support the "bourgeois" as against the "socialist" parties.

9. V. L. Meller (ed.), *Rabochee dvizhenie v 1917 godu* (Moscow: Tsentroarkhiv, 1926), pp. 150-51.

10. *Rabochaia Gazeta*, no. 142, 25 August 1917.

11. The Declaration and the list of organizations that endorsed it are in *Gosudarstvennoe soveshchanie*, Ia. A. Iakovlev (ed.) (Moscow: Gosizdat, 1930), pp. 77 ff., and in Robert F. Browder and A. F. Kerensky, *The Russian Provisional Government, 1917: documents* 3 (Stanford: Stanford University Press, 1961): 1480 ff.

12. P. N. Miliukov, *Istoriia Vtoroi Russkoi Revoliutsii* 1 (Sophia: Rossiisko-Bolgarskoe knigoizd-vo) part 2 (1921), p. 117, and part 3 (1923), pp. 63 ff.

13. A. A. Bublikov, *Russkaia Revoliutsiia* (New York, 1918), p. 81.

14. *Rabochaia Gazeta*, no. 149, 1 September 1917.

15. *Revoliutsiia 1917 goda (Khronika sobytii)* 4 (Leningrad, 1924): 143.

16. The Democratic Conference was convoked by the Soviets, not the government. The notice about its convocation was signed by N. S. Chkheidze for the CEC and N. D. Avksent'ev for the executive committee of the All-Russian Soviet of Peasants' Deputies.

17. *Izvestiia VTsIK*, no. 160, 2 September 1917, quoted in *Revoliutsiia 1917 goda (Khronika sobytii)* 4:149.

18. *Rabochaia Gazeta*, no. 150, 2 September 1917.

19. *Izvestiia Moskovskogo Soveta*, no. 161, 13 September 1917, cited in P.O. Gorin (ed.), *Organizatsiia i stroitel'stvo sovetov rabochikh deputatov v 1917 g.* (Moscow: Kom. Akad., 1928), pp. 374-76.

20. F. Dan, "K istorii poslednikh dnei Vremennogo Pravitel'stva," *Letopis' Revoliutsii*, no. 1 (Berlin, 1923).

21. They wavered only for a few days after the Kornilov uprising, because of the conduct of the Kadet ministers and press. Tsereteli thought that "all the live forces in the country" would understand if the Kadets were "severed from power," and Skobelev, that "Kadets can no longer expect cabinet posts." *Vpered*, no. 147, 1 September 1917.

22. The tragedy of Bolshevik dictatorship may have retrospectively colored the pre-October views of the most truthful writers. On the other hand, some ideas expressed at the time by experienced politicians strike us as fantastic. For instance, a lead article in the main SR paper argued that if the bourgeois groups made a coalition government impossible and the Bolsheviks made a socialist government "from NSs to Bolsheviks" impossible, then "the Bolsheviks will have to form a cabinet." It actually warned the Bolsheviks against "vain attempts to hide behind hasty ad hoc theories that it is impossible for them to take power. *Democracy will not accept these theories.*" "Puti soglasheniia," *Delo Naroda*, no. 160, 21 September 1917 (italics added). And Potresov said in the pre-Parliament, two days before the overturn: "If we are unable to combat this elemental urge [for immediate peace at any price] then let the Bolsheviks assume power and pay for it in history." A. N. Potresov, *Posmertnyi sbornik proizvedenii* (Paris: Dom knigi, 1937), p. 263.

23. Browder and Kerensky, *The Russian Provisional Government...* 3:1667.

24. See Skobelev's speech in *Vpered*, no. 149, 3 September 1917, and in Browder and Kerensky, *The Russian Provisional Govern-*

ment . . . 3:1663. Soon Tsereteli also began to argue that one could not exclude an entire party just because some members or parts of it had been mixed up in the Kornilov affair. Ibid., p. 1683.

25. This was also stressed in the report of the CC of the PSR to the International Socialist Bureau, written by Inna Rakitnikova, *Kak russkoe krest'ianstvo borolos' za Uchreditel'noe Sobranie* (Paris: 1918), p. 15.

26. *Vpered*, no. 153, 8 September 1917.

27. *Vpered*, no. 154, 10 September 1917.

28. *Vpered*, no. 155, 12 September 1917.

29. S. Belen'kii and A. Manvelov, *Revoliutsiia 1917 goda v Azerbaidzhane* (Baku: Istpart TsK i BK AKP(b), 1927), p. 172.

30. In the Moscow *Vpered* this resolution had already been published on 12 September.

31. Membership data are available for 1,200 delegates at the Democratic Conference, of whom 172 registered as Mensheviks, 38 as Menshevik Defensists, and 29 as Bund members. There are no party data for more than 300 representatives of the CEC, trade unions, and cooperatives, many of whom were Mensheviks. Nearly one-third of the Menshevik delegates registered with the Menshevik Internationalist faction, which comprised 94 members. *Iskra*, no. 3.

32. N. N. Sukhanov, *Zapiski o revoliutsii* 6 (Berlin: Grzhebin, 1923): 113.

33. *Rabochaia Gazeta*, no. 161, 15 September 1917.

34. *Rabochaia Gazeta*, nos. 160-64, 1917; *Iskra*, no. 2.

35. See Pavlo Khristiuk, *Zamitki i materialy po istorii ukrainskoi revoliutsii, 1917-1920 gg.* 2 (Vienna, 1921): 191; on the voting in the peasant section see Oliver H. Radkey, *The Agrarian Foes of Bolshevism* (New York: Columbia University Press, 1958), pp. 412-14. Rakitnikova (see n. 25) explains the votes against a purely socialist government mainly on the basis of the fear of isolating the socialist leadership from nonsocialist circles among which support could be found: the advocates of coalition "failed to take into account *the result of the Kornilov uprising—*the working masses' natural mistrust of nonsocialists, of all who were not directly with them, who *stood even a little more to the right than they*" (italics added).

36. *Den'*, no. 168, 20 September 1917. *Den'* specifically accused Bogdanov of having aborted and compromised the idea of coalition.

37. The appeal was signed by one member of the CC, F. A. Iudin; two alternates, I. N. Dement'ev-Kubikov and P. Ia. Golikov; the CEC members E. A. Maevskii, I. Emil'ianov, M. S. Binasik, and I. V. Zakhvataev; contributors to *Den'*, beginning with A. N. Potresov; a number of other prominent Right Mensheviks, such as G. E. Breido,

D. Kol'tsov, V. Levitskii, M. Kheisin, and A. Shneerson; and E. Kuskova, who did not participate in party work at all.

38. The Revolutionary Defensists had the majority in the CC. Obviously many of them shared Bogdanov's views and voted accordingly. Bogdanov himself was an alternate member and probably did not vote. We read in *Den'*, no. 210, 1 December, that Liber favored a "purely socialist government without Kadets" at the time.

39. *Izvestiia VTsIK*, 9 September, reprinted in Gorin, *Organizatsiia i stroitel'stvo Sovetov* . . . , pp. 382–84.

40. *Revoliutsiia 1917 goda (Khronika sobytii)* 4:240.

41. Against P. Golikov, a Potresovite.

42. *Revoliutsiia 1917 goda (Khronika sobytii)* 4:406.

43. Chkheidze, Tsereteli, Dan, and Kuchin.

44. *Vpered*, no. 166, 26 September 1917.

45. *Iskra*, no. 2, 3 October 1917. The text of the resolution, ibid.

46. The CC's resolution is in *Rabochaia Gazeta*, no. 170, 26 September 1917.

47. *Vpered*, no. 190, 24 October 1917. An interview with Nikitin had appeared in the Moscow *Russkoe Slovo* on 8 October. The CC's decision that the three ministers must "immediately leave the Party" no doubt underlies Dan's story in *Letopis' Revoliutsii* (see n. 20) that Nikitin was expelled from the Party while still a minister. Actually there had been no expulsion. Three weeks after the overturn, Nikitin declared his intention to leave the Moscow organization of the RSDRP. At the time this was by no means the same as leaving the Party. Nikitin's notice is in *Vlast' Naroda*, no. 161, 15 November 1917. See also *Vpered*, no. 226, 6 December 1917.

48. Skobelev's visit to Kerensky is reported in *Edinstvo*, no. 168, 20 October 1917.

49. Speech on 13 October at a plenary session of the CEC of the Soviets of Workers' and Soldiers' Deputies and the executive committee of the Soviet of Peasants' Deputies. *Rabochaia Gazeta*, no. 187, 15 October 1917.

50. Resolution of the Moscow committee, printed in *Vpered*, no. 168, 28 September, and no. 169, 29 September 1917.

51. *Revoliutsiia 1917 goda (Khronika sobytii)* 4:171.

52. *Vpered*, no. 157, 14 September 1917. Reprinted from *Izvestiia Moskovskogo Soveta*, no. 161, 13 September 1917, in *Organizatsiia i stroitel'stvo sovetov* . . . (see n. 19), pp. 374–76.

53. S. P. Mel'gunov, "N. V. Chaikovskii v gody grazhdanskoi voiny," in A. A. Titov (ed.), *Nikolai Vasil'evich Chaikovskii* 2 (2 vols.; Paris: 1929): 30.

54. Letter to the editors, *Vpered*, no. 200, 4/17 November 1917.

55. Sir George Buchanan, *My Mission to Russia* 2 (London: Cassell, 1923): 176.

56. See Mel'gunov, "N. V. Chaikovskii . . . ," (see n. 53), p. 32; and D. A. Chugaev (ed.), *Triumfal'noe shestvie sovetskoi vlasti* 1 (2 vols.; Moscow: Izd-vo ANSSSR, 1963): 261, in series *Velikaia Oktiabr'skaia Sotsialisticheskaia Revoliutsiia—Dokumenty i materialy.*

57. *Vpered*, 12 October 1917. Italics added. Another Moscow leader of the Revolutionary Defensists, G. A. Kipen, also maintained (at the Extraordinary Party Congress) that "no tactics could have prevented the collapse that had been approaching all the time." *Novyi Luch*, no. 2, 2 December 1917.

58. In the June elections to the City Duma, the Bolsheviks had received 75,000 of the 645,000 votes cast, that is, one in every nine; in the September elections to regional dumas they received every second vote (198,300 out of 390,000). In the army, over 80 percent voted for them. We have data on the voting in nineteen units of the Moscow garrison: 19,398 for the Bolsheviks, out of 23,079. By that time many people who had voted for Mensheviks in June had lost confidence in them. In comparison with June, they had lost 60,000, and the SRs 320,000 votes; the Bolsheviks had gained 123,000. *Vpered*, no. 167, 27 September 1917; *Soldat-Grazhdanin*, no. 162, 28 September. See also V. I. Lenin, *Sochineniia* 21 (3d ed.; Moscow: Partizdat TsK VKP(b), 1928), n. 98.

59. *Vpered*, no. 184, 17/30 October 1917.

60. The resolution is in *Revoliutsiia 1917 goda (Khronika sobytii)* 5 (1926): 268. On p. 168, the initiative is mistakenly credited (with a reference to *Armiia i Flot Svobodnoi Rossii*, no. 245) to Menshevik Internationalists supported by Menshevik Defensists and "both groups" of SRs. Dan's authorship of the resolution is confirmed by himself and by Stankevich. See Browder and Kerensky, *The Russian Provisional Government . . .* 3:1780-82. Dan subsequently recalled that he had lost confidence in Kerensky's government somewhat earlier and had hardly any personal contact with its members any more. Yet, with this resolution, he made a last attempt to persuade the provisional government that a radical change in its policies was imperative. He had managed to round up a majority in the pre-Parliament—something Bogdanov and Martov had vainly tried to do at the Democratic Conference. Both the Menshevik faction in the pre-Parliament and the SRs had approved the text of his resolution.

61. Popov, *Oktiabr'skii perevorot* (see n. 5), pp. 174-76.

62. Ibid., p. 177.

63. *Revoliutsiia 1917 goda [Khronika sobytii]* 5:175.

64. *Arkhiv Russkoi Revoliutsii* 7 (1922):290; or G. N. Golikov (ed.),

Oktiabr'skoe vooruzhennoe vosstanie v Petrograde (Moscow: Izd-vo ANSSSR, 1957), p. 340.

65. *Krasnyi Arkhiv* 23:149-50.

66. *Krasnyi Arkhiv* 25: 51.

67. S. P. Mel'gunov, *Kak bol'sheviki zakhvatili vlast'* (Paris: La Renaissance, 1953), p. 86.

68. A. Denikin, *Ocherki russkoi smuty* 2 (Berlin, 1924): 135.

69. Miliukov, *Istoriia Vtoroi Russkoi Revoliutsii* 1, part. 2, p. 157.

70. Mel'gunov, *Kak bol'sheviki. . .*, p. 205.

71. *Krasnyi Arkhiv* 24:78.

72. There are repeated references to such a directive in the testimony of former minister V. N. Lvov about his role in the Kornilov affair. D. A. Chugaev (ed.), *Revoliutsionnoe dvizhenie v Rossii v avguste 1917 g. Razgrom kornilovskogo miatezha* (Moscow: izd-vo ANSSSR, 1959), pp. 426-27, in series *Velikaia Oktiabr'skaia Sotsialisticheskaia Revoliutsiia—Dokumenty i materialy.*

73. The protocols of the meeting of 20 August are in ibid., pp. 371-77, with a reference to Arkhiv TsK K-D partii. The record was apparently edited after the fiasco of the Kornilov uprising, probably in connection with the investigation by the inquiry commission set up in September 1917.

74. *Rech'*, 16 September 1917.

75. Browder and Kerensky, *The Russian Provisional Government. . .*, 3: 1758.

76. Quoted in S. A. Piontkovskii, *Oktiabr'skaia revoliutsiia v Rossii; ee predposylki i khod* (Moscow: Gosizdat, 1923), p. 59.

77. V. L. Meller, *Rabochee dvizhenie v 1917 godu*, pp. 113, 199.

78. *Revoliutsiia 1917 goda (Khronika sobytii)* 5:27.

79. *Revoliutsionnaia Rossiia*, no. 21/22, p. 6. On the mood in conservative circles see Mel'gunov, "N. V. Chaikovskii. . ." (n. 53), pp. 30-32; and P. N. Miliukov in Browder and Kerensky, *The Russian Provisional Government. . .* 3: 1524, 1803.

80. Speech at a closed meeting of the pre-Parliament commission, 13 October. V. Maliutin, "Nakanune oktiabr'skogo perevorota," *Byloe*, no. 12, (1918), pp. 13-41. It must be said that responsible Revolutionary Defensists had already begun to see the situation more realistically. F. A. Cherevanin, a Defensist member of the Menshevik CC and head of the economic section of the Central Executive Committee, said on 4 October that continuing the war "threatens Russia with economic death."

81. Mel'gunov, *Kak bol'sheviki zakhvatili vlast'*, p. 82.

82. Popov, *Oktiabr'skii perevorot*, pp. 174-75.

83. *Voprosy Istorii KPSS*, no. 1, (1963), p. 153.

84. In his 1923 article in *Letopis' Revoliutsii* Dan recounts how he tried to persuade Kerensky that many Bolsheviks opposed the uprising and that the provisional government could bolster the opposition to Lenin by promising immediate reforms. There is a comment on this in S. A. Alekseev (ed.), *Revoliutsiia i grazhdanskaia voina v opisaniiakh belogvardeitsev* 2, *Oktiabr'skaia revoliutsiia* (6 vols.; Moscow-Leningrad: Gosizdat, 1926), in which Dan's article is included: "It has to be admitted in fairness to the Gotsliberdans that this was not a bad plan. Sowing dissent among the leaders of an uprising is half the job of aborting it." However: "luckily," Dan overestimated the Bolsheviks' hesitations; and even if he had prevailed upon Kerensky, the confusion in Bolshevik ranks would "probably" not have been sufficiently "serious" (130, n.).

3. The First Days of Soviet Rule

1. *Rabochaia Gazeta*, nos. 189, 190.

2. *Revoliutsiia 1917 goda (Khronika sobytii)* 5 (Moscow-Leningrad: Istpart pri TsK VKP 1926), p. 249. With minor changes, this appeal was also published in Moscow, in *Vpered*, no. 186.

3. *Edinstvo*, no. 170, 22 October 1917.

4. *Revoliutsiia 1917 goda (Khronika sobytii)* 5:270.

5. R. Abramovitch, *In tsvey revolutsyes* 2 (Yiddish; New York: Workmens Circle, 1944): 160 (italics added).

6. *Den'*, no. 198, 25 October 1917.

7. *Rabochaia Gazeta*, no. 199, 29 October 1917.

8. *Rabochaia Gazeta*, no. 196, 26 October 1917. The committee of the Petrograd organization usually supported Martov, but in the Menshevik faction of the Soviet Revolutionary Defensists dominated until October. In the elections to the executive committee of the Petrograd Soviet in late September, the Menshevik Internationalists polled only 15 percent of the Menshevik vote in the workers' division, and not one of their nominees was elected. The Menshevik Defensists got three seats. *Rabochaia Gazeta*, no. 144, 27 August and no. 170, 26 September 1917; *Den'*, no. 173, 26 September. No Potresovites were on the executive committee despite their considerable influence among workers: they had the majority, for example, in the small Menshevik faction of the conference of factory committees, convened by the Bolsheviks just before the overturn; and although its Bolshevik organizers had picked Martov as coreporter with Trotsky, it was not Martov who spoke but his brother V. Levitskii, a Potresovite and at the time

his political opponent. P. N. Amosov et al. (eds.), *Oktiabr'skaia revoliutsiia i Fabzavkomy* 2 (Moscow: Izd-vo VTsSPS, 1927): 142, 163, 165.

9. See *Revoliutsiia 1917 goda (Khronika sobytii]* 5:191.

10. S. A. Piontkovskii, *Sovety v Oktiabre. Sbornik dokumentov* (Moscow: Izd-vo Kom. Akad., 1928), p. 33 (italics added).

11. V. F. Morozov, *Penzenskaia organizatsiia bol'shevikov v period podgotovki i provedeniia Velikoi Oktiabr'skoi Sotsialisticheskoi Revoliutsii* (Penza: Penzenskoe knizhnoe izd-vo, 1959), p. 44. Savitskii left the Bolshevik party in December 1917.

12. Statement by S. M. Zaretskaia, a member of the CC. *Rabochaia Gazeta*, no. 204, 5 November 1917. The decision to form the committee was reached about 3:30 A.M. Then, or perhaps even a little earlier, the Menshevik V. Sher informed the Stavka that a Committee to Save the Revolution was in session at the City Duma. S. A. Alekseev (ed.), *Revoliutsiia i grazhdanskaia voina v opisaniiakh belogvardeitsev* 2: *Oktiabr'skaia revoliutsiia* (Moscow-Leningrad: Gosizdat, 1926): 402. The Menshevik Internationalists had just announced at the Congress of Soviets that they were leaving it "in order to organize a government." *Rabochaia Gazeta*, 27 October 1917.

13. For example: The Petrograd City Duma, warning in a resolution of 24 October against armed demonstrations, stated that as a democratically elected organ it was itself "the only legal representative" of civil government, and it did not even mention the provisional government. A. L. Popov, *Oktiabr'skii perevorot* (Petrograd: Novaia èpokha, 1918), p. 348. Stankevich, chief army commander and Kerensky's comrade-in-arms, thus recalled the mood of 26 October: "... with the government so unpopular in the country, better not mention it at all." V. B. Stankevich, *Vospominaniia 1914-1919 gg.* (Berlin: Ladyzhnikov, 1920), p. 272.

14. V. I. Ignat'ev, *Nekotorye fakty it itogi chetyrekh let grazhdanskoi voiny (1917-1921)* (Moscow: Gosizdat, 1922), p. 4. The author, a member in 1917 of the NS party, is one of the few participants in the meeting and the committee who have published memoirs.

15. *Rabochaia Gazeta*, no. 197, 27 October 1917.

16. Ignat'ev, *Nekotorye fakty* ..., pp. 4, 5. At a meeting of Menshevik Internationalists on 26 October, Martov spoke in favor of participating in the committee. *Novaia Zhizn*, no. 164, 27 October. On Menshevik Internationalists' participation see also Martov's speech at the Party congress on 4 December. *Novyi Luch*, no. 6, 7 December 1917.

17. The CC rejected a proposed amendment to the resolution,

which would have reduced the committee's role to "creating a center" of struggle for a homogeneous government—in the line of succession to the provisional government. *Volia Naroda*, no. 155, 27 October 1917.

18. The CC's resolution of 26 October is in *Rabochaia Gazeta*, no. 197, 27 October 1917, and in *Revoliutsiia 1917 goda* (*Khronika sobytii*) 5:293. The "city" mentality of the Mensheviks is very apparent in this resolution, hastily composed in an atmosphere of crisis. Transfer of land to land committees is not included among the pressing tasks. "Local" refers only to *Komitety Spaseniia* in cities, with the participation of organs of *city* self-government.

The CC's resolution speaks of *Komitet obshchestvennogo Spaseniia*, not *Komitet Spaseniia Rodiny i Revoliutsii*. Apparently the second name was adopted later in the day. On 26 October, the CC as well as the Potresovites used the first (cf. *Edinstvo*, no. 174, 29 October), originally proposed by the committee's initiators. It appears in Dan's resolution adopted by the pre-Parliament on 24 October, and it continued to be used interchangeably with the official later name. In the illegal protocols of the provisional government for 8 November, even *Komitet Obshchestvennogo Spaseniia Rodiny i Revoliutsii* is mentioned; protocols of the MRC repeatedly refer to *Komitet Obshchestvennogo Spaseniia*. M. Fleer, "Vremennoe Pravitel'stvo posle oktiabria," *Krasnyi Arkhiv* 6 (1922): 216; and *Dokumenty Velikoi Proletarskoi Revoliutsii* 1 (Moscow: Gosizdat, 1938): 136, 166.

19. Popov, *Oktiabr'skii perevorot*, pp. 345-47.

20. On 19 November, a conference of Menshevik Defensists in Petrograd passed a resolution offered by Potresov, which stated that the ministers of the provisional government who were still at liberty were the only legal government. *Klich*, no. 1, 23 November 1917.

21. Popov, *Oktiabr'skii perevorot*, p. 321. The same appeal, suitably modified and with a reference to the arrest of "some of the people's ministers," was reissued after the occupation of the palace. On 26 October, a large meeting of "Menshevik Defensists of the RSDRP" stressed in a resolution: "The only recognized government is the provisional government headed by Comrade Kerensky." In the appraisal of the overturn—"betrayal of our country to the external foe and abolition of freedom"—as in all other utterances of this group at this time, the dominant motif is the threat of defeat in the war and its consequences. *Edinstvo*, no. 174, 29 October 1917; Popov, *Oktiabr'skii perevorot*, pp. 329-30.

22. *Edinstvo*, no. 174, 29 October 1917 (italics added).

23. The article "Mertvye dushi," *Den'*, no. 215, 7 December 1917.

24. Speech at the Party congress, *Novyi Luch*, no. 2, 2 December 1917 (italics added).

25. *Novyi Den'*, 4/17 February 1918, in A. N. Potresov, *Posmertnyi Sbornik Proizvedenii* (Paris: Dom knigi, 1937), p. 279.

26. The Presidium of the pre-Parliament issued an appeal without any programmatic demands. Being a combined effort, it dealt only with a few matters on which all the groups represented in the pre-Parliament could agree: Everyone should rally around the new committee, which would "depose" the Bolsheviks and then organize a government "capable of seeing the long-suffering country through to the Constituent Assembly." Popov, *Oktiabr'skii perevorot*, p. 335.

27. *Revoliutsiia 1917 goda (Khronika sobytii)* 5:294; Popov, *Oktiabr'skii perevorot*, p. 324.

28. *Land*: "The Constituent Assembly will allot the land to the people forever" did not exclude its temporary transfer to land committees that the SRs advocated. *Peace*: "The Bolshevik uprising delays the peace desired by all." *Succession*: "Preserving the continuity of . . . state power, the All-Russian Committee to Save the Country and the Revolution will assume the initiative in recreating the provisional government"—a formula to satisfy those who considered the committee a sovereign organ qualified to create a government not necessarily "inherited" from Kerensky as well as those who felt that the new government must have Kerensky's blessing, and even those who expected the committee to restore the very provisional government that the Bolsheviks had locked up in Petropavlovsk Fortress. *Coalition or homogeneous government*: "A government that will be based on the forces of democracy."

The text of the declaration is in *Rabochaia Gazeta*, no. 197, 27 October 1917; also in *Revoliutsiia 1917 goda (Khronika sobytii)* 5:293, and in Popov, *Oktiabr'skii perevorot*, p. 339.

29. L. Trotskii, *Oktiabr'skaia Revoliutsiia* (Moscow-Petrograd: Kommunist, 1918), p. 84.

30. The above-cited appeal of 26 October, "Vas podlo i prestupno obmanuli," and the instruction (27 October) of the Central Committee and the military commission of the Central Committee of the Party of Socialist Revolutionaries, "Vsem grazhdanskim i voennym organizatsiiam partii," are in Popov, *Oktiabr'skii perevorot*, p. 324; the slogan in *Delo Naroda* of 28 October 1917: "a homogeneous socialist cabinet without Bolsheviks and census people [*tsenzoviki*]."

31. *Revoliutsiia 1917 goda (Khronika sobytii)* 6:4; "Oktiabr'skii perevorot i Stavka," *Krasnyi Arkhiv* 8:157. The expectation of Kerensky's imminent return is reflected in the resolution of the Menshevik CC of 28 October, which insists on the immediate reconstitution of the provisional government, the surrender of the MRC, and guaranteed

immunity for the participants in the uprising. *Rabochaia Gazeta*, no. 199, 29 October 1917.

32. The telegram is reproduced from Vikzhel archives in G. N. Golikov (ed.), *Oktiabr'skoe vooruzhennoe vosstanie v Petrograde* (Moscow: Izd-vo ANSSSR, 1957). p. 643.

33. *Dokumenty Velikoi Proletarskoi Revoliutsii* 1:116.

34. D. A. Chugaev (ed.), *Triumfal'noe shestvie Sovetskoi Vlasti* 1 (2 vols.; Moscow: Izd-vo ANSSSR, 1963): 153, in series *Velikaia Oktiabr'skaia Sotsialisticheskaia Revoliutsiia—Dokumenty i materialy*.

35. For the appeal of the Petrograd Committee of Menshevik Defensists to soldiers, "Vy pomogli v fevrale," see *Volia Naroda*, no. 157, 29 October 1917; also Popov, *Oktiabr'skii perevorot*, pp. 331-34.

36. Ignat'ev, *Nekotorye fakty* . . . (see n. 14), p. 5; S. P. Mel'gunov, *Kak bol'sheviki zakhvatili vlast'* (Paris: La Renaissance, 1953), p. 190. At the trial of the SRs, Gots admitted that he had been responsible for directing the military activity under the flag of the committee: "The CC [of the PSR] had authorized me to organize the resistance, and I decided to do this in the name of the largest and most influential organization in Petrograd at the time," the Committee to Save the Revolution. *Revoliutsionaia Rossiia*, no. 21/22, p. 7. For safety, the organ directing this work apparently had no formal name. Participants call it *Voennyi Komitet* (Stankevich), *Voennyi Sovet* (Kerensky), *Voennyi Otdel* (telegram in *Kievskaia Mysl'*), and *Voennyi Shtab* (Colonel Mufel')—all with the addition "of the Committee to Save the Country and the Revolution." See also *Oktiabr'skoe vooruzhennoe vosstanie v Petrograde*, pp. 819, 822.

37. Krasnov's telegram is in *Krasnyi Arkhiv* 24:204 (from A. I. Koz'min's collection); the testimony of the cadet Duke of Lichtenberg, in *Oktiabr'skoe vooruzhennoe vosstanie v Petrograde*, p. 820.

38. Both appeals—that of the SRs, mentioning Chernov but not the provisional government or Kerensky, and that of the Potresovites, not mentioning Chernov—are reprinted in *Volia Naroda*, no. 159, 31 October 1917, and in Popov, *Oktiabr'skii perevorot*, p. 341 and pp. 330–31.

39. Mel'gunov, *Kak bol'sheviki zakhvatili vlast'*, p. 196.

40. P. Vompe, *Dni oktiabr'skoi revoliutsii i zheleznodorozhniki* (Moscow: Istproftran, 1924), p. 28; *Rabochaia Gazeta*, no. 198, 28 October 1917; Ignat'ev, *Nekotorye fakty* . . . , p. 5.

41. "Oktiabr' na fronte," *Krasnyi Arkhiv* 24:91; Voitinskii's testimony, *Krasnyi Arkhiv* 9:187.

42. *Revoliutsiia 1917 goda* (*Khronika sobytii*) 5, 25 October.

43. N. I. Podvoiskii, *God 1917* (Moscow: Gos. izdat. polit. lit-ry, 1958), p. 162.

44. V. A. Antonov-Ovseenko, *Zapiski o grazhdanskoi voine* 1 (Moscow: Vysshii Voennyi Redaktsionnyi Sovet, 1924): 9.

45. A. F. Il'in-Zhenevskii, *Ot fevralia k zakhvatu vlasti*, (Leningrad: Priboi, n. d.), p. 135. See also Mel'gunov, *Kak bol'sheviki zakhvatili vlast'*, p. 182.

46. Mel'gunov, *Kak bol'sheviki zakhvatili vlast'*, chap. 5.

47. *Oktiabr'skoe vooruzhennoe vosstanie v Petrograde*, p. 827 (italics added).

48. Abramovitch, *In tsvey revolutsyes* 2:169.

49. *Rabochaia Gazeta*, no. 200, 1 November 1917.

50. *Revoliutsionnaia Rossiia*, no. 21/22, p. 8 (italics added).

51. *Den'*, no. 205, 11 November 1917.

52. "Protokoly zasedanii TsIK i Biuro TsIK Sov. Rab. i Sold. Deputatov 1-go Sozyva posle oktiabria," *Krasnyi Arkhiv* 10:101-5.

53. *Pechatnik*, no. 7/8, 28 November 1917. Quoted in V. L. Meller (ed.), *Rabochee dvizhenie v 1917 godu* (Moscow: Tsentroarkhiv, 1926), p. 301.

54. This appeal was published in *Edinstvo*, no. 178, 3 November. On the same day, *Rabochaia Gazeta*, no. 202, merely noted: "The editors have received an appeal of the executive committee of Menshevik Defensists in which they sharply protest against the CC's decision and declare that they will not submit to it but will continue to strive, not for a 'homogeneous,' but an 'all-nation' government." More ordinary announcements of Potresov's group continued to be printed in the Party press.

55. Articles by Stepan Ivanovich in *Drug Naroda*, which briefly replaced *Den'* when the latter was closed by the Bolsheviks (quoted in *Rabochaia Gazeta* no. 204, 5 November, and in *Den'*, no. 201, 7 November 1917). *Drug Naroda* came out with the subheading "Organ of the Group of Menshevik Defensists."

56. At the same meeting, Dan told the garrison delegates that if Russia perished, the Petrograd garrison would be the chief culprit. Reported in *Den'*, no. 206, 12 November 1917. The commissar for the northern front, V. Voitinskii, simply appealed to Krasnov's Cossacks to do their duty regardless of malicious outbursts from "deserters entrenched in the rear." From A. I. Koz'min's collection, *Krasnyi Arkhiv* 24:204.

4. Vikzhel

1. The declaration read by Khinchuk is in *Rabochaia Gazeta*, no. 196, 26 October 1917; the Internationalists' declaration, in A. L. Popov, *Oktiabr'skii perevorot* (Petrograd: Novaia èpokha, 1918), p. 382, and in *Revoliutsiia 1917 goda* (*Khronika sobytii*) 5 (Moscow-Leningrad: Istpart pri TsK VKP, 1926): 192.

2. *Rabochaia Gazeta*, no. 198, 28 October 1917.

3. *Rabochaia Gazeta*, no. 200, 1 November 1917.

4. Popov, *Oktiabr'skii perevorot*, p. 383.

5. "Revoliutsiia v opasnosti," *Novaia Zhizn*, no. 166, 29 October. It also appeared in several other newspapers.

6. One representative of Vikzhel, Mamaev, even left the pre-Parliament together with the Bolshevik faction. *Revoliutsiia 1917 goda* (*Khronika sobytii*) 5:44.

7. The data on membership are taken from Osip Piatnitskii's article "Vikzhel', do, vo vremia i posle oktiabr'skikh dnei," in *Put' k oktiabriu* (Moscow: Gubernskii Istpart, 1923), pp. 175-80. Piatnitskii was the head of Vikzhedor, set up by the Bolsheviks to replace Vikzhel. There is no reason to put greater faith in the data usually cited on the basis of P. Vompe, *Dni oktiabr'skoi revoliutskii i zheleznodorozhniki* (Moscow: Istproftran, 1924), p. 10: 3 Bolsheviks, 9 Left SRs, 5 right SRs, 2 *mezhraionsty*, 1 Menshevk Internationalist, 6 Mensheviks, 3 NSs, and 11 in the nonpartisan "bog," mostly of the Kadet type. Vompe counts himself among the *mezhraiontsy*—an obvious anachronism since they had merged with the Bolshevik party earlier. His own stand at the time was closest to the Menshevik Internationalists'. Cf. his telephone talk with Bel'batov on 29 October in V. Storozhev, "Iz arkhiva Moskovskogo V. R. Komiteta," in *Oktiabr'skoe vosstanie v Moskve*, N. N. Ovsiannikov, ed. (Moscow: Gosizdat, 1922), p. 190.

8. G. D. Kostomarov, comp., *Oktiabr' v Moskve* (Moscow: Ispart MOK VKP, 1932), p. 186. Referring to Vompe, Radkey states that Malitskii was a *Left SR*. This is doubtful, at least for this period.

9. *Revoliutsiia 1917 goda* (*Khronika sobytii*) 5:283.

10. Railroad unions must take "all available measures" to stop troops moving against one another in the socialists' struggle; "firm measures" to stop reinforcements to one of the sides; "the firmest measures" to stop troops sent to demolish socialist parties and democratic organizations. Although both sides, sincerely or not, later blamed Vikzhel for delays and failures, it is doubtful that local railroad workers could have seriously impeded the movements of armed units if these had been at all determined to proceed. Krasnov's Cossacks traveled almost

four hundred kilometers from Ostrov to Gatchina. Troops conveyed by railroad from Petrograd decided the outcome of the street fighting in Moscow. Vikzhel's own representative at the Stavka failed to delay Krylenko's detachment, which took over the Stavka.

11. Popov, *Oktiabr'skii perevorot*, p. 402.

12. *Rabochaia Gazeta*, no. 199, 29 October 1917. Italics added.

13. Storozhev in *Oktiabr'skoe vosstanie v Moskve* (see n. 7), p. 190.

14. Telegram of 29 October. *Revoliutsiia 1917 goda* (*Khronika sobytii*) 6:436.

15. Letter to the editors, *Volia Naroda*, no. 159, 31 October.

16. "Bol'sheviki dolzhny kapitulirovat'," *Rabochaia Gazeta*, 29 October 1917.

17. A. Martynov argued in *Iskra*, no. 7, that "the fighting organizations—the Soviets of Workers' and Soldiers' Deputies—and the organizations brought forth by universal suffrage—the city dumas—must participate *equally* in creating the government." Italics added.

18. *Rabochaia Gazeta*, no. 200, 1 November 1917.

19. *Revoliutsiia 1917 goda* (*Khronika sobytii*) 6:30; R. Abramovitch, *The Soviet Revolution 1917-1939* (London: George Allen & Unwin, 1962), p. 109.

20. Appeal of the Committee of the Petrograd Organization of the RSDRP, *Rabochaia Gazeta*, no. 198, 28 October 1917.

21. *Professional'noe dvizhenie v Petrograde v 1917 godu*, A. Anskii, ed. (Leningrad: Izd-vo Leningradskogo oblastnogo Soveta profsoiuzov, 1928), p. 301 (the appeal of 27 October) and p. 55 (the resolution of 31 October.

22. On Tsentrorek (river transport workers' union) see T. Krylova, 'K istorii soiuza vodnikov," in ibid., pp. 221-22; on the leather workers' union, Popov, *Oktiabr'skii perevorot*, p. 393.

23. *Professional'noe dvizhenie v Petrograde v 1917 godu*, p. 120.

24. *Rabochaia Gazeta*, no. 203, 4 November 1917; Popov, *Oktiabr'skii perevorot*, p. 394. The duma consisted of 39 Bolsheviks, 12 Mensheviks, 10 SRs, 1 NS, and 5 Kadets. See B. D. Gal'perina and V. I. Startsev, "Sovety Rabochikh i Soldatskikh Deputatov Petrograda v bor'be za ovladenie apparatom gorodskogo obshchestvennogo upravleniia," in *Rabochie Leningrada v bor'be za pobedu sotsializma* (Moscow-Leningrad: Izd-vo ANSSSR, 1963), p. 73. The authors note "waverings" in this mainly Bolshevik duma of a typical working-class neighborhood, which spoke out for an all-socialist government (p. 81, with a reference to archive materials).

25. *Rabochaia Gazeta*, no. 200, 1 November 1917; *Revoliutsiia 1917 goda* (*Khronika sobytii*) 6:39; S. An-skii in S. A. Alekseev, ed., *Re-*

voliutsiia i grazhdanskaia voina v opisaniiakh belogvardeitsev 2: *Oktiabr'skaia revoliutsiia* (Moscow-Leningrad: Gosizdat, 1926), p. 304.

26. S. P. Mel'gunov, *Kak bol'sheviki zakhvatili vlast'* (Paris: La Renaissance, 1953, p. 232. R. Abramovitch, *In tsvey revolutsyes* 2 (Yiddish; New York: Workmens Circle, 1944):181.

27. *Biulleten'*, no. 6, in G. Lelevich, *Oktiabr' v stavke* (Gomel: Gomel'skii rabochii, 1922) (appendixes, p. 16).

28. *Krasnyi Arkhiv* 9:169.

29. Lelevich, *Oktiabr' v stavke* (appendixes, p. 29).

30. D. A. Chugaev, ed., *Triumfal'noe shestive sovetskoi vlasti* (Moscow: Izd-vo ANSSSR, 1963), part 2, p. 75. In series *Velikaia Oktiabr'skaia Sotsialisticheskaia Revoliutsiia—Dokumenty i materialy.*

31. In the program of the all-socialist government they now favored, the Odessa Mensheviks included convocation of the Constituent Assembly "on schedule"; immediate transfer of land to land committees; an "active foreign policy" for quick peace. *Rabochaia Gazeta*, no. 211, 12 November 1917. When the Odessa Menshevik paper *Iuzhnyi Rabochii* printed the declaration of the CC members who had left in late October, the editors commented that they agreed with the CC.

32. *Revoliutsiia 1917 goda (Khronika sobytii)* 6:34.

33. M. E. Dziuba et al., *Bor'ba trudiashchikhsia Orlovksoi gubernii za ustanovlenie Sovetskoi vlasti v 1917-1918 g.* (Orel: Orlovskaia pravda, 1957), p. 102. Ibid., a more "rightist" laconic resolution drafted by the minority of the Menshevik faction: instant termination of the civil war, which was "clearing the way" for extreme reaction; a "democratic government" that would "fight for the speediest conclusion of peace" and the speediest convocation of the Constituent Assembly, but also "for immediate transfer of land to land committees."

34. *Revoliutsiia 1917 goda (Khronika sobytii)* 6:9; *Rabochaia Gazeta*, no. 207, 8 November 1917.

35. *Bol'sheviki Urala v bor'be za pobedu oktiabr'skoi sotsialisticheskoi revoliutsii* (2d ed.; Sverdlovsk: Istpart pri Obkome, 1957), p. 29.

36. Ibid. At the time, Trotsky opposed any agreements with socialist parties "from the trash barrel of history." In 1957 the Soviet historian nevertheless wrote that on 28 October 1917, the Ufa Mensheviks and SRs, "supported by Trotskyites, managed to have the activity of the Revolutionary Committee restricted."

37. Ibid., p. 42. Also K. Ia. Votinova, "Bor'ba za pobedu oktiabr'skoi revoliutsii v Permskoi gubernii," in *Ustanovlenie Sovetskoi vlasti na mestakh v 1917-18 g.* 1 (Moscow: Gos. izdat. polit. lit-ry, 1953): 245 ff.; and *Revoliutsiia 1917 goda (Khronika sobytii)* 6:35.

38. The Rostov organization and the Don Committee of the

RSDRP(O) had very popular leaders such as B. S. Vasil'ev (chairman of the Rostov Duma), I. M. Grossman (member of the Council of Trade Unions), P. S. Petrenko, and A. S. Lokkerman. After the elections to the Rostov SWD just before the overturn, the Menshevik faction was the most numerous: 76 Mensheviks, 66 Bolsheviks, 30 SRs. *Vpered*, no. 191, 25 October 1917. Soviet studies confirm the Mensheviks' leading role until October in Rostov and Novocherkassk trade unions, Soviets, and city governments. See, for example, P. Moskatov et al., *Rabochii klass Dona v bor'be za Sovetskuiu vlast'* (Rostov, 1957), p. 33.

39. *Rabochaia Gazeta*, no. 211, 12 November 1917.

40. Moskatov, *Rabochii klass Dona* ..., p. 37; V. A. Antonov-Ovseenko, *Zapiski o grazhdanskoi voine* 1 (Moscow: Priboi, 1924): 195.

41. "Rol' partii proletariata," *Novyi Luch*, no. 18, 22 December 1917.

42. For example, Piatnitskii in *Put' k oktiabriu* (see n. 7), pp. 179-80: "This slogan was very popular with the masses; [the Vikzhel leaders] thought they could give the power back to SRs and Mensheviks in this way and isolate the Bolsheviks in the 'socialist government' itself."

43. Lelevich, *Oktiabr' v stavke*, p. 24. Quoted from the newspaper *Mogilevskaia Zhizn.*

44. In this category are also some lists of candidates for the Constituent Assembly, such as the one drawn up by the S-D organization of the Sixth army: Tsereteli and Chkheidze side by side with Martov, Gorky, and Lunacharskii (*Rabochaia Gazeta*, no. 197); and the decision of the executive committee of the United organization of the northern front on 30 October: to approve joining the Comittee to Save the Revolution "so as to insist there...that the Central Committee to Save the Revolution invite the Petrograd Military-Revolutionary Committee to merge for common work [!?]." Lelevich, *Oktiabr' v stavke*, appendixes, p. 4.

45. *Edinstvo*, no. 182, 8 November.

46. *Rabochaia Gazeta*, no. 200, 1 November 1917.

47. The Left SR Lap'er and the S-Ds Antonevich and Seniushkin.

48. *Biulleten' Obshchearmeiskogo Komiteta*, no. 5, 1 November, quoted in Lelevich, *Oktiabr' v stavke*, appendixes, p. 9.

49. Ibid., appendixes, p. 11. Yet only two days earlier, on 30 October, the army committee had demanded that the Bolsheviks submit to the decision "of the sovereign organ of democracy—the All-Russian Committee to Save the Country and the Revolution." Ibid., appendixes, p. 5. The army committee consisted of twenty-five members:

one from each front, each army and fleet. Radkey says, without giving his source, that its chairman, S. V. Perekrestov, was a Menshevik. Oliver H. Radkey, *The Sickle under the Hammer* (New York: Columbia University Press, 1963), p. 73. This fits his theory of "Menshevik shepherds and SR sheep" but contradicts Stankevich and Mel'gunov, who call Perekrestov an SR. See Stankevich in *Oktiabr'skaia revoliutsiia*, p. 223, and Mel'gunov, *Kak bol'sheviki zakhvatili vlast'*, p. 234.

50. Data on the composition of the "cabinet" are in An-skii's report to the City Duma, *Rabochaia Gazeta*, no. 201, 2 November 1917; also in *Revoliutsiia 1917 goda* (*Khronika sobytii*) 6:39; and in Lelevich, *Oktiabr' v stavke*, appendixes, p. 16. On the agreement see *Rabochaia Gazeta*, no. 201.

51. Abramovitch, *In tsvey revolutsyes*, p. 183.

52. *Biulleten' OAK*, no. 6, quoted in Lelevich, *Oktiabr' v stavke*, appendixes, p. 16.

53. The telegram to Vikzhel is in E. N. Gorodetskii, comp., *Iz protokolov i perepiski V. R. K. Petrogradskogo soveta 1917 g.* (Moscow: OGIZ, 1938), p. 334, n. 44; the telegram to Dukhonin, in G. N. Golikov, ed., *Oktiabr'skoe vooruzhennoe vosstanie v Petrograde* (Moscow: Izd-vo ANSSSR, 1957), p. 800. The commissar of the northern front, V. Voitinskii, a Revolutionary Defensist, went much farther in his conclusions. On 1 November he telegraphed: "Agreement has been reached on the basis of *deposing* Kerensky." He suggested stopping all troops that were on their way to Petrograd. *Krasnyi Arkhiv* 24:91. Italics added. His statement on 2 November sounds even more categorical: "Now that the truce has put an end to the civil war and a *new government has been recognized*, I am no longer commissar of the northern front." *Krasnyi Arkhiv* 9:186. Italics added. In both cases, Voitinskii spoke for himself, not for the Menshevik organization.

54. *Krasnyi Arkhiv* 24:97.

5. The Consolidation of Bolshevik Rule

1. Lenin had written in the CC's resolution of 2 November: "One cannot renounce a purely Bolshevik government without betraying the motto of Soviet power." This phrase, and a reference to "the dictatorship of the proletariat and the poorest peasants that has already begun," did not appear in the resolution as printed in *Pravda* at the time. V. I. Lenin, *Sochineniia* 35 (5th ed.; Moscow: Gosizdat, 1958): 44.

2. Lenin bolstered his attack on Vikzhel with an ad hoc theory: Vikzhel was not a Soviet type of organization, not a "voluntary union" of the masses' revolutionary vanguard struggling to overthrow landlords and capitalists. Ibid., pp. 43-45, and D. A. Chugaev, ed., *Triumfal'noe shestvie sovetskoi vlasti* 1 (2 vols.; Moscow: Izd-vo ANSSSR, 1963): 15-19, in series *Velikaia Oktiabr'skaia Sotsialisticheskaia Revolutsiia—Dokumenty i materialy.*

3. *Revoliutsiia 1917 goda (Khronika sobytii)* 6 (Moscow-Leningrad: Istpart pri TsK VKP, 1930): 38.

4. Ibid., pp. 46-47.

5. Speech of 3 November, *Rabochaia Gazeta*, no. 204, 5 November 1917.

6. *Rabochaia Gazeta*, no. 202, 3 November 1917.

7. *Sotsialistcheskii Vestnik*, no. 6, May 1960, p. 122, and R. Abramovitch, *The Soviet Revolution 1917-1939* (London: George Allen & Unwin, 1962), p. 116. *Rabochaia Gazeta* of 5 November devoted its entire front page to the four "preliminary conditions," under the heading W E DEMAND.

8. *Revoliutsiia 1917 goda (Khronika sobytii)* 6:68.

9. G. Lelevich, *Oktiabr' v stavke* (Gomel: Gomel'skii rabochii, 1922), appendixes, pp. 27, 33. Between 1 November, when eleven Revolutionary Defensists left the CC, and 8 November, when most of them rejoined it, the Internationalists had an absolute majority of votes in the CC. The statement sent to Vikzhel expressed their position: "Since the Central Executive Committee has not met the preliminary demands and since the Party considers it possible to conclude any agreements only if they are fully met, the RSDRP(O) is obliged to refrain from further negotiations." And it was the Menshevik Internationalists who returned to Vikzhel when signs of crisis in the Bolshevik CC seemed to justify renewal of the negotiations. The statement about refraining from further negotiations is in A. L. Popov, ed., *Oktiabr'skii perevorot* (Petrograd: Novaia èpokha, 1918), p. 406.

10. Quoted in *Revoliutsiia 1917 goda (Khronika sobytii)* 6:83.

11. Ibid., p. 89.

12. Lozovskii's letter was published in *Rabochaia Gazeta*, no. 204, 5 November 1917. He was to fall victim to another personality cult in a later era.

13. Lenin, *Sochineniia* 35:44, 70.

14. Ibid., p. 48.

15. Ibid., p. 49.

16. E. Iaroslavskii, ed., *Istoriia VKP(b)* 4 (Moscow: Gosizdat, 1929): 268.

17. A. F. Il'in-Zhenevskii, *Ot fevralia k zakhvatu vlasti*, p. 162.

18. P. G. Bogdanov in D. A. Chugaev, ed., *Ustanovlenie Sovetskoi vlasti na mestakh* 2 (Moscow: Gosizdat, 1959): 150.

19. *Bol'shaia Sovetskaia Èntsiklopediia* 43:320.

20. M. E. Dziuba et al., *Bor'ba trudiashchikhsia Orlovskoi gubernii za ustanovlenie Sovetskoi vlasti v 1917-1918 g.* (Orel: Orlovskaia pravda, 1957), pp. 47, 84.

21. Ibid., p. 119, citing *Golos Truda*, no. 178, 28 November 1917, with list of Mensheviks elected to the executive committee: Glukhov (the first chairman of the Soviet), Gnesin, È. M. Kagan (Defensist, Bund member, chairman of the Party committee and editor of the Party paper), Klokov (Internationalist), Marks, Miks, Panevin, V. F. Pereverzev (mayor, and until 25 November chairman of the Soviet of Workers' and Soldiers' Deputies), and Talyzenkov.

22. E. I. Bugaev, *Vozniknovenie bol'shevistskoi organizatsii i obrazovanie kompartii Belorussii* (Moscow: Gos. izdat. polit. literatury, 1959), p. 169.

23. *Pervyi legal'nyi Peterburgskii komitet bol'shevikov v 1917 godu. Sbornik materialov i protokolov* (Moscow-Leningrad: Gosizdat, 1927), p. 340: and Lenin, *Sochineniia* (5th ed.) 35:550.

24. *Revoliutsiia 1917 goda (Khronika sobytii)* 6:74.

25. Abramovitch, *The Soviet Revolution*, p. 111.

26. Cf. letter from N. Angarskii, *Proletarskaia Revoliutsiia*, no. 72, 1928, pp. 177-78.

27. *Krasnyi Arkhiv* 23 (1927): 128.

28. *Vpered*, no. 202, 6 November 1917.

29. The notorious A. Vyshinsky, later chief prosecutor at the show trials but at the time a Menshevik, was arrested by a patrol of pro-Bolshevik soldiers while distributing this issue of *Vpered. Vpered*, no. 202, 6 November 1917.

30. G. D. Kostomarov, comp., *Oktiabr' v Moskve* (Moscow: Gos. sots.-ekon. izd-vo, 1932), p. 152; *Krasnyi Arkhiv* 23:124, 128. Italics added.

31. *Revoliutsiia 1917 goda (Khronika sobytii)* 6:73. After the CEC's endorsement of Lenin's dictum the Left SRs branded it "a clear manifestation of a system of political terror" and announced the recall of their representatives from the MRC; and Nogin announced the departure of the Bolshevik opposition from the Sovnarkom. We can see how swiftly Lenin dealt with opposition in his party. His "decree on the press" had appeared only eight days earlier, on 27 October. On that day he had vowed that the measures against the bourgeois press were "temporary and extraordinary," to be revoked as soon as the new regime was consolidated. He had solemnly declared that restriction of

the press was "admissible only insofar as absolutely necessary"; newspapers could be closed only by order of the Sovnarkom; the right to free speech was curtailed only temporarily—a special order would restore it when circumstances became normal. Popov, *Oktiabr'skii perevorot*, pp. 262-63. The decree does not appear in Lenin's *Sochineniia* 35.

32. *Vlast' Naroda*, no. 156, 8 November 1917.

33. S. Piontkovskii, ed., *Sovety v oktiabre* (Moscow: Kom. Akad., 1928), p. 44. Italics added.

34. The letter, of 7 November 1917, to the commander of the Red Guard unit is in Kostomarov, *Oktiabr' v Moskve*, p. 152: "The Military-Revolutionary Committee of the Soviet of Workers' and Soldiers' Deputies expresses its gratitude to your unit for services rendered, and invites you, since military operations in Moscow have been ended, to remove the unit from the Alexander School and take it back to Petrograd." The letter was signed by A. Lomov (Oppokov), a member of the Bolshevik CC, in his capacity as member of the Moscow MRC.

35. D. Erde, *Gody buri i natiska* (Kharkov: Gosizdat Ukrainy, 1923), 1:63-64. Italics added. The same author repeated in 1927 that the local Bolshevik leaders "maneuvered too much, trying to seize power as painlessly as possible." D. Èrde, *Revoliutsiia na Ukraine*, p. 164, quoted in *Istoricheskie Zapiski*, 73:283.

36. N. N. Popov, *Ocherki revoliutsionnykh sobytii v Khar'kove*, pp. 19-20.

37. V. Morgunov, "Soobshchenie," taken down in 1927. *Istoricheskii Arkhiv*, no. 5, 1957, pp. 208-9.

38. Èrde, *Gody buri i natiska*, 1:116.

39. "Obshchedemokraticheskaia vlast'," *Vpered*, no. 206, 10 November 1917.

40. F. I. Dan, B. I. Gorev, F. A. Cherevanin, and the representative of the Bund, G. M. Erlich; possibly also L. M. Khinchuk or K. G. Gogua.

41. Iu. O. Martov, A. S. Martynov, R. A. Abramovich, I. S. Astrov, Eva L. Broido, D. Iu. Dallin, S. Iu. Semkovskii, and possibly either N. A. Rozhkov or Anna P. Krasnianskaia.

42. Report on Dan's speech of 3 November, *Rabochaia Gazeta*, no. 204, 5 November 1917.

43. Resolution of the electoral committee of Menshevik Defensists and sector representatives, *Edinstvo*, no. 176, 1 November 1917.

44. The Party's list was registered as no. 16, in the name of the committee of the Petrograd Organization of the RSDRP(O). The Potresovites' list as no. 17, in the name of the electoral committee of Menshevik-Defensists of the RSDRP. Potresov headed it. The other candidates were K. A. Gvozdev, P. P. Maslov, I. N. Dement'ev (Kubi-

kov), V. A. Maevskii (Gutovskii), I. I. Emel'ianov, G. E. Breido, M. L. Kheisin, V. O. Levitskii, G. G. Trifonov, I. V. Vasil'ev, I. I. Ladyzhenskii, N. N. Andreev, B. A. Ginzburg (Kol'tsov), and M. V. Myskov. *Den'*, no. 202, 8 November 1917. The appeal of the electoral committee is in *Edinstvo*, no. 170, 22 October 1917. Transgressing the CC's decision about lists separate from the Party's, the electoral committee had combined its list with those of the NSs, the SR-Defensists, *Edinstvo*, and the Equal Rights for Women League. *Edinstvo*, no. 175, 31 October 1917.

45. In Kharkov Province the official Menshevik list got 11,978 votes, and the Menshevik Defensists' list 5,797. Èrde, *Gody buri i natiska*, 1:111. Gvozdev and Potresov headed it, followed by A. A. Poddubnyi, R. F. Tkachenko, M. F. Kuznetsov, N. V. Chernyshev, P. S. Odor, N. D. Bogdanov, S. L. Sirota, M. Ia. Babin, and V. Ia. Desiatov. *Rabochaia Gazeta*, no. 193, 22 October 1917. In Ekaterinburg Defensists formed a bloc with the same groups as in Petrograd. Dan headed the official Party list for Ekaterinburg. *Rabochaia Gazeta*, no. 193. It is known that the Menshevik Defensists' list for the Black Sea fleet was in fifth place in number of votes, and the official list, in fourth place. *Klich*, no. 1, 23 November 1917. The Defensists did better in Petrograd: 16,834 votes, as against 10,531 for the official list of the Menshevik organization. *Rabochaia Gazeta*, no. 214, 16 November 1917.

46. B. S. Baturskii, P. A. Garvi, K. A. Gvozdev, L. I. Goldman, K. M. Ermolaev, S. M. Zaretskaia, P. N. Kolokol'nikov, V. N. Krokhmal', M. I. Liber, A. N. Smirnov, and F. A. Iudin.

47. *Edinstvo*, no. 176, 1 November 1917.

48. Both were signed, besides the eleven members of the CC, by three alternates: B. O. Bogdanov, P. Ia. Golikov, M. I. Skobelev.

49. *Volia Naroda*, no. 159, 31 October 1917.

50. *Rabochaia Gazeta*, no. 201, 2 November 1917.

51. *Rabochaia Gazeta*, no. 204, 5 November 1917.

52. See the discussion of this resolution on p. 75.

53. A report on the meeting of 3 November is in *Rabochaia Gazeta*, no. 204, 5 November 1917. The Menshevik Internationalists were not present, having by this time formed separate factions in the pre-Parliament and the Soviet. However, Abramovich spoke at this meeting defending the CC's resolution. Unlike Dan and the more skeptical Internationalists in the CC, he viewed agreement and a government from NSs to Bolsheviks as an immediate need. He insisted on attempting to agree, at whatever cost, on a short-term government with a minimal mutually acceptable program. This view, too, was grounded

in pessimism: the pro-Bolshevik workers and soldiers, Abramovich said, conceived of the revolution and socialism only "in the guise of bolshevism"; with the regime removed, the country would find itself amid the ruins of sans-culotte socialism and a raging reaction of the "Black forces" of the right.

54. "K sozdaniiu vlasti," *Rabochaia Gazeta*, no. 206, 7 November 1917.

55. *Novyi Luch*, no. 2, 2 December 1917.

56. Martov's speech at the Extraordinary Congress is in *Novyi Luch*, no. 1, 1 December; his closing speech, in *Noyi Luch*, no. 2, 2 December 1917.

57. *Rabochaia Gazeta*, no. 206, 7 November 1917. No steps were taken to organize such a committee. There is, however, an account in *Novaia Zhizn* of another conference, which met at midnight on the same date to discuss the idea launched by the Menshevik CC. Present were oppositional Bolsheviks (Zinov'ev and Riazanov spoke), Left SRs, United Social-Democrat Internationalists, members of Vikzhel, and (by some mistake?) a representative of the CC of the Soviet of Peasants' Deputies. The left Menshevik Internationalist Ermanskii also spoke at this conference. The Menshevik CC had not sent anyone—it was under the impression that this meeting was still about a central government in agreement with the Sovnarkom, which was already impossible or not yet possible. Later during the night the meeting did get hold of a representative of the CC, G. M. Erlich, who confirmed the Mensheviks' refusal to take part in negotiations until terror was abolished. *Revoliutsiia 1917 goda (Khronika sobytii)*, 6:90.

58. M. Rafes, *Ocherki po istorii Bunda* (Moscow: Moskovskii rabochii, 1923), p. 422.

59. *Rabochaia Gazeta*, no. 210, 11 November 1917.

60. *Sotsial-Demokrat* (Kharkov) of 11 November, cited in *Rabochaia Gazeta*, no. 214, 16 November 1917.

61. *Rabochaia Gazeta*, no. 208, 9 November 1917.

62. Twenty-nine members of the CEC voted for this resolution, thirteen against it, and seven abstained. *Rabochaia Gazeta*, no. 202, 3 November 1917.

63. S. A. Piontkovskii, *Oktiabr'skaia revoliutsiia v Rossii: ee predposylki i khod* (Moscow: Gosizdat, 1923), p. 89.

64. Popov, *Oktiabr'skii perevorot*, p. 359; *Revoliutsiia 1917 goda (Khronika sobytii)*, 6:49. Another organization in which right SRs and NSs predominated, the Union of Post and Telegraph Workers, even threatened to strike unless an all-socialist government was formed. Lelevich, *Oktiabr' v stavke*, appendixes, p. 22.

65. *Rabochaia Gazeta*, no. 200, 1 November 1917.

66. *Den'*, no. 205, 11 November 1917.

67. Ibid.

68. Tsereteli's speech at the all-Russian congress of representatives of local self-governments and executive committees of Soviets of Workers', Soldiers', and Peasants' Deputies is in *Rabochaia Gazeta*, no. 210, 11 November, and *Den'*, no. 205, 11 November 1917. The congress was convoked by the Petrograd City Duma; seventy-five delegates from twenty cities attended it. Tsereteli's 12 November speech in the CEC of the First Convocation is in the post-October protocols of that body in *Krasnyi Arkhiv*, 10:101-5.

69. *Rabochaia Gazeta*, no. 209, 10 November 1917.

70. *Rabochaia Gazeta*, no. 208, 9 November 1917.

71. *Novyi Luch*, no. 2, 2 December 1917.

72. *Novyi Luch*, no. 1, 1 December 1917.

Part II. The Period of War Communism and the Civil War

Introduction

1. *Partiinye Izvestiia*, no. 8 (15), 10 June 1918, pp. 16-17. B. I. Nicolaevsky's archive, now at Hoover Institution (ABN in future references).

2. V. I. Lenin, *Sochineniia* 26 (4th ed.; Moscow: Gosizdat): 429.

3. A. N. Potresov, *Posmertnyi Sbornik proizvedenii*, B. Nikolaevskii, ed. (Paris: Dom knigi, 1937), pp. 278-79.

4. Stepan Ivanovich, *A. N. Potresov. Opyt kul'turno-psikhologicheskogo portreta* (Paris, 1938), p. 183.

5. The Petrograd Social-Democratic weekly *Delo*, no. 2/8, 7 April/25 March 1918, p. 7.

6. A. F. Deviatkin, A. B. Bogdanov, I. M. Buksin, and others.

7. Martov to P. B. Axelrod, 19 November 1917. ABN.

8. Martov to N. S. Kristi, from Petrograd, 30 December 1917, in the collection *Martov i ego blizkie* (New York, 1959), pp. 48-49.

9. *Stimmen aus Russland.* Herausgegeben von der Delegation der "Sozialdemokratischen Arbeiterpartei Russlands" und der Partei "Sozialisten Revolutionäre": P. Axelrod, N. Russanoff, W. Suchomlin. Stockholm. no. 1, 20 June 1918, p. 8.

10. In his (untrustworthy) book *Iz perezhitogo (1887-1925)* (Moscow: Gosizdat, 1927), in a distorted account of the Menshevik Congress of December 1917, O. A. Ermanskii blames his failure to be elected to the CC on rightists' intrigues and stresses his agreement with Martov, Actually, Martov was one of his chief opponents.

11. Referring to the dissolution of the Constituent Assembly, Martov writes: "At that time the political bloc of our Party with the Party of Socialist Revolutionaries, which had lasted throughout the first year of the revolution, fell apart". . . . "Beguiled by the Entente's armed intervention, the Party of Socialist Revolutionaries began to organize a mass uprising of workers and peasants against the Bolshevik dictatorship, in the name of the Constituent Assembly and republican freedoms. The CC of our Party vainly advised the SRs against this course. . . . The CC forbade Party members to participate in any way in uprisings organized under the banner of the Constituent Assembly with the help of foreign troops." *Sotsialisticheskii Vestnik*, no. 7 (49), 4 April 1927, pp. 4 and 6.

12. In February 1919, a resolution of the All-Russian Conference of SRs in Petrograd rejected "overthrow of the Soviet government through armed struggle; Allied intervention in Russia's internal affairs; and blocs with bourgeois parties."

6. From the Dissolution of the Constituent Assembly to the Outbreak of the Civil War

1. In the collection *Martov i ego blizkie* (New York, 1959), p. 49.

2. N. Zhordania, *Moia Zhizn'* (Stanford, California: Hoover Institution on War, Revolution, and Peace, 1968), p. 83.

3. "Zashchita Vserossiiskogo Uchreditel'nogo Sobraniia," in *Arkhiv russkoi revoliutsii*, 12:56. Sokolov fantastically exaggerates the chances of armed defense. There is, however, no reason to suspect that his citations were invented or consciously distorted.

4. Ibid., p. 31.

5. *Tretii Vserossiiskii S"ezd Sovetov* (Petrograd, 1918), p. 59.

6. *Novyi Luch*, 10 December 1917. The final version of the appeal had been formulated by a commission that included Martov, Martynov, Kolokol'nikov, Gorev, and Dan.

7. On 1 February a new calendar, the so-called New Style, was introduced, differing from the "Old Style" by thirteen days.

8. *Partiinye Izvestiia*, no. 6/7, 20 May 1918, p. 15.

9. It is impossible to ascertain the number of casualties. At the Third Congress of Soviets, Sverdlov announced that twenty-one persons had been killed, among them "two workers and one soldier." The Mensheviks challenged this statement in *Novyi Luch*, 13 January 1918.

10. The funeral is described in *Novyi Luch*, 12 January 1918.

11. Iu. P. Denike, "B. O. Bogdanov v nachale 1918 goda," *Sotsialisticheskii Vestnik*, February/March 1960.

12. Ibid.

13. *Novaia Zaria*, no. 2, 1 May 1918, cols. 55-56.

14. *Delo*, no. 2, 7 April 1918, p. 16.

15. G. Ia. Aronson, "Dvizhenie upolnomochennykh fabrik i zavodov v 1918 godu," Inter-University Project on the History of the Menshevik Movement (New York, 1960), p. 12.

16. *Martov i ego blizkie*, p. 64.

17. *Novaia Zaria*, no. 2, 1 May 1918, col. 57.

18. Article by G. Kuchin [Oranskii] in *Novaia Zaria*, no. 3/4, 20 May 1918, p. 27.

19. L. Martov, "Rabochie i gosudarstvennaia vlast'," *Novaia Zaria*, no. 1, 22 April 1918, p. 15.

20. *Novaia Zaria* was the organ of the Central (Moscow) Region of the RSDRP, but everything the editors wrote also applied to the rest of the country.

21. *Novaia Zaria*, no. 1, col. 3. I was one of the editors of this periodical from its second issue, together with Kuchin. The declaration had been written by Kuchin and cleared with the contributors who were members of the CC, in particular with Martov.

22. *Novaia Zaria*, no. 1, 22 April 1918, pp. 13-16.

23. Ibid., pp. 62-63.

24. *Novaia Zaria*, no. 2, 1 May 1918, p. 64.

25. *Novaia Zaria*, no. 3/4, 20 May 1918, p. 33.

26. *Novaia Zaria*, no. 5/6, 10 June 1918, p. 95.

27. F. Dan, "Bol'shevistskii bonapartizm," *Novaia Zaria*, no. 3/4, 20 May 1918, p. 17.

28. *Novaia Zaria*, no. 1, 22 April 1918, p. 8.

29. *Delo*, no. 3 (9), 14 April 1918, p. 15.

30. The Moscow organization itself was not part of the Central Region organization.

31. *Drug Naroda*, organ of the Group of Menshevik Defensists, 5 November 1917.

32. *Drug Naroda*, 4 November 1917.

33. I could not obtain this issue of *Novyi Luch* and I am quoting from Potresov's reply.

34. *Novyi Den'*, no. 4, 17 (4) February 1918.

35. *Novyi Luch*, 19 (6) February 1918.

36. *Novyi Den'*, 21 (8) February 1918.

37. *Novyi Den'*, 28 (15) March 1918.

38. *Novyi Den'*, 21 (8) April 1918.

39. *Novyi Den'*, 17 (4) and 20 (7) 1918.

40. *Novyi Den'*, 17 (4) April 1918.

41. In the foreword to *The Peasant War in Germany*. He wrote on the same subject more concretely in a letter to Bebel on 24-26 October 1891. This letter was not yet known. Engels' letters to Bebel were published much later.

42. *Novaia Zaria*, no. 3/4, 20 May 1918.

43. S. Schwarz recalls that he had written an article, "Back to Capitalism," and that Dan had objected: Why "back" and not "forward"?

44. *Novaia Zaria*, no. 3/4, 20 May 1918.

45. A reference to the German occupation of Belgium.

46. *Novaia Zaria*, no. 5/6, 10 June 1918.

47. Broadly speaking, these were the conclusions of the commission entrusted by the CC of the Party in December 1917 with drafting the future constitution. I was a member of that commission, with Tsereteli, Abramovich, and Semkovskii. The commission did not finish its work on several other points.

48. *Protokoly zasedanii VTsIK. Mart-iiun' 1918 g.* (Moscow, 1920), pp. 239-40.

49. Ibid., p. 291.

50. Quoted in Kuchin's article "Itogi," *Novaia Zaria*, no. 5/6.

51. *Den'*, 2 April (20 March) 1918.

52. We cannot discuss the coalitions of 1917 here. Let us merely note that they failed to produce a workable government and that their partisans argued that a bourgeois revolution could not be "made" without the bourgeoisie.

53. My personal recollection. I was a member of the conference.

54. Only this can explain the otherwise incomprehensible voting on "The Present Situation and the Tasks of Our Party" at the plenum of the regional committee of the Central Region just before the Party conference. The committee, in which Defensists predominated, passed the resolution I had offered by only six votes against four, with two abstentions. *Novaia Zaria*, no. 5/6, gives only the text of the resolution and the results of the vote. My preceding pages are largely based on my own recollections, to which I resorted, however, only when I found direct or indirect confirmation in the contemporary press. I do not clearly recall the debates at the plenum, but careful textual analysis of the resolution makes me 90 percent sure that only the mention of "national tasks" could have evoked criticism.

55. G. Kuchin [K. Oranskii], "Itogi (Obshchepartiinoe Soveshchanie)," *Novaia Zaria*, no. 5/6, p. 22.

56. My personal recollection.

57. There had been sixty-four delegates (fifty-two with a vote from

forty-seven Party organizations. At the December congress, there had been 130 delegates with a vote.

58. *Novaia Zaria*, no. 5/6, p. 90. Nevertheless, the bureau managed to subsidize local organizations to some extent.

59. See above, p. 120.

60. Iu. Denike, "Bor'ba za nezavisimost' i edinstvo Rissii," *Novaia Zaria*, no. 5/6.

61. "Itogi," *Novaia Zaria*, no. 5/6.

62. R. Abramovich says that, for instance, he himself and the well-known worker *intelligent* A. N. Smirnov entertained such thoughts.

63. Reported in *Novaia Zhizn*, 12 June.

64. *Sotsialisticheskii Vestnik*, no. 7/8, 25 April 1926.

65. Quoted in B. I. Nikolaevskii, "RSDRP(M) za vremia s dekabria 1917 g. po iiul' 1918 g." (Unpublished study, Archive on History of Menshevism, Columbia University), p. 31.

66. I attended this meeting as representative of the bureau of the Central Region. Nicolaevsky believed that Maiskii knew of the SR plan to organize an uprising in the Volga and Ural regions: even before the Czech insurrection he had proposed that the CC detail some of its members to Samara "to act as a fully empowered Party center in the event of an uprising." Ibid., p. 43.

7. The Outbreak of the Civil War

1. Iu. Martov, *Doloi smertnuiu kazn'!* (Berlin: Sotsialisticheskii Vestnik, 1923), pp. 4, 5-7, 8, 9.

2. *Krasnaia Gazeta*, published by the Petrograd Soviet, 21 August 1918.

3. *Utro Moskvy*, no. 21, 4 November 1918.

4. *Novaia Zaria*, no. 1, 22 April 1918, p 32; no. 2, 1 May, pp. 36, 40; no. 5/6, 10 June, pp. 71-72.

5. *Saratovskii Sovet Rabochikh Deputatov (1917-18]*. *Sbornik dokumentov*, V. P. Antonov-Saratovskii, ed. (Moscow-Leningrad: Gos. Sots.-Èkon. Izd-vo, 1931), p. 486.

6. Ibid., p. 514. The Saratov Menshevik committee consisted of D. Chertkov, L. Maizel, V. D''iakonov, B. Guterman, R. Ginzberg, and others.

7. Ibid., p. 523.

8. *Nash Golos*, no. 13, 9/22 June 1918.

9. *Novyi Mir*, no. 9, September 1958, pp. 156-57.

10. Martov's speech at the twentieth session of the Central Executive

Committee, 14 June 1918 in *Protokoly Zasedanii Vserossiiskogo Ispol-nitel'nogo Komiteta 4-go Sozyva, Stenofraficheskii Otchet* (Moscow: Gosizdat, 1920), p. 426.

11. V. I. Lenin, *Sochineniia* 23 (2 ed.; Moscow: Gosizdat): 578.

12. "The question of expelling SRs from Soviets apparently met with no objections among the Bolsheviks—all of them were for expelling the SRs, whose party was in favor of armed struggle against the Bolshevik government and later formed the so-called front of the Constituent Assembly. The Mensheviks, who were against armed struggle and participation in the civil war, were a different matter. About the Mensheviks there apparently was no unanimity among the Bolsheviks, and this made itself felt at the session of the Moscow Soviet of Workers' Deputies of 5/18 June, that is, four days after the CEC's resolution. During those four days, the 'moderate' elements à la Kamenev among the top Bolsheviks must have won out. Hence, when the question of 'counterrevolutionary' parties in Soviets was discussed at the meeting of the MSWD, the chairman, Smidovich, after an ominous reminder about the Terror of the Great French Revolution, which had erected guillotines in public squares—[a point] 'we have not yet reached'— after these and other frightening words, Smidovich proposed expelling the right SRs from the Soviet but said nothing about the Mensheviks. This ran counter to the resolution of the CEC." B. Dvinov, *Moskovskii Sovet Rabochikh Deputatov 1917-1922 g.* (*Po lichnym vospomina-niiam i dokumentam*), paper no. 1, Inter-University Project on the History of the Menshevik Movement, p. 37.

Dvinov may be right that there was dissent about the Mensheviks— but the difference between their and the SRs' views was already well known when wholesale expulsion was decided on.

13. *Iskra*, Moscow, no. 3, 15/28 June, and no. 4, 16/29 June 1918.

14. *Iskra*, no. 3, 15/28 June 1918.

15. Toward the end of 1918, the Party came to accept the idea of a "transition period": socialism could be built in Russia only in collaboration with both the Bolsheviks and the moderate socialist groups— that is, through "agreement" rather than war.

16. On the legion, see Denicke's account in this volume, pp. 152-53.

17. L. B. Genkin, *Iaroslavskie rabochie v gody grazhdanskoi voiny i interventsii (1918-1920 g.g.)* (Iaroslavl: Iaroslavskoe knizhnoe izd-vo, 1958), pp. 29-30.

18. *Boris Savinkov pered voennoi kollegiei Verkhovnogo Suda SSSR* (Moscow: Litizdat N.K.V.D., 1924), p. 176. After the Iaroslavl and other uprisings on the upper Volga, Savinkov left for France.

19. Ibid., p. 40.

20. Ibid., pp. 39-40.

21. Ibid., pp. 181-82. It is impossible at this time to check the authenticity of this account.

22. Ibid., p. 69.

23. Grigor'ev perished in November 1919 in Vladivostok where he had taken part in General R. Gaida's uprising against Kolchak.

24. *Proletarskaia Revoliutsiia*, no. 10 (22), 1923, pp. 215, 216.

25. *Boris Savinkov pered voennoi kollegiei* . . . , p. 60.

26. The Soviet literature uses the word *miatezh* ("riot") for anti-Soviet uprisings. *Vosstanie* ("uprising") is reserved for "progressive" movements.

27. S. and M. Broide, *Iaroslavskii miatezh. Po zapiskam generala Perkhurova* (Moscow: Gosiurizdat, 1930), pp. 126, 127; *Proletarskaia Revoliutsiia*, no. 10 (22), 1923, p. 231; the verdict in Perkhurov's case, 19 July 1922, is in *Istoriia Vserossiiskoi Chrezvychainoi Komissii 1917-1921 g.g. Sbornik dokumentov* (Moscow: Gos. izd-vo polit. lit-ry, 1958), pp. 159-61; L. B. Genkin, *Iaroslavskie rabochie v gody grazhdanskoi voiny* . . . , p. 49. This author says that Bogdanov-Khoroshev was one of Perkhurov's principal assistants. Although Genkin had access to Soviet archives, his account contains little that is new. All workers are "Communists"; partisans of the Constituent Assembly are imperialist agents; a White officer in Iaroslave is "Trotsky's stooge." And this was written in 1958!

28. *Proletarskaia Revoliutsiia*, no. 10 (22), 1923, pp. 219, 224-25.

29. *Rabochii Internatsional*, organ of the Petrograd Committee of the RSDRP, no. 11, 14 August 1918.

30. According to Bogdanov-Khoroshev's testimony at his trial five years later, Martov had suggested that he leave for abroad, but he, Bogdanov, had already realized that "a democratic republic could not offer freedom" and felt duty-bound to work in his own country. Martov was dead by then, and Bogdanov could safely tell his unlikely story. His death sentence was commuted to three years and four months of forced labor.

31. *Rabochii Internatsional*, Petrograd, 7 August 1918. ABN.

32. L. Martov, "Sobiraiut materialy," *Sotsialisticheskii Vestnik*, no. 16 (38), 16 August 1922, p. 7.

33. *Rabochii Internatsional*, Petrograd, 7 August 1918.

34. Resolution of 2 August 1918. *Rabochii Internatsional*, 7 August 1918.

35. Trotsky, commissar of war at the time, writes that the German

military envoy in Moscow, fearing a reopening of a true German-Russian front, made it clear to him that if the Whites approached Moscow, the Germans would approach it from the east, from Orsha and Pskov. "We were caught between hammer and anvil." L. Trotskii, *Moia Zhizn'. Opyt avtobiografii* (Berlin: Granit, 1930), part 2, p. 124. This suggests that the Germans demanded more energetic Soviet operations against the Czechs.

36. L. Martov, "Vospominaniia renegata," *Sotsialisticheskii Vestnik*, 9 December 1922, pp. 15-16. Maiskii confided his plans to a few rightist Mensheviks he trusted. He told an old friend, Simon Wolin, that he hoped to work in the new government, obviously expecting Wolin to join him. Wolin did express such a desire, and Maiskii promised to try to arrange a pass for him, but apparently did not succeed. Wolin never heard from him again.

37. I. Maiskii, *Demokraticheskaia Kontr-Revoliutsiia* (Moscow-Petrograd: Gosizdat, 1923), pp. 38, 39. Later Maiskii asserted: "Until the day of my departure from Moscow there had been no resolution of the CC forbidding Party members to take part in governments in territories reconquered from the Bolsheviks by the counterrevolution" (ibid., p. 38). It is true that no resolution had been worded in exactly this way, but the CC had repeatedly condemned uprisings against Moscow.

38. "First an SR came to see me [in Moscow]," recalls S. Schwarz, "a young girl had arrived from Saratov with the message from Samara. After a while a Menshevik woman came, also from Saratov, on the same errand. I refused."

39. Il. Vardin, *Revoliutsiia i men'shevizm* (Moscow: Gosizdat, 1925), p. 91.

40. I. Mints, *Men'sheviki v interventsii* (Moscow: Gos. Sots.-Èkon. Izd-vo, 1931), pp. 83, 87.

41. Vardin, *Revoliutsiia i men'shevizm*, p. 92. Vardin quotes from *Vecherniaia Zaria*, organ of the Samara Mensheviks, but gives no date.

42. Maiskii, *Demokraticheskaia Kontr-Revoliutsiia*, pp. 145, 162. Maiskii's book, written after his expulsion from the Party and in part after he had joined the Communist party, should be used with caution.

43. Sometimes illegal Bolsheviks used this name.

44. Maiskii, *Demokraticheskaia Kontr-Revoliutsiia*, p. 178.

45. *Bor'ba Kazan'. Sbornik materialov o chekho-uchredilovskoi interventsii v 1918 g.*, no. 1 (Kazan: Kombinat Izdatel'stva i Pechati, 1924), pp. 170-71. ABN.

46. Ibid., p. 176.

47. *Russkii Istoricheskii Arkhiv* 1 (Prague, 1929); 83-84.

48. G. K. Gins, *Sibir', Soiuzniki i Kolchak* 1, part 1 (Peking, 1921): p. 274.

49. This letter is in ABN.

50. *Utro Moskvy*, 21 October 1918. The revised Menshevik policy is discussed below, pp. 182 ff.

51. He wrote a contrite letter to *Pravda* in October 1920 and later joined the Communist party.

52. I. Mints, *Angliiskaia interventsiia i severnaia kontrrevoliutsiia* (Moscow-Leningrad: Gos. Sots.-Èkon. Izd-vo, 1931), p. 114.

53. *Interventsiia na severe v dokumentakh*, prepared for publication by I. Mints (Moscow: Partiinoe Izd-vo, 1933), pp. 44, 53.

54. Ibid., p. 43.

55. Ibid., pp. 42-43.

56. Mints, *Angliiskaia interventsiia i severnaia kontrrevoliutsiia*, p. 104.

57. "Inostrannoe vmeshatel'stvo i proletariat," *Rabochii Internatsional*, Petrograd, no. 11, 14 August 1918, p. 2.

58. M. S. Kedrov, *Bez bol'shevistskogo rukovodstva (Iz istorii interventsii na Murmane)*. *Ocherki* (Leningrad: Krasnaia Gazeta, 1930), p. 28.

59. Ibid., p. 32.

60. Ibid., pp. 28-32, 53; *Istoriia Diplomatii* (Moscow: Ogiz, 1946): 377 ff.; *Iz istorii bor'by sovetskogo naroda protiv inostrannoi voennoi interventsii i vnutrennei kontrrevoliutsii v 1918 g. Sbornik statei* (Moscow: Gos. Izd-vo Polit. Lit-ry, 1956), pp. 142–70; George F. Kennan, *The Decision to Intervene* (Princeton, N.J.: Princeton University Press, 1958), pp. 31–57.

Trotsky's telegram had undoubtedly been dispatched with Lenin's consent. In the Stalin era it was, however, cited as evidence of Trotsky's work as an "agent of British imperialism."

61. *Rabochii Internatsional*, Petrograd, 7 August 1918. ABN.

62. In 1919 he returned to his family in Saratov but kept away from the Party organization.

63. *Sotsialisticheskii Vestnik*, no. 3 (241), 9 February 1931.

64. For lack of primary sources, I am using excerpts quoted in anti-Menshevik Soviet publications. They may have been distorted, curtailed, or put in the wrong context. I have exercised great caution, using only excerpts that seemed authentic to me. At present there is no other way of writing a history of the Russian revolution. Despite valuable work by foreign scholars, much is still unclear.

65. Quoted from *Iuzhnyi Rabochii* of 26 October 1918 in *Men'she-*

viki-interventy. Sbornik statei (Moscow-Leningrad: Gos. Sots.-Èkon. Izd-vo, 1931), p. 34.

66. Ibid., p. 35.

67. Ibid., p. 24.

68. Mints, *Men'sheviki v interventsii*, p. 71. Quoted from *Priboi*, no. 536, 20 August/2 September 1919. At a zemstvos' and cities' conference in December 1919, Crimean Mensheviks declared that Allied armies could help restore a democratic Russia only if they did not interfere in her internal affairs. Ibid., p. 69. Mints refers to *Priboi*, no date.

69. Ibid., p. 91. Quoted from *Golos Rabochego*, no. 162, no date. It was late September or early October 1918.

70. Ibid., p. 92. Mints refers to *Zaria*, no. 22 (and its supplements), 4 September/22 August 1918.

71. Stepan Ivanovich, *A. N. Potresov. Opyt kul'turno-psikhologicheskogo portreta* (Paris, 1938), pp. 158–59.

72. This letter was largely a reply to the news about the Ufa conference.

73. The complete text of "Tezisy i Rezoliutsii Tsentral'nogo Komiteta ot 17–21 oktiabria 1918 g." could not be found. I had to quote from excerpts in *Pravda* of 29 October 1918 and in Vardin, *Revoliutsiia i men'shevizm*, pp. 99-100.

74. *Utro Moskvy*, no. 19, 21 October 1918. ABN.

75. Letter of 25 October 1918. ABN.

76. Letter of 23 January 1920. ABN.

77. Both these documents are in ABN. The first is in German.

8. Between the World War and the NEP

1. Since 10 November 1918, Germany had had a socialist government, the Council of Peoples' Commissars, consisting of three Majority and three Independent Socialists. There were workers' and soldiers' councils throughout the country. These held a congress (16–20 December), at which the Majority Socialists had the majority. Because of disagreements within the government, the Independents left the Council of Peoples' Commissars on 29 December—that is, during the Menshevik conference in Moscow. Martov could not foresee these developments from the incomplete and sometimes garbled news that reached Moscow. (*Ed.*)

2. *Partiinoe Soveshchanie R.S.-D.R.P., 27 dekabria 1918 goda-1-go ianvaria 1919 g. (Rezoliutsii)* (Moscow: Biuro Tsentral'nogo Komiteta RSDRP, 1919), pp. 8, 9, 10, 12.

3. Ibid., p. 24.

4. Ibid., p. 14. The wording "freedom of most of the laboring masses" (rather than "freedom" generally) shows how the concept of freedom had been narrowed to adapt to Russian conditions. Martov's resolution (pp. 000–00) contained no such restriction.

5. Ibid., p. 15.

6. Ibid., p. 3.

7. Ibid., p. 5.

8. At a meeting of Moscow party workers on 27 November 1918, Lenin had spoken with resentment of a letter from Adler: "Just today, as it happens, I received [by hand] a letter from Friedrich Adler—a man well known for his revolutionary conduct in Austria. . . . Written in late October, . . . [it] contains only one request: Couldn't the imprisoned Mensheviks be released? He has found nothing more intelligent to say at such a time. . . ."

9. V. I. Lenin, *Sochineniia* 28 (4th ed.): 426.

10. Ibid., pp. 191-92.

11. Lenin, *Sochineniia* 29 (4th ed.): 131.

12. *Delo Naroda*, organ of the Moscow Bureau of the CC of the Party of Socialist Revolutionaries, no. 5, 25 March 1919.

13. *Delo Naroda*, no. 4, 23 March 1919, p. 3.

14. Leaflet of the CC of the RSDRP, April 1919. ABN.

15. For details about Martov's arrest, see *Sotsialisticheskii Vestnik*, no. 7/8, 4 April 1924, p. 16.

16. This letter was reprinted in the collection *Sotsialdemokratiia i revoliutsiia* (Odessa: Gruppa Sotsial-Demokratov, 1920), pp. 17-19.

17. *Pravda*, 5 July 1919.

18. Lenin, *Sochineniia* 29 (4th ed.): 428.

19. Quoted from B. Nikolaevskii, "Men'sheviki v period voennogo kommunizma (1918-1921 g.g.), p. 37 (unpublished; Archive on History of Menshevism, Columbia University). The resolution was not printed anywhere. (*Ed.*)

20. Although in those years "agreement with the Bolsheviks" had been the Mensheviks' idea of a favorable outcome of the revolution, there had been no actual negotiations since the Vikzhel ones in 1917. Rumors of negotiations arose several times; second- and third-rank Bolsheviks sometimes tried to sound out the Mensheviks about it; upon hearing such rumors, the Right Mensheviks accused the CC of "negotiating" with Lenin. The fact is that no negotiations took place. See Martov's letter to Axelrod, p. 211 of this book.

21. *Oborona Revoliutsii i Sotsial-Demokratiia. Sbornik statei* (Petro-

grad-Moscow: Kniga, 1920), p. 14. (This was no. 1 of the series *Voprosy sotsial-demokraticheskoi politiki* under Martov's editorship.)

22. Ibid., pp. 12-13 (and *Ivestiia* of 4 October 1919).

23. Ibid., p. 14.

24. Ibid., p. 16.

25. Ibid., p. 20.

26. Ibid., pp. 21, 22.

27. Ibid., p. 24.

28. See the collection *Martov i ego blizkie* (New York: 1959), p. 104.

29. R. Abramovitch, *In tsvey revolutsyes* 2 (in Yiddish) (New York: Workmens Circle, 1944): 265, 267.

30. Letter of 23 January 1920. ABN.

31. Before discussing ideology, the conference heard reports from local organizations, which indicated considerable Menshevik influence, and electoral successes where Menshevik candidates were able to run: "In *Tula* up to 50 S-Ds were elected to the Soviet, 95 percent of them in the workers' division. In the elections to the Consumers' Association, 8,000 votes were cast for S-Ds (39 representatives), 9,000 for the Bolsheviks (41 representatives), and over 3,000 for nonpartisans. S-Ds gained control of a number of trade union boards (chemicals, food processing). In *Smolensk* the S-Ds got 30 Party members and 20 sympathizers elected to the Soviet; and to the Consumers' Association, 73 representatives, while only 51 went through on the Bolshevik ticket and 56 on the nonpartisan ticket. And it was in the working-class quarters that the S-Ds drew their greatest support. Thus, in *Kremenchug* at an all-city nonpartisan conference, the S-Ds got 340 votes and the Bolsheviks 390; to the trade union congress, 3 S-Ds and 2 Bolsheviks were elected; with the exception of the tobacco workers' union, all the trade unions were in the hands of the S-Ds. In the reelections to the Soviet, 71 S-Ds went through, and 62 Bolsheviks. Finally, in *Kharkov* our Party got 200 deputies elected." From the foreword to *Sbornik Rezoliutsii i Tezisov Tsentr. K-ta RSDRP i Partiinykh Soveshchanii* (Kharkov: Glavnyi Komitet RSDRP na Ukraine, 1920). ABN.

32. Ibid., pp. 9-10.

33. Ibid., p. 11.

34. Ibid., p. 17.

35. Ibid., p. 29.

36. *Sotsialisticheskii Vestnik*, no. 1, 1 February 1921 (*SV* in future references).

37. B. I. Nikolaevskii, "Sorok let tomu nazad," *SV*, no. 2/3, February/March 1961, p. 30.

38. I am forced to cite Martov's letter from two articles in *Pravda* (5 and 10 April 1921) by I. Vardin, who somehow got hold of the original text. The excerpts in Vardin's articles are apparently authentic; compare Martov's letter to Axelrod cited on p. 211.

39. *SV*, no. 2/3, February/March 1961, p. 30.

40. Martov's letter to S. Shchupak, 5 February 1921. ABN.

41. Martov's speech at the second session of the Seventh Congress of Soviets, 6 December 1919, in *Sed'moi Vserossiiskii S"ezd Sovetov Rabochikh, Krest'ianskikh, Krasnoarmeiskikh i Kazach'ikh Deputatov. Stenograficheskii otchet* (Moscow: Gosizdat, 1920), pp. 57–59. All quotations on the next two pages are from the same speech.

42. I have been unable to find Martov's speech in Russian. The text is from *Sowjetrussland und Polen. Reden von Kamenev, Lenin, Trotski, Marchlewski, Sokolnikov, Radek und Martov in der vereinigten Sitzung des Allrussischen Zentral-Exekutivkomitees des Moskauer Rates der Arbeiter- und Bauerndelegierten, der Gewerkschaftsverbände und der Betriebräte am 5. Mai 1920.* Herausgegeben von der Redaktion Russischer Korrespondez, 1920. S. 35.

43. Martov's letter to Stein, 26 June 1920. ABN.

44. Martov's letter to K. Kautsky, 27 June 1920. ABN.

45. "Tezisy TsK RSDRP k avgustovskoi konferentsii 1920 goda." ABN. Since the conference did not take place, these theses were published as resolutions of the Central Committee.

46. Speech on 2 October 1920 at a convention of employees in the leather industry, in Lenin, *Sochineniia* 31 (4th ed.): 281.

47. Speech on 22 September 1920, at the Ninth All-Russian Conference of the Russian Communist party, in ibid., p. 251.

48. *Volia Rossii*, Prague, 20 and 22 October 1920 (speech of 15 October).

49. A long unsigned letter to French socialists, written in September 1920 and apparently stemming from rightist Menshevik circles, criticized Martov's stand and favored a defeatist policy: "According to official sources, scores of Russian officers, including regimental commanders, have gone over to the Poles. Isn't this reminiscent of '63 [1863]? Honest Russian people did not support their official fatherland, especially when its actions went against their conscience and against the interests of mankind. Why cannot the Mensheviks in the CC and L. M. see this. . . ." ABN.

50. Some accounts may create a false impression of the Mensheviks' policy. For example, R. Abramovich writes in *In tsvey revolutsyes*: "We made an official declaration at the Congress of Soviets to this effect [expressing support of the Soviet government in the war with

Poland]. We had the idea that if the Red army defeated Pilsudskii's legionnaires, it would meet at the German-Polish border with a renewed German revolution. This would mean that Russia, Germany, and all Central Europe would be united on a large revolutionary territory reaching the Rhine on the German-French border. The Russian revolution would be at the door of France and of all Western Europe. True, it would be going on under the banner of the Red army. But at that time we still hoped, first, that in the course of events the Bolshevik dictatorship would change and, second, that the enormous democratic force of organized European workers would prove politically, ideologically, and economically stronger than the weak semi-peasant Russian bolshevism, so that the leadership of the European revolution would not remain in the Bolsheviks' hands when the general European revolution began" (pp. 328-29). These ideas had some currency in leftist Bund circles, but they clashed with Martov's policy. Misapprehensions may arise because Abramovich fails to mention that these were his personal views, differing from the Menshevik party line.

51. Letter no. 9 of the CC of the RSDRP, 30 June 1920, *Volia Naroda*, Prague, no. 4, 16 September 1920.

52. G. Aronson, "Anglichane v Moskve," *Novyi Zhurnal* 11 (1945): 339. Photostats of the documents given to the British delegation are in the Archive on History of Menshevism, Columbia University.

53. S. Volin, *Deiatel'nost' men'shevikov v profsoiuzakh pri sovetskoi vlasti*, paper no. 13 of the Inter-University Project on the History of the Menshevik Movement (New York, October 1962), p. 163.

54. F. Dan, *Dva goda skitanii (1918-1921)* (Berlin, 1922), pp. 13, 14.

55. *Pravda*, 2 June 1920.

56. P. B. Axelrod to A. Chkhenkeli, 22 February 1919. The letter is at the International Institute of Social History, Amsterdam.

57. 18 June 1919. ABN.

58. Letter of 28 December 1919. ABN.

59. Letter of 30 May 1920. ABN.

60. *Martov i ego blizkie*, p. 105.

61. Letter of 20 June 1920.

62. The above correspondence is at the International Institute of Social History, Amsterdam.

63. Axelrod to S. M. Ingerman, 14 August 1920. ABN.

64. *SV*, no. 5, 5 April 1921, p. 10.

65. Martov's letters to S. Shchupak and E. L. Broido of 26 June 1920. ABN.

66. Ibid.

67. Ibid.

68. *SV*, no. 4, 18 March 1921, p. 6.

Part III. The Mensheviks under the NEP and in Emigration

9. The Opposition to the NEP

1. The journal launched by the Mensheviks in Berlin. See p. 243.
2. F. Dan, *Dva goda skitanii* (Berlin, 1922), p. 113.
3. Lead articles in *SV*, nos. 4 and 5, 1921.
4. Boris Dvinov, *Ot legal'nosti k podpol'iu* (Stanford, Calif.: The Hoover Institution on War, Revolution, and Peace, 1968), p. 30. According to these valuable reminiscences, written in 1924 soon after the author left Russia, the Menshevik Central Committee consisted at the time of F. Dan, B. Nicolaevsky, I. Rubin, O. Ermanskii, A. Pleskov, A. Troianovskii, I. Iudin, A. Iugov, S. Ezhov, and F. Cherevanin as well as Iu. Martov, R. Abramovich, D. Dallin, and E. Broido, who were already abroad. In August 1921 B. Bèr had been included in the CC as representative for the main committee for the Ukraine. The CC's secretary was K. I. Zakharova.
5. Martov's letter to S. Shchupak, 30 March 1921. B. Nicolaevsky's archives (ABN in future references).
6. Martov's letter to S. Shchupak, 7 January 1921. ABN.
7. Unpublished report on the activity of the CC in 1921 and the first half of 1922, p. 4. ABN. See also lead article in *SV*, no. 17, 1921.
8. Lead article in *SV*, no. 20, 1921.
9. See David Dallin, p.p. 213-14 of this book.
10. Iu. Martov, "Na puti k likvidatsii," *SV*, no. 19, 1921.
11. Lead article in *SV*, no. 6, 1921. Martov visualized the following postrevolutionary situation: "The rapprochement between proletariat and peasantry will not last forever. Further economic development and [greater] stratification of the peasantry itself are bound to increase the area of friction between the interests of significant strata of it and the interests of the proletariat. Under certain conditions the interests of the peasantry as sellers of agricultural produce, receivers of ground rent, and hirers of manpower clash with the interests of the proletariat so strongly that the combination peasant-bourgeoisie against the proletariat is much more likely than the combination peasantry-proletariat against the bourgeoisie. So far, such a situation does not exist in Russia." Martov, "Na puti k likvidatsii," *SV*, no. 19, 1921.
12. Martov's letter to S. Shchupak, 30 March 1921. ABN.
13. Letter no. 16 of the CC of the RSDRP to Party organizations. ABN.
14. The full text of the theses is in *SV*, no. 21, 1921.

15. On intraparty controversies on this subject see David Dallin's part of this book.

16. G. Aronson, "K peresmotru partiinoi platformy," *SV*, no. 22, 1922.

10. The Party's Activities in Russia

1. Unpublished report on the activity of the CC in 1921 and the first half of 1922. ABN.

2. B. Dvinov, *Ot legal'nosti k podpol'iu* (Stanford, Calif.: Hoover Instution on War, Revolution, and Peace, 1968), pp. 65-66.

3. Protocols of the Delegation of the RSDRP Abroad (unpublished), meeting of 11 October 1922.

4. G. Kuchin, "Rabota partii, nachinaia s oseni 1922 g.," p. 12. ABN. This work is particularly interesting in that it was not written for publication but to inform the delegation abroad of the true situation of the Party in Russia.

5. Kuchin's letter to the delegation abroad, 16–17 October 1922. ABN.

6. Kuchin, "Rabota partii ...," p. 12.

7. Ibid., p. 10. Dvinov, *Ot legal'nosti k podpol'iu*, p. 124.

8. Resolution of the bureau of the CC, 23 October 1922. ABN. Italics added.

9. See the letters of the bureau of the CC to the delegation abroad, 27 December 1922 and 14 March 1923. ABN.

10. Kuchin, "Rabota partii ...," p. 15.

11. Resolution of the bureau of the CC; 15 November 1922. ABN.

12. Letters of the bureau of the CC to the delegation abroad, 27 December 1922 and 14 March 1923. ABN. Also the protocols of the delegation abroad, meetings of 27 December 1922 and 21 February and 1 March 1923.

13. Resolution of the bureau of the CC, 19 January 1923. ABN.

14. Report on the activity of the CC (see n. 1), p. 11.

15. The full text of the statement is in Dvinov, *Ot legal'nosti k podpol'iu*, pp. 133–36.

16. *SV*, no. 15, 1922.

17. Report of the activity of the CC ..., pp. 14–15.

18. Interview with L. O. Dan, New York, 6 May 1962.

19. Report on the activity of the CC ..., p. 19.

20. See Dvinov, *Ot legal'nosti k podpol'iu*, p. 80.

21. Kuchin's letter to the delegation abroad, 16 February 1922. ABN.

22. Kuchin, "Rabota partii ...," p. 11.

23. Dvinov, *Ot legal'nosti k podpol'iu*, pp. 74-75, 127. The author

was in charge of the secret distribution of *SV*.

24. Letter to the bureau of the CC to local organizations, 23 August 1922. *SV*, no. 18, 1922.

25. V. Lenin, *Sochineniia* 32 (4th ed.): 171, and 33:253.

26. *SV*, no. 1, 1923.

27. Dvinov, *Ot legal'nosti k podpol'iu*, p. 111

28. *SV*, no. 6, 1922.

29. *SV*, no. 21, 1922.

30. Kuchin's letter to the delegation abroad, 16-17 October 1922. ABN.

31. Undated theses drawn up by the bureau of the CC, probably in late 1922 or early 1923. ABN.

32. *SV*, no. 7, 1921.

33. *SV*, no. 11, 1921.

34. *SV*, no. 1, 1922.

35. Letter of the bureau of the CC to local organizations, 7 September 1922. ABN.

36. Leaflet of the bureau of the CC, "Vybory v Sovety. Ko vsem rabochim, ko vsem trudiashchimsia v Rossii," September 1922, ABN.

37. Unpublished protocols of the delegation abroad, meeting of 9 September 1922.

38. *Zaria*, Berlin, no. 6.

39. B. Sapir, "Andrei Kranikhfel'd," in the collection *Martov i ego blizkie* (New York, 1959), p. 143.

40. *SV*. no. 23/24, 1922. See also *SV*, no. 8, 1921.

41. Kuchin, "Rabota partii . . . ," p. 33.

11. The Evolution of Ideology

1. Iu. Martov's letter to P. Axelrod, 30 January 1921. ABN.

2. F. Dan, *Dva goda skitanii* (Berlin, 1922), p. 70.

3. Martov's letter to A. Stein, 26 June 1920. ABN.

4. See David Dallin, pp. 233-34 of this book.

5. Martov's letter to Axelrod, 5 April 1921. ABN.

6. Letters to the delegation abroad written in the name of the CC by B. Dvinov, 30 August 1921, and I. Rubin, 25 September 1921. ABN.

7. I. Rubin's letter to the delegation abroad, 25 November 1921. ABN. Rubin, a member of the CC, was arrested after the conference, talked with Dan in prison, and reported the conversation to the delegation abroad.

8. See B. Dvinov, *Ot legal'nosti k podpol'iu* (Stanford, Calif.: Hoover Institution on War, Revolution, and Peace, 1968), pp. 71–72.

9. F. Cherevanin's letters to the delegation abroad, August and October or November 1922 (undated). ABN.

10. G. Kuchin's letter to the delegation abroad, 16-17 October 1922 reporting on the conference in detail. ABN. See also B. Dvinov's resumé (*konspekt*) for the period of August to October 1922. ABN.

11. Protocols of the delegation abroad (unpublished), meeting of 7 October 1922.

12. Ibid., meeting of 26 April 1923.

13. *Zaria*, Berlin, no. 4, 1922.

14. See G. Aronson, "K istorii pravogo techeniia sredi Men'shevikov," paper no. 4 of the Inter-University Project on the History of the Menshevik Movement (New York, 1960; mimeographed), p. 120.

15. Martov's letter to S. Shchupak, 8 June 1921. ABN.

16. When Metropolitan Benjamin was shot in Petrograd in 1922, Martov wrote in *SV*, no. 15: "We assert that neither in Petrograd nor anywhere else in Russia can you find twelve jurors freely elected by the people or freely picked from among the people, from among workers and peasants, who would agree to condemn to death a minister of the church, guilty only of agitating against the confiscation of church property—[jurors] who over such a picayune matter would want to challenge their believing fellow citizens, trample their innermost feelings. . . . One cannot help thinking that, backstage, the hands of the idiots who sign or prescribe these insane bloody sentences are guided by the satanic will of [the revolution's] most reactionary enemies."

17. Martov's letter to K. Kautsky, 28 January 1920. ABN.

18. Martov's letter to Shchupak, 14 December 1920. ABN.

19. Martov's letter, without name of addressee or date, apparently written in March 1922. ABN. Isolated as it was from the West, the bureau of the CC put greater hopes than the delegation abroad in the International's pressure and urged more decisive action. A. Pleskov, the extreme leftist in the CC, wrote the delegation on 28 April 1922: "It is imperative that Vienna force 'the Nine' to put the Russian question on the agenda. If this fails, try again at the congress itself, and it looks as if an ultimatum cannot be avoided there. However, we do not want to hamstring you. We realize that you can see better." And Dvinov wrote the delegation from Moscow on 2 May that its tractability at the conference of the three Internationals had made "an unpleasant impression" in the CC. Dvinov, *Ot legal'nosti k podpol'iu*, p. 112. Yet F. Adler, the secretary of the Vienna Union, considered that the Mensheviks had taken "a well-nigh perfect stand" at that conference.

20. Lead article in *SV*, no. 11, 1922.

21. *SV*, no. 1, 1923.

22. Resolution of the bureau of the CC, 26 January 1923. ABN. See also the protocols of the delegation abroad, meetings of 2 and 15 December 1922.

23. David Dallin discusses Axelrod's stand on the policy of the socialist parties toward bolshevism (pp. 228-34 of this book).

24. Letter of 4 February 1921. ABN.

25. Axelrod's letter to Stepan Ivanovich, 22 April 1923. International Institute of Social History, Amsterdam.

26. Protocols of the delegation abroad, meetings of 26 April, 29 March, and 13 March 1923.

27. Report on the activity of the CC during 1921 and the first half of 1922 (unpublished), p. 12. ABN.

28. Kuchin's letter to the delegation abroad, 16-17 October 1922. ABN.

29. The full text of this resolution is in *SV*, no. 4, 1921.

30. Martov's letter to Shchupak, 5 March 1921. ABN.

31. Axelrod even insisted that recognition should be granted only on certain conditions. One condition became very topical in 1924, when the Soviets had been recognized by England and several other European countries, and France was considering the same step. Axelrod wrote: "In my opinion the British Labour Party has taken much guilt on its conscience in recognizing the Soviet regime. But it would be much worse in a moral-political sense if the French workers' party let the French government recognize the Bolsheviks' military annexation of Georgia without making a resolute protest and demanding the restoration of Georgia's independence as a condition for recognizing the Soviet government." Axelrod's letter to Dan, 7 December 1924. International Institute of Social History, Amsterdam.

32. Dvinov, *Ot legal'nosti k podpol'iu*, pp. 79, 121.

33. Martov's letter to Axelrod, 30 January 1921. ABN.

34. *SV*, no. 5, 1922.

35. Dvinov, *Ot legal'nosti k podpol'iu*, p. 96.

36. On the Genoa conference see the following articles in *SV*, 1922: R. Abramovich, "Predely Genui," no. 8, and "Rossiia v Genue," no. 10; F. Dan, "Itogi Genui," no. 11.

37. Leaflet "Sobytiia v Rure," February 1923. ABN.

12.   *Two Party Centers*

1. In 1926 Dan still thought that the 1920 theses "represent even now the ideological basis of our Party's tactics." F. Dan, "Bol'shevistskii opyt i sotsializm," *SV*, no. 4, 1926. See also his article "Lintsskaia programma," *SV*, no. 22, 1926.

Stepan Ivanovich wrote in his article "Sokrovishche miatezhnykh," *Zaria*, no. 3, 1924: "Shortly before his death Martov began to revise his theoretical premises. . . . Perhaps, if death had not cut short this work of revision, it would have reached the point at which the various currents in social democracy could have converged." This exaggeration of Martov's shift evidently had to do with tactical considerations in the struggle against "the Martov movement." In particular, there are no indications that Martov had become less hostile to the extraparty right.

2. The first quotation is from D. Dallin, "Gosudarstvennyi kapitalizm," *SV*, no. 12, 1923; the second, from P. Garvi, "Bonapartizm ili demokratiia," *SV*, no. 23/24, 1923. See also A. Iugov, "Levyi kurs i chastnyi kapital," *SV*, no. 19, 1924.

3. See pp. 266-70, above.

4. R. Abramowitsch, *Die Zukunft Sowjetrusslands* (Jena, 1923), p.56.

5. The theses were printed (without their authors' knowledge) in *Zaria*, nos. 3 and 4, 1923.

6. The letter is in *SV*, no. 21, 1923.

7. Protocols of the delegation abroad (unpublished), meeting of 26 April 1923.

8. Ibid., meetings of 27 September 1923; 11 May, 14 June, and 22 November 1924.

9. G. Kuchin's letter to the delegation abroad, 16 May 1924. ABN.

10. Letter of the delegation abroad to the bureau of the CC, 28 October 1923. ABN.

11. Protocols of the delegation abroad, meeting of 12 November 1923.

12. Lead article in *SV*, no. 12, 1923.

13. Lead article in *SV*, no. 6, 1924.

14. Lead article in *SV*, no. 2, 1924. Potresov, who knew Lenin closely in the early years of the century, described him as a person who had never been young and who looked like a "typical middle-aged shopkeeper," not an *intelligent*. According to Potresov, Lenin's inner strength and simplified approach to life were strikingly evident even then. The Party leaders did not attach much importance to his idiosyncratic views, expecting him to mature. In 1901, Lenin, "though not sentimental by nature, spoke of Iu. O. [Martov] with an unconcealed feeling of almost rapturous admiration." In the inner S-D group, "Plekhanov was revered, Martov was beloved, but Lenin alone was unquestioningly followed as the only undisputed leader"—because of his iron will and faith in himself. A. N. Potresov, "Lenin," in *Posmertnyi sbornik proizvedenii* (Paris, 1927).

15. Letter of 28 October 1923. ABN.

16. F. Dan, "'Mertvaia's.-d. i 'zhivoi' kommunizm," *SV*, no. 21/22 1923.

17. R. Abramovich, "Rabochii Internatsional i sotsialisticheskie

partii," *SV*, no. 4, 1924, and "O putiakh Internatsionala," *SV*, 17/18, 1925.

18. P. Axelrod's letter to F. Adler, *SV*. no. 21, 1924.

19. The prominent rightist Menshevik Voitinskii disagreed: "Evolution nearly always encompasses a broad political process; only certain critical points in this process are marked by revolution." He held that the dichotomy revolution-evolution was significant only in that it ruptured legal continuity. V. Voitinskii, *Sily sovremennogo sotsializma* (Paris: Biblioteka Demokraticheskogo Sotsializma, 1929), p. 113.

20. R. Abramovich, "'Edinyi front' v Germanii," *SV*, no. 23/24, 1923. See also A. Kurinskii, "Germanskii krisis," *SV*, no. 14, 1923.

21. R. Abramovich, "K voprosu o Gruzii," *SV*, no. 22/23, 1924.

22. The text of the resolution in in *SV*, no. 1, 1925.

23. The text of the resolution is in *SV*, no. 15/16, 1925.

24. Letter of the delegation abroad to the bureau of the CC, 28 October 1923. ABN.

25. Letter of 14 September 1923. ABN.

26. Copies of all the leaflets cited are in ABN. All carry the taunting imprint "Press of the Bureau of the CC of the RSDRP."

27. More about Kuchin's role in Boris Sapir's chapters in this book, pp. 377-88.

28. G. Kuchin, "Rabota partii, nachinaia s oseni 1922 g.," pp. 23–24, 26. ABN.

29. Ibid., p. 42.

30. Ibid., pp. 37, 39, 27.

31. *SV*, no. 13, 1923.

32. Letter of 14 September 1923. ABN.

33. Kuchin, "Rabota partii . . . ," p. 38.

34. Letter of the bureau of the CC to the delegation abroad, 20 April 1923. ABN.

35. Protocols of the delegation abroad, meetings of 17 October 1923 and 3 February 1925.

36. In 1923–24, *SV* always noted the appearance of these printed or mimeographed publications. The bureau of the CC put out its organ, *Sotsialdemokrat*, and its bulletin, *Iz Partii*; the Petrograd organization, *Rabochii Listok* and *Mezhdunarodnyi Biulleten'*; the Central Bureau of the Youth League, *Proletarskaia Molodezh, Biulleten'*, and *Nashi Zadachi*; the Kiev Youth League, *Molodoe Delo* and *Molodoi Sotsialdemokrat*; the students' bureau of the Petrograd committee, *Golos Sotsialdemokrata*; and so on.

37. G. Aronson, "Obzor nelegal'nykh s.-d. izdanii v Sov. Rossii," *Slavianskaia Kniga*, no. 2, 1926.

38. D. Dallin's letter to the bureau of the CC, 31 December 1923. ABN.

39. *SV*, no. 1, 1924.

40. Kuchin's letters to the delegation abroad, 5 and 14 August 1924. ABN.

41. Letter of the bureau of the CC to the delegation abroad, 28 June 1924. ABN.

42. Letter of the abureau of the CC to the delegation abroad, 3 April 1925. ABN.

43. Ibid.

44. Letter of 18 November 1924. ABN.

45. Letter of the bureau of the CC to the delegation abroad, 8 March 1926. ABN.

46. *SV*, no. 19, 1926.

47. See pp. 254-55, above.

48. Letter from Russia to the delegation abroad, 12 April 1926. ABN.

49. Letters from Russia to the delegation abroad, 20 March and 15 February 1928. ABN.

50. Letter of the Leningrad organization of the RSDRP to the delegation abroad, 30 January 1928. ABN.

13.   The Platform of 1924

1. On the rightists' theses see pp. 290-91, above.

2. Communication to Party members from the bureau of the CC, "Ko vsem chlenam partii," January 1924. ABN.

3. Letter of the bureau of the CC to the delegation abroad, 14 September 1923. ABN.

4. The text of the platform was printed in *SV*, no. 12/13, 1924, and also published as a pamphlet, *Platforma RSDRP* (Berlin: Sotsialisticheskii Vestnik, 1924).

5. G. Kuchin's letter to A. Iugov, 25 April 1924. ABN.

6. D. Dalin, "Èkonomicheskaia platforma RSDRP," *SV*, no. 14, 1924.

7. See G. Aronson, "K istorii pravogo techeniia sredi men'shevikov," paper no. 4 of the Inter-University Project on the History of the Menshevik Movement (New York, 1960), p. 123. After the acceptance of the platform, the delegation abroad published its resolution to coopt a rightist, in the same issue as the declaration of the five rightists, *SV*, no. 12/13, 1924.

8. Five years later, a prominent rightist still thought the advent of

socialism "quite close" in western Europe, though not in Russia. V. Voitinskii, *Sily sovremennogo sotsializma* (Paris: Biblioteka Demo-kraticheskogo Sotsializma,1929), p. 128.

9. *Problemy revoliutsii* (Berlin: Zagranichnaia Delegatsiia RSDRP, 1926).

10. See Aronson, "K istorii pravogo techeniia . . . ," pp. 125, 126.

11. Protocols of the delegation abroad (unpublished), meeting of 20 October 1925.

12. Ibid., meeting of 19 June 1925.

13. Ibid., meeting of 10 March 1929.

14. Th. Dan, "Die Sozialdemokratie Russlands nach dem Jahre 1908," an appendix to J. Martow, *Geschichte der russischen Sozial-demokratie* (Berlin: Dietz, 1926), pp. 320–26.

15. Quoted by B. Nicolaevsky in his foreword, "A. N. Potresov," to *A. N. Potresov. Posmertnyi sbornik proizvedenii* (Paris, 1937), p. 85. About Dan's article in *SV* on the tenth anniversary of the Soviet regime, Potresov wrote: "I realized, to my extreme vexation, that my old comrade, the present leader of the Party majority, still has not learned enough from life to move away by as much as one step from the road [he followed] in the era of revolutionary crisis and full-scale maximalism." A Potresov, *V plenu u illiuzii* (Paris, 1927), p. 93.

16. Potresov, *V plenu u illiuzii*. One chapter of this book deals with the platform of 1924.

17. I. Tsereteli's letter to P. Axelrod, 25 July 1927. International Institute of Social History, Amsterdam.

14.   The Party in Emigration

1. In the late twenties and early thirties, the delegation abroad consisted of R. Abramovich, G. Aronson, D. Dallin, F. Dan, B. Dvinov, M. Kefali, B. Nicolaevsky, S. Schwarz, A. Iugov, and I. Iudin. Iudin died in Paris in 1937. From 1933 to 1941 Dallin lived in Poland and did not work in the delegation.

2. Protocols of the delegation abroad (unpublished), meeting of 9 June 1925.

3. Gonikberg had been leader in the Moscow Union of Chemists, the last independent trade union in Russia, and had gone abroad after its closure. The relative idleness of émigré life weighed on him, and he probably missed the popularity his work had won him in Russia. In 1926, in Berlin, he saw the chairman of the All-Russian Union of Trade Unions, Tomskii, and the chairman of the Moscow Council of Trade Unions, Mel'nichanskii, both of whom he knew well. They probably

persuaded him that he could safely return to the USSR. Gonikberg notified the delegation abroad of his decision, promising not to make anti-Menshevik statements in Russia. The delegation ruled that no Party member could go to Russia to work in the Union of Trade Unions without carrying on Menshevik work. Gonikberg left nevertheless and soon published a recantation in the trade union paper *Trud*, whereupon the Central Committee expelled him from the RSDRP. (His later fate is unknown.) The resolution of the delegation abroad stated: "Having taken cognizance of G. Gonikberg's letter in the official organ of the All-Russian Union of Trade Unions, *Trud*, of 31 August, about his withdrawal from all political activity, the CC finds that G. Gonikberg 1) has broken the obligations he had contracted toward the Delegation of the RSDRP Abroad and 2) has committed a crime against the Party by publishing such a statement. The CC of the RSDRP resolves to consider G. Gonikberg expelled from the Party." Protocols of the delegation abroad, meetings of 7 March and 12 September 1926.

4. Ibid., meeting of 12 September 1926.

5. Ibid., meeting of 6 April 1927. One such organ was the journal *Katorga i Ssylka*, published by the Union of Political Forced-Labor Convicts and Deportees.

6. Protocols of the delegation abroad, meeting 18 January 1926.

7. G. Aronson writes in *Bol'shevistskaia revoliutsiia i men'sheviki* (New York, 1955), p. 34: "What did the right wing of social democracy bring with it into emigration? An implacable anti-Bolshevik crusade, rejection of dictatorship in principle, mistrust of despotic socialism in any form, a determined protest against the terror that was corrupting the government and the people, a call to fight not only the dictatorship but also every variety of capitulationism."

8. *SV*, no. 15/16, 1925. In the same issue, F. Dan wrote that in Russia "the soil has been prepared for Social-Democratic sowing . . . the seed that our Party will sow in it are his, Axelrod's." P. Garvi: "At a time of doubt and vacillation, 'back to Axelrod' means ahead, for a determined Europeanization of the Russian labor movement, for the victory in it of the ideas of internationalism, democracy, and socialism." I. Tsereteli: "His spiritual makeup became especially dear and close to me in 1919," when the makeup of bolshevism became clear. K. Kautsky: "Axelrod and Plekhanov are among the founders of Marxism not only in Russia but in the world. The German and French schools did not exist before the Russian school." Kautsky also noted that "Axelrod never was a sectarian. For a Russian, this is not easy" so long as there is no mass movement.

9. F. Dan, "K 10-letiiu smerti G. V. Plekhanova," *SV*, no. 11, 1928.

10. G. Osipov, "Eduard Bernshtein," *SV*, no. 1, 1925.

11. F. Dan, "Neispravimyi marksist," *SV*, no. 19, 1929.

12. F. Dan, "V plenu u proshlogo," *SV*, no. 15, 1927, and Potresov's answer in *SV*, no. 20, 1927.

13. Potresov wrote Kautsky on 5 April 1928: "The question arose, could I continue [writing on politics] in *Sotsialisticheskii Vestnik* within the Party framework? To my regret, I had to answer in the negative. Before my eyes was the example of the Party opposition (Garvi, Voitinskii), showing that in this situation I should be condemned to eternal silence and could express my disagreement only in exceptional cases." The letter is at the International Institute of Social History, Amsterdam.

14. F. Dan, "Pamiati A. N. Potresova," and P. Garvi, "A. N. Potresov—chelovek i politik," *SV*, no. 14, 1934.

15.   Socialism and Stalinism

1. Lead article in *SV*, no. 10, 1925; and F. Dan, "Bol'shevistskii opyt i sotsializm," *SV*, no. 4, 1926.

2. O. Bauer, "Die Zukunft der Russischen Sozialdemokratie," *Der Kampf*, Vienna, no. 12, 1931.

3. O. Domanevskaia, "Piatiletka i ee perspektivy," *SV*, no. 13, 1929.

4. A. Iugov, "Èkonomicheskie posledstviia otmeny Nèp'a," *SV*, no. 21, 1929.

5. A. Shifrin, "Konets reformistskoi linii," *SV*, no. 1, 1931.

6. F. Dan, "Perspektivy general'noi linii," *SV*, no. 12/13, 1931.

7. O. Bauer, "Evropa i men'shevizm," *SV*, no. 6, 1925.

8. O. Bauer, *Kapitalismus und Sozialismus nach dem Weltkriege* (Vienna: Wiener Volksbuchhandlung, 1931), p. 223.

9. Ibid., p. 220.

10. Bauer replied in his article in *Der Kampf* (see n. 2) that he was not advising the Mensheviks to commit suicide—he thought they would play an important role in the future in helping to democratize the Soviet regime and transform into complete socialism the elements of socialism introduced by the regime. Such a prospect did not satisfy the Mensheviks.

11. Protocols of the Berlin organization of the RSDRP (PBO in future references) for 21 April 1932. Carefully composed by V. Schwarz, these extremely valuable protocols cover all of 1931 and the first half of 1932. All summaries of speeches were authorized by the speakers concerned.

12. PBO for 21 May 1931.

13. PBO for 1 April 1932.

14. For example, Iugov argued that the theses took it for granted that nationalization should be the rule and denationalization an exception, whereas the 1924 platform took the opposite view—and that it was necessary to return to the principles of the theses. PBO for 21 May 1931.

15. PBO for 16 June 1932.

16. In 1905, "the peasantry marched in step with the liberation movement of the time only in the context of direct struggle for land, which put it face to face with the authorities," wrote Martov in the symposium *Obshehestvennoe dvishenie v Rossii v nachale XX veka* 1 (Petersburg, 1909): 672. During the 1905 Revolution, "the peasantry was shaken to its very depths by the war, yet basically it remained *outside sociopolitical life.*" E. Maevskii in ibid., 2:62. But according to a Menshevik expert on agrarian problems, the peasants' economic struggle of 1905 "gave them the idea that they must participate in the country's political life. . . . Ideas about a democratized social order have penetrated deep into the peasant milieu, and this cannot be wiped out by any repressions." P. Maslov, *Agrarnyi vopros v Rossii* 2 (Petersburg, 1908): 451. F. Dan wrote that even in 1917 "the fate of the Constituent Assembly showed how little the peasant masses really cared about the future organization of the state, and to what extent economic interests—the seizure of landlords' estates—predominated in their minds over political interests, the establishment of political freedom." In combating Stalinism, the peasants were again "in a passion over economic but not political freedom." Dan's appendix to K. Kautsky, *Bol'shevizm v tupike* (Berlin, 1930), p. 179.

17. "In Russia, individual farming, for all its backwardness, remains dominant in the villages for the entire historical period." O. Domanevskaia, "Piatiletka i ee perspektivy," *SV*, no. 13, 1929.

18. The memorandum of the delegation abroad and the appeal of the International are in *SV*, nos. 8 and 9, 1930.

19. A. Iugov, *Piatiletka* (Berlin: Sotsialisticheskii Vestnik, 1931), p. 97; and PBO for 9 April 1931. Iugov began to revise his views on the general line before Dan did.

20. PBO for 10 March 1932.

21. PBO for 16 June 1932.

22. In 1930, he had written: "We regard the [kolkhozes] experiment, which is undoubtedly going to fail, as the greatest setback for Russia's economic development and a stimulus for the blackest kind of counterrevolution. The revolution must perish if millions of peasants

are driven to despair and to mortal hatred of the working class and the revolution." R. Abramowitsch, "Revolution und Konterrevolution in Russland," *Die Gesellschaft*, December 1930.

23. PBO for 29 March and 5 May 1932.

24. PBO for 26 March 1931.

25. Nicolaevsky remarked: "On the basic question of the attitude toward the peasantry, the views dominant in the camp of the rightist comrades are very close to mine." PBO for 16 June 1932.

26. The drafts for the letter and the platform are in an appendix to G. Aronson, *Bol'shevistskaia revoliutsiia i men'sheviki* (New York, 1955).

27. PBO for 26 March 1931.

28. PBO for 9 January 1932.

29. Nicolaevsky mentioned the possibility of a schism over political disagreements. PBO for 22 January 1932.

30. *SV*, no. 1, 1928.

31. Protocols of the delegation abroad, meeting of 10 March 1929. Only one member voted against this resolution, and one abstained.

32. Dallin's letter to the bureau of the CC, 31 December 1923. ABN.

33. Lead articles in *SV*, nos. 7/8 and 9, 1925.

34. D. Dalin, "Shuitsa i denista pravoi oppozitsii," *SV*, no. 22, 1929.

35. PBO for 23 June 1932.

36. Interview with B. Nicolaevsky in New York. Dan considered it harmful to express pessimistic views of the revolution publicly, but in private he often did. Abramovich remarked that a bloc with the left Communist opposition would "only mean perishing together with them on the next day after 'Thermidor.' That is what the . . . line of Fedor Il'ich [Dan] amounts to." PBO for 26 February 1932.

37. F. Dan, "Razgrom trotskistov," *SV*, no. 3, 1929.

38. P. Garvi, "Novyi ètap diktatury i nasha taktika," *SV*, no. 3, 1930.

39. The theses were discussed in the delegation on 23-25 August 1934. They are in an appendix to the protocols of the delegation abroad.

40. *SV*, no. 7/8, 1929.

41. Tsereteli writes that in 1917 "the national question was one of the basic questions on whose solution the fate of the Russian revolution depended." I. Tsereteli, *Vospominaniia o Fevral'skoi Revoliutsii* 2 (Paris: Mouton, 1963)'; 69.

42. *Rabochaia Gazeta*, organ of the CC of the RSDRP, 31 August 1917.

43. *Rabochaia Gazeta*, 25 October 1917.

44. *Rabochaia Gazeta*, 7 December 1917. Until 1917, Lenin too had been against federalism, though willing to compromise if the political

situation required it. He wrote in 1914: "Other things being equal, we are definitely in favor of centralization and against the petty-bourgeois ideal of federative relations." V. Lenin, *Sochineniia* 21 (4th ed.): 87.

45. A resolution of the 1925 congress of the International also said that the International expected all member parties to "actively defend the rights of national minorities . . . autonomy for territorially compact minorities, and equality, free use of their own languages, free development of their schools and culture, for scattered minorities." *SV*, no. 17/18, 1925.

46. In connection with Abramovich's article, Tsereteli wrote Axelrod: "Of course I completely agree with you . . . [it is] absurd to demand that we engage in propaganda which in principle rejects . . . a revolutionary attitude toward the Bolshevik dictatorship." There was, however, "the point, unquestionable for all in the International, that military-nationalistic methods of struggle are inadmissible for socialist parties." Letter of 21 November 1927. International Institute of Social History, Amsterdam.

47. Abramovich's speech in the executive committee of the International, 3 August 1928. *SV*, no. 18, 1928. See also his article "Palestinskie sobytiia i sionizm," *SV*, no. 16/17, 1929.

48. Sidney and Beatrice Webb, *Soviet Communism: A New Civilization?* 1 (London: Longmans, Green, 1935): 431–40; 2:554.

49. Harold J. Laski, *The Webbs and Soviet Communism*. Webb Memorial Lecture No. 3 (London: Fabian Publications 1947), p. 11. Laski did recognize that Russia was a police state as well as a dictatorship of the Communist party, in which "the vital initiative belongs to the Political Bureau" (pp. 12–13).

50. G. D. H. Cole, *The Development of Socialism During the Past Fifty Years*. The Webb Memorial Lecture, 1951 (London: Athlone Press, 1952), p. 31. In all fairness it should be noted that Cole said a little earlier in his lecture: "I hate, as much as a man can hate, the developments of 'Soviet centralism' and power-realism which George Orwell satirized in *Animal Farm*" (p. 30). (Ed.)

51. Laski, *The Webbs and Soviet Communism*, p. 16.

52. *SV*, no. 15/16, 1931.

Part IV. Notes and Reflections on the History of Menshevisim

16. The Mensheviks Before the Revolution of 1917

1. Publishing a declaration by some Zimmerwaldists exiled to Siberia (Dan, Tsereteli, and others) in *Izvestiia Zagranichnogo Sekretariata Organizatsionnogo Komiteta*, no. 3, 5 February 1916, Martov

wrote: "The group that has composed this declaration includes several comrades very influential in *our part* of the Party."

2. Th. Dan, "Die Sozialdemokratie Russlands nach dem Jahre 1908," in J. Martow, *Geschichte der russischen Sozialdemokratie* (Berlin: Dietz, 1925), p. 255.

3. Ibid., p. 234.

4. N. Trotskii, *V zashchitu partii* (Petersburg, 1907), p. xvii.

5. *Protokoly Ob"edinitel'nogo s"ezda* (Moscow: Gosizdat, 1959), p. 267.

6. Copies of this correspondence have been preserved; they were in the custody of B. Nicolaevsky and are now at the Hoover Institution. I believe the originals were acquired by Gosizdat for inclusion in the second volume of the work on social democracy in Russia, the first volume of which came out in 1928: A. N. Potresov and B. I. Nikolaevskii, eds., *Sotsialisticheskoe dvizhenie v Rossii. Materialy* (Moscow-Leningrad: Gosizdat, 1928).

7. I have read the whole correspondence but unfortunately was unable to copy from letters dated later than 4/17 April 1910.

8. See Axelrod's letter to Martov of 3 October 1910 in *Pis'ma* P. B. Aksel'roda i Iu. O. Martova (Berlin, 1924).

9. A. Potresov, *P. B. Aksel'rod. 45 let obshchestvennoi deiatel'nosti* (Petersburg: Nakanune, 1914).

10. See Dan's letter to Axelrod of 12/25 November 1906 in Axelrod's archives at the International Institute of Social History, Amsterdam.

11. See Dan's appendix to Martov, *Geschichte der russischen Sozialdemokratie*, pp. 242-45.

12. Iu. Martov, "Kuda idti?", *Golos Sotsial'demokrata*, no. 13, April 1909, pp. 4–5.

13. F. Dan, "Burzhuaziia i sovremennyi rezhim," *Golos Sotsial'demokrata*, no. 13, April 1909, p. 6.

14. F. Dan, "K sovremennomu polozheniiu," in the Menshevik collection *Otzvuki* (Petersburg, 1907), pp. 4, 5.

15. *Golos Sotsial'demokrata*, no. 13, 1909, p. 8.

16. *Otzvuki*, August 1907, p. 6.

17. His letter of resignation was printed in no. 14, May 1909. The article in question was "Evoliutsiia obshchestvenno-politicheskoi mysli v predrevoliutsionnuiu èpokhu." B. Nicolaevsky analyzes the conflict in the collection *A. N. Potresov* (Paris, 1937), pp. 56–61.

18. Letter of 3 May 1909. Axelrod's archives at the International Institute of Social History, Amsterdam.

19. Martov's letter to Potresov, 27 October/9 November 1908.

20. Letter of 4/17 December 1908.

21. *Golos Sotsial'demokrata*, no. 13, April 1909.

22. *Pis'ma P. B. Aksel'roda i Iu. O. Martova* (Berlin, 1924), p. 338.

23. Ibid.

24. Ibid., pp. 312, 330.

25. An attempt to synthesize the two "truths" was made in the theses published in the journal *Zaria*, nos. 3 and 4, 1923, in Berlin. In G. Aronson's opinion, they were drawn up in Russia by the so-called right opposition within the Party, though their authors remain unknown. Nor do we know how the émigré rightist group headed by P. Garvi reacted to them. They are interesting but are couched in terms too general to give us an idea of the concrete policies their authors had in mind. Even in this form the theses probably did not express the views of the majority of the right opposition.

17. The Conception of the Bourgeois Revolution

1. A. F. Kerensky, *Russian History's Turning Point* (New York, 1965), p. 207.

2. V. M. Chernov, *Pered burei* (New York, 1953), p. 334.

3. I. G. Tsereteli, *Vospominaniia o fevral'skoi revoliutsii* 2 (Paris-La Haye, 1963): 416.

4. Appendix to J. Martow, *Geschichte der russischen Sozialdemokratie*, p. 303.

5. L. M. [Martov], "Na ocheredi," *Iskra*, no. 93, 17 March 1905.

6. Appendix to J. Martow, *Geschichte der russischen Sozialdemokratie*, pp. 238–39.

7. See Martov in *SV*, no. 23/24, 9 December 1922, p. 15; and David Dallin, pp. 173-74 of this book.

8. I. M. Maiskii, *Demokraticheskaia kontr-revoliutsiia* (Moscow-Petrograd: Gosizdat, 1923), p. 8.

9. *Sbornik rezoliutsii i tezisov TsK RSDRP i partiinykh soveshchanii* (Kharkov: Glavnyi Komitet RSDRP na Ukraine, 1920), p. 32.

10. *SV*, no. 1, January 1946, p. 6. Italics added.

11. D. Dallin, "Griadushchaia èpokha," *Mysl'* (Kharkov), no. 11, May 1919, pp. 403–10.

12. Martov had not intended to remain abroad. The Menshevik CC informed Party organizations in its letter no. 12, 28 September 1920, now at the International Institute of Social History, Amsterdam: "Comrade Iu. Martov, delegated abroad by the CC for contact with the European socialist parties, has left Moscow on 21 September. His

trip will take two to three months." The CC even scheduled a Party conference to take place upon his return (ibid.), instead of the one that had been canceled because of the August arrests.

13. F. Dan, *Proiskhozhdenie bol'shevizma* (New York: Novaia Demokratiia, 1946).

14. *SV*, no. 8/9, 24 April 1923.

15. Ibid.

16. The Russian S-Ds enjoyed the sympathy and assistance of such figures as Karl Kautsky, Otto Wels, Paul Hertz, Rudolf Hilferding, and Ströbel in Germany; Bracke, Leon Blum, Longuet, and Renaudel in France; Friedrich Adler and Otto Bauer in Austria; Ijzerman, Albarda, and Jan de Roode in Holland; Vandervelde and De-Brouckère in Belgium; Vladek, Dubinsky, Khanin, and Hillquit in the United States; and such friends and, in effect, Mensheviks in Latvia as Klara, Paul, and Bruno Kalnins, Vishnia, and Menders. Mention should also be made of the following, who in the twenties were still in the youth movement and came to power, so to speak, only in the thirties: the Hollander Koos Forrink, the Germans Max Westphal and Erich Ollenhauer, the Dane Hans Hedtoft Hansen, the Austrian Karl Heinz, and the Sudeten Germans Karl Kern and Ernst Paul.

Of great help to the delegation abroad were the Mensheviks who had settled in foreign countries and become involved in local labor movements. They served as direct channels for the influence of Russian social democracy. In France, there was Orest Rosenfeld, Leon Blum's associate and one of the editors of *Le Populaire*; in Germany, Alexander Stein, first one of the editors of *Freiheit*, the organ of the Independent party, and later head of the Department of Culture and Education of the Central Committee of the United Social-Democratic party (S.P.D.); Alexander Shifrin-Werner, one of the editors of a Social-Democratic paper in Mannheim; Iurii (George) Denicke, a member of the Research Institute of the German labor movement; and Paul Oldberg, journalist; in Sweden, M. D. Shishkin and Mer; in Czechoslovakia, Arkadii Stoilov, settled in Prague and connected with both the Czech and the German S-D parties; in the United States, I. M. Minkoff, S. M. Levitas, Ingerman, and James; in Latvia, Gofenberg and Shapiro.

For personal and other reasons, Dan was closest to the French socialists and the socialist movements in Latvia and Austria, while Abramovich was most popular in Germany, Holland, Denmark, and especially the United States. His American connections proved very valuable when *SV* found itself in financial straits: thanks to lecture tours arranged for him by American Jewish labor organizations, *SV* was kept afloat during the last years of the Berlin and throughout the Paris period. The same organizations, with the Jewish Labor Committee at their head and with the support of the American Federation of Labor, obtained American visas for the European S-Ds fleeing from Hitler—the delegation abroad and all Menshevik émigrés among them.

17. B. Dvinov describes this period in detail in his book *Ot legal'nosti k podpol'iu* (Stanford, Calif.: Hoover Institution on War, Revolution, and Peace, 1968).

18. V. I. Lenin, *Sochineniia* 43 (5th ed.): 242.

19. *Pis'ma P. B. Aksel'roda i Iu. O. Martova*, pp. 147, 148.

20. This letter is in the Axelrod archive at the International Institute of Social History, Amsterdam.

21. Letter of 21 January 1913 in *Pis'ma P. B. Aksel'roda i Iu. O. Martova*, p. 259.

22. G. Aronson in the collection *Protiv techeniia* (New York, 1952), pp. 66–77.

23. G. Kuchin, "Ot starogo k novomu," *SV*, no. 1 (47), 1 January 1923.

24. G. Kuchin, "O nashei partii," *SV*, no. 18 (40), 21 September 1922.

25. See appendix to Dvinov, *Ot legal'nosti k podpol'iu*.

26. I should like to mention here that Kuchin cannot be classed with the right intraparty opposition as G. Aronson does in "K istorii pravogo techeniia," paper no. 4 of the Inter-University Project on the History of the Menshevik Movement (New York, 1960).

27. Letter of 6 August 1921. The Axelrod archive at the International Institute of Social History, Amsterdam.

28. I remember this high-minded, dedicated man with personal gratitude. It was he who sent me abroad to report to the delegation on the illegal work in Russia. After an accident in 1921, Kononenko was bedridden for a long time, and remained lame. He was also suffering from tuberculosis but kept going thanks to the devoted care of his wife and Party comrade Ida Efremovna Pisterman. Not wishing to burden the Party budget, he eked out a living by writing. One of his books, published under the pseudonym V. Semenov, deals with the history of socialism in England. In the fall of 1925, Kononenko lived in a rented room in a Moscow suburb, posing as a salesman preparing to enter a *rabfak*. The camouflage was so good that it was very difficult to find him through Party channels. He was not yet forty when he died.

29. See *SV*, no. 7, 16 April 1932, and no. 9, 10 June 1933.

30. Martov, "Otvet kritikam," *SV*, no. 2 (48) 17 January 1923.

31. F. Dan, "Voprosy platformy," *SV*, no. 23/24, 9 December 1922. The last italics added. Someone in Russia—Kuchin or one of his collaborators, perhaps Mikhail Kononenko—sent in a sharp reply to Dan's criticism, a statement entitled "Pobol'she iasnosti, pomen'she illiuzii" (a copy of it was preserved in the archives of the delegation abroad). It disagreed in particular with Dan's remarks about the form and composition of the government: "The political value of the resolution [that is, the theses]. . . lies precisely in the fact that, from the direct assessment of the *capitalist* relations in Soviet Russia and of the *new* developmental stage of the government itself, it draws *new* political inferences. The burden of these inferences lies in *revising* the so-called tactic of agreement and furling up the old slogans of 'socialist coalition' and a 'common front' with the mutating regime. Instead, the theses formulate [a Party] position [that is] independent politically and in the class sense. . . . At the same time the slogans of political freedom and a fully democratic regime are put at the center of the Party's policy."

32. G. Kuchin, "V polose obshchestvennoi reaktsii," *SV*, no. 6 (76), 24 March 1924.

Appendix A. Some Statistics of the Unification Congress, August 1917

1. *Rabochaia Gazeta*, nos. 139 and 144, 22 and 27 August 1917. The CC was supplying literature to about three hundred party organizations. *Novy Luch*, no. 4.

2. There are no precise figures. One hundred delegates representing 110,000 members attended the opening. *Shchit*, no. 1, 30 November 1917. By 4 December, 120 delegates had registered with the credentials committee. *Novyi Luch*, no. 6, 7 December. The paper gives no details on the membership of the organizations represented.

3. Among the others were Ber (Kharkov); Sandomirskii (Donets Basin); Viliatser, who had arrived from Rostov shortly before the Congress; and Sumskii, the only delegate from Kiev.

4. *Kievskaia Mysl'*, 15 December, and *Novyi Luch*, no. 16, 20 December 1917.

5. The other fourteen members of the CC from the faction of Revolutionary Defensists were B. S. Baturskii, P. A. Garvi, L. I. Goldman (Akim), B. I. Gorev, F. I. Dan, K. M. Ermolaev, S. M. Zaretskaia, I. A. Isuv, M. I. Liber, A. N. Smirnov, L. M. Khinchuk, I. G. Tsereteli, N. S. Chkheidze, and A. I. Chkhenkeli.

Appendix C. The "Menshevik" Trial of 1931

1. An American journalist who attended such a trial later explained his uncritical reports as follows: "I readily accepted the great trial for

what it was: a revolutionary gesture in which the concept of justice did not even enter. It was a court-martial in the midst of a strenuous social war, where ordinary notions of fairness must be suspended. We wrote of evidence and witnesses and judicial rulings, fortifying the illusion that this was, in a rough and strange way, a tribunal of justice." E. Lyons, *Assignment in Utopia* (New York: Harcourt Brace, 1937), p. 120.

2. *Protsess kontrrevoliutsionnoi organizatsii men'shevikov. Stenograficheskii otchet* (Moscow, 1931).

3. Protocols of the Delegation of the RSDRP Abroad (unpublished), meetings of 2 and 3 March 1931.

4. *SV*, nos. 4 and 5, 1931.

5. Protocols of the delegation abroad, meeting of 3 March 1931, and *SV*, no. 5, 1931.

6. *SV*, no. 5, 1931.

7. N. Jasny, "A Soviet Planner—V. G. Groman," *The Russian Review*, January 1954.

8. According to *Bol'shaia Sovetskaia Entsiklopediia* 35:37, *Prompartiia* was "an espionage and sabotage organization of the top bourgeois intelligentsia." One of its leaders was the eminent scientist Ramzin. In December 1930 *Prompartiia* leaders were sentenced to be shot, but this was commuted to ten years of imprisonment. In reality, no such party existed. It had been invented to persecute the intelligentsia and stage a trial.

9. Krylenko spoke of Ikov with irritation and ill-concealed respect: "Ikov is reserved, taciturn, knows the value of words, says no more than is necessary . . . has not in the least disarmed and remains an enemy."

10. We can get an idea of the line of self-defense of the accused (after the GPU had worked on them) from Ginzburg's statement: "I agree entirely with the prosecutor's description of this organization [the fictitious 'bureau']. I cannot think of any words that would more adequately express my present feelings about this organization, even though I was one of its initiators and leaders in the past." Yet "this organization" had never existed!

11. Groman, Sher, Iakubovich, Ginzburg, and Sukhanov.

12. At a general meeting of the All-Russian Association of Old Bolsheviks, E. Iaroslavskii said: "The proletarian trial of Mensheviks will disclose to the world proletariat the full extent of the treachery and venality of the leaders of the Second International." Typical of the many resolutions passed at factories in connection with the trial was the one of the Neva Engineering Works: "Let the Western proletarians hold a trial of the Second International and the Menshevik traitors of their own countries." *Pravda*, 1 March 1931.

The International in turn said in its 1931 May Day proclamation that the current duel between the forces of fascism and those of the working class made it "doubly painful" for socialists of all countries to witness "the abuses of revolutionary justice committed by the Soviet government in order to sharpern the divisions in the working class with the aid of an infamous trial and a campaign of filthy slander." *SV*, no. 8, 1931.

Name Index

Abramov, 168
Abramovich, Rafail A., 352; in 1917, 9, 44-45, 48, 55, 390; and negotiations on homogeneous government, 64-79 passim; under Bolshevik rule in Russia, 105, 117, 136, 147, 192, 215-17, 226-27; in Menshevik party abroad, 231-32, 245, 250, 254-55, 269, 279, 285, 343, 374-75, 377-78, 387; on common front, 273-74, 281, 290, 298; and new Socialist International (1923), 282, 295-99, 344-45, 348, 375; in new Menshevik center group (1927), 321, 328, 332; and "Menshevik" trial, 383, 395-96, 398-99, 400-402
Adler, Friedrich, 231, 294-95, 326, 328
Akhmatov, 97, 106, 190
Aleksandrova, V. A., 352
Alekseev (General), 166
Aleksinskii, Grigorii, 101
Anan'in, E. A., 352
An-skii, S., 65-66, 68
Antonevich, 62
Antonov-Ovseenko, V. A., 54, 70, 82
Antonov-Saratovskii, V. P., 159-60, 395
Aronovich, 299
Aronson, Grigorii Ia., 352; in Menshevik party abroad, 251, 254-55, 274-75, 292, 320-21, 328, 338, 374-75
Astrov, Isaak S., 105
Avilov, 10
Avksent'ev, N., 38, 171, 173, 191, 249
Axelrod, Pavel Borisovich, 116, 151, 216, 351, 380, 383; in the years 1905-14, 354-56, 360-61; and theory of bourgeois revolution, 373-74; position in Menshevik party in 1917 and after,

104-5, 228-33, 318, 322, 375; as Menshevik representative abroad (1917-20), 99, 102, 105, 178, 225, 228-32; and Socialist International, 229, 231-32, 278-79, 282-83, 295, 339, 345; on Bolshevik regime, 105, 233-34, 267, 269, 283, 291, 295, 316-17

Bakunin, Mikhail, 295
Balabanov, M. S., 378
Baturin, Boris, 101
Bauer, Otto, 233, 297-98, 324-28, 347
Bebel, August, 142, 295
Bèr, Boris, 378; in extreme left of Menshevik party, 106, 183, 214-15, 256, 268, 338
Berlatskii, B., 395, 401
Bernstein, Eduard, 322, 399
Bernstein, Iakov, 384
Bienstock, Grigorii O., 382
Bogdanov, B. O., 355, 378; on issue of coalition government in 1917, 22-31 passim; on Bolshevik seizure of power, 56; in right wing of Menshevik party (1918-22), 84-85, 115, 254
Bogdanov-Khoroshev, 168
Boldyrev, V. (General), 173
Branting, 189-90
Braude, 395, 400
Braun, 70
Breitscheid, 401
Breshko-Breshkovskaia, 171
Broido, Eva L.: CC member (1917-18), 171, 390; member of delegation abroad (1921-27), 250, 320, 374-75; and "Menshevik" trial, 397
Broido, M. I., 45

Subject Index